DEVOUR US NOT

SHORT STORIES OF AFRICAN AMERICAN HISTORY

Arnold P. Powers

To order additional copies of this book, contact:
Xlibris LLC
1-888-795-4274
www.Xlibris.com
Orders@Xlibris.com
110291

1821

Powers

This book is dedicated to my beloved, Melinda Juana De Leon Altar
The year of the photo was 1973, "The Marine Corps Ball"
Olongapo City, Republic of the Philippines

My Difference Makers, Movers & Shakers & Unsung Heroes List

1. Hero-**Ali, Muhammad**
2. Hero-**Angelou, Maya**
3. Hero-**Ball, Krystal**
4. Hero-**Bashir, Martin**
5. Hero-**Belafonte, Harry**
6. Hero-**Brazile, Donna**
7. Hero-**Carver, George Washington**
8. Hero-**Chaney, James Earl**
9. Hero-**Chavez, Cesar**
10. Hero-**Clark, Dick**
11. Hero-**Collins, Addie Mae**
12. Hero-**Cosby, Bill**
13. Hero-**Davis, Angela Y.**
14. Hero-**Defrancesco-Soto, Victoria**
15. Hero-**Douglass, Fredrick**
16. Hero-**Elliott, Jane**
17. Hero-**Evers, Medgar**
18. Hero-**Goodman, Andrew**
19. Hero-**Hall, Tamron**
20. Hero-**Harris-Perry, Melissa**
21. Hero-**Hayes, Chris**
22. Hero-**Hechler, Kenneth William**
23. Hero-**Height, Dorothy**
24. Hero-**Holder, Eric**
25. Hero-**Jackson, Jesse**
26. Hero-**Jolie, Angelina**
27. Hero-**Jordan, Senator Barbara**
28. Hero-**Kennedy, Bobby**
29. Hero-**Kennedy, John Fitzgerald**
30. Hero-**Kennedy, Ted**
31. Hero-**King, Jr., Martin L**
32. Hero-**Kornacki, Steve**
33. Hero-**Lee, Spike**
34. Hero-**Lewis, John Robert**
35. Hero-**Lincoln, Abraham**
36. Hero-**Maddow, Rachel Anne**
37. Hero-**Maher, Jr. William "Bill"**
38. Hero-**Mandela, Nelson Rolihlahia**
39. Hero-**Marshall, Thurgood**
40. Hero-**Mathews, Chris**
41. Hero-**McNair, Carol Denise**
42. Hero-**Miller, Doris**
43. Hero-**Newton, Huey Percy**
44. Hero-**Obama, II President Barack Hussein**
45. Hero-**O'Donnell, Lawrence**
46. Hero-**Parks, Rosa Louise McCauley**
47. Hero-**Powell, Adam Clayton**
48. Hero-**Powell, Colin**
49. Hero-**Powers, Mary Alice Carroll**
50. Hero-**Powers, Juana "Melinda" Altar**
51. Hero-**Robertson, Carole**
52. Hero-**Robinson, Amelia Boynton**
53. Hero-**Robinson, Jackie**
54. Hero-**Rodriguez, SgtMaj. Joe A.**
55. Hero-**Roosevelt, Anna Eleanor**
56. Hero-**Sarandon, Susan**
57. Hero-**Schultz, Ed**
58. Hero-**Schwerner, Michael**
59. Hero-**Sharpton, Al**
60. Hero-**Till, Emmett**
61. Hero-**Toure'**
62. Hero-**Truth, Sojourner**
63. Hero-**Tubman, Harriet**
64. Hero-**Wagner, Alex**
65. Hero-**Walkowiak, Linda K.**
66. Hero-**Washington, Booker Taliaferro**
67. Hero-**Wells-Barnett, Ida Bell**
68. Hero-**Wesley, Cynthia**
69. Hero-**Wilberforce, William**
70. Hero-**X, Malcolm**

My Difference Makers, Movers and Shakers & Unsung Heroes List   I

1. #   2. #   3.*   4. *   5. *

6. *   7.*   8. *   9. *   10. *

11. *   12. *   13.#   14. *   15. @

16. *   17. *   18. *   19. *   20.*

1.   Hero-**Ali, Muhammad** - *Born Cassius Marcellus Clay, Jr. World Heavy Weight Champion Boxer.*   **2.**   Hero-**Angelou, Maya** - Born Marguerite Ann Johnson. an American Author and Poet.   **3.**   Hero-**Ball, Krystal** - Born Krystal Marie Ball, MSNBC Co-Host of, " The Cycle."   **4.**   Hero-**Bashir, Martin** - MSNBC Host of a political opinion show named "Martin Bashir."   **5.**   Hero-**Belafonte, Harry** - An American Singer, Songwriter, Actor and Civil Rights Activist.
6.   Hero-**Brazile, Donna** -Author, Academic, and Political Analyst. Vice Chairwoman of the Democratic National Committee.   **7.**   Hero-**Carver, George Washington** American Scientist, Botanist, Educator/ Inventor. Allegedly castrated by his White Master.   **8.**   Hero-**Chaney, James Earl** - Murdered Freedom Rider near Philadelphia, Mississippi June 21, 1964 by the KKK.   **9.**   Hero-**Chavez, Cesar** - Mexican-American Farm Worker, Labor Leader and Civil Rights Activist. **10.** Hero-**Clark, Dick** - Born Richard Augustus Wagstaff Clark, Jr., radio and television personality, "American Bandstand Host."   **11.** Hero-**Collins, Addie Mae**- Born April 18, 1949 died in the 16th Street Baptist Church bombing, on September 15, 1963.   **12.** Hero-**Cosby, Bill**- Born William Henry Cosby, Jr. American comedian, actor, author TV producer, educator, musician & Activist.   **13.** Hero-**Davis, Angela Y.** - American Political Activist, Scholar, Author & once on the FBI's Ten Most Wanted Fugitive List.   **14.** Hero-**Defrancesco-Soto, Victoria** - Doctor, MSNBC Contributor & Political Analyst.   **15.** Hero-**Douglass, Fredrick** - Born Frederick Augustus Washington Bailey, American Social Reformer, Orator, Writer & Activist.   **16.** Hero-**Elliott, Jane** - Educator, Author of the infamous   "Blue-eyed / Brown-eyed Exercise."   **17.** Hero-**Evers, Medgar** - Murdered Civil Rights Activist in Jackson, Mississippi, June 12, 1963 by the KKK.   **18.** Hero- **Goodman, Andrew** - Murdered Freedom Rider near Philadelphia, Mississippi June 21, 1964 by the KKK.   **19.** Hero-**Hall, Tamron** - MSNBC Host of, " News Nation with Tamron Hall."   **20.** Hero-**Harris-Perry, Melissa** - Born Melissa Victoria Harris, MSNBC Host of, " Melissa Harris-Perry Weekend News."

Also Heroes are the 26 victims of Newtown, Connecticut, whose lives were stolen on Friday, December 14, 2012 and Trayvon Martin who was gun down February 26, 2012, only guilty of "walking while Black."
* Artistry by Arnold P. Powers   # Artistry by Arnold P. Powers, Jr.   @ Artistry by Newspaper articles or photos

My Difference Makers Movers and Shakers & Unsung Heroes List II

21. *   22. *   23. *   24. *   25. *

26. *   27. *   28 .*   29.. *   30. *

31.*   32. *   33. *   34. *   35.@

36. #   37. *   38. #   39.*   40. *

21. Hero-**Hayes, Chris** - Born Christopher L. Hayes, MSNBC Host of, "All In with Chris Hayes." **22.** Hero-**Hechler, Kenneth William** - Born 1914, the Only Congressman in 1965 to walk with MLK at Selma, Ala. (Democrat, W. Va. 1959-1977) **23.** Hero-**Height, Dorothy** - Educator, Civil Rights Activist, African-American Rights Activist & Family Reunion Activist. **24.** Hero-**Holder, Eric** , 82nd & 1st African-American Attorney General of the U.S. (2009-2016) **25.** Hero-**Jackson, Jesse** - Born Jesse Louis Burns-A Baptist Minister, Civil Rights Activist, Founder of Rainbow / PUSH. **26.** Hero-**Jolie, Angelina** - Born Angelina Jolie Voight-Actress, film Director, Screenwriter and Humanitarian **27.** Hero-**Jordan, Senator Barbara Charline**-My Congresswoman in 1970-1st Afro-American elected to Texas Senate (1967-1973), & US House of Rep. (1973-1979). **28.** Hero-**Kennedy, Bobby** - Born Robert Francis Kennedy-Senator-Assassinated in 1968-Humanitarian, 64th Attorney General 1961-1964. **29.** Hero-**Kennedy, John Fitzgerald** - 35th President of the US - Assassinated in Dallas on November 22, 1963 - Beloved by All. **30.** Hero-**Kennedy, Ted** - Born Edward Moore Kennedy, Senator of Massachusetts for 49 yrs (1962 - 2009). Backed Barack Obama for President **31.** Hero-**King, Jr., Martin Luther** -Born Michael Luther, A Baptist Minister., Civil Rights Activists, Assassinate in Memphis, April 4, 1968. **32.** Hero-**Kornacki, Steve** - Born Stephan Joseph Ko rnacki, Jr., MSNBC Host of, " Up With Steve Kornacki." **33.** Hero-**Lee, Spike** -Born Shelton Jackson Lee- Film Director, Producer, writer & Actor. Heads his own Production Co. named 40 Acres & A Mule Filmworks. **34.** Hero-**Lewis, John Robert**- Senator D-GA (1987 - Present), Civil Rights Leader, Survivor "Bloody Sunday" 1965 Selma to Montgomery march. **35.** Hero-**Lincoln, Abraham** - (1861 - 1865) 16th President of the United States and Emancipator. **36.** Hero-**Maddow, Rachel Anne** - MSNBC Host of, " The Rachel Maddow Show." **37.** Hero-**Maher, Jr. William "Bill"**- Comedian, Political Commentator ,donated 1 million dollars to President Obama's Campaign. **38.** Hero-**Mandela, Nelson Rolihlahia** - 1st African President of South Africa, Civil Rights Activist, Forgiveness Champion. **39.** Hero-**Marshall, Thurgood** - First African-American Justice. Argued victoriously Brown v. Board of Education, (Supreme Court 1967 - 1991). **40.** Hero-**Mathews, Chris** - Born Christopher John Matthews, MSNBC Host of Hardball with Chris Matthews.

* Artistry by Arnold P. Powers   **# Artistry by Arnold P. Powers, Jr.**   **@ Artistry by Newspaper article or photo**

My Difference Makers Movers and Shakers & Unsung Heroes List III

41. *   42*   43. *   44. *   45. *

46*   47. *   48. *   49. #   50. @

51. *   52. @   53. *   54. *   55. *

56. *   57. *   58. *   59. #   60. #

41. Hero-**McNair, Carol Denise**-Born Nov 17, 1951 died in the 16th Street Baptist Church booming, September 15, 1963. **42.** Hero-**Miller, Doris** - 1st African-American to receive the Navy Cross for an Heroic act at The Pearl Harbor Attack, December, .1941. **43.** Hero-**Newton, Huey Percy** - Civil, Political & Urban Rights Activists, co-founder of the Black Panther Party in 1966. **44.** Hero-**Obama, II President Barack Hussein** - 44th President of the United States & 1st African-American President (2008-2016). **45.** Hero-**O'Donnell, Lawrence** - Born Lawrence Francis O'Donnell, Jr., MSNBC Host of The Last Word with Lawrence O'Donnell **46.** Hero-**Parks, Rosa Louise McCauley** - Civil Rights Activists, "First Lady of Civil Rights." **47.** Hero-**Powell, Adam Clayton**- First African-American Politian to be elected to Congress from New York (Harlem 1945-1971). **48.** Hero-**Powell, Colin**- Born Colin Luther Powell-First African-American & 65th Secretary of State (2001-2005) . **49.** Hero-**Powers, Mary Alice Carroll**, My Mother, Educator, my biggest motivator and supporter. **50.** Hero-**Powers, Juana "Melinda" Altar**- My only Wife who was a faithful, beautiful companion and Mother. **51.** Hero-**Robertson, Carole**-born April 24, 1949 died in the 16th Street Baptist Church booming, on September 15, 1963. **52.** Hero-**Robinson, Amelia Boynton** - 101 yr old Civil rights Activist and "Bloody Sunday Survivor in 1965." 1st female from Ala to run for Congress. **53.** Hero-**Robinson, Jackie** - Born Jack Roosevelt Robinson, Broke the color barrier in MLB, Activist for Racial Justice. **54.** Hero-**Rodriguez, SgtMaj. Joe A.** - One of my oldest friends & Best SgtMaj in USMC during my tenure. Saved my mil career. **55.** Hero-**Roosevelt, Anna Eleanor** - First Lady from 1933-1945, Human Rights Activists, Champion for Justice. **56.** Hero-**Sarandon, Susan** - Born Susan Abigail Tomalin- Actress, Social and Political Activist. **57.** Hero-**Schultz, Ed** - Born Edward Andrew Schultz, MSNBC Host of, " The Ed Show." **58.** Hero-**Schwerner, Michael** - Murdered Freedom Rider near Philadelphia, Mississippi 1964 by KKK **59.** Hero-**Sharpton, Al** - Born Alfred Charles, Jr. MSNBC Host of Politics Nation, Baptist Minister, Civil Rights Activists. **60.** Hero-**Till, Emmett** - KKK murdered this 14 year old Chicagoan youth for whistling at a White woman, August 28, 1955.

* Artistry by Arnold P. Powers   # Artistry by Arnold P. Powers, Jr.   @ Artistry by Newspaper article or photo

My Difference Makers Movers and Shakers & Unsung Heroes List IV

61.*   62. *   63. *   64. *   65. *

66. @   67. @   68. *   69. *   70. #

61. Hero-**Toure'** - Host of The Cycle, Born Toure' Neblett, Novelist, music journalist, Member of Rock & Roll Nominating Comm. **62.** Hero-**Truth, Sojourner** - Born Isabella Baumfree, Abolitionist & Women's Rights Activists and Famous *"Ain't I a Woman?"* speech. **63.** Hero-**Tubman, Harriet** - Born Araminta Harriet Ross, Abolitionist, Humanitarian, Union Spy, Underground Railroad founder. **64.** Hero-**Wagner, Alex** - Born Alexandra Swe Wagner, MSNBC Host of, " NOW with Alex Wagner." **65.** Hero-**Walkowiak, Linda K.** - My Therapist, Brought me back from the brink of despair. **66.** Hero-**Washington, Booker Taliaferro**, Educator, Author, Orator, Advisor to Republican Presidents, Founder- Tuskegee Univ. **67.** Hero-**Wells-Barnett, Ida Bell** - American Journalist, Newspaper Editor, Suffragist, Civil Rights Activist, Anti-Lynching Crusader. **68.** Hero-**Wesley, Cynthia**-Born April 30, 1949 died in the 16th Street Baptist Church booming, on September 15, 1963. **69.** Hero-**Wilberforce, William**-English Politician-Headed the Parliamentary Campaign that passed the Slave Trade Act of 1807. **70.** Hero-**X, Malcolm,** Born Malcolm Little, AKA El-HajjMalik El-Shabazz. Assassinated on February 21, 1965, Muslin Minister of Black Supre.

* Artistry by Arnold P. Powers   **# Artistry by Arnold P. Powers, Jr.**   **@ Artistry by Newspaper article or photo**

Excuse me If we don't apologize

Excuse me if we don't apologize,
Ye thieves of forced family good-byes;
In retrospect that opened thine-eyes;
To all the atrocities you've tried to hide.

Yet to say the suffrage was justified;
And "mea culpa," Not thy!
Stolen from our native land and expecting us to be obliged,
Without cause, take us across the ocean and call it a ride,
And for your profits, while millions of souls died.
Woe, and you wish not to be reminded or openly criticized,
But you gladly took the wealth and all that it implied.
Yet, we're expected to be happy as a watermelon high.

This something, you tell the world thru innocent cries,
Suggesting you did us a favor and we'd be lost without your guides,
Unlike the ostrich, our heads are not buried, no we will not hide,
Degrade our women and say they're not icandy for your eyes,
Yet Beauties of Michelle Obama and Tamron Hall, that can't be denied,

Awaken from years of oppression, education and no liberty supplied,
Lynched, burned and beaten, all in an effort to take away our pride.
Ye fools, God gave these Black Souls a strong will to survive,
Be gone you nothings and no one can ever put that aside.
Kept us down with laws, and voter suppressions, Nye, Nye, Nye!

O' yea O' yea, we're the apple of our fathers eyes,
Strong, soulful, can't hold us back but God knows you've tried.
Assassinate our Leaders, burn our churches as history has surmised,
But we're still here, struggling, but we won't compromise or apologize.

We've got a second term Black President, Koch bros ain't you surprised
Yeah, we can tell how much you tried to marginalize and scrutinize;
No we're not shy, for we know who lives beyond the skies,
Our Father in heaven, and that's no tale of lies,
No we ain't ashamed, and will not apologize,
We're precisely, and wondrously made and children of the
most high,

Carroll / Melton Family Reunion
Houston, Texas
August 15-17, 2008

Carroll / Melton Family Reunion
Tuskegee, Alabama
July 15-18, 2010

Introduction

Short Stories contained in this book are a combination of survival, triumph and defeat of African-American and White-American movers and shakers that have made a difference for the betterment of America. As the importance of their stories pictured amongst these pages will forever remind us of their heroism and their lives. The mere existence of these tales are equally unforgettable. But because of it, today's America has been reborn. For this project was more important because of the everlasting memory of purposely hidden written facts, illustrations and photographs for our understanding of how this country was formed. What sights must have graced their eyes in the recordation of this history. Noticeably, some of the stories, pictures and illustrations appearing on these pages, one might, find objectionable, due to the graphic nature of its content. But, to uncover and review these stories; of which little has previously been reported since its occurrence, compelled me to dust off the time of obscurity for the reviling of these unwarranted atrocities. Stories, viewed faithfully without the absence of blind truth, opened mine eyes for a more appreciation for how far we have come as a people. Word usages of *"Negro," "Nigger"* and *"Colored,"* were used in the content of these pages as a measure of the limited dialog of that period in describing African-Americans and not for glorification of the past. Its purpose moreover, is not to offend anyone or make any suggestion that these are politically correct word usages today. Rather, a commonality of degrading rhetoric used to further the worthlessness of a people and keep the oppressed in their so called, *"place,"* are not acceptable by today's standards.

"The Appeal," of June 3, 1899

American exceptionalism seems to have gotten lost in the translation towards all Americans as Plutocrats attempt to manipulate and whitewash the country to further the big divide between the demographics. Because of the tales of how a right-winged fanatical element of America, set out on disenfranchising African-Americans from any advancement opportunities or successes, is a prominence in today's headlines. The subject of race odious in today's climate is an issue that has almost removed itself from our defining vocabulary until an honest and genuine American of bi-racial descent was elected President. The commonsensical approach to race tolerance is a factor in bettering America's greatness, but how much is fear apart of it? Radical conservative right winged element of today, like the, *"Tea Party,"* a **"Loud-mouth,"** radio talk-show host, named Rush Limbaugh, a trio of **"racist,"** Billionaires named Karl Rove and the Koch Brothers (*David H. & Charles G. Koch*), an **"ill-informed,"** Millionaire named Donald Trump, a Pulitzer Prize-winner named George Frederick Will, a former **"Disgraced, thrice adulteress,"** *X*-Speaker of the House named Newt Gingrich, a sitting Senator who was apart of a like group who set out on making President Obama a, *"one term President,"* named Mitch McConnell and a **"Disgraced,"** political surrogate named John Henry Sununu are examples of this element by virtue of their, *"talking points"* and spoken *"dog whistles."* How this fear factor has poisoned our ability to just get alone is no secret. But some of the stories contained in this book displays how whites and blacks working together over a 100 years ago in concert for a better America. To combat such stories are virtually unknown, appear now in these chapters to reveal how America has changed. Many of whom gave their lives to ensure proper justice was served, so we would not be denied our fundamental rights to Life, Liberty and the Pursuit of Happiness. A nation so conceived in its liberty would be so hypocritical as to deny anyone the same is the creation of the essence of right wing rhetoric and hate both then and now. But it's

"Semi-weekly Interior Journal," Mar 10, 1903

a debt of unjustness will never be repaid for the many souls who sacrificed all with their lives. A system dominated by people who deem themselves as judges despite so much opposition toward the success of us as a people; how did so many of our forefathers do it, the humblest of Americans? I recalled living in Hawaii where a local band had recorded a song called, *"I'm in love with the local boys."* This set off a fire storm among the whites, which were a minority in Hawaii at the time. But the white's so out raged by the song, requested local radio stations not to air the song. The local group was appalled at the reaction expressed by whites; they, the local band, being proud of their island heritage; was unconscionable for whites who had rejected others far too long now find themselves rejected for love of local boys. But, in recalling the incident, it wasn't the song title that upset the whites, rather it was but one verse that went like this, *"Blonde hair and blue eyes don't thrill me, because I'm in love with the local boys."* It was as if the locals had insulted the gods of Anglo-purity. Amazing considering the shoe being placed on the other foot and how the need to be love and accepted effects everyone; as in the case of the Jane Elliott's experiment contained among these chapters.

The significance of written articles such as the one to the left and cartoon illustrations shown on many pages throughout the body of the book is to further illustrate the perception of negativity endured constantly by people of color. Each illustration displays the Negro in either some type of servitude or with the exaggerated feet sizes, big crusty white-lip sizes, to the darkest of midnight black of faces appeared in almost every newspaper in America for many years. An example of the constant stains of racism that has mock this nation and restrict its prosperity for some. These cartoons would also convey the Negro either in some type of mischief or just looking like an idiot with unfashionable clown-like clothing or appearing lazy. No matter what the African-Americans did during our struggles, there was always a constant reminder of put-downs and derogatory poisonous element of hate nearby. Whatever become of evildoers in my opinion, with respect to the evils they commit without punishment? A theorizes synopsis of the opinion that life has a pattern of balances that allows for *"payback,"* even when justice appear to be invisible. Life's biblical principals are where this theory of payback and balance derives from; Galatians 6:7 which simple reads, **"Be not deceived; God is not mocked: for whatsoever a man soweth, that shall he also reap."** A pattern that is guaranteed, according to the principals of God's law. There is also another pattern, sometimes called history repeating itself; if the lessons were not learned or history is not properly recorded, it will repeat itself. Or, unexplainable patterns such as, the four Presidents of these United States assassins chosen dates to commit their crimes. Abraham Lincoln (*16th President*), James A. Garfield (*20th President*) William McKinley (*25th President*) and John F. Kennedy (*35th President*), all have patterns of commonalities other than being POTUS. However, there were more attempts made unsuccessfully that far exceeds the successful occurrences. But of the four white men assassins, three of the four killers committed their evils on a Friday. Lincoln's killer, John Wilkes Booth committed his act on Good Friday, April 14, 1865. Garfield's killer, Charles J. Guiteau committed his act on Saturday, July 2, 1881, McKinley's killer, Leon Czolgosz committed his act on Friday September 6, 1901 and Kennedy's alleged killer, Lee Harvey Oswald, (*if you believe that lie*), committed his act on a Friday, November 22, 1963. So whether it is a pattern of God's law as clocks repeating time every 12 hours, change and balance will apply. African-America history from 200 years ago until today, the measure of racial prejudice has moved about an inch. The only change is the renaming or characterization of institutionalized racism which is and will always be an element of this country's history. But, for anyone or any nation, to underestimate the spirit of an oppressed people or the heart of their hopefulness, will be done at that person and or nation's own peril. And it should be noted that evil or any and everything we do in this life, repeatable or not, these evil circumstances have payback consequences. To the least of these evils to the most macabre, what goes around will come back around, *"Karma."* The hunter being captured by the game! But not in an evil turnaround, because evil doesn't correct evil. Only good can correct evil and justice for all only applies to whom all can afford it. And the moral compass of doing what is right and what is done to the least of these.... So if a break-through of accomplishments is preceded by the word *"first,"* then karma has entered the picture. The University I attended, Prairie View A&M, had the dubious distension of having an 80 football game consecutive losing streak from 1989-1998. But in 2009, they won the Black College National Championship, *"karma."* But, we people of color love America, even though at times she didn't love us back. Our home is our home; otherwise we'd be making an exit in haste to leave her. To the millions of Americans whose suffrage was as great as our own, is the reason for our love for America, despite a small minority group who set out on preventing the inedibility of nation pride. We are a hopeful people, Diasporas, re-rooted in the fabric of America, mindful of our ancestral pass, yet loss of nostalgia will not bear witness to our displacement. We too, now here, carry the pride and love for a country we all share, regardless of color or gender, as home. Tom Brokaw made a statement on, *"Meet The Press,"* one fall Sunday morning, *"This is the Century for Women."* A bold yet accurate statement on September 2, 2012, in

which only time will have more merit to that statement than those mere words can suggest. To the upper left is a somewhat unknown but very outspoken component of labor unfairness named Mary Harris Jones aka *"Mother Jones."* She, being obscure and not nationally known was a loud voice heard by many whose interest she advocated. Mother Jones, after losing all her children and husband to yellow fever, became quite vocal in her latter years. Like Mother Jones, *"Aunt Rachel,"* aka Mrs. Rachel L. Harris was virtually unknown, but she was an Army Nurse during the Civil War and responsible

"Mother Jones, aka Mary Jones"
"The Courier," of October 6, 1900

Mrs. Rachel L. Harris aka, "Aunt Rachel"
"The San Francisco Call," of August 16, 1903

for saving many lives. Without nursing training, Aunt Rachel, got involved after her husband as a member of the 12th Illinois Infantry was nursed back to health by his wife, Aunt Rachel. Women all over the world have been denied their rightful placement. In the history of the Supreme Court, there have been only four female Judges appointed in its 224 (1789) year history. The first appointee was Justice Sandra Day O'Connor, (1981-2006) appointed by President Reagan, a Republican. Justice Ruth Bader Ginsburg (1993), became the second, appointed by President Clinton, a Democrat and two more female Supreme Court Justices have been appointed within the last four years by President Obama, a Democrat. Their names are Justices Sonia Sotomayor, (2009) who became the first Hispanic male or female to be appointed and Justice Elena Kegan (2010). And just as the ceil was broken on the Supreme Court selections, likewise will the glass ceiling controlled by white men in

American Presidential politics will be broken come 2016. And let us not forget the double standards and the victimization women face. Case and point; who can forget the **Recy Taylor** incident, where a 24 year old married black woman, employed as a sharecropper in Abbeville, Alabama was gang raped in 1944. The incident occurred while Recy and two others were leaving church services walking along a dirt road. Six white men were never brought to justice for the crime. And the Sheriff of the town stated to Recy's husband, *"Nigger, ain't $600.00 worth it for the rape of yo wife?"* An offer made by the six rapist (*$100.00 each rapist proposed*) to the Taylor family to prevent a high profile trial. But an all white male jury in 5 minutes of deliberation, dismissed the case. The driver of the vehicle, identified by a witness who was with Recy, was fined only $250.00. The driver admitted to the rape and named the others involved. So, the journey for women, and in particularly women of color has been as horrific a journey as what the entire black race has endured.

So it is conceivable that, both parties in 2016 could have females as their representative for the presidency post of the United States. Everyone concluding that Hillary Clinton will be the presumptive Democratic nominee. I think not, but someone like a brilliant Elizabeth Warren who became the first female Senator from Massachusetts or equally bright and well informed is a Rachel Maddow, who host her own show (*TRMS*) MSNBC. Better yet, Tamron Hall by virtue of her beauty along as well as the other two could become the first female President of the United States in 2016. And to use beauty as a measure of characterizing a female's qualification to the highest job in the land is not, in my humble opinion, a chauvinist method of defining females as my Christian faith guides me per Proverb 11:17. Complimentary only without sexism or animalism brio. There's nothing more pleasing to a man's eye as a beautiful woman. But back to Hillary, it is not to suggest that she is not beloved by us all, worldwide other factors will control her decisions. One, I just don't believe she'd want the job at 69 years of age and considering the level of her involvement or noninvolvement in the Benghazi saga in 2016. So, with the cycle of God's balancing law system that includes the progression of women is imminent. Women have played a major role in shaping world affairs and not only in this country for which they should receive their just due. It's only fair that their time has also come. They and we will not be denied or devoured.

More evident of this upward female mobility can also be viewed through a mythical legend of Santa's flying Reindeers. Since the male reindeer losses their antlers by December while the females maintain theirs, adds a little irony to the female contributions that alludes historical memory, suggesting that all of Santa's reindeers were female. But more realistically, the 2012 Olympics, where America sent 530 athletes to the London Summer Games, a total of 46 Gold medals were awarded to American athletics of which 29 were women and only 17 were men. A total of 29 Silver medals were awarded, 15 to men and 14 to women. There were 29 Bronze medals awarded, 13 to men and 15 to women. And for the first time in American Olympics participation history, the 2012 London games, our nation sent more women than men, 530 total athletes, 261 men and 269 women. The trend of change and pattern of balance for the betterment of America and the world, contributes to God's plan for balance. Look at the 2012 historical female election where a record of 20 females are now Congressional Senators. And the inevitability of efforts to hold one back, depravity will always be weaken by time. Injustice will soon give way to tolerance, respect and love and the recordation of hidden shameful pass will no more show itself. And let us not forget

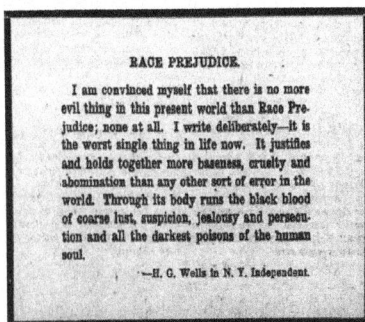

RACE PREJUDICE.

I am convinced myself that there is no more evil thing in this present world than Race Prejudice; none at all. I write deliberately—it is the worst single thing in life now. It justifies and holds together more baseness, cruelty and abomination than any other sort of error in the world. Through its body runs the black blood of coarse lust, suspicion, jealousy and persecution and all the darkest poisons of the human soul.

—H. G. Wells in N. Y. Independent.

"The Appeal," of May 2, 1914

"Lady Liberty," the statue of Liberty, where a broken chain lies at her feet indicative of what women as well as

other demographics are freed as a result of time. In contrast, and despite all that has been done to devour us as a people from this nations' enriched history, we're still here. Not all good though, when we are about 12% of this nations population yet we out populate every race in prison population. Even though a lot of the incarcerations are unfair and unjust would lessen the total but not enough to change the percentage. Where blacks are given the opportunity to participate in athletics, we far out perform all races. The NFL once boasts about 85% white participation, now approximately 65% are black participants. The NBA boosts a 79% black roster participation now as the overwhelming evidence of black participation dominance. So in step with God's balancing plan for life and everything it entails, the cohabitation of the races is a must despite the much opposition to the contrary. And to fight against the inevitability of race and gender fairness will ultimately lead to a dismal finish. The demographic of America is changing, until angry white men can get pass their own devour at all cost persona, they'll be left behind as we become more diverse. Case and point, President Barack Obama was reelected President of the United States on Nov 6, 2012 while his challenger, Willard Mitt Romney received 80% of the white vote and lost. President Obama received 93% of the African-American vote, 71% of the Hispanic vote and 73% of the Asian-American vote and less than 30% of the white vote and a resounding victory. He also won the popular vote while receiving 332 Electoral Votes to Mitt Romney's 206 Electoral votes. African Americans represent about 12% of a white dominate country.... Same could be said of then President Bush and Vice President Dick Chaney at the beginning of the Iraq war, their war. Remembering, based on the predication that Iraq had *"WMD's"* (W*eapons of Mass Destruction*)." Only to determine later, he didn't, only because no weapons were **found**. Didn't Saddam Hussein have two years to hide or send these weapons to Syria or some other Middle Eastern country, since he would not allow inspectors to enter his country? If you have nothing to hide, why not allow inspectors to enter. Rather than delay the inevitable and be labeled as a non-compliant country, or was this revenge or greed about interest of profitability for Halliburton Corporation of which Dick Chaney was a board member, supposedly. Or, was this a revenge factor for Saddam Hussein's role in the supposed assassination attempt on daddy Bush? But things that appear so obvious in appearance don't necessarily rain truth when realized. And hence, everyone tends to blame President Bush and his administration for the supposed lie on the WMD, but was it lie? Or, was this karma and balance for stealing the election from Al Gore in 2000 to add insult to injury. And not to exclude the Katherine Harris significant influence and involvement in its outcome, assuring a Bush victory as a major conflict unrealized. And 911 prior knowledge theory by the Bush Administration? We won't go there, but time will always reveal truth as truth will always prevail in time.

So what do the following *"haters, or dream killers,"* mentioned at the beginning of this introduction all have in common with hate being the rudiment of commonality? *"Donald Trump born 1946 (67), "Newt" Gingrich (Newton Leroy McPherson) born 1943 (70), Charles G. Koch born 1935 (78), David H. Koch born 1940 (73), Rush Limbaugh born 1951 (62), John Henry Sununu born 1939 (74) Mitch McConnell born 1942 (71) Karl Rove born 1950 (63) and George Frederick Will born 1941 (72),"* all are angry white men over the age of 60. These individuals observing their America that once favored their demographic now changing in favor of the very ones they stepped on in their route to the top. But the 2012 Presidential election changed all the hate as it represented the demographic change of a nation whose time for change has finally come. The balance of change yet again giving way to time. But this element of hate that has dringest our country must rid itself from its atmosphere. Statements of *"Taking our Country back, or One Term President,"* are not elements of a united body of people; mainly because the demographic change in numbers helps dilute the majority grip on hate.

But these pages will reveal some rather unknown & known factors of hopefulness; will of a people; movers and shakers who persevered to cercumvent the devouring of African-Americans. So, can sorrow be measured? Can hate be generational? Is forgiveness hereditary? But don't get it twisted; this is not a book of African-American victimization or victimology. Rather it's a theme acknowledgement of a *"Paradigm Shift,"* of all whom endured these atrocities that must be given omen for their sacrifice. Unlike the 1849 book by Charless Carroll, who wrote, *"The Negro a Beast" or "In the Image of God,"* that tries unsuccessfully to tie bibical responsibility to the creation of the Negro as a beast and less than the white man. As to give some authority to suggest even God hates them, adds in that period a sort of superiority that is undeniable. So the devaluing proceess has been a point of focus for as long as man could read. So putting in focus the devalued life's African-Americans faced and the process that would impede its repeat. And yes the Bible is a good source of fair accessment if read without biases. But, if we expect people to view us as people based on what they have seen, observed or been taught of us to change; should not we as a people share some responsibility in that characterization? A resounding No! It is my belief that an entire race of people should not be judged on a negative characterization of a minority number within that race, rather, each person should be devalued on the merit of their individual character. Unlike a Larry Elder, who is black, makes a statement of Jesse Jackson, Al Sharpton and Louis Farrakhan, commonality other than their blackness is their screams of racism; racism in describing what's wrong with Black America. He concludes his remarks with *"racism,"* in their minds is a result of being raised in a household without the presence of their own fathers. A major factor, in the opinion of Mr. Elder in his own surmise of what's really wrong with Black America, or more specifically, black males in America. Also, try the likes of a Dr, Thomas Sowell or Justice Clarence Thomas, both of whom are black, but share a very negative view of educational opportunities like *"Affirmative Action,"* just because it supposedly didn't aid them in their success. Then why are so many *"uppity blacks,"* whose very existence directly or indirectly are examples of the very fruits of such actions, failed to acknowledge its importance to their success. That's like a CEO saying, *"I built this company all by myself with no help from anybody or any source."* And of course, *"they didn't build that!"* not all by themselves anyways.

This is what I mean by, *"getting it twisted."* Surprisingly, among our so-called smartest African-Americans in their characterization of what's wrong with the state of Black America are more self-critical rather than offering a vision of hope. And just like the Republicans wanting a smaller government with little or no entitlements, yet refuses to raise the, *"minimum wages,"* which would allow the poor to release themselves from the dependency of these programs, but then there would be no justification to criticize the poor. So then comes some prominent figures in the African-American community as Harvard graduate Dr. Cornel West, who states, *"President Obama is a white man with black skin"* & *"America has been niggerized."* Let us also not forget the once 2012 Republican Candidate Campaign front leader, Herman Cain, who stated, *"If you're black and poor, blame nobody but yourself."* And once first African-America Mayor of a southern city, Andrew Young, lost in their criticism of blackness with comments like, *"Bill Clinton is every bit as black as Barack Obama and he's probably gone with more black women than Barack."* And this was somehow an effort of trying to show that the President didn't have enough *"dogg"* in him to be labeled black? And further denied the blackness of President Obama as not bearing the heritage of slave ancestries also disqualifies him of his blackness? Have we not as a people slept long enough in the darkest of self-criticism and hate. So hasn't the light of love placed the light of justice within our vision long enough for us to have clear vision? Then hate, seems to be the center piece of parallels linking us together to those that hate us. This division in the face of others should be removed from our visionary destiny as a people. As serious as a Chaplain Barry Black's prayer, living by the sword, in this case hate; will invariably causes one to perish by it and become defeated by its commonality with its emergence. *"Is the silence of Justice on wordless paper the fault of the author if the thought doesn't agree with ours? Or does the reader bear some responsibility in promoting the volume of Justice for righteousness if the subject matter is really bias. So then, who better knows of us as a people for the sake of Justice or can true Justice be felt by one it doesn't touch? If not us, in recognizing this injustice, then who?"* SPEAK UP!

Table Of Content

Chapter I... 1
Short Stories of all our struggles, triumphs, defeats and successes for we people of color that has shaped this nation.

Chapter II 223
Stories of my family's contributions in shaping this nation.

Chapter III 250
Stories of my life.

Chapter IV 277
Index

C hapter I

"Our mostly forgotten short stories as a people"

"The Republic" of, September 13, 1903

"We The People" Who determines who *"We"* are?

If *"We,"* as describe by the Constitution are for all Americans, as the forefathers intended, then why the initial exclusion of the African's who were slaves born in America. The intent of dismissing the American born African descendants was a nothing short of a selfish act. But, "We," too **are** Americans, and more specifically African-Americans. So Americans who have Biblical principals, *"Karma,"* as the biblical explanation states, *"Whatsoever a man soweth, that shall he also reap."* Then denial of American citizenship solely because of race rather than birth origin is not constitutional but biblical denial. But, life has a principal karmic balancing sheet that knows no boundaries as time is the enemy of age. Constant evolvements and changes of what was first is now last, adds more prudence to that theory. Hope is another commonality, oppressed people can look forward to as a measure of promise; *"that this too shall pass."* As if a continuing trial case, the inevitability of opposite changes is assured. When the principals of law and the value of moral law so inexpliticitly destroys the spirit of all what's right, then assuredly, *"karma"* is almost guaranteed. America, in part, in its attempt to bury its horrific pass, yet again will the balances of morale law reveal with inevitability of what goes around comes around. Ask many Americans who are not apart of the group of Americans that can not enjoy the amber waves of grain, might object the primmest of acknowledging any truth to the theory of maltreatment of any citizen is nothing but Justice realized. Rather, the shift of position to justifying any action directed at another as merely following the laws of righteousness for the lawlessness is a weak defense. Yet the morale argument of justice for all is for the most part a feared position for America. For your sins will always return to you to collect! A biblical principal.

"Los Angeles Herald," of January 17, 1909

A self proclaimed nation of non-barbaric citizens at times will allow the arrogant nature of its too many secrecy to cloud the history of recordings. But the deniability of recorded facts without accepting responsibility of its pass with acts of silence applicable to their own principals; points the finger at the oppressed as a common practice enjoyed by the blameless. But the balances of life for righteousness has one, and only one path. Where the path to corruption has many paths with many more complications and most likely to be traveled by many. Why is that? Is it because of less guilt in the eyes of the doer, assuming he's in the right simply because he has the power. Genuinely, the feeling of right in ones head, caught up in the moment, while the heart constantly reminds each of us of how wrong, subconsciously, we really are as reality sets in. So, people, for better or worse know right from wrong. And it's that ambivalent sense of human-like behavior, unlike the animal kingdom that just instinctively knows when the path of righteousness is not taken. Ironically, there are times when animals act more like human-beings should act with all the intellect we possess over the animal kingdom. The statement suggesting us, being our brother's keeper's, almost seems like a metaphor. Yet knowledge, seemingly is considered to be the root of our prosperity and power, in most cases is not the definitive answer, or is it? Or is it the root of destruction that the power of knowledge brings? For invariably, the more a human-being knows, or thinks he or she knows, makes them wiser or egotistical to the point of thinking they've never been or will be wrong on anything. Timing, one would also argue, the success factor or a component of the

1

Devour Us Not

success factor as opportunity being a source of timing regardless of kill set, knowledge, opportunity, race or environment. Or is its opposing any and everyone's views that are contrary to our own. When we feel a superiority base over one that is woven in the fabric of less than human treatment, dare dream or deem equal to our own, is that humanistic? Reiteration of generational instilment of hate does not make one more knowledgeable for the sake of being dominate in a world controlled by power. These lens in which we humans view life's daily path, the inability to perfect what is essentially imperfection, are a constant. To attempt to build a world unlike that in which is described in our Constitution is but another example of the unattainable for periods in our history that is forever prominent then and now. But as our history has documented the pass of attempted *"Maafa" (Swahili word meaning chaos or holocaust);* we as a people are still here. Even though we now view a nation endless in its hate, that now has watched our numbers dwindle in population for unknown reasons. As Hispanics now occupy what once was our solidified second place in population numbers as the ever evolving cycle of change has indeed changed us in number, but has not eliminated us. We as people of color have endured, despite all efforts to the contrary. So our appreciation of being the benefactors of hope, this mighty gift of indescribable strengths are what have made us, despite all endeavors to the contrary, permanent fixtures without apologies of this nation, this world. But with this eagerness of acceptability, the path to equality would find a trail of detours not by our own choosing. Rather, a forced too often in a suburbia metaphor of exclusion, applicable to all those dominant facets of an intuitive orphanage. Being invisible at heart while desecrating the appearance of obvious reality is wrong. An intelligent progressivism view that harbors no responsibility and harbors no fault. And to satisfy an inevitability of removing a race of people from obscurity, by hostility and indifferences and claim right for your actions, is mostly obscured. But in an effort to receive your just reward for Justice and for the good of the commonwealth of these United States, one would think the level of considerate forethought would be first place in the minds of the aggressors. Yet, the overwhelming imbalance of numbers committing these atrocities against a minority people would find no reward; rather, it's a down payment for future generations or current ones to seek pay back. Benefactors of these atrocities against a people remind a principal and moral certainty given historical patterns. There will never be social justice when any type of strong hold, blood thirsty, barbaric prone heathenish types has zero regard for the well-being of another human-beings. The principals of life for that type of behavior will never be allowed in the principles of biblical thinking. Rather, the efficiency of life and the life of all working towards a common goal is the ideal will of a socially just society as a whole. As not to single out these United States as a stand along country, guilty of such atrocities would be a major injustice to world societies as a whole. For, every country, third world, democratic, communist or otherwise, social injustice is always a certainty. But with most other countries, there is rarely hypocrisy, an unquestionably entity as wide spread as it is in this country. Which makes the fork tongue theory of justice that much more easily to defend? The Civil War defeat and purpose, one might surmise and even sympathize with the anger and revengeful nature in which these crimes appear to lend its rage to the extent of severely punishing the obvious. Then by some miraculous notion of nobelium, a veil is then placed over the unmentionable past as to metaphorically hide its ugliness from the world. While the dust of denial seems to age and generations mount and recollects fade from memory. If we're so eager to conceal the past from the future generations, then, shouldn't that be a light bulb moment of suspicion, worthy of investigation? A moment that suggest if it's so hideous of an element in which a nation murders itself, or prostituted itself into self deprivation, why hide. But as an act of moral justification in an effort to undermine its own impervious acts, makes fools of noble men. Unchanged by the accumulation of dust from the old that will rise again in the clearest of the new.

But the transformation what seemingly would be for the betterment of their, then perfect America, at the expense of the least unfortunately among equally patriotic Americans be the solution that deprives one of the dream? So, these justifications for punishing a race of people for what one like person of that race may or may not have committed is not reminiscences worthy. Yet these volumes of violence are neither remote nor mythical events from the nameless faces and human-less souls. Each victim was born from some woman's womb and had a father and families. So in the aftermath of any alleged crimes that were committed, what was so often overtly missed were these factors of humanism? With the number of centuries this lawless behavior added depth to this unforgivable sin, it's no wonder the stench still lingers. It should have been without celebration, the imbrued evils of ethic cleansing or race purification that grasp the hope of a people that this would someday end, but without consequences. And repercussions of those acts of evil would inevitably face the wrath of God is our continued prayers. Since processing the superior knowledge complex, placing one in a god-like, picturesque status surely in hindsight finds this a relevant fact to the unconscionable disregard for human life and its biblical principals.

Even times before the Joplin, Missouri, Chicago and Springfield, Illinois, massacres of the early 1900's, the slave trade conversely displayed millions upon millions of non-reportable lost souls. Not to mention the millions of freed slaves during the Reconstruction Period where slaves were allowed to starve to death in retaliation of emancipation. Unspeakable crimes of lawlessness soaked the minds of all profiteers seeking enormous financial gains at all cost regardless of human intolerability. Inherited generational murderous acts, none the less, still carry the barbaric devil like behavior of inflicting hell here on earth of the unexpected. Acts recognized only by the devil as unparalleled wretchedness, lost under the spell of the unconscionable. Common place of having no regard for a people of the world and by some accounts, the first people of civilization; gives a thought as to and by what reasons are these afflictions placed on this group of people. Or, what we as a people have and or experienced is no different than what any other group of oppressed people have experienced for generations. Is it then the **hair** or the **color** that makes us more exclusively different than any other ethic group? Or, is it because of both hair and color, undeniably, sets us apart and seems to have a major effect on how the world and all societies judge us as unworthy? Sometimes we are our own worse enemy by the phrases, *"the white man's ice is colder"* or *"the white man's gasoline is better because it doesn't contain water."* A narrow minded view or an inexcusable reason to bring hate into the equation when race dominance is a matter of discussion is no justification for evil or self hatred. Arguably, committers of such acts of evil could use any reason to inflict it. Examples of the total disregard for the lives of we people of color is what happened in Fredericksburg, Virginia, reported by *"The Richmond Planet,"* the Saturday edition dated *September 16, 1899*, describes the trial of Edward H. Conway, a white man, receiving a $10 fine for murdering Clarence Scott, a black man in Spotsylvania County. Or the hanging of Noah Finley, a Negro, for highway robbery and **attempting** to kill a white man named Major Darst.

Devour Us Not

This curse from some form of viewed birth defect that somehow makes us targets of unjustifiable lawlessness was the inexcusable tactic often used. The equal justice under the law is but another hypocritical fact that makes a mockery of the judicial system and the robe wearing appointees as equally flawed for not exercising right justice. To suggest compromise as the reason to satisfying the winds of injustice for the betterment of all, is but a cloud of despair continually darkening our less than perfect image of our America, our country. The natural order of things, *"That's just the way it is and how its been for as long as I can remember." "Mm-hmm."* Statements of following the status quo are nothing short of a cop out for a nation of on-lookers that voice their objections, if there were any, in silence. Harmonious living is the inarguable goal of any society. But for centuries, this factor of desires and hopes have gone unnoticed or unchallenged. It is almost inconceivable, that human-beings in a nation that has been be blessed with so much promise and wealth would have a pandemic like civil rights violations and hate that the pursuant for change would have to come from the oppressed. How well do I remember seeing Martin Luther King, Jr. walking in protest among hostel crowds while objects were being hurdled in his directions as I watch the rapidly blinking of his eyes, signifying in my opinion, total fear denied in the face of hate. But despite the blinking, soon thereafter he'd be relentless within a few days anticipating more violence directed at him as he yet again walked back to the non-violent efforts he'd later give his life for. Many people of color were fearful at all times for MLK's life considering where he'd display his fearlessness in the hotbed of the south which made our concerns viable. It was as if his protection at those times where God's blanket of protection upon him, not visible to the naked eye. Mainly because his purpose or the cycle of patterns for his journey was not realized as his acceptance of his calling would soon liberate a people, a nation, for the good of America. Such a young person in age, who was murdered before he was forty, carried the weight of an entire race of people and all its history on his back once he accepted his calling. There was no other person in America, in modern history would challenge a corrupt system of race-hate like Rev. Dr. Martin Luther King, Jr.

Almost every person of color has seen or heard of the movie, *"Rosewood"* and how horrified in disbelieve of its realism we all felt at its viewing. Unbeknownst to many Americans, that was only a small incident in parallel to the frequency of occurrences or the multi-numeric totals these incidents played out in American history. Imagine, literally, you are your brother's keeper. Because in almost every incident, one person of color would have allegedly commit a crime and the whole community in a blood-thirsty frenzy would be blamed for the crime and pay for it with the taking of their properties, burning of their homes, massacring their families, animals and ultimatums issued to leave everything behind or die. Given the same circumstances committed by an Anglo would have yielded very different results with no guilt associate with these atrocities. Mainly nothing of the magnitude inflected on the blacks was ever inflected on the whites. Which makes the hypocrisy of the *"amber waves of grain,"* obscure. Not only that, these massacres often went unpunished and unpublicized, only through sometimes bias newspaper articles that used the slaughters as a chastising for keeping one in line or someone stepped out of their place. And denial would render a permanent spot in the perpetrators minds to their uncompromising quest for an all white society in justifying their rage. The constant vengeances that had to be paid back double fold or sometimes triple or quadruple. But what wasn't considered was the failure to realize, the judgment and answering to a higher power, an uncalculated misstep when enraged. The assumption of right being a constant to the majority makes the swallowing of evil slide down the throats of hatred like a hot knife slides through butter. And one who will seek proper justice and not allow the drought of silence to be the final outcome is wishful thinking. For every debt of wrongdoing, must be satisfied with proper justice from one generation to the next.

Chicago, Illinois, where one versus many was common, but also like many other cities within our shores. Common among our shameful history is a known fact of terrible crimes against humanity in the form of mob violence that went unpunished and particularly during the summer of 1919. During that year, there was more violence against blacks in the form of riots and lynching than any other time in our history. But, the race riot that occurred in Chicago, Illinois on July 27, 28, 29, 30, 31 and August 1, 1919 had a very different conclusion. The honorable **Mr. Augustus L. Williams**, (Negro) Attorney at Law, as recorded by the *"The Broad Ax,"* Saturday, *July 8 & 15 1922*, describe the first of its kind against some of the best (white) Lawyers in the State. According to Peter M. Hoffman,

the coroner of Cook County, stated only thirty-eight were killed as a results of the riots, fifteen whites and twenty-three blacks. Also a 1,000 were left homeless by the burning of residences and over 365 blacks injured. Contrary to the rumors of several hundred bodies of both black and white citizens of Chicago, to reduce the total count and embarrassment that would be bestowed upon a great city, bodies were being tossed into the Bubbly Creek waters. But coroner Hoffman is expecting us to believe that a mob of about 5,000 whites walking the city looking for any person of color to reap havoc upon, only murdered twenty-three. All of the tensioned had been brewing for years. Many of the blacks were newly arrived immigrates from the south in seek of a better life.

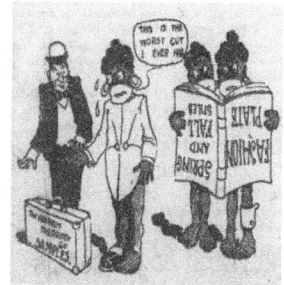

And because Chicago was a prosperous metropolitan city with no color lines drawn for black neighborhoods, Irish communities soon observed an over-populated city with job opportunities becoming scarce. Then came the drowning of Eugene Williams, a Negro, plus the anger from whites over the great migration that triggered the riot. After three years

of gathering support and cooperation from the black communities, money contributions, and using over $2,000 of his own money, Attorney Williams decided to sued the city of Chicago for the injustice. Because the enormity of property value and lost of life was so hard felt, Attorney Williams made the proper decision for the sake of justice in seeking compensation for the surviving family members. The St. Louis Republic, June 26, 1904

Devour Us Not

these cases were unprecedented and especially for a black lawyer. On Wednesday, May 25, 1921 he presented his first case known as Ada Dozier, widow, vs. City of Chicago, before Hon Judge Samuel C. Stough, Superior Court Judge of Cook County. Prosecuting attorney was a very brainy and very competent Hon Charles Pease and a team of equally competent legal heads that gave Hon Williams all he could handle. In the end, an all white man jury of 12 rendered a victorious verdict and awarding her a twenty-three hundred dollars settlement. The greatest legal victory of its kind in the United States. Then on Tuesday, October 25, 1921, Mr. Williams began to try a second and third case before the Hon Thomas G. Windes, Dean of the Circuit Court of Cook County, who was coincidently for any surviving citizen black or white that lost life or property was to be compensated by the city of Chicago. The second case of Mrs. Carrie Lovings, widow vs. The City of Chicago

"The Richmond Virginia Times," of December 7, 1902

was about Joseph Lovings who was ever as loved as his name suggested. He worked in a white barber shop. Riding his bike home from work on July 29, he encountered the evils of about 5,000 heathenish mobsters that fired fifteen to twenty bullets into all parts of his body. Then if that wasn't enough for the cowardly blood thirsty mob, they then began to deface his lifeless body by caving in his face and crushing in his skull with unknown objects. This was all witnessed by several white citizens that testified to include a Roman Catholic Priest. He testified that he kneeled down right in the presence of the mob, not knowing how they'd react to his religious obligation of offering prayer for his

"The Republic," of September 13, 1903

WHITETRASH AND NIGGERS.

Whenever you see in THE VOICE the terms "Whitetrash" and "Nigger," you can know that we are not referring to MEN but to that off-scouring of the Caucasian and Negro race from which Fat draws the Scabs and Suckers and Gunmen he uses against working MEN. For instance, Fellow-worker Gaines is a Negro, but he is not a *nigger*—he is a MAN. Reversing the races, Defective Harrel is not a MAN—he is *whitetrash*.

"The Voice of the People," of New Orleans, LA., April 2, 1914

"The Washington Herald," of June 22, 1913

soul, did so without incident. It was said that Mr. Williams was eloquent in his presentation and closing remarks that mesmerize the jury in rendering a favorable verdict, while awarding her a $3,500 settlement. Mr. Williams successfully tried twenty-six cases before the Circuit Courts with claims totaling more than $100,000. But the history of race issues even though now may be in racial fatigue, that has a slow down of the pulse of racial concern-ment, be not dismayed. For this permanent fixture of race is so heavily woven into the fabrics of our society until it will not change the hopeful

gestures we as a people will forever believe in. The year of the riot in Chicago according to *"The New York Tribune,"* dated, *October 19, 1919* admits to over 39 other cities erupted in race clashes. And from **1889-1918** some **2,472** black men, **50** black women, **690** white men, and **13** white women were lynched in America. The worst reported violence of race relationships in this America ever was recorded in Chicago and Joplin, Illinois.

But unlike what Mr. Williams achieved in Chicago, rarely were the thugs prosecuted for their actions, hence karma, for whatever a man soweth, that shall he also reap. And for the number of people who will find the reiteration of these stories a bit picayune, I say too long has our history been buried among the quietness of our forefathers hearts, as they walked the path deserving of recognition previously or partly touched upon. In a collective effort to disarm ones mind to the recollection of passed events of a shameful American past, unconscionably, African-American History Month, was given of the 12 months of the year, February, the shortest month of the year.

Progenitor is **President Thomas Jefferson** to a number of inquires most famously, **Sally Hemings** children's claim of what was told to them by their mother. And that was the third President of the United States was their father has been the subject of much debate since its initial reporting. And the constant dispute by the Monticello Society, denials and their consistent avenues to draw away from the theories into these allegations have been on going since the awareness of this relationship became public. As not to taint the reputation of a good name as prominent a figure in American history as Jefferson was. And not to dance around the hypocrisy of his own words, *"The presence of two elementary races in America is a menace to our physical and morale characters; to our happiness and to our safety,"* would dare have a sexual encounter with the very second class citizen he so eloquently defiled. But, many studies that include the denial of actual DNA to dispel any such rumor to the contrary. Many, movies and books have been written and made denouncing a common practice for most slave-owners of that era. And yet again the concealment of factual evidence is still not a convincer.

Ms Lucy Evans   Mrs. Evelyn Erskine   Mrs. Julia A. Harris   President Thomas Jefferson

But according to the, *"The San Francisco Call,"* newspaper article dated *August 26, 1909,* makes yet another claim about then President Thomas Jefferson. Pictured above is Lucy Evans, whose story of kinship to Jefferson was reported to the newspapers by her great-grand daughter, Mrs. Evelyn Erskins, as told to her by her mother Mrs. Julia A. Harris, who was the daughter of Ms. Lucy Evans. Accordingly, Ms. Lucy Evans was supposedly the known daughter of President Thomas Jefferson, as told to her by her mother, Priscilla, an African slave, while living on the plantation of Monticello. Mrs. Julia A. Harris, who was 80 years old in 1909, states her mother was born when Jefferson

Devour Us Not

was becoming Vice President. Apparently, Priscilla was an attractive young African Slave that gained favor with Jefferson at some point during her enslavement. Also, noticeably from the article and by the number or lack of information about any forbidden relationship from the grounds of Monticello among the some 154 slaves living there. It was a cult like loyalty atmosphere that impeded any such gossip from becoming known. But, explained by *"Aunt Lucy,"* as she was affectionately called, detailed life on the plantation as bothersome, filled with jealousy from other slaves who associated her Caucasian-like features as an offspring of Jefferson. Aunt Lucy also mentioned being a personal slave to one of Jefferson's daughter's who was married to Colonel Carr. Her sizing of Jefferson describes him as being a very kind man and treated his slaves very well. He had schools of learning where the training of

skilled labor such as cabinet making, bricklaying, masonry and others were a constant. But the amount of scrutiny surrounds Thomas Jefferson as his relationships with women of pure and mixed African blood remain as secretive as any fog of creditable evidence to the contrary. Ms. Lucy Evans died in San Francisco, California, on November 4, 1897 at the age of 101, sincerely, without any doubt believing in her kinship to the third President. So for whatever reason the craving of *"Dixie Sex,"* as it was sometimes called when sex between a white man and an African-American woman was performed was unclear to define. But clearly, adds myth to the notion of complete hatred of the white race towards his brother of the darker race. Or was it perhaps the easy availability of an oppressed race and the dominance that prompted these interactions. Of course thinking that Negroes could receive knowledge but could not impart knowledge adds to the theory of no respectability. I think the latter adds way more so to the argument mainly because of a point brought out by a minister named Rev. J.E. Kirby, who was the President of the Atlanta Georgia Theological Seminary and reported by the *"Seattle Republican,"* newspaper article of *December 2, 1904*. Nothing unusual about this article which expresses the sentiments of almost every red-blooded white American both then and now. But to employ the words of God as to give some biblical authentication to an argument of justified lawlessness is a bit disconcerting and disturbing. But to permanently secure our fear as African-Americans and the notion of a weaker race was an ill-fated gamble of pure wishful thinking. But somehow overwhelming numbers will always trump a stronger race. Case and Point; and so many similar cases of its comparison happened in Duluth Minnesota, June 14, 1920, where a mob of 5,000 stormed the jail and lynched **Isaac McGhie, Elmer Jackson** and **Nate Green** of an alleged rape of a nineteen year old white girl. The story as told by the young lady's escort, James Sullivan, who was watching the loading of animals behind the tents of a circus performance about ten o'clock that night. About that time several Negroes with a gun approached the couple. The Negro with the gun placed it at the escort's head while pinning his arm behind his back. The other two grabbed the girl, placing their hands over her mouth in a desperate and cautious manner, took her to a bushy area near the Misasbe tracks and assaulted her one after the other. The escort bitterly complained of being helpless to assist his companion as he was made to watch the entire assault. The Negroes, after the assault, must have given warning to revealing the act

as they were watched after their release through a ravine, a path different than back to the circus grounds. As the word spread around town about six Negroes being held at the county jail for the rape of a white girl, the blood-thirsty frenzy and the events that followed are all too familiar for that era. Just like the movie, *"Rosewood,"* justice would not be served. Storming the jail to gain access while **slightly** injuring six policemen has no contrast to what was to follow. Supposedly, the mob taking control of the situation conducted a mock

trial, found three of the six Negroes being held, guilty, all the while the three taken, screamed out their innocence were immediately taken from the jail and lynched from a telephone pole. After the lynching, the heathenish, cowardly mob disburse, while the other three Negroes, Louis Williams, John Thomas and Harry Richardson where quickly taken from the jail, relocated to a safe place out of town fearing a reoccurrence. Now, supposedly, as to the next day, a Grand Jury was convening immediately to bring the matter of the mobs action to justice. Since most of the guilty parties were identified and well "L known within the community by the Police Chief, it would appear not to have a problem establishing guilt, after all there were by their own boosting admission of facts, about 5,000 witnesses and later acknowledged photos and post cards of this lynching were printed. But by some consolation of acknowledged sanctity, their bodies were not traditionally mutilated or riddled with bullets. Also, there were two Catholic Priest present, Fathers Powers and Howard. Father F.J. Howard climbed some 15 feet up a telephone pole to plead with the mob that their actions were wrong, but to no avail. As shouts of *"think of the girl"* and *"lynch him,"* of some 5,000 was no match for one voice of reason. It was stated that both the frail Irene Tusken and James Sullivan were taken to the circus train about to take off for Virginia, was halted by police to identify the alleged 12 perpetrators, and was then taken from the train and rushed to police headquarters. The news of the lynching spread like wild fire as also in a similar case in Omaha, Nebraska where one Negro, Will Brown, pictured below, was lynched and burned, upon further investigation found the white girl, Agnes Loebeck, also pictured below of Omaha was lying. An innocent soul, lost at the hands of an angry mob. So the N.A.A.C.P. in the Tusken case reported by *"The Appeal of St. Paul Minnesota," (The Circus Negroes)* dated *July 10, 1920,* held a meeting at the St. James Church. Irene Tusken, a school age white girl who made the allegation of assault against two Negroes were conducted and read a second investigated by Dr. Valdo Turner and Attorney J. Louis Ervin that actually went to Duluth for a further investigation into the Tusken incident. Attorney W. F. Francis also reports of a special detective that was sent by the association left no doubt in the minds of all at the meeting to the innocence of the three murdered circus workers of the crime of rape. Additionally, for this crime, there were still fourteen Negro men incarcerated, even though the knowledge of the Physician examination was known. The NAACP then took up a collect to financially support of the efforts of this injustice in the amount of $159.19. The investigation revealed that 12 members of the mob were also indicted for their involvement into the lynching.

Burned remains of Will Brown, before he was hung, body riddled with bullets, then his body was dragged throughout the streets before the body was mutilated "The Omaha Daily Bee," of Sep 25, 1919

"Will Brown" "The Bee," of Sept 25, 1919

"Agnes Loebeck" "The Bee," of Sept. 25, 1919

Devour Us Not

Then on June 19th rumor of Irene Tusken had died as a result of the rape, caused another frenzy to brew but was quickly denounced by her Physician Dr. David Graham and orders from Sheriff Magie of, *"shoot to kill,"* if any attempt to storm the jail again. Nefarious desires of white men sometimes called, *"blacksnaking,"* is only but a guilty path of like thinking and then stigmatized to every black man with being a crazed white woman rape fiend. A trial for three of the twenty-one men charged with murder of the three Negro circus hands on June 14, 1920 was held on August

"Postcard of the Duluth lynching of Circus hands"

31, 1920. The three were, **Henry Stephenson, Leonard Sheldon and William Rosen.** According to *The Appeal* dated *December 11, 1920* reports that the NAACP had hired Attorney F. L. Barnett, Jr. of Chicago, who was the stepson of the infamous Ida B. Wells-Barnett who was well known for her fight against lynching. William Miller, Negro, was acquitted by a jury where Max Mason, a Negro, was found guilty as reported by *The Appeal of December 4, 1920*, briefly suggested, Mr. Mason will receive another trial while being granted a 40-day stay. Also, Henry Stephenson, a white man was found guilty according to, *"The Bemidji Pioneer,"* dated

"Public Sale—State of Missouri, county of Pike. To whom it may concern: The undersigned will, on Tuesday, September 29, A. D., 1849, sell at public outcry, for cash, on premises where Coon creek crosses the old Mission road, the following chattels, to-wit: Six yoke of oxen, with yokes and chains; 2 wagons with beds, 3 nigger wenches, 2 buck niggers, 3 nigger boys, 5 prairie plows, 23 steel traps, 1 barrel pickled cabbage, 2 hogshead tobacco, 1 lot nigger hoes, 1 spinning wheel, 1 loom, 3 fox hounds, a lot of coon, mink and skunk skins, and a lot of other articles. Am gwine to California.
JOHN DOE.

September 1, 3 & 11, 1920, where it was reported that Nate Natelson, a defendant, testified against Henry Stephenson to ceil his fate while the jury only took 40 minutes to deliberate. Bryson Olson, a white man was founded not guilty, while Louis Dondino was founded guilty but only served about a year in State Prison. Carl Hammerberg, a white boy was found guilty and serve about a year and a half in a State Reformatory because of his age. Despite all the compelling arguments of so called justifications, was the smoking gun theory that came from the accuser's own Physician the night of the alleged circus assault. Dr. David Graham stated unequivocally, that no rape or assault had taken place. So in all likelihood of those circus hands, all in their twenties, all murdered and then place in unmarked graves were innocent. Victims of someone's imagination in a Christian land, died for no other apparent season other than being black. Yet the alleged victim, Irene Tusken,

unlike the innocent circus hands, lived a long life, dieing in 1996 at the age of 94. She never spent a day in prison or ever made a statement as to what caused her to fabricate such a story that took the three innocent lives and destroying the reputation of a people of that city. Of course, it really didn't take much for the formulation of the negative thought to be instilled. For the deepest of hatred in that community and elsewhere was a way of life as far back as most could recollect. So, in examining Rev. J.E. Kirby's theory of the amalgamation of the races which always result in chaos as a result of one dominant race over another, he failed to realize an important factor of realization in the ever evolving cycle of God's balance. The almost promise of turnaround and fair-play element as no deed of any kind will ever escape the eyes of justice, even when the human eyes look blind in an effort of justification. Even generational, time is not of the essence as much as the inevitably of payback.

The previous examples of lawlessness where it appears to be race dominance, is more number driven than stronger, weaker race driven. It doesn't matter how strong a person claims to be one man could never over power five thousand. And even more so when that same five thousand is filled with rage and hatred. So, when Rev. Kirby's misguided explanation of depicting a greatly inferior civilization, meaning people of color coming from a heathenized jungle atmosphere, then hypocritically omit's the cowardly and heathenized action of a mob, might want to reconsider a different analysis. But he was merely echoing the sentiments of his constituents in an effort to rid America of its so called problem of African Americans living in America as free an equal as whites. Which was incidentally stolen from the native Indians. And the bow and arrow theory being of no match for the shotgun as a means of driving home the point of modern civilized dwellings vice an undeveloped one…. So his bold solution of saving the poor, socially unmatched, educationally challenged Negro from being completely devoured by this so called dominate race theory was nothing short of hypocrisy. It is also the Christian thing to do most in their justification and that is **Segregation**. And there it is the second best word, other than the *"N"* word, that is most pleasing to the white man's ears. As echoed by the 45th Alabama Governor, George Wallace, *"Segregation ta-day, Segregation da-mar, Segregation fa-ev-va."* I recalled in 1960 when the Dallas Cowboys first came to town. There was already an American League Football (AFL) team hear called, the Dallas Texans. Most noticeably, were the fact that the AFL, that the Dallas Texans were apart of, had a lot of African-American's on its team as well as most other AFL teams. Whereby, the National Football League (NFL), considered, the pinnacle of football supremacy had mostly all white players on their teams. Giving some argument to the selection process was that most of the players from the NFL were from *"Big-Time,"* college football programs, such as USC, Notre Dame, University of Alabama, University of Texas, and thereby restrictive in their permission of black athletics. So the AFL, because of *"segregation,"* players came from predominant all black football programs such as

The carpet-baggers ask me to cast my vote to keep the white folks down. Now all I ever wanted was to get on a level with the white man. I never wanted to get above him. They say that a nigger is better than a white man in Cincinnati. Well, that may be true--in Cincinnati, but it ain't true down here. It is my interest to stand by the Southern man, and it's my wish to. Whatever law is made to affect the white man's plantation also affects my little cotton patch in the same way. The three cent tax on cotton hurts me worse than it does the white man. But it puts money in the Yankee's pocket.

They want to disfranchise the white man, and make the nigger put them into office, that they may have taxes and things their own way. They never would have passed a law allowing niggers to vote if they hadn't thought the niggers would vote the Republican ticket. Never! never! never! Who believes otherwise? Not this nigger, certain. The Yankee brought the nigger here from Africa for selfish purposes, set him free for selfish purposes; and now they want to vote him for selfish purposes.

Grambling, Southern, FAMU, Howard University and Prairie View, etc. So the measure of football talents, based on a restricted college affiliation, dominated by racial prejudice was no justifiable measure of talent at all. Rather, it furthered, in its attempt to keep the races separate, denied the opportunities for millions to showcase their individual talents, solely based on school affiliation. This barrier, signifying the obvious racial lines drawn even in sports, was used as a means of also deciding race dominance in a competitive world. Also remember the Washington Redskins were the last NFL team to integrate. So hypnotically, present a picture of any NFL team in 1960; then place a 2013 photograph of the same two teams or any other team in the NFL today. There will

Devour Us Not

"Los Angeles Herald," of November 25, 1906

be an overwhelming, but very noticeable observation......race representation disproportionate to this nation's population. But, to a certain degree, whites could point to this disproportion as it relates to Swimming, Tennis, Ice Hockey, La Crosse and Polo. In response to that analogy, consider talent minus opportunity equals nothing. Or, in other words, opportunities where the availability of these sports is not accessible to inter-city kids or any child of a minority or impoverished group. So the likelihood of these groups excelling in these sports is remote. So given even access, availability and opportunity favors an imbalance of race distribution not equated to this nations population percentage. But a person of color rarely resonates to the race superiority theories. However, blacks, excepted into a white dominated workforce, elitism, tends to adopt that superiority complex, placing them in a category that is contrary to its traditional. An inherited value which makes us more tolerable and less judgmental than most races surmises our view of Justice. So the ethical ambition of ones accomplishments, particularly if you're black, does not sway the argument that all people of color have achieved the same plight or less are more agreeable of being narcissistic. Rather, joining in on the bashing of like race successes of life, that hold banners of accomplishment over ones head while erasing historical struggles, all in an effort of tailored sacrifices that makes us relentless, is another issue.

So, Rev. Kirby, in his lackluster attempt to glorify the independence of people of color being separated in hundreds of miles of independent land own and operated by blacks among their own people is much more gratifying than being woven into a society that hates you is his lie. But in the eyes of the majority, of course, right? So, people of color, particularly black males, will not have to worry about the white man's evil attempt to use his obvious superior wit to oppress, falsely accused and judge him unfairly, right? So, then the black man would have no one to give fault to his failures while rendering him equally viewed for how much intellect his own initiative will reward him or view him as whites view him now, right? As a mental note and a reminder, this opinion was written in 1904, Rev. Kirby quickly acknowledges and confirms the Supreme Court decision ruling about the Dred Scott decision, particularly the words, **"free or slaves, Africans could never become American citizens and therefore have no rights that any white man would be bound to respect."** And therefore, making a point that a black man would never be able to hold public office, or receive equitable treatment.

Only if the Reverend had foresight regarding that comment about public office and fast forward to the year 2008. He like many then and now who dare think this negative thought would be amazed. And, in further expressing the sentiments that there will never ever be fair treatment from white men towards black men. This statement, however holds some true value even today. But then, Rev. Kirby concluded his article by favorably acknowledging how the white man would be so sadden by the complete separation of the black race by virtue of the establishment of the mulatto race. And continuing that this blow by far would create a hardship towards the white man's happiness. To the dare mentioning of the mulatto race, was as if it were a badge of honor or cravens of equal thoughts for what is preceded that of a black man's feelings towards a white woman. So how could a race of people crave the females of that race and genuinely despise its male counterparts. Or, is it more fear than genuine hatred? Fear of generational teachings that you're better than, and God loves you more, only to find out the myth of that hypocrisy rather than excepting the truth of God's balancing system of life. A concept written so eloquently by Thomas Jefferson, **"We hold these truths, to be self evident that all men are created equal."** Fundamental, principals, seemingly a man of God would focus on rather than allow secular and popular views to cloud his opinion of a race and a people. But speaking like the *"son of the morning,"* in an all-out effort in impeding their efforts to grab equality, seek the American dream like every other naturally born and

naturalized American living in this country. What harm is there in a race wanting that for themselves and their people without the concerted efforts of another race set out on the impediment of that feat, even if by and most commonly, illegal and barbaric means. Is it really that gratifying to hinder the efforts of one race, and then assume the balances of life will not reward your ill soliciting efforts?

Walhalla, Mississippi, December 17, 1888, was one of the very worst days of race rioting in that town's history at that time. In the end, twelve white men and one hundred and fifty black men laid dead. An inevitable conclusion after years of small mishaps as reported by the *"Fort Worth Daily Gazette,"* of *December 18, 1888.* The cause of the 1888 incident started when a farmer had his gin house and eight bales of cotton burned. The incident was reported and an assumption was made; it had to have been the Negroes for whom the white farmers had had trouble with. An attempt, by a law officer was made to arrest the alleged gang leader when the tables were turned and the officer received a severe beating after the suspect resisted arrest. After details of the beating were widely known, a posse of white men was formed from Walhalla to settle the score. As the posse approached the cabin of the suspects, they were met with a volume of gun fire from reportedly about fifty well armed Negroes. When the smoke cleared, four white men were killed, eight wounded and three of them mortally. As results of that gunfight created a blood-thirsty frenzy mob to form from nearby Meridian which lead to the forming of about seventy-five well armed white men. But, the inconsistent and exaggerated news of the gun battle and a well-armed black mob was formed, went out all over the state of Mississippi and reportedly, every city were sending well armed white men to guarantee a massacre. Given the climate of the times and the area in which this occurred, it really didn't take much to insight a heathenish mob of a revengeful nature to reap havoc upon a supposedly mob of blacks. Reportedly, after the white mob was formed, a hunt throughout the county was in pursuit. A shootout did ensue at some point leading to the

enormous lost of life. Even though the complete information of what happen will probably never be known, because of reporting biases and racial prejudices, key elements of the story was purposely averted. Consider, also the lawmakers were as crooked as the citizens of that county. So, if a mob scene was witnessed by at least a thousand and the lawmakers wanted the crime to disappear, which is what happened in the case of Joe Coe or George Smith, on October 10, 1891 in Omaha, Nebraska, then *c'est la vie.* The incident was recorded by a Saint Paul, Minnesota newspaper article from *"The Appeal,"* of October 24, 1891. Although it is unclear how the two names equate to one person, but his lynching as a result of what was apart of court records as to how he died is what's so significant about corrupt lawmakers. This is so far-fetch from the realization of lawfulness, until it bears mentioning as to the extent the disgrace of a flawed system will do to justify a crime cover-up. An analysis

Devour Us Not

was used as this case was beyond precedents. Whether you are smothered by roses or drowned in honey, a death at the hands of another is a death of the obvious. This incident, as reported by the, *"Perrysburg Journal of Ohio,"* *October 17, 1891,* states, Joe Coe was accused of assaulting five year old Lizzie Yates. According to *the "Abilene, Kansas Weekly Reflector,"* newspaper article dated, *October 15, 1891* stated he, Joe Coe, had been invited to the Yates residence on North Eighteenth Street, identifying himself as a garbage man there to inspect the premises. Shortly thereafter, Lizzie Yates, five years old, came into the house in agony with noticeable blood streaming down from her person. Authorities were notified after his description was made and he was found hiding in a hay mow not far from the Yates residence. The night in questioned as the news of the assault became public was the day of the public lynching of Ed Neal (*white*) for which the crowd was already ignited. At about 9:30 pm, that night, the crowd then demanded Joe Coe's release to them. Even though a brief stand by Captain Cormack with a revolver in hand, confronted the so called, *"loud mouth,"* of the mob. This strategy temporarily caused the mob to abandon the Harvey Street entry to the county jail. But the crowd was relentless as former Governor Boyd made his way through the crowd. He eventually managed to speak with the crowd in an attempt to reason with them, advising them of the wrongness for lawlessness and the consequences they face. Notwithstanding, was his words when they were cut off by the impatient blood-thirsty crowd seeking Joe Coe with unison cries for his immediate death. An unyielding crowd became very innovative when they used steel street car rails to gain access to the jail, where Joe was seized, dragged and beaten while trying to make their way to the street. By the time he reached the streets, he was clothes-less as they strung him up over an electric railway trolley wire. Joe Coe was only 20 years old, with never a discussion as to whether the crime was actually committed by him. And in the aftermath of this incident, a trial was attempted by the mob leaders. The case was eventually dismissed by the Judge who took the sole statement from the coronary expert as to the cause of Joe's death. He determined and used the theory of a *"heart attack,"* or being merely frighten to death at the thought of being hanged as the cause of Joe Coe's death and not being lynched. And supposedly, he was already dead before the rope was placed around his neck. Of all the many participants in this young man's death, no one was ever legally charged for it, mainly because his death was theorized as a heart attack.

December 11, 1921, a *"New York Tribune,"* newspaper article, reports another lawless act for which no one was punished. Fort Worth, Texas, a packing house employee, involved in a strike was beaten by strike sympathizers and hospitalized. Fred Rouse, 30, a Negro, had been involved in an altercation in which Rouse had shot and wounded two strikers that were brothers. A phone call was made inquiring into his location after the altercation. It was reported that about thirty men took Fred Rouse from his hospital bed, after a brief struggle, placed him in a car and drove off. Fred Rouse's lifeless body was found about twenty minutes later, dangling from a tree.

"The Groesbeck Journal," August 19, 1921, a newspaper article, reports the story of a thirty year old Negro named Alexander (*Alex*) Winn. His crime was an alleged attempt to assault a nine year old white girl at Datura, Texas. Soon thereafter a mob was involved that took the law into their own hands. All that was mentioned in the article, was the fact that the little girl was playing in the barn where Alex was supposedly working. The mother heard a scream coming from the child inside the barn. She frantically ran towards the barn to investigate.

Reasons for the screams or questioning the girl or the Negro never happened. A decision was made that, white girl screams, black man nearby, "guilty!" She could have been screaming because of a spider or an accidental fall. I'm assuming, fearing for his life, Alex began to run and as a result of that he was shot twice, allowing the men to catch up with him. Within minutes of the reported screams, a rope was requested but none was available. So a chain was then placed around his neck until he died. In the newspaper article, as to appease the readers of the necessity for dignity, a statement was made of its orderly proceedings, witnessed only by neighbors and parents of the little girl. They were nearby with guns available in the event of such an occurrence would take place, their justice would be swift. No further investigation was made nor was there any diabolical heathens charged with this crime. The deceased body was then taken to Coolidge, Texas and burned vice cremation. What makes this story so bazaar, is the imbalance of justice or punishment to fit the alleged crime. God in his infamous wisdom has a balancing system in place for which he sometimes outsources or subcontracts. For whatever the rationale behind wanting for a rush to justice, the severity of the punishment and the taking of ones life are not justified in any circumstances without due process. More importantly, the child was not harmed, unclothed or touched, only the alleged attempt. So, for this event, the balance of justice will be an outsourced matter for God, for its unnecessary taking of his greatest gift on August 15, 1921 in Datura, Texas. For mankind, some generation will one day yield the brunt of this aggression to balance this injustice.

Will Godley and **French Godley** were lynched on August 19, 1901 in Pierce City, Missouri. And, the aftermath of this event lead to another case of lawlessness in that region. Accordingly, *"The Minneapolis Journal," August 20, 1920* newspaper article, there was the murder of Ms. Gazelle Wilde that triggered the violence. Bloodhounds were put on the trail that went to a George Lark's residence that was a porter on the St. Louis and San Francisco railroad and was also named by Will Godley as the murderer. After the news of murder was known, a mob of hundreds to a thousand were formed and the burning of every Negro homes in the area. All Negroes in the area fled in all directions to include Joplin about 34 miles away and Springfield in the opposite direction of about 50 miles away. Peter Hampton, who was seventy-five years old, was reported to have been burned alive inside the house of Ike Carter that was surrounded by the

mob to ensure the death of everyone in that residence guaranteed. Meanwhile, George Lark was arrested in Springfield, Missouri, the following morning, suspect in the throat cutting of Ms. Wilde. The *"Wichita Daily Eagle,"* dated, *August 22, 1901*, with all its misspelled words describes a *"No Negroes Allowed,"* city controlled by a band of thugs. The mission was to rid the city of all Negroes in Pierce City, Springfield and Joplin where most blacks attempted to resettle after the lawlessness. Some Negroes in Marionville, about 23 miles away, tried to resettle there they were asked to leave. These migrations were completed out of fear, on foot, with no money or food. An ideology of a nationalize nation of Immigrants and natural born Americans, in this case by chance happen to be of African descent, had no place of want by any city in that region unwilling to look beyond their ethnicity. In an effort of devouring a race without conviction. A problematic issue of race blaming much the same way the Japanese-Americans were treated after the Pearl Harbor attack and the Muslims after 911.

Devour Us Not

It was said that every white person in the city of 3,000 attended the funeral of Ms. Gazelle Wilde as reported by *"The St. Louis Republic,"* dated *August 21, 1901.* The city of Pierce City, now the wishful all white, is a result of random criminal acts committed by Negroes in the pass 10 years. About 5 miles away in Monett, Negroes were not welcomed there either. In 1894 when Ulysses Haydon was taken from the Sheriff's office and hanged to a telegraph pole, after being accused of murdering Bots Greenwood, a white man working as a brakeman for the railroad as reported by *"The State Republican,"* newspaper article dated, *July 5, 1894.* Because of the railway system and the employment of Negroes as porters of descent pay for a person of color prompted the migration to those mid-west cities. But so many incidents of violence associated with people of color, guilty or not, being your brothers keeper, whites used that excuse to get their wishful, *" all-white,"* communities. This was welcomed news to satisfy those desires of hate. After the hanging of William Godley, the initial alleged culprit of the crime and his elderly grandfather just because he was related were strung up. It was later determined that William and his grandfather were both innocent. But naturally, no response of guilt was expressed by the citizens in that city once the news of their innocence reached reasonable ears. There was never a question of what would become of a people, already living below the poverty line on minimal income comparative to their white counterparts. The local hardware store was sold out of both ammo and weapons while every application for weapons by Negroes was refused. In search for the Negroes, the orders was given to remove all weaponry from the Negro homes, allowing them no defense. It is unclear how many homes were burned or families forced to flee. Most of their involvement was innocently and unprovoked. Thirty was a number given by the newspaper but could have been much higher. Governor Dockery of Missouri received a telegram of the incidents in Pierce City and offered a reward for the capture of the responsible parties. Also mentioned in the telegram about all the violence and lawlessness, of which the governor had no sincere response other than to get more definitive information and punish all responsible. No one ever paid for that crime.

To top that as reported by *"The Daily Ardmoreite,"* of April 16, 1906 newspaper article reports three Negroes being hung and burned in Springfield, Missouri on April 15, 1906. Allegedly, Ms. Mable Edmonson, who had recently moved from Monett to Springfield, Missouri, hired a Negro domestic driver and was riding in her buggy with the young man named Charles Cooper when they were stopped by two Negroes. The young man accompanying Ms Edmonson were beaten unconsciously and Ms Edmonson was dragged in the woods and assaulted. Horace and Jim were soon arrested on suspicion with little or no evidence linking them to the crime in anyway. As word spread of the assault, the frenzy of blood thirsty thugs quickly formed into a mob of nearly a 1,000 white citizens about 8'oclock.

"The San Francisco Call," of June 18, 1905

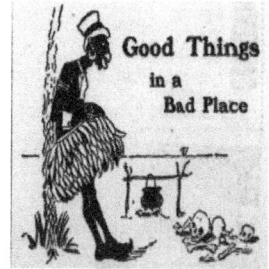

"Evening Star," of January 22, 1902

First going to the city jail demanding their release only to find out they were in the county jail. Now the death crazed mob figuring they'd never be able to gain access to the county jail, went to the residence of the sheriff to obtain the keys. The success of that mission which claimed the destruction of the sheriff's home by smashing in doors, breaking windows and smashing furniture. All of this freighting his wife to hysteria and unconsciousness. They eventually located the keys and headed back to the county jail. The mob then had grown to about 3,000 at about midnight, as they proceeded to take Horace Duncan and Jim or James Copeland from the county jail and hung them from an electric light tower in the town square. After that, the mob completely unsatisfied, set fire to the two young Negroes, both under the age of 21 as all of 3,000 whites watched and cheered. Soon the crowd disbursed as the charred remains of the two victims continue to be consumed by fire and smoke lay lifeless in view of all humanity. But that wasn't enough for the crowd. I'm sure fearing that they may not have lynched the right suspect, went back to the county jail two hours later and in the same manner dragged William Allen to his death. With still smoke from Horace and Jim still smothering, young William's body was soon ashes and riddled with bullets. The following day, Governor Folk had called in 266 extra deputies and seven companies of militia troops to protect the Negro residences and preserve life. As the black community of about 2,000 began to return to their homes, fearing a repeat of the pass, some had fled to the nearby woods for safety. With no means of protecting themselves and no weapons either by law or lack of affordances, could ill afford to become victims yet again. Now infuriated with the events from the previous night began to demand for justice. As this once peaceful town settled down, reactions denouncing the mobs outrageous act began to increase in volume, particularly when Ms. Edmonson herself stated that Duncan and Copeland were not her attackers. Governor Folk, unlike his predecessor, sent the Assistant Attorney General from Jefferson City to begin a process to bring to justice all involved in the innocent slaying of three of its citizen when so little evidence was known about the crime for which they were charged and without due process. April 16, 1906, Judge Lincoln of the criminal courts announced a special grand jury to began on Tuesday, April 17th, to convene into the lynching saga. Governor Folk also issued instructions that all the leaders of the mob, that was citywide known, be arrested and placed in the jail surrounded by troops for their protection as soon as possible. Soldiers, commanded by General H.C. Clark, sympathy for the mob from obviously those who participated, were now verbally walking the streets denouncing the presence of troops and jeering the old adage of ridding the city of all its Negro citizens and to starting another uprising if a single person were to be indicted or jailed.

GEORGIA MOB LYNCHES NEGRO, BURNS CHURCHES

EASTMAN, Ga.—The charred body of Eli Cooper, a Negro, was found to-day in the ashes of a Negro church, burned by incendiaries this week. Three other Negro churches and a Negro lodge in this section were burned Tuesday night. The acts of violence followed reports that the Negroes planned to "rise up and wipe out the white people," and that Cooper remarked the Negroes had been "run over for fifty years, but this will all change in thirty days." The burned churches and lodge rooms were said to have been the scenes of mass meetings recently during which the uprising of Negroes was discussed.

"The Broad Ax," of August 30, 1919

Devour Us Not

During the chaos of removing the alleged rapist from the county jail, all but 6 of the 50 criminals escaped according to the *"Warren sheaf,"* dated, *April 26, 1906* newspaper article. The so-called frustration the white citizens of Springfield expressed was a continued act of violence prone to that of the Negro community. Two months before all the violence, the article paints a pattern of criminal behavior by blacks. Describing the assassination of T. M. Kinney, a prominent tailor, for which two Negroes were jailed. An old peddler; name unknown was killed and another unknown Negro who was accused and jailed for that crime. Moreover, the protest of an anti-Negro Play that was viewed by the white citizens undoubtedly fueled the anger in many that didn't need very much to precipitate. But no where in the article does it mention white crimes. Of the some 50 prisoners that were housed in the county jail, not all were black that made the daring escaped in the mayhem. So, where was the parallel of consistency or justice for that matter?

But, April 17th four white men were arrested for being leaders of the mob from that Saturday night. According to *Richmond Planet, dated, September 1, 1906*, show cases the supposed ring leader of the mob was Daniel D. Galbraith on August 20, 1906. After taking the stand for over two hours in his own defense, later in the trial dispelled all previous testimonies fingering him with the one who was among the first to enter the jail. He was identified as the one carrying the rope and showcasing later, a piece of the rope, a piece of one of the Negro's trouser leg as souvenirs and making a number of outlandish statements during the chaos. Even the wife of the sheriff, Mrs. E. V. Horner, who testified it was Daniel who entered their home in search for the keys forcing she and her kids outside in their sleeping attire was not enough to convict him. His young son, Virgil Galbraith, age thirteen, also testified on his father's behalf. And several of his obvious friends claimed he was an innocent on-looker, neither offering or attempt to impede the efforts of the law. Out of some four thousand witness to these crimes who also some returned the following morning to take pictures, unrepentant or unremorseful, rather, glorifying in their heinous crime with pride as they posed for the cameras for their own amusement. It was also proven, the assault of Ms. Edmonson never took place and no one was ever charged and found guilty of the murder of three of its young innocent citizens after so many first hand eye witnesses would turn a blind eye to justice. In the aftermath of the trial's injustice to its Negro citizens, fearing once again that no one would ever protect their rights or freedoms would best seek refuge elsewhere, began to leave the city in quick and mass numbers. Much to the delight of most of the wishful whites who like their surrounding community was far removed from compromising to giving equal respect as they felt they deserved. Even to this day, that region of the country still host a large percentage of white population and small black populations as to what the original plan was over one hundred years ago. So, who is really the criminal element here? Then who should really be run out of town for lawlessness? This concerted fear factor of wanting an all white America that will never be, because of God's balance of justice and legally responsibilities, some generation will have to give an account of the number of lawless acts often based on false information, purposely or not.

NEGRO WHO SLEW WHITE GIRL IS BURNED AT STAKE

Moultrie, Ga.—John Henry Williams, Negro slayer of Lorena Wilkes, 12 year old white girl, was burned at the stake here by a mob after he had been convicted of first degree murder and sentenced to be hanged July 8.

The prisoner was taken from the officers as he was being escorted from the courtroom and was rushed to the scene of his crime, where he was tied to the stump of a tree.

Williams calmly smoked a cigaret as the match was applied to the fuel around him, and he made but little outcry as the flames slowly burned him to death. It was reported that he made a full confession.

"The Broad Ax," of June 25, 1921

Ironically, as reported by, *"The Day Book," of June 09, 1913*, on the very same block where, Duncan, Copeland and Allen were brutally hung, burned and shot on Goddess of Liberty Tower Square some seven years prior on Easter Sunday, was consumed on June 8, 1913 by fire. The phenomenon of combustion manifested in light, flame, and heat was non other than fire, that totaled anywhere from $700,000 to a million dollars of property damage. An entire block, which started in the basement of the Heer Dry Goods Company that covered the northeast corner of the square *"Karma."*

As reported by the, *"Scott County Kicker,"* dated, *November 13, 1909*, in Charleston, Missouri, George Jackson, a nineteen year old Negro was arrested in Bird's Point, Missouri about 296 miles from Pierce City, Missouri, for an alleged attack on Mrs. Phenia Henderson, a sixty year old widowed woman who's age and lack of close proximity to neighbors made her a prime target for an assault. George Jackson waited for her as she returned from a visit to a neighbor's home where he alleged to have assaulted her by beating her unconscientiously. Rumors of the assault swirled around town as a mob was imminent. But, because of lack of leadership or spokesman, the mob never materialized. Fast forward as reported by, *"The Times and Democrat,"* of July 7, *1910*, about the lynching of two Negroes. The two Negroes were Robert Coleman and Sam Fields for the alleged murder of a Mississippi County farmer named William Fox. A pistol was used to shoot the farmer dead and rob him. After swirls and rumors of a mob and lacking the front leader to take charge, finally about four in the evening an unidentified man began to ignite the mob and the force to retrieve the men from the jail was successful as the police officers offered little resistance to the fiery tone of the mob as they were brushed aside while the hammering of metal manage to secured first Robert Coleman as he was strung up to the cheers of white men, women and children. After his obvious death was apparent, the mob went into the jail and dragged out Sam Field who indicated for leniency, he'd show them where he and Coleman hid the pistol in the assault. With the rope still around his neck with some members yanking on it, loaded Sam Fields in a wagon as the mob walk and rode in cars accompanying Sam to the location of the pistol. After

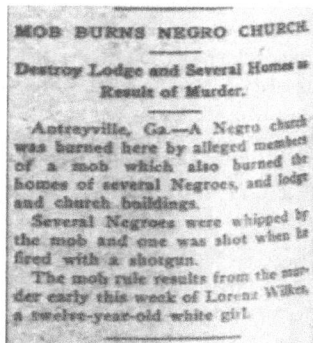

MOB BURNS NEGRO CHURCH

Destroy Lodge and Several Homes as Result of Murder.

Anstreyville, Ga.—A Negro church was burned here by alleged members of a mob which also burned the homes of several Negroes, and lodge and church buildings.

Several Negroes were whipped by the mob and one was shot when he fired with a shotgun.

The mob rule results from the murder early this week of Lorenz Wilkes a twelve-year-old white girl.

going part of the way, it was reported, Sam used the words, *"I guess,"* at such time the mob being impatient with his stuttering and babbling, stopped the charade after his inability to find the pistol. They jerked him from the carriage and strung him up much to the delight of the crowd of several hundred who cheered yet again. Rumors of the mob violence caused the Negroes of Charleston to flee the area for their own protection and safety. No one was ever charged for the murder of Robert Coleman and Sam Fields. In Springfield, Illinois, August 14, 1908, an attempt to lynch a black man who had allegedly assaulted a white woman was refused protection by the Police. To everyone's surprise, as the men had already been removed from the jail and taken

Devour Us Not

to a safe place. The mob tried to visit the black residence and was chased away by troops with bayonets. The mob then managed to lynch William Donnegan, an 80 year old elderly black man living in a conservative white neighborhood married to a white woman for many years. Conclusion, 40 homes and 24 businesses were destroyed, 2 blacks were killed several others beaten and 5 whites killed. A grand jury brought about 107 indictments and almost 80 who were implicated in the riots that included 4 police officers.

But only one man was convicted, a 20 year old Russian Jew named Abe Raymer, the alleged ring leader of the mob. The small-time vegetable peddler of the Springfield, Illinois riots was acquitted for

his involvement of the murders of all who died in the riot. No one has ever paid, legally for the deaths and destruction of property, some estimated 1,500 families effected and believed to have left the city, all from the city of Springfield, Illinois and the riot of 1908. Springfield, mindfully, the home town of **President Abraham Lincoln**.

In Springfield, Ohio, **Richard Dickerson**, aka *"Dixson,"* a Negro, was lynched by a mob of about 1,500 on March 7, 1904, for the murder of Police Officer Bailiff Charles Collis and the wounding of Mamie Corbin his mistress, in the left breast just above the heart. As reported by, *"The Washington Times,"* March 9, 1904, five Negro Juke-joints had been set a fire to include the *"Levee,"* and a number of Negro Saloon in the district that included the Mantoles Saloon, Les Thomas Restaurant, Charles C. Burke Saloon and Thomas Saloon. Oddly, Charley Bray, a white owned Saloon in the same district was not touched. Later, Mr. Bray admits to not even calling the fire or police department after adjacent black owned businesses were in flames. Yet the mob, in a self-justified cleansing effort to rid against evils, which causes irrational behaviors from its black and white citizens, targeted the Levee district for its total destruction. Mainly because in the pass eighteen months, the district boost 12 murders, for which no case ended in death of the murderer. It was even rumored that the Dickerson

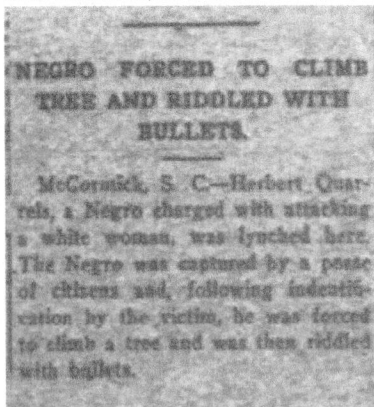

murder was premeditated. Mainly because, supposedly, Dickerson had made a bet of a quarter, two hours before he murdered Officer Collis, someone he'd had prior troubles with, that he'd kill a white man before noon that day. Then lured him *(the Officer),* allegedly, to his room to go with him to Mamie Corbin's place to get his clothes. There had been a fallout between Mamie and Richard that was allegedly the reason he went to the police station. There he filed a complaint about getting his clothes back that required an officer of the law. Officer Collis was that Officer that accompanied Richard to his mistress room to circumvent any type of altercation. An argument did brake out and Dickerson allegedly shot his mistress, then Officer Collis four times, after which he turned himself in at the local police department after being chased by Officer Collis where he was immediately jailed. The *"Honky-Tonk,"* frequent by Negro and known for its Patron drunkenness,

nightly violence, gambling and *"lo women,"* also known as prostitutes, was a next day target to be torched according to mob-rumor. And to add insult to injury, all the insurance companies cancelled all policies of the black owned establishments that were torched and refused to pay damages for the fires. Dickerson, after rumor of his murderous rage spread throughout the town, was taken from the jail by the mob, shot to death, and then strung him up on a telegraph pole in front of the Troup's Drug Store. After his lifeless body dangled in the air, it was then riddled with bullets by the mob, as reported by, *"The Evening Bulletin,"* of January 15, 1904. Their section of recent lynchings includes the following commonalities: January 15, 1904, in Vicksburg, Mississippi, Butch Riley, a Negro, allegedly killed C.C. McMillian, taken to jail where a mob over-powered the Sheriff, took Riley from the jail and lynched him. January 15, 1904, Gainesville, Florida, Jumbo Clark, a Negro, allegedly assaulted a 14 year old white girl, taken to jail where a mob of 50 hoodless men in broad daylight, took Jumbo from the jail, where he was lynched and his body was riddled with bullets. January 15, 1904, in Petersburg, Virginia, Elmore Moseley, a Negro, was lynched by a mob of Negroes for allegedly murdering another Negro that was friends of the victim before his wife and child. Moseley, after he was acquitted, was taken from his home, lynched and his body riddled with bullets all by the Negroes who disagreed with the acquittal verdict.

One astounding comment was made about the Richard Dickerson that was reported by *"The Washington Times,"* March 9, 1904, that before he, Dickerson, was hung, an estimated 2,000 bullets were put into his body. After which he was strung up and the mob began to riddle it with bullets for at least half an hour. As his body swayed from side to side at the force of each bullet's impact to his body, occasionally his arms would twitch upwards at a bullet hitting a nerve connected to the muscle of the arm, much to the cheers of the heathenish blood-thirsty mob for their amusement. Richard Dickerson's body left in the winds of a disgraceful county for four hours before being cut down. His body was then prepared for shipment to his hometown of Cynthiana, Kentucky for burial. So, when a bad seed is planted, a bad harvest is always assured. Soon, after a two day mob-controlled city and total destruction of 20 Negro buildings and homes, a special grand jury was form by Judge Mower to investigate the riot violence. The first indictment was made against Earle Sulkins, a baseball player, for his involvement in both the lynching of Dickerson and the burnings most of the Negro businesses and homes.

"The Minneapolis Journal," February 28, 1906, reports that a riot of about a thousand was targeted for the district in the Negro community called, *"The Jungle,"* of Springfield, Ohio. Even though there were no lives lost, six Negro houses and one saloon was damaged by fire. The cause of the unrest stemmed from the shooting of Martin Davis, a white man, by two Negroes and the fact; relationships had not been the same since the 1904 merciless hanging of Richard Dickerson for which no whites served any time. So looking for any glimpse of any

Devour Us Not

reason to destroy black properties and take black lives were imminent. All in a collective effort of keeping the already impoverished blacks from becoming equally, financially and politically powerful. That would then be unconscionable and causing respect to be given to a race considered inferior. A fear factor, some were unyielding to give, yet according to the *"Daily Arizona Silver Belt," March 15, 1907,* reports of flooding throughout the state of Ohio. As the Madison River waters swelled above its banks near Springfield that left two hundred families homeless and causing about a half million dollars in property damage in 1907, *"karma."* The *"Palestine Daily Herald," June 23, 1908,* reports of race problems in Sabine County, Hemphill, Texas, June 22, 1908. Two weeks prior, a white man named, Hugh Dean of Geneva was murdered in between a black School and Church, while holding a bottle of whiskey in his hand. Much conspiracy surrounding this murder where the frequent exchange of whiskey was a constant and silence of available facts being concealed by the Negroes were a certainty. Mrs. D.H. Dean, his mother, already a widowed woman was sadden by the death of her prominent son who's lifeless body was believed to have been taken to a spot near the school in an effort to conceal the true murder location. Allegedly, Dean was murdered at the Negro church and then taken to the school where eight Negroes were arrested for the conspiracy. Williams, age 26, Jerry Evans age 22, Will Johnson age 24, Moses Spellman age 24, Cleve Williams age 27 and Will Manuel age 25, where six of the Negroes taken from the city jail after over powering the jailers for the keys and hung five from a single tree branch and three more Negroes were hung the following day.

One of the Negroes was shot to death as he attempted to run while another Negro escape and was still at large while a reward of more than a thousand dollars have been offered for his capture. The brutal shotgun murder of Aaron Johnson in his home while sitting near his wife and child had his head and brains splatter over both of them as her screams echoed so loudly that the nearest neighbor a half mile away could be heard. Johnson, a 24 year old newly wed white man all of 15 months ago, allegedly was shot by Peter White, a 19 year old Negro, that was a farm hand of Johnson. This murder and the Dean murder 2 weeks prior caused the frenzy of the mob of about 150 men. Bob Wright, allegedly paid Peter White $5.00 to murder Aaron Johnson. Both men had been arrested. Wright was taken to San Augustine while White was taken to jail in Rusk for safe keeping. There were rumors reportedly of a mob unsuccessful attempt to take Wright from the jail but was spoiled by the protection of State Militia. Sometimes during the mayhem of swarming violence, the school, which is about one hundred yards from the Rockwall church where Dean was murdered, was burned down to the ground by the mob. Then the collection of all weapons from the Negro citizen of Hemphill was confiscated. Among the collection of weapons taken from every Negro's residence were loaded shotguns, pistols and rifles leaving each black household weaponless, while all white households were allowed to keep their ammo and weapons. No residence of Sabine County was ever charged and convicted for the murders of the Negroes or for the involvement in the two suspicious murders of white men. And just like this nation could appropriate 40 billion dollars immediately to bring justice to all responsible parties for 9 / 11, yet we as a nation can't find 1 dollar to stop the cycle of poverty in America. One dollar can't even be appropriated to increase the level of education to make us more globally superior. A nation with the title, *"riches nation in the world,"* still have ghetto's, homelessness, starvation, illiteracy, unfairness and where

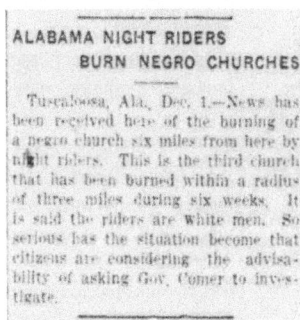

ALABAMA NIGHT RIDERS
BURN NEGRO CHURCHES

Tuscaloosa, Ala., Dec. 1.—News has been received here of the burning of a negro church six miles from here by night riders. This is the third church that has been burned within a radius of three miles during six weeks. It is said the riders are white men. So serious has the situation become that citizens are considering the advisability of asking Gov. Comer to investigate.

2% of the population controls about 90% of the wealth. The *"Bisbee Daily Review,"* May 23, 1902, reports the burning at the stakes of **Dudley Morgan** in Longview, Texas on May 22, 1902. Allegedly, Dudley was involved in an assault and robbery of Mrs. McKee, who was the wife of a Texas and Pacific section foreman of Lansing, Texas. Dudley, a Negro, just before the disgrace, he supposedly implicated another Negro as a coconspirator and in his confession named Franklin Heard that was to receive part of the stolen monies. Once the news of a Negro at large, a mob was ensued and Dudley was captured and positively identified by the victim. After the capture, Dudley was transported to Marshall, Texas by train with a large crowd of blood-thirsty thugs and battleaxes waiting for a merciless killing greeted him. First, Dudley's eyes were burned out as he yelled to be shot to alleviate the pain. A red hot burning timber was then placed to his neck, after that the mob burned off all his clothes and then began to burn other parts of his body to a slow an agonizing death. This method of torture was much preferred by the crowd as they expressed their approval verbally with each cry of mercy from Dudley in broad day light. A punishment unfitting of the crime, were of no concern to all that witness this atrocity with gladness. The horrific actions of that day never concerned the crowds for what they had inflicted upon another human being, nor where there any indictments or convictions handed out for this crime against humanity. Given the equal committed crime by an Anglo would never have become such a spectacle. But even an inkling of unsubstantiated rumor would still have yielded the same results as history has recorded. As what seemingly would be a forever mark upon a race of people *"Diaspora,"* and all the elements associated with its meaning has cast this spell of clouded injustice of unadulterated sins *"Maafa,"* will not lean its permanent fixtures upon us, so we declared. But moments of stigmatized dishonor, are generational instilled and were so deeply woven into these American

NEGRO CHURCHES BURNED BY WHITES

Enraged Mob at Grays, Ga., Commit Depredations After Failure to Find Negro Murderer.

Grays, Ga. Special. After witnessing the destruction by fire of two negro churches and the negro schoolhouse and lodge building, which they had applied the torch after failing in an attempt to secure possession of George Clarke, the negro prisoner charged with the murder of L. S. Mitchell, of Wayside, members of the mob of several hundred men who swarmed upon the county seat of Jones county dispersed and quiet was restored. The negro Clarke, together with three other negroes, is in jail at Macon, where they were hurried in an automobile by Sheriff John Brooks, of Jones county, ... he was apprised of the approach of the mob.

. . . . surrounding the jail and finding the prisoners gone the mob proceeded to set fire to two negro churches and a big wooden building . . . by negroes for a schoolhouse and lodge meetings. The building was completely burned, and during the fire the residence of E. H. Bonner, ordinary of the county, caught fire, but the mob allowed the flames to be extinguished here. Mitchell was shot down near his home a week ago, and the negro Clarke, accused of the murder, was captured Tuesday.

values for centuries, until generational time reversals of change would be used to rid this nation of its curse. Like in all changes, because the deepening of this form of evil is so enormous, its taken on a different approach, but systemically and principally the same. The challenge now is to just recognized the evil and systematically adjust accordingly. Social awareness will eventually destroy social injustice, just as protest in any form will expose it. Fortunate for a generation of young Americans living in a world with a broad perspective, being able to judge a person on character content, rather than stereotypical behaviors or skin color. Having modernized our thinking of living in a nation of harmony is better than a nation of race dominance, hatred and resentment, one would think. The team-work concept is better than individualism, when viewing the larger and broader picture of the teams' accomplishments. Mainly, because no country or team is no better than it's most vulnerable or susceptible link; a valid argument. Even though this link may be the constant target to any opposition, rightful or not, a team will never allow such improprieties. And why not? Mainly because, then the ornery or resentment becomes the team's definer and not the link. Therefore, pride in team or nation becomes the rallying cry, rather than the link of vulnerability, because all are needed if the success of the team, the nation is the main priority focus, not self. So why attempt to devour the vulnerable knowing the cycle of change will itself, its an

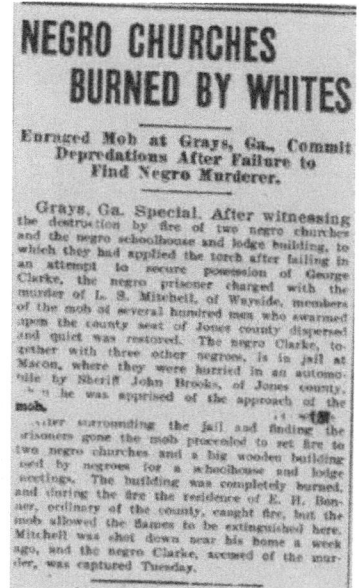

Devour Us Not

inevitability, regardless of time tables. *The San Francisco Call, November 19, 1900*, newspaper article discusses the burning at the stakes at Limon, Colorado, located about sixty miles from Denver, November, 18, 1900. Governor Thomas discussed the execution by the mob citizens of that town. John Porter supposedly confessed to the killing of eleven year old Louise Frost. Prominent members of the city to include the Mayor denounced the murder, calling it *"Limon's Atrocity." "Oh my God, Let me go, men I have something more to tell you, Please let me go: Oh my God, My God,"* were some of the final words spoken as the flames from a kerosene lit wood would consume his body. The screams and groaning of the worst kind were uttered in agony as he begged for mercy and request to be shot, among 500 barbaric excited

"New-York Tribune," of Sep 5, 1915

citizens as they watched with no remorse. It was about 6:23 in the evening when Robert W. Frost, father of Louise, whose decision it was in favor of burning, vice

mutilation or hanging, lit the stacked wood on the very spot where Louise's body was found a week prior. Porter was offered an opportunity to kneel down and pray, which he did just prior to having his arms and legs secured by being chained to the stake by a dozen men to ensure he was firmly secured

"Louise Frost" - "Louise's Father-Robert W. Frost"
"The San Francisco Call," of November 17-19, 1900

Preston "John" Porter, Jr.
"The San Francisco Call," of November 17-19, 1900

without any possibility of escape. He was also given a Bible in which he consumed himself viewing the gospel of St. Luke where just before he kneel to pray. He had detached pages from this chapter and distributed to his executioners. The crowd stared until the entire body was consumed with fire. Then the crowd was orderly as a church exit as they then performed the heartless task of bidding each other good night as they departed for their own residences. Allegedly, on Thursday, November 8, 1900, Louise left her home in a buggy in route to the post office. When night fell and she had not returned with the distant being only a mile and a half from her residence, thoughts began to dominate the family's concern of something tragic must had happened. A search party was organized and she was found at dusk on

BLOODIEST AFFAIR ON RECORD.

Three Men Murdered at Door of Tennessee Baptist Church.

Jellico, Tenn., Sept. 28.—One of the bloodiest affairs in the history of East Tennessee occurred north of Anthras post office yesterday. The scene was a Baptist church, within fifty yards of which a "blind tiger" has been operated for months. Services had closed, and nearly all the congregation had emerged from the church, when a crowd of drunken men, who had visited the blind tiger, began firing into the worshipers with pistols.

John Bonnett, J. W. McKinney and Edward Thomas were shot down at the church door and died almost instantly. The preacher was mortally wounded. Another worshiper was also shot down in front of the church, but is not dangerously wounded.

"Keowee Courier," of September 30, 1908

NIGHT RIDERS APPLY FIRE.

Thirteen Negro Churches and School Houses Burned.

Albany, Ga., Sept. 28.—A special to the Albany Herald to-day says that thirteen negro churches and school houses were burned in the neighborhood of Kestler by a band of unknown night riders Saturday night. Every negro church and school house the corners of Early, Baker and Calhoun counties were destroyed.

Among the burned buildings were the New Salem church and school building, belonging to the best class of negroes in that section.

The cause of what is generally regarded an outrage is not known, but the recent attempted criminal assault of a white woman by a negro near Kestler is supposed to have been one of the causes which led to the application of the torch to the property of the negroes.

In the country visited several negro lodge rooms were dynamited. Several lynchings have taken place in this same community within the past few months. A reign of terror exists among the negro population.

"Keowee Courier," of September 30, 1908

Friday. Charles E. Wamsley was the researcher who first discovered Louise, with her body submerged in blood, his first question was did she recognize her attacker. She then asked him to lift her up before she became unconscious. Dick Biestline and Mr. Jewel, attempting to aid Mr. Wamsley when it became apparent that her lifeless-like body was slowly nearing death. Only the utterance of whispered words of nothingness from Louise were heard. Wamsley knowing the nearness of her death, tried to secure the answer to who had stabbed her as

the area was observed as signs of an obvious struggle. The men manage to get her to her home where she died an hour later. Even though she was unconscious she was re-

called shouting out, *"Don't!, don't!"* But Louise never regained consciousness to give details into who had committed this horrific crime against her. After she passed away, an examination was performed that revealed sixteen stab wounds. Almost immediately, horses and bloodhounds were rounded up for a man hunt. Footprints leading from the crime scene to a cabin occupied by a gang of hired railway workers near the railroad post were tracked. Significance to the shoe print was the heel where four nails projected a unique structure unidentifiable with any other shoe print. In the cabin, the shoe was identified with sixteen year old Preston *"John"* Porter, as the word went out for all Negroes working on the railway to leave the state. On that Monday, November 12, 1900, John Porter, his Father and brother were all arrested in Denver. Under constant interrogation, after they were transported from Denver to Limon by train, John confessed on Wednesday the 14th by saying, *"Well, I done it!"* As if the weight of the interrogation had altered his steadfastness when he, uttered those fatal words. Then he gave a graphic detail of the events as lying and waiting, securing the horses by the bridle, forcing her from her buggy at knife point then drugged her in the bushes where he assaulted her. When asked if she said anything or screamed, he replied, *"She cried a little,"* in an unremorseful tone. And so by those alleged words ceiled his fate as Sheriff Jones allowed with little resistance, for the mob to take John Porter from his custody and torch his body. And this so called smoking gun of the shoe print and confession in a court of law would probably have yielded a verdict of guilty. All-be-it, this is of the opinion of a one sided interrogation tactic from a number of various methods to a probably scared immature 16 year old. A kid looking in the face of the enemy would almost assuredly agree to or say anything not understanding what would result in his immediate death. Many Americans and African-Americans at that time spoke out against this cruel and unusual punishment of burning another human being. Most notably was Mrs. Ida B. Wells-Barnett, a champion for a law against such cruelty towards any human being. No one ever paid for this crime nor were there a trial depicting what really happened and the motivation behind the assault. Undoubtedly, the stigmatized manner in which people of color are depicted then and now gives some measure to the degree of punishments and views blacks face in a world of being their brother's keeper.

During the 2012 Republican campaign debates, one of the candidates became the subject of some unwanted racial rhetoric as it relates to property of family ownership. The pejorative word in question was located on a rock visible to the entry of the property had been known and was an acknowledged as a common fixture of that property. One of the property work hands, an African-American, did give a contrary response to when the name was painted over after probably centuries of common knowledge of its existence. The word was, *"Niggerhead,"* a word commonly used to degrade in an era that criticized anything unusually unattractive as being like the head of a Negro. The Negro head being usually abnormal or even disfigured unlike the symmetrically round head of an Anglo. So, add this word in a series of insults directed at people of color for the purpose of self-hatred and denial of self-proclaim beauty. Like the word, *"Nigger-Heaven,"* though unrelated to beauty, it's still an exclusion element of a society of race separation. But the term meant the upper deck of a movie theater or courtroom as the only seating arrangement for blacks so they could not be in close proximity to whites. Another issue that did divide us in more ways than one. As reported by, *"The Arizona Republic," Mar 16, 1911,"*

Devour Us Not

reports the United States and Mexico as being nine miles from Douglas, Arizona of Cochise County. As to the origin of how these names were considered in the United States, more than a hundred *"Niggerheads,"* and other place names now considered racially offensive, were changed in 1962. The United States Board on Geographic Names made these changes, but many local names remained unchanged today. Lady Bird Johnson was even instrumental in making efforts to change the name in Burnet, Texas. Whether talking of stylish and eloquent clothing, that clearly is an

"The Day Book," of January 11, 1913

advertisement of *"Niggerhead Suits,"* as a component of dressing for success is overlooked by the mere presence of a century old painful word is by itself, regardless of complimentary intent, reflective of derogatory

"The Princeton Union," of Oct 20, 1921   "Pittsburg Dispatch," of Sep 3, 1892   "The Evening Herald," of Oct 26, 1896   "The Appeal," of June 30, 1917

rhetoric. Even in an industrial setting, is also announcing to the highest value of coal as *"The Pride of Tennessee."* So the question still remains, as positive as these ads below appear to symbolize, symbolization is the key to the rejection of the word *"Nigger,"* that has mauled its people of color. But without ever walking in our shoes, the reality of significant on all understanding, the depth of pain this word has had in our culture as well as country. It reminds me of a discussion that was presented in one of several Leadership Class conducted by the Federal Government for which I was employed. The class, being racially and gender diverse, the question of racial tolerance and racial sensitivity came up. An Anglo-Manager explained she was not aware how she at the time was not being sensitive to racial issues. One day a white employee, friends with a black employee, all ended after over ten years of mutual respect in the workplace. The incident occurred when the white employee played as a practical joke, took a miniature rope and made a hanging noose and placed it in the black employee's cubicle in view of all in that department. The black employee was so offended by this action, went to the female Anglo-Manager attending the Leadership Class with me and expressed his disapproval of his former friend's action. The Anglo Manager stated at the time, being insensitive toward the incident took no actions, other than asking the white employee to explain what had happened and nothing more. Like the Anglo-Manager, the white employee didn't understand the black employee's anger and frustration. Long story, short, the black employee ended up filing an EEO complaint against the white employee and Management for which the Manager was floored and later apologized. After several discussions and only after these discussions and sensitivity training was she educated about the history of hangings in America. A topic she later admits to being completely ignorant of. Valued lessons learned in a cultural awareness and racial sensitivity world for which most Americans, not black can identify with. And like the Leadership Class incident, the word *"Nigger,"* as popular as it may appear in the hip-hop culture, particular with how it resonates with the younger generation who has lost the significance of its meaning as it relates its derogatory implications. This should never lose its meaning for the horrific history many die never knowing or being called anything else. But, as the newspaper article from, *"The Appeal," June 30, 1917*, where only Negroes and dogs were not allowed in a public elevator in Houston, Texas

"The Bourbon News," of September 16, 1910

further illustrates the lack of respect human-beings and the Negroes of that era faced. Impervious to equal valued in American history, is the fact that some of our most popular and most valued hero's had Negroes as their body guards or being politically correct, *"body-servants."* As to why, with all the typical stigmatizations of negativity associated with Negroes, would these famous men and women chose with all the liberties at their exposure, pick a then *"second-class citizen,"* maybe they missed the memo. Accordingly, reported by *"The Houston Daily Post," December 17, 1899,* pictured Tom Blue, a Negro, and a Houstonian at the age of ninety. Mr. Blue was Samuel *"Sam,"* Houston of Texas, body servant. He was even present during the battle of San Jacinto, April 21, 1836. The battle led by General Houston defeated General Antonio Lopez de Santa Anna in about 18 minutes which led to the signing of a treaty that paved the way for Texas to become an independent country. Today, there is a bigger than life statue of Sam Houston, sixty-seven feet tall located off highway 45 just outside Huntsville, Texas. Sam, twice President of the Republic of Texas, before Texas joined the union in 1845 as the 28th State. Sam Houston also became the seventh Governor of Texas and is buried in Huntsville where he died in 1863. But very little is known about **Tom Blue**, a Negro, his body Servant.

| Tom Blue | Ferdinand Shavers | James H. Jones | Elizabeth Keckly | Thomas Cross | William Henry Crook | Fred Ebiling |

Tom Blue, Gen Houston's Body Servant * Ferdinand Shavers, Abe Lincoln's Body Servant * James Jones, Jefferson Davis's Servant * Elizabeth Keckly, Mrs. Lincoln's Seamstress * Thomas Cross, Abe Lincoln's Servant * William Crook, Abe Lincoln's Security Guard Servant * Fred Ebiling, Abe Lincoln's Barber - *"The Houston Daily Post," Dec 17, 1899, "The Salt Lake Herald," Aug 9, 1909, "The Washington Times," Jun 12, 1921, "The Washington Times," Sep 4, 1904, "The Morning Times," of Oct 17, 1896, "New-York Tribune," of April 17, 1893, The Evening World., May 22, 1888.*

Thomas Cross, was a servant to President Lincoln who wrote a letter on his behave that helped him avoid the draft during the Civil War. He and **William Crook** accompanied Mrs. Lincoln to Chicago after the assassination of President Lincoln. **Ferdinand Shavers** was the first body servant of Abraham Lincoln even four years before his election to the Presidency. *The Morning Times, February 9, 1896* reports President Lincoln's wearing of his beard and the reaction from the public. A written request from a little girl named Grace Bedell convince the President to continue the wearing of whiskers for no other apparent reason other than admiration in 1865. But in portraits from 1853, 1861, 1863, 1864, Lincoln had a full beard which was also admired by many vice being clean shaving. So a petition about Ferdinand Shavers was eventually made on his behalf to be appointed as the official body guard during Lincoln's Presidency. But, when the civil war broke out, fearing for his safety as a black man, President Lincoln released him from his custody as he then requested he be assigned to the Black Regiment. He eventually began working for the Indiana recruiting station where he rose to the rank of Captain in the regular Army in Indianapolis, Indiana. He lived out his final days in Leavenworth, Kansas and Colorado. **Elizabeth Keckley,** a Negro, was the seamstress and dress maker to many socialites in Washington; one of whom was Mary Todd Lincoln, the wife of President Abraham Lincoln. Elizabeth Keckly was born a slave, around 1822, but developed a mastery in needle workings to secure her own freedom from slavery. The

Devour Us Not

news of her dressmaking became a populist among high society women to include Mrs. Jefferson Davis and Mrs. Abraham Lincoln, Mary Todd Lincoln at the recommendation of a mutual friend, General McLean's wife. Through her association with fashion, linking her with Mrs. Lincoln, she soon became what was deemed in that era as a Modiste, Companion and friendly relationship with Lincolns during their four years in the White House. From the first inauguration to the assassination, every dress worn by Mrs. Lincoln during her years in the White House was made by Elizabeth Keckly. But, then there's the book, titled, *"Behind the scene,"* written by Elizabeth, supposedly in New York mostly about her four years in the White House and all that took place during that period. The book was described as a treacherous friend out for revenge for financial gain against a hated master. Both blacks and whites condemned her actions in writing such a personal account of

activities taking place for a beloved President such as Abraham Lincoln. Needless to say, to exonerate herself from being blamed as a bad omen among black servants, the book's revenues were never made to Elizabeth; she never received a cent from its sales. Then the book was mysteriously suppressed after word of its content spread. In an interview, Elizabeth Keckly stated about the book, that she just wanted to write a simple story about her life and particularly about the Lincoln's with the proceeds going towards the rebuilding of Wilberforce University. Wilberforce was the first University for Negroes in the United States and was burned after the Lincoln's assassination. Much was also stated about the many personal gifts of pictures and blood-stained garments worn by Mrs. Lincoln the night of the assassination that aided in collaborating her story of facts that were all gladly given to her. The book essentially marked the end of her relationship with Mrs. Lincoln as Elizabeth passed away in 1907 at nearly 90 years old, defending her position on her memoirs to the very end.

James H. Jones, a Negro, was servant to Jefferson Davis, President of the Confederate. Jim as he was affectionately called by President Davis was with Jefferson Davis the night he was captured, May 10, 1865 in Irwinton, Georgia as reported by *"The Washington Times," of June 12, 1904*. Ironically, Davis was wearing a waterproof wrath or ragian made by none other than Elizabeth Keckly, for Mrs. Davis, that was inadvertently given to him by Jim as he was attempting in a hast to escape the Yankee approach on horseback. That attempt to escape had failed as Mr. Davis realized he was surrounded and essentially gave up and wondered back to the tent still occupied by his wife. A month before

Richmond failed, Jim was entrusted with about $12,000,000 dollars of silver, gold and other valuables that included the Confederate Seal. His trustworthiness was assured for the Seal was never collected by the Yankees. Being a captive, Jim was eventually released back to Raleigh, N. C. where he never saw the Davis family

again. One of the most valued gifts given to Jim was the walking cane of Mr. Jefferson Davis after his death. Given to him by Mrs. Davis with engraved silver trimmings that read, *"To James Jones, in grateful memory, from Mrs. Jefferson Davis."* The cane handle was made from a deer Mr. Davis had killed while holding the post of Secretary of War on a hunt in Mississippi. Senator Blackburn had commented on the wood for which two canes were made, his and Mr. Davis, was of the highest value and the only two from that piece of wood. The secret of the Confederate Seal was secured by James Jones and was never ever recovered from the day the seal was placed in his hands by Mr. Davis until the day James Jones died. The supposed $12,000,000 dollars in coins and other treasuries were taken by Jones to a train bound for South Carolina and turned over to Captain Parker where he initially buried the monies and then dug it back up after it was deemed safe from attack. When asked of the question as to; of all the people, why Jefferson Davis did entrusted him with such a magnanimous responsibility, Jones offered no explanation. Jones lived out his life with his son, Doctor William Jones in the suburbs of Deanewood, about four miles out from Bennings Line near Washington.

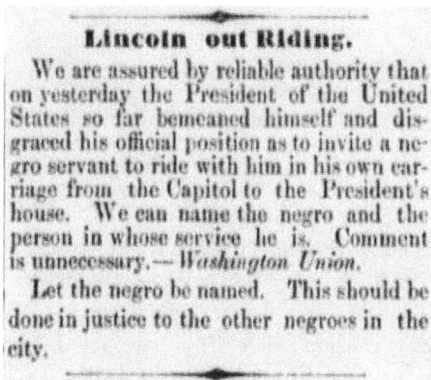

Lincoln out Riding.

We are assured by reliable authority that on yesterday the President of the United States so far bemeaned himself and disgraced his official position as to invite a negro servant to ride with him in his own carriage from the Capitol to the President's house. We can name the negro and the person in whose service he is. Comment is unnecessary.— *Washington Union.*

Let the negro be named. This should be done in justice to the other negroes in the city.

President Lincoln, once while walking in a park was approached by an unknown pitifully dressed Negro with one leg who extended his hand for help according to *"The Morning Tulsa Daily World," of February 12, 1922.* Mr. Lincoln, who banked at the Riggs and Company of Washington bank, handed the helpless Negro without knowledge of his name a check. Mr. Lincoln simply made the check out to, *"Colored Man with one leg,"* knowing the customer service relationship at the bank was assured and the needs of the Negro would be sufficient enough to satisfying his needs without question. To the right is an article about the President's relationship with an unknown Negro, an act viewed by the public then as despicable and demeaning. But Mr. Lincoln's association with Negroes were many unbeknownst to the public for obvious reason of that era. *"The National Tribune," December 10, 1891*, reports of a Negro barber coming with President Lincoln from Illinois to Washington, D.C. in 1861. And for two years, William H. Johnson, a Negro, shaved and cut the President's hair until his death from small-pox in 1863. A disease initially attracted by the President from which he recovered, but Johnson wasn't as fortunate. Then the job was given to Samuel H. Williams who held the position until Lincoln's assassination in addition to having his mother as the cook. Adding little merit to the mischaracterization of relationships between all whites and blacks as somewhat of a myth. A mischaracterization of justice and denial.

The story of **James Benjamin Parker** in 1901 received enormous press coverage that for lack of a better word, got lost in the eyes of justice for his contribution to an heroic act. It should be noted that if the contribution of James Benjamin Parker had been sustained and admissible in court documents, would have caused series credibility flaws into the secret service ability to protect the President of the United States in public. As reported by, *"The Washington Times," September 7, 1901, was* the events into the assassination of President McKinley. Still dealing with the devastation of a hard blow to this nation as the Lincoln assassination and still feeling

James Benjamin Parker

that sorrow of a beloved President some thirty-six years earlier. September 6, 1901, after being introduce to the crowd by John Milburn, President of the exposition, tragedy was but seconds away. While standing in the Temple of Music at the Pan-American Exposition at 4 o'clock in the afternoon, Buffalo, New York waiting to meet the public with many watching. Also in attendance among three thousand people inside and another ten thousand or so outside, was Leon Czolgosz from Detroit who fired two bullets into the President's body with a 32-calibre derringer, concealed by a handkerchief. The first bullet struck the sternum in the President's chest, deflected to the right, and then traveled beneath the skin to a point directly below his right nipple. The second bullet struck him in the abdomen that left a hole in the President's stomach but no bullet was found by physicians during the examination and operation from these wounds. Before a third shot could be fired an Ireland, a secret serviceman, George A. Foster, a detective named Gallagher, James Benjamin Parker, a Negro who was directly in front of Czolgosz and a sailor, named Frances F. O'Brien from the United States Artillery Corps grabbed Czolgosz and wrestle him to the

ground. James Parker, was described as a giant of a man, standing erect at six feet six inches tall, worked as a waiter in the exposition café. Parker was originally born into slavery in 1845 in Atlanta and had recently moved from New York to Buffalo. Parker, being the closest in proximity to Czolgosz, was the first to give him a terrific blow and bring him to the ground, knocking the pistol from his grasp before he could fire another shot as others later assisted him according to "The Hocking Sentinel," September 19, 1901. Leon admitting during the trial that he would have fired more shots had he not been stopped. Also during the trial,

artilleryman member O'Brien testified that he was the first to attack Czolgosz and bring him to the ground. His testimony was collaborated by his fellow artillerymen, Neff and Bertschey. George A. Foster, the secret service-man testified he was the one who grabbed the gun that prevented Czolgosz from firing again. He also stated there was a colored man nearby that never offered any assistance in apprehending Czolgosz. Harry T. Henshaw, superintendent of the Temple of Music was next to testify which collaborated all previous testimonies given to establishing the sequence of events. John Branch, a colored employee at the exposition testified he was an eye witness to the assassination and pretty much described almost in rehearsed like fashion that matched all previous testimonies. Detective James F.H. Vallelley and Superintendent of Police Bull, both collaborate each others testimonies as to how the interrogation went. When the testimony phase of the trial ended, there was no mentioning of James Benjamin Parker's valor, nor was it mentioned in an official report filed by the secret service. And now as apart of the Official Court documents, no mentioning of James Parker's contributions. It was believed that District Attorney Penny, in conjunction with the secret service, embarrassed by the amount of the initial publicity and heroic acts by James Parker received nationwide, saw an opportunity as one of many "old Dixie tricks," for people of color to be excluded from any positive opinions. On October 29, 1901, Leon Czologosz was electrocuted, as 1,700 volts of electricity entered his body as reported by, "The Salt Lake Herald," October 30, 1901. Many of the Negro Press bitterly complained as well as other United Press organizations released confusing information about the inconsistency of reporting of facts by witnesses. It should be known that James Benjamin Parker is the real hero in this story of "Dixie Trickery." James Parker died April,

1908 in a mental hospital for the insane in Philadelphia. No one came to claim his body, so it was then given to a medical college. He never recovered from the negative publicity.

President Abraham Lincoln at one point of his life was a postmaster, appointed to his postmaster's position by President Andrew Jackson, on May 7, 1833. In Lincoln's 1860 autobiography, he pointed out that the office was *"too insignificant,"* to make politics an objection and ended up being indebted to the office while seeking employment elsewhere. Williamsburg County, Lake City, South Carolina, February 22, 1898, Frazier B. Baker was appointed as Postmaster, for the county with a large Negro population. Accordingly, the

Abraham Lincoln - 1854
"The San Francisco Call," of Feb 7, 1909

Frazier Baker's Family
"The Colored American," of Dec 2, 1899

trouble started about the time of the appointment when he was fired upon while leaving the office one night. It was reported that Baker was rude, obnoxious, ignorant and insensitive to customer's needs, particularly white women while forgetting his place after his appointment. This mischaracterization of Frazier was used in an effort of justifying reasons for taking the law into their own hands. Fearing for the safety of his family after the first incident, Mr. Baker moved into a house on the outskirts of town near to where he had established the post office. A week prior to the horrific crime, what was used to convey a warning to Baker, was the riddling of bullets into the post office building. Word of this incident was reported to Senators B. E. Tillman and Mc Lauren.

Congressman Horton then asked the Postmaster General to intervene. The discussion of removing Baker because of the impending violence against he and his family was immediately rejected by Baker. Acknowledging Washington's supposedly protection rights as a Federal employee gave him this false sense of security. Security that was short lived because within days, a cowardly mob of about three to four hundred well armed angry white men with shot guns, pistols and torches in hand, set fire to the post office. Then they proceeded to the Baker's home where he and his family were sleeping on February 22, 1898 and set fire to it. It was reported that Frazier was first to reach his front door with his infant child in his arm in an attempt to flee the burning house. When the door was opened he was met with volume of bullets striking him and the child several times rendering him and the child dead before they fell. Still inside the burning house door way, one by one the wife and children begin to exit. His wife was shot several times as well as two of the girls in the arm near the shoulder. Other reports reveal that of the seven occupants of the home all were shot but only Frazer and his infant child were killed and were allow to be burned while on-lookers watched with no attempt to secure their safety. The wounds the two girls suffered were so severe until it appears their arms may have to be severed. District Attorney Abial Lathrop was appointed to assist the postal inspectors, Maye and J.W. Bulla in gathering information on all responsible parties for justice as reported by, *"The Laurens Advertisers,"* of March 1, 1898, *"The Salt Lake Herald,"* of February 23, 1898 and *"The Watchman and Southron,"* of March 2, 1898. Thirteen citizens of Williamsburg County, Lake City, South Carolina were on trial for the murder of Frazier B. Baker and his infant child. The seriously wounding of members of his family with intent to kill, the burning of the post office and the home of the Baker's. The case resulted in a mistrial. No one was ever found guilty of the murders as his remaining family

Devour Us Not

was rescued by a young white woman and taken to Boston. Only minor postal restrictions were put in place on the county but nothing more was done for the senseless murder of a citizen just because he was a person of color. The lawlessness of criminal mischief against people of color had a variety of unjustified solutions without remorse.

As reported by *"The Salt Lake Herald," March 14, 1901* in Corsicana, Texas, John Henderson, a Negro, allegedly murdered a white woman, Vallie Younger, on March 6, 1901. After her husband return home from farming and find his wife missing. His three year old daughter supposedly stated, *"A Nigger hit mama."* Bloodhounds were then called out, a posse ensued which lead them to Henderson. Before a cowardly mob crowd of about five thousand watched; John Henderson was brutally murdered by being burned alive, after supposedly he made a full confession. After the word had gotten out about Henderson's arrest, fearing the worst, law officials moved Henderson to Hillsboro. Then the night before, with the mob in pursuit while Henderson was in the process of being transferred to Ft. Worth by train, when the train stopped in Itasca, the mob overpowered the officers and secured the prisoner by force. Many car loads from all around nearby communities assisted in this act of barbarity by taking Henderson to the courthouse yard where an iron pole was immediately erected. Several good Samarians attempted to appeal to the blood-thirsty mod to no avail. A committee was quickly formed to secure the confession which was immediately signed an attested by the justice of the peace, H. G. Roberts. The confession statement read as follows: *"I, John Henderson, Colored, 22 years old murdered an unknown white lady, three miles north of Corsicana, on the 6th of March, 1901. There was no one present but myself, the woman and two little children. I murdered her and left her in the house without any intention of robbing her. I don't know why I did it. (Signed.) JOHN J. HENDERSON.* At that point, the announcement of his execution was scheduled for 2pm. To allow for more witnesses to come to Corsicana as it was reported all seats were over packed aboard the trains coming into Corsicana. When word of U.S. Marshalls and troops from Dallas were in route to Corsicana, a speedy rush to carry-out their intended purpose began. Henderson was then taken from the jail in handcuffs surrounded by law officials in route to the burning site. Quickly after Henderson had been attached to the pole with wire, oil was then placed on the wood and Henderson's clothing. Just before the flames got too great, Conway Younger, the husband of the murdered woman launch at Henderson with a knife and slashed him across his face. Conway made another attempt to cut Henderson but the flames were too great as the crowd yelled with excitement. Remarkably, as the crowds were ecstatic, Henderson never said a mumbling word, much to the crowd's disappointment. In about ten minutes or so, Henderson was believed to be dead, having slightly moved his hand, rolled his eyes at the angry mob and a groan. Justice of the peace, Roberts, acting coroner, held an inquest over the remains and gave the following verdict: *"I find that deceased came to his just death at the hands of the incensed and outraged feelings of the best people in the United States, the citizens of Navarro County and adjoining counties. The evidence as well as the confession of guilt by the deceased, shows that his punishment was fully merited and commendable."* No one was ever charged or an investigation into the brutal murders of John J. Henderson or Mrs. Vallie Younger of Navarro County, Corsicana, Texas.

"The Mighty Voice Few Have Heard Of, But the Truth Of Her Message Still Lives On." Ida B. Wells, ahead of her time as her significant contribution to the struggles for people of color deserves some recognition

in this family's journey as well. But, who was this extraordinary woman who was constantly criticized by the opposition? During a period in American history when speaking out against the placate hatred of the south and its unfair treatment of African-Americans by whites was not only dangerous for your family but could cost **you** your life. A lot is to be said about the contributions of males during our struggles as people of color, but rarely is there any mentioning of black female contributions. I think, as apart of our history, her story is worthy to be told. *"Ida B. Wells-The Broad Ax," of July 14, 1917*

"The San Francisco Call," of March 26, 1901   **Ida B. Wells** had many titles, but a journalist by trade. She was a fearless, anti-lynching crusader as her lecturing took her to far away places; such as The United Kingdom after being denied in her own country to speak out against lynching. She was born July 16, 1862 as a slave to James and Elizabeth Wells in Holly Spring, Mississippi. Both parents were literate when 90% of blacks were illiterate after the civil war. She was the second eldest of eight children where her parents; by slave standards were skilled as a cook and a carpenter, living on different plantations. Ida accepted the family-leadership responsibilities at the age of fourteen when both of her parents and several of her siblings were tragically killed by an epidemic of yellow fever that devastated their town. Ida took the weight of caring for her siblings by teaching school and attending college at Rust College to support them. With the burden of keeping the family together, teaching and attending school, she made a choice to move to Memphis, where it is told her Aunt helped her with the family. Perhaps it was the incident of 1884 when Ida was 25 years old that sparked the fight in her. The incident occurred when she defiled a conductor's orders to give up her seat aboard a train to a white man *(does this sound familiar?)*. Ida really put her teeth into this event, literally, as she bite the conductor who was trying to remove her. Accordingly, Ida was eventually removed by force from the train after paying the same amount as every other customer aboard. So the conductor with the assistance from other men, took action, much to the applauds of every seated white person, both male and female aboard the train. Even though the Civil Rights Acts law of 1875 had been passed, southerners refused to acknowledge any law benefiting equality. And least of all to one so daring as to defy the idea that they are equal. But Ida's unfortunate incident that day only fueled a burn-ing and a yearning, that if only one voice, *"hers,"* then this voice shall speak for all who can't for fear or lack of knowledge remain in silence. Ida didn't, and so she won an out of court settlement. Another real turning point in Ida's life was the 1892 lynching of three of her friends in Memphis. It was not a joyful period for African Americans between 1890 and 1910 and in this country because there were 2,600 black men, women and children lynched that were reported. Yet, realistically one can consider that not all incidents were reported or observed other than the cowardly mobs that conducted them.

While Ida was a partner in the local black newspaper, *"The Free Speech and Headlights Newspaper,"* she wrote a very reviling article into the lynching incident. The atrocity of that incident involved her three friends being taken from the county jail by several hundred heathenish, cowardly mobsters and lynched. Her friends, one of which she was the god-mother to one of their daughters, had a very successful and competitive local grocery store. To eliminate the competitive edge their store had over the white owned similar business, prompted the whites to eliminate the competition through fear and intimidation. Remember, the faulty southern laws prevented blacks from violence of any kind against whites and it prohibited gun ownership of blacks, while whites could get ammo/guns without payment. But in the blacks defense to protect their property against damage, a fight broke out during an altercation and a white man was injured. They were then arrested and charged with a crime of violence against a white person who initiated the incident. Proclaiming liberation from the injustices of

Memphis, Ida encouraged all her readers to save their money and move west or anywhere, as she eventually did. So, in the aftermath of the lynching, she moved away after threats were made where she continued her quest for justice on their behalf. Ida used the experience from the Memphis incident and surmised whole editorials that suggest the issue surrounding the animosity between the races was the southern whites using a stereotypical characterization of black male's sexual aggression as the justification for their lynching's, as sort-of- an *"eye for an eye"* parable. And these lawless acts were somehow based on some fundamental notion that make black men natural-born rappers of white women in particular and therefore the need to be severely punished for their action or the mere thought. Moreover, Wells suggestion that white men need look no further than the morality of their own white women as the essence of the falsehood that black men are responsible for the misconduct of their women. Wells first pamphlet in 1892 gives a parable into the sexual cravens of white men toward black women as being the bases for their assumption of equal thoughts for that of

black men, hence the creation of the mulatto race by their one-sided acts of hypocrisy. Of course this set off a firestorm as the truth general does, for which her newspaper office was completely destroyed by fire and consequently made a clear passage for her relocation to Philadelphia, and New York before settling in Chicago. On, June 27, 1895, at the age of 33, Ida married a prominent 41 year old Lawyer named Ferdinand L. Barnett in Chicago, Illinois. Ferdinand was a widower man with two young sons, with the eldest about 10 years of age. During the first eight years of her marriage,

Hon. F.L. Barnett
"The Broad Ax," of February 10, 1917

Hon. F.L. Barnett (Older)
"The Broad Ax," of December 27, 1919

Ida gave birth to two sons and two daughters named Charles born in 1896, Herman in 1897, Ida, Jr. in 1901 and Alfreda born in 1904. Wells wrote many pamphlets exposing white violence, lynching and defending blacks against wrongful prosecution. In 1896, Ida helped organize the **National Association of Colored Women.** She also opposed the policy of accommodation advocated by Booker T. Washington and had personal, if not ideological, difficulties with W.E.B. Du Bois, her co-founder of the National Afro-American Council and **National Association for the Advancement of Colored People (NAACP)** in 1909. She was one of the first black females to run for public office as she ran for the Illinois State Legislature. She once said*: "One had better die fighting against injustice than die like a dog or a rat in a trap."* Her fearless journey, fueled by her motivation into her own experiences and the experiences of others whom she knew and did not know, caused for world wide admiration and recognition for what she had accomplished in her lifetime. Her drooling schedule left little time for her family but the benefits from her actions help bring notice to an American epidemic. For without the voice of a woman once physically thrown from a train for attempting to exercise her fundamental rights as a paying customer aboard pubic transportation, was eventually heard and the world listened. One can only wish they were born in a time to have grace her presence with a listening ear. As the many *"Unsung Hero's"* of our civil rights struggles did. Her gripping acts of defiance, her uncompromising efforts of unjust normalcy of opening the windows for this tainted glass of injustice proved to be yet again, one of the few untold heroic stories of our civil rights era. No finer words could have been written of her than that of the above left Salt Lake City newspaper article dated September 15, 1894. Where by the hands of God would she be raised up article titled *"God Has Raised Her Up"*, and thought of as a savior for the cause of placing an end once and for all the barbaric gestures of lynching. Also, at that session and the first speaker at the event was the first president of the NAACP or first known as The National Afro-American Council was Bishop Walters. Like many of our other

clergymen, denouncing the lynching of black men for the simplest or alleged horrific crimes had an explanation to the oppositional criticism of promoting crime. Being quick however to dispelled the notion of condoning crime by Negroes in an effort to cease lynching as a means of punishment for and exclusively for

"The Appeal," of Jan 30, 1892- A Young Ida B Wells

1909-Ida B. Wells-Barnett, Charles, Herman, Ida & A Alfreda

Ida B Wells-Barnett's Family-"The Broad Ax," of December 22, 1917

Reading from L/R of the Group Family photo, Top: *Hulette M. Barnett, Herman Kohlsaat Barnett, Regiment Supply Sgt. F.L. Barnett, Jr., Ida B. Wells Barnett, Jr., Charles Aked Barnett, Albert G. Barnett. **Reading from L/R Bottom:** Hulette E. Barnett, Ferdinand L. Barnett, Beatrice J. Barnett, Audrey V. Barnett, Ida B. Wells Barnett, Alfreda H. Barnett and Florence B. Barnett.*

Ida was called the Joan D'Are of the African-American Race.

*"Uncle **Jerry Lord Chesterfield**"*
"Ft. Worth Gazette," of Mar 12, 1893

Negroes. Their struggles would continue long after both their deaths. Gifts of voices that has lasted a life time, Ida B. Wells-Barnett died, March 26, 1931. A lost felt in not only the black community but around the world. A very special and unique child of God who's passionate words of justice eventually lead to the disbandment of lynching as a means of cruel and unusual punishment throughout the south and all other states. A fighter that never gave up her fight to end mob law violence to awaken this nation of its blind eyes of justice. Her relentless and tireless effort to the anti-lynching movement changed this oppressed people, while notifying the world of the hypocrisy that had run wild like feathers

on an open plain. Hypocrisy that has caused a nation to default on its guarantee of life, liberty and the pursuit of happiness. Her voice now silent, still reminds with us evermore. Many unknown slaves were apart of the White House employment team. And many Presidents that were slave-owners brought their slaves with them when they occupied the White House. George Washington was the only President that was a slave-owner that never brought his slaves to Washington, only because the White House was located in New York and Philadelphia during his presidency. These Presidents that were slave-owner were Thomas Jefferson, James Madison, Andrew Jackson, John Tyler, Zachery Taylor and James Polk. **Uncle *Jerry*,** as he was affectionately called, began working within the White House during 1873. Soldier, President Ulysses S. Grant being a frequent visitor to a Baltimore Hotel where Jerry was a waiter, was an admirer of Jerry by the manner in which his mannerisms of politeness and bearing convinced the President to invite Jerry to come to Washington. After about thirty years Uncle Jerry's ghost stories became legendary about as much as his courtly bows and polite mannerisms. His

Devour Us Not

proclaim that the White House was haunted were often the scenes for attentive White House occupants to be entertained by these intriguing tells from Uncle Jerry's ghostly goons from the attic. On July 25, 1904, according to *"The Washington Times," July 26, 1904,* newspaper article, Uncle Jerry Chesterfield, a long time employee of the White House that served eight Presidents, died. Originally hired by Ulysses Grant, he fatefully served Rutherford Hayes, James Garfield, Chester Arthur, Grover Cleveland, Benjamin

Uncle Jerry

"Los Angeles Herald," of December 17, 1905

Harrison, William McKinley and finally Theodore Roosevelt. Uncle Jerry some-

"The Washington Times," of July 26, 1904   times would travel with President Grant to San Francisco, California while rejecting the invite to travel beyond our shores as his body servant. President and Mrs. Roosevelt would often visit Uncle Jerry during his illness at his then modest home in gratitude for his service and to cheer him up. The President along with Chairman Cortelyou had brought flowers only two weeks before his passing which according to the attending Physician, says help Uncle Jerry hang on to life a little bit longer. Uncle Jerry was initially hired in 1873 as a cleaner and helper. A job that Uncle Jerry took very seriously, allowing no dust to accumulate at any time. Shortly after he had been hired by President Grant, Mrs. Grant chose Jerry as her footman for her carriage servant. A footman's duties included the lighting of the carriage and in the house at dusk. He goes out with the carriage in the evening and valets any member of the family. A footman dresses in livery and is well mannered tall and nice-looking. When one footman is employed, the butler assists in his duties. Uncle Jerry also hoisted and lowered the American flag and was described as the hardest working employee on the payroll. The only blunder ever made by Uncle Jerry shortly before his illness, was raised the American Flag upside down, which is the sign for distress. Needless to say, a number of frantic phone calls broke out all over Washington D.C. as the job from that day on was given to an Army serviceman. Uncle Jerry often commented about his love for President William McKinley and how he would have his room and cabinet chambers as clean as possible. Rheumatics made his work responsibilities in winter difficult but, Jerry admittedly enjoyed summer the best as he'd showcase his vocal styling of old Negro songs while he worked that could be heard throughout the corridor. Uncle Jerry was born in the eastern part of Maryland as a slave, but little else is known of his pass. His official title at the White House was black major-domo, which means a confidential family slave, treated like family, rather than a traditional slave. But Uncle Jerry was no slave at the White House, that title was an old term used during slavery to distinguish a Negro slave of a white family who was treated and regarded as a regular family-member. An honorary term not one of disgrace as *"slave,"* would suggest of that era. But, Uncle Jerry died in honor, beloved by all who knew him as a kind and gentle soul.

Arthur Simmons, an escaped slave from an Aristocratic family in North Carolina was employed about the same time as Uncle Jerry in the White House. Resident number 1739, Arthur was President Cleveland's private Messenger, with an annual salary of $1,200.00. Arthur was the former doorkeeper for Secretary Loeb to POTUS for about forty plus years. Secretary Loeb had commented that Arthur had forgotten how to treat people. Before being transferred to the position with the Department of the Interior, because of some complaints according to, *"The Washington Times," of February 1, 1905,* Arthur was replaced by William B. Dulaney of Alexandria, Virginia. The new position caused a reduction in salary to $845.00 annually. Arthur died August 23, 1907. He also had a son named, Arthur Simmons, Jr., residential number 1820, who was also employed as a bookbinder at the Governments Printing Office, according to, *"The Washington Times," of March 20, 1895.* Uncle Jerry and Arthur's relationship was described as total resentment. Uncle Jerry would always comment, *"Look at him over there pretending to be well rounded as if he knows what those pages are trying to tell him."*

It was said of Uncle Jerry, that he would often comment on Arthur's inability to read as he would be often seen with a newspaper in his hands. Sarcastic exchanges were often expressed between the two. Arthur's wife was named Alice and they had seven children, Arthur, Jr., Samuel, Henrietta, Hannah, Alice, William and Catharine. His estate at his death was valued at $5,000.00.

"Los Angeles Herald," of July 9, 1905

"The San Francisco Call," for November 27, 1898, reports of a major riot in Wilmington, North Carolina, November 10, 1898 where fifteen Negroes were killed. It was suggested that political superiority caused the frenzy among the whites. North Carolina unlike other southern states which had major restrictions to the 14th and 15th amendments and voting rights was not the case in North Carolina. Our system of democracy depends solely on majority rule. Majority works well if you're the majority and such was the case in the state of North Carolina where the Negro population of registered voter was 210,000 whites to 100,000 Colored. But then scramble these numbers away from color lines into party affiliations and here's where the problem became unbearable for some citizens who felt by the crossing of party lines gave the advantage to the Negroes.

Governor Russell, a Republican was from Wilmington where the population regarding racial lines was two to one Negroes over whites. In the last election which still saw a majority main office holders as white, but saw an increase in government jobs such as the police force, fire department and postal service being heavy populated by the majority like in every other American city where the majority ruled. This meant that a majority black town now saw a black government essentially in place. Enforcing the law with authority most assuredly angered most whites. Additionally, consider the fact that the majority of the taxes were being paid by the whites who owed the majority of the land. So now the dilemma of having the three percent tax paying population collecting taxes in an aggressive manner from the majority taxpayers. A system in place long before the elections. Both black men and women, still remembering the years of slavery and reconstruction, ceased the opportunity to flex their political might to the very sensitive whites. Now while beginning to see the shoe on the other foot and less desirable than the previous strong hold of making life for Negroes as difficult as possible, found the likings unbearable. Where during the times of reconstruction, both black men and women when traveling and encountered a white person, the Negroes were required by law to yield the sidewalk, even if it meant walking in mud. Young white girls before, wound often tease black girls by having their hats snatched from their heads in a reversal of devious acts, had their hats then thrown in the streets of mud. Many complaints were then filed and pointed a finger at Governor Russell's management as the cause of the city's white strong hold being reversed. By the time for the next election, the whites were set on tilting the election in their favor. In many counties around the state were being armed by white's six months before the election had begun to arm themselves by the purchasing of Winchesters, Springfield rifles and ammunition. All in an effort to win the election by force, intimidation and any other means was the intent of the mob. Soon after the election, the plan was to rid the city of all black leaders by forcing them to resign, leave town or face violence. The Colored editor of the Republican paper, Alexander L. Manly, was the first to depart the county as the records building was burned by a mob of angry whites one night. The mob numbers had grown to at least two thousand as the beginning of the shooting allegedly started by a black man that wounded a white man who then returned fire, killing the black man in Brooklyn, a suburban community. Gun battles were being reported throughout the county where it was reported that fifteen blacks were killed and many more wounded as most of the Negroes were without weaponry. Soon the forceful take over began. Silas P. Wright, the Mayor had left town and Justice of the Peace, Bunting was directed to leave as

Devour Us Not

"Carrizozo News," of Nov 20, 1908

well as other city officials. But, before Bunting could leave both he and his Colored assistant were hanged in front of his house. The mayhem of violence forced Mayor Wright to resign or face the wrath like Bunting. Then Colonel A.M. Waddell was elected as Mayor and sworn in by M. Newman, Justice of the Peace. It was reported that all the old properly elected officials went to Washington to request an investigation be initiated into the hostel takeover and murder of innocent blacks. Blacks who had exercised their right to vote caused an element of the opposition to take the law into their own hands. The so called reported fifteen murdered Negroes was a very modest number that was contrary to the reports of the streets running run red with innocent black blood. And for this lawlessness and murder, no one was ever charged for crimes against humanity.

A Chicago newspaper article from, *"The Day Book," of July 22, 1913*, reports a fire that burned alive thirty-three Negro convicts. The Oakley Convict Farm where these thirty-three men were serving time was located twenty miles southwest of Jackson, Mississippi. A prison farm which had no fire fighting equipment, housed prisoners on the second floor of a wooden building built with old lumber, in 1903 from the old prison in Jackson, Mississippi. A wooden building which had all windows heavily barred, a wooden caged that was locked and the fire happen at midnight, on the first floor near the stairway landing, which was the only entry to that floor that also housed hay, corn and molasses. Sergeant S.T. Byrd of the penitentiary guard was in charge of the prison as he first called his wife who then reported the incident to Mrs. O. M. Spickard, secretary of the prison board and acting warden of the penitentiary. Accordingly, Sergeant Byrd claimed to be very concerned and destruct about the incident and his inability to circumvent the inedibility of total catastrophic chaos. The fire was first discovered by two guards who explained that the fire was too far gone to attempt to unlock the only way out door to where the reported fire started. No one within supposed ear volume could hear thirty-three trapped men yelling for their lives. Eventually, other inmates were freed to attempt to save their fellow inmates by the use of buckets of water with little results. Sergeant Byrd could not explain why the thirty-three Negroes were in the **locked caged liked so-called sleeping quarters building** at **midnight, unsupervised** in which the ignition of a very **suspicious fire** was initiated at the **only entry and exit** to the building and the, *"can't be explained,"* theory is an outraged of total incompetence or purposely planned murders. Despite what criminal activities these men were serving time for, their untimely deaths were murder and nothing more. No one was ever reprimanded, disciplined or investigated for these murders.

The following details of their crimes are as follows: Dudley Reed, 1909 was sentenced to life for criminal assault with the death sentence commuted. George Baker, 1908 was sentenced to life for murder. Will Suggs, 1911 was sentence to life for murder. St. Clair Collins, 1913 was sentenced to life for criminal assault. Ezekiel Frances, 1907 was sentenced two years for assault and battery and twenty years for criminal assault. Tom Barnes, 1908 was sentenced ten years for attempted criminal assault. Alvin Rutherford, 1912 was sentenced for life for murder. Tom Haynes, 1911 was sentenced twenty years for manslaughter. Ed Lewis, 1913 was sentenced seven years for burglary. Walter Sykes, 1910 was sentenced seven years for burglary, Peter Butler, 1910 was sentenced seven years for burglary. Ernest Brown, 1913 was sentenced one year for crime against nature. J. Sheppard, 1912 was sentenced four years for grand larceny.

The remaining names of the dead and their crimes were not mentioned in the article mainly because of the

elemental nature of their significance: Sam Todd, Robert Jackson, Jesse James, Mannie Washington, Isaac Smith, Willie Marson, Andrew Jackson, Anderson Smith, Lenox Lewis, Henry Davis, Ernest Richardson, Frank Allen, Ed Brown, Greevy Havis, Tony Clark, Charles Shows, John McDonald, Will Union, Jesse Young and John Hays. The Sergeant in a supervisory capacity was never charged or never convicted of dereliction of duty or negligence for the brutal burning of thirty-three human beings; neither were any officers under his supervision.

According to, *"The New York Tribune," of July 31, 1910*, a race riot or more appropriately a massacre broke out in Anderson County, Texas where as many as fifty men reportedly were killed. Slocum and Elkhart, small Texas towns located about fifteen miles south from Palestine, Texas in Anderson County where the troubles began. The total correct number will probably never be realized but the reported total was twenty-one Negroes mostly unarmed and four whites killed. The problem started in the village of Slocum when James Alford, a crippled white farmer, killed James Spurger, a Negro farmer who owed a note that was questioned and or refusal of the Negro to pay the debt in question. Conflicting reports state that perhaps Spurger slapped the white man or may have been in some manner overpowered by the Negroes in an insulting approach where he took advantage of the situation and a cripple. One fact can't be denied, was the number of innocent dead Negroes on the sides of the roads, shot in the back and unarmed. Four Negroes found in a house, that were all shot to death and one near death with 13 shotgun bullets in his body. And the mob acknowledging going around looking for Negroes to murder. Many Negroes left the area for which the whites gladly took over their land and property without properly acquiring it. Many conflicting reports that were reported by a number of newspaper reporters of over a thousand Negroes, well armed were killing whites. This effort was probably used to start a frenzy within the surrounding white communities to tilt the armed citizens of whites toward a guarantee massacre for that reporting. Eight white men were eventually charged with the murders and placed in the local jail. For concerns about receiving a fair trial, the case was transferred to Houston, Texas but never went to trial. There were even rumors of wire cutting to circumvent the worldwide report networks from receiving the severity of the situation for historical fact and impervious guilt.

"The Broad Ax," of November 22, 1919, newspaper article speaks of a commonality of lawlessness that occurred in Helena, Arkansas. While trying to understand what caused the riot in Helena, addressing the Thirteenth Amendment to the United States Constitution would be the starting point. Like so many counties in the south, as apart of releasing the strong hold the south set out on depriving all people of color their rightful share of justice, wanted a new system tilting the levels of injustice and the impediment of black progress to a minimum. Essentially, the Amendment outlawed slavery and involuntary servitude, passing both the Senate and House in 1864 & 1865 respectively. Phillip County, Arkansas, where the center city is Helena, is also located in the Delta region of the lowlands of southern states. The identity of peonage rolls in this system of crop sharing, debt, and farm operators caused in part the riot. The black farm operators hired a white Lawyer to go before an all white jury to complain against fair wages for their products. During that era of 692,000 square miles of farm land of mostly cotton in the region with a population of 78% Negro owning about one third of the farms in the region. All the white plantation owners system of fairness with their Negro tenants where to furnish the sharecroppers and tenants their supplies. These supplies include such things as food, farming clothing and materials used in the performance of ones duty, housed in what was called a *"commissary."* Contrary to what would be over looked as the most profitable aspect of this system, is the fact that, with adding another element

"The Day Book," of May 22, 1915

to the profitability of farming, the commissary, with no direct link to farm product itself went unnoticed as a major ripe-off. Supply and demand as it relates to the commissary issue is like having a today's standard local 7-11 store that is open when traditional stores are closed. The close proximity to neighborhoods requiring special need items at ridiculous prices. In parallel, there appears to be then and now an elements sole purpose is to prevent people of color from forever having achievements due him. Case and point, in 2011, the Commandant of the Marine Corps, General James Amos as a gesture to commemorate the achievement of blacks in the Marine Corps proposed a medal. The Marine Corps being the last branch of the services to integrate, paid omen to all the, "Black Montford Point Marines," who were the first to join their ranks, with a Congressional Gold Medal. This set off a fire storm of oppositions not wanting any recognition of Marines who broke the color barrier among its rank. A barrier that was felt by the expense of being spit upon and having their uniforms ripped off their bodies while being beaten for impersonating a Marine. All for the right just to wear the uniform of a Marine. Even Hispanics not natural born American citizens were accepted before American born that were black. So in the efforts of accomplishments with this much restrictive element fighting against you, how did the Negroes overcome, after already having endured 244 years of slavery?

But the system in Helena, Arkansas was apart of a nation wide effort to forever keep the Negro ignorant of a system that takes the cotton product the Negroes would break their backs for by using their very expensive gin-tech machines, giving the Negroes a less than a favorable market price. Then sell the newly ginned cotton at a higher and more profitable price in the marketplace was an insurmountable tactical move against any fairness the Negroes were seeking. Even though it wasn't widely known, the word eventually got out and initially all Negroes questioning the profitability of the whites were either beaten, hung or both to keep the rebellion from spreading. A tactic that worked for many years before 1919, when the Government was doing an investigation in another issue of peonage realized it was more prominent within the Negro communities, hence the hiring of a Little Rock, Arkansas Lawyer named Bratton to represent the 86 Negroes to combat this injustice. As a result of the efforts of this Attorney and his victories, the shackles of debt for a vagabond labeled people was released. Monthly accurate statements were then being given as the whites then attempted to find another avenue to oppress the blacks and keep them in their place. Cotton prices then begin to rise as the *"Dixie trickery,"* effort was exposed for the betterment of all in the community.

In the riot that killed four white men and twenty-five black men as reported by *"The Evening World," of October 2, 1919.* The riot started when supposedly, propaganda was spread by white men in the black communities of posses in search of victims to kill. Victims as a result of the Negro cotton pickers, planters and tenants who were feed-up with low and unfair wages as it relates to the business of being ripped off by white plantation owners. Whites being fed propaganda rumors of blacks arming themselves, made the whites paranoid from their own guilt. Four of the Negroes killed were four Johnston brothers. Dr. D. A. Johnston, a druggist, along with three of his brother's were stopped by Mr. O. R. Lilly, a city councilman and a mob of armed white men. The brothers walking together after a white friend told them to getaway for trouble had started away from Helena and headed for their neighborhood. But, in reality, Helena was where the trouble started. After the four brothers were apprehended by the mob, headed by Lilly, supposedly a gesture to take the gun from Mr. O.R. Lilly by one of the brothers occurred. Then the brother fired three shots into his body, killing him. The mob realizing what had happen open fire on the brother, riddling all of the four brothers with bullets, killing them all.

"The St. Louis Republic," of May 10, 1903

Depending on who was speaking like almost every similar story of this era, only five whites were killed and between twenty-five and 200 Negroes where killed in the riot of Helena, Arkansas. It was rumored that the stench of dead bodies could be smelled for miles. About a thousand Negroes were arrested with over a hundred indicted. This so-called gathering of

"The Pensacola Journal.," February 18, 1906

evidence as the Negro being the instigators and initiators of the rioting and murders were gathered by some white planters, a white Merchant, the white Sheriff, Bankers and the Mayor of Helena. When the trial was concluded twelve of the indicters received a death sentence and about fifty-four other Negroes received penitentiary sentences. During the kangaroo courts in which no whites were on trial for murder, no Negroes in the jury, no venue of change, no defense witness were called and each trial for the sixty-six Negroes which lasted 5-10 minutes each was a major blow to justice everywhere. The whites were alleged to have been merely defending themselves against the Negro aggression. Much to the silent applauds of whites set out on ridding the county of anymore trouble makers set out to impede the county by interfering with their flawed domineering business practices. In a collective effort for a defense of the Negroes, white Lawyers over-priced fees lined up to further add to this tragedy as their efforts were not for the defense of their clients, the Negroes, rather, it was for the lining of their pockets and alleviating the Negroes from whatever wealth he had acquired. A simple plan of placing them back to a level as a vagabond. Many Negroes seeing the injustices of the south, in wake of the kangaroo proceedings, begin to leave in record numbers as a part of the great migration. Lawyers received warning from Governor Brough that if any white Attorney in court or elsewhere should feel a need to help the Negroes against their way of life in the south would be jailed, suffers business depravity and social isolation. The evils of injustice and the miscarriage of righteousness as a county proudly repudiated any factual evidence that was omitted from these proceedings now had been issued threats. As the *"Cayton's Weekly," of January 17, 1920*, tried to give some logical explanation into a white man fake manufactured, *"Negro up-rising,"* that nullified the Negro his birth right under the constitution. President Theodore Roosevelt, acutely aware of the manner in which black men were perceived, makes a December 7, 1906 statement regarding its national status and the black issue. Approximately, 436,000 slaves once occupied Mississippi before Emancipation. Certainly, whites in southern states were devastated that the Emancipation Proclamation had passed, coupled by feeling the anger of losing the War Between the States and the lost of some 48,000 Mississippians war dead, were still on the minds of every southerner and particularly, the Mississippians and Alabamians. Why Mississippi one might ask, plantations and slave labor that made Mississippi one of the nation's richest and most productive states during the slave period. With a multitude of steam and flatboat activities through the over 1,000 streams and rivers made Mississippi the import state of the region. So Mississippi was ill-prepared to function, once that, meaning slavery, was taken away. Furthermore, having the arrogance to think they'd always be able to control an oppressed people and the conditions created by their enslavement factored more into its depression.

One of the most horrific tales of lawlessness started in Meridian, Mississippi, Monday, March 6, 1871. The then ostracized Mayor, William Sturgis wrote to the editor of the, *"New York Tribune," Thursday, March 16, 1871* describing complete mayhem of historical proportion in the Meridian incident. Let me describe some of the main characters or victims of this tragic saga: **Mayor William Sturgis**, originally from Connecticut was appointed an Alderman, May of 1869. On July 3, 1869 Sturgis was appointed to the office of Mayor of Meridian by then Governor **Adelbert Ames**. **Daniel Price**, a Negro teacher, was arrested. Mayor Sturgis had no aspirations to

"The St. Louis Republic," of May 10, 1903

become Mayor but later recalls' coming to Meridian only to assist his brother, **Theodore**, with his business. **Robert J. Mosley**, the white Sheriff of Meridian and also a Republican. **Adam Kennard**, a white Sheriff from Alabama and the leader or spokesperson for the Ku-Klux and a bounty-hunter. **Daniel Price**, a black school teacher and contractor originally from Livingston, Alabama, now teaching school in Meridian. Price was also known as an outspoken spokesperson for the rights of former slaves. **William Clopton**, one of Mayor Sturgis advisors, a black man, the alleged arson of Theodore's store and an agitator. **Aaron Moore**, a Republican member of the Mississippi Legislature of Lauderdale County, originally from Jackson, Mississippi and **Warren Tyler**, a black men, defendant witness, Mayor Sturgis advisor and an agitator. **James Brantley**, a white man called to testify. **Judge William Bramlette**, the white Judge presiding over the trial of Daniel Price and the riot.

By the end of the Civil War and Emancipation, the Ku Klux Klan and other hate groups such as the *"red shirts, "rifle leagues"* and the *"white owls"* were creating havoc all over the southern states. Since most of the political leaders in the south were either sympathetic towards the Klan and other groups of hate or were members of these groups. Crimes against people of color and others attempting to aid in their new adjustments were going unpunished. In an effort to slow down this aggression and maintain a since of order, in 1870, Congress passed a series of Criminal Coded Enforcement Acts. These acts were aimed at protecting the rights of all Americans. The criminal portion was added as a result of the Ku Klux Klan's efforts in intimidations and the murder of many blacks and some whites when they attempted to vote, hold public office, jury selection and involved in any educational process of ex-slaves. Alabama, notorious for many injustices and non-punishable criminal violence by the Klan, forced many ex-slaves to leave the state and travel west to the near-by state of Mississippi. And Texas like other southern states was equally up to task of black hate. Case & point: The University of Texas, coach Darrell Royal in 1963, as he was opposed to integration, commented that UT didn't need black players on its rooster to win a National Championship and went on to do just that in 1963 & 1969. Yet, UT has had only two Heisman Trophy winners in their football dominant history, Earl Campbell (1977) and Ricky Williams (1998). And why the reference; both Heisman Trophy winners are black.

One very outspoken Alabamian, ironically was the first for the state of Mississippi to be arrested under the new enforcement act designed for his protection. Daniel Price, the very outspoken school teacher was rumored to be educating the blacks of the law and their rights. Many whites, still enjoying the ignorance of many of their farm help became aggravated with Mr. Price's motivation. A committee was formed by white Meridians mainly to silence Daniel Price and removed any sympathetic ears like Mayor William Sturgis. Mayor Sturgis, was rumored to be attending rallies by mostly blacks upset by unfair treatment was cause for the Meridians to feel the advice and support he offered showed partiality that would give the ex-slaves an unfair advantage into justice for them. The word of Daniel Price's arrest reached Alabama, so Sheriff Adam Kennard and 50 other well armed men showed up for the trial. After hearing the news of this unexpected quest, knowing the history of their involvements caused the city official's of Meridian to cancel Price's trial three times and suggested it might be wise for Price to leave the city. Before the arrest of Price and the idiotic manner in which the alleged charges were brought about, prompted Price to make a number of predictions by the black community of civil unrest if the allegation stood. These remarks and later the knowledge of Sheriff Kennard's arrest of several ex-slaves that migrated to Mississippi with Price were fueling into the inevitable. After a deal was made with the prosecutors to free Price on the condition he leave the city was sealed, then he left the city. This act infuriated the white community that they organized a petition to remove Mayor Sturgis from office which the black community then counters with their own petition that was sent the Governor who had appointed the Mayor. There had been recently a gubernatorial election in which Republican **James L. Alcorn** won. After receiving the petition from Meridian and a personal plea from Major Sturgis for Federal troops, newly elected Governor Alcorn sent federal troops to keep order. By this time the state funds were limited so the troops left after a few days of occupancy. It was then Mayor Sturgis attempt to single-handedly challenge all the whites citizens who by then began a slow intimidation campaign against the Negroes. Another effort was made by the Mayor as he then sent several advisors

(***William Clopton*** *and* ***Warren Tyler***) to the Governor's Mansion in Jackson, Mississippi to further illustrate the need for Federal intervention before the escalation of violence become imminent. This prove to have some weight into the Mayor's plead, because the advisors returned to Meridian with a member of the Mississippi Legislature for Lauderdale County named **Aaron Moore**, a Republican.

Before long the word was out and Republican Moore held a rally at the steps of the county courthouse to discuss the events of unrest and peace negotiations for the citizens of the city. There, several speakers spoke at this event and an estimated 200 Meridians showed up both black and white to take in the plan. However, after the meeting, it was reported that William Clopton, one of the advisors sent to Jackson had organized a military type group to fend off any further attacks against people of color. Soon the word of this group hit the white community who had also heard this group was armed with guns, sticks and sword policing the town by walking around looking for trouble. So, the whites formed a mob and began walking about town also to force the Mayor and all his advisors to leave town.

The circumstances resulting from these events caused an unsuspected fire in the business district. The first fire supposedly started on the second floor of the Mayor's brother, Theodore's, business. Even though no one claimed responsibility, the Mayor and all his sympathizers were believed to be the culprit's. During the fire and attempts to secure the rest of the district, William Clopton was hit in the head upon suspicion of being the arson responsible. So strongly were these allegations, caused Sherriff Robert J. Mosley to arrest Clopton, Tyler and Moore and charge them with inciting a riot. He further encouraged all black citizens to disarm for their own safety. With that thought in mind, the Sherriff then permitted Tyler to go and get a haircut, unescorted where he was frisked by the Sherriff and reportedly had no weapons. However, later the barber who cut his hair noticed seeing a weapon on him after his hair was cut. Mayor Sturgis, before the trial began, was noticed giving one of the three men a note while the other two were held in a room later visited by Mayor Sturgis who alleged gave both Clopton and Moore a pistol before returning to the courtroom. It was reported the tension was high with most of the whites seated in front and were heavily armed with anticipating a shoot-out. The blacks were seated in the back as was the rule of order for that period. Mayor Sturgis having an inkling into what might occur never reentered the court room. As the trial began with Judge William Bramlette presiding, the calling of the witnesses began. The second witness was **James Brantley**, whose testimony so infuriated Tyler until he alleged to have jumped up and called the witness out as a liar. This in turn aggravated the witness until he grabbed the walking cane of the nearby-posted Marshall and gesture to attack Tyler with it. The alert Marshal then grabbed the witness and restrained him as Tyler moved toward the door in an effort to avoid being hit. It was at this point that Tyler was seen reaching for a pistol that was later reported by the barber that he had. Ironically, Sherriff Mosley stated he had frisked Tyler before the barber visit and there was no weapon, also the Marshall said he did not see Tyler with a weapon nor did he see him fire one. But it was at this point, all agreed the first shot was fired in the courtroom coming from that general vicinity. And all the witnesses that later testified that Tyler fired the first shot were all white. When the first shot rang out, several weapons were then drawn and fired within the

courtroom that lasted seemingly from 2-5 minutes. During this exchange of bullets flying throughout the courtroom, Judge Bramlette was hit in the head and killed instantly. Clopton was also injured by gun fire while Tyler raced to another floor and was spotted, conveniently by the barber who cut his hair, tossing a weapon while fleeing the courtroom. Tyler was later found with several gun shot wounds in his body as he had been shot by a multitude of bullets not sustained in the courtroom.

Clopton was seriously wounded in the aftermath of the courtroom shoot-out and was supposedly placed in law-officers protection. A witness reported seeing Clopton being thrown from the two-story room onto the streets. The next morning he too was found dead with his throat being cut and no witnesses. Moore, more fortunate than the other two, played dead next to the slain Judge for a white and then ran for his freedom in a wooded area near a railroad track where he hopped a train back to Jackson followed by an angry mob set out on his capture and most assuredly lynching to no avail. After several miles, the mob gave up and Moore returned back to Jackson, Mississippi.

Meanwhile, an angry mob began a deadly campaign of mass destruction of black owned properties, churches, homes and businesses. More devastating than that were the many lives of innocent people of color that were not armed and had nothing to do with any of the events of that day, slaughtered. The only commonality that existed was the color of their skin which happens to be different from that of the cowardly mobsters. The reported number was recorded to be about thirty blacks killed. But other blacks that managed to tell their story stated the numbers mounted into the hundreds. Mayor Sturgis, after an agreement had been reached for his alleged involvement, optioned him safe passage out of the city in exchange for his resignation. It was then, that this incredible story of lawlessness and cowardly actions hit the world wide press as Mayor Sturgis told his amazing story to the, *"New York Daily Tribune," of March 16, 1871.* The aftermath of the ostracized Mayor's article, a national investigation was initiated on March 21, 1871, resulting in only 6 men indicted. Although, many blacks in that southern town knew who the killers, rappers and destroyers of property were, but much too afraid to come forward publicly. So the silence of their knowledge were taken to their graves as the guilty yet again walked free. For all the countless and needless deaths and repeated pleads from Congressman's in Washington after a second investigation, one man was found guilty of rape of a black woman. For I believe in every debt there must be a payment made. For some generation within all the guilty parties that participated in those murders, and rapes will give an account for their actions.

During President Obama's major affordable health care speech on Wednesday, September 9, 2009 (9-9-9), South Carolina Representative Joe Wilson (*Republican*) yelled out *"You lie!"* when the President said the legislation would not mandate coverage for undocumented immigrants. Never before in modern day history has a sitting President been so disrespected. The aftermath of that incident prompted a private citizen to send that representative a check for a million dollars...... Jesse Helms tried to discredit Martin Luther King, Jr. in 1983 when the National Holiday was being discussed and President Reagan vetoed the bill initially to make it a holiday but eventually signed the bill after much debate. And a freshman Senator named Ted Cruz stated we needed a 100 more like Jesse Helms in the Republican Party. The state of South Carolina being the last state of the union to adopt the National Holiday speaks for itself. The many elements of hate, code words and dog whistles that exist in this country that labels a race and despises any accomplishment people of color make, is not a recipe for a cohesive nation. Yet, there's an element so insistent for fear of blacks achieving compatible triumphs that any

"The Marion Daily Mirror," Nov 6, 1909

and everything goes. A Newspaper article from *"The Washington Times," of May 26, 1911*, reports, twenty-eight year old **Laura Nelson**, one of the most famously known female lynching postcard scenes and the erroneous characterization of her sixteen year old son, Lawrence. But Lawrence or *"LD"* as he was called was only **twelve** years old. The Nelsons had been married for thirteen years according to the 1910 Federal Census. Both were lynched in Okemah, Oklahoma, May 26, 1911. They were taken from the county jail through an unlocked door the night before and dragged to a wagon, taken six miles to the Canadian River bridged and lynched. Laura being first to be lynched and then her son. The actions of lynching a Negro woman or *"Negress,"* as the newspaper article described her, was the first known of its kind in the state of Oklahoma. The mother and son

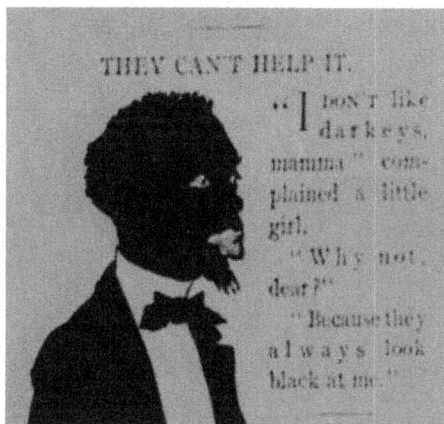

THEY CAN'T HELP IT.

".. I DON'T like darkeys, mamma" complained a little girl. "Why not, dear?" "Because they always look black at me."

"The York Tribune," of December 20, 1896

were arrested on charges of murdering deputy Sheriff George H. Loney who had gone to the Nelson's home and discovered stolen goods. The article also reports of there being no further investigation into this lawless act for the mob had answered justice in their perverted minds and they had gotten what they deserved, according to onlookers. There was also a famous postcard printed of the lynching showing Laura in a long southern style dress with the bonnet still upon her head hanging three quarters of the way down and her son several feet from her, that was partially clothed and probably had been sexually assaulted. LD was *"high yellow,"* a gene probably taken from his father. While living in Texas, Austin was listed as *"white."* There were reports of Laura having a small nursing child in jail with her. The Federal Census does record a daughter named Sarry that would have been about two years old in 1911. Laura was also reportedly

rape before she was hanged. Reports of her husband, Austin, had been involved with the illegally acquiring of an animal, sheep or a cow depending on reports from the Okemah Ledger newspaper article. The twelve year old son of Laura supposedly fire the shot at deputy Loney hitting him in the leg and he bleed to death during a long gun battle that ended only because the Nelson's ran out of bullets. The daughter was reportedly taken from the

1910 Federal Census of Laura Nelson and her family of Okfuskee County, Oklahoma

Devour Us Not

jail, after the fate of her mother was realized and raised by an unknown residence of Okfuskee County. No one from Okfuskee County, Oklahoma ever paid for the lawlessness and violation of Laura Nelson and her son. Her husband received a short prison term of 2 years after he supposedly confess to theft. But he lost his entire family. Had Officer Loney not been obsessed over getting his man, could have lived. The obvious attempt of the leg shot was to wound him otherwise one would think a head or body shot in the chest would be more

Laura Nelson-Photograph by G.J. Farnum, 1911

towards an attempt to kill. And why was it necessary to jail both parties since only one could have fired the shot. Known by the officers who were there during the arrest and to drag a woman away from her nursing child.....

The newspaper article, *"The Mt. Sterling Advocate," of January 18, 1911,* reports of the attempted lynching of two Negroes on charges of assaulting white girls and one for murdering his wife in Shelbyville, Kentucky. A mob of about 100 men stormed the jail early the morning of January 15, 1911 for the purpose of carrying out their evil. Hanging from a bridge near Eminence Pike only minutes from the county jail was Eugene Marshall who was sentence to hang for the murder of his wife whom he had beheaded. Jim West, a chauffeur, body was also found hanging from the bridge for his alleged crime of assaulting a white woman, who was the daughter of a Shelbyville farmer. And Wade Patterson's body was found in a creek after he was shot while attempting to flee the mob. After a weak investigation in which no persons were indicted, Edward Thompson, a jailer stated he hid the keys to the cells after the mob of about a hundred men, some hooded became more demanding. Lawman Hornback was the one who let the mob in the jail office after becoming fearful they'd blow the jail up with him in it, after commands were being made to light the dynamite to blow them and the three Negroes up together. The mob use sledge hammers to break open the cell locks while Hornback and Thompson did absolutely nothing. No one was ever charged nor an investigation for these murders despite knowledge of most of the perpetrators.

Three Negro men and one Negro woman were murdered in Valdosta, Georgia as reported by, *"The Washington Times," of May 20, 1918.* Apparently, a white farmer named Hampton Smith was shot to death while he ate supper with his family. An attempted murder of his wife in Barney, Georgia, found near a creek, alive, after being attacked by some Negroes and shot. A mob of armed men with bloodhounds were looking for what was known as a fifth suspect, a Negro, named Sydney Johnson in connection with the Smith murder. Heavy guards were surrounding the jail where the entire Johnson family was being held for their protection. Haynes Turner, a Negro, married to Mary Turner was one of the men hanged at Okapilco River in Brooks County, Saturday, May 18, 1918. Later, Mary, 8 months pregnant was hanged at the Folsoms bridge, over little river located about 16 miles from Valdosta, Georgia. Mary was hang just for voicing her opinion about the lynching of her husband, after which her body was then riddled with bullets. The alleged murder plot to kill Hampton Smith was planned by the Johnson family at the Turner's house. Among some very incriminating evidence was a gold watch belonging to Smith, found in the possession of Mary Turner. Another incriminating effort was made by Will Head, a Negro, who supposedly made a willful confession before he was strung up to a tree near Troupeville about four miles from Valdosta on Friday night, May 17, 1918. Eugene Rice aka, James Isom was also hanged the same night after Head's confession implicated him by the Camp Grounds Church at Morven. Some 18 Negroes were found days later that had been lynched and about 500 residents of Brook County left for good fearing the violence. Many more mysterious disappearances were recorded but unsubstantiated because of the mass exiting. There were so many reports written about this lynching, yet details of its horror remain a mystery.

Two newspapers among several hundred with all different variations report the following. *"The Watchman and Southron," of June 29, 1912, and "Keowee Courier," of June 26, 1912,* one reports the headlines as, *"Negro cook ran*

amuck," list the Negro woman's name as **Anna Boston**. She also was known as Ann Barksdale or Anne Bostwick, working as a cook in a wealthy white Mistress home named Mrs. Jennie *(Barlow)* Jordan, wife of the very wealthy planter, R.F. Jordan in Pinehurst, Georgia. He owned one of the largest plantations in the county and employed many Negroes. Some type of dispute broke out and Anne allegedly used a kitchen knife to stab the woman in the back before slitting her throat. When law officers, headed by Sheriff Bennett went to Hawkinsville where Anne was living with full knowledge of a trail of angered white's with guns in hand and in a frenzy following behind him. It was no surprise after they had made the arrest and were transporting her to jail, that the mob would take her from the officers. They did eventually take her back in front of the Jordan home where she wound be hanged on a tree. Anne was reported to have been pregnant and very visibly so. There was never an investigation or anyone charged for this crime.

Another familiar tale as reported by, *"The Ogden Standard," of October 6, 1919.* Lincolnton, Georgia, two Negroes named **Jack Gordon** and **Will Brown** were hanged and their bodies riddled with bullets before being cut down and their bodies were then burned. They were allegedly accused of shooting Deputy Sheriff Roy Freeman, who later died and wounding Boyce Fortson his deputy. Another Negro named **Mose Martin** was killed by the mob after he and several other Negroes where being whipped into confessing the whereabouts of Gordon as the mob was in a frantic looking for him. The mob of about a thousand well armed white men captured Brown first. Gordon however, was being held for suspicion by Sheriff Kelly of Wilkes County awaiting an investigation when the mob with little resistance from the law officers took Gordon from the county jail and proceeded to the outskirts of town. Brown was being held purposely to be hanged together with his co-conspirator. Within minutes the mob carried out the evil deed which took its course in a matter of minutes. No one was ever investigated or charged for this action despite full knowledge and addresses of the leaders of these cowardly followers.

In Monroe, Louisiana, January 30, 1919 as reported by the, *"Keowee Courier," of February 5, 1919,* after being found guilty of murdering Blanchard Warner, a white man in Columbia by a jury, **Sampson Smith's** fate was sealed so he thought. But, the jury specifically recommended no capital punishment, rather, time for his crime, considering the evidence presented in the trial of an all white jury. Sampson Smith, a Negro, was immediately being transferred after the trial, to Monroe for safe keeping by the Sheriff of Caldwell Parish. Fearing for the safety of the Negro and the unfavorable verdict in the eyes of the mob that thought the Negro was getting away with murder. News of the verdict being spread as rumors for, *"the ole familiar,"* mob organizers whose names and faces were all well known was in a frenzy over a Negro getting off light for murdering a white man was too much for the mob to comprehend. Before the Sheriff could get to the outskirts of Columbia, he was supposedly overpowered by a mob of many loud and angry well armed citizens of Monroe and believed other surrounding communities. Smith was taken from his custody by force to a remote location near the adduction and lynched.

"The Appeal," of July 15, 1916

Smith's dangling body was found the next morning by law officers who returned his body to the undertakers. No one was ever charged, no one was ever investigated for this lawlessness, despite in full daylight hours of the incident.

May 8, 1916, Monday, the rape and murder of Mrs. Lucy Fryer by allegedly **Jesse Washington**, a 17 year old Negro who's trial was scheduled for Monday, May

"The Saint Paul Globe," of Mar 5, 1905

15, 1916 in Waco, Texas. The District Judge of the Criminal Court was R. I. Munroe, who had to wiggle his way through the crowd of so many people to start the trial. Washington who was brought in from Dallas by Sheriff Fleming in the middle of the night and lead into the court room. Like many blood-thirsty crowds looking for a one way justice, began to yell obesities at Washington as an attempt to strategically control the trial outcome. With appeasing to the overwhelming crowd, the Judge allowed the expedition of the proceedings to be rushed. Before one could blink, the jury brought in a verdict of *"guilty,"* much to the delight of over 2,000 citizens in the court yard outside and another 1,500 in the courtroom. With that reading of guilty and the assessment of death as a punishment, all within one breathe and less than an hour in record time. Washington had supposedly waived his rights and would have been hang that afternoon complying with the speedy trial demagoguery. During this time, both the Sheriff and the court stenographer snuck out the courtroom side door, unwilling to witness or intervene any actions which were surely forthcoming. Before the Judge could conclude the proceedings with his gavel, the crowd, after a thug in the back of the courtroom yelled, *"Get the nigger!"* did so. The Judge did nothing to protect Washington and it probable would not have brought much favor anyway with this already angry crowd. They then grabbed Washington and led him down the back stairs to the waiting blood-thirsty mob clawing at the bits with the frenzy of a newly disturbed beehive looking for prey.

The chain that was around his neck was then placed in his mouth adding a dual purpose to this gesture of silence of what was to be a painful last hour of his life. This also would impede and slow down the death effect to be prolonged. In route to the City Hall Lawns where by this time news of the trial had touched, it appeared every corner of the city. The crowds had risen by this time to an estimated of over 10,000. In broad daylight in front of the whole city, before God and all, the unashamed mob with and entourage of onlookers hanging from trees, looking out windows of office buildings nearby. Without the least bit concern of the evilness of the crime they were about to be participants of, went about the calculated plan of a heathenish crowd by positioning the boys body and lighting the fire. Washington was reported to have been castrated before being doused with coal oil and soon the body began to burn to a crisp. The crowd quite jubilant and well pleased of what had occurred without due process. As Washington's body left smoldering for sometimes as people began to come and go, taking pictures without a one showing any remorse for what they had just witnessed. One man with his young son on his shoulder commented to a reporter that his young son was never too young to know the proper way to treat a nigger. A *"nigger,"* was all any member of that crowd saw that day and not a human being with a soul. Regardless of what he may have committed and the unmitigated gull of the citizens and officials of the city of Waco, Texas in 1916 could rest comfortably that night while some mother and family's hearts were being ripped apart. And to the crowd thinking they had rendered proper justice is, unbelievable. Why did Waco, a population of 40,000 mostly Christian citizens, with 39 white churches and 24 Negro churches allow such a travesty. And to add insult to injury, while Washington's corpse was still smoking, a cowboy on a horse through a lassoing around the corpse and dragged it all over town. At one point, the head was detached as a little boy grabbed it and placed it on a doorstep and extracted the teeth that were loose for sale as souvenirs. Being unofficially

"The Saint Paul Globe," of Mar 5, 1905

auctioned by the boy and everyone who gathered these items with pride as everything associated with Washington's death had become a most sought after commodities for bragging and showing-off rights. By the time night had fallen, gave an opportunity for the undertaker to gather just a few fragments of ash large enough to put in a small ash jar to present to his next of kin. There were a series of postcards printed of the burning of Washington and several inquires into the lynching but it was proven that there was never a rape. The woman's Physician confirmed this by examination. There were reports that Jesse Washington was mentally challenged and employed by the Fryer's as a farm hand. But because the only evidence linking Jesse to the murder was blood on his clothing and a forced signed confession written not of his own hand, many had doubts. Despite the broad-daylight appearance of this murder and the hundreds of pictures taken at this shamed event, no one was ever charged or convicted of any crime. Some years later a theory was derived that possibly, the husband murdered his 53 year old wife and Jesse later found her lifeless body and attempted to help her, but later felt panic and ran. Being mentally incapable of comprehending his then involvement probably caused him to be silenced with fear. *"The Kansas City Sun," of July 8, 1916,* comments that during the burning, people were singing and having such a good time as if attending a sporting event. Young, Jesse's clothing were snatch from his body and passed around for souvenir purposes and one individual wanting a souvenir so badly that he cut off one of Jesse's ears as the clothing had all been all distributed. Others having seen this also cut off all his fingers. One of the office buildings in plain view of all was the Mayor of the city's office who was seen viewing the lynching as everyone else without the slightest attempt to intervene. Until this day Waco seems to have never forgiven itself for that infamous day and likewise for the rest of the world.

Wagoner, Oklahoma, **Marie Scott** became the second Negro female to be lynched in the state of Oklahoma since it became a state in 1907. As reported by, *"The Tulsa Star," of April 4, 1914*, about a hundred white men stormed the county jail Tuesday morning, March 31, 1914, overpowering the jailer and took Marie Scott and lynched her almost in the heart of the town. She was alleged to have murdered Lemuel Peace, a white man, by cutting him to death, Sunday night, March 29, 1914. The pagan mob entered the jail well armed and rope in hand, pointed their weapons at the jailer, took his keys, open the cell housing Ms. Scott, placing the rope around her neck and leading her outside in full view of many on-lookers to a block away and lynched her. Marie Scott never uttered a word in the mayhem and the swiftness manner in which the mob conducted its evilness; there was little time to attract thousands. The Sheriff's whereabouts at the time were unknown but he did manage to go to the spot and remove the body of Ms. Scott from public view. Supposedly, without provocation, Ms. Scott attacked Lemuel, a very popular family man while he walked the streets of a known segregated prostitute area. Ms. Scott, a recent immigrant of only two weeks to Wagoner and was known as a prostitute by virtue of her residence location. Also known that the area in which Lemuel was killed was frequent by white men that crave the sweet nectar of black-sex in plain view without regard to color influence. Even, so called family men, big business men, all white men rather taste the sweetness of black sugar than their own pure white sugar. So, the so called shock to his family of where he was killed was no shock to well over half the white male population of that city and throughout the south of the goings-on behind close doors in a hypocritical era. In part, because of the parables of attempting to compete with his despised black brothers and become the brute he so admires silently about the black male and penis envy. This prompted many white males to veer toward this curiosity to pursue black females and to improve their skills as a lover. So, Judge Allen, the criminal Judge in the circuit court never called for an investigation into the crime. In cases like these, no one is held accountable for the crime and no official sworn to up hold the law of the land, equally were not held responsible. Also shared in the guilt of

Devour Us Not

failed justice was ever punished. Bulloch County, Georgia during the month of July, 1904 *"The Washington Times," of August 28, 1904* reports the fire of Henry Hodges and surrounding area. The Hodges home like all residence in that area where miles apart like most normal farm communities were. The fire was noticed by nearby neighbors who rushed into action to offer assistance. Pictured to the right are **Will Reed** and **Ed Cato**. By the time the neighbors arrived the building was so engulf in flames until the notion of savaging anything became unmentionable. The intrigue was then focused on the location of the Hodges family who were believed to be home but no one was initially sure. Neighbors begin calling each members names with no response. There were five members in this family to include their three small children, a 10 year old girl, a two or three year old boy and a toddler, months old. By the time the heat subsided, neighbors approach the entry way and discover an awful sight of pools of blood and ax with pieces of hair fragments on and near the ax. This information spread like a wild Santa Anna wind as the community began to get suspicious of a number of minor incidences of aggression becoming bolder with each occurrence. After the confirmation of death for the entire Hodges family, a deep sorrow was felt as the community became enraged as to with evil could have killed this family in cold blood. Since all the whites were very close nit, the focus then pointed to non-other than it had to have been, *"the niggers."* Their main conclusion of suspecting the Negroes were the manner in which the sloppiness of evidence weren't even concealed. So, knowledge of the cause of death was visible and first indication of foul-play. Apparently, white men would use more intelligence while committing their crimes as to alleviate any possibility of their involvement. Almost immediately Reed and Cato became suspects by the mere fact of trouble with the two in the pass. They were subsequently arrest on suspicion. In gathering information as to their whereabouts the evening in question, both men began to conflict their stories in an apparent fib-like manner. But the most damaging evidence was from the wife of Cato who acknowledged his guilt and involvement. Before the word could get out to the mob that had already begun to form, Sheriff Kendrick of Bulloch County rush the two men to the nearby Chatham County at the Savannah jail for safe keeping.

Constant interrogation tactics were used to motivate a confession, since they could not understand what could have cause this much hate. Soon the two began to sing like Cockatoos. Reed acknowledged the organizing of some secret black society named the, *"Before Day Club."* The auspicious naming of this club was in part for the time of day their crimes would be carried out. This secret club was being organized by the blacks, reasons being; feed-up with white wealth, superiority behavior, treatment of bad business dealing and low wages. All whites in their efforts to keep the Negroes in their place and poor for life. Bulloch County, boost to having one of the riches counties in the country, mainly because of the cotton corp. Cotton crop that was being picked solely by Negroes, but the whites were the ones celebrating in the wealth of this success, while the blacks saw no improvement in their lives since slavery. So, bandits would take the wealth from all the whites in protest and kill all witnesses regardless of age to conceal their crimes by burning up any evidence linking the perpetrators to these crimes. Reed then began to give names that included preachers, deacons and other well respected members of the community. The Sheriff then convinced Reed to describe his crime. Reed told of Cato being the look out man as he approach the front door with the ax. Mr. Hodges whom Reed admits he had no beef with, but was apart of the plot organized by the preachers acknowledging Mr. Hodges well known tendency to keep large

"The San Francisco Call," of April 2, 1911

amounts of cash in his home. He describes his next murderous act as when Mr. Hodges came to the door, he struck him in the head with the ax. The noise of the blow aroused Mrs. Hodges who then headed for the front door only to be axed herself by Reed in almost identical fashion. Reed then entered the house knowing the total amount of adults had been silenced. This left the innocence of a child at the mercy of a cult like follower set out on accomplishing his intended purpose. Then Reed describes the conversation he had with the eldest child who was hiding behind a trunk. The child ask of him what he wanted to do and Reed's reply was *"money,"* the child then extended her trembling hand forward which contained a silver nickel and murmured, *"Please take this, its all I have."* Reed's cold bloody reply was a blow to the head with the ax. After that both Reed and Cato's stories began to conflict. Reed states that after the triple murder he went back to Cato to explained what he had done, he then requested matches to burn the house down so the evidence of the murder and the gruesome manner in which he describe it, would be hard to detect. Needless to say the house was eventually set on fire consuming the entire family within minutes. Soon the confessions were known throughout the county and the community had already made up its mind regardless of any jury verdict would render, hanging then burning and not necessarily in that order would be the course of their fate. Anything less than that would cause for the total humiliation around the world in the eyes of the Georgians.

With the knowledge of all law officials and government officials, the leaders of the mob were widely known as they were very vocal about expressing their voices as to how this trial wound unfold and no other way would be accepted. Holding true to form, Judge Daley's effort for exercising a speedy trial was an understatement in its rush to judgment. Troops were called in from Savannah and twenty-five located inside the courtroom and eighty or ninety located throughout the community and camped near the jail house. But while in the courtroom it was reported in retrospect to the Judge that these soldiers had no ammunition in their weapons. And it was widely known that the soldiers would shoulder no resentment towards the mob and would not challenge any aggressive nature on behave of the mob up to and including surrendering their weapons. Some weapons were taken from some soldiers but returned to them only after the deed of its intended purpose had been completed. Contrary to that soldier concept was the fact that all the mobsters were heavily armed. Despite the large boisterous crowd, there were many ministers and highly respected Georgians speaking loudly against the lawlessness that was being discussed by the majority of the residence.

With little resistance from the soldiers guarding the courthouse back stairs where some very young and inexperienced soldiers were posted had obvious intentions. Probably, purposely plan in sympathy for the mob and majority of the citizens of the county to allow the mob to gain access to the two prisoners without incident. The prisoner were taken from the court house and then preceded for the three hour parade of angry mobsters surrounded Reed and Cato down Main Street while eventually ropes being placed around their necks that excited the crowds. Loud discussion of the method of death was being address during the walk much to the howling cries from Cato who pleaded with crowd to be hanged vice burning him. When the question was put to Reed, he was defiant and requested to be burned and Cato to be hanged. Hanging closely to the two convicts were newspaper reporters questioning the two throughout the three hour march of dead men walking. Upon reaching their destination only pausing monetary to capture the moment by photographers, before the two were tied together back to back then drenching the pine wood and their bodies with ten gallons of kerosene. The match was set and the two were in flames almost immediately. Cato screamed in agony for several minutes before being hit in the head which seem to end his pain. Reed however was silently defiant till the end as the wind favored him as he was quickly swallowed up in flames and probably died within seconds. But not Cato as his yells were awful to hear much to the crowds delight as they jeered with every outburst. The role of the soldiers, the Judge, Sheriff and others in official capacities should face an investigation into sympathizing with the mob and should have lean a hand to prevented the mob violence against the Negroes. This was written by several newspapermen as a suspicious act, but did acknowledged that the firing of one bullet would have ignited a blood bath of innocent lives. Because the details of the so-called confession told in the confidence to the law officers that was leaked to the citizens, caused the overwhelming support of total destruction of the two

"The San Francisco Call," of April 2, 1911

Negroes. As if an excuse would be needed to give reason for whites to totally destroy the Negroes anyway. Whatever was going on in the minds of Cato and particularly Reed for his brutal attack of innocent lives, was only predicated by the senseless beatings of so-called disrespecting whites which was an enforced law. Performing all the hardest work of one of the richest farm lands in the country but reaping less of the benefits than before slavery, all the while being told that they're place is second class citizens and nothing more. Certainly, Cato and Reed should have been punished for their acts, but under the law by sworn officials governing proper due process and not taken the life of two human beings by a host of thugs. No investigations, no one held accountable for the events of that day as if two wrongs equal a right. So as a result of the burnings, the efforts for fairness was lost as the whippings for insubordination were still being conducted, wages were stagnate with the chance of fair wage distribution was lost and the willful mistreatment in general would continue. Several notices were posted as a warning to other blacks after the Reed and Cato's death that they'd best behave or face a similar fate. As a result of these warnings, many blacks left the area creating a strand in labor force of the cotton industry. Also not receiving much publicity was the fact the two blacks were kill near Statesboro for no other apparent reason other than being black. Albert Roberts, an aged Negro and his son were also shot but did recover and did receive the best of medical attention. Both Roberts and his son were unarmed, never a troubled person to anyone and was but one more victim of racial hatred in that region for many years afterwards.

By 1917, the city of East St. Louis, Illinois, like many other cities in the north and Midwest states were flexing its industrial might of offering good manufacturing plant jobs. World War I and the then segregated military, caused many vacancies for lack of an all white male labor workforce. To satisfy this void, Negroes were sought after for what would seem fair and equal wages and benefits for all comers. Many Negroes from the south in search of a different kind and better work, other than field hand, began to arrive in large numbers. When word of the differential pay status became known to the newly migrant workers, they sought and demanded equal pay. Several days before the riot, there had been clashes between Negroes, whites and the authorities boiled over with mayhem. A mayhem that was fueled by the killing of a laborer named Cappage, a white man. As a result of that killing, whites began to work themselves into a frenzy as mobs were being formed to ripe havoc in the black communities. Reports of mobs headed by white women were even seen with their clothing drenched with blood, kicking and stumping Negroes that had been shot that laid lifeless in the streets. Hundreds of thugs had forced about a hundred Negroes into a house then set the house a blaze. When the fire began to consume the house, the Negroes attempted to escape from the fire. As they exited, target practice began as they were being shot as quickly as they exited while the crowds laughed and made fun of, in their opinion, *"like picking off rabbits,"* ritual of target practice. A group of about ten white girls in the mayhem, were pulled off an elderly Negro woman who could barely walk by a group of sympathetic white on-lookers. The woman was so badly kicked and beaten until she was unconscious and later was reportedly died from her injuries. Martial Law by this time was declared on July 3, 1917, by Major Mollman. Despite many threats for him and his family's own safety had been declared on behalf of the out-of-control mobsters. The Mayor, disregarding threats against his life

placed the security of the city above his own safety. He made the necessary decisions to protect the Negro citizens of East St. Louis, Illinois as reported by *"The Bemidji daily pioneer," of July 3, 1917.* The streets ran red with Negro blood as they became easy prey for a number of easily 10,000 men and women thugs, set out on ridding the city of its Negro population who would have the audacity to demand pay equal to that of whites. It was reported that over a 100 to 200 Negroes, men women and children were murdered and at least 500 seriously injured. There was over a million and a half dollars of property damage also recorded. There were 8 Illinois National Guardsmen units called into the city that received praise for restoring order. In the aftermath, the streets were littered with dead Negro bodies. Negroes were seen hanging from trees and poles as smoke filled the air from Negro homes and properties that had been destroyed by fire. Several investigations were conducted into the worst race riot in the United States history where President Theodore Roosevelt never condemned the actions of the mob or even discussed the issue in a public setting. There were no indictments from the Federal investigation that lasted only a month. But, black leaders and individual black organizations begin to pressure Congress with equal rights under the law for all. They made it known, that the intolerable manner in which the lawlessness of mobsters that occurred in black neighborhoods would be a thing of the pass.

Unsung heroes in an era of race invisibles saw the strength of a people reflective on the backs of the least of them. Black women and their nurturing abilities have for centuries been the caregivers of child-rearing for both hers and others. Such is the case of a remarkable woman and the matter of childcare. **Jane Collins**, a Negro caregiver, never drew any attention from the high society of whites who walked around her with the invisibleness of a vehicle blind spot. With the recognition of motherless child caregivers, white society types often hired black Nannies that normally spent more time with their kids than the biological mother's did. So it was not unusual to see black Nannies walking with white children or picking up or taking white children to and from school in 1911. New York City in 1901, came a young white girl at 15, who had left her southern town and headed for the lights of a big city seeking stardom. And like all stories of this sort as reported by *"The Sun," of March 3, 1911,* things did not work out, mainly because of immaturity and inexperience. The young white girl was taken advantage of and left pregnant, jobless and homeless. With a child, penniless, jobless and homeless, this young white girl roamed the streets looking for assistance while carrying too much pride to return home. Not having reached her goals of becoming a star, brought desperation into her thought process when she came upon Jane Collins. It's unclear as to how the girl happen to make the acquaintance of Ms. Collins but what she ask of her was the possibility of her taking care of her 6 month old child until such time as she could secure employment. Having the instinctive characteristic known for women of color as nurturers, Ms. Collins accepted the child in her care from this stranger. Having raised three daughters of her own and now grown and married, qualified her as a suitable candidate. Ms. Collins lived on the second floor of 226 West Thirtieth Street and had four rooms. Over seven years went by with no word from the stranger who happened to have arrived at her doorstep in dire straits, seeking mercy for her child she named as Margaret Clemens. The understanding was, she'd be in good hands with Jane. In fact, the young white girl was never heard of again. Like most Nannies on the society streets of New York, Ms Collins went about her daily routine as though she was the child's Nanny. And the normalcy of this activity was viewed like any other Nanny would without any consideration for what really was a foster-mother case. With each passing day, Jane Collins becoming increasing more fond on the child, teaching her of Santa Claus to the boogieman. She also would take her to church, not being permitted to enter herself or fearing any suspicion of taking her by curious whites never impeded her efforts to ensure a strong religious base. Each night Jane would teach the child to say her prayers, an act of religiousness that became a nightly ritual

most enjoyed by the child. Being invisible to society while going to and fro to school, church and elsewhere, brought no attention until one day. Perhaps it was the manner in which the child being a bit to reactive towards an obvious mother-daughter relationship or mother-like figure that arouses the attention unlike before. But Jane was very cautious in public not to display so much attachment emotionally for fear she'd be questioned as to the identity of the child's true parent. As her suspicion became a reality, an inspector arrived at her doorstep just as the stranger had over seven years prior. Someone had noticed the consist absents of white parents that this organization of investigation requiring proper documentation authenticating the child's rightful parentage. After Jane could not explain her story, the inspector removed the child from Jane's custody with a violent protest from Margaret. Margaret was then taken to a temporary children's home overnight until the court date the next day. Jane Collins was devastated, having

learned to love this child as her own, was not even permitted to see the child to put her to bed with their nightly ritual of prayers. It was told in the court proceedings that the child had cried herself to sleep, not understanding why she had been taken from what she considered her mother. For in the process of her upbringing, Jane admits to not allowing the influenced of black culture entirely to taint the child's development. As to the common use of black lingo, Jane admits to using words appropriate to her culture as to ward off any dialog that would suggest nothing less. Jane, also mindful, yet fearful of not having to alter her natural white culture that was necessary as she even chose her companions carefully. Yet, oddly color and race was never apart of any curiosity from Margaret as to why she couldn't play with the black kids

(Pictured above is Little Margaret, behind her is Jane Collins and with the hat is a daughter of the Latter's from Long Island, New York)

in the neighborhood or why was supposedly her mother was black. The methodically manner in which Jane constructed Margaret's life was not base on self hatred, rather to eliminated any possibility of being detected by nosy battleaxes in wondrous curiosity as to her white heritage upbringing.

The next morning when Jane Collins went to court, the first person she saw was an arrogant Mrs. W.K. Vanderbelt, and Mrs. J. Howard Wright heads of a high-society group that called themselves, "Big Sisters," and Virginia Young, a deaconess with the St. George Church and also acting as one of the child's guardians. Generally these women had a hand with society issues that kept blacks in their places inside a child court-arena. As the high-society madams showcased their might in characterizing the excellent manner in which Jane Collins had taken such good care of Margaret, as she then used a dagger of a punch line thrown in when the mentioning of her long golden hair and denouncing the improperness for a white child were being raised solely by a Negro woman as unnatural. Eluting to the tainted black culture as second rate that would scare the child's life forever. As Judge Wyatt also reiterated the role Jane Collins played in the rearing of Margaret, only once was the consideration for the child's feeling taken into account. When the Judge called for her to come before him as he explained in the most elemental manner equal to her level of understanding that it was best for her in the long run and that her "Mammy" would be allowed to see her from time to time. As the Judge also, in an attempt to gain some acknowledgement from the child as to his words of assurance satisfying the void of her Mammy's absence by compounding the necessity of these proceedings. The child replied when asked would she ever forget her Mammy, she stated, as she turned to look at Jane, "No Mummy dear, I will never forget you. You've been so

"The San Francisco Call of Feb 25, 1912

good to me." With those words, Margaret's emotions succumb her as she began to sob uncontrollably. To Margaret, Jane was the only mother she knew. And like a child, they see no color, only their pureness of heart makes that distinction. Finally the decision was made that Jane Collins was unfit to further care for Margaret. Unfit by New York Society standards, solely because of her ethnicity. So, the courts would then allow the millionaire Latter's, who are white, from Long Island or Mrs. Bush of Great Nock, also rich and white from Long Island as well to adopt Margaret. The Bush lady had one special requirement before her family would adopt Margaret and that is that she be pretty. As the society people took Margaret from the openness of the courtroom, with the tears of fright flowing down her rosy cheeks, her one free hand extending to Jane in her bluest of eye's, her true mother was being punished for loving and caring for a child not of her own body. Margaret never knew Jane was not her biological mother and to what does it matter anyway.... Jane herself, as the pain of her sorrow became overwhelming like a blanket of steel wrapped around her shoulders, caused her to kneel on one knee with also one hand extend to what had become, *"her child."* She had asked of the Judge, *"Why did it take so long?" "Why did you give me a chance to love her?"* As the words from her trembling voice distorted by the moisture of tears that had left her eyes and reached her lips, she then dropped her head as the sounds of Margaret's cry had faded then vanished from view of her ears. She continued her cry on one knee before accepting the inevitable. The Judge being a sensible minded man could only scratch his head in misunderstanding of how a woman of color could love a white child so much. Then as he exited the courtroom and Jane's cry, which by then had become as silent as the visibility of Margaret. He looked back slightly once more as he swaged his head from side to side in amazement as if her true emotion was unlike anything he had ever seen. But Jane Collins dream of forever being with Margaret was soon realized as eventually she and Margaret were reunited as her official Nanny. Only when the Latter's didn't have an answer for the depression and resentment Margaret had developed for them in the aftermath of the separation. It was unclear if the true story of her relationship with Jane was ever reviled to Margaret as Jane was the Nanny until Margaret reached adulthood and beyond. What a lesson from a child's love as an example adults could learned from the purest of innocence. But color more than anything has tainted the image of this country. With race and color being a major component of who we are as Americans good and bad can be surmised as a race sensitive nation.

Traditionally, any American Championship Team that wins a championship gets invited to the White House to receive congratulations from the sitting President of the United States. In 2011 the Dallas Mavericks went to the White House for their congratulatory ceremonious event from President Obama. Not invited was newly acquired guard Delonte West for a troubled passed with drugs which made him illegible to a White House visit, but technically he was not apart of the championship run anyways. So his no show was expected with controversial ties. Yet, when the 2011 Hockey Stanley Cup Championship was rewarded to the Boston Bruins, a strange thing happened on the way to the White House. Their visit had a notable absence, the Goalie, Tim Thomas, the playoff MVP a year before, was the **ONLY** one who chose not to attend the event hosted by President Barack Obama for political reasons. Which is code for; because he's black, and his invite would not beneath him to attend. But, in all fairness, this is not the first time an athlete has shrub the invitation to the White House by a sitting President. Famously, Michael Jordan during one of the Chicago Bulls Championships refused to visit the White House under President George Bush 41. Somehow having the parables of Michael Jordan and Tim Thomas are not the same; similar but there is a vast contrast. Both however were champions in their respective sports, both key components for their teams success, both MVP's, one black who rejected a

Devour Us Not

sitting President's invite when the President was white and the other one white who also rejected a sitting President's invite when the President was black. But Jordan's no show was not about race, where Thomas was and that's where the parables ends. Symbolically in an attempt to substitute race for politics, is used mostly to disguise the race hate makes the issue stupid. Imagine code language even in today's climate which has no place in a united country. And for people who promote this hate are less noble than others.

The extraordinary roles of black females in our history are also apart of us as a people. **Julia Hanson**, a Negro, Philanthropist and wealthy woman dies in Washington D.C. September, 15, 1902 and was buried at **Mount Olivet Cemetery.** Mrs. Hanson, born in 1804, was 98 years of age when she passed as her funeral services were held at St. Patrick Church. Julia secured her freedom from her master in 1823 and moved to Washington D.C. when she began working in industry where she built an enormous amount of wealth. Her estate valued about $75,000.00 in 1902, but had many controversies into its distribution. Julia had only one brother named Henry Grindle and he had two daughters named Eliza Murphy and Julia Ashe that essentially became heirs of her estate with much drama behind the reading of her Will. Annie O. Talbott in 1905 filed a lawsuit against the Julia Hanson's estate for lost wages. Eugene Carusi and Charles Frances Carusi, executors of the Julia Hanson estate received notice that $10, 710 in back wages for services rendered were being challenged. Annie claimed to have been a member of her household staff making about $180.00 yearly while performing nursing and cooking among other domestic duties. The period she was employed by Julia was from January 1880 to September 15, 1902. But, Chief Justice Clabaugh in Circuit Court Number 2 dismissed the charges and likewise was the case when the two nieces protest the Will. The bulk of her estate did eventually go to the two nieces with the following charitable organizations receiving portions of her estate; Oblate Sisters, Little Sisters of the Poor, St. Joseph's Male Orphan, St. Ann's Orphan Asylum for Girls, and several small gifts to personal friends. Few other details

are known about this entrepreneur; against all odds achieve what even some white men could not.

Mrs. Alma Boone little, pictured on the left was sued by her husband, Arthur C. Little, a druggist from Detroit, Michigan on the grounds that she concealed the fact that she had Negro blood in her veins before he married her. What was obvious during that era, before DNA, he was probably right. But more importantly, she could have made the same claim. During centuries of race mixing, willfully or not, it was happening. Mrs. Little had obvious fair skin, natural sandy colored straight hair, thin lips, but had very noticeable ethnic eyes. Yet, visual observation was not enough to definitely identify a person under one umbrella of race recognition than another. Actress **Victoria Rowell**, who is black

but has a white mother by ethnicity mainly because her father is black, she is classified as black. She has a daughter that has blonde hair and blue eyes, by her previously married with her then husband, Tom Fahey. But to use an element of obvious racial hatred as a means of denouncing a person as your spouse for whom you've chosen, and suddenly finds it distasteful after an ethical identity question is raised is just ludicrous. Genes are not all proportioned inconclusively recognizable when race mixing occurs. Case and point, the **President of the United States, Barack Obama's** mother was white and his father of African descendant. Yet the President has more of his African characteristics from his father in his facial outline than his Caucasian characteristic outer

"The Washington Herald," of Aug 3, 1913

appearance. But in 1915, before a more scientific details about the origin of our descendants, logically an unproven argument of an unlikable component, despite the unproven fact of authenticity that her mother was said to have been a full-blooded Negro. In proving that his wife was a Negro did not stand up in court, for lack of scientific sophistication. However, because of the implications implied, the marriage failed without proof of purity for her race or his. A simple concept, of race, heavily woven in the fabric of our culture that decides what the heart wants and what society dictates is incalculably American. For Arthur Little to assume he's of the purest of his race without heredity Negro blood visible in his own outline features which may or may not present itself in himself was a cultural barrier used to place people in categories subject to inferior treatment. Even in the manner of twins as reported by *"The Day Book," of July 21, 1916* describes the birth of twin born in Denver, Colorado July 21, 1916. A Caucasian woman gave birth to the twins where the one baby was described as having a perfectly oval shaped head with Caucasian like features was a girl while her brother was described as having a slopped head, dark skin and Negro liked features. The father was of mixed blood that was described as Spanish-Negro descent. The mother, Mabel Owen failing to believe the children were hers and gave them up to the State. There was another story of interest where a wealthy Caucasian couple was married in the south around the turn of the century. A very high-society types where a grand wedding was performed and all dignitaries attending and all was grand until a year later. The couple's first born child was a Negro by all race classifications of the period. It created such a bad impression on a great family name with whisperings of disgrace all about. As the husband accused his wife of infidelity by all appearances of having an affair with a Negro. The wife's family was devastated as the husband began to disassociate himself from his wife by filing for a divorce and eliminating her from the high-society social class with the rumors. He suggested to her that if not an affair then there was somewhere in her blood line, Negro blood or to phrase it more appropriately, she was then considered damaged goods. A charged the wife vividly denied to no avail. A thought that just enraged the husband for his total contempt for the Negro race. About six months later, the husband's wealthy parents paid him a visit, a visit that would just devastate the husband. What they discussed with him that caused him to be so distraught was the fact that he was adopted because his wealthy parents could not have children. And not having children as a society couple somehow would have made them less desirable as a social equal. So out of desperation they knew they had to adopt. Knowingly, at the time that the only child available to them that would have been about the time they should have had a child, was the existence of the a slave girl's pregnancy. But because the nature of his biological heritage that wasn't visible by appearances, was the fact that his mother was from that African slave. This was once considered an act of flawed heritage and disgraceful, undesirable by most society types at the time. The slave girl that had been forcefully impregnated by her white master and was later killed for it. But the master managed to save the child by placing the child in the care of a convent headed by Nuns. He was that child, as he became inflamed with anger, calling his parents liars after their chilling truth had been reveled to him with written documented proof. The pain was much too great as he, the husband, had often looked down on the very people that he, himself was apart of. And for all the things he had called his wife, in response to the assumption that it was her flawed heritage that caused the marriage breakup. But now, it was he that now had the flawed black blood of Negro heritage. The irony is to be careful in how you hate, because the very thing you hate, you may soon become. But this method of deep racial hatred and discrimination is not all exclusively American. Every region of the world has its own method of classifying people. The only despicable thing about this unilateral discriminatory method is the hypocrisy of it all. But the will of the African woman is one of endurance, perseverance and strong willed. Without their significant role in our American history that has been overlooked far too long, who knows how this devoured plan of a people might have played out otherwise.

Devour Us Not

"Sojourner Truth"

Isabella Baumfree or as all know her as **Sojourner Truth** was a major player in the racial inequalities that exist then and now in America. Isabella Baumfree was her birth name and according to Sojourner Truth, that name came about as an answer from God, after her escape from her master when she was first ask her name she stated God told her name would be Sojourner Truth until the day she dies. Sojourner was describe as being six feet tall and muscularly built that stood erect with a deep masculine voice. She was born approximately 1797 in Ulster County, New York and died November 26, 1883 in Battle Creek, Michigan as reported by *"The Deseret Evening News, Saturday, November 29, 1902."* Sojourner, being one of the first to receive her freedom in the state of New York after the 1817 act of New York which emancipated all slaves over the age of 40, and all slaves regardless of age were freed in New York in 1827. Sojourner had a saying related to her receiving her freedom, *"I only count my age from de time dat I was 'emancipated. Den I begun to lib."* She was mother to five children and admitting, three were sold from her by her master. Sojourner was promised her freedom one year earlier than the required date for displaying loyalty towards him and family. But when the time came to release her, the master refused to acknowledge any such agreement which prompted her to take matters into her own hand and run away with the remaining two of her children. During the walk to New York, which took all day, she sought shelter with a Quaker family where she remained for the year requiring her natural freedom by law. After her forty years as a slave, Sojourner landed in New York where she worked for her wages and providing for her children while maintaining a home for ten years. On November 17, 1864 as reported by, *"The Washington Times," of October 5, 1902*, President Lincoln invited Sojourner to the White House and on December 1, was commissioned by the National Freedman Relief Association. The position was *"counselor"* to the newly emancipated Negroes that formed a colony in Arlington Heights. As a part of her year teaching assignments were to teach all familiar domestic work to the women about cleanliness and other domestic values that would enable gainful employment. She then used her experience to become a Nurse at the Freedman Hospital. Her duties afforded her the opportunity to visit many parts of the city. Distances that required her use of public transportation for which she was denied. So Sojourner was then coupled to file a complaint that made significant changes to public cars in their elimination from public use. Only after her complaint to the president of the transportation company was this acknowledged. Sojourner's efforts made the Negro more industrious and more qualified to the level their education would provide. Both white and black's benefited from her efforts which lead to a more respectable ethnical professional. Sojourner died with her name remembered as Sojourner. Her birth name of Isabella Baumfree was never mentioned after her freedom was acquired. An old fashioned red brick house that hung a sign at 2007 Vermont Avenue in the city which read *"Sojourner Truth Home,"* where she died was established as a school for a small group of Negro women for training in domestic matters for many years. And her most famous line *"Ain't I a woman,"* identifies her feelings on women suffrage.

When a rioting mob was turned on in Evansville, Indiana July, 1903 as reported by, *"The Bourbon News," of July 10, 1903,* which started when Officer Louis Massey, a white man, became the first officer to die in the line of duty in Evansville. Lee Brown, a Negro, was alleged to be the culprit. When the news of the murder became known to the citizens of Evansville, a mob first attacked the black community. The mob looted a white owned hardware store of its weapons and ammunition that caused the store owner to place an ad requesting the return

The Connubial Yoke, as Viewed in Darktown.

"The Evening World," of October 11, 1904

the then stolen goods. Finally, Governor Winfield Durbin from Indianapolis called in the Militia after the destruction of homes and businesses owned by Negroes were being burned. The Sheriff had mentioned he'd protect the Negroes but failed in his efforts. As most of the Negroes began to flee to the woods for safety, left an already frenzy crowd opportunities to have its way. The State Militia troops, Company A, First Regiment, National Guard that had about 400 armed soldiers, commanded by Colonel McCoy were called out to protects the Negro citizens and property of Evansville, Indiana. After the four days of destroying black businesses and wild lawlessness something needed to done. Also assisting in guarding the jail was one hundred Deputy Sheriff's under the leadership of Sheriff Chris Kratz that positioned them in a manner that would have protected what the mob assumed was the murderer of Officer Massey. But, 16 out of the 46 prisoners were Negroes who began to sob and yell for fear of the inevitable of being black and helpless to defend themselves in their cells. But Brown as he was called, was swift away to Vincennes, Indiana for fearing what was all too familiar and common throughout this country, was the mob rushing the jail and taking the law into their own hands. Without fear of penalties imposed by law, the mobs actions were that of fearless anger. During the gun battle of Brown and Massey, Brown was seriously wounded and eventually visited by three doctors who gave him up for dead. Later on Brown did eventually died from those wounds. Some of the white citizen that were killed on that Monday fight with the Militia was twenty-three year old Frank Lamble, shot in the back running away and died from his wounds on Tuesday. Also killed was Charles Taylor, twenty-five years old also shot in the back and was reported as an innocence on-looker awaiting a lynching. August Jordan and Hazel Allman, little white girls hit by ricocheting bullets as they sat in their parent's buggy in wait for a lynching was also killed and buried on Wednesday. There was an element of secrecy surround the funeral of young Hazel as not to infuriate the mob further. John Barrett was another victim who was killed. In the aftermath of the violence, the police department arrested ten citizens of Evansville for carrying concealed weapons; nine of the ten were Negroes that were fined $100 each. Negro fireman were asked to leave the city during the violence at the advice of the Mayor, their jobs were then given to white men. Of all the Negro citizens in Evansville were invisible from view in fear of what had occurred in other cities throughout the country began leaving the area by any means necessary. Reported were some Negroes being killed by so called accident shooting, while fleeing. Ironically, one was the wife of Lee Brown who was accidentally shot while trying to board a moving train. There were five grand jury indictments for the rioting; Richard Grosbeck, who was a socialist for the clerk, A.P. Cardwell, a furniture merchant, J.T Ziegler, William Trimble and James Steele were all released on bond. All of the troubles started when Lee Roberts or Lee Brown as what little was known about the Negro, was drinking five cent beer at Ossenberg's saloon at 10th and Mulberry Street. An argument broke out between Brown and the Negro bartender, Thomas Berry, over whether the five cent beer had been paid for. Brown, as explained by patrons of the saloon claimed Brown was drunk and probably didn't pay for the drink. Finally, the bartender had Brown thrown out of the saloon, at which time Brown made a loud threat against the bartender saying, *"I'm gon' get him."* The bartender then noticed Officer Massey walking his beat and notified him of the threat Brown had made. True to his word, Brown showed back up with a pistol in hand and after a brief discussion with Officer Massey, gun fire was exchanged between Massey and Brown. Massey loosing his life at the hands of a Negro is what ignited the white citizens of Evansville to riot. The gun battle that occurred between the white mob citizens and the militia that cost nine lives was unwarranted and unnecessary. With the loss of two innocent children, brought to the scene by their parents to witness what most were assured of was to witness a lynching of a Negro, America's favorite pass time. Several provoking attempts to intimidate the militia were initiated by the mob first by yelling, *"Tin soldiers, nigger lovers, and puppets,"* which didn't faze the soldiers. One of the leaders of the mob

Devour Us Not

then began to ride a bike near to where the soldiers were positioned close enough to see if he could penetrate their lines. The one bold mobster came close enough to grab one of younger-looking soldier's weapons in an attempt to secure it from him. A wrestling match then ensued as the other mobsters began to inch closer to the militia while yelling more louder obscenities as if a prize fighter testing the courage of his opponent. In the panic of loud voices matched by the already mayhem, a shot was fired from the mob. A shot the mob vehemently denied. But after careful examination of one of the dead bodies at the morgue was a pistol that had three bullets missing from its chamber. The militia had returned fire and a volume of shots were fire, several hundred leaving nine white mobsters dead and about fifty more wounded as bodies began to fall like leaves from a tree on a winters day. Lost in all of the innocence, the mob claimed for protecting their way of life in trying to take vengeance for the killing of one of their own by a Negro was in some bazaar manner giving the advantage to the Negroes. What failed to be realized and uncovered were the innocence of the Negroes who lost their life's savings. With nothing to fall back on and no monies or help from anyone in restoring these life's in what was preventable and unnecessary, a perfect hatred. But this was the all too familiar plan in not allowing the Negroes to achieve too much for fear he just might surpass them in their efforts to achieving equality.

Mr. & Mrs. Henry Black
"The Colored American," of July 18, 1903

Mr. Henry *(born in 1844)* **and Mrs. Cornelis Black** *(born in 1853),* were proud and prominent Hotel owners, formerly of Evansville, Indiana pictured left. They were some of the innocent victims of mob violence against their property. The Black's Hotel, valued at about $2,000.00, was the best hotel in the area for Negroes. After years of struggling, and placing all their hard earned monies and effort into their hotel, that was the Black's sole livelihood and source of all their wealth and income. A structure that was completely destroyed by the mob without provocation. The Black's reportedly had no insurance and was left penniless as a result of this cowardly act. Since they were up in age, they agreed to leave the city of Evansville for St. Louis and start life all over again not knowing how or where their sources of income would come. An all too common cry for too many Americans just simple being of the wrong color in a country that neither valued their already contributions nor their rights as citizens. Their businesses were targeted by the mob solely because they were black, as many of their neighbors who had nothing to do with the murder of Officer Massey nor did they frequent the Ossenberg saloon. Most were law-abiding citizens and devout Christians, yet, with no compensations and the law officer's inabilities to properly secure protection of its citizen's, their lives and property were lost. A constant reminder of the number of lawless events within its city limits made life unbearable and intolerable. A descent city where all white owned homes and businesses were left in tacked with no fear of retaliation. Many business owners like the Black Hotel owners could not sustain the high cost of insurance, which was higher than insurance of similar value and likeness for that of whites. But they and people like them lost everything while the irresponsible guilty parties were allowed to walk among them free and build more wealth. While most Negroes were constantly relocating and rebuilding throughout their entire lives. This form of the Negroes way of life is a testament as to the constant survival instincts that has made us so resilient and steadfast both then and now and shall not and will not, be devoured! An echoed cry for a people of limited means who despite all the love for a country who often did not return the same, continues to try and prove its worthiness and acceptance evermore.

"The Times," of Dec 7, 1902

The Supreme Court decision; Dred Scott vs. Sanford where Dred Scott first attempted to sue for his freedom in 1847. After about ten years of back and forth through decision reversals and court appearances; only to see his dreams shattered with the Supreme Courts infamous decision much to the chagrin of the anti-slavery movement. The story of Dred Scott is significant to all people of color, because the effect it had on President Lincoln and the lives it shaped for every American in this country then and now. The ruling by the Supreme Court stated that, **"All people of African descent (***Because of their beliefs that blacks were inferior to that of whites***), free or slaves could never become American citizens and therefore have no rights that any white man would be bound to respect."** The Supreme Court; upright and incorruptible; our finest institution of honor and the only court established by the United States Constitution. So what about the interpretation of the following words need explaining; **"We hold these truths to be self-evident, that all men are created equal, that they are endowed by their Creator with certain unalienable**

"Sam" Dred Scott   *Harriett Scott*   *Daughter's Eliza & Lizzie Scott*
Frank Leslie's Illustrated Newspaper, June 27, 1857

"Judges In The Dred Scott Decision" - *Judge-James Moore Wayne (1835-1867), Judge-Benjamin R Curtis (1851-1857), Judge-John Archibald Campbell (18-1861), Judge-John Catron (1837-1865), Judge-John McLean (1830-1861), Judge-Peter Vivian Daniel (1842-1860), Judge-Robert Cooper Grier (1846-1870), Judge-Samuel Nelson (1845-1872), Chief Judge-Roger Brooke Taney (1836-1864). Library of Congress.*

Rights, that among these are Life, Liberty and the pursuit of happiness." Also, bear in mind; those words were written by a man who owned as many as 150 slaves, and also created a free system of tax-supported elementary education for all except slaves that was defeated; so in his efforts to show mercy to his fellow man, the main focus of his plight seem to have been focused on trying to appease his constituents rather than nobility to all. But the linger state of equality would be an everlasting document that would be written later by the very same thoughts. Let's not forget he had impregnated a 14 year old mulatto girl named Sally Hemings, half sister to his late wife which is all a bit hypercritical. So how is it then that a body of honorary appointee's, entrusted with maintaining the consistent and orderly development of Federal Law could have bias and sinister motives? The Supreme Court of that era was more than just full of controversy and biases regarding slavery. Their moral characters were suspect as well as their opinion. The appointment processes where Southern Presidents who oppose the abolishment of slavery would select appointees whose views agreed with their own and some even had family ties to slave ownership which also gave strength to their views. And their general philosophy of taking a barbaric savage, living in African and bring him to a Christian country, treat him like a barbaric savage is better in the eyes of the unjust if the latter is considered just. But the latter of the two options proposed by the majority; a people set out on profiteering from the free labor of hard work not their own is the consensus argument. So their decisions certainly understandably, but morally reprehensible, violated the very honor and

Devour Us Not

"The Washington Herald," of Jan 3, 1915

code of the African slaves that their sworn appointment guaranteed to uphold. About Dred Scott and his life: Born approximately 1800 in Southampton County, Virginia, he was owned by Peter Blow who passed away and was sold to Major Tellaferro and then subsequently purchased by an unmarried Army Surgeon named Dr. John Emerson around 1832. By this time, some of the states had established themselves as Free States and laws granting freedom with certain time lines were being offered to all slaves.

Illinois and Wisconsin were the two such states of freedom. During the 1836 year, Dr. Emerson had traveled to Illinois and stayed for a period of time and then to Wisconsin. Dr. Emerson, while in Wisconsin had befriended a local justice of the peace who had a female slave named Harriet Robinson that caught the eye of Dred and soon they were married. Dred and Harriett had two sons (*Both died as infants*) and two lovely daughters named Eliza and Lizzie (*Madison*). In 1838, Dr. Emerson received orders to go to St. Louis, Missouri. Sometime during the Missouri post of duty and shortly before his death in 1843, Dr. Emerson's was married. It is believed that Mrs. Emerson had lent the Scott family to an Army Captain as hired hands. Then there was considerable ownership claims when the Scott's were sold to Dr. Emerson's brother-in-law, (Mrs. Emerson's brother) John F. A. Sanford of New York. June 1847, Dred Scott first sought and lost his right to freedom in court. After several attempts with the Missouri Supreme Court, the St. Louis Circuit Court, The United States Circuit Court in Missouri and ultimately to The United States Supreme Court where the final decision of the Supreme Court was read on March of 1857 by then Chief Justice Roger B. Taney of Maryland. A staunch supporter of slavery because of his prior ownership of slaves. While this decision was well received in the South, Northerners were outraged. This decision alone, in the opinion of most would further divided the views of slavery in the Republic and made for a life changing debate about the legality of rights for people of color and the inhuman-like treatment they received. This further divide also leads to the War Between the States by some accounts. Bitter sweet ending was that Peter Blow, the originally owner of Dred Scott had a son that befriended Dred at childhood and was responsible for his legal fees throughout the years and then secured his freedom through purchased on May 26, 1857. Dred would only see freedom for a few months after Taylor Blow purchased the family and set them free, Dred Scott died of tuberculosis on September 17, 1857. But, he died a free man, having tasted the sweet liberty he was denied almost his entire life while maintaining the alluring silence of hope.

The Douglass Family

L/R: 1st Wife-Anna Murray-Douglass, Frederick Douglass, 2nd Wife-Helen Pitts-Douglass, Lewis Douglass, Frederick Douglass, Jr., Charles .R. Douglass and Rosetta Douglass Sprague.   The Frederick Douglass Family - "The Appeal," of Sep 3, 1892

Frederick Douglass was born as reported by, *"The Broad Ax," of February 16, 1907*, in the latter part of February, 1817 at Tuckahoe near Easton, Talbot County, Maryland. Born a slave on Colonel Edward Lloyd's plantation of a Negro mother and a white father. As a child, Frederick moved around as his master sent him to Baltimore in 1825 to live with one of his relatives. In 1833 he was sent to St. Michael's, Maryland to live again with his master and worked as a field-hand. In January, 1834, Frederick was sent to live with Edward Covey, a so-called slave-breaker, for a year mainly because Frederick Douglass had a strong will of which Edward was

very good at breaking the bravest of slaves down. But, Frederick was not to be broken, as he'd stand tall and fight everyday against the technique of whipping as a means of breaking him. Between the years of 1835-36, feed-up with the 270 plus years of the barbaric system of slavery, he made his first unsuccessful attempt of tasting the right of a free man while being employed by William Freeland. This first attempt of tasting that liberty only fueled the passion in Frederick to continue his pursuit of freedom at all cost. During this period in Baltimore, he learned a trade of ship-calker for which he was hired. In the year of 1838, September 3rd, Frederick Douglass at the age of about twenty-one, he made his successful attempt of ac-

quiring his freedom by escaping to New York City. He had acquired a sailor uniform and impersonated a sailor without suspicion in acquiring his freedom. Shortly after arriving in New York City he meet and married Miss Anna Murray for whom he was married for forty-four years until her death. During their marriage, they had four children, Frederick Douglass, Jr., Rosetta, Charles and Lewis. It was shortly after his freedom he adopted the last name of *"Douglass,"* and he and his new wife, Anna, moved to Bedford, Massachusetts. In 1841, Frederick attended his first Anti-Slavery Convention in Nantucket Island and so compelling was his argument against the institution of slavery that he was hired as an Agent of the Massachusetts Anti-Slavery Society that required his lecturing skills in denouncing slavery. In 1847 Frederick was responsible for establishing the weekly newspaper in Rochester, New York called Frederick Douglass' paper that was later changed to The North Star. The North Star stayed in production until the abolishment of slavery which was the core of its existence to discredit. Mr. Douglass later became the editor of the National Era that was continued by his sons Lewis and Frederick, Jr., after his death. In 1859, the John Brown riot in which Mr. Douglass was supposedly the instigator prompted Governor Wise to make requisition for his arrest. It was suggested that Mr. Douglass went to England and stayed for six or eight months to avoid any association with the riot. An when the civil war broke-out in 1861, Mr. Douglass was an advent component of addressing Negro soldiers employment with then President Lincoln as well as a proclamation of emancipation on the slavery issue. After careful consideration of Mr. Douglass' proposal of Negro troops, he was a major player in the recruitment process in starting the infamous fifty-fourth and fifty-fifth Massachusetts. Frederick Douglas among his many accomplishments such as being an honorary

member of Washington Benevolent and Literary Societies as well as the author of a number of books that include, *"A Narrative of my Experience in Slavery," "My Bondage and My Freedom."* February 20, 1895, Frederick Douglass died a few minutes before seven in is home of Anacostia Heights of heart failure. His net worth at the time of his death was valued at between $100,000 and $200,000. After the death of Frederick first wife, Anna of 44 years, he then married **Helen Pitts**.

Helen was a white lady of middle age living in New England, working as a clerk in the recorder of deeds for the District of Columbia when Mr. Douglass was appointed to the office. It was later in 1886 Mr. Douglass was removed from that position by the President Cleveland. Helen Pitts family initially disapproved of the relationship with Mr. Douglass. Not only because of his ethnicity because her family appeared to be against any involvement with people of color. But, Helen was adamant about the relationship which forced them to yield to her insistence that her happiness and separation from them would be at risk. The amount of criticism Frederick received as being hypocritical from Negroes and whites were much greater than any of the rejections Helen's family had proposed. In 1871, President Grant appointed him Secretary to the Commission to San Domingo and also territorial counsel for the District of Columbia. In 1872 he was elected Presidential Elector At Large for the State of New York and simultaneously being appointed to carry the electoral vote of the state to Washington. In 1876 he was appointed United States Marshal for the District of Columbia. And in 1889 he was appointed

Devour Us Not

Minister of Haiti by then President Harrison. Ironically the country had recently experienced a revolution and a new government in place refused to accept Mr. Douglass arrival solely because of his color in a country of mostly black people. That position was the last of all the appointments Mr. Douglass held during his life. But of all criticism surrounding Mr. Douglass life, he was the most influential African-American of his time and beloved by all Americans.

Who was **John Mercer Langston** and what part did he play in African-American history, pictured on the left & right? The New York newspaper article from *"The Sun," of November 21, 1897*, gives some incline into the life of this remarkable American who was 1st of his race to be accepted to the Bar. Mr. Langston was born a slave on his white father's farm in Louisa County, Virginia, December 14, 1829. Mr. Langston describes his mother as a slave on Captain Ralph Quarles plantation, but lover to his wealthy father on a nearby farm. Also the

uncharacteristic manner in which he catered to and acknowledged the half-breed children he had by his black-Mistresses by making financial investments into describing his unusualness, was his fathers belief in the abolishment of slavery on a volunteer bases only, despite owning many slaves himself. The manner in which his treatment of his slave was more in tune with employer with employee without the obvious exchange of monetary values vice principal and developmental values. But where does one draw value to his or her life? Freedom of choice or opportunity to choose is far more valued than any monetary accomplishments that are tangible to the eye yet blinded by the spirit of the soul's desire. Needless to say of his father describing his attitude toward his slaves that was not looked upon unfavorably by surrounding farms and plantations caused unnecessary social ostracizing. What it indelibly shaped was the thinking of Mr. Langston. His white slave-owner father in describing his then slave mistress as the following; *"The woman for whom he discovered special attachment and who finally became really the mistress of the great house of the plantation, reciprocating the affection of her owner. Winning his respect and confidence, was the one whom he had taken and held, at first, in pledge for money borrowed of him by her former owner, but whom at last he made the mother of his four children, one daughter and three sons. Her name was Lucy Langston. Her surname was of Indian origin and borne by her mother, as she came out of a tribe of Indians of close relationship in blood to the famous Pocahontas." "Of Indian extraction, she was possessed of a slight proportion of Negro blood: and yet she and her mother, a full-blooded Indian woman, who was brought up on the plantation and remained there up to her death were loved and honored by their fellow slaves of every class. Lucy was a woman of small stature substantial build, fair looks, easy and natural bearing even and quiet temper, intelligent and thoughtful, who accepted her lot with becoming resignation, while she always exhibited the deepest affection and earnest solicitude for her children. As early as 1806 as her emancipation papers show, Captain Quarles set Lucy and her daughter Maria, then her only child, at liberty. Subsequently, three other children, son's were born to them; and though it maybe in his last will and testament."* As recorded by *"The Sun," of New York, November 21, 1897.* But in describing the wealth he'd provided to his slaves children that included stock, live stock, cash and land, he described as illegitimate offsprings by the restrictive law prohibiting race mixing and without the sanctity of marriage made for a more compelling argument. Both Captain Quarles and Mr. Langston's mother died in 1834, when he was four years of age. The executor of Captain Quarles Will was Captain Gooch, who then moved the family to Chillicothe, Ohio. In 1844, when Mr. Langston was 14 he entered Oberlin College where he remained 8 years, graduating in 1852. Wanting to become a Lawyer but understanding the limitations for his race ever to be admitted to any University that would accept any other course for his life. Even though Mr. Langston had background studies in Theology, he had no interest in pursuing it but as fate would have it, then came Mr. Philomon Bliss of Elyria. Despite restrictive laws prohibiting admission of Negro's, opportunity granted him only because of his ethnicity closely resembling an Anglo. By the time Mr. Langston finished his law degree program and was accepted to the Bar as a white man, he married a North Carolinian. Her name was Miss Caroline M. Walt, also a graduate of Oberlin College. *"The Washington Times," of March 16, 1911,* states there were five children born to their union two daughters and three sons. Mr. Langston eventually built-up a lucrative law practice and his lecturing on anti-slavery sustained a descent

living and domesticated lifestyle that was neighborhood friendly. His home also became the popular attraction for most anti-slavery lectures and Leaders throughout the country. The eloquent manner in which Mr. Langston convey his passion for the contempt of slavery, contrary to the way he was raised made him more effective in denouncing the disrespect his race was being depicted in a society of civilized people. His level as an Orator was being compared to such renowned prolific speakers as Frederick Douglass. Mr. Langston was on the Board of Education for Oberlin College for eleven years. Because of Mr. Langston's humble beginnings, few knew of his slave connections and how his witness to the treatment of others paved his approach against the institution of slavery. Acknowledged during board meetings to white propaganda around the entire country of the inferiority of the black race or not having the intellect or cooping skills to compete with whites would bring out such rage and anger from Mr. Langston. During some of his lectures, that anger felt from slavery would manifest itself first in his eyes as they filled with such tears of hurt, most noticeable by his constituents and all viewing audiences. He was very compassionate about the restrictions of race prohibiting access to life based on Negro-blood in ones veins. He, like Frederick Douglass was apart of the recruitment and enlistment efforts for the fifty-fourth and fifty-fifth of Massachusetts. After the law was made for this provision in 1867, Mr. Langston was offered a position as General Inspector of the Bureau of Refuges, Freedman and Abandoned Lands by General O. O. Howard. This position considered highly regarded, caused Mr. Langston to leave his Ohio home. His important efforts involved in the reconstruction period of the Freedman's Bureau as his relentless and tireless efforts of educational works particularly in southern states where it was mostly needed. In 1868, he was made Dean of the Law Department of Howard University as well as Acting President at Washington, D.C. campus. He was credited with turning out the first wave of African-American Lawyers in these United States. Mr. Langston was also a member and Attorney of the Board of Health of the District of Columbia and a trustee of the Freedmen's Savings and Trust Company for seven years. In 1877, Mr. Langston was appointed Minister Resident and Consul-General to Haiti and served until 1885 when he resigned. Also in that same year, he was made President of the Virginia Normal and Collegiate Institution at Petersburg, Virginia for three years. His tenure was only interrupted by his election to the Fifty-First Congress as a Republican for which he did one term, after a defeat when his re-election bid failed. Mr. Langston's law practice in Washington D.C. began in 1891 after his political aspirations failed. But considered the biggest disaster of his life was the publishing of his autobiography in 1894, titled, *"From the Virginia Plantation to the National Capital."* The book did irreversible damage to his reputation and credibility by its content. Too much boasting and painting an overly magnified narcissistic view to his accomplishments that also had a hand in the breaking of friendship between him and Frederick Douglass. John Mercer Langston, it was said, had a competitive spirit about him as he allowed this edge of competitiveness to make his unyielding argument about who was the better or greater man. It was also said, only after the death of Mr. Frederick Douglass, that John Mercer Langston then considered the greatest man of his race. On November 15, 1897, Mr. Langston died. He was also the great-uncle to Langston Hughes, a Howard University

graduate and renowned poet and Charles Henry Langston, his brother, also an abolitionist.

Booker Taliaferro Washington born in a slave cabin on a plantation in April 5, 1856 according to a, *"New York Daily Tribune-Sunday,"* of May 3, 1903, newspaper article. Product of a Negro slave woman plantation cook and her white male slave-master from a neighboring plantation. Earliest memories of slavery-time, was rumor talk among the quietness of night as slaves describing ill-treatment of slaves by whites to a long-ship rides from Africa. Mr. Washington recalls his sobbing mother kneeling by he and his brother, John's bed on a dirt cabin floor praying for a victory of Lincoln's Army, *"so we, the slaves, can be free,"* she remarked. As repetitively as she voiced that prayer, her belief was assured that

"Bisbee Daily Review," of Mar 6, 1902 -*Booker T. Washington*, "The Colored American.," of December 28, 1901-1st wife *Fanny Norton Smith*, 2nd wife *Olivia America Davidson*, 3rd Wife *Margaret James Murray Washington*, "The Appeal," of April 22, 1905-*Miss Portia M. Washington-Wood* (Daughter of Fanny & Booker T.), "The Appeal," of April 22, 1905-*Prof. Charles Winter Wood* (Husband of Portia Washington).

God would someday hear the voices of his people for freedom. That powerful belief in God was then instilled in Mr. Washington from that point on as it became a rallying cry for prosperity. His mother's defiance of plantation rules for the caring for her children were unprecedented. Mr. Washington, of all the subjects related to slave life was his description of meal choices partaken by slaves. Meals were of the simplest of content unless for special holidays where meat would be plentiful. Because of the unavailability of meat, occasionally the discussion of menu selection was a matter of planning for months. He recalls however, late one night his mother, Jane, cooking up a chicken dish in somewhat of a secrecy. Knowing the limited amounts proportionally given to her children that day, prompted his mother to prepare that dish late one night. The whereabouts of this chicken was a mystery, but only the thoughts of opportunity warranted its necessity, or so it was thought. As he recollect in hindsight, the word theft in that circumstances did not apply as that day's standard for theft. But, Mr. Washington, being cognizant of the stereotypical avenues directed towards the struggles of Negroes in the era of trustworthiness never gave mentioned to his mother. To him, by whatever means any avenue of opportunities for a hand up was rare and most welcomed. And most assuredly not bordering theft when the ill-treatment of slaves ran rapid just like being malnourished. So, Mr. Washington's, lessons of life, he gives credit to his mother as his white father was a none factor. He like most, a victim of a flawed system of oppression, dominated by injustice so making provisions for a sometimes starving family was a matter of survival. But this element of theft, for no beneficial legitimacy of survival is nothing but theft and made a negative stigmatized element of black culture that we people are criticized even today. Despite all the disfranchisement attempted by bias southern legislature, the denial of Dr. Booker T. Washington's efforts in establishing Tuskegee Normal and Industrial Institute would not hamper his diligence, rather, brought national notoriety for his intellect. Undeniable is how Dr. Washington revolutionized the educational system in the south. For one of many quotes given by Dr. Washington was, *"There can be no liberty without intelligence; no independence without industry, and no power for man and no charm for woman without character."* The educational machine of Tuskegee changed the economical structure

in the south during Dr. Washington's tenure. But most critical of his works were outsiders of his own race in labeling him as an *"old school Negro,"* which was very respectful toward whites and not demanding more political power based on his influence. Moreover, whites weren't too far off of their criticism as to the how's and why's Negroes would be expected to self sustain themselves without handouts from them. After all, they were, a not so distant past totally ignorant as slaves. But with all its criticisms about Dr. Washington, his vision of creating a learning environment where on the grounds which once stood of that day, plantation dominances now housed architecturally modernization applicable for its time.

Aligned the landscapes with buildings designed and labored by people of color who were descendants of slaves. A planned effort by Dr. Washington in Macon County, Alabama's Black Belt district to the surprise of most whites and blacks in the area. And the assumption of the Negro always relying on a superior races for guidance was but wishful thinking. Efforts, justifiable was the first of its kind in the south giving equal ploy to skilled and professionalism work solely for non-blacks. All of this started in 1872 when Dr. Washington entered Hampton Institute, where it is believed the influence for Tuskegee came from. Hampton Institute that stated with just 50 cents was an example of what greatness could achieve with such meager means. While trying to secure a location for his

Dr. Booker T. Washington- "The Appeal," of March 12, 1892

school, he purchased 100 acres of what was considered worn-out land, a mile from Tuskegee for $500.00 total and requiring $200.00 down payment. Dr. Washington having many associates at Hampton Institute wrote for a financial assistance. Having been a graduate in 1874, returned as a teacher in 1881 and where he met and married his first wife, Fannie Smith summer of 1882. The monies and the needs were being spread like wild fire as monies from all sources begin to come in on behaves of Tuskegee and its hope and intent. Also instrumental in fundraising was Miss Davidson who later became Dr. Washington's second wife. In a few short years saw the expansion of land for the school to 3,500 acres valued at nearly a half million dollars while free of any encumbrances. Scholarship monies of the donations that were used to acquire quality teachers as an old farm house were initially used as the school. In 1883 a significant part of Alabama legislation was being proposed to cut of appropriation to the school, but the Speaker of the House, Colonel W.F. Foster, and an ex-Confederate Officer from Tuskegee saved the appropriation. Colonel Foster had to leave the chair to protect the institution that not only save it but increased the appropriation to $3,000.00 a year which later gave wings to a financial summary boosting in a ten year period of $28, 000.00 from the State of Alabama in addition to the $3,000 a year, which $34,121.32 in volunteer donations, $7,486.33 in student payments and $25, $550 in labor cost. All these increases allowed for the rewarding of more student scholarships as well as building expansions. A price tag of only $8.00 a month just for board per student, none of which his 150 students could afford even after half of was paid by work at the school. A start in a rented shanty church to the great institution of learning of today is quite an accomplishment. Then like a volume of downhill rushing waters, the expansion of this school began to take off as blacks realized the success of a people will come from the people. As the students and teachers began sharing the responsibilities of building the *"Porter Hall,"* the first of many buildings built by the people. Being self-reliant, they began to plant its own food and raise its own livestock as the vision of self-reliance grew. Which was lesson to be learned particularly in the south that solely relied on the product of cotton as the primary source of income rooted in black labor? Dr. Washington's band of students and teachers showed the Black Belt what could be done if the liberties to expand could be exercised without preventive legislature set out on

Devour Us Not

disfranchisement. Dr. Washington's example also showed America what the Negro could do was but an ocean of possibilities given to him with equal opportunities denied for fear of the inevitable. For the most part initially, there were no white men or women involved in the management of the school.

But there were two white men on the Board of Trustee as by law required but only as advisories. The fulfillment of a dream; for Negroes to control the running, management of a school for higher learning when most of the students, parents could neither read nor write was immeasurable to Tuskegee. All of the teachers even though at first glance one would suggest white, were indeed all Negroes with graduating certificates from the likes of Universities such as Fisk and Harvard. Even though this was purely coincidental, Dr. Washington being of fair skinned as a white man himself, opened the haters debate of what has resonated in the Negro communities for centuries of the *"light & dark-skin"* and *"good-hair, nappy-hair,"* divisions.

"Some of the First Teachers of Tuskegee," *Wm V. Chambliss-The Colored American, July 20, 1901, Chas Greene, The Colored American., January 19, 1901-Mr. H.E. Thomas, Superintendent of Engineering Dept-1901, The Colored American., March 24, 1900-Mrs. B.K. Bruce-Lady Principal-1900, The Colored American., June 29, 1901-James D. McCall-Director Academics Dept.1901, The Colored American., April 6, 1901-Architectual and Mechanical Drawing-W.S. Pittman, The Colored American., April 6, 1901-Architectual and Mechanical Drawing-W.A. Rayfield, The Colored American., April 6, 1901-Architectual and Mechanical Drawing-Robert R. Taylor, The Appeal., August 25, 1906-Landscape and Gardening-Elmo Turner, The Colored American., June 20, 1903-Head of Academics-Roscoe Conkling Bruce, The Appeal., March 12, 1892-Nursing Dept-Dr. H. T. Dillon, The Colored American., December 28, 1901-Lady Principal of Girls Dept.- Mrs. Margaret Murray Washington, The Broad Ax., May 31, 1913-Lilla Washington, Niece of Booker T. Washington, The Appeal, March 9, 1912-Mr. Emmett J. Scott-Secretary to Booker T. Washington, Rev. E.J. Penney-The Appeal., March 12, 1892.Mr. Robert W. Taylor-The Colored American, October 10, 1903. Prof. William H. Councill-The Colored American, July 18, 1903. George Washington Carver-The Colored American,*

Booker Taliaferro Washington was one of the most influential African-Americans in history as to his accomplishments for his race. It is also said he was the last generation of Negroes born in slavery that had an immeasurably effect on attitudes of both races as

to what could be accomplished if only the availability of opportunities. Dr. Washington was married three times and had three children. After attending Wayland Seminary School in 1876, he returned to Malden, West Virginia. While attending the African Zion Baptist Church as a Sunday School teacher, he met and married his first wife, Fannie N. Smith in 1881. They had one child, a daughter named Portia M. Washington. Shortly after a brief teaching assignment at Hampton, he went to Tuskegee, Alabama to spread his vision of success. In May 1884, Fannie died. He then married one of the teachers at Tuskegee named Olivia A. Davidson in 1885. They had two sons named Booker T. Washington, Jr. and Ernest Davidson Washington before she died in 1889. The year of 1893 he married Margaret James Murray and they stayed married until his death November 14, 1915. Dr. Washington received so many awards and prestige during his life time it's too numerous to list. He was also invited to the White House several times. But among some of honors was an Honorary Masters of Art degree from Harvard University in 1836 and an Honorary Doctor of Law degree by Dartmouth College in 1901. July 4, 1881, Tuskegee begins and established so many traditions. One of the most colorful and Pageantry ones was, at the start of each class day, there would be a parade of all students attending class in a student body unit. There would be a band and all its glitter to celebrate the proudest of being a student of Tuskegee and being a part of an historical event each starting day. There was also another tradition of every graduating class to march in line throughout the campus on Graduation Day singing *"Auld Lang Syne,"* not ever knowing whether or not their returns would be. Washington became the first Negro to be pictured on a U.S. stamp (10 cent) and from 1951-1954, his image appeared on the back of a half-dollar coin.

This is the story of fifty-one year old **Anthony Crawford**, a Negro, pictured on the right. The incident occurred in Abbeville, South Carolina, October 21, 1916 when Crawford got into an argument with a shopkeeper named W.D. Barksdale about the price of cotton seed. It was reported by the, *"The Appeal," of January 6, 1917,* that Barksdale called Crawford a liar and in reply, Crawford commenced to cursing him out. Due to the loud comotion and old laws prohibiting such activities from a Negro, prompted a clerk from within the store to come out bearing an ax handle, to put Mr. Crawford in his place with a good beating. After striking Crawford, Sheriff Burts walking his beat observed the ruckus and preventing the beating while arresting Crawford, hauling him off to jail, much to his humiliation of all the white onlookers. Crawford was released on $15 bail as he attempted to return to his home. Only after a number of agitators fueling the anger of combustible rhetoric eager for a showdown with Crawford continued. Anthony Crawford was a proud and well respected farmer of the community. He was married with sixteen sons and daughters and a net worth of about $20,000. So proud was he that he remarked to a friend previously, *"The day a white man hit me is the day I die."* A frenzy of Barksdale's friends headed towards the whereabouts of Crawford after he was seen fleeing the jail after he had posted bond. The severity of punishment for humiliating a white man in front of his own place of business with his mouth was grounds for a lynching according to Barksdale. Crawford sensed trouble wondered into a boiler room of a nearby cotton mill. He had gathered a four-pound sledge hammer in defense of his honor. By

Devour Us Not

the time the crowd reached him there was no dialogue, as Crawford struck the nearest agitators. McKinney Cann was struck in the head fracturing his skull. Someone from the crowd hurled a rock, knocking out Crawford as the crowd then consume is body with kicks and a knife stabbings in the back. Apparently the Sheriff was nearby as he then arrested the semi-unconscious Crawford and made a promise that he would not transfer him out of town until the conditions of Cann were known, *"wink-wink, Mum-hum."* About four in the afternoon while

"Anadarko Daily," of May 17, 1902

Crawford had gain his consciousness sitting in the county jail cell, the mob still angered over what they believed was a Negro gone amuck, was set out on settling up the score. As they then approached the jail in a frenzy pushing the sheriff and jailor to the side, with little resistance from either, acquired their guns and keys, open the cell where Crawford was housed, took him out and first dragged him into the streets. The condition of Cann was known and he would recover from his blow from Crawford. The dragging of Crawford's, by this time, partially mutilated body through the Negro part of town with a rope around his neck, and infuriated the Negro community. The mob then hung his body to a pine tree near the entrance to the fair grounds and fired about two to three hundred rounds of ammunition into his body.

Federal 1910 Census of Abbeville County, South Carolina

The following Monday, the mob flexing its muscles called a meeting at the Abbeville County Courthouse. A decision was made to issue an ultimatum to the remaining Crawford family to leave the state of South Carolina by November 15. This meant abandoning their $20,000 property for the thugs of the city to confiscated and divide among the criminals who had committed the crime. After unanimously passing this resolution they proceeded to the Negro part of town to close all Negro businesses. After careful reconsideration of what would effect the profitability of farm life without Negro labor, and the laziness of White farmers to performed such tedious labor task, and not to mention the ever increasing boll weaver problem, caused another meeting on November 6th and the following resolution was unanimously pass: *"We the citizen of Abbeville in mass meeting assembled, do hereby express in unqualified terms our disapproval of the recent violent acts of certain persons committed in our community, and the spirit of lawlessness that seems rite in the county resulting in continued acts of lawlessness it is,*

RESOLVE: *That the Sheriff of Abbeville County, the Mayor of Abbeville County, the Police Force, and every officer of the county and city be urged to use every effort to enforce the law and to protect the citizens of the town and county regardless of condition or color.*

RESOLVED FURTHER: *That we do hereby pledge ourselves as individuals to give to the officers of the law our physical support in maintain the law.*

RESOLVED FURTHER: *That if it is necessary to carry out this determination that the aid of the State and Federal Government be called in order that every citizen may enjoy his rights under the constitution.*

TOM HALL

"The Bismarck Tribune," of Jan 10, 1917

RESOLVED FURTHER: *That a committee with Captain J.L. Perrin as Chairman, be appointed for the purpose of ascertaining what can be done towards the organization of a local military company for the protection of the citizens of this county and for maintaining order in our midst. That this committee be empowered to act in the premises.*

RESOLVED FURTHER: *That EVERY CITIZEN OF THE TOWN OF ABBEVILLE BE ASSURED the protection of the men of this meeting as long as he obeys the laws of-the state, and pursues only his own legitimate business.*

RESOLVED FURTHER: *That a meeting of the law-abiding citizens of Abbeville County be called to meet in this Court House on next Monday at noon to perfect an organization for enforcing law and order this county, and that every community in the county be represented at this meeting, and that steps be taken to show to the people of the state and United States that the men of Abbeville county will defend the law, and protect the citizens of the commonwealth in the enjoyment of all rights guaranteed by the law."*

On the next meeting held by the citizens of Abbeville County endorsed the resolution and established a twelve man committee to be observance and watchful of all lawlessness activities against any citizens. Furthermore erasing the threats made towards the Crawford family whom had already suffered a major blow to their three generations of hard-work and wealth accumulation end so senselessly. Also Governor Manning wrote a letter to Mr. Oswald Garrison Villard, Vice-President of the N.A.A.C.P. the following: *"I realize the gravity of this offense and am determined to do everything in my power to bring the offenders to justice. I have called on the Sheriff of Abbeville County to take the necessary steps to prevent any unlawful action with regard to the expulsion of the family of Crawford. I am giving serious consideration to this matter with a view to making recommendations to the Legislature, so as to be able to deal with such conditions when they arise."*

Roy Nash, secretary for the N.A.A.C.P. conducted an investigation into the lynching of Anthony Crawford. Additionally Governor Richard Irvine Manning, III, who quickly denounced the murder also called for an investigation to be conducted by solicitor Robert Archer Cooper and Sheriff R.M. Burt. Like in most cases of this sort, the south remain solid and no one would testify against the guilty, not even one known victim who was struck by Crawford. Mc Kinney Cann who was struck first must to have been in the lead since he was the first and only victim of the sledge hammer attack. He had a number of brothers and they had a reputation of hell raising and using intimidation tactics. The boldness of the mobsters were defiant as an article collectively written for and by the whites directly involved placed in a local newspaper article suggesting that all Negroes were to submit to the whites are face a justifiable death then proclaimed themselves, *"Not guilty."*

There were also political battles within the white race about Sheriff Burt's appointment and the whites resenting his inherited wealth from his grand-father Armistead Burt and influence of appointment fraud at the highest level of State government. There was a local favorite with law enforcement experience that should have carried all the votes in the county but lost to Burt much to the suspicion of all the locals. And the Negroes didn't trust any law officer or whites in the region for that matter because of continued efforts to rob them of their liberties and any part of profitability's they would have worked hard to earn. So any given opportunity to embarrass the attempt of Burt to force his non-lawful might, would receive no local support. So Burt was like an enemy in his own backyard. Many Negroes after witnessing Crawford's murder for standing up for his rights to fair pay for his labor, left Abbeville County, South Carolina creating an economical down slide of wealth for lack of cheap labor taken for granted. No one ever paid for the murder of Anthony Crawford even though almost everyone in the whole town knew and were privy to all what happened in that town that day.

Devour Us Not

Harriet Tubman is one of the most incredibly courageous women of our culture. Born around 1820 in Dorchester County, Maryland as a slave and at an early age was made a field-hand. She was also a Union Army spy at the request of Governor Andrews of Massachusetts and nurse during the Civil War. She performed these duties while under fire from the enemy many times. This position had she been white and male would have granted her a military pension. But initially she was denied her pension but persistent won her small pension. She managed to escape from the oppression of slavery around 1849. In a bio of her life, it was said of her that she intervene by knocking down the plantation overseer who was about to thrash a slave. When the overseer gathered himself off the ground, he struck her so hard with an iron weight until it crushed her skull. For years she would suffer from somnolence, (*a state of near-sleep or a strong desire for sleep*). The issue of slavery and all its cruelty consumed her every thoughts from the crack of the overseer's whip, to the sounds of dragging chains of clatter that bound a human-being to them. Auction blocks and combinations of numbers being barked out like the commands from a Marine Drill Instructor screaming at a newly arrived recruit. Results that wound try and make properties of human-beings. As to break any family ties, that would otherwise erase the spirits of all whom were sold. Tallying, sun risings and sun sets, not allowing for pity for tomorrow had no hope yet they still persevere. Harriet would free over 3,000 Slaves at a risk that placed a $40,000 bounty on her head an assured hanging to start the, *"underground railroad."* Given the name of General Tubman during the Civil War because of her maneuverability through swamps and jungles without detection, showcased her diligence towards her mission. Secretary of State Seward had given land to Harriet or was it from the proceeds of a book written by Sarah H. Bradford that allowed her to purchase the land and establish the Harriet Tubman Home for indigent aged Negroes in Auburn, New York. A building that was first known as the Zion A.M.E. Church. Suffering from pneumonia, Monday night on March 10, 1913 at the age it was believed to be 95, Harriet Tubman dies in the *"Harriet Tubman Home."* Of the many escape tales as explained in the, *"New York Sun of June 7, 1896,"* of Harriet's life on the run was an incident in which she was nearly captured by one of her old masters. As apart of her abilities to maneuver, all of slaves seeking refuge had nothing. She being the caring and very hospitable would manage to acquire food. This particular day she visited a village to secured some live fowl and rope to tie around their legs to secure their escape and attacks on her. When she saw her old master bearing down on her location on horseback with a sense of evil in his eyes, her instinctive notion of quick action she released those chickens. This caused the chickens to fly right in the path of the horse, causing her narrow escape. Harriet often mentioned in her travels was her ability to go undetected. She would often hear people reading aloud, though she couldn't read herself about billboard postings announcing her capture dead or alive, as they unknowingly walked amongst them. Harriet spoke well of a Quaker named Thomas Garrett. Garrett had a safe house that was used by Harriet and her band of run-away-slaves. One night while crossing the river over a bridge at Wilmington, Delaware, with a team of Army Officers waiting for her and her slaves, Garrett sensing trouble had

sent across earlier in the day two wagons filled with bricklayers whom he knew and trusted for a make-believed job on the other side. All in clear vision of the Officers that had staged themselves in an attempt to capture Harriet. By nightfall their loud jubilant songs and laughter from intoxication drew no attention to the Officers as at the bottom of the wagon was Harriet and her band of slaves. Included in that band was a very well-known slave named *"Joe,"* whose master so desperately wanted him back, offered up $2,000 for his capture and return. Thomas Garrett was eventually found-out and fined so heavily that it left the 60 year old Quaker penniless. In that trial at sentencing the United States Judge commented to Garrett, *" Let this be a lesson to you that you'd best not ever interfere with the cause of justice by the helping of runaway Negroes."* Garrett replied, *"Judge, thee hasn't left me a dollar; but I wish to say to thee that if anyone knows of a fugitive who wants shelter and a friend, send him to Thomas Garrett."* The Fugitive Slave Law of 1850 was a major blow to Harriet, her trusted Quakers friends and all others who aided her in her efforts. After that Harriet said, *"I'll never trust Uncle Sam with my people again, I'll just tak'em straight to Canada."* Harriet's last expedition to the south was in 1860. On her way to Boston to attend another anti-slavery meeting at the request of Gerrit Smith, she'd fight the greatest single battle of her life. While in route to Boston she made a planned stop to visit a cousin in Troy. While there, a lot of excitement was being discussed about a captured slave named Charles Nalle. His master, also his younger brother was in town making arrangements to take him back to Virginia. Harriet, without a clear plan, just a loud boisterous voice of command like brio that had a following of equally motivated citizen ready for a challenge with her.

She rushed to the Office of the United States Commissioner. Shouldering her erect muscular figure and manly leadership strength; though short in statue, the volume of her voice more than compensated for the height initially halted the deportation. Minutes before, with an awaiting wagon, the large crowd, now numbering hundreds dared the Officers to bring down the fugitive. The more time went by the larger and louder the crowds got and the more the Officer hesitate. Once again, without skipping a beat, Harriet knew she had to do something even more courageous to cause a chaos in the streets. So she went and asks some little boys who were just standing around to shout, *"Fire,"* as loud and emotionally as they could possibly. And they did just that, causing fire alarms to go off, people running around like chickens being chased by a fox in a hen-yard. As the streets were being prepared to be blocked gave an opportunistic Harriet to put on one of her many disguises as a very old woman at the foot of the stairs near to where a path had been cleared to the wagon. Again and again the Officer's would clear a path only to have it close right back with new onlookers. While the ignorance of Harriet's old lady routine caused for respect of her supposed age left her in tact, assuring she pose no risk of interference. By then the crowd becoming anxious with no new excitement with some still looking for the fire cause some to assume some type of slave auction. As bids began to ring out from the crowd, his master thinking it would probably be less of a hassle to just except money and be on his way, start excepting the bids. One bidder shouted, *"$1,200 for him,"* almost immediately another shouted, *"$1,500."* By this time a gentleman from across the street raised his window high enough to stick his head out and yelled, *"$200 for his rescue and not a penny for his master."* That comment excited the crowd with laughter as the whole ordeal was making a spectacle of a very serious situation from which has brought death to some. Noticing the growing out-of-control situation mounting, prompted the officer to try and force Nelle in the wagon with the zealous crowd in close proximity. With the master and several Officers in and near the wagon as a Marshall and another Officer on either outer shoulder of Nalle began their daring walk to the wagon, Harriet sensed the opportunity. As soon as

73   *Devour Us Not*

The Paducah Sun," of Sep 10, 1903

she made visual contact, she yelled out, *"Here he comes, Take him."* She then threw herself upon the Officer nearest her with her strength pulled him down. This action created mayhem as everyone began to join in and freeing the fugitive. Harriet managed to free him momentarily from the other Officers grasp as she attempted to get away while dragging him down the street. She yelled to her friends who were near by, *"Drag us out!" "then drag him to the river," "drown him, but don't let them have him."* By this time an Officer noticing the upper hand this loud mouth woman was proposing, struck her over the head with his club as this released part of her gripe on Nalle forcing him back into the grabbing and pulling of the crowd. Harriet made a recovery as she leap again; knocking over people secured him around the neck, then threw him over her shoulder like a bail of cotton she had performed so many times before. Then she was dragged down by the crowd but still managing to keep her grip on him. The crowd, Officers, the master, Nalle and Harriet all moving and repositioning themselves now far from the steps and the wagon as she managed with help from a majority crowd sympathizers, pushed him into an awaiting boat on the river bank. She then escaped to a ferryboat on the other side of the river for a short ride to a nearby safe house. With the Police in hot pursuit, they reached the safe house before Harriet. As she approach the stairway where Nalle was in hiding in a room, she observed two people already shot by Officers lying in the stairway. Harriet, along with some of her friends marched up the stairway where some officers were in the processing of apprehending Nalle again. When she kicked in the door to the room where Nalle was being held, knocked over one Officer who first attacked her, followed by throwing another Officer out the 2 story-window. After gaining her composure, she then threw Nalle over her shoulder like before, headed down the stairway and out the door. With the Officers still trying to recall what had happen to them by a woman half their size and weight, but unknowingly that she was from the Ashantee Linage of African tribes known for their warrior mentality. After clearing the house and headed for the road she saw a man approach them with what looked to be a very strong and fast horse with a carriage. He asked Harriet what the commotion was all about, when she pleaded with the man that the man she was carrying was a fugitive slave and was about to be forced down south back into slavery. Had this been a southern man, the results would have been the total opposite. He immediately jumped out of his carriage and said with gladness, *"This is a blood horse, drive him till he drops."* With the gratefulness of a person who has just been given a million dollars, she thanked the kind gentleman as she then lifted Nalle into the carriage making a clean getaway. He was then driven to Schenectady County, New York, another safe house drop off point and later made his way to Canada. With his freedom being owed to the heroics of Harriet Tubman, he vanished in the mixed of free Canadians and was never heard of again. As so many of the hundreds of slaves Harriet help secure their lives and their freedoms, acknowledgement of her role was not her reward. She sorts out her gratification in pulling one over the alleged smartest ones with her God given maneuverability's. Harriet soon thereafter made her way back to Auburn where she made her home and was her last great adventure before the Civil War. The faster than light horse assumed to have made his way back to his home as his instinct would have suggested. But Harriet never made it to that all important meeting in Boston; for her services were much too needed in Troy, making one more triumphed effort for Liberty.

The Moses of her people was but one of many titles given to her. John Brown, a white man and abolitionist known for his unsuccessful raid at Harper's Ferry, and was later hanged in 1859 for his views, once said of her, *"one of the bravest and best persons on the continent."* Wendell Phillips, a white man, Harvard grad and abolitionist also stated, *"she has done more for the loyal cause than many Captains and Colonels."*

Devour Us Not   74

Mrs. Annie Sherwood Hawks was born May 28, 1836 in Hoosick, New York. She is most famous for her 400 Hymns and many poems which started at an early age. Most notably of her Hymns is *"I Need Thee Every Hour,"* and *"My Soul Is Anchored."* She died on January 3, 1918 in Bennington, Vermont where she was living with her daughter, after surviving her only husband's death, who passed in 1888.

Rebecca B. Spring, born in 1811 and died 1911, (*At age 98 pictured on the left and right with one of her butt naked grandchildren hanging on*) reported by, *"The Tacoma Times,"* of June 24, 1909, newspaper article explained in an interview when she was 96 years old, about her affiliation with fellow abolitionist John Brown. Mrs. Spring and her husband, Marcus were both abolitionist as she visited John Brown while

he was in prison at Charlestown, Virginia. In her procession was a letter he had written to his wife that she hand delivered to her in Philadelphia. She spoke fondly of John Brown and as she recalls his last days before his hanging, words as acknowledged that he had made some great errors, I'm assuming alluding to the Harper's Ferry disaster and was deserving of being hung. Mrs. Spring was also requested to nurse the wounded of John Brown's band after the Harper's Ferry disaster. Aaron D. Stevens and Albert E. Hazlett, both white men of Brown's band were captured at first, but then escaped to wonder in the woods before turning themselves in and were the last two to be hanged. In their cells they requested Mrs. Spring bury them on free soil. Mrs. Spring, being true to her word, after their deaths buried them on their estate in Eagleswood, New Jersey where their bodies are surrounded by a picket fence with no visible headstones. Her famous words back to John Brown during her visit at Charlestown prison were, *"Well it is better to die of a big idea than of a fever."* And for that response he appeared pleased. As this significant figure in the abolishment movement, remains virtually unknown, hero's non-the-less behind the abolishment of slavery. The list of who's who in American and the world of abolitionist included frequent quest like the following; John Brown, Margaret Fuller, John G. Whittier, William Channing, Fredrika Bremer, Lydia Maria Child, Ralph Waldo Emerson, The Carolyle's of London, England, Gerrit Smith, Wendell Phillips, Horace Greeley, Elizabeth Palmer Peabody, Hans Christian Anderson, Admiral Wolfe and his daughter. Marcus Spring, being a very wealthy man and vehemently opposed to slavery, during the 1860's as reported by, *"The Wichita Daily Eagle,"* of June 20, 1891, made his mark

toward ending slavery. Rebecca, daughter of a Quaker added a good match of equal beliefs by both. Marcus and Rebecca founded the estate and city of Eagleswood located to the west of Perth Amboy, New Jersey. Known as cultured socialites and was the Headquarters for the Abolitionist movement of that day. Both Marcus and Rebecca founded the Eagleswood Military Academy that was very privileged and private. As a result of the Civil War caused many students and teachers to abandon the school for the war causing its inevitable closure.

In 1847 Frederick Douglass met **John Brown** (*Pictured on the left*) for the first time in

Devour Us Not

his life of that meeting Douglass stated that, *"Though a white gentleman is in sympathy of a black man, and as deeply interested in our cause, as though his own soul had been pierced with the iron of slavery."* John Brown, a white man, gave his life for the cause of Negroes. Brown was a Christian man, joining Hudson Church in 1816 and the place he grew-up when his father and mother moved there. One afternoon in prayer meeting, John accepted his calling. It was at this meeting that Brown first outlined his plan to lead a war to free the slaves. Praying about the murder of Rev. Elijah Lovejoy in 1837, John stood to pray after his father had prayed that John made the chilling statement, *"I pledge myself that I will devote my life to increasing hostility towards slavery."* John Brown's first wife, Dianthe Lusk died in 1832 from an epidemic of fever leaving him with five children to raise. They had a total of seven children, five surviving and they were: **John Brown, Jr.**(1821), **Frederick** (1827-1831), **Owen** (1824), **Jason** (*January 19, 1823*) and **Ruth** (1829). John Brown in about 1857 established a school of military instructions after an unsuccessful hard fought campaign of fighting the pro-slavery movement in 1836. The school became known as the Lecompton Constitution that initially included ten of his well known men from Lawrence and Topeka plus his son Owen. *Captain Brown* or *"Oasawatomie Brown," or Isaac Smith,* as he was sometimes called, retired momentarily to get more organized. In 1833, a year after the death of his first wife, John then marries a sixteen year old girl named **Mary Day** who took care of John Brown's five children by Dianthe Lusk and she had thirteen more children of her own.

The infamous Harper's Ferry, West Virginia raid led by John Brown as recanted by, *"The Record-Union,"* of *December 27, 1897,* by some accounts lead to the Civil War. Under one of his alias, Isaac Smith, rented a farmhouse on July 3, 1859 from a man named John Cook whom Brown had made acquaintances with earlier in the spring of 1859. John Cook was a school teacher on the height of Maryland, opposite of Harper's Ferry. The storing of rifles, pistols and pikes were placed in and around the school and his place would be used to store other weapons. With him were the following 21 men (14 whites & 7 black): **John Brown**, **Watson Brown** (*son of John Brown*), **Oliver Brown** (son of John Brown), (** indicates Negro participants*) **John Henry Kagi***, **Adolphus Thompson***, **Stewart Taylor***, **Sherrerd Lewis Leary**, **Dangerfield Newby***, **Jeremiah Anderson***, **William H. Leeman** (*Murdered while crossing the Potomac river*), **William Thompson** (*Murdered when taken prison*), **John Copeland***, **Shields Green***, **John E. Cook**, **Edwin Coppock**, **Aaron Dwight Stevens**, **Charles P. Tidd**, **Francis Jackson Merriam**, **Osborn P. Anderson**, **Albert Hazlett**, **Barclay Coppock**. In August, Brown met with Douglass to discuss the Harper's Ferry Plan with reservation and tried to discourage the use of Negroes. **Mary "Mammy" Ellen Pleasant**, (*pictured right*) died Monday, January 4, 1904, according to, *"The San Francisco Call,"* of *January 13, 1904,* describes Mammy's involvement with John Brown. When John Brown was captured he had a

letter in his possession, a letter signed, *"W.E.P."* and read, *"The ax is paid at the root of the tree. When the first blow is struck there will be money to help."* The author of the letter after years of searching was Mammy Pleasant who had purposely made her *"M"* appear like a *"W."* Mrs. Pleasant inherited a large sum of money from her first husband and in 1858 and moved to California. Hearing about the freeing of the slaves in the south, and the already infamous John Brown, she headed east with the $30,000 of United States Treasury drafts. Mrs. Pleasant had already procured drafts through the aid of Robert Swain, John W. Coleman and William Alvord. She arrived in Boston where she had the drafts exchanged for Canadian papers and then converted the papers into coins before her prearranged meeting with John Brown in Canada. Mrs. Pleasant a seasoned Abolitionist explained to Brown to delay any attempts to start the revolution until her contacts in the south are aroused and properly notified in a simultaneously rebellion. As what seem to be a mutual understanding as her travels to the south months later, learned the fate of John Brown. Mammy had written a letter pledging her support to Brown for the cause and blamed him for acting prematurely. But before she died she requested on her grave stone; her name, age, nativity and the words, *"She was a friend of John Brown."* The Harper's Ferry plan called for many more men than were available. Brown's 21 band of men ranging in age from 21-49 that were poorly trained for a complex military operation. The town of Harper's Ferry was surrounded by mountains on all sides and a bridge to cross the Potomac. Leaving some men back as guards, John led his band of 18 to the attack. The premise behind the raid was to acquire more weaponry to recruit more fugitive's slaves or free Negroes to join their band. Harper's Ferry Armory housed over 100,000 rifles, muskets and ammunition and considered a very large facility in size. October 16, 1859, Sunday night, Brown and his band of 18 men guided by Cook executed the element of surprise which caught a single watchman guarding the armory as the cutting of the telegraph wires prevented communications to other military complex sources. Just before entering Harper's Ferry, they had to cross the bridge. There they spotted a Negro named Haywood who begins to run unknowingly this raid was for his liberation. He was shot and killed before he could sound an alarm. During the trial it was admitted that Brown almost lost all his Negro following because of their superstition in seeing one of their own being first to be killed marked a doomed for the raid. Things were then going according to plan as the rounding up of cooperative hostages from a nearby farm were collected as well as local slaves on a plantation. They were told to join the fight for their liberty. One of the hostages was Colonel Washington whom had entertained Cook at his home on several occasions and was a descendant of President George Washington. He bitterly complained at the trail about the thief of a sword of President George Washington that was given to him by Lafayette.

Brown, having secured the armory, spent the night there and took in more hostages the following morning. The fighting went on and off all day Monday as later visions of Brown could be seen directing his men while holding one dying son in his arms and another son already dead at his feet. And with the other hand he would get off a round or two in total defiance. Also in their collection of hostages were city officials, which then began to spread like wild fire throughout the valley. Before the Marines could arrive, local citizen took matters into their own hands and began to attack Brown's band in a fire fight. Of the Negroes Brown had taken into custody none would raise arms to shoot against their masters. It is believed it was there on a Thursday workers began showing up for work that Brown would continue to take in more hostages. The rumors reach as far away as Washington where Colonel Robert E. Lee dispatched 1,500 Marines. Trouble really begins when the unplanned arrival of a passenger train approached the town. After repeated warnings from Brown's men to stop a firefight broke out. After the Negro baggage master was shot and all hell broke out with bullets flying every where the train did stop. In retrospect Brown admits stopping of the train wasn't consequential to the mission. By allowing it to be stopped and not continue its normal routine, caused the conductors to notify authorities. An unexplained theory that seem to puzzle Brown and his men. The firefight got so intense after the word spread until Brown and his men had to move to a nearby engine house where they barricaded themselves willing to fight to the death. The engine house would be later classified as Brown's fort. Soon there after the Marines had arrived as positions were established until sealing all the exits in and around the small valley town to include the

Devour Us Not

bridge across the Potomac River sealing off any and every escape route. Tuesday morning, October 18, 1859, Lieutenant J. Stuart, who had accompanied General Lee was to request of Brown his unconditional surrender. A signal of Brown's decision would be relayed to General Lee some distance away by the waving of a handkerchief. Brown, had some stipulations to the initial proposal and requested he and his men be given at least a half hour head start to cross the river and if he were then caught; all would be fair, but no deal otherwise. A second request was asked of Brown in which he flat-out refused. Stuart then gave the signal and the Marines took a large nearby latter rushed and crushed in the barricaded door killing two Marines in the process. Brown who was wounded and several of his men were seized then taken to

Charlestown jail. It was reported that about eight of his men had managed to escape. But in pursuit John Cook and Albert Hazlett were captured. William Thompson had been previously taken from the engine-house by citizens of Harper Ferry, taken to the river, his body riddled with several hundred rounds of ammunition and then thrown in the river. The

"The National Tribune," of Sep 28, 1893-**John Brown** at age 59 in 1859- "The Spanish Fork Press," of Mar 5, 1908
Jason Brown at age 85 and **Ruth Brown-Thompson** at age 71, last surviving children of John Brown, "The San Francisco Call," of Oct 5, 1900

town's people had allowed for one of Brown's men, a Negro's body to remain in the streets for several days until the hogs began to eat the decomposed, horribly smelling corpse that remained unburied. Of the men placed in jail with Brown were Shields Green and John Copland both Negroes and John Cook who was recaptured. Brown was charged with conspiracy to produce insurrection, murder and treason in Judge Parker's old courtroom in Charlestown. John Brown's Lawyer was Mr. Hoyt from Boston. The trial lasted only six or seven days with a return verdict of guilty. During the trial it was said that John Brown was as composed as if to say my work here on earth is done. December 2, 1859, John Brown was driven to the place of execution by a common farm wagon. As he and his men were hanged. He made very little commits first saying, *"The ball is now put in motion and will never stop until every Negro is set free,"* while in route to his final destination. "A beautiful morning," was his commits as he looked up into the clear sky. *"A fine display of soldiery,"* as he briefly gazes at the soldier nearest him. After exiting the wagon and the ire silence of the crowds presence to witness the hanging in some opinions a great man. He lifted a Negro child by the arms of his mothers grasp and kissed his forehead before handing him back to her. And with a blank calm he walked to his execution station as if previously rehearsed. Being ask by the executioner, if he had any last words, John Brown, Abolitionist, with his last breathe said yet again, *"The ball is now put in motion and will never stop until every Negro is set free,"* and asking to have the black cape placed over his head quickly. John Brown's body dangled for about forty minutes. Normally a source of loud jeering from the crowd acknowledging proper justice was the silence of nothingness that day. A slight blowing of wind as the crowd witnessing the ending life of a man who gave his life for a race of people not his own in man's law, but was his own in the eyes of God. And just as silence had sealed the lips of the crowd, the silence of shuffling feet leaving the site was as orderly as a Church exit after your sins had been forgiven. Among the attendee's was John Wilkes Booth. John Brown's lifeless body was taken down and carried to Elba, Essex County, New York, accompanied by his wife for burial. His wife, Mary Ann considered by this time to be a very large woman, stayed at a nearby hotel and did not attend the hanging. Having buried two sons from the raid, Mary Ann soon moved her family to Rohnerville, California and had a house built for her

"The Republic Sunday," of Sep 13, 1903

two remaining daughters, Sarah and Ellen and grandchildren. Also traveling with them and moved in next door was one of her adult son's and his family. **John Brown** and **Mary Day** had 13 children with only 6 lived to adulthood. These children were: **Annie** (1832-1926), **Watson** (1835-1859), **Salmon** (1836-1919), **Charles** (1837 - 1843), **Oliver** (1839-1859), **Peter** (1840 - 1843), **Austin** (1842-1843), **Amelia** (1845-1846), **Sarah** (1846 -1916), **Ellen** (1848-1849) and **Ellen II** (1854-1916). John's son Frederick from his first wife, died in the Osawatomie raid in 1856. He lost two more sons, Watson and Oliver in the Harper's Ferry raid.

Annie married a man named Adams, lived in Cape Mendocino, California and they had one child. John Brown, Jr. died and left his wife a widow with a son and daughter, while Ruth married Henry Thompson and lived in Pasadena, California. Jason and Salmon did not take part in the Harper's Ferry raid. *"The Washington Herald," of November 14, 1909* reports that Jason by John's first wife was one of the last surviving children of the infamous John Brown and he only had one child named Charles P. Brown. Jason explained in an interview, that he was called by his father and asked him to join his band at Harper's Ferry, but he refused stating, *"Father, I cannot go. I have seen too much. I have a horror of war."* Had he not made that decision, Jason Brown would have died in Harper's Ferry raid on Dec. 2, 1859; instead Jason Brown dies, December 25, 1912 at the age of 90.

"Black Churches and Preachers are the cornerstone of the Black community and our heritage."

"The Colored American," of Jan 20, 1900-**Rev. Robert Johnson**-Metropolitan Baptist Church Washington DC, "The Colored American," of Jan 20, 1900-**Bishop Henry M. Turner**-6th Episcopal District, Atlanta, GA., "The Colored American," of Feb 10, 1900-**Rev. M.M. Moore**-African Methodist Episcopal, Washington DC "The Colored American," of Apr 6, 1901-**Rev. John Jasper**-Fluvanna County, Virginia once baptized 300 members in 2 hours, "The Colored American," of Apr 25, 1903-Financial Secretary, African Methodist Episcopal, Washington DC ,"The Colored American," of Jun 2, 1900-**Rev. L.J. Coppin**-Elected Bishop of A.M.E.

"The Salt Lake Herald," of Jul 21, 1895

Nathaniel "Nat" Turner was a slave in Virginia, according to, *"The Minneapolis Journal," of January 4, 1902.* In explaining Nat's beginning as being able to read, he was taught by his master's children. His ability to read caused him to be involved in an abolished organ that inflamed his mentality about slavery. Having the ability to read also furthered his reasoning and foresight abilities that sealed his fate. Almost immediately, with the liberal manner in which Nat was regarded caused him to organize all the Negroes in the nearby farms that eventually spread beyond local boundary lines. Nat had arranged for a barbeque meal in the woods and far from any acknowledgement of white interferers or over-seers. They came with every weapon imaginable, guns, axes, pitchforks, knifes, swords and machetes. Nat was considered a religious fanatic, even though he was a slave, he was thought to be a very intelligent young man. There were reports that he was a self-proclaimed messenger of God and God had commanded him to kill his oppressors, sparing no one. Nat's mere presence caused the other Negro slaves to fear and regard him as having the persona equal to that of whites. A trait necessary for his destiny that was to follow. Besides, it was a breech of southern law to teach a Negro anything that would allow him to gain any superior advantage over his oppressor. So the more he discussed his plans and the necessity of his version of ending slavery, the more the majority slaves feared him. This made the execution of his plan of a

Devour Us Not

murderous rage in his mind easier. Nat made the below confession to Mr. T. R. Gray of Jerusalem, Southampton County, Virginia according to *"The Salt Lake Herald," of July 21, 1895:*

"Since the commencement of 1830, I had been living with Mr. Joseph Travis who was to me a kind master and placed the greatest confidence in me; in fact, I had no cause to complain of his treatment of me. On Saturday evening, the 28th of August it was agreed between Henry, Hark and me to prepare a dinner the next day for the men we expected and then to concert a plan as we had not yet determined on any. Hark on the following morning, brought a pig and Henry brandy and being joined by Sam, Nelson, Will and Jack they prepared in the woods a dinner where about 3 o'clock, I joined them."

"I saluted them on coming up and asked Will how he came there; he answered his life was worth no more than others and his liberty as dear to him. I asked him if he thought to obtain it. He said he would or loses his life. This was enough to put him in full confidence. Jack, I knew was only a tool in the hands of Hark. It was quickly agreed that we should commence at home (Mr. J. Travis) on that night, and until we had armed and equipped ourselves and gathered sufficient force neither age nor sex was to be spared. We remained at the feast until about two hours in the night, when we went to the house and found Austin; they all went to the cider press and drank, except myself."

"On returning to the house, Hark went to the door with an ax for the purpose of breaking it open. As we knew we wore strong enough to murder the family if they were awakened by the noise; but, reflecting that it might create an alarm in the neighborhood we determined to enter the house secretly and murder them whilst sleeping. Hark got a ladder and set it against the chimney, on which I ascended and hoisting a window, entered and came downstairs unbarred the door and removed the guns from their places. It was then observed that I must then spill the first blood. On which, armed with a hatchet and accompanied by Will. I entered my master's chamber. It being dark, I could not give a death blow; the hatchet glanced from his head. He sprang from his bed and called his wife. It was his last word. Will laid him dead with a blow of his axe and Mrs. Travis shared the same fate as she lay in bed. The murder of this family, five numbers, was the work of a moment; not one of them awoke. There was a little infant that was sleeping in a cradle that was forgotten until we had left the house and gone some distance, when Henry and Will returned and killed it. We got here four guns that would shoot and several old muskets, with a round or two of powder."

"We remained some time at the barn, where we paraded: I formed them in a line as soldiers and after carrying them through all the maneuvers I was muster of, marched them to Mr. Salathul Francis, about 600 yards distance. Sam and Will went to the door and knocked. Mr. Francis asked who was there. Sam replied it was him and he had a letter for him. On which he got up and came to the door. They immediately seized him and dragged him out a little from the door; he was dispatched by repeated blows on the head. There was no other White person in the family."

"We started from there to Mrs. Reese's maintaining the most perfect silence on the march where finding the door unlocked, we entered and murdered Mrs. Reese in her bed while sleeping. Her son awoke, but it was only to sleep the sleep of death; he had only time to say, "Who is that," and he was no more. From Mrs. Reese we went to Mrs. Turner's a mile distance which we reached about sunrise on Monday morning. Henry, Austin and Sam

went to the still where finding Mr. Peebles, Austin shot him and the rest of us went to the house; as we approached the family they discovered us & shut the door. Vain hope! Will, with one stroke of his axe opened it and we entered and found Mrs. Turner and Mrs. Newsome in the middle of the room, almost frightened to death. Will immediately killed Mrs. Turner with one blow of his axe. I took Mrs. Newsome by the head and with the sword I had when I was apprehended, I struck her several blows over the head, but not being able to kill her, as the sword was dull. Will turn round and discovering it, and dispatched her. A general destruction of property and search for money and ammunition always succeeded the murders. By this time my company amounted to fifteen, and nine men mounted, who started for Mrs. Whitehead's (the other six were to go through a byway to Mrs. Bryant's and rejoin us at Mrs. Whitehead's). As we approached the house we discovered Mr. Whitehead standing in the cotton patch, near the lane fence; we called him over into the lane and Will the executioner, was near at hand with his fatal axe, to send him to an untimely grave. As we pushed on to the house I discovered some one running around the garden, and thinking it was some of the Whitehead family, I pursued them but finding it was a servant girl belonging to the house. I returned to commence the work of death, but they whom I left had not been idle. All the family was already murdered but Mrs. Whitehead and her daughter Margaret. As I came round to the door I saw Will pulling Mrs. Whitehead out of the house, and at the step he nearly severed her head from her body with his broad axe."

"Miss Margaret, when I discovered her had concealed herself in a corner formed by the projection of the cellar stoop from the house; on my approach she fled, but was soon overtaken, and after repeated blows with a sword. I killed her by a blow on the head with a fence rail. By this time, the six who had gone to Mr. Bryant's rejoined us, and informed me that they had done the work assigned them. We again divided, part going to Mr. Richard Porter's and from thence to Nathaniel Francis', the other to Mr. Nowell Harris and Mr. T. Doyle's."

"On my reaching Mr. Porter's, he had escaped with his family. I understood there that the alarm had already spread and I immediately returned to bring up those sent to Mr. Doyle's and Mr. Howell Harris's, the party I left going on to Mr. Francis having told them I would rejoin them in that neighborhood. I met those sent to Mr. Doyle's and Mr. Harris returning, having met Mr. Doyle on the road and killed him; and learning from some who joined them that Mr. Harris was taken home. I immediately pursued the course taken by the party gone on before; but knowing they would complete the work of death and pillage at Mr. Francis' before I could get there. I went to Mr. Peter Edwards expecting to find them there, but they had been there and left."

"I then went to Mr. John T. Barrow's, they had been there and murdered him. I pursued on their track to Captain Newitt Harris, where I found the greater part mounted and ready to start. The men now amounting to about forty, shouted and hurrahed as I rode up; some were in the yard loading their guns, others drinking. They said Captain Harris and his family had escaped, the property in the house they had destroyed, robbing him of money and other valuables. I ordered them to mount and march instantly, this was about 9 or 10 o'clock Monday morning. I proceeded to Mr. Levi Waller's two or three miles distant. I took my station in the rear, and as it was my object to carry terror and devastation wherever we went, I placed fifteen or twenty of the best armed and most to be relied on in front, who generally approached the houses as fast as their horses could run; this was for two purpose to prevent their escape and strike terror to the inhabitants- on this account. I never got to the houses after leaving Mrs. Whitehead's until the murders were committed except in one case."

Devour Us Not

PICKANINNY IN A SATCHEL.

"I sometimes got insight to see the work of death completed viewing the mangled bodies as they lay in silent satisfaction and immediately started in quest of other victims. Having murdered Mrs. Maller and ten children, we started for Mr. William Williams having killed him and two little boys that were there. While engaged in this, Mrs. Williams fled and got some distance from the house, but she was pursued, overtaken, and compelled to get up behind one of the company who brought her back and after showing her the mangled body of her lifeless husband. She was told to get down and lay by his side, where she was shot dead. I then started for Mr. Jacob Williams where the family was murdered. Here we found a young man named Drury who had come on business with Mr. Williams. He was pursued overtaken and shot. Mrs. Vaughn's was the next place we visited, and after murdering the family there I determined on starting for Jerusalem. Our number amounted and armed with guns, axes swords and clubs."

"The Evening World," of New York, NY, June 10, 1901

"On reaching Mr. James W. Parker's gate, immediately on the road leading to Jerusalem and about three miles distant, it was proposed to me to call there but I objected, as I knew he was gone to Jerusalem and m object was to reach there as soon as possible, but none of the men having relation at Mr. Parker's it was agreed that they might call and get his people. I remained at the gate on the road with seven or eight, the others going across the field to the house about half a mile off. After waiting some time for them I became impatient and started to the house for them and on our return we were met by a party of white men who had pursued our blood-stained track and who had fired on those at the gate and dispersed them. Immediately on discovering the whites, I ordered my men to halt and form as they appeared to be alarmed. The white men, eighteen in number approached us in about one hundred yards, when one of them fired (this was against the positive orders of Captain Alexander Peete who commanded and who had directed the men to reserve their fire until within thirty paces) and I discovered about half of them retreating. I then ordered my men to fire and rush on them. The few remaining stood their ground until we approached within fifty yards when they fired and retreated. We pursued and overtook some of them whom we thought we left dead (they were not killed). After pursuing them about two hundred yards and rising a little hill, I discovered they were met by another party and had halted and were reloading their guns. (This was a small party from Jerusalem who knew the Negroes were in the fields and had just tied their horses to await their return to the road, knowing that Mr. Parker and family were in Jerusalem but knew nothing of the party that had gone in with Captain Peete. On hearing the firing, they immediately rushed to the spot and arrived just in time to arrest the progress of these barbarous villains and save the lives of their friends and fellow citizens)."

"Thinking of those who had retreated first and the party who had fired on us at fifty or sixty yards distant had all only fallen back to meet others with ammunition as I saw them reloading their guns and more coming up than I saw at first and several of my bravest men being wounded the others became panic-stricken and squandered over the field. The white men pursued and fired on us several times. Hark had his horse shot under him and I caught another for him as it was running by me. Five or six of my men were wounded, but none left on the field. Finding myself defeated here I instantly determined to go through a private way and cross the Nottoway River at Cypress Bridge, three miles from Jerusalem and attack that place in the rear. As I expected they would look for me on the other road and I had a great desire to get there to procure arms and ammunition.

After going a short distance in this private way, accompanied by about twenty men, I overtook two or three who told me the others were dispersed in every direction. After trying in vain to collect a sufficient force to proceed to Jerusalem, I determined to

COLORED SCHOLARS EXCLUDED FROM SCHOOLS.
"If the *free* colored people were generally taught to read, it might be an inducement to them to remain in this country. WE WOULD OFFER THEM NO SUCH INDUCEMENT."—*Rev. Mr. Converse, a colonizationist, formerly of N. H. now editor of the Southern Religious Telegraph.*
In those parts of the country where the persecuting spirit of colonization has been colonized, such exclusion has ceased.

The Slave Almanac of 1839 where Negroes were refused education

return as I was sure they would make back to their old neighborhood where they would rejoin me, make new recruits an come down again. On my way back I called at Mrs. Thomas's, Mrs. Spencer's and several other places the white families having fled we found no more victims to gratify our thirst for blood. We stopped at Major Ridley's quarters for the night and being joined by four of his men with the recruits made since my started for Mr. William Williams having killed him and two little boys that were there. While engaged in this Mrs. Williams fled and got some distance from the house, but she was pursued, overtaken, and compelled to get up behind one of the company who brought her back and after showing her the mangled body of her lifeless husband. She was told to get down and lay by his side, where she was shot dead. I then started for Mr. Jacob Williams where the family was murdered. Here we found a young man named Drury who had come on business with Mr. Williams. He was pursued overtaken and shot. Mrs. Vaughn's was the next place we visited, and after murdering the family there I determined on starting for Jerusalem. Our number amounted and armed with guns, axes swords and clubs."

"The New York Correspondent," of Aug 23, 1831

The True Confessions of Nat Turner by Thomas Gray, 1831

Devour Us Not

"The San Francisco Call," of Mar 24, 1912   The Nat Turner Massacre   "El Paso Herald," of May 4, 1918

After going a short distance in this private way, accompanied by about twenty men, I overtook two or three who told me the others were dispersed in every direction." "After trying in vain to collect a sufficient force to proceed to Jerusalem, I determined to return as I was sure they would make back to their old neighborhood where they would rejoin me, makes new recruits and come down again. On my way back I called at Mrs. Thomas's, Mrs. Spencer's and several other places the white families having fled we found no more victims to gratify our thirst for blood. We stopped at Major Ridley's quarters for the night and being joined by four of his men with the recruits made since my defeat, we mustered now about forty strong. After placing our sentinels I laid down to sleep but was quickly roused by a great racket. Starting up I found some mounted and others in great confusion, one of the sentinels having given the alarm that we were about to be attacked. I ordered some to ride around and reconnoiter and on their return the other being more alarmed, not knowing who they were fled in different ways so that I was reduced to about twenty again. With this I determined to attempt to recruit and proceed on to rally in the neighborhood I had left. Dr. Blunt was the nearest house which we reached just before day. On riding up the yard, Hark fire a gun. We expected Dr. Blunt and his family were at Major Ridley's as I knew there was a company of men there, the gun was fired to ascertain if any of the family were at home; we were I immediately fired upon and retreated leaving several of my men. I do not know what became of them as I never saw them afterwards."

"Pursuing our course back and coming in sight of Captain Harris's where we had been the night before we discovered a party of white men at the house on which all deserted me but two (Jacob and Nat). We concealed ourselves in the wood till near night when I sent them in search of a Henry, Nelson, Sam and Hark and directed them to rally all they could at the place we had had our dinner the Sunday before. Where they would find me and I accordingly return there as soon as it was dark and remained until Wednesday evening when discovering White men riding around the place as if they were looking for some one and none of my men were joining me. I concluded Jacob and Nat had been taken and compelled to betray me. On this I gave up my hope for the present and on Thursday night after having supplied myself with provisions from Mr. Travis's, I scratched a hole under a pile of fence rails in the field where I concealed myself for six weeks never leaving my hiding place but for a few minutes in the dead of night to get water which was very near Thinking by this time I could venture out, I began to go about in the night and cavesdrop the houses in the neighborhood , pursuing this course for about a fortnight and gathering little or no intelligence afraid of speaking to any human being and returning every morning to my cave before the dawn of day. I know not how long I might have led this life if accident had not betrayed me. A dog in the neighborhood passing by my hiding place one night while I was out was attracted by some meat I had in my cave and crawled in and stole it and was coming out just as I returned.

Few nights after, two Negroes having started to go hunting with the same dog passed that way. The dog came again to the place and having just gone out to walk about discovered me and barked on which thinking myself discovered I spoke to them to beg concealment. On making myself known they fled from me." "Knowing then they would betray me I immediately left my hiding place and was pursued almost incessantly until I was taken a fortnight afterwards Mr. Benjamin Phillip in a little hole I had dug out with my sword for the purpose of concealment under the top of a fallen tree. On Mr. Phillips' discovering the place of my concealment, he cocked his gun and aimed at me. I requested him not to shoot and I would give up, upon which he demanded my sword. I delivered it to him and he brought me to prison. During the time I was pursued I had many hair breadth escapes which your time will not permit me to relate. I am here loaded with chains and willing to suffer the fate that awaits me." Subsequent to Nat Turner's surrender, several Negro sympathizers knew of his whereabouts but refused to give him up. The way he was allowed to survive was food and drinks were brought to him or made it available for him during his period of hiding. The aftermath deeply effected Virginia and the South. It was the largest lost of life before the Civil War. There were sixty whites, half children, hacked to death and about 100 Negroes who may or may not have been involved. There was a $5,000 reward for his capture that was given to Mr. Phillips when he brought Nat in and turned him over to the authorities at gun point. November 11, 1831, Nat Turner was publicly hanged by having him stand in a wagon and have the wagon drive off. Farmers near and far received the date of the public hanging as masters would bring all their slaves to see the execution. From that day, the District of Columbia and the state of Virginia imposed strict laws prohibiting Negroes from public assembly of two or more. The Black Church's, the backbone and source of hope and strength in the black communities were prohibited. One of the laws even permitted the shooting on the spot of the gathering of Negroes of three or more if their explanation is even remotely questionable. This meant open season for all who were Negro slaves based on the vague nature in which the law was purposely written. And the innocent slaves and free blacks left after the massacre paid by enormous suffrages of more strenuous workloads, food rationings and other privileges of denial. All backed and enforced by unjust laws.

I recalled in 1971 while stationed at Camp Lejeune, North Carolina, where a racially incident occurred between blacks and whites. Prior to my arrival, the incident involved supposedly a hanging. Basically, when I reported there it was explained to us blacks; only that no more than 2 blacks could be seen in a public place of assemble or we would be charged with inciting a riot. Blacks were not allowed to carry around wooden canes which was more of a fashion statement than preceded as a weapon. Popularized by civilian culture of African pride, angered many whites. These canes were made in any number of Far Eastern or African countries, but whites feared the mere thought of it as an equalizer. Whites gathered in six to ten men packs and nothing was said. That order didn't last very long, but yet again the element of fairness to tilt the favor always away from a person of color was prevalent in 1971, and equally today but it's more disguised.

Joplin, Missouri, the largest city in Jasper County, Missouri. Scott Joplin, a ragtime composer from Missouri, is not for whom the city is named. The city was named for a prominent Methodist Minister named Reverend Harris Joplin, founder of the first Methodist congregation in 1873. One of several tornados' to touchdown in Joplin, Missouri throughout its history did so recently on May 22, 2011. A Sunday afternoon around 5:41pm where about 75% of the city was reported to have been destroyed. An EF5 (*Enhanced Fujita Scale 5*), yet again,

85

"The Colored American," of April 4, 1903

devastated the town of Joplin covering six miles long, half a mile wild through the middle of town eastward across Interstate 44 into a rural portion of Jasper County and Newton County. Final death count for the 2011 tornado, 162, with property value lost totaling three billion dollars while flatting some eight thousand structures. A city proudly boosting it's motto of: ***"Proud of Our Past...Shaping Our Future."*** This motto, obviously unbeknownst to the current citizens of this city's pass, will be unveiled for the world to see its true past. Aftermath of the devastation, many signs read, *"God Loves Joplin," and "We Support You Joplin."* Suggesting God's mercy despite the devastation, but clearly undermining his golden rule. As a midwest city, Joplin's current population percentage is African American at about 3% with whites averaging about 87% and 10% make up of Asians, Hispanics and Native Americans.

As many in this country were drawn to the enormity of destruction and lost of life, sympathy poured in from all over the world. President Obama, having recently returned from Europe, visited Joplin first hand rather than reading or viewing the results from afar, made some rather heart felt comments. As he walked around greeting the survivors with words of this action not being just a Joplin problem, but rather a national problem, seemingly, temporarily comforting the weary and hurting. The President also among his many comments were praised prompted to recognize the number of volunteers from all over this country as well as around the world as the concerns of the devastation resonated with all offering their assistance. But the fog of impaired clarity related to this city's motto, became absent due to the current tragedy, *"what you have done to the least of these,"* also lost in a time capsule of history untold or forgotten. So whatever you don't remember, you are condemned to forget and more likely to repeat. The property damage coupled with EPA's effort in beginning a massive cleanup effort in and around Joplin that started in the early 1990's added more seriousness to the clean up effort as it relates to the lead problem. It was reported that about 2,400 properties of lead and cadmium contaminations, mostly in northwest Joplin were being eventually cleaned up by hauling out contaminated soil and replacing it with clean soil less the contaminants. Now, the wind velocity that assuredly makes a double action clean up effort, adds insult to injury and compounds the clean-up effort.

Let us now regress to earlier times in Joplin's checkered pass. April 15, 1903, Officer Theodore Leslie in carrying out his law-enforcement duties attempted to arrest several Negroes for alleged theft who had taken hidding positions inside a boxcar of the Kansas City Southern Railway Yard. The officer gave several word warnings to no avail; he drew his revolver and fired several shots into the box car. During the warnings shots, a Negro alleged to have slipped out of the box on the other side, blind-siding the officer and shot him in the head from behind. The following afternoon Lee Fullerton located Thomas Gilyard, A Negro, age 20, known as a tramp or drifter, located Gilyard in a slaughterhouse armed with a rifle. Fullerton alone with another deputized individual managed to force Gilyard to surrender and give up the rifle before hauling him off to jail in Joplin. In many such racist issue of the period, word of the arrest and his association with the murder of Officer Leslie spread like flood waters in a valley with no banks on all sides. Within a short period of time the jail was surrounded by a mob of thugs wanting to take the law in their own hands with yells of threats and racial rhetoric.

Devour Us Not   86

Efforts by City Attorney H.H. Decker for calm and justice fell on deaf ears. For thirty minutes with Gilyard in close proximity, just when it appeared racial rhetoric filled the airs. Just when it appeared the city attorney was winning the argument, a group of angry citizen would not accept anything but their own blood-thirsty vengeances of gratification. They dragged Gilyard from the jail down two blocks of the street to a nearby telegraph pole on Second and Wall Street. With the rope already around his neck, efforts for the purpose of a quick death, one group of the party trying to string him up and another party trying to pull him back down in a tug-of-war effort like prating fools. Despite all the mayhem, chaos, the cry for his own innocence of one man could be heard the loudest among the hundreds of yelling heathens. Within minutes more of the thugs who wanted him hung, won out and the ever so loudly voice heard only moments before was silenced. This jubilated the crowd of about 500 white men with excitement as if a touchdown had just been scored at a sporting event without being cognizance to lose of life. Unsatisfied with the hanging of Gilyard, and no resistance from law-enforcement, caused these

"The Washington Times," of May 28, 1922

vigilantes to then head to the Negro session of town and burned almost every Negro home in the session. Warnings were then given for every Negro to leave their homes, live stock and all their possessions behind and never return to Joplin. Being out numbered, under-supported by arms or ammunition, forced the Negroes from their generational rightful homes and head for the woods. Hickory Bill, a white man, known as a hot-head trouble maker and Negro hater, was released at the demands of burning down the jail if not complied with. Hickory Bill was under arrest for assaulting a Negro. This in terms gave Hickory Bill an opportunity to legitimize his actions as he then joined the mob in reaping havoc on all Negro residences. Mayor Trigg and some rightful residences tried every effort to control the mob but their efforts like that of their law-enforcement team were ignored. So the expectations of the wicked continued with little regard to the wrath for their deeds that waits.

That night, every Negro had left his home with many of them fleeing to nearby *"Bisbee Daily Review," of October 8, 1903* Springfield. The Mayor of Springfield now faced with the overflowing of Negroes made most of the white citizens of Springfield uncomfortable. As efforts were used to show the Negroes they were not welcomed in Springfield either. A committee was formed by the Mayor that did not contain the keys to the city, rather a boot of unwelcoming. As the word in the entire state of Missouri was received nearby towns also began to rid their towns of long time Negro residencies and drifters from Joplin and Springfield. Most of the Negroes in Joplin in 1903 had recently arrived from nearby Pierce City, Missouri, roughly 30 miles away where a similar incident drove all the Negroes away. This was during the month of August in 1901 when Will Godley, a Negro, was lynched (*A 2003 tornado devastated the town of Pierce City*). Supposedly, Godley had assaulted Caralle Wild, a white woman, by assaulting her and slitting her throat, leaving her in the woods. The mob then headed for the jail after rumors of his arrest, dragged Godley out and lynched him even though the so-called evidence were weak and circumstantial, followed by evidence proving Godley's innocence. With Gilyard's body hanging in view high above the eye levels, his body was then riddled with bullets in the aftermath. Somehow one bullet missed its intended target and struck an innocent white boy killing him instantly. There was no documented recorded evidence as to whatever happened to all the Negro residences of Joplin. God only knows where they all ended up with nothing but the clothes on their backs and an entire state covering some 69,704 square miles in distance rejecting them. Even by today's standard, the population of blacks living in Joplin, Missouri is 3% of its population. After Gilyard was cut down and buried the next day, forensic test were performed on all the bullets they extracted from his body. Lodged in his leg was a match of the same bullet that was extracted from Officer Leslie skull. Some how this gave justification to Gilyard's innocence. Completely obvious to their thinking

Devour Us Not

was that Gilyard had no bullet wounds while he was incarcerated. And the weapon, a rifle, confiscated from Gilyard the night of his arrest, forensic test were run with the bullets of that rifle neither matched the bullet found in Officer Leslie skull or any other victim. It was later determined that Officer Leslie was killed by a pistol.

But Joplin would not be finished with its checkered past. As time went by since the 1903 horrors, small amounts of Negro business men began to infiltrate the county lines of Joplin, but quite mindful of only seven years prior the ever mindful of *"Jim Crow,"* was alive and well. On November 27, 1912, a seventeen year old stenographer named Pearl Nugent, white, alleged committed suicide in the office of her thirty-five year old Negro

"The Columbus Journal," of Feb 17, 1909

employer, named Minister J.N. Brownlee. Brownlee was known as a well educated man and very wealthy having made money in real estate. Sometimes during 1911, Brownlee, being new to the area had placed an ad in the local newspaper of a position being offered for which Pearl applied. Pearl never mentioned to her parents that her employer was a Negro. Instead she reportedly mentioned to them that she was accepted for a position working for a white Real Estate businessman. They had only recently been aware of his ethnicity after their daughter's death. Upon her first encounter with Brownlee at his office on 521 ½ Virginia St., Phone # 1259, as she had mentioned to her friends, she had become immediately infatuated with him. Perhaps it was the uncommonly charm and wit, contrary to what she had either been taught or observed that transfixed her mind to his appeal. It was rumored that Charles Houston also a Negro and J.N. Brownlee would entertain many white women and orgies would be performed in his offices without the slightest amount of suspiciousness from white citizen who most were even unaware of Brownlee's presence in the city. Apparently these midnight suppers of wine drinking and later turned into wild parties were all geared towards black men and white women only as were reported during the inquest. Both Brownlee and Houston were secretly sent to a nearby location as mobs were beginning to form despite overwhelming evidence of suicide and friends response to the inquest. Eventually the fear of danger subsided as Brownlee was eventually allowed to continue his successful real estate business of acquiring homes and properties. But the evils of Joplin would continue with its string of mystery murders. Clarence Roundtree, an 18 year old Negro, decomposed boby was found in a nearby river and the case was never resolved. A.C. Stone and his Negro family of four were found murdered in their home that included

his wife and two children in Joplin. Their murders were never solved.

Pictured from left to right, **Roscoe Conkling Bruce, Jr.**, and his parents, **Roscoe Conkling Bruce, Sr.**, and **Mrs. Blanche K. Bruce.** Roscoe, Jr., was chosen as class Orator at Harvard University in 1901. Both parents are on staff at Tuskegee Institute in Alabama.

*Pictured L/R: "Akron Daily Democrat," of Dec 24, 1901-**Roscoe Conkling Bruce, Jr.**, "The Colored American," of Jun 20, 1903, "Head of Academic for Tuskegee Institute,**" Roscoe Conkling Bruce, Sr.**, "The Colored American.," of Mar 24, 1900-**Mrs. Blanche K. Bruce-**Lady Principal-1900 at Tuskegee Institute, Alabama.*

Born in 1879, Washington, D.C. where he received his initial education by attending Phillips Exeter Academy

before entering Harvard in 1898. He gained much attention as a freshman in a debate against the sophomores. He was awarded the Coubertin Medal, (*also known as the True Spirit of Sportsmanship Medal*) an award presented by Baron Coubertin for the first time in Harvard's 300 plus year history, that this medal had been award to a Harvard Student. The fall of 1899 he was nominated as a candidate for the Princeton debate. After three trials, he was the first chosen to represent Harvard on the debate team. Roscoe also received the Greenleaf Scholarship award as a freshman. He had written several papers for the college newspaper as among his strongest attributes; his literary talents such as the Orator appointment of **Glement G. Morgan**, pictured above right, Harvard Class of 1890. Harvard, in the early 1900's seemed to be on the cutting edge of diversity when it comes to allowing talent to trump over racial discrimination. President Eliot, President of Harvard University, as reported by, *"The Broad Ax," of March 13, 1909*, as he explained what he classifies, *"The Democracy of Education."* The assimilation of the races in an educational platform where as each excepted race will receive the highest quality of education on a professional bases. That premises would then afford the representative of that race who will then go and educate his or her race whom are less fortunate, would be receiving quality training and have professional influences. Hence making the race tolerance levels more expectable for all races and ending race isolations which breed race discrimination.

Memphis, Tennessee, has had a long history of social and civil unrest. From Mayor Henry Loeb's and all authoritarian figures in Memphis of racist actions in the 1960's before and after the day Martin Luther King, Jr. death and beyond. Wednesday, March 9, 1892, *"The Times," of Richmond, Virginia, March 10, 1892,* reports the ambush shooting of four deputies in an area of Memphis Negro section known as, *"The Curve."* With warrant in hand, Saturday night, March 5th the white officers in a black community drew much attention but never had there been anything like this. About 3 o'clock in the morning of the 9th, seventy-five hooded violent starved mobsters headed down the street for which no one saw or heard a thing, in route to Shelby County jail. Watchman O'Donnell was on duty at the outer gate of the jail speaking with a friend while jailer Williams was up-stairs asleep. Hugh Williams of a White Haven, so he claimed had a prisoner in his possession, after acknowledging the watchman's request to the nature of his quest. In this fibbed attempt to gain jail access became successful, watchman O'Donnell unlocked the entry gate and was rushed by several men. Being over-powered by the rush, O'Donnell reaches for his pistol, as to defend his position of responsibility. When one of the masked men suggested he'd best rethink that decision which he gladly complied with while addressing the numbers against him. Some of these men seized O'Donnell's weapon and asked for the keys which housed the Negroes. Watchman O'Donnell was then bound with rope as his clothing was search in an effort of securing the keys. Unsuccessfully in obtaining them from his person, men were then placed over him for guard as the office was searched. Soon the cry of *"All right boys, here they are!"* Within seconds, the masked men had gained access to the Negro Department of the cells where some twenty-seven Negroes were being held in connection with the Deputy ambush case. Alice Mitchell in jail in another part of the building on charges of murdering Freda Ward recalls how silent and seemingly orderly the masked men were in going from cell to cell knowing exactly what they were looking for. Alice soon recalls the shuffle of feet stopped and a small scuffle broke out before Moss was seized and his mouth was silenced with tape followed by similar task for McDowell and Stuart was last.

Devour Us Not

"El Paso Herald," of January 18, 1913

Soon the three are dragged, push and hurried out the jail. Down the street, they turned the corner into Auction Street headed for the Mississippi river. They stopped by the tracks of the Chesapeake and Ohio railroad before turning and at a quicken pace along the track before stopping in a field near Wolfe river. The men were allow to voice their opinion as they were unbound for that reason.

Moss supposedly made a request that their faces be allowed to face the west. It was said before he could get those words out, the folly of firearms could be heard for miles as their bodies were riddle with so many bullets, it literally tore their bodies apart with even parts of their head and others missing. When the bright spring morning of the 9th of March with their bullet riddled bodies of the three Negroes, **Calvin Mc Dowell, William Stuart** and **Theodore Moss.** A mail-carrier word spread and about 200 Negroes showed up to retrieve the bodies. Long before, in the silence of night, the mob had split and all went their separate ways. Nothing was said among the crowd aloud as murmuring could be observed and they cursed and mumbled surrounding the jail. Around 10 o'clock, the riddled bodies were given to the Negroes to take back to a home in the curve. About 7 o'clock in the evening a large crowd began to throw rocks at the house. News reached Sheriff Mc Lendon who gathered a posses of white men and headed for the curve. Upon his arrive he found a large crowd of armed Negroes and a large crowd of whites as Sheriff Mc Lendon pleaded for their disbursement riding back and forth on his horse. It was reported that 200 of the Negroes had armed themselves with rifles from the old Tennessee Riflemen, a Colored Military Organization. It was also reported that a gun maker named Frank Schuman was making weapons and selling it to the Negroes. Judge Dubose then ordered about 20 deputies to the armory to protect the guns and ammunition from the hands of the Negroes. Word of the selling of weapons to the Negroes by Frank Schuman reached Judge Dubose who was promptly summoned. Upon the arirval of Mr. Schuman before the Judge who demanded he stops selling weapons to Negroes. In which Mr. Schuman replied, *"I'll sell to whom ever I want."* Which then prompted the Judge to throw him in jail. Memphis remain on high alert for more trouble as the crowd of Negroes vield to defind themselves against anymore violence involving hangings or any other lawless acts. Hugh Shields was next to be hanged or violated as rumors from the mob had spread. Even the thought of another act of lawlessness, the Negroes of *"The Curve,"* had had enough.

Frank Embree *(pictured left, nude)* of Higbee, Missouri before he was murdered by a lynch mob of estimated over a thousand on July 22, 1898 in Fayette, Missouri. Paraded through the town prior to the lynching in a wagon, with his hands bound, was striped of all his clothing which revealed so many deep knife cuts and lashes on his body from being whipped for over half an hour prior to lynching. This muscular young 19 years old Negro, had his life cut short after being accused alone with his brother of criminal assault of a 14 year old white girl named Millie Daugherty in Howard County, Missouri. He had written a letter to his brother explaining his fear of after the courts releasing him from the alleged crime, he'd be hunted by the mob. While aboard the Chicago & Alton train, the mob stopped the train near Higbee and over-powered the Sheriff and two Deputies taking matters into their own hands. The unknown photographer that snapped the picture prior to his murder, shows the eyes of defiance and angry, but no pain or shame; victim of mob injustice. The Embree case received national attention by the Fred Douglass Literary Society of Saratoga Springs, N.Y., condemning the acts of Gov. Lon V. Stephens of Missouri, yet commending the actions of Gov. Stanley of Kansas. Embree was arrested in Garnett, Kansas whereby an agreement was made for his safe return back to Missouri between Governor W. E. Stanley of Kansas and Governor Stephens. Once Embree reached Missouri, Sheriff G.D. Gibson

Frank Embree Unknown photographer 1898

of Howard County and the law officials offered no defense to protect Embree from the mob. A newspaper article by *"The Evening Times," of August 2, 1899*, reports a public reprimand by Governor Stanley to Governor Stephens as follows: ***"Governor Stephens has been guilty of a gross breach of faith. He failed to furnish Embree protection as he promised me he would do, and is therefore culpably responsible for his murder. Hereafter I will refuse to honor any requisition coming from the Governor of Missouri."***

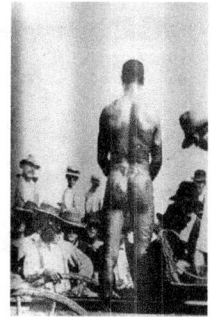

Gov. William E. Stanley of Kansas
*" Kansas City Journal,"
of January 10, 1899*

No one ever paid for his (*Frank Embree*) death or the three (*Calvin Mc Dowell, William Stuart and Theodore Moss*) massacred, bullet riddled bodies in Memphis. No one heard a thing; mob was ever so silent in their attack and the dead don't have words to speak.

Rose Carson and her sister, Negroes, were arrested in Orangeburg, South Carolina according to *"The Anderson Daily Intelligencer," of July 14, 1914.* Rose Carson worked for Mr. & Mrs. D.F. Bell. They had a 12 year old daughter and it was known that problems existed with the family and Rose. The child was reported missing on Saturday, July 11, 1914, after earlier had left home to bring home the cows. Immediately, the family suspected fowl-play and notified the authorities. Rose and her sister were arrested on suspicion and taken to Elloree County jail on Sunday. After a hunt, the child's body was found early Sunday morning. Then the mob was formed and approached the jail and took both women from their cells with no resistance from law-enforcements. The women were taken back to the crime-site and supposedly Rose confessed to the crime as well as her sister confirming it, but claiming her own innocence. It was reported also that there were about thirty Negro men present, not among the mob, but did not offer any protest to the hanging. Rose was hanging by her neck and over two to three hundred rounds of ammunition riddled into her lifeless body. After the word spread nationally, there were many criticisms to the thirty Negro men who stood by and did nothing as reported by, *"The Appeal," from Saint Paul, Minnesota, July 18, 1914*, newspaper article, calling the Negroes *"cowards and a disgrace to their race."* And yet in that same article summarizing the lawless act of that day, nothing was mentioned about, *"Serve and Protect,"* as to the responsibility of the law-enforcement officers cowardliness in offering no defense in protecting these women or the hundred or so mobsters for their disgrace in carrying out the disgrace. How ironic of ones inability to see the forest but not the trees!

In one of the most horrific and barbaric incidents of lawlessness recorded was reported by the, *"Marietta Daily Leader of Marietta, Ohio" of April 25, 1899.* Sam Hose, Negro, **supposedly** confessed to killing Mr. Alfred Cranford, a white man, but did not assault or rape his wife, Mattie. He continued by saying he was paid $12 dollars by a 60 year old Negro Preacher named, *"Life,"* or *"Lige,"* Strickland of Palmetto. After the word of this alleged confession was known, a mob went scouring the countryside looking for him as he returned home. But he was found within 24 hours swing from the limb of a persimmon tree, one mile from town with a note pinned to his chest that read, *"We must protect our southern women."* Both ears and all fingers had been removed from his body. The word had reached his employer, Major Thomas as a small band of mobsters took him from his cabin on the plantation of Major Thomas after pleads from his wife and five children for his

Devour Us Not

life. Strickland was taken to Newton where an impromptu trial was performed with several citizens giving testimony to the Minister's character as a law-abiding citizen. The blood-thirsty mob unconvinced, took him to his death place where he was strung up repeatedly and released in an effort to force a confession, but each time he refuse to give up his innocence. Shortly after Sam Hose's arrest, a mob of about 2,000 had formed from the community of farmers of Griffin, Palmetto, and Newman and other surrounding small towns. Sam had been apprehended initially in the swamps where he was in hiding near his mother's house. He was in route by train, guarded by the *"Jones Boys,"* until he was forcefully

Honorable William Yates Atkinson
"The San Francisco Call," of Apr 24, 1899

apprehended by the mob at gunpoint from the law-enforcers. The mob then preceded in route to their designated killing place when they were met by a former Governor named the Honorable William Yates Atkinson. He then addressed the mob with the following words of caution, *"Some of you are known to me, and when this affair is finally settled in the courts, you may depend upon it that I will testify against you."* It was noticed that a member of the mob then drew a revolver and aimed at the former Governor, but he was met by a larger mobster who then over powered this fool and secured the pistol from his grip, possibly saving the life of the Governor. After the size of mob and the violently taking of Sam from law-enforcers prompted then current Governor Candler, to ask for federal troops. There were also rumored reports that the Negroes were arming themselves for the possibility of protecting themselves and their property from an enraged majority aggression.

By the time the loud and jubilant crowd reached where they carried out their evilness, some of the most uncivilized acts against a human-being began. First a stake was implanted into the ground for which their intent was to burn him alive first. Before the torch was lit, several knifes were presented and in a copy-cat act of barbaric cowardliness, one by one the mobsters severed each ear, his nose, each finger and thumbs and even his gentiles. Then those items were passed around like priceless items at an auction house. But their attempt was not for the highest bidder, rather, it was for souvenirs and trophies of disgrace at bargain prices. Sam was initially in complete agony, much to the delight of over 2,000 men, women and children. They witnessed this disgrace with all the pomp and circumstances with the lifting of every separated part of his body. Finally, his body was doused with kerosene and the torch was lit. As his body burned with not a one of the over 2,000 pacified blood-thirsty evildoers lifting a hand in stopping this atrocity against humanity. As his body continued to burn and even push back into the fire when it appeared some of his body portions had been missed. Sam never uttered a word in agony much to the disappointment of the heathens who had rejoiced at the misplay of agony he'd shown during the mutilation. But very silent were three words he did speak in finality, *"Oh, Lord Jesus."* But after the body had burned to a crisp and even before it could cool, some of the heathens risked getting burned themselves; yet again to begin the favorite part of these acts by continuing to dismantling of his body. The selling of souvenirs, some of them for money as little as 5 cent for small bone parts were being auctioned as at a land sale. His heart was also removed as well as pieces of his liver which sold for 10 cents a small piece. Once the body had reasonably cooled, the crowd then turned into the likes of a pack of wild dogs over road-kill.

Scraping, screaming, pulling as if 100 dollar bills were on the ground for the taking. W.E.B. Du Bois, living in Georgia at the time recalled passing a grocery store which was selling the knuckles of Sam Hose was appalling to him. It was also reported that the mob also cut large portions of flesh from his

face, cut open his stomach and began to pull his body parts out for sale like almost every inch of his body

was. A nation wide investigation was conducted and it was proven that Pastor Strickland was a godly man and never had $12 or $20 ever to pay anybody, according to his employer, Major Thomas who did so voice fully the night he was lynched. **Governor Allen D, Candler** (*Pictured in the upper right corner*) blame the characteristic behavior of the citizens of Georgia on the carpetbaggers and scallawag's who filled the Negroes head in the post emancipation era of boldness. And that the government would give them liberty and protect them right or wrong in their endeavor. Bearing the assumption that a black man could ever be considered equal to whites caused all the friction in Newton of whites unwillingness to surrender their strong hold on the necks of the Negroes.

The Negro citizens of Chicago hired Detective Louis P. Le Vin, white, to investigate the Hose murder. Detective Louis described his experience in investigating the incident and detailed his finding in the, *"Richmond Planet," of October 14, 1899.* Sam Hose aka Samuel Wilkes worked for Alfred Cranford (26) for over a year. Louis found no creditable evidence to suggest Sam killed Alfred at the dinner table by cowardly sneaking up behind him and axing him before his family. This was an all so common attempt to infuriate a murderous mob. There was an attack on Mattie Cranford (25), Alfred's wife, but she had to identify the assailant. Sam was well known to the family. In asking white members of that community about the Hose incident, Louis recalls here's were some of their responses:

"A nigger had killed a white man that was enough." "The young niggers did not know his place and that they are getting to much education and being influenced by the Northern niggers." One Newman resident named W.W. Jackson explained, *"If I had my way, I would lynch every Northern nigger that comes this way. They are at the bottom of this."* While another white man was interviewed from Lincoln, Alabama named John Low said, *"My Negroes would die for me simple because I keep a strict hand on them and allow no Northern Negroes to associate with them."* All the above comments give one a clear picture as to the bias mentality of whites who were fearful of Negroes becoming wise as to their unbalanced treatment of fairness. Whites wanted to forever keep Negroes down to the lowest level of the poverty ladder, uneducated and a constant low-life of unworthiness was the ideal America.

When Sam was captured, after running for his life after the incident, he gave the following statement as his version of what happened. He stated the trouble started about a week prior. Sam explained of his mother's illness and that he wanted to go home to visit her. He then asked Mr. Cranford for some advancement on work already performed in which Cranford refused. I'm assuming based on some previous agreement in frequency of payment that was established. Cranford, known for his quick temperament provoke harsh words at Sam. But nothing else transpired that day. The next day it was said that Cranford borrowed a revolver from a friend and said that he'd kill Sam if he mention the money issue again. On the day of the murder, Sam explained that

Devour Us Not

"The Day Book," of Mar 1, 1917

Cranford fired at him first, followed by the throwing of the axe and then he ran. Sam also acknowledged that at the time he through the axe, Mattie, his wife, was in the house without visual sight of Sam. When Sam ran, he headed for the woods to mother's house where he was captured. After the killing was discovered by Mattie, she immediately went to Alfred's father's house and told him that Sam had killed her husband, but never said anything about an assault. The Cranford family was an old well known aristocratic and wealthy family of Georgia. The burning of Sam was a premeditation advocated forcefully by a prominent member of the community named E.D. Sharkey who was the Superintendent of Atlanta Bagging Mills. But the premises were to make an example of Sam for others to remain in their place. Sharkey had mentioned that he had spoken with Mattie the day after the murder and she told him then she had been assaulted. An obvious falsified statement to infuriate the bias community into a frenzy. It was also a known fact, that Mattie was unconscious for two days after the death of her husband. John Haas, President of Capital Bank also added to the advocacy of the burning of Sam by his prominent status. W.A. Hemphill, President and business manager, Clark Howell, editor of the Atlanta Constitution newspaper was also out front promoting burning. Clark Howell also wrote in his newspaper a summary of known to be falsehoods about the killing in a necessary furry of to enrage his readers to include the offerings of $600 for his capture, never once suggesting a trial or allowing the law to run its course. Then Governor Candler added to the non-protection of Sam by his issued words of blame as he requested Sam to be taken to Atlanta. But for ten hours of day-light and the words having spread all over Georgia, knowledge of the change in safe keeping, did reach the Governor, but offered no assistance to save his life. Sam was captured in Griffin and brought to Newman while in the custody of the "Jones Boys," J.B. Jones and J.L. Jones. R.A. Gordon, William Matthews, P.F. Phelps, Charles Thomas and A. Rogowski were also assisting the Jones boys. These men were well aware of a mob totaling more than a 1,000 awaits them in Newman. Logistically, Griffin was closer to Atlanta than Griffin to Newman, so this was purposely planned and ignoring the Governor's orders, all in an effort to seek mob justice. Another noticeable factor was there were no scheduled trains scheduled to go from Griffin to Newman. This news traveled all over the state of Georgia as people came from far and near of evil-doers set out on viewing what their hearts desires; death to the least of these. It was even reported that the conductor announced these words before the train took off, "All aboard the Special train to Newman!" "All aboard for the burning!"

Some very prominent presence at the witnessing of this barbarity was William Pinton, Clair Owens and William Potts of Palmetto; W.W. Jackson, H.W. Jackson, Peter Howson and T. Vaughn of Newman, John Hazlett, Pierre St. Clair and Thomas Lightfoot of Griffin. R.J. Williams ticket agent at Griffin who made up the special Central of Georgia and vocally advertised the burning at Newman. While B.F. Wyly and George Smith of Atlanta made up special Atlanta and West Point Railroad trains to accommodate as many heathens wanting to view what would be an immeasurably disgrace. Minister Strickland of Palmetto was never involved as he claimed with his dieing breath. Minister Strickland's body left hanging in the sun for ten hours before it was cut down and taken to calaboose in Palmetto and locked up. Detective Louis Le Vin mentioned in all the interviews conducted, **no one** ever heard Sam mentioned or anyone else mention Sam's affiliation with the Minister Strickland. The white-haired 60 year old noble man of God with a wife and five kids was innocent. The Detective went to visit the minister's employer, Major Thomas. He would try his best to save him to no avail. At the time the Strickland family still resided, he mentioned that Minister Strickland never had over five dollars to his name at any given time in his life. This was a creative way to increase and infuriated the already amount of blood-thirsty killings

the mob could add to their favorite pass time of inflicting as much fear in the Negro community as possible. Just as hardly anything was mentioned only a few days prior to the Sam Hose incident was the killing based on suspicion, of five Negroes, **Bud Cotton, Henry Bingham, Tip Hudson, Ed Brown** and **John Bigby** and the wounding of **Clem Watts, George Taylor, Isham Brown** and **John Jamison**. All apart of the commonality of life as a Negro was to be forever at the mercy of no justice and no trial. Of those men, none had reputations of crime; no one could indicate why these men were targeted for arson in burning two buildings in the community. The mob then ordered all the families of the nine Negroes to leave the area and all did, taking everything with them. Included in all the lawless efforts of the mob, no one was ever brought-up on charges for murder nor were concerns of the seventeen fatherless children and five widows of lost innocent blood ever challenged. Many more unsolved deaths, missing Negroes was endless with no one to protect them. The detective Le Vin left that part of the country totally convinced this would continue as long as the Negroes were left impoverished, uneducated and without outside impartial interference. Mrs. Mattie Cranford, by her own admission was never sexually assaulted by Sam Hose, the mob simply made that up to infuriate the mob into the frenzy heathens of sanguinary acts they eventually became. Their diabolical drama displayed a since of rage that wasn't human-like. Many Negroes were warned by the note attached to the dead chest of Minister Strickland to leave town and many Negro families did so. Also one of the most hunted afterwards was the hunt for Albert Sewell for talking bad about the whites of Palmetto in seeking revenge for Hose's death. He was finally caught and hanged April 24, 1899 for expressing his opinion or *"Speaking ill of white people,"* in proper era terms.

In almost synchronized unity, most newspaper articles, Ministers, government officials and many white citizens tended to justify the diabolical nature of the crime by targeting Hose's crime as fitting for what he received. Addressing him as a *"Brute,"* is an indicator of bias reporting. A conclusion based solely on his initiation as well as other Negro acts of violence in Leesburg and Griffin by drunken Negro soldiers is what leads to the feed-up emotions of whites. By batch justification of accounting for everything a representative of that race does as an indication to mutilate ones body as even keel was their justifiable logic. **Former Georgia Governor, William J. Northern** (pictured on the left) as reported in, *"The Evening Bulletin," of Maysville, Kentucky, April 25, 1899*, states, *"My first suggestion is that all homes (white) should be made miniature arsenals at least to the extent of one good Winchester and one good pistol; that women (white) be allowed to carry weapons upon their persons, concealed, if so desired, and that they be taught the use and handling of firearms, so that they may become their own protectors in the absence of their husband's or masters of the house. An occasional Negro lying dead in the backyard, shot by a brave woman in defense of her honor, will do more to stop this awful crime than all the lynching that may occur in a year. I would have every county supplied with at least half a dozen well trained bloodhounds."* A statement made on the falsehood that Hose had sexually assaulted Mattie. Bishop Henry M. Turner, a leading figure in the African Methodist Church residing in Atlanta, had for many years advocated Negroes going back to the, *"motherland."* His views however, did not resonate with the majority of Negroes because his tendency to equate master-slave theories in peaceful resolutions that could satisfy the differences between the races. He further added that a black man will never receive equal justice in American and will always be stigmatized in a negative light. As one of the trains departing from Newman with hundreds of jubilant white passengers,

Devour Us Not

HEY THERE HENRY, WAKE UP !!
DO YOU WANT TO
EARN A QUARTER?

"The Day Book," of August 23, 1915

boasting as if having just won a major sporting event in the backyard of their opponent. With trophy pieces of body parts and wood splinters from the Hose burnings were suddenly stoned at McPherson, Georgia near Atlanta, presumably by young angry Negroes. Several passengers were injured from scattered broken glass as the jubilance then turned to screams of fear and ducking for cover. Changing the victorious atmosphere into one of defeat in the backyard of their opponent. But, concluding that lynching, regardless of how great, horrible, small or insignificant the crime, if you're a Negro, the punishment most likely would be much more severer than the crime act committed, or not. Reverend Gilbert Ellison of Waynesboro, Georgia was inside his church on April 9, 1899, when he was shot to death for no other apparent reason except being a Negro. According to, *"The Watchman and Southron," of Sumter, South Carolina, April 19, 1899,* James Robinson, a young white man knocked on the Church doors, Sunday night, April 9, 1899 shot and killed the Pastor. A Special Grand Jury was form on April, 11th and the murder was considered willful and deliberate with no accomplices, but nothing further was derived from the murder.

"The Houston Daily Post," of August 3, 1900

Houston, Texas in 1900 had about 75, 000 residences. A lot of strange characters which made the largest city in Texas very unique. Adding to its uniqueness was a character named Sam Pictured on the left by a Houston Daily Post artist. Sam was born January 25, 1844 at 4 o'clock in the morning in Louisiana according to his mammy. **Sam Stuart** was the only Colored or white chimney sweeper in Houston in 1900. As he walked the streets in route to his next job, with the instrument of his trade strapped over his shoulder and a horn in his hand, you'd here his famous songs. Resembling by appearance, a Negro Uncle Sam, added the prideful steps as he strut along the sidewalks of Houston. Like a banker who just deposited a million bucks in his pockets, Sam had just that kind of step. With his pride higher than any dollar that would escape his pockets, life accordingly, was good. Sam boast about marrying a young wife who had eight children but only three lived. He gave his address proudly as, 14 German Street, as though it was a corner lot on millionaire's row. Everyone knew Sam was a poor man but his spirit would not allow him to dwell upon it. A man of meager means, Houston's finest who had accepted his role in American and Houstonian history as though it had an IOU waiting for him just around the corner. But seemingly around every corner was a group of kids who would be following Sam around as if he were the Pied Piper. They'd ask him to blow his horn right in the middle of one of his songs. And as obliging as he was spirited, the kids would be just as joyous as if a special request had been granted by their favorite recording artist at a major concert. Sam bragged once about a white lady had given him $2.25 just to have him sing one of his songs in a phonograph machine that broke and he then had to record it again for her. His songs was described as unique, had political meaning, blues emotions, soulful rhythms, gospel lyrics with a happy childlike melodies. The only time any despairing remarks came from his lips was when he mentioned as reported by, *"The Houston Daily Post," of August 3, 1900,* which mentioned when he joined the federal Soldiers and was mustered out in Galveston, Texas in 1867. He was promised and scheduled to receive a pension for his service. This never did materialize, much to the anger of Sam who pursue this effort, to no avail, for years. It would be a sad day in Houston, Texas and America the day the vocal styling's of the Uncle Sam like-man with the dusty stove top hat,

that walked around as if he were the drum-major of a marching band that would not be around forever for all Houstonians to joy their ears with his songs and spirit. Giving complete silence to his predicament without fear or short of his unstinted recognition of dignity; would have a void of the quietest of silence to this man of indissoluble entity of American culture shared by the likes of many.

Mme. C.J. Walker died May 25, 1919 at her home in New York according to *"The Kansas City Sun," of May 31, 1919.* Her last public act of kindness was to write a check for $5,000.00 for the National Association at the Anti-Lynching Conference. Among her many titles in describing her life's accomplishments are Philanthropist, Lecturer, Traveler, Entrepreneur and very successful business woman just to name a few. Recorded to have been the first woman millionaire in the country. Known for her famous culturist hair products, Mme. Walker was born December 23, 1867 in Delta, Louisiana to the slave parentage of Owen and Minerva Breedlove. At the age of six, Sarah Breedlove, her birth name was an orphan along with her older sister Louvenia and four brothers, Alexander, James, Solomon and Owen, Jr. To escape the death of yellow fever, all the children packed up and moved to Vicksburg. Louvenia's husband, because of the necessity to survive, was married young. So in an attempt to secure her own freedom perhaps or to escape cruelty, at the age of 14, Sarah also found herself going down the isle of holy matrimony. She married Rev. J.J. Walker and later became a young widow at 20. From her marriage to Rev. Walker, was one child born, her daughter Lelia Walker Robinson Wilson (She later married John D. Robinson and then Wilson). The only means of support was a washtub. With the worrisome of trying to support a child with no education, the stress caused her hair to begin to fall out. Madam Walker recalls praying to God to allow her to at least keep her hair as she tries to keep up appearances. And in mythical-like fashion, a man appeared to her in a dream and told her what ingredients to mix in an effort to save her hair. She admits, some of the ingredients came from Africa and was sent for to completion of her product. Within weeks her hair began to come back. Not convinced the growth was a result of the product, she tried it out on her friends with the same results. Hence, began the elements that would create her empire. Soon (Sarah) Madam Walker moved to St. Louis where she attempted to educate herself. Her dreams and aspiration always included the beautification of her race and in

"The Kansas City Sun," of February 23, 1918

particularly the hair. In 1905 her dreams became a reality, she began manufacturing a hair produce that would revolutionize the unmanageable, *"kinky hair."* She moved her business to Denver and arrived with a dollar and a half in her purse. She found a job as a cook until she saved enough money to buy her ingredients to manu-facture. Her first lab was in an attic where she worked two days out of the week on this *"cure to baldness in*

97   *Devour Us Not*

"The Washington Bee," of October 17, 1908

women formula."

Admittedly, having an eye for business, Madam Walker at one point owned a newspaper named *"The Afro-American,"* where she would use the source of advertising as a means of promoting her product. Traveling all over the country as another means of promoting her product, she then moved to Pittsburg in 1908. And with every stop in the various cities she visited, she established agents that would also spread the word locally of her product. By 1910, after more traveling and Lelia now able to shoulder some of the business responsibility, she moved the business to Indianapolis, Indiana. By this time the popularity of her products caused the business to leap to South America and all over the continental United States. She had over 15,000 employees and a $100,000 net worth annually. Madam Walker conducted a beauty course schools, turning out many graduates in the New York school system every six weeks. She also maintains support for six students each year at Tuskegee Institute in her interest in promoting education as a means of goal achievements.

It was reported that she had purchased a 34 room house in Irvington village, a New York wealthy suburb division worth a quarter of a million dollars. The three story, red tile roof top home located on Broadway near Fargo Lane with a spectacular view of the Hudson River. The home also boasts the architectural genius of the Italian Renaissance style period, designed by a Negro Architect named V.W. Tandy. Mme. Walker supposedly was married three times all ending in either death or divorce. Needless to say at the time of her death, her daughter inherited an estate supposedly worth about $800,000 in 1919 making her as reported by *"The Appeal,"* of June 21, 1919, *"The Richest Colored Woman in the United States."*

"The Kansas City Sun," of December 15, 1917

Annie Minerva Pope Turnbo Malone pictured on the left is the founder of Poro College in 1900 despite never having graduated from High School. The construction of her school was located in the heart of the Negro neighborhood, 3100 Pine Street, St. Louis, Missouri and was once known as the greatest institution of its kind in the world. When asked why she didn't erect the school's buildings in the business district so that the whites could marvel at the success of blacks, she modestly replied with a smile, *"We are not working among the white people, we strive for our own, Poro College. An industrial effort of the Colored People, by the Colored People, for the Colored People and the education of example. Undismayed by the century or more of handicap that we labored under, we mean to catch and then keep up. You cannot help the Jews*

by dwelling among the Gentiles."

Pictured on the right, enjoying the fruits of their labor are Mr. and Mrs. A.E. Malone. Proprietors and manufactures of then the world's famous Poro College with them is Mrs. Malone's private secretary and book keeper, Miss Maudelie McMurray and

their chauffeur. With the founding of Poro College, Mrs. Malone became the largest hair product for women manager in the country. Once, the Malone's made a $5,000.00 donation to the Y.M.C.A. as an example of their generosity in paving the way for the support of the Negroes and its communities. The product called Poro that allowed the Malone's to have over 25, 000 agents country wide. And one of their students and agents at one time was the infamous Madam C.J. Walker. For many years before the development of Mrs. Malone product, Negro women use a variety of home remedies to make their hair more manageable. They used soap, heavy oils, goose fat and other animal greasy body parts to straighten their hair. Before her Poro products, many chemical agents were introduced which in part created scalp and hair follicles. So Mrs. Malone's product was safe, made by a person of color and had no chemical after effects or damaged hair results. Malone's interest in hair came from her own experiences while preparing her sister's hair which prompted her to develop her product. Annie was born August 9, 1869 in Metropolis, Illinois, the tenth of eleven children to the parentage of Robert and Isabella Cook Turnbo. The children moved to nearby Peoria after both parents died. The older syblings took responsibility for keeping the family together, but Annie having a number of childhood illnesses caused her to miss a number of days and eventually dropped out completely. Her pattern of initial business savyness, caused many African-American women to gain self respect through financial independence. However, due to mismanagement and over extending her generosity caused the business to collapse with no chance of recovery. Annie died in 1957.

Phillis Wheatley-"The Appeal," of July 16, 1892

Phillis Wheatley was named the, *"Great Negro Poetess of the Last Century,"* according to, *"The Appeal of St. Paul and Minneapolis, Minnesota," July 16, 1892* of that year. Phillis Wheatley, born Nov. 19, 1753 in Senegal West Africa and was brought directly from Africa and sold on the Boston Slave Market in about 1761. A kind white lady known as Mrs. Susanna Wheatley purchased her as Phillis sat among the other naked slaves waiting for ownership to be established through price bidding. The name *"Phillis,"* was the name of the ship that brought her from Africa to the shores of America. And hence became her chosen American name that was used all her life. Recalling the disgrace of that moment of slave auctioning, Phillis having the frame of mind to keep a piece of the enslaved cloth to cover her loin after being striped of all her clothing. This act in displaying a defiance, impressed Mrs. Wheatley so she came to her rescue and made a bid for her.

Mrs. Wheatley in describing Phillis, at the age of eight, states she exhibited a desire to learn despite the male dominated culture in Africa she had arrived from. With this eagerness, Phillis was reading from the Bible, mastering the English language in a little over a year's time frame. Obviously, treatment of slaves was considered very differently from their southern counterparts. Within two or three years, social society types, as apart of their daily routines of stimulating talks would permit Phillis to join in with amazement. Soon, her reputation was known all over Boston as her unusual grasp change many opinions to the contrary with race stereotypes. Phillis also learned Latin and made a translation to English, of an Ovid story from an English magazine. It was suggested perhaps this was her love for poems must have come from as she began writing and publishing poems. There was even a poem addressed to George Washington who publicly praised her work. That poem became the first according to the, *"Perrysburg Journal," of February 16, 1895,* ever written in honor of President George Washington, written October 26, 1775. Later, the poem appeared in the Pennsylvania Magazine for April, 1776 and reads as follows:

"Celestial choir; enthroned in realms of light, Columbia's scenes of glorious toils I'll write. While freedom's cause her anxious breast alarms, She flashes dreadful in refulgent arms; See mother earth her offspring's fate bemoan, And nations gaze at scenes before unknown. Fam'd for thy valor, for thy virtues more, hear every tongue thy guardian aid implores. Proceed, great chief, with virtue on thy side, Thy ev'ry action let the goddess guide. A crown, a mansion, and a throne that shine, With gold unfading, Washington, be thine!"

At age 21, and after the death of Mr. John Wheatley, the Boston merchant, and the husband of Mrs. Susanna Wheatley, Phillis was emancipated. However, Phillis continued to live with Mrs. Wheatley under a different sort of arrangement other than ownership. Soon thereafter, Mrs. Wheatley began having health issues, causing her to be sent to Europe for a cure, accompanied by Nathaniel Wheatley, her son. America, still relatively new as a country, lack the experience, medically to satisfy her problems. And just like America, Phillis was creating quite a reputation for herself with her intellect and her humbled mannerisms abroad. It wasn't long before Mrs. Wheatley became seriously ill and sent for Phillis. She arrived just before the death of Mrs. Wheatley in 1773. Phillis eventually married a man named Dr. John Peters. Two children were born to this union, but they never lived beyond infancy. It was believed that her husband was cruel to her and not appreciative of the manner of attention paid to her for her popularity and partiality treatment. He was eventually jailed for debts, leaving Phillis in financial ruins. And on December 5, 1784, at the age of 31, Phillis Wheatley suddenly died. When the news reached all over the world, all who knew her mourned her passing. One of her famous poems title *"On being brought from Africa to America:"*

> *"Twas mercy brought me from my Pagan land, Taught my benighted soul to understand*
> *That there's a God, that there's a Saviour too: Once I redemption neither sought nor knew.*
> *Some view our sable race with scornful eye, "Their colour is a diabolic dye." Remember,*
> *Christians, Negroes, black as Cain, May be refin'd, and join th' angelic train."*

William Edward Burghardt Du Bois was born February 23, 1868 in western Massachusetts. For many years Du Bois dedicated his life to sociological investigations of Blacks in America by his powered lectures of the injustices. And for his strong views, many deem him as an anti-American. In 1951 he was indicted as an unregistered agent for a foreign power. A move for which he was acquitted, but forced him to be exiled from the country. He moved to Ghana where he remained until his death August 27, 1963. He was the author of *"Soul of Black Folk,"* a history of John Brown, *"The Suppression of the Slave Trade," "The Philadelphia Negro," "Litany of Atlanta"* and many pamphlets on the race question and injustice. He was also the Director of Publicity and research for the National Association for the advancement of Colored People. Graduate of Fisk University, received his PhD from Harvard University and also attended Berlin University. Du Bois was instrumental in forming the N.A.A.C.P. after his vocal opposition to Booker T. Washington's conservative views on reasonable accommodation. Du Bois more radical views began to resonate with many blacks who were fed-up with the oppression. Washington's theory of excepting discrimination for the time being, infuriated Du Bois and divided the nations blacks. Becoming wide spread among black intellectuals caused the labeling of Washington as a *"Tom,"* which caused the N.A.A.C.P. to interject views from both sides in a collective effort of seeking justice. Du Bois was the first Negro graduate of Harvard University to receive a PhD.

Owen Lovejoy, Abe Lincoln and **Elijah Lovejoy** pictured on the left were ministries and abolitionists. Owen was born in Albion, Maine in 1811 and ended up in Alton Illinois in 1836 joining his brother Elijah in studying for the ministry. Elijah already established in Alton as the editor of the local anti-slavery

newspaper, a position that would cause much animosity between the local establishments and would later cost him his life. All for the right of justice against the evils of slavery. Abraham Lincoln in 1856 wrote a letter about Owen Lovejoy, after the formation of the then new Republican Party which included all the abolitionists, which altered the thinking of the old South Republican Party. Owen was elected to the Illinois Legislature in 1854. Two years later, by one vote, he was nominated to the United States House of Representatives. So, when the Ottawa convention nominated Owen Lovejoy for the 1856 Congressional nomination over Leonard Swett, a

President and Mrs. Abe Lincoln
"The North Platte semi-weekly Tribune," of February 11, 1916

Criminal Lawyer and personal advisor to President Lincoln, he then wrote a letter to Henry Clay Whitney, an Illinois Lawyer on July 9, 1856 that read as follows: *"It turned me blind when I first heard Swett was beaten and Lovejoy nominated; but after much anxious reflection I really believe it is best to let it stand. This of course, I wish to be confidential."* Lincoln initially did not sympathize with the abolitionists of the new Republican Party and not wanting to disturb the direction the party was going agreed not to challenge Lovejoy's nomination for the sake of the party. Lovejoy consistently denounced slavery and was feared by many Politian's when he was nominated to Congress; feared the violate of all Southern Laws protecting slavery; essentially forever was their plan. On the floor of Congress, Owen was criticized and stigmatized as a, *"Nigger-Stealer"* for promoting slaves to escape and being linked to the Underground Railroad. After the death of his brother, Owen on the floor of Congress stated, *"I do assist fugitive's slaves. Proclaim it, and then upon the house-tops; write it on every leaf that trembles in the forest; make it blaze from the sun at high noon,*

and shine forth in the milder radiance of every star that bedecks the firmament of God; let it echo through all the arches of heaven, and reverberate and bellow along all the deep gorges of hell, where slave-catchers will be very likely to hear it." Owen, according to *"The Omaha Daily Bee,"* of January 15, 1881, stated also: *"Thou invisible demon of slavery, dost thou think to cross my humble threshold, and forbid me to give bread to the hungry and shelter to the houseless? I bid you defiance in the name of God!"* Slaveholders then tried to intimidate him with threats in an effort to silence his message, to no avail.

Elijah had exactly the same views that were expressed in his weekly newspaper articles called, *"The Alton Observer,"* regarding the evils of slavery. Elijah's home in Princeton was even believed to be one of the stations in the Underground Railroad. Elijah Parish Lovejoy at the age of 34 was murdered on November 7, 1837 as reported by, *"The Valentine Democrat,"* of November 18, 1897, by an angry mob in Alton, Illinois. Elijah, born November 9, 1802 owned a newspaper in the Godfrey and Gilman warehouse that focused on destroying the institution of slavery through his editorials from the distribution of his newspapers. After facing enormous pressure from pro-slavery citizens in St. Louis and having his equipment destroyed three times, caused him in 1836 to move across the river to Alton, Illinois. Despite the fact that at the time Illinois was a free state, even though elements of slavery were alive and well in Illinois. A gun battle between Elijah's supporters and a mob opposed to the abolishment of slavery broke out. Unable to gain access to the warehouse because of its strong windows and doors, the mob resulted to throwing burning brands upon the roof. In a brave attempt to save the lives of his friends and himself, Elijah was seen climbing from a window twice to remove the debris and was wounded the second time. Elijah was hit in the exchange and died from that wound, leaving behind a wife and two children. His supporters got together an The Lovejoy Monument, located at the Grand View Cemetery in Alton, Illinois at a cost of $30,000.00 was created. The architect was Louis Mulguard of St. Louis, and the sculptor was Robert P. Bringhurst, also of St. Louis.

"The Valentine Democrat," of November 18, 1897

The efforts of Senator C. A. Herb of Alton, proposed an appropriation of $25,000, made by the State Senate that was rejected. Then Governor Altgeld would refuse to sign the bill until the citizens of Alton raise $12,000. The citizens of Alton then organized the *"Lovejoy Monument Association"* and raised about half of the requested amount by the due date. The Governor then allowed the appropriation to pass favoring control be given to the

"The Intelligencer," of May 11, 1915

Association. The seventeen feet high monument was dedicated in 1897.

Luther Holbert and his wife, Negroes, were burned at the stakes in Doddsville, Mississippi, February 8, 1904, for the alleged murder of James Eastland, a prominent white planter and John Carr, a Negro. All the trouble supposedly started Wednesday, February 1, 1904 at the Eastland's Plantation. John Carr, a worker for Eastland had a cabin on Eastland's farm, where he, Holbert and another Negro named John Winters where all inside when Eastland entered. Apparently something had occurred earlier that caused Eastland to enter the cabin armed. Upon entering, supposedly, Holbert opened fire on Eastland fatally wounding him as he returned fire killing Winters, according to *"The San Francisco Call," of February 8, 1904*. When the news reached Doddsville, a posses was formed and left for the Eastland's Plantation. Being partly motivated by a $1,200 reward offered by relatives of the Eastland family, a family well known for their wealth in Mississippi. When the posse of about a 1,000 reached the Eastland Plantation, more shooting erupted and an unknown Negro was killed. Holbert had left the scene for his home to inform his wife for a getaway, and vowing never to be captured alive. He and his wife, dressed in men clothing, heavily armed headed for their escape. The posse on horseback and hounds began the pursuit. A pursuit which started on Wednesday morning the 1st ended late Tuesday night the 7th when they were found asleep in a heavy belt on timber three miles east of Shepard's town. Their travel on foot had taken them 100 miles through the swamps and canebrakes. In Yazoo County, near the town of Belzoni, two unknown Negroes, supposedly one bearing a striking resemblance to Holbert, *"by being a Negro,"* were shot down by the posse. Supposedly, a call for surrender was given by a mob of about a 1,000, some on horseback with about two packs of bloodhounds, were ignored and the immediate chase begin which by the mob's justification caused their actions. In the interim, Holbert's 16 year son was captured Friday, the 3rd and arrested on suspicion but later released after his innocence had been established. Luther Holbert and his wife *(the wife being nowhere near the crime)* where brought back to Doddsville and burned at the stakes in view of a Negro Church. Before Holbert and his wife were brought back to Doddsville, three other Negroes were lynched apparently; the mob became impatient waiting on the arrival of the Holbert's couple. Before Holbert and his wife were burned, each finger, ear and other body parts were severed from both, much to a joyous crowd who gave their approval with claps and loud jeers derisively. No one was ever charged for these crimes, nor was there any investigation.

The *"Cayton's Weekly," of May 24, 1919*, reports the lynching at Shubuta, Mississippi. Lynched was 2 brothers and 2 sisters, Negroes, named Andrew & Major Clark and both pregnant sisters, Maggie & Alma Howze. The alleged murder of a retired wealthy Dentist named E.L. Johnson, white, who was also the father of both Maggie and Alma Howze's unborn children. Supposedly, Major confessed after being tortured almost to death after all four were arrested. An unknown or unnamed white man had openly bragged about killing the Doctor in a plot because of some grudge he had against him. The killer then seized the opportunity to kill the Doctor and blame it on the Negroes. So gruesome for its time, papers were delayed in its release of this story. Without remorse, the mob started bragging about how tough it was to lynch one of the women by these words in describing her as, *"That big black jersey heifer."* The mob's justification, surprisingly, knowing they would not receive any

"The Marion Daily Mirror," of December 17, 1910

punishment for their crimes and the fact that the next term for the courts would not convened until March the following year. Here's their story: Dr. E.L. Johnson was a thirty-five year old prominent Dentist of Shubuta, Mississippi. Dr. Johnson had inherited a large farm after the death of his father. Soon thereafter, his dentistry business failed forcing retirement. Living on the farm as hired hands paying off a debt incurred by their father was two Negro brother's named **Major** and **Andrew Clark,** ages 20 and 15. Also living on the farm as lovers of the Doctor was two Negro sister's named **Maggie** and **Alma Howze,** ages 20 and 16. Maggie was between four and five months pregnant and Alma, her younger sister was also eight and a half months pregnant. Supposedly, Dr. Johnson had impregnated both girls but Major had fallen in love with Maggie and had disagreements with the doctor once the affair had been acknowledged to him. It was believed that Maggie and Major had planned to get married despite the known father of her unborn child by Dr. Johnson. In the mist of this acknowledgement, plotted by supposedly Maggie and Major, a quarrel broke out and Major supposedly shot and killed the doctor early one morning near his barn. News of the murder hit the rumor mill and **all four** were arrested for murder and taken to Shubuta jail for trial. Word of the murder caused a frenzy among some of the locals and soon a mob proceeded to the jail for mob justice. They secured the keys from the Deputy Sheriff in charge without incident, took all four from the jail and drove them to a covered bridge over the Chickasawhay River. Four ropes were produced and four ends were tied to a girder on the under side of the bridge while the four ends were made into nooses and fastened securely around their necks while they were standing on the bridge. Each one vehemently denied their involvement with the murder of Dr. Johnson. Maggie Howze screamed out the loudest, *"I ain't guilty of killing the doctor and you oughtn't to kill me."* So loud and annoying until one member of the cowardly mob in an effort to silence her cries, picked up a monkey wrench and struck her in her mouth knocking out her teeth and then in the head leaving a large gash. Then one by one each one was thrown over the bridge killing Alma, Major and Andrew instantly while Maggie manage to catch herself twice and had to be pulled up and the third time she died. Before Alma was buried, it was reported that her baby was still moving around inside her womb. But no attempt was made to save the child's life as Alma and the others were all buried on a Sunday, after the Friday's hanging. No one was ever charged in these murders.

Voter restrictions have been a major part of the disenfranchising of Negroes in America every since emancipation, particularly to whatever party Negroes supported. In 2012, there have been 34 states that have introduced new laws in my opinion to further hold back the progression of Negro citizens. In Vicksburg, Mississippi, December 7, 1874, a similar thing happened to encourage voter suppression. Limited information is known about this massacre, mainly because the whites were reportedly collecting deceased Negro bodies and literally tossing them in the Mississippi River to suppress the numbers slaughtered. In the South, Reconstruction period was worse and offered more violence towards Negroes then during slavery. President Ulysses S. Grant was reluctant to use Federal Troops for reasons unknown initially, much to the approval of angry whites which left the Negroes defenseless. And in counties where Negroes out numbered whites caused a political nightmare for whites who wanted Negroes to be a people of suffrage forever. In the mayhem of civil unrest reportedly, only fifty Negroes were killed. But the Negro hiding in the woods saw wagons of dead Negroes being

"The San Francisco Call," of July 28, 1907

tossed in the river and based on the missing; the number was more like 300. It was reported that all communication wires were cut in an effort to impede the true severity of the slaughtered from reaching the American public. Several well known white supremacy groups such as the *"red shirts"* and the *"KKK"* whose sole purpose was to intimidate and slaughter the defenseless Negroes. The *"Nebraska Advertiser,"* of December 24, 1874, detailed the political angle in the 1874 massacre. The premise of *"clean-out,"* the office holders that didn't share the radical white's views was the plan. Three office holders were even indicted by the Grand Jury. Sheriff Crosby, being one of the main focuses to taking over his position. The Wednesday before the slaughter, the Board of Supervisors held a meeting requiring Crosby to give a good bond which he failed to do. The white citizens, headed by a hot-headed white supremacy group member, mustered a meeting of their own on the same day. Their purpose, in the mist of five Lawyers was to examine the legal ramifications of ousting Crosby and replacing him with one of their own. During the decision making, *"time for action,"* conclusion was made and this meant by force would these replacements take place if not willful in demanding the resignations of the targeted officials. Feeling the resentment from a vocal supremacy groups, all old officials fled the county except Crosby. But Crosby fearing for his life did sign his resignation. He then proceeded to Jackson, Mississippi, to inform the Governor of what was being done by force in an effort to suggest the inappropriate manner in which his job was taken. He also requested the support of the militia for his and the safety of the Negroes. Crosby realizing the enormity of the situation wanted to inform the Negroes of the potential violence headed their way as a result of his meeting in Jackson.

Crosby made an announcement for the Negroes to come to the court house for a meeting. Knowing it was the Negroes who placed him in office legally, felt compiled to solicit their support again. The following day, Judge Brown attempted to hold court and was refused by a mob. Another meeting was then scheduled the day the Negroes were to meet at the court house but they were met at the city limits by the white supremacy groups who open fire, slaughtering and butchering all Negroes in view. All the Negroes were said to be unarmed and after being chased, most gave up on their knees begging and expecting mercy. They were then met with a volume of bullets, mowing them down like newly cut grass blades. The streets and country-sides were being patrol by whites and anyone not apart of the supremacy group was massacred. Captain Cowan, one of the main killers was observed directing an old Negro named Ambrose Brown. Being unable to move as quickly as one of much younger age was shot down by Cowan in cold blood. Some Negroes were taken prisoner, only because the killing became like saving a meal for left-over's. The very next day, they were released and shot down like dogs. The only reason fifty deaths were recorded was because the day the news became aware to the world, reporters only counted the physical bodies minus the hundreds of bodies that were tossed in the Mississippi. Very few Negroes survived that massacre and the numbers were suspiciously recorded but noticeable were the empty properties unoccupied by the missing and unidentified dead.

The Anderson Intelligencer of April 24, 1873 reports another political massacre. Grant Parish, Colfax, Louisiana long before April 1873, there had been trouble between the races. A contested election for Governor of Louisiana and local offices precipitated the troubles. Many of the Parish's in Louisiana were not emancipated so most of the Negroes, who were dependent and illiterate, were considered a volunteered systemic slavery system. In Grant Parish, Negroes out numbered the whites. In a political fight to gain control, the whites were driven from the city of Colfax. Barriers and fortification stations were set up all over the city as word reached other Parishes of the Negroes taking over the city. The Grant Parish Sheriff plus a hundreds of other surrounding counties of whites, headed toward the town on Easter Sunday, April 13, 1873. Upon their arrival,

Devour Us Not

a flag of truce was sent to the Negroes urging their surrender. A demand was made specifically for the initial black posse. Also was a warning that if they intended to fight, that everyone would be fair game to include women and children. The Negroes were defiant and refused the offer of surrender. The gang of whites then charged the barriers and the Negroes retreated to the Court House where an intense fire fight broke out for some time. Supposedly, it was a friendly Negro who was bribed to set fire to the Court House. After attempts from the Negroes inside failed, a white flag was seen from the Court House by the Negroes inside. In view of the white flag, two white men rushed toward the door of the Court House and were immediately shot to death. With the smoke becoming overwhelming, the Negroes began to exit the building in mass. As soon as they became visible to the whites, they immediately opened fire killing most who attempted to exit until the Sheriff gain control of the whites. When the dust and smoke had subsided, there were sixty-five dead Negro bodies accounted for that was badly mutilated with bullet holes. Another thirty who had surrendered were also shot and killed and then thrown into the river to conceal the true massacre numbers. Even though the total official count varies, the historical marker dedicated in 1950 gives the count of dead as three whites and one hundred and fifty Negroes. There was never any arrest made for the events of that Easter Day.

MRS. A. THORNTON.

Few outside of Cincinnati, Ohio had heard of **Mrs. Anna Thornton** in 1900. But the community and that city knew of a Dermatology Parlors, largest of its kind in Cincinnati, located in the Malta Building on W. 5th Street. Starting from humble beginnings as reported by, *"The Colored American," of November 17, 1900*, Mrs. Thornton was born a slave in February 1856 in Kentucky, where her mother was also born while her father was born in England. After emancipation, illiterate, as most all Negroes were, Anna had a passion to be independent and an entrepreneur. Her hard work and determination made her who she was. Anna Thornton, by 1900 was forty-four years old, divorced with one adult child. Though somewhat hampered by the divorce and lack of opportunities available to women and especially Negro women, she persisted in developing a technique of being a, *"professional scalp specialist."* A profession catering not only to black scalps but all scalps. Located in the heart of the business district, her tenacity in her abilities to successfully teach and inspire others in the city of Cincinnati made her a hero of her era and a champion among all women.

- As reported by the, *"Fort Worth Daily Gazette," of March 5, 1884*, **Ellen Sherwood**, a Negro woman was found in the woods near Chappell Hill, Texas hanging from a tree. She was about 25 years old and leaves behind three children. No one indicted, no investigation conducted.
- As reported by, *"The Morning Tulsa Daily World," of April 11, 1921*, **Rachael Moore**, a Negro woman was found hanging from a tree 15 miles from Jackson, Mississippi, on April 9, 1921. She was the mother-in-law of Sandy Thompson who a week prior was also lynched for the murder of E.B. Dodson. No one indicted, no investigation conducted.
- As reported by, *"The Daily Ardmoreite," of December 29, 1902*, **Oliver Wideman** and his wife, **Patrina**, who lived on the farm of W.C. Jay in Greenwood, South Carolina. W.C. Jay, came home and found Oliver

- abusing his wife, Patrina. William C. Jay, coming home one Friday, went to the cabin where the commotion was and ordered quietness. Soon thereafter, Mrs. Eva Jay heard a gun shot, went out to investigate and saw both Mr. & Mrs. Wideman running. By the time she reached him he was dead in a pool of blood. Soon the alarm went out and a posse was formed scouring the countryside for the two Negroes. They were soon captured and allegedly both blaming the other for shooting the gun that killed Mr. Jay. While in the custody of the constable on the way to the jail, the mob stopped the constable near Winterseat Bridge and both were lynched. They had a 19 years old daughter named Conilia. No investigation performed.

- As reported by, *"The Roanoke Times," of March 21, 1895*, **Harriett Talley**, a Negro woman was hanged by a mob near Petersburg, Tennessee, March 20, 1895. She was accused of burning the dwellings of a Bayless Marshall a few months earlier. No other details were known or investigated.

- As reported by the, *"Daily Evening Bulletin," of August 21, 1886*, a Negro woman named **Eliza Woods** was accused of poisoning her employer, Mrs. J. P. Wooten the week before August 21, 1886 in Jackson, Tennessee. Many rumors had swirled around for years in which 11 children in the neighborhood of Eliza were suspiciously poisoned. This 57 year old woman was also linked to the poisoning of Mrs. Wooten's toddler sometimes during 1885 but could not be proven. Eliza was contained in the county jail that was over-powered by the mob and dragged in the streets. The mob consisted of both hooded and non-hooded participants, white men and women and Negro men and women on the side. Supposedly, many Negroes in the community in which Eliza lived, were afraid of her and appeared to show no emotion into the activities of the mob. At the ringing of a bell, signaling the charge to the jail that was met with little resistance by law enforcers. Before she could reach the court square, the mob had stripped her of all her clothing as her hands were tied behind her. As she was strung up, her completely nude body dangling from the rope attached to her neck, only five bullets were shot into her body as the crowd gazed up at her until she appeared lifeless. The contents of Mrs. Wooten stomach was sent to a Nashville chemist for analysis. The results came back positive for arsenic poisoning. After investigation of Eliza's home, a box of rat poison was found as well as stolen dresses and jewelry for the Wooten household.

- As reported by, *"The Paducah Evening Sun," of May 25, 1909*, **Mary Rufus**, a Negro woman was charged with breach of peace in police court of Paducah, Kentucky. She was given hours to leave the city or fined $50.00. Market building is a frequent gathering place in the city which caused a law to be placed in that general area for loitering. Supposedly, The Market Master named Clark had instructed Mary Rufus to move along at which time she was reportedly made threats to knock down the Market Master if he addressed her again. Near the building where she had made her commits, her body was found hanging a day later. No witnessing, no investigation was conducted into her death.

- As reported by the, *"Bisbee Daily Review," of February 16, 1912*, **George Sanders** and **Mary Jackson** in Marshall, Texas were lynched by a mob to the same tree for allegedly living in the house where Jennie Sneed lived that shot and killed Paul Strange a white man. No investigation and no trials were conducted.

- As reported by, *"The Coalville Times," of July 31, 1903*, **Jennie Speer**, a Negro, allegedly administered poison to a 16 year old white girl named Jennie Dolan in Shreveport, Louisiana in 1903. John Dolan the child's father reported the death and a posse were formed to search for Jennie Speer. She was found crouching in a hay stack, proclaiming her innocence when she was dragged to a nearby tree and hanged. No

Devour Us Not

DON'T LET ANY VISITORS FEED OR ANNOY THE ANIMALS.

"The Minneapolis Journal," of May 13, 1905

investigation and no one indicted.

• As reported by, *"The Montgomery Tribune,"* of June 24, 1904, **Mrs. Maria Thompson** of Lebanon Junction, Kentucky, allegedly killed John Irwin, a wealthy white man with a razor. John Irwin had allegedly had some type of altercation with Mrs. Thompson's son for which Maria disagreed with. She allegedly met John Irwin in a melon patch and slit his throat. On June 16, 1904, Maria was taken from the jail by the mob and attempted to lynch her. Because Maria weighted 255 pounds, when they tried to lynch her, the rope broke. After the rope broke, Maria fell to the ground and began to run from the mob. Before she could place too far a distinct from the mob, her body was riddled with bullets. No investigation and no one indicted.

• As reported by the, *"Brenham Weekly Banner,"* of April 26, 1878, an unknown Negro woman was brutally lynched for being involved with burning down of a barn in Virginia. Allegedly, the unknown Negro woman had somehow convinced an unknown Negro boy to burn down the barn. The unknown Negro boy was later identified and questioned and proven to be innocent as well as the unknown Negro woman who was hung.

• As reported by, *"The Roanoke Times,"* of May 13, 1897, **Mollie Smith** and **Amanda Franks**, two young Negro women of Huntsville, Alabama were lynched by a mob the morning of May 12, 1897. Their alleged crime was poisoning the Kelly family for whom they worked.

• As reported by, *"The Muskogee Cimeter,"* of September 11, 1908, **Elwell Smith**, a white man disguised as a Black man in Des Moines, Iowa on September 8, 1908 was nearly lynched by a number of white men. Suspicions of his wife's affair followed her one night. In Des Moines, there had been several reports of assaults against white women by Negroes in the pass several months. Elwell, all decked out in black-faced by applied burnt cork, was following his wife when she stopped and told a white man that a Negro was following her. Elwell, being infuriated with her talking to a stranger, began to chastise his wife, and assaulting the white man she was speaking with. Her cries were heard by a number of white men who rush to her defense. Their over-powering voices of *"lynch him"* made Elwell's attempt in explaining his disguise almost mute. It wasn't until Elwell manage to free one hand to wipe his face was his true identity known. A comical end to an otherwise serious event. But this was not an isolated incident. Many Negroes have been falsely lynched when white men disguise themselves as Negroes to commit a crime knowing the blame would be avenged against an unsuspecting Negro. What ended up as comical could have cost Elwell his life.

• As reported by the, *"Keowee Courier,"* of July 15, 1914, Essie Bell, a twelve year old white girl was murdered by a thirty-five year old Negro woman named **Rosa Richardson**. July 11, 1914 in Orangeburg County, Elloree, South Carolina, Essie Bell daughter of Daniel Bell was lured in the woods by Rosa who purposely beat her head in with a lightwood knot. Rosa Richardson was employed by the Bell's and it was on their place, Rosa's house resided. There had been some friction between the Bell's and Rosa for which she was alleged to have refused to work for them any longer. Essie was assumed to have gone to graze the cows, but after her lengthy absence, the alarm was sounded and immediately Rosa and her sister were held as suspects. Bloodhounds were summoned from the nearby penitentiary but were delayed because of previous obligations. Sherriff Salley was notified that Columbia would make available their hounds for the

search. Before the hounds arrived, the body of the young girl was discovered. Supposedly ever effort was made to secure the prisoner's safety, but the mob managed to secure the prisoner, place her in a waiting automobile and taken back to the crime scene. After blood was found on the clothing of Rosa and her alleged confession with no apparent motivation given, other than vengeances, based on prior altercations. The mob now convinced of their role for mob justice, lynched her from a tree and riddled her body with bullets. Supposedly, there were several Negro families present that offered no resistance to the crime. Instead, they consoled the grieving family after the ordeal, as Rosa's body swayed back and forth after the hundreds of rounds entered her lifeless body.

- As reported by, *"The Daily Ardmoreite," of March 20, 1907*, two unnamed Negro women allegedly assaulted Mrs. Ella Rheaton, a white woman and her daughter and son while they were walking along a public road. The Negro women for no apparent reason sliced Mrs. Rheaton and her daughter with a razor then kicked her son in Stamps, Arkansas on March 19, 1907. The two Negro women were soon arrested and placed under guard at a school house. As with the rapid pace of wild fires, rumor of the assault hit the rumor mills and a mob was formed. Needless to say, the two women were removed from the school house and their bodies riddled with bullets.

- As reported by, *"The San Francisco Call," of August 2, 1901* & July 30, 1901, Mr. and Mrs. R.T. Taliferro were brutally murdered in Carrollton, Mississippi. Arrested, and taken to the Carroll County jail for the alleged murder were **Betsie McCray**, her daughter, **Ida McCray** and her son **Belfield McCray**, all Negroes. The rumor flourished and a mob was soon formed and marching towards the jail. Meeting them was Judges W.F. Stephens and W.H. Hill who stood at the steps appealing to the 500 men crowd of unmasked well known prominent citizens in broad daylight demanded with persistence the release of all involved with the murder of the Taliferro's. Supposedly, the daughter, Ida McCray made a full confession naming her mother, who refused to acknowledge or confirm any involvement in the murders. Her brother and others were all named and implicated in knowledge of the crime. The mob over powering the Judges and other law-enforcement officials, secured the keys from Jailer Duke, took all three from the jail and took them to a public place outside the city to a public road, lynched them followed by riddling their bodies with several hundred rounds of bullets. Governor A. H. Longino arrived after the lynching from Jackson, Mississippi and addressed the crowd on the Court House steps, still feeling the excitement of the lawless act express the importance of maintaining civil order and allowing obedience for the law. No one was ever charged for this crime and no investigation conducted.

- As reported by, *"The News-Herald," of Highland County, Ohio of April 26, 1888*, on April 19, 1888 in Gallatin, Tennessee, Jim McCollough found the bodies of two Negroes and reported it to local authorities. In the area, a series of house burnings were being conducted by unknown sources. But, a Negro woman named **Puss Kirkpatrick** was arrested and charged with incendiarism. What Jim McCollough reported was while taking a walk alone a country road stumbled over the body of Isaac Kirkpatrick, husband of Puss, shot to death alone the road. Within close proximity was the dangling body of Puss Kirkpatrick, dressed in a

"The Rising Son," of September 30, 1904

night dress hiding behind a tree invisible from the road at first glance and her feet within inches from the ground. The parties involved in these murders of Puss and her husband was never brought to justice.

• As reported by the, *"Kansas City Journal," September 30, 1897*, in the Massanutten mountains, six miles east of Cowan's Depot, Virginia. The body of Peb Falls was found dangling from the limb of a tree in the woods on September 29, 1897. Peb Falls, a white woman, married, but supposedly lived a very loose life and was driven out of town where she wondered in the woods and was allegedly associating with Negroes. Peb was also linked in a notorious tar-and-feathered case, where she was alleged one of the ring leaders. It was believed that Peb was hung by the Negroes in the woods where she slept and lived or angry whites. No investigation or other inquires were conducted into her murder.

• As reported by, *"The Washington Times," of May 9, 1919*, the lynching of a nameless Negro man and woman on May 9, 1919. The Negro man was recently *"Honorably Discharged,"* from the Army, admits to hiring the Negro woman that had a relationship with the white woman of his interest. The Negro man of Durant, Mississippi was to dictate a letter that was to be given to the white woman for some type of romantic encounter. Once the information reached the wrong hands, a mob was formed and both the Negro woman and man were hung on the outskirts of Pickens, Holmes County, Mississippi. No investigation or other inquiries were made into this matter.

• As reported by the, *"Daily Press," of September 3, 1910*, Deputy Sheriff Allen Burns went to the home of Edward Christian to make an arrest for the alleged theft of a watch from a local Physician in Graceville, Florida. Accompanied by the Physician making the allegations, both approached the home of Christian with the Deputy Sheriff called for Christian to come out and be confronted by his accuser. The Physician states, a volley of shots rang-out two hitting the Officer in the chest and arm. The Physician then fled the scene and spread the word throughout town and soon a posse was formed. There was a Negro woman, named Hattie Bowman, still in the house of Christian that was arrested and taken to jail. Christian had made an escape and got as far as Dothan, Alabama before he was captured and brought back to Graceville. As soon as that word had been published, another posse was formed. Both Hattie and Edward were taken from the jail with little resistance, taken to the outskirts of town and hanged. Their bodies were found the next morning hanging from a trestle and no one could offer an explanation as to whom the guilty parties were. The coroner's death report simple read, *"death met by parties unknown."* While the Editor of, *"The Broad Ax," of September 10, 1910*, concluded that, *"Let it be remembered that neither of them were charged with raping a white woman."*

• As reported by, *"The Broad Ax," of June 10, 1916*, that the body of **Mary Glass**, a 15 year old Negro girl and her newly born white baby was dragged from the river in Coffeyville, Kansas during June of 1916. It is alleged that the son of David Cline, one of the most prosperous and influential white men in the County, was in a forbidden relationship with Ms. Glass. His son was charged with the murder and locked up.

• As reported by, *"The Evening Bulletin," of April 22, 1895*, 40 miles south of Greenville, Alabama, five Negroes was lynched near Buckalow Plantation as reported by a Sheriff of the county. The murder of Watts Murphy, a popular young white man and the nephew of Governor Watts. Allegedly, the three males and two female Negroes murdered Murphy; they placed his body in a brush and set fire to it. Initially, three Negroes were arrested, but intense interrogation, two more Negroes were identified. Soon without the names of the Negroes given, they were jailed and securely protected at the county jail. The five were taken from

the jail by the mob and hanged.

• **As reported by the, *"Cayton's Weekly," of December 21, 1918 & June 21, 1919*, an unnamed Negro woman in Alexandria, Virginia, just blocks from the White House was this woman disemboweled and her unborn child torn from her flesh in broad day-light without an ounce of concern from on-lookers who did nothing, not even reporters who could not even get her name. The woman allegedly was protesting the**

hanging of her later proven innocent husband, when she was strung-up by her heels, the unborn child, torn from her womb, as it rolled from her open stomach, was stumped like mincemeat and kicked down the street like a common dog.

The **"Black Patti"** or **Madame Sissieretta Etta Jones** was known as the greatest female soprano vocalist of her generation, endowed with the voice of an angel. Born, Matilda Sissieretta Joyner in Portsmouth, Virginia on January 5, 1868 and died June 24, 1933. Her father, an African Methodist Episcopal Minister married Henrietta Beale. The family then moved and settled in Providence, Rhode Island. The name *"Black Patti,"* was first given to her by an overly enthusiastic New York newspaper reporter that used it in describing her talents which comes from the Italian Opera singer Adelina Patti Jones. Her Agent heard it and began using it. In an interview, Black Patti states her beginnings started as a child in Church at Providence when she nailed a high *"C,"* note.

Several people impressed upon her mother to allow her to study the love of her life; music. Ms. Jones was described as being tall, well-built with copper colored skin tone. Her style of performances that included comedy, burlesque, vaudeville and opera was marveled by all. This Prima Dona's Company was known as the *"Black Patti Troubadours Show."* Her ensemble of colorful costumes with era period, *"darky fun," "the cake walk," "coon songs" and "the buck dances"* creates a great operatic olio for her listening and visual audiences. The adage of her performance broadens the musical culture of all American people with pride. And for periods of performance is the fact that she was of African descent escapes the minds of all within a listening ear. Among the some forty dancers and comedians in her company act were considered some of the most talented Negroes in the world. The phenomenal popularity of her show was notably assembled the largest audience ever in 1911 at the famed Madison Square Garden, New York City. Madame Jones also boost of being the first Negro singer to entertained The Prince of Wales and King Edward VII of England, audiences in Paris, Berlin and all over Europe.

Despite all the popularity Black Patti possessed, she could not escape the cruelty of racism. The Richmond, Virginia, *"The Times,"* of September 18, 1902, reports the refusal of Miss Elizabeth Kennedy, a Southern white lady, star in the Captain Jinks of the Horse Marines, to occupy a dressing room that had been occupied a week prior by Black Patti. The Academy of Music Theater, was even halted because Miss Kennedy requested the star

Devour Us Not

"The Day Book," of May 20, 1915

dressing room is fumigated, deodorized and finally pacified. Oddly, Miss Kennedy made no objections to the room initially; it was only after seeing a poster of Black Patti on a wall in the room did she asked the stage manager if in fact Black Patti had occupied the room previously. Miss Kennedy refused to even place her trunks of wardrobe changes in the room fearing odor contamination. An employee had to be sent to the drug store twice to acquire enough smelly cologne to satisfy Miss Kennedy's complaint. However, the excessive smelly stuff did delight front row sitters who were seen from time to time sniffing the aroma of sweet smell. In wanting to avoid the pettiness of her complaint, Miss Kennedy refused to also speak with the press concerning the saga. Black Patti last performed around 1915 when she moved back to Providence to care for her elderly mother. It was reported that Ms. Jones used all her wealth just to survive and care for her mother that left her penniless when she died.

Blakely Durant, who sang songs for Ulysses Simpson Grant, William Tecumseh Sherman, James M. McPherson and other Generals at Army Headquarters of the Tennessee. Camp sobriquets of *"Blake," "Old Shady,"* a Negro, named Blakely Durant entertained at the request of Generals aside from his regular duties as a cater for the mess. Using his twanging guitar to serenade the entire camp was his specialty. First employed as an Officer's mess-cook, for the Seventy-first Ohio Regiment and was even reported being on the field at Shiloh. He was also apart of the Vicksburg campaign at Grant's Headquarters. He was soon assigned to the steamer Magnolia that was used as a transporter. Around the camp fires, melody soulful music became popular campaign songs

such as *"Suwanee River," "Ole Virginny," "John Brown's Body"* and many others that delighted the moments of war and calm the spirit.

"The Princeton Union," of May 25, 1893

Mrs. Laura Belle Durant Hickman *(pictured left)* was born December 31, 1861 in the countryside near Carthagenia, Ohio. Mrs. Hickman moved to St. Paul Minnesota with her parents in 1866 and lived in St. Paul her entire life where she died July 4, 1918. One of her parent was the infamous Blakely Durant, *"Old Shady."* Laura, married John H. Hickman, Sr. son of a minister and was the mother of seven children with four of them living until adulthood. Two of her sons, Maurice A. and John H., Jr., for years were proficient clerks in the St. Paul Post Office and her third son, T. Lloyd was

"The Appeal," of July 13, 1918

considered a renowned singer like his grandfather. Having performed patriotic work as a Y.M.C.A. secretary his songs reminded many of spiritual songs of his grandfather. Laura inherited the love for country from her father and devoted her life working to commemorating the patriot acts. She was President of the Ladies of the G.A.R. (*Grand Army of the Republic, Union Army members between April 12, 1861 - April 9, 1865*), President of the West End Branch of the Young Men Christian Association (*Y.M.C.A.*) and President of the Monday Art Club, a local community group. She was also a State Organizer of the Minnesota Federation of Colored Women's Club. Laura, a devout Christian since the age of 14 when she joined the Pilgrim Baptist Church. The church of her husband's father who was the founder where she served in

JUST LIKE A WOMAN

many capacities. Using her inherited vocal stylings of her father, she sang soprano in the choir for five years, was on the deaconess board, a church clerk, a Sunday School Teacher and a financial worker. Laura later joined the Memorial Baptist Church, May, 1914 where she was very active until her health began to fail her. At her funeral she was masterfully eulogized by all as her husband and three of her sons and a brother left to morn her passing. Her tireless work was praised as to the hundreds of people her efforts touched.

Edward M. Bannister according to the, *"The Sun," of November 8, 1896*, was born in St. Andrews, New Brunswick around 1833 or 1827. Parents of Indian, African and French origins, received a

practical education from the local village schools. Edward, known for his art work before the age of ten, created a reputation of drawing excellent portraits of his classmates and the neighbors of his father. Much to the disappointment of family and friend, who wanted Edward to become a great artist, took an apprentice job with one of, the most successful cobblers in St. Andrews. Being complacent living there under the British rule of fair play, regardless of skin color which played no role in his success, felt the bite of prejudice once he left the security of that environment. Black and white race differential became the forever constant. Being humiliated with a reminder of his mixed race, with one third dominating by skin pixels, placed him in a category as totally Black. This consumed Edward's artist thoughts that changed his talents of drawing landscapes and scenic views from his childhood to focusing on human features, and more particularly the face.

While studying art in Boston under Dr. Rimmer, his classification of genius became widely known among all viewers of his work. He was also a member of the Boston Art Club where he was a contributor of his exhibits at the annual exposition of the Boston Art Club. After completing his art studies in Boston in 1871, he then moved to Providence, Rhode Island. After moving to Providence, finding most class of painter was devoted to the French School as illustrated by Bougueread. So, Edward feeling the pressure of demands changed his style yet again to landscapes where he studied the Nacragansett coast with much success. Painting title, *"Under the Oaks,"* received a first award medal at the Centeninial Philadelphia in 1876. An interesting story surrounds the winning of that award. Edward recalls finding out the news of his first-prize gold medal winnings through the newspaper. As he did in the most expedient manner, rush to the committee room to verify there wasn't a misprint in the paper. As he approached, like all present ahead of him, excited about the newly announcements of awards, upon viewing his presence; within the range of his hearing comments were being made about his prresence in the room. Asuming, no person of color would dare have talents that any white man would be bound to respect; received more stares and comments than most. As he reached the inquiry desk, the insulting remarks did resonate into an all familiar surrounding of his pass by suggesting what his presence at his desk was. The excitement of news from the paper eased the insults as Edward acknowledged inquiring about the, *"Under the Oak"* painting. A continuation of insults carried forward as he suggested what that title had to do with him. Edward recalls when the excitement fizzled as the reality of the obvious became apparent, Edward quickly analyzed the communication through their eyes as they viewed him not as an artist but an overly aggressive

and inquisitive Negro seeking information for gossip purposes only. Edward though angered by the negativity, refused to allow himself to become angry. By not receiving a confirmation of his winnings Edward remained calm. This intelligent strategy worked for when Edward stated he painted the, *"Under the Oak,"* painting an apology immediately went from the clerk at the desk. This set off a chain reaction from on-lookers over hearing the inquiry began to gravitate toward Edward. Where once eyes of suspicion filled the room, congratulatory comments were then being offered to extending of handshakes and overly excitement filled the atmosphere. The painting was eventually sold to Mr. Duff of Boston for $1,500.00. That notoriety gave clot to Edward's paintings as he continued to make the annual exhibits while making more than a modest income. He was reported to have made a purchase of fine sailing yacht which consumed most of his leisure time sailing around Newport and adjacent points for his own amusement. Edward's range of figure pieces which mostly were Scriptural eventually caught the attention of the Roman Catholic Church of Providence which then invited him to entertain the original conception of the invitation he called *"Come unto Me all Ye that are Weary and Heavy laden."* Edward's paintings was often described by all viewer and critiques alike was so brilliant and ahead of his time. Until trying to determine his ethnicity, it was impossible until one visited his studio which showcased lovely paintings of his wife, Christiana Carteaux, famous in her own right.

Ms. Bannister, Christiana Carteaux, whose popularity and beauty was famously known and considered the Hub's most successful hairdressers. Mme. Carteaux, as she was known to Boston's "400," descends from a well known Narragansett Indian Chief. Her hair oil cosmetics and perfumes, formulated from her own design were most popular and world renowned. Mrs. Bannister's soft voice and strong Christian character, long flowing hair, tall in statute and stately posture made her a stand-out, as a unique and exotic diva. No doubt the influential in her appearance as well as her profound oration, caused Mrs. Bannister to be instrumental in establishing an *"old Age,"* home for Negro women in Providence. When the Fifty-fourth Massachusetts, a Colored Regiment of the Union Army, gained knowledge of the pay difference became widely known, a number of protest of all who's heart was on the side of justice began to take shape.

White Soldiers were receiving $13.00 a month while it was initially proposed $10.00 a month to the Colored Soldiers. Mrs. Bannister sprang into action immediately upon hearing the news of the disparaging gesture by contacting people of influence to include Governor Andrew of Massachusetts. Christiana contacted several of her influential friends and raised over $4,000.00. Her passionate words were remember for many decades when she address the Fifty-Fourth. *"Stand on your rights," "and the God of Hosts will raise to aid you in your struggle for Justice."* It was known that her words were taken into the battles of history by all its members. But for many years the Fifty-Fourth of Massachusetts were purposely excluded from the pages of history by whites set out on its obscure contributions in military significant during the Civil War. Edward Bannister, her husband credits his success totally to his wife and love for New England. Both he and his wife, charismatic and creativity made them the power couple of their generation. Edward died January 9, 1901 of a heart attack, while

the passing a year later of Christiana in 1902.

Blanche Kelso Bruce *(Pictured on the right)* was appointed Register of the United States Treasury first by President James A. Garfield short term and served from May 21, 1881 to June 5, 1885 and then by President William McKinley from December 3, 1897 to March 17, 1898. The Honorable Mr. Bruce was the only Senator to be an ex-slave, and was also the only Negro at the time to serve a full term as a Representative from Mississippi. He was also the first African-American to serve as Register of the United States Treasury. His period of service as Senator was under the Garfield-Arthur administration and for several months under the Cleveland administration. His widow, went on the serve as Assistant Principal at the Tuskegee Institute Normal School in Alabama until her death in 1923. Blanche was born March 1, 1841, as a slave near Brunswick, in Chariton County, Virginia. His mother, Polly Bruce was a house-slave and Blanche was the product of his slave-owner as his father. Blanche was treated very well and freed by his father once he became of aged and educated him alone with his legitimate children. He then moved to Missouri where he was a printer's apprentice, a trade he had learns from a trade school as apart of his educational development arranged by his father. When the Civil War broke out, Blanche put in an application to join the Union Army, but he was rejected for obvious reasons. He went to school and became a teacher before becoming a porter aboard a steamboat on the then popular Mississippi River routes. After the Civil War and during the Reconstruction Period, Blanche had become a wealthy landowner. Blanche held positions as Sergeant-at-Arms of the State Senate, member of the Levee Board, Sheriff and tax collector of Bolivar County, County Superintendent of Education and newspaper editor. He was a Senator during the Reconstruction period and was succeeded by General J.Z. George on March 4, 1881. He was the District of Columbia recorder of deeds from 1891-1893. Blanche met and married Josephine Beal Wilson in 1878 and had one son Roscoe Conkling Bruce born in 1879. Roscoe bearing the name of Blanche's mentor, Senator of New York, Roscoe Conkling. Blanche Kelso Bruce died March 17, 1898 in Washington, D.C.

Judson Whitlocke Lyons, *(Pictured left)* was born in Burke County, Georgia, on August 15, 1858 as reported by, *"The Washington Bee," of March 26, 1898.* Before and after the Civil war, he attended a local country

school until 1871. Soon thereafter, he was taken to Augusta Institute, later called the Baptist College under the directions of Dr. James T. Robert to study for about six years. It was there he taught some night courses and worked on campus to support himself. In 1880, he became a delegate to the Republican National Convention. He also worked for the Internal Revenue Service for about two years, while studying Law for the very distinguished Law Firm of Gibson and Brendt of Augusta, Georgia. In 1883, Lyons came to Washington D.C. where he attended, Howard University Law School. Needing only a few hours to graduate, did so in only nine months, with honors. In November, 1884, after being admitted to the bar by ex-Judge George Hook Shoemake, Miss Bogkin Wright and Fred T. Lockart. Judson Lyons, allowed him to practice successfully

Devour Us Not

became the first African-American to do so in the state of Georgia. Being the first in 1884, by 1898 that figured of African-American Lawyers being admitted to the Bar in Georgia had risen to fifty. Lyons was soon elected President of Haines College in Augusta, Georgia. He became one of the youngest Politian's ever and nationally known as a prolific speaker. He was appointed as Register of the United States Treasury by President William McKinley becoming the 2nd Negro to hold that post from April 7, 1898 to April 1, 1906. He died June 22, 1924 in Augusta.

William Tecumseh Vernon, a Republican, who became the Register of the United States Treasury, at that time, was the nations highest Governmental post occupied by a Negro and the third Negro ever served at that post. His signature, pictured above, appeared on all United States currency from June 11, 1906 - March 14, 1911. Appointed by President Roosevelt in 1906, Vernon was born in a one room cabin as a slave on July 11, 1871, in Lebanon, Missouri. Lebanon, a Southwest Missouri city in the Ozark Mountains, as reported by, *"The Kansas City Sun," of April 24, 1920*. His parents were Adam, an African Methodist Preacher and Margaret Vernon. Adam who passed January 30, 1916 in Quindaro, Kansas, his home at the time according to, *"The Kansas City Sun," of February 5, 1916*. After receiving his Bachelors degree at Lincoln University in Pennsylvania, he soon became a teacher in the Bonne Terre, Missouri school system for two years. He was later the, principal of an African American school in Lebanon, Missouri for four years. Vernon received his PhD of Divinity and Doctor of Laws from Wilberforce University, Ohio. After resigning from the post as principal to become the first President of Western University at Quindaro, Kansas as apart of a then growing and innovative system of the A.M.E. Church. Western University, being new had but one building, half a dozen students and the only teacher was W.T. Vernon. He remained at post from 1896 to 1906, acquiring 130 acres of land, a faculty of twenty teachers and nearly four hundred students. Formally known as a pulpier, a platform lecturer, commencement orator and writer, Dr. Vernon was also President of Campbell College, a church school in Jackson, Mississippi. He was also pastor of Avery Chapel at Memphis, Tennessee. He also held a position of President of the Colored Anti-Tuberculosis Society of Tennessee. In 1920, he was consecrated a Bishop of the A.M.E. Church and

assigned to the 17th Episcope District of West Africa. He then returned to the United States in 1924 where his serves were required in the South and Midwest and in 1933 he returned to Western University. Bishop Vernon passed away July 25, 1944 and was succeeded in death three days by his wife, Emily.

James Carroll Napier born in Nashville, Tennessee on June 9, 1845 to William C. and Jane E. Napier who were both free Africa-Americans.

"Evening Public Ledger," of September 29, 1915

President William H. Taft appointed Republican James C. Napier to the post of Register of the United States Treasury, making him the fourth African-American in a row to hold that position. He occupied the position from March 15, 1911 to September 30, 1913. James was President of a local Bank in his home state of Tennessee and had to resign to except the appointment. According to, *"The Appeal," of March 25, 1911*, James was considered a man of great wealth and was married to the former Ida Langston, daughter of the Honorable John Mercer Langston. He was the first African-American elected to the United States Congress from Virginia in 1888. Honorable Langston was also the younger brother of fellow abolitionist Charles Henry Langston and the great-uncle of renowned poet Langston Hughes (*James Mercer Langston Hughes*).

In Dallas, Texas, March 3, 1910, as recorded by, *"The Daily Capital Journal," Salem, Oregon, Thursday, March 3, 1910*, the police of Dallas warned Negro residence of impending violence against all Negroes in the city. And quite obvious that the police could not guarantee their safety in light of the recent out breaks. Allan Brooks, a Negro, was accused of sexually assaulting a two and one half year old white girl, named Mary Ethel Buvens who was the daughter of Henry J. Buvens. Brooks initially taken to Sherman and return to Dallas the early morning of the third of March. When rumors spread throughout town that the accuser was to be at the courthouse for trial that morning, an estimated crowd of about 2,000 angry white men ascended to the court-house to invoke their form of cowardly justice. Surrounded by police officers, Allan Brooks was lead in the courtroom that was filled to capacity by spectators and on-lookers that quickly turned into mobsters. Two court appointed Lawyers were initially assigned to defend the Negro, but both refused because of his color. Two more were in agreement to defend the Negro. A pre-planned signal of a whistle-blow was sounded as seemingly every available on-looker leaped towards Brooks, pushing aside the weak surrounding officers. As officer's made their weak attempt to protect Brooks, they were more interesting in securing their own safety in an out-of-control chaotic scene in the courtroom. Brooks was eventually hurled out a two story window to a cement pavement below plus a thousand or more waiting for his in flight body to hit the turf. When his body reached the ground, immediately a swarm of loud, cowardly mobsters descended upon him and began kicking and stomping his already bruised body. A rope was eventually placed about his neck as he was dragged 12 blocks to Elks Arch in the downtown section and he was strung up from the center of arch as the crowds had swelled to over 2,000. The mobsters were so infringed until officers, already intimidated by the large number, dared to interfere in taking him down after he swung back and forth long after his apparent demise. The mob then issued bold warnings to the police department not to attempt any form of rescue for Brooks as the police, out armed and out numbered, retreated. The mob continued their presence at the corpse of Brooks and were prolonged by the continued cat calls directed at the body as if they were awaiting a reply. Getting bored and still thirst for Negro blood, headed for the county jail. Being held in custody were thirty-six year old Burrell Oates who was convicted 7 times for murdering and robbing Sol Aranoff, a white man. Strange enough was the fact that a white man named Holly Vann was convicted by virtue of the evidence against him and his confession, was hang for this crime in 1904. Bob *"Blubber"* Robinson, a Negro, convicted of murdering Frank Wolford, a white man, both detainee's were incarcerated, so the cowardly mob demanded their release to them. The county jail authorities attempted to pacify the crowd by speaking rationally to the them by suggesting the Negroes were not in the county jail rather, they were taken to Ft. Worth by order of Mayor Hay. The crowd still refusing to disburse, so a company of militia had assembled to assist the police officers which had little effect in convincing the

Devour Us Not

"The San Francisco Call," of September 7, 1905

crowd of what had happened earlier in the day would not reoccur. The fire department was eventually called in and soon used streams of cold water on to by then had mounted to about 3,000. The mob so intimidated the firemen of being lynched themselves, rolled up their hoses and departed the area. Then Sheriff Ledbetter by then made his attempt in trying to reason with the crowd, when they turned on him and caused him to flee for the nearest vehicle. After being convinced the prisoners were probably not being held in Dallas, the crowd finally dispersed. The quick thinking of Mayor Hay and Sheriff Ledbetter, making provisions for the prisoners to be taken to Cleburne and eventually Waxahachie saved their lives from the mob that day. But on November 29, 1912 in Waxahachie, Texas, Burrell Oates was hanged after 7 trials with little or no evidence for the murder of Sol Aranoff.

The *San Francisco Call of June 1, 1901*, Modoc County, California reports years of suspicion of the Hall's and Yantis families for thefts in and around the surrounding communities for barbed wire, pieces of harness and articles taken from clothes lines of Lookout, California. Lookout is a small town 10 miles west of Adin. **Calvin Hall**, a Negro of 72 years, had 3 sons from a relationship he had with an American-Indian woman. His sons, **Frank Hall** age 26, **James Hall**, age 19 and **Martin Hall** age 16 all lived and were accused in Lookout. With search warrant in hand, Constable Carpenter, approach the residence of the Hall's ranch and after a period all was arrested. Several incriminating articles were found in the search. Immediately, rumors of threats were directed at the Hall and Yantis (*white*) families. Calvin was charged with petty larceny, consisting of pilfering of several hayforks only and initially set free. His sons of Frank, James and Marin, plus B.D. Yantis, a 27 year old white man were charged with burglary and remained in custody. A bond of $300 procured by the Justice of the Peace was set for which the four were unable to acquire. Supposedly, there were no jails in Lookout so the four were taken to a Lookout Hotel. Constable Carpenter, assisted by R. Nichols, J.W. Brown and S. Goyette were assigned in two guard teams to guard the detainees. Calvin was allowed to stay at the hotel as a quest so he could be near his son's until their trial which was scheduled in a few days. At 2 o'clock in the morning, without warning, and as silent as the calm of night, between thirty and fifty masked men appeared in front of the hotel, rushed inside and pointed barrels of loaded guns at the guards Brown and Goyette, then advised them not to interfere in their actions.

The guards later acknowledged, there was no need to swift the four in custody away, so they though for petty theft and offered no aggressive move towards impeding these thugs from carrying out their evil plan. Brown and Goyette were disarmed and told them to assist them. The mob then broke into the rooms of all to include Calvin, who was not under arrest and dragged them into the street. The mob headed for the Pitt River, particularly the bridge that spans the river. It was said of Frank, the eldest son of Calvin offered the most resistance as the mob nearly chocked him to death before the lynching for his defying efforts. The mob attributed his spicy mannerism to his Indian heritage acquired from his mother. Calvin, the 72 year old was hanged first at the north end of the bridge followed by the other four one by one. And just as quick and silent were their efforts in carrying out these needless crimes, were their presence at the scene. As they quickly and silently disbursed without leaving a trace of evidence. When the bodies of the five victims were discovered the next day, news spread as thrill-seekers rushed to the bridge from far and near in a craved effort to see the mobs work. Sheriff Street of Modoc County, the Coroner and District Attorney Bonner left Alturas to conduct an investigation once the news was wired. No one offered any information to include the two guards accompanying the mob of the responsible parties.

Amanda Smith, (*pictured on the right*) a famous Negro Evangelist was born at Long Green, Maryland, January 23, 1837 to the parentage of Samuel Berry and Mariam Matthews. Born a slave on the Darby Insor's Plantation who was her father's master while a nearby farm of Shadrach Green is where her mother resided as a slave-housemaid. Her father purchased his own freedom and the freedom of his wife and all his children according to, *"The Colored American," of May 2, 1903*. Soon after purchasing the entire family, they moved to Pennsylvania. Because of slavery, Amanda's education totaled to only three months. She was converted to her religious

beliefs in March, 1856. Furthering her religious growth was fueled by the teachings of Bishop Taylor of Africa and Bishop Thoburn of India who molded her into the profound lecturer she became. In 1893, Amanda wrote a book titled, *"The Story of the Lord's Dealings with Amanda Smith,"* which was about the story of her life. She was also the founder and manager of the Chicago Industrial Orphanage bearing her name for Colored children. The orphan home at 305 147th St., was well received in the city of Harvey, Illinois near Chicago by rich and poor, black and white. Sister Smith as she was affectionately known, June, 1901 was seriously when injured she was thrown from a carriage. A temporary set back of internal injuries but it wasn't long before Sister Smith was back to her Christian gospel while traveling to Africa, England, India, Scotland and many other countries where she was warmly received. She also lectured at the World's Fair in 1893. Her unctuous ability to expound on Biblical scriptures was captivating to all listening ears. One of her quotes was, *"There are just two things in the Bible: "It shall come to pass," and "It came to pass."* Amanda was so compassionate about people and always offered her assistance to help the needy. Beverly Payne, a Negro, former General in the Liberian Army and former vice consul of the United States at Honrovia. Mr. Payne died September 24, 1900 in the home of Amanda at Harvey, Illinois. The family was not financially able for his final arrangements. Amanda used her influence to raise the amounts necessary to satisfy the final bill of her friend, before the undertaker would release his body to the family which took four months. Amanda died March 1915 in Sebring, Florida at the age of 78.

A crowd of about ten thousand to include women, gathered and danced for joy at the lynching of a Negro as reported by, *"The Times and Democrat," of November 13, 1909*. The crowd was so large that it scoured the entire counties from Karnak to Vienna, Illinois, a distance of about sixteen miles. The body of Ms. Annie Pelley, a white woman was found, bruised and gagged in an alley of Cairo, Illinois, resulting from a fierce fight and struggle. **Will James**, a Negro who had recently come from the south was allegedly targeted and supposedly confessed to the murder. In his confession, Will also named Arthur Alexander, a Negro as apart of the attack on Ms. Pelley. Governor Deneen appealed to Sheriff Davis after he reported strong mob activity that stormed the jail with massive numbers requested militia troops. Sheriff Davis anticipated the violence, only with James and a Deputy was on the run for more than 24 hours before the evitable. Driven from town to town in avoidance of the mob, Sheriff Davis took to the woods but was eventually found between Karnak and Belknap, Illinois, lying on the banks of a creek. With little resistance from the officers, the mob took James from them after some type of consequential dialog of their decision was made. James was then taken back to Cairo and lynch in the most

—New York Times.

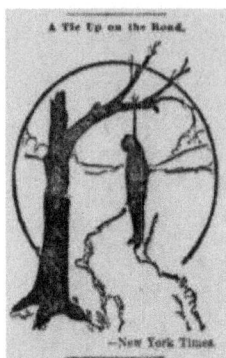

"The Paducah Sun," of January 6, 1904

prominent part of the city to a telegraph pole. Women were invited to first pull the rope which broke and James hit the ground. The mob so dissatisfied by that outcome was then compelled to fill his body with over estimated 500 bullets, literally ripping his body in pieces. The remaining parts of his body were then dragged for more than a mile to Twenty-Sixth and Elm street in an alley and burned his body near to where the assault had taken place. The mob, still unsatisfied with brutal murder of Will James and feeling invincible towards any law-enforcement officer to interfere, stormed the jail and gained access to Henry Salzner, a white man, and photographer, accused of murdering his wife of two years with an axe. Mrs. Salzner's bloody body was found under the bed and their two children were playing in their mother's blood. Henry was then arrested at his mother's home where he often spent the night. The mob already resentful of Salzner's alleged crime was more than eager when it was suggested he be the next lynched victim. After a half an hour of blows to the steel structured door, Salzner was apprehended by the mob and taken out the back door. He was taken to Twenty-First Street and Washington Avenue, with a rope around his neck was allowed to make a statement, when he involved his sister as the culprit in his wife's death. Crying most piteously for his life, the mob allowed him a short religious moment before their impatience ran out. A strange white man stepped forward and acknowledged his feelings of declaring the innocence of Salzner. And before he could utter an explanation of his theory, he was met with volume of screams, kicks and blows that removed him from the platform. He was only saved because of a few level headed mobsters that pleaded with the others that spared his life. After Salzner was strung up, his body was then riddled with bullets which some inadvertently cut the rope causing Salzner's body to hit the ground. When the body hit the ground, the shooting stopped and the mob then disbursed leaving the bullet filled body on the ground where it had fallen. No investigations were ever launched for either crime of the lynched Illinoisans' despite being unmasked.

"Col. Robert Reed Church" *"Mary Church Terrell"*
"The Colored American," June 9, 1900 *"The Colored American," of January 3, 1903*

Mary Church Terrell (September 23, 1863 – July 24, 1954), according to record keeping, Mary Church Terrell was one of the first African-American women after emancipation to receive a college degree. Daughter of a former slave, she became an activist of several suffrage groups in America, representing both males and females and blacks and whites. Born in Memphis, Tennessee to the parentage of **Col. Robert Reed Church** and Louisa Ayers. Robert Church was known as a mulatto and more likely the son of his white master,

Charles Church. He became a millionaire from his dealings in real-estate investments in the Memphis and surrounding areas and was rumored to have been married twice. When Terrell was six years old, her parents sent her to the Antioch College Model School in Yellow Springs, Ohio where she completed her elementary and secondary education. Mary Terrell's nick-name within her family circle was *"Mollie,"* and her brother was born during their father's first marriage, which eventually ended in divorce. Their half-siblings, Robert, Jr. and Annette, were born during their father's second marriage, to Anna (*Wright*) Church. Mary was excepted to Oberlin College where she majored in *"Classics."* Most of her classmates were white males. Despite the large

Mary Church Terrell   **Judge Robert H. Terrell**
"Richmond Planet," of Aug 27, 1910   "The Colored American," of Oct 24, 1903

racial and gender gap, Mary was nominated as class poet, and then elected to two college's literary societies. Mary Terrell also served as an editor of the Oberlin Review. Mrs. Mary Church Terrell graduate from Oberlin in 1884, to become one of the first African-American women to accomplish that honor. She also received her Masters from Oberlin College in 1888 and studied abroad in both Berlin, Germany and Paris, France. Mary Terrell was the first President and honorary President of The National Association of Colored Women. She was Trustee of Public Schools for the District of Columbia for eleven years, a delegate to the International Congress of Women and visited Berne, Switzerland in May, 1919. She was also Vice President of The Booker T. Washington Memorial Association, that erected a monument for Booker T. Washington. She then became Trustee of the Hartsborne Memorial College of Richmond, Virginia. She Spoke fluent Italian, German and French, and had 3 daughters die in infancy and 2 adopted daughters named Mary and Phyllis Goines who was married to Lt. William C. Goines. Mary attended the conference in Berlin, Germany in 1904 where she was a keynote speaker. On October 18, 1891, **Mary Church Terrell** married Republican **Judge Robert Heberton Terrell**, who became the first African-American Municipal Court Judge in Washington, D.C. who was nominated three times by Presidents to include President Roosevelt. He was first nominated by then President William Howard Taft in 1910 and later reappointed in 1914 by then President Wilson and Attorney General McReynolds. He was also confirmed five times in 18 years by the Senate, despite stiff opposition from Southern Senators. It was suggested that Senator Vardaman of Mississippi, one of the biggest racist in Washington at the time, who had previously tried to block the appointment voted no objection to the reappointment. In 1901, then Attorney's Terrell and Hewlett were appointed with eight white men as civil magistrates. In 1905 Congress reduced these ten Justices of the Peace to just six and that number include Judge Terrell. In that same year, the Peace Courts were abolished by Congress and five Municipal Courts were established with jurisdiction amounting to $500.00 and Judge Terrell was the only one of the originals retained. Judge Terrell also graduated *cum laude* from Harvard University and Howard University Law. Mrs. Terrell, a Republican was appointed at the National Republican Headquarters in New York City where she was in charge of campaign work in the Eastern Division among Colored women. Though, having no vote, she was picked by Henry Lincoln Johnson whom was also a vote-less participant of the Republican Party 1920. *"The Appeal," of November 2, 1907,* during one of her noted lectures stated:

"By a continual exaggeration of the Afro-American's vices; by a studied suppression of the proofs of his marvelous advancement; by a malicious use of epithets, such as the scarecrow of social equality, the bugaboo which mislead and poison the skepticism with respect to evidence of his marvelous advancement along all lines, but with a convenient credulity with respect to every report or tradition which can be used to prove his inferiority and depravity, the South has almost succeeded in persuading the whole world that it is a martyr and the Afro-American a brute. "The rapidity with which the South has poisoned the mind of the North against the Afro-American, and has actually alienated the sympathy and support of thousands who were formerly our good friends, is a splendid tribute to the persuasiveness, the plausibility, the persistency, and the power of the South, while it resembles nothing so much as a skillful trick of legerdemain."

Every word of the foregoing is absolutely true, yet a number of *"good Negroes,"* at once came

121   *Devour Us Not*

forward and denied Mrs. Terrell's statement, one Dr. Childs of Washington, D.C. who stated: *"The fate of the Colored people rested upon merit, and was judged by much the same standards as those applied to the white man."* It was later suggested that Dr. Childs ought to travel through Georgia or Texas, and he would soon learn that he was not, *"judged by the same standards as those applied to the white man,"* was Mary's pointed reply. Mary Church Terrell died July 24, 1954 at the age of 91. Judge Robert Terrell suffered a stroke in 1921, followed by another stroke a year later leaving him paralyzed. Judge Terrell died in Washington, D.C. in December 1925.

Phillips County, Arkansas as reported by the, *"Cayton's Weekly," of January 17, 1920,* the troubles that occurred the year before in Phillips County, where the Negroes outnumbered the whites, four to one was the constant rumors that the Negroes would someday organize and massacre the whites. Based on this premise of fear, anytime a gathering of Negroes were spotted the assumptions by suspicious white on-lookers were the uprising was imminent. Out of this panic, caused the riot of September 30, 1919 in Elaine, Arkansas where five whites and some two hundred Negroes by some estimation were killed. Initially, the reporting of bias newspaper articles by white sympathizers reported Edward Ware, the supposed ring leader of an organized effort to raise the price of cotton. The hike from forty to fifty cents in several counties that included Phillips was widely rejected. Ware and a preacher, named Will McFarland were eventually caught in Algiers, Louisiana, after rumors of $100 bounty for the two being implicated in an up rising had surfaced as reported by a Louisiana paper, *"The Era-leader," of November 13, 1919.* The initial killing of O. R. Lilly, a white man member of the board of alderman for the city of Helena, Arkansas was killed by a number of Negro men as reported by, *"The North Platte Semi-Weekly Tribune," of October 10, 1919.* That death in retaliation of several other Negroes was the beginning of the riot. White Federal troops were called in because of the out numbered whites in the area. The mob of whites along with Federal troops being mislead into thinking the Negroes were the instigators; as ill-equipped and passive as most Negroes were; made a "turkey shoot," of a massacre for most Negroes who were simple on their way by foot somewhere. Some 200 Negroes were eventually rounded up and placed in a stockade for interrogation.

After a year of investigative reporting by the NAACP discovered that the Negroes had organized themselves, however it was to protect themselves against exploitation by certain white farm-owner's. These whites were either descendants of slave-owners or slave-owners themselves, were set out on taking advantage of the Negroes assumed lack of knowledge. The NAACP also helped raise about $50,000.00 for proper counsel for the *"Elaine Negroes."* There were even rumors of civil law suits being proposed for the blatant disregard of the Negroes civil and Constitutional rights. Guilt seems to side with ones own thoughts, if the honor of integrity was not followed. Oddly enough, there had been similar protest by white tenants, if the unfairness of the mulcted of their product was questioned with little or no protest from the white land-owners. Yet the Negroes for decades had taken it without protest, mainly because of the lack of knowledge and fear of the evitable. And like most gatherings by Negroes, assumingly, they'd be left alone, generally occurred in the local Church. Even during slavery days, the only hollowed sacred grounds where Negroes could gather without the watchful eye of a white overseer was the Church. Apparently, it was at one of these meetings in Hoop Spur, when a party of white

"The Paducah Sun," of February 18, 1903

men on horseback were riding by when one of them fired a shot into the crowd of Negro gatherers. Eventually arrest was made of all Negroes involved in the so-called uprising. They were Robert Knox, Ed Colman, Ed Hicks, Franks Hicks, Frank Moore and Paul Hall, as their case went as far as to the United States Supreme Court after the State Supreme Court found them guilty and sentenced them to die in the electric chair. Also, Edward Ware, Will Wordlow, Albert Giles, Joe Fox, John Martin and Alf Banks, Jr., were also charged and were appealing their sentences at the State Supreme Court level. But, most noticeable during the trial after the indictments, were no Negro jurors, because all Negroes had been purposely disenfranchised in Arkansas. The indictment of about 122 Negroes with false charges of murder, conspiracy and insurrection were set in motion for a quick execution. Few whites were indicted that were apart of the so-called uprising contributors and generally shared in similar circumstances. These 122 were subject to beatings, death threats, torture and electric shock in an effort to force a confession. A supposed deal was eventually made for some of the 122 to be set free if they were to testify against the others and also, have them work for an unspecified period of time without wages, overseen by white land-owners. For those accepting that proposal was then set free, others refusing were labeled as ring-leaders or trouble-makers and indicted. During each trial of the 12 Negroes indicted as ringleaders, were the swiftness of the case, with each taking less than an hour and sentencing less than eight minutes. That sixty or so others who expected to claim guilty to second degree murder were not brought to trial, rather they were given various jail sentences up to 21 years. Many of the Southern bias newspaper reporting's applauded the efforts of the jury in having compassion in not recommending hanging and the decisive manner they performed their civic duty by quick rendering of their so-called justice. But, bottom line in Moore v. Dempsey, the United States Supreme Court vacated six of the twelve guilty verdicts convictions in 1923 on the grounds that the bias manner in which the mob-dominated atmosphere of the trial and the expedient manner in the trial itself lean prudence to the argument of less than fair-play. And the use of testimony coerced by torture denied the defendants' due process required by the Fourteenth Amendment to the United States Constitution shed light into the Southern standard court proceedings conducted for the Negroes. The other six men went back to trial and received sentences of 12 years. The legitimacy of the NAACP received much praise for their efforts in coming to the aid of the Elaine Negroes which help promoted a since of not being all alone in a corrupt system of Southern non-justice.

Amanda America Dickson, was known as one of *"the wealthiest Negress in the country,"* according to, *"The Anderson Intelligencer," of June, 14, 1893.* Amanda died suddenly, June 11, 1893 at 5 am in the morning at her home, 542 Telfair St., a very affluent mixed neighborhood in Augusta, Georgia. Amanda was buried the following day at the Colored Trinity Methodist Church grounds in Augusta. She had the finest metallic coffin, laced in mouse colored plush as she was laid in an eternal rest dressed in her wedding dress. The 43 year old, mulatto was the product of a white slave-owner father, named **David Dickson** and a mulatto slave mother named Julia Frances Lewis Dickson. David (*pictured on the right*), was known as one of Georgia's most wealthiest and successful farmers ever.

"The Orangeburg News," of December 4, 1869

Devour Us Not

LOST

"Mose, I hear that your son Pete is a good for nothing darkey?"
"Yassah. Deed he is. Dat boy tryin' ter make two wild oats grow whar one grew befo'?"
————o——o————

"The Day Book " of Jan 10, 1916

in Hancock County, Georgia to the parentage of Thomas and Elizabeth Sholars Dickson. His father, a native of Virginia served in the Revolutionary Army when after the war he settled his family in Georgia. His mother, Elizabeth, was born in North Carolina in 1777 and lived with her son David after her husband passed away. She eventually died in 1864. It was said that she was very fond of Amanda, the only child David would have, despite being illegitimate and forbidden by law. David Dickson's wealth was acquired through hard work that started in 1835 when he entered into a partnership with Col. Thomas M. Turner and opened a store in Sparta, Georgia for some years. In 1846, concluding his mercantile business he returned to the place of his birth, with about $25,000 in capital he acquired in his trade. When the Civil War broke out, his property, located on the Little Ogeechee River in adjoining counties of Hancock and Washington where his property was then value at

$500,000.00, covering some 15, 600 areas. He also owned another 13,000 areas in Texas and over 500 slaves at one time he freed before the Civil War. David's method of crop planting was the envy of every farmer in the south. Many agriculture advisers and farmer from far and near would visit his showcase plantation with amazement what he was able to accomplish. A rotation of crop, fertilizering and cultivating were keys to his success in addition to his savvy business sense. David Dickson died a millionaire on February 13, 1885 and left his only, yet illegitimate daughter by one of his slaves, a reported $487,000.00.

Amanda America Eubanks Dickson Toomer
November 20, 1849 - June 11, 1893

Amanda America Eubanks Dickson was born November 20, 1849 as a slave on the plantation of her white father slave-owner, David Dickson, Hancock County Plantation of Georgia. Her mother, Julia was believed to have been about 12 years of age, when Amanda was born. David was believed to be about 40 years of age. According to, *"The San Antonio Light," of December 3, 1885,* David lived most of his life as a bachelor and only married in 1870 to Clara Harris, a white woman, who lived as his wife for only two years before dieing childless. Much to the debate of the majority of his white relatives, mainly the children of his brother and sister living in New York, Texas and Georgia. Normally, the entire estate would have gone to them but Amanda

had Colonel Charles W. Du Bose of Sparta, one of the best Lawyers in the country, hired by David before he passed. The family disputed the sanctity of David Dickson for leaving Amanda $487,000.00 and hiring several administrators to ensure it was carried out as he wished. He made it perfectly clear with several Attorneys' because he knew there would be challenges not only from his blood relatives but others thinking it were too much money for a Negro. He even made provisions for Amanda to live with one of his siblings and supposedly cousin of Amanda named the *"Eubanks."* They also questioned his supposed infatuation with Negro women and being single most of his adult life. David did however, make provisions for his favorite blood Niece and Nephew, to receive $5,000.00 each of his sister's children $2,000.00 to each as well as his brother's children. He gave a $1,000.00 to a half a dozen others and $25,000.00 to Julia, Amanda's mother. No sooner than the Will was offered for probate did the bickering begin. Amanda and her mother immediately moved to Augusta. The case was tried before the Hancock Superior Court, Judge Lumpkin presiding. Of course the unmitigated gual of a *"Negress,"* description made by all newspapers and surrounding communities, to think she'd be entitled to the estate of a white man when she was illegitimate. With the Superior Court, the jury ruled in favor of honoring the Will of David, regardless of what bloodline, race or any other factors may suggested otherwise.

The case then went to the Supreme Court where Amanda's case was upheld to much protest to no avail, making Amanda the wealthiest African-American woman in the world reported by the, *"Fort Worth Weekly Gazette," of July 1, 1887.* Sometimes during 1886, she purchased her residence at 452 Telfair St. A double brick house, three stories high, containing twelve or fifteen rooms, shaded in front by three mammoth oaks, a large yard surrounding the property in a very sophisticated community. Amanda owned a business in Augusta named Howard & Co.

Nathan Toomer

"The Breckenridge News," January 30, 1907

Amanda eventually married and divorced her white cousin, Charles Eubanks in 1866 after he returned from fighting in the Civil War. Amanda and Charles had two sons, Julian Henry born in 1866 and Charles Green born in 1870 and soon there after Amanda divorced Charles Eubanks. Julian eventually married Eva

"The Day Book," of January 22, 1914 Walton, daughter of Isabella and George Walton of Augusta. Charles married Kate Holsey, daughter of Harriet and **Bishop Lucius Holsey** from Augusta also. Amanda married Nathan Toomer, as a mulatto boy during slavery; he was sold in Chatham County, North Carolina to a man named

Toomer as his body servant. He later became a Lawyer, who was first married to Harriet and had two daughters before marring Amanda August, 1892. Nathan later became the wealthiest Negro in the south after his wife of less than a year, Amanda suddenly died of nervous exhaustion, June, 1893, without a will. Her son's reportedly received $100,000 each and her husband apart of her estate as well as apart of their grandfather's will. Amanda and Nathan had three sons, Henry born 1876, Walter born in 1877 and Fred born in 1879. Nathan Toomer later married Nina Eliza Pinchback. Nina was the

"The Washington Bee," of Aug 29, 1908

"The Colored American," Oct 6, 1900

daughter of the first African-American Lt. Gov. and Governor Pickney B.S. Pinchback of Louisiana, elected December 1871(*Pictured left & right*). To this marriage a son was born named Nathan Eugene Pinchback Toomer (*His adopted Professional name of Jean was later used*) born December 26, 1894 and later became a famous author of the 1923 best seller book titled *"Cane."*

April 20, 1893 an attempt was made to kidnap Mamie Toomer, an heiress and the daughter of Nathan Toomer. Dunbar Walton, Carrie Wilson, and Jacob Calhoun all Colored men and Louis E. Franks a white man were all arrested on kidnapping charges. There was even a bribe offered to Squire John Gensler to issue a fictitious summons for the subjected girl to appear before the court in an effort to secure her. In having the girl appear by summons would allow the authorization to pick her up from the Asylum and

"The Washington Times," of March 16, 1911

hence a so called legitimized kidnapping. Franks was to be the cab driver and Calhoun was to use the court ordered summons to pick her up. The strange and twist of this alleged kidnapping by Calhoun and Frank was that the 14 year old beautiful Mulatto girl was as white as an Angelo and was recently placed as a student at St. Francis Colored Catholic Orphan Asylum. Her Stepmother, who was none other than Amanda America *"Marie"* Eubanks Dickson, who had recently received a fortune of $487,000.00 through the bequest of David

"The New York Sun," of May 20 1894

Dickson, a white man and her father from Augusta. Mrs. Eubanks, through the Georgia Legislature, had her name changed to Dickson, her biological white father's last name from her married name of Eubanks who was the nephew of father. After that unsuccessful marriage, she then was engaged and eventually got married to Nathan Toomer in 1892. A suit was filed on Mamie Toomer's behalf and she received $50,000.00. Charles Dickson, son of Mrs. Amanda Toomer and a stepbrother of Mamie Toomer by marriage, desired to marry her. Mamie didn't object and appeared to be in love. Her Stepmother, Amanda, was also in favor of the marriage to her son. Objections were displayed by Mr. Nathan Toomer, who then brought her to the St. Francis Colored Catholic Orphan Asylum on March 10, 1893. The Stepmother, Amanda, it was said that she offered Mr. Toomer $15,000.00 to let the girl go free to marry whom she wished. Mr. Toomer told police Captain Baker that his primary objection of Charles Dickson to marry his daughter in Canada was related to a rumor that had surfaced that Charles Dickson was already married to Kate Holsey. A trial was held by Judge Dennis in the Criminal Court, Baltimore, Maryland without a jury to render a verdict. According to, *"The Stark County Democrat," of March 28, 1895* each defendant in their participation in the conspiracy kidnapping case was fines $100 each while Franks, the lone white cab-driver was fined $25.

Toomer then filed a $100,000.00 law suit against Pullman Palace Car Company. On June 5, 1893, Colonel Toomer engaged a section of sleepers from Baltimore to Augusta accompanied by his wife. But the sleeper switched at Columbia where the Toomer's claimed for 24 hours they were trapped in the freight yard exposed to the elements of heat from the sun and the smells of diesel engines oil which made his wife very ill. Reportedly a Physician had to be called in for Amanda. Mrs. Amanda Toomer eventually returned to Augusta, but within 2 days died. According to the purchased ticket by the Toomer's, there were no previsions for a delay or switch. The delay and subsequent over exposure to the elements were contributing factors to Mrs. Amanda America Dickson Toomer's untimely death according to, *"The Evening Bulletin," of July 31, 1893.*

1880 U.S. Census. Toomer, Nathan . Georgia, Houston County, Upper 14 Dist. Age: 41, Race: Mulatto, Born: NC; Wife-Amanda age 25 & 3 Sons-Henry age 4, Walter age 3 and Fred age 1.

After the death of Amanda America Eubanks Dickson Toomer in 1893, Nathan Toomer married Nina Eliza Pinchback in 1894. Nathan Toomer soon abandon his family in September 1895, as Nina Eliza Pinchback Toomer filed for divorce in 1898 after only four years of marriage. He was then ordered to pay Alimony by Judge Cox, a claim of no support offered by his then wife Nina. Nina later married a painter and decorator named A. Combs in 1905. Nina dies at her home in New Rochelle, New York on June 9, 1909 after an operation for appendicitis. She was buried at Beechwood Cemetery, New York; she was 38 years of age.

Louisiana laws are peculiar in nature as a commonwealth. Unlike many other systems not influenced by France or Spain, America is a country of immigrants. Their laws clearly based on the civil laws of Rome and a one race system, under minds the multi-cultural system of America regardless of class. The arrest of Homer Adolph Plessy on June 7, 1892 for violating the Louisiana 1890 Separate Car Act because he didn't move to the car designated for *"Colored Passengers"* started a landmark doctrine of *"Separate but Equal."* Completely hostile to the Constitution of the United States of justice for all, the ruling adopted mostly by Southern states to clearly disenfranchise African-American citizens of America, did so for over sixty years. A ruling that would plague the minds of all American until 1954 when the Supreme Court overturned the decision in the *Brown v. Board of Education* and set the plate form for the Federal Civil Rights Act of 1964.

Obviously, *Plessy v. Ferguson* case wasn't based on education but the premise of generalizing the racial issue of keeping the races separate as a Jim Crow policy was the intent. The Plessy

"Akron Daily Democrat," of August 3, 1901

Supreme Court Justices who made the decision on Plessy v. Ferguson in 1896

Stephen J. Field- *(R) Appointed by Abe Lincoln* , **Rufus W. Peckham**- *(D) Appointed by Grover Cleveland* , **Horace Gray**- *(R) Appointed by Chester Arthur* , **Melville W. Fuller**- *(D) Appointed by Grover Cleveland* .
* *Newspaper Article photo appears: "The San Francisco Call," October 15, 1897, "Los Angeles Herald," October 25, 1909 , "Richmond Dispatch," August 12, 1902, "Richmond Dispatch," November 21, 1902.*

David J. Brewer- *(R) Appointed by Benjamin Harrison,* **Henry B. Brown**- *(R) Appointed by Benjamin Harrison,* **George Shiras, Jr.**- *(R) Appointed by Benjamin Harrison* , **Edward D. White**- *(D) Appointed by Grover Cleveland* .
* *Newspaper Article photo appears: "The Ogden Standard," February 17, 1910, " Deseret Evening News," April 7, 1906, " Pittsburg Dispatch," October 11, 1892, "The Citizen," December 15, 1910.*

Devour Us Not

case named in part for Judge John Howard Ferguson who first rejected the racial argument of as long as things were equal but separate no violation for Homer Plessy's Fourteenth Amendment rights were violated. Equal protects under the law set the bases for defending whites rights not to associate with races other than their own in schools, buses, railcars, churches etc. So this enshrined doctrine would be the cornerstone argument for keeping the races apart in any setting. African-Americans fought this law in Louisiana for years to no avail. So an arrangement was planned for Homer to challenge the law legally in 1892 followed by his assured arrest and conviction. The Citizens Committee of New Orleans recruited Homer for this purpose of challenging the appearance of the law or the letter of the law. A first class ticket was purchased for the route from New Orleans to Covington. Through whatever curiosity caused the conductor to question Homer's race may have been a plan of the committee as well. Because it was rumored that there was a committee Detective on board purposely to arrest Homer for the challenge. After several defeats in local courts, the case was then sent to the Supreme Court in 1896 as *Plessy v. Ferguson*. Homer, as described by many as appearing *"7/8 white,"* and could have unnoticeably ridden the car seated as a white man. Born, March 17, 1862, to the

parentage of reportedly 2 free African-Americans, must have undoubtedly had some Creoles, French or Spanish in his blood-line. The committee's plan to gain recognition from the highest court in the land was a risk understood by the committee but they were willing to risk it all. Challenge not only the Dred Scott decision but put an end to all law changes that hampered any American from their birth given entitlements of justice for all.

John M. Harlan- Supreme Court Judge(R) Appointed by Rutherford Hayes
Newspaper Article photo appears: "The Colored American," December 22, 1900.

Albion Winegar Tourgee- Lawyer of Homer Plessy
"The Washington Times." of July 20, 1902

Justice John Marshall Harlan (*pictured above*) was born in Boyle County, Kentucky, June 1, 1833 and died at the age of 78, at 8:15 am, the morning of October 14, 1911 as reported by, *"The Tacoma Times,"* of October 14, 1911, of an acute attack of bronchitis that started as a cold. He had gained a Nobel title of *"Lone Dissenting Member"* for his vote in the infamous *Plessy v. Ferguson* case, May 18, 1896. The Honorable Mr. Harlan was married to the daughter of John Shanklin of Evansville, Indiana, Malvina F. Shanklin on December 23, 1856. His parents named him after Chief Justice John Marshall, unbeknownst at the time how his life would turnout and be influenced by the inevitable. Upon Mr. Harlan's death, he was one of the longest sitting Judge's on the Supreme Court bench in the United States history, totaling 33 years, 10 months and 25 days. Appointed By then President Rutherford Hayes, November, 1877 at age 44. Justice Harlan had 3 son's named, John Maynard Harlan, Rev. Dr. Richard D. Harlan, James S. Harlan and 2 daughter's named Ms. Laura Harlan and Ms. Ruth Harlan. During the Civil War, he served for three years as Colonel of the 10th Kentucky Regiment of the Union Army.

In the Supreme Court decision, the vote was 7 to 1 against the plaintiff, Homer Plessy. Most of the southern judges so far removed from the interest of fairness and equal rights for all under the Constitution were common place. Their failure to see the injustice and violation of civil and legal rights for Negroes was directly related in part to the Dred Scott decision of 1857. All but one voted for Plessy, the Honorable Mr. Harlan, who was

"The Mercur Miner," of February 12, 1908

ahead of his time, or was he? Justice Harlan voted against the abolishment of slavery, the Thirteenth Amendment, and was a slave-owner himself at one time. But Justice Harlan in his defense, being witness to the atrocities of post emancipation and the Reconstruction Period which was worst than slavery itself, in his own opinion. There were even reports of an alleged illegitimate child born to a Negro woman, fathered by Justice Harlan. But Justice Harlan believed in, "all citizens are equal before the law." Justice Harlan then wrote: *"I am of the opinion that the statute of Louisiana is inconsistent with the personal liberty of citizens, white and black, in that state and hostile to both the spirit and letter of the Constitution of the United States."* But, all others except Associate Justice David Josiah Brewer who did not rule because of his daughter's death the day before, was not in attendance. Justice Henry Billings Brown wrote the majority opinion for The Supreme Court in Plessy v. Ferguson, 163 U.S. 256: *"Laws permitting and even requiring their separation in places where they are liable to be brought into contact do not necessarily simple the inferiority of either race to the other, and have been generally, if not universally, recognized as within the competency of the state legislatures in the exercise of their police power. The most common instance of this is connected with the establishment of separate schools for white and Colored children, which have been held to be a valid exercise of the legislative power even by courts of states where the political rights of the Colored race have been longest and most earnestly enforced."* According to the, *"Richmond Planet," of May 23, 1896*, editorialized the decision that public sentiments influenced the greatest judicial body in the world. It went on to say that the decision ignored the equal rights of Negroes and will help promoted discrimination, persecution and murder. In hindsight no truer words were realized in determining that, that decision in its bringing evil days and divide the country along racial lines.

Rosa Louise Parks died October 24, 2005, at the age of 92. When Rosa Parks died, millions in America and all around the globe mourned her passing as her casket was honorably placed in the **rotunda** of the United States Capitol for two days. This was the highest and most historic gesture this country had ever bestowed upon a woman and lest of all a woman of color. If you can imagine for a moment, how many times had a person of color been ask to remove themselves from a seat, normally paid for like every other riding customer, and commanded to move to the rear to the delight and satisfaction of every white person aboard. Refusal of such a command could have very easily resulted into much more harm than just a simple arrest. Such an honor, given to Rosa Parks had been previously reserved for Presidents of the United States **only**. This country and all its citizens owe this remarkable woman a debt of gratitude for; if nothing else, her courage. I purposely started her story with the ending to give some perspective into this courageous woman's life. Somewhat like the Ida B. Wells-Barnett incident that occurred in 1884; December 1, 1955 was the day of the Rosa Parks triumph. At that time, living in Montgomery, Alabama, working as a seamstress, more than likely tired from a long hard days work for pennies, literally, refused to give up her seat to a well-able-bodied white man. The aftermath of her defiance lead to her arrest and fined, but also eventually, ended legal segregation in America. As her case, reluctantly went all the way to the Supreme Court. Much the same way Ida B. Wells-Barnett did some 71 years earlier, the Rosa Parks fight and the bus boycott lasted 382 days. This was the starting point for desegregation and the modern day civil rights movement and

Devour Us Not

the emerging of, "Black Justice." Rosa was born February 4, 1913 as Rosa Louise McCauley in Tuskegee, Alabama to James McCauley, a carpenter, and Leona McCauley, a teacher. Rosa's early life as a child was filled with visual thoughts of the silence of night calm, interrupted as she would hear the rumbling of Klansmen horses, riding in the night while living on her grandparents farm in Pine Level, Alabama. Her visions would take her to recollections of these horsemen riding in the night in search of **"Dixie Sex"** and unsuspecting victims for lynching parties. As the cry of fear stopped on deaf ears of their victims; much to the mobs delight that quenched their blood thirsty desires for their own amusement continued for generations. But that fear which was a common occurrence for people of color in that part of the country resonated itself in her heart and mind for a life time. Recalling the good parts of her life in retirement, Rosa suggest her felling of unhappiness to the thought of the forever reminder that the klan and people like them would always make the life for people of color miserable.

And to the unprovoked victims and their families, that sense of lawlessness with no protection, was hopeless. But acknowledging her felling of fear on the bus that day, seem to have eluted her. She recalls the pain of fear that day, just for that brief moment of defiance was purposely and instinctively, ignored. For the forthcoming consequences of her actions unbeknownst to her at the time would make world history. It was as if a blanket of protection by God himself had been placed on her tired body; the tone of an entire race of people's hope had finally arrived in the body of a slender, middle-aged, tired seamstress that cold December day. And this would be her calling, a continuous workload of injustices while working with the NAACP. Serving on the staff of U.S. Representative, John Conyers, the Southern Christian Leadership Council establishing an annual Rosa Parks Freedom Award in her honor, and the boycott also led to the formation of the Montgomery Improvement Association, led by the young pastor of the Dexter Avenue Baptist Church, Rev. Dr. Martin Luther King, Jr.

Rosa Parks soon founded the Rosa and Raymond Parks Institute for Self-Development. A *"Pathways to Freedom"* was the name of the Institute that sponsored the annual summer program for teenagers. President Clinton presented Mrs. Rosa Louise Parks with the **Presidential Medal of Freedom** in 1996 *(Medal given by the President of the United States for especially meritorious contribution to the security or national interests of the United States, or world peace, or cultural or other significant public or private endeavors. It is awarded to individuals selected by the President or recommended to him by the Distinguished Civilian Service Awards Board)*. She also received a Congressional Gold Medal *(A **Congressional Gold Medal** is an award bestowed by the United States Congress along with the Presidential Medal of Freedom, the highest civilian award in the United States)*. The decoration is also awarded to an individual who performs an outstanding deed or act of service to the U.S. and was awarded in 1999 to Rosa for her tireless acts of civil rights services.

March 6, 1903 was supposed to have been the last official hanging in Duluth, Minnesota and the state. The old jail designed by Oliver Traphagen in 1889, housed Charles Ernest Lafayette Henderson, a 32 year old Negro who had the dubious distinction of being known as the last person to be hanged, officially in the state of Minnesota. Capital punishment was outlawed as cruel and unusually punishment in 1911, officially. But as time marched on, there would be more unofficial hangings most noticeably by mob violence in 1920. Sheriff W.W. Butchart, affectionately nick-named *"Ole W.W.,"* the executioner, gave a thirty minute talk before the hanging. And all day prior to March 6th, the day before the hanging, Henderson was singing old Negro gospel hymns. Only interruption was when the Officer's came into measure him for his coffin and the writing of final letters was the

final full day of his life. His two sisters Mrs. Bessie Lapseley and Mrs. Josephine Heard was with him right up until just before the hanging, they later admitted could not witness. Henderson was hanged at 2 pm in court room number 1 where he had been sentenced. Henderson first presented Sheriff W.W. Butchart with a testament acknowledging the Sheriff's sworn duty and his no malice felt feelings for what he had to do by law. He then handed roses to each deputy, supposedly, thanking them for their kind treatment

Charles Ernest Lafayette Henderson & Ida McCormick

Of him ,according to, *"The Minneapolis Journal," of March 6, 1903.* The flowers had been brought in earlier by his sisters before the hanging. Without any quiver in his voice, admitted to the crime, however expressing no sorrow of the act as being premeditated. But, went on to say he had entered her room unbeknownst to her the

night of June 21, 1902, in their rooming house on 319 W. First Street, after his suspicious was getting the best of him over his thoughts of love lost. He over heard Ms. McCormick, who was later determined to be his biological daughter, no longer loved him and that a new younger lover had entered her life she had met in the restaurant. Unable to contain his anger, he burst from the closet of his hiding and brutally butchered her by stabbing her seventeen times. He was then charged with first degree murder. Her employer, Mrs. Celestine Brown, described her as being born in Kansas, very young and beautiful, very popular and well liked as a waitress at her restaurant on 405-7 Fifth Ave S. **Charles E.L.**

Henderson pictured above left was a veteran of the Spanish American War where he was quartermaster sergeant in the Illinois Volunteers and honorably discharged. He was also considered to be very well spoken attributed to his education and equally well traveled from his military experience. He was also a Bible verse quoting man, and could be often heard humming and singing spirituals. He and Ida had recently arrived in the city from Chicago.

Corinth, Mississippi, August 19, 1902, according to the, *"Corinth-Burlington Weekly Free Press of October 2, 1902,"* Mrs. Carrie Whitfield, the wife of a very prominent local citizen was found dead in her home. An investigation was conducted and it was determine that she was assaulted and her head was practically severed her head from her body. A group from Chicago detective team was sent in as well as surrounding communities of mobsters set out on lawlessness in an effort of bringing harm to an alledged crime of murder. Soon the name of Tom Clark alias Will Gibson, a Negro, who lived near the Whitfield's had been heard making threats to his wife. Supposedly, Clark became a person of interest. It was also determined that Clark had had trouble with his wife and a secret she privy to about a crime was know and she threaten to divulge the contents concerning a crime. The detective team got wind of this information and questioned the woman and she told enough to make Clark a primary suspect. Clark was soon arrested on the information optained from his wife. While in custody, Clark allegedly confessed to murdering Mrs. Whitfield in addition to murdering two other men aboard a train in Mississippi and some type of outrage imposed on a Negro woman that he ingeniously covered-up to confuse police authorities. A citizen committee team had been formed in the search for the guilty party and just

Devour Us Not

gathering information heard the supposed confession and recommend hanging. Clark insisted the execution be delayed so he could give final good-byes to his mother and brother. By telegraph messaging was his request sent for the two parties. In the interim, like water rapids down a slippery slop, word of the violent confession reach far and near throughout Mississippi. People came by the hundreds on trains, horseback, wagons, and by whatever means possible in an effort to see pain inflected upon a guilty Negro. Knowing the impending violence vastly approaching, law authorities did absolutely nothing to secure the prisoner in their custody.

At about 3'oclock, Clark was taken by force from the jail and dragged to the east gate of the Negro cemetery, located in the western part of the city. He was securely fastened to an iron rod embedded in the ground. The loud crowd asked if he'd like to give a statement and Clark handed a letter to one of the mobsters and ask if he'd deliver it to his mother and brother. There was never an opportunity for his relatives to attend his final moments as he *(Clark)* requested. In the letter he appealed to his brother to raise his children properly and with specific advisement to be mindful of evil and disloyal companions. Soon the call was announced to light the torch. His body was soaked with a flammable liquid before the husband and son of Mrs. Whitfield lit the torch. And as quickly as he was taken from authorities, fire spread all over his clothing as Clark moaned and cried before his head went forward and the voice of a human-being was silenced. Then only the cracking of fire on wood was heard. After his charred body was completely burnt to a crisp, the crowd disbursed and walked away from it appearing disappointing because Clark didn't cry out. No one was ever charged or investigated for this crime.

On September 4, 1875, Clinton, Mississippi, considered a dry county, meaning a law prohibing the sale of alcohol was in place. A political rally was being held Saturday where some young white men from Raymond, Mississippi, brought liquor during the meeting. Bare in mind, this was during the period of Reconstruction in America, where Negroes were quickly exercising their right to gain political powers throughout the South. Particularly in Mississippi where there were 170,000 more Negroes than whites as reported by the, *"National Republican," of March 26, 1884.* White League organizations began to submerge themselves all over the South but particularly in Mississippi and Louisiana, its headquarters and origin. Set out on the four major principals of their missions, (1) make census and the enrollment of all white men in their State; (2) incorporate into the interior of any military organizations, local or Federal; (3) set aside to impede, by whatever means necessary, legal or not the election of Negro men to office and nullify the Enforcement Act (4) allow only white men to be elected to office.

As one can imagine, this did not set well in a climate less than a generation before where whites ruled. *"Yasum and No-sa mis-a boss-main,"* was the norm from the Negro's submissive and servitude manners. These changes in the minds of every white were inexorably exacerbating. The Governor of the state of Mississippi was then Governor Adelbert Ames, a carpetbagger and known to have resentment towards Freedmen, was elected as Governor, which set the tone for the hatred in the state. The Governor made every attempt legislatively to kill or slow down the emerging political might of the Freedmen. A native of Maine, Ames was sworn into office January 4, 1874. And with no delay he sanctioned a property tax law in an effort to disenfranchise the Negroes. Because of the political turmoil and racial riots attributed directly to his tenure as Governor, the Democratic legislature made it possible for his Lieutenant Governor, Alexander K. Davis to be impeached. Governor Ames would have also been impeached had he not made a deal to protect his political record. But the deal forced him

"The San Francisco Call," of April 28, 1901

to resign in disgrace, a little over two years in office on, March 20, 1876. Most of the crowd at the political rally of September 4, 1875 was Negroes, to include an armed Negro Marshall. Martin Sively, a white man was identified as the one with the bottle of liquor as he called for his friends over a short distance away to join him for a drink. Noticing what had transpired prompted the Negro Marshall to confront Martin who became defiant and struck the Marshall over the head with the bottle. A Negro Senator named Caldwell observed the incident, went over to control it. By then such a commotion had erupted until about some twenty Negroes went with him. To defuse the incident, Senator Caldwell ordered the Negroes to stay back which only directed the attention of almost everyone at the meeting to rush towards the excitement. Then a shot ring out that cause pandemonium. Upon hearing the shot, Martin Sively emptied his pistol into the crowd. With no more bullets, the crowd angered by the random unprovoked shooting, requested he give up his pistol. Being out numbered did so when someone from the crowd shot him in the head. By this time chaos had over taken the crowd and Martin was then striped of his clothing and his finger was cut off for his ring. The crowd then wondered from the meeting place where Charles Chilton was shot dead in his yard right before his family. About a mile and a half away from that scene, Frank Thomasson, a young promising Lawyer was shot off his horse, after which the crowd then plunged their knifes into his body. John Neal was then fatally shot in the left lung then Waddy Rice was shot in the hand. Four Negroes were found in a field mortally wounded, while six other Negroes were found dead throughout Clinton. Colonel Harding hearing of the shootings and killings organized the whites within the cities of Clinton and Edwards then telegraph for assistance to Jackson and Vicksburg. As soon as the wire reached its intended audience, armed white men hit Clinton like the excitement of a lottery win.

Under the direction of Captain W. H. Andrews, street patrols were established, supposedly to gain order and peace. White men who came by train acknowledged they were fired upon and debris was placed on the tracks in an effort to delay or derail the train. By Sunday, September 5, 1875, still fresh on the minds of the 1874 Vicksburg slaughter of as many as a hundred and fifty Negro citizens, a crowd of over 2,000 mostly from Vicksburg as reported by, *"The Arizona Sentinel," of September 11, 1975*, began déjà vu in Clinton. When daylight hit and the litter of Negroes bodies filled the spaces where land previously occupied, it was an unbelievable sight. In the fields and on roads totaling to at least 500 by some accounts. Negroes who manage to escape in the woods and nearby swamps said it was like the 4th of July for keeps as they witness the slaughter of family and neighbors alike in cold blood. The night air was filled with gun smoke, yells and screams as the rumbling of horses and gunshots echoed the normally quietness of night air and country insect noise. Conflicting accounts from the Government and City Officials were down played in reporting these slaughters. But for the hundreds who could not be accounted for, whose homes were left unoccupied, their livestock left unattended to, and no justification could suffice from what was the truth and fact. The blind eyes of injustice like the year before in Vicksburg, the devouring intent rages on.

- **Case / Point** 1968, in a small all white town in Iowa, **Jane Elliott**, a thirty-five year old third-grade white teacher at Riceville Community School, wanted to teach her all white students about civil rights in

"The San Francisco Call," of June 4, 1911

Jane Eliott

America. Right in the middle of all what was going on with racial prejudice in 1968, she wanted to increase their knowledge and broaden their perspective on racial awareness and tolerance. The idea to her came after watching yet another assassination on TV in a hate society and recalling a novel she had read earlier concerning Germany and the Holocaust. The determination of who (*The Jews*) were chosen to be gassed in their chambers of death first was based on something as elemental as the grade she taught. Germany's obsession in World War II with eye color, was one of the bases for the death sentence to be numerically sequenced. Jane being a native of Iowa, wanting to stop the generational *"cycle of hate,"* decided on the day after Martin Luther King, Jr. 's assassination to give her students a lesson in discrimination. America, in her estimation was obsessed with skin color, having no African-American's in the city to draw a reality test from, needless to say having diversity in her classroom, used eye color as her base. To get a consciousness of where her class was intellectually, she posed the question when one of her students address the issue of Rev. Dr. Martin Luther King, Jr.'s assassination as *"Why did that King get shot?"* Jane in heart was an anti-racism activist and felt compelled to place herself in the middle of much controversy as a result of her experience. Ms. Elliott understood if a question was proposed to give an analysis of what her students thought of *"Colored People,"* she'd get a variety of responses tailored along what they'd heard from their parents or other family members. Colored People was purposely inserted by Ms. Elliott knowing the term besides the *"N"* word was most associated with African-Americans by whites in an area of black absences.

Like Ms. Elliott, these children had not seen any blacks in and around their communities. So, when she received their responses, this is mostly what she heard: *"ignorant, unemployed, lazy, thieves,"* and other stereotypical views plaguing the black race even today. Realizing where their mind set was, Ms. Elliott proceeded with her exercise with the student's approval. What came next was unbelievable and awakened the disease of hate in all of us as a nation in 1968. Ms. Elliott received national notoriety both positively and negatively. After her appearance on the Johnny Carson show, each day, some of her own colleagues walked out of the teacher's lounge when she entered. Hateful glares and other displays of disapproval were faced by Ms. Elliott when in public. I was an eighteen year old sophomore in college when I first became privy to the exercise. My first thought was what a trailblazer of a woman to risk racial isolation and scrutiny which was the initial response. But as time went on, her exercise revolutionized diversity training in this country for the better. What a powerful lesson of race tolerance was imposed by a small framed, high-pitched loud voiced, thin-framed white lady with glasses who stood at the door of controversy, opened it up and told the world, *"Let's fix this now, before another generation passes!"*

- **The Exercise:** First day, Ms. Elliott made a very compelling and convincing argument that the blue-eyed kids were the superior group of kids. Much better than than their brown-eyed peers.
- She had the blue-eyed kids place a brown material fabric around the necks of their brown-eyed peers, as to easily identify them from most distances, thereby planting the seed of hate that the brown-eyed kids were the minority kids.
- The blue-eyed kids were given extra privileges much to their delight, never considering the effect their peers

- were feeling while watching in amazement and envy. They were given second helpings at meal time, access to a new Jungle Jim and 5 extra minutes at recess.
- The blue-eyed kids were allowed to sit in the front of the classroom while the brown-eye kids were seated in the back rows.
- Blue-eyed kids were encouraged not to play or associate with the kids in the brown collars who represented the brown-eyed kids.

"New-York Tribune," September 5, 1915

There were designated water fountains for the blue-eyed kids and a different fountain for the brown-eyed kids. Brown-eyed kids were publicly chastised in full view of the purposely watchful blue-eyed kids when the rules were even forgotten or were not followed per her initial instructions. Ms. Elliott would purposely single out brown-eyed kids and use negative rhetoric, embarrassing them before the entire class.

- Ms. Elliott, within the first fifteen minutes of the experience noticed the students' change in their personalities, particularly with previous friends and the esteem of the minority brown-eyed kids. She was mindful of the resistance among the minority kids in respect to the thought of knowing, per Ms. Elliott's exercise, that blue-eyed kids were far better than brown-eyed kids. This statement caused some resistance from the brown-eyed kids initially, but Ms. Elliott used an unsubstantiated theory of the higher intelligence of blue-eyed kids over their peers of brown-eyed kids, to justify the process.
- Completely buying into this theory like any other eight and nine year olds would, when a convincing teacher expressed her opinion, they'd lived up to her expectations. She also noticed that after the brown-eyed kids accepted the premise of being less intelligent than their blue-eyed peers, they acted the part, and lived down to her expectations. While the blue-eyed kids became boastful, border-line completely arrogant and disrespectful to their minority appointed classmates, a noticeable decline in enthusiasm was observed by the deemed minority kids. The simplest of task previously dominated before the exercise by class leaders became frustratingly problematic for the minority brown-eyed kids. She also recorded grade improvements, mathematical skills were less challenging and reading task reached far beyond what had been observed only a day before for the majority blue-eyed kids.

The following day the roles were reversed. Individually, the previously minority brown-eyed kids did taunt the blue-eyed kids, but collectively, the intensity of the taunts were less and less frequent. It was as if their very inquisitive minds recalled only the day before how they felt, must to have been a contributing factor. When Ms. Elliott ended the exercise by having the blue-eyed kids remove their collars and reiterating the purpose of the exercise, she reassuring each child how special and uniquely different each one was. The kids hugged and cried and removed all boundaries that had been placed on them days before. She had all the children write letters to Coretta Scott King expressing freely what they had learned from the exercise on discrimination. Ms. Elliott explained what was more shocking than the students was the racial insensitivity on behalf of her all white collogues. One female teacher even stated, *"I thought it was about time somebody shot that son-of-a-bitch."* Her first thought was pure amazement; how a well-educated colleague would express such a negative opinion. The responses expressed by the students who were subjected to the exercise were posted in the local newspaper. The nature of Ms. Elliott's exercise has stayed with me all my life and allowed me to understand what we can become as the products of our environment. And constant put-downs can govern your abilities as well as marginalize your potential for life. She and many others like her are trailblazers and will remain my heroes for

Devour Us Not

life.

Mrs. Alice Strange Davis was born in Lynchburg, Virginia, April 21, 1861 as recorded by *"The Colored American," of August 11, 1900*. In 1876, Alice Strange entered the Normal Department of Howard University and graduated as Valedictorian of her 1880 class. Excelling in every area of her

"St. Louis Republic," of August 18, 1901

Mrs. Alice Strange Davis
"The Colored American," of August 11, 1900

studies and her major, of music. According to, *"The Appeal," of April 19, 1890*, Mrs. Davis' mother, Isabella was a Negro slave working for a very influential well-to-do white family in Lynchburg, Virginia. Mr. J.V. Strange, the slave-owner and biological father of Alice. In almost every case of this sort, promises were made on behalf of a white father to an illegitimate child and their Negro mothers for support and acknowledgement of kinship. Alice was treated and accepted by the family as long as Mr. Strange was alive. Provisions were initially made by Mr. J.V. Strange when he sent Alice to Washington D.C. to get her education for which was financed by Mr. Strange. He also gave her some property in Washington D.C. and $10,000 worth of land in Virginia. But his married white daughter named Ann found out, she became infuriated and demanded her father resend his gifts to Alice. Reluctantly and feeble, gave into his daughter's unreasonable demand and requested she give up the property. Alice, understanding it wasn't Mr. Strange but his selfish daughter who wanted Alice to benefit nothing from her father's wealth. Mr. Strange offered Alice $250.00 and a week later in 1889 he died. Unlike the promises made, his Will, influenced by his daughter, contained nothing about Alice who was not even mentioned. The deed of reconsideration was set aside by the Supreme Court because of undue influence. Alice and her Attorney husband brought the suit to the Supreme Court. Because the Circuit Court's decision decided against her, when the Supreme Court viewed the complexity of the case, unanimously ruled in Alice's favor. To include the land, much to Ann's disappointment was restore back to Alice by the Supreme Court.

Alice was particularly motivated by her love for music, her major, which set the course for her life. Upon graduating, she was employed by the Washington D.C. public schools for eight years. She was married in 1888 to Joseph S. Davis, a practicing Attorney in the city of Baltimore where they resided during their marriage. After a short marriage of four years and a daughter named Edith, Mr. Davis suddenly died in 1892. Mrs. Davis then moved back to Washington D.C. where her music ambitions started with music lessons in 1874. This element source which continued all her life, became her passion and avenue to her motivation. Mrs. Davis began systematic and thorough courses of training in both instrumental and vocal music under such famous teachers as Professor's J. W. Bischoff, Waldecker, Richard Burmeister and Dr. Kimball. Mrs. Davis taught more than four hundred pupils, many of whom were white in her private sessions. In 1896, Mrs. Davis was appointed Director of Music in the Washington D.C. Pubic Schools by the Trustee's Rev. Sterling M. Brown and Mrs. Mary Church-Terrell with much protest. Mrs. Davis was also an active member of the World's Women's Christian Temperance Union, (W.W.C.T.). The success of her gifts afforded her a very lucrative life style and social graces where she earned as much as $2,000 a year from these sessions. Both of her homes in Washington and Baltimore were the center of cultural music, social circles of literary art and charm. Mrs. Davis died August 7,

1900 at a treatment center in Battle Creek, Michigan, leaving her mother, Isabella, a brother, Charles and an eleven year old daughter, Edith. Her services where held where she was Director of Music, the First Congregational Church, pastorate directions of Dr. J.E. Rankin and also at that time President of Howard University. When a memorial services at Park Temple in honor of Mrs. Alice Strange Davis was held on September 30, 1900, Mrs. Mary Church Terrell, Mr. W.B. Hayson, Mr. Edward Knight and Professor Kelly Miller all gave Addresses.

"El Paso Herald," of October 24, 1916

Isaiah T. Montgomery, Negro, pictured on the right, according to, *"The Washington Times," of November 24, 1901* became a Mayor. What's so unique with this story about Mr. Montgomery is where he started. President of the Confederate was President Jefferson Davis, who at one time owned about four hundred slaves before the Civil War. Montgomery was one of those slaves and here's his story. The Davis's plantation was located on Davis Bend in Warren County, Mississippi, comprised of many thousands of acres lying in a huge bend of the Mississippi River. Accordingly, there were two plantation houses named *"Brierfield" and "Hurricane."* Hurricane was a name given to one of the houses because of the devastating and damaging storm at one time had hit the plantation and Brierfield was the name of Joseph original plantation house. The overall day-to-day management of the plant-ation was made by the older brother of Jefferson named Joseph or, simply, *"Mr. Joe," and "Mr. Jeff,"* for Jefferson Davis. Jefferson Davis, for obvious reasons spent a lot time away from the plantation mostly in Washington. Isaiah's father was a foreman on the plantation which gave some clout to young Isaiah as he was being trained to be a *"house servant,"* in the big house

"The Colored American," of Jan 25, 1902

and other light outside functions. When Jefferson Davis was to be inaugurated in Montgomery, Alabama, Isaiah was one of two men who rowed him down to take the steamer. As a result of this environment, Isaiah learned to read, write and became business savvy. He also became a trusted business apprentice of sort, and a favorite of Mr. Joe. This meant he would use a row boat to travel down river to a bigger dock to pick up the mail daily. Of the some four hundred slaves who lived on the plantation, two groups were formed, called *"upper" and "lower."* Isaiah stated that the slaves were treated very well on the plantation and both the upper and lower sections had two overseers and were very competitive in crop accomplishments and management. No overseer was allowed to punish a slave on his own and almost like a court proceedings, when a case was up for possible punishment, generally, a Sunday would be set aside for that purpose and resolve. Only in retrospect did most of Davis's slaves, to include Isaiah admitted by comparison; appreciated the treatment of their times as slaves by the Davis family. Isaiah's description of Mrs. Davis as having a religious character and as descent a human-being in heart, as he'd ever encountered. Her concerns for all slaves was more alone the line of employee rather than slave. She was observed for hours out among the plantation giving her take on what would be best for the people as well as the most efficient manner to run the plantation for the betterment of all. After the Civil War ended and the plantation became just the property of the Davis family, Isaiah's father was hired as the foreman. This benefited Isaiah into managing a large plantation. Isaiah then acquired land and pattern it after the Davis

WUZ YOU SPEAKIN' TO ME MISTAH DUFF?

"The Day Book," of April 9, 1915

plantation. After the Civil War, Joseph Davis sold Benjamin Green, Isaiah's cousin a tract of his land to start a community. He and Isaiah made more large purchases for a track of Land in Yazoo River Valley for that continued dream. The colonization of Negroes in this area of happiness and prosperity proved to be a winning success for the Montgomery's attributing it to the lessons they learned while living on the Davis plantation. As reported by, *"The Washington Bee," of August 21, 1909* describes Mound Bayou consisted of over 30,000 acres of land and a thousand or fifteen hundred inhabitants. Homes were being built, a cotton seed oil mill was built costing $40,000. Competitive crop sharing were established and soon land expansions were made, and more homes built. Then the community determined the political aspects of being a legitimate town. Isaiah was elected as the first Mayor and the all-Negro city was named Mound Bayou, Mississippi. The town grew to several stores and other businesses and even a school. Some of the cities most famous residence was **Medgar Evers**, a 37 year old Negro Civil Rights Activist , that was assassinated on June 12, 1963 by the KKK. He was also employed as an Insurance Representative for the Magnolia Mutual Life Insurance Company. Also during the 1955 trial of **Emmett Louis Till** (*Till, the 14 year old Negro boy, who was murdered for whistling at a white woman and his body tossed in the Tallahatchie River*), Mound Bayou, Mississippi was where the majority of Negro journalist covering the trial were living as the other surrounding communities almost but had signs unwelcoming Negro reporters. And who could ever forget **Mose Wright**, the great Uncle of Emmett on the witness stand identifying one of the murders and his chilling words, *"Dair he."* Mound Bayou at one time was on of the most prosperous town in Mississippi and the south. But as soon as their wealth and popularity became known, laws and exploration of it inhabitants begin to weaken the core of previously marked success. And in the 1920's and 30's a lot of the previously owned black land and businesses were then taken over by whites and *"the Dixie trickery,"* in a collective effort to rid the town of all black success and prosperity.

Theodore Parker, many came to appreciated the grandeur of his spiritual intellect and council. Son of a farmer and mechanic, Parker was born in Lexington, Massachusetts, August 24, 1810, a reformer and abolitionist, his teachings was Love. From among his papers, was this song:

> Oh Brother! Who for us didst meekly wear,
> The Crown of Thorns about thy radiant brow;
> What Gospel from the Father didst thou bear,
> Our hearts to cheer, making us happy now?
> 'Tis this alone, the immortal Savior cries,
> To fill thy heart with ever-active love;
> Love for the wicked as in sin he lies,
> Love for thy Brother here, thy God above;
> Fear nothing ill, 'twill finish in its day,
> Live for the Good, taking the ill thou must;
> Toil with thy might, with manly labor pray,
> Living and loving learn thy God to trust,
> And He will shed upon thy soul the blessings of the just.

Theodore Parker- "New-York tribune." of May 2, 1920

It was said of Parker that because he was born in toil to humble parents was reasons he had so much sympathy for people of suffrage. Parker was educated at Harvard College and Harvard Divinity School graduating in 1836 and was ordained June 21, 1837. He was installed the same day as pastor of the West Roxbury Unitarian Church. In 1846 the 28th Congregational Rev. Parker became its minister. Until 1859, he preached in the Music Hall to the largest congregation in Boston until his health begins to fail. He died the following year in Florence, Italy, May 10, 1860, reported by the, *"Bisbee Daily Review," of August 25, 1910.* His lectures and quotations which he popularized would inspire speeches by President Abraham Lincoln and Rev. Dr. Martin Luther King, Jr. When Theodore Parker lay on his dying bed in Florence, Italy he commented, *"There are two Theodore Parker's now: one is dying here in Italy, the other I have planted in America."* Just by his words suggest, his indelible words, some controversial has made Rev. Parker's words concrete among intellectuals. The *"Memphis Daily Appeal," of March 7, 1857,* reports the Clergymen of Manchester, New Hampshire in 1857 protested against Theodore Parker for his employment as a lecturer before the Manchester Lyceum. Apart of the pastors were Rev. C.W. Wallace, H.H. Hartwell, S.C. Bartlett, J. Milton Coburn, I. G. Hubbard and G.W.H. Clark which contains the following words: *"We not only maintain that one who has published to the world his unqualified denial of the binding authority of God's word, and his sneers at the sinless character of Jesus Christ, and who is thus directly undermining the foundation in society, ought not to receive your official and public endorsement as a fit guide of public sentiment, and thereby gain additional influence to spread his skepticism. We urge another and even more decisive reason: "Mr. Parker is bold and unscrupulous. By frequent implication or assertion, he violates the neutral ground of the lecture-room, and thus insinuates his skeptical views. One of the last lectures before you--his lecture on Progress-- contains sentiments directly in conflict with its contents." "Whatever may be his qualifications in other respects, we think that such a man has forfeited his claim to be employed as a lecturer by the chief literary association of a Christian city."* Regardless of some criticisms, Rev. Parker lecturing skills were sought after as knowledge thirsty American crowds poured into halls where he would be speaking to hear his views with great enthusiasm. His profound views against slavery were worldwide known. The Fourteenth Lecture of the New York Anti-Slavery Society's Second Annual Course as recorded by the, *"New-York Daily Tribune," February 21, 1855,* was delivered by Theodore Parker on a cold February day. But when Oliver Johnson, one of the founders of the New England Anti-Slavery Society and Abolitionist introduced Parker, hear is how he summed up his characterization. *"Ladies and Gentlemen__ The gentleman invited to address us this evening has been charged with entertaining and promulgating some pernicious heresies but I believe he has never been charged; even by his worst enemy, with torturing either the Old or New Testament into an apology or defense of American Slavery. His religious creed may be as deficient and erroneous, by the popular standard, as that of the Good Samaritan; but I ask you when he was ever found on the side of the slaveholder? When has the America slave, plundered, outraged, forsaken, lifted up his cry to him in vain! I have great pleasure in introducing to you one who has been thought worthy of an indictment in a United States Court for his fidelity to Freedom, and to freedom of speech is the old cradle of Liberty."* Parker's attack on the idolatry of George Washington's crime and his blundering, with the following words which sums up his underling thoughts that he gave in a speech on July 4, 1857 in Washington D.C. *"The acceptance of the U.S. Constitution, which seemed suited to advance the cause of liberty, really gave that cause a deadly wound, by incorporating with it the support of slavery. Of all those who, by signing that instrument, aided in this recognition of slavery as a thing proper to be continued under the law. I blame Benjamin Franklin and George Washington most. I*

would sooner have cut off my right hand than given its signature to that Constitution." "Washington was born a slaveholder, and married slaves. Although he joined in a resolution against the slave trade and offered to La Fayette to join him in emancipating his slaves, he continued a slaveholder through his life. He even tried to recover fugitive slaves from Florida and directed a seizure of one of his own in New Hampshire. If it could be done without confusion or popular tumult. Not until his death were his slaves emancipated. This slaveholding was the greatest blot on Washington's character; there is no excuse for it." Theodore Parker had many quotes that lasted through the ages. From, "The Commonwealth," article of September 25, 1913, fifty-three years after his death, it states: "Did the mass of men know the actual selfishness and injustice of their rulers, not a government would stand a year; the world would ferment with revolution." And one of my favorites from, "The Times and Democrat," article of July 29, 1909 titled, "Mans Ideal of Character." "Every man has at times in his mind the ideal of what he should be, but is not. This ideal may be high and complete or it may be quite low and insufficient, yet in all men that really seek to improve it is better than the actual character. Man never falls so low that he can see nothing higher than himself."

The, "Industrial Freedom," of September 17, 1898, records yet another quote: "Give me the power to labor for mankind; Make me the mouth of such as cannot speak; Eyes let me be to groping men, and blind, And conscience to the base, and to the weak. Let me be hands and feet, and to the foolish, mind." Parker, a vigorous thinker, and a ripe scholar of Unitarianism caused his suspicious religious beliefs to be profoundly questioned throughout his lifetime. An author of infallibly and miraculously inspired in his mind, tried to move Unitarianism toward transcendentalism to no avail within his lifetime. But as the transcendentalist movement gained in popularity, only after Parker's death for which he was given influence as a key component to its liberal teachings. His quote regarding this even resonates today, "The authority of Jesus, as of all teachers, one would naturally think, must rest on the truth of his words, and not their truth on his authority."

Tar and Feathers according to, "The Morning Call," article of August 5, 1894, about Dr. Ricketts take on tar and feathering as starting with the Greeks. This type of punishment of an offending victim was even considered a punishment worst than hanging and most repulsive. The aerating of blood through naked skin pores take when tar hardens and it becomes extremely difficult to remove. The feathers are then added in cement like fashion to the tar, anchoring it to the skin. Which is generally where the internal suffering occurs? Contracting as it cools, with each vein pulling causing enormous pain of a sweat less body. Since the body skin is an absorbent agent. The irritation of the skin and hair can not be disengaged and must be detached along with the removed tar if time permits before death. If an individual has kidney disease, the likelihood of his avoidance of quick death is almost a certainty otherwise; the survival rate is good but painful.

A small town of West Liberty, Ohio located about eight miles north of Urbana, November 18, 1899 three people were tarred and feathered as reported by, "The Watchman and Southron," article of November 29, 1899. A similar incident occurred, December 1892, in West Liberty when John Jackson, a Negro eloped with a white waitress named Lessie Hinklep were jailed and subsequently taken from jail and tarred and feathered. The involvement with Nell Jackson occurred when reports of Marshall Daniel Krabill's barn was burned on a Friday, November 17, 1899, with a cow inside. Mrs. Nell Jackson, his nearby neighbor, a thirty-five year old white woman, who married Grant Jackson, a thirty-four year old Negro twelve years prior, was accused of the barn burning. Grant Jackson, known as a *"tough-guy,"* and notorious for insulting white women and feared by some white men. Grant was shot to death in a fight leaving Nell a widow with two children (sons) several years before this incident. Also included in that arrest warrant was her father-in-law, **Ed Jackson**, a seventy-one year old Negro and **David Rickman**, a forty year old Negro cement contractor. Ed and David who was living with Nell Jackson when lawmakers attempted to arrest all of them for the barn burning. Word of the arrest spread like fallen winter leaves on an open plain with high winds. Just after midnight, there were about one hundred and fifty masked men gathered and headed for the town. Marshall, Krabill, was the

"The National Tribune," of August 22, 1901 only lawman that had keys to the jail after dark. After Krabill refusal to give the keys to the mob, a scuffle broke out between he and some of the mobsters. Apparently a large man was Marshall Krabill as he reportedly knocks down several of the mobsters in their scuffle. Even though he was outnumbered, Marshall Krabill stood his ground. They left the Marshall's home after it was understood he would not be intimidated. The Jackson's house and barn became the next target by the mob. The house still contained Ed Jackson's wife and Nell Jackson's two children did not phase the thugs intensions of completely demolishing their home and barn and releasing of all their horses and live stock to run wild. All their furniture was dragged into the middle of the street and smashed to bits and pieces. All doors were knocked down and windows smashed. Now feeling their oats, the mob headed for the county jail to demand the prisoners. After refusal from law-enforcements Sheriff Bell and Besler, the fearless mob organized into three groups and battered down the jail-house doors. The mob then stoned the jail seriously injured the Sheriff's in defending their prisoners. The mob soon gain access to the prisoners despite the Sheriff gallant efforts to prevent.

First prisoner taken from the jail was Mrs. Nell Jackson, as they dragged her to the nearby mill stream, beat her, thrust several knifes into her breast, tossed vitriol in her eyes, stripped her naked, then covered her with a combination of turpentine mixed in with roof paint and tar and feathers. She was then placed in three feet of water and made to march back and forth through the stream while dodging pistol shots and stones being directed her way. Much to the amusement and delight of the viewing crowd that was growing by the hour. The second group of mobsters soon arrived with David Rickman. Nell Jackson was then taken from the stream, placed on the banks to dry while David's term of like treatment took place. In addition to the identical treatment, David was whipped and pounded several times before being tarred. His marching up and down the stream continued until the third group of thugs arrived with Ed Jackson.

Ed received no preferential treatment because of his age as his sequence of events started and ended just like the previous two. When the amusement of Ed were no longer entertaining, all three were forced back into the stream and made to, *"play possum"* in the stream submerging their tarred bodies in cool stream waters. The three were then gather together and marched through several streets naked, tarred and feathered while being whipped on body parts where no tar had covered. With onlookers viewing the display of humiliation without pity or interference, the three were released. It was said that David had walked several miles towards Bellefontaine while Nell and Ed Jackson walked three miles before finding clothing. Keeping a watchful eye was the mob when two Negroes made an attempt to aid the released victims, the mob viciously attacked them causing them to flee partly clothed for their efforts. After news of their release reached the Sheriff, Nell and David were re-arrested and taken back to jail until their court appearance. The three victims eventually had their day in court as Nell explained that she had nothing to do with barn burning and further reiterated she would never set a

"I'se in town, Honey"

"The St. Joseph Observer," of February 16, 1918

fire in so close proximity to her own residence where her 2 children were. Nell also said she was in bed and was only awaken by the light and cracking of wood shingles in flames that awaken her. Ed Jackson unfortunately died shortly after the tar and feathering incident the following day from injuries suffered at the hands of the mob. In 1901 after proven no involvement with the burning, the two remaining victims filed a lawsuit against the citizens of Logan County for damages. County Prosecutor Sam H. West summoned a Special Grand Jury calling also fifty witness bring the whitecapping thugs to justice. A judgment awarding David Rickman $3,000 deceased, Ed Jackson descendants $1,000 and Nell Jackson $7,000 was rewarded as recorded by the, "The Appeal," article of June 1, 1901. Even in rendering justice, the white citizens of Logan County, Ohio couldn't be depended on to be impartial. Ed Jackson's life was shorten as a result of the treatment he received on behalf of the mob and his home was completely demolished and live stock let loose. Yet his award was less than all victims. Nell Jackson, white, received the highest award, while David wasn't half of her award. Amazing how blind justice can be silenced by obscure hatefulness.

Blackwell, Oklahoma. Blackwell was established following the September 16, 1893 Cherokee Outlet of some 12,000 area's of land run by Col. Andrew Jackson Blackwell, a white man married to a half-breed Cherokee Indian, as recorded by the "The Times," of February 11, 1898. Having built a number of towns in Kansas and the Indian Territory, Col. Blackwell decided to go south to Oklahoma. In 1898, there were about 2,000 residences in Blackwell. With a history of never ever allowing a Negro to live there, Col. Blackwell, the founder, made an incentive to a colony of Negroes to settle there to change that image which was no reflective of his views. He offered them protection, and a sufficient lot of land to each family plus enough land for eventually a schoolhouse and a church. Soon, the word spread and Negroes

"The Jennings Daily Record," of August 6, 1902

came from far and near. According to Cherokee Laws, for his land dealings in 1894, Col Blackwell was arrested and sentenced to death for high treason for the selling of known Indian land to the white man. Blackwell admits to leasing land for coal mining purposes for which he would receive $250,000 and 3% of all coal taken as profit. As recorded by, "The Herald," of December 8, 1894, members of the Cherokee Council took Col. Blackwell from his family on a Friday in December of 1894 and brought him to Claremont where he was confined on bread and water for violation of the Cherokee Law. The following Monday, Col. Blackwell was stripped of all his clothing, shaved clean and brought before Chief Ohaha to confess. Col. Blackwell admitted to having nothing to confess about and acknowledged it was some type of conspiracy. And for his response he was then taken to a place called, "The Needles," a notorious Indian ran prison where he was reportedly treated horribly. Indian dances were performed while sharp objects were being jabbed into his naked flesh while he was chained both hands and feet. After the dance, Col. Blackwell was taken back to his cell. One night an odd thing happened which was later verified by the Indian guards. Blackwell claimed an Angel came down from heaven and unlocked his chains from his hands and feet as he fled the next morning. Col. Blackwell, claimed to have been sent by God, was a known religious man when he first arrived in a city call David of Oklahoma Territory. His faith was fashioned after the Mormon faith of Salt Lake City and a temple was built with donations from

"The San Francisco Call," of August 6, 1911

various local Indian tribes and from Col. Blackwell himself, who reportedly was worth over 2 million dollars. The purpose of the temple, according to the reporting of, *"The Wichita Daily Eagle," of April 28, 1895*, it was Col. Blackwell's dream to have a central location where all Indian tribes could come to perform their individual tribal dances and rituals and devotions. In the interim, Col. Blackwell had also built a church in Blackwell called *"The House of God,"* for all other denominations to come in harmonious worship. The night before his execution his half-breed Cherokee wife named Rosa and several white man from David, liberated Blackwell from Indians. Blackwell remained in hiding for a year. The Cherokee Nation soon filed a suit with the United States Northern Judicial Courts, claiming the white residence of David be treated as intruders for illegally acquiring land on known Indian territory. Several court battles ensued and the Indians eventually won out. But to avoid losing their houses, the wife of Blackwell, as a half-breed Indian, took possession of the properties to prevent what the whites had work hard to built from losing. But, the colony of Negroes was forced to leave because whites, who were deemed as intruders by the courts didn't want the Negroes in Blackwell. They refused to hire them for work, both men and women, boomed Col. Blackwell's barn as a warning to leave, and many Christian whites offering to help was threaten and businesses boycotted. So one by one, nearly starving to death trying to survive and with no sympathy from their townsmen. This left the once vision of a harmonized community of Col. Blackwell without fulfillment, he died June 19, 1903 as recorded by, *"The Wichita Daily Eagle," of June 21, 1903*, leaving a wife and three children. Blackwell was a native of Mississippi, responsible for forming three towns, Blackwell Rock, later changed to Blackwell, David and Chelsea. Even today, 2012, the population of African-American's in Blackwell is less than 1% of the total residences.

Oklahoma wasn't the only region of the country that restricted Negro inhabitants from settling or remaining in an area where cohabitation had worked. Until either an unforgivable offense general against a white woman or some form of criminal element forced deportation of Negroes. As recorded by the, *"Daily Evening Bulletin," of July 31, 1886,* the case of Mrs. Benjamin Stevens at De Leon, Texas in Comanche County 1886, where a Negro was hung for her murder. The citizens of Comanche County in lieu of that incident and similar incidents in months prior to the Mrs. Stevens incident, posted signs throughout the county, *"No Negroes allowed in this town."* When this word was posted in De Leon, Bibbs, Snipe Springs, Whittells and Fleming, Texas, Negroes began leaving their homes and any acquired land behind for fear of their lives. Interviews were conducted for some of the fleeing Negroes were Luke Jefferson, Joe Butler who communicated that they'd lived in the area for 16 years and soon as a few bad Negroes commit a crime of the forbidden fruit, (*white women*) all people of color will pay the price for a few. Texarkana, Arkansas as recorded by, *"The Progress," of September 17, 1898* where the posting of *"Negroes Leave or Else,"* in Grayson and other counties. Near Mount Pleasant in 1898, two Negroes were ambushed in the cotton fields causing many Negroes to flee to Texas only to return claiming sign being posted in Texas for Negroes to leave also. A meeting soon held by Sheriff Dixon to combat the trouble set in place by some prejudice residences. District Attorney R.D. Hart of Texarkana acknowledged warning being placed for whitecaps under the law for intimidation by any means in causing the disenfranchising

Devour Us Not

of the local Negroes. Many of the cowardly ambushes continued with many Negroes being picked off while in the fields until the realization of economic downfall in profitability and not finding a suitable replacement workforce eventually caused the cease of the ambushes and intimaedations. Needless to say, the whites were much too lazy to endure the pain of back breaking works themselves. The Negroes of Henrietta, Oklahoma had their Christmas of 1907 interrupted by warnings to leave the city as reported by, *"The San Francisco Call," of December 26, 1907.* The trouble started when James Garden, a Negro was lynched for the alleged murder of Albert Bates, a prominent white businessman. Negroes were then given 48 hours to get out of town or face a similar fate themselves, which most did.

Texarkana, Arkansas, March 23, 1898, seven Negroes including three brothers was lynched. According to, *"The Sun," of March 24, 1899,* the citizens in Little River County lynched Ben Jones, Moses Jones, Joe Jones, Edward Goodwin, Adam King and two unidentified others. These seven supposedly friends of *"Gin"* Duckett who was lynched previously for the alleged murder of James Stockton, a wealthy white planter in the county. Dockett, before his lynching had supposedly, bragged about killing a white man and urged others to follow him. Duckett's lynching was to be avenged by local Negroes that infuriated the whites to rid the county of these troublesome Negroes. Two mouthy Negroes named Joe King and John Johnson were rumored to have been making unfavorable comments about whites were taken in the woods and whipped. In light of all rumors and violence, many Negroes began to flee the county fearing for their lives.

Indianapolis, Indiana, September 30, 1904 as recorded by the, *"New-York Tribune," of October 1, 1904*, where a Republican meeting was being held and where an all male Negro Glee Club had been advertised to be the singers at the meeting were viciously attacked. Stones and clubs were thrown in their direction as they exited for their lives. No one could pin point the motivation for the attack since the Glee Club was favorably announced with no reservations. But the violent crowd supposedly was from Van Buren, a nearby county who came to Landisville with trouble on their minds. Pistols were soon being fired and reportedly, Orrville Ramsay, a white man of Landisville was shot and killed. Seventeen other persons were injured before order was restored. A determination was never made why this unprovoked attacked was directed at this popular Glee Club but most residence in Landisville suggest it was racially and politically motivated.

April 25, 1910 in Coleman, Texas, twelve Negroes were badly beaten and one white man seriously injured according to, *"The Daily Ardmoreite," of April 26, 1910.* Between 150 and 200 men women and children were driven out of town. Admittedly, there were no Negroes in and around Coleman, Texas until the Santa Fe railroad began hiring black labor. The whites acknowledged that just the appearance of Negro faces and the seemingly wanting fair and equal treatment was more than what they were willing to give up. A confrontation between two white youths and a Negro broke out. The youths reported the shellacking they had received from the Negro and the fact he attempted to purposely run them over with a carriage caused a posse of about a thousand men and boys to form. They began scouring the Negro neighborhoods stoning and clubbing every black face in sight. The crowd had become so infuriated, that law enforcements could not penetrate their ranks. Every Negro by the hundreds were forced to flee. After every black residence was completely demolished, the

crowd dispersed. In Montgomery, Alabama on October 23, 1899 as recorded by, *"The Times," of October 25, 1899,* three Negroes were shot near a small lumber town called, Searight. Employed by the Turpentine Stills, a large company who's major workforce were Negro men and women. It was stated in the article, payday was on a Saturday and widely known was a place called Falk's bar, where after a payday weekend, Negroes behavior of drunkenness was common place. Shots were fired after hours of drinking and whites got together, armed themselves and the Negro hunt was on. Every Negro in that generally area was forced in the swamps. And after a day or two, the Negroes began returning to their homes only to be forced back into the swamps. Only after law-enforcement got involved, after weeks of hiding in the swamps were Negroes allowed to return to their homes and resumed their lives.

Arriving in by train to Harrodsburg, Kentucky October 7, 1904, from South Fork was eighty Negroes of which thirty were women according to, *"The Nebraska Advertiser," of October 7, 1904.* A disturbance was created when a white farmer's wife was stabbed and died at the hands of a Negro. Allegedly, a Negro woman went to the farmer's house asking for a sandwich for her lunch. While the farmer's wife was preparing the lunch, the Negro woman was supposedly looking for things to steal. So when the woman handed the sandwich to the Negro, she snatched the sandwich and some clothing and ran out the door. In hot pursuit was the farmer's wife who eventually caught the Negro woman but was stabbed to death either by the woman or a coconspirator. The farmer's wife lay in the woods until she was found by a white man who reviled to him her story before dieing. Baring any false or made-up portions to provoke the obvious.

As reported by, *"The Paducah Sun," of September 15, 1902,* a grand jury assembled in which witnesses were unwilling or did not bear any knowledge of what had transpired at John Bean's house, a Negro farmer the week before by the mob. A riot trouble broke out in El Dorado, Illinois after the John Bean incident. He had lived in Saline County, Illinois for many years and had accumulated much of his wealth there which was near to the dwellings of a number of well-to-do Negroes. John Bean's barn was burned down with two horses and 1,000 pounds of tobacco. Also lost along with about forty Negro families was the forced abandonment of their homes.

The terror was caused for soldier's to be called in by Governor Yates to guard John Bean and Reverend Peter A. Green's houses, who was the pastor of the African Methodist Church. The guards were surrounded and the fight continued with wagon-loads of mobster's for more than a month. John Bean and his wife, Nancy eventually moved out and leased their farm property for a year. The guards were then moved to Mr. Parson Green's house only. Sheriff Samuel Baxter widely criticized for his lackadaisical attention to the continued aggression of whites, wanting to rid the county of its wealthy Negroes. Governor Yates soon sent Adjutant General Col. Theodore Ewert to investigate the allegations from Negro citizens. On July of 1902, Governor Yates wrote the following message to the Sheriff: *"I deem it my duty, upon the strength of what I have myself learned during the past two weeks about the disorderly occurrence in your county, to censure you severely, hoping thereby to awaken you to a sense of your duty and to repair, as far as possible, any harm done. You deserve censure, in the first place, for failure to comply with your duty to respond when called upon, as an executive officer of the law, to aid and inform the chief executive; but you are much more deserving of censure for the plain breach of duty to inhabitants of your county."* As reported by, *"The St. Louis Republic," of July 5, 1902* to Col. Ewert's

Devour Us Not

"What'd you git dat chicken, Mose?"
"Sh-z-z-z me, Mandy; I can't tell a lie an' I don' wanter commit myself."

report to General James E. Smith his findings. Col. Ewert describes normal classes at the Industrial College founded by Dr. J. D. Alston where the all Negro students and teachers were in attendance. The school house was stoned by supposedly unknown lawless white thugs in which the Sheriff, after two days and complaints advised the Negroes to just close the school house doors and depart. Since the college was very successful in educating Negroes, the mob then proceeded to wreck the El Dorado African Methodist Church and dispersed the congregation while in service. The Negro school was eventually closed and most Negro residences were sent fleeing into nearby Harrisburg. Notices begin appearing all over the county that all Negroes must leave the county at once and never return. Result of all this hostility towards the Negroes were not the traditional reasons whites use to rid it's communities of all its Negroes of no offenses had been committed by the Negro residences. Some morons even suggested the rationale behind the prejudice was what most stated as an inevitable of assured crime if the Negro presence remained. His (The Sheriff) conduct as described by Col. Ewert as being reprehensible and intolerable, suggested the Sheriff immediately gather-up all responsible parties involved in the meeting and assure them of a complete and secure immunity from any future disturbances. Governor Yates then sent a demanding letter to Sheriff Baxter reiterating what Col. Ewert had recommended and requesting an immediate response to that letter as a demand and not a request.

During all the commotion against the Negroes, a special meeting was held by the Afro-American Protective League in nearby Harrisburg, denouncing the President of the Industrial School at El Dorado, Dr. Jefferson D. Alston. Charges stemming from unworthiness, weak and lack of confidence in his ability by members of the community he served. Dr. Alston, a Negro, was influenced by the radical right to condemn his own race or perhaps it was fear and intimidation or money mismanagement. Other resolutions were adopted against James Mitchell, an Attorney of Mt. Vernon, Illinois who was hired by the State to prosecute B.B. Barrett of El Dorado and known leader of the rioting mob. The case was thrown out because of an unverified alibi that was uninvestigated by Mitchell of Barrett's whereabouts. The deliberation by the jury took only three minutes. The targeting of John Bean's house and barn on two occasions was first thought to drive he, his wife and Mother-In-Law out of town. Also was the fact that he was one of the wealthiest Negroes in the county and major contributor, financially was another motivating factor. A major theory buster of equality that most whites resented and feared for their power-hold might be in jeopardy. While Rev. Green became a target which was visited by the mob and demanded compliance with all the signs posted, he fought back. A fire fight broke out and a mobster reportedly had been hit by Rev. Green, a claim denied by the Pastor. Negro houses were stoned and fired into by whitecap thugs. The troubles in El Dorado lasted from May 29, 1902 until the end of that year when the presence of military troops roam the area and later sent home for supposedly, time to vote. Some of the residence of El Dorado never did return and that included John Bean. A Grand Jury was formed and nearly 200 witnesses were called according to, "The Appeal," of October 18, 1902, but failed indict any of the forty men who were reported to have formed a secret organization sworn to eliminate the African American population from Saline County. Supposedly, for political purposes in wanting the county to be run on a Democratic ticket and Negroes generally during that era were all Republicans. But we all know that was just a more civil reasoning behind what was really going on and that was to rid the county of its black occupants in an effort to establish an all white county. And because there was the lack of support from the county, all troops begin establishing winter quarters fearing what ended ultimately in December, 1902.

Rev. Dr. Martin Luther King, Jr. was born January 15, 1929 as Michael Luther King, to a preacher father named Martin Luther King, Sr., pastor of the Ebenezer Baptist Church. His mother, Alberta (*Williams*) King who was by trade a former school teacher. Rev. Dr. King, Jr. at the age of about six had his name changed to that of his father, who also changed his name. At the age of 15, in 1944, young King entered Morehouse College in Atlanta. It was told that Rev. King initially had reservations about a career in the ministry. But reluctantly or not he entered Crozer Theological Seminary in Pennsylvania where he graduated winning the Plafker Award as the outstanding student and the J. Lewis Crozer Fellowship award of his

"St. Paul Daily Globe," of July 24, 1890

graduating class. Rev. King later married Coretta Scott, June 18, 1953 and later became the pastor of the Dexter Avenue Baptist in Montgomery. This is where he mobilized the black citizens of that city to participate in the city bus-line boycott after the Rosa Parks incident. Rev. King, now an active participant in the civil rights movement became the subject of a series of threats to the Jim Crow laws of the south. It was then, that Rev. King adopted the non-violent tactics and became the subject of numerous arrests, harassments, the booming of his home and eventually his life taken at the age of 39, April 4, 1968, on the balcony of the black-owned Lorraine Hotel. Rev. King was standing next to Ralph Abernathy, when he was shot in the neck by a rifle bullet. Because there were so many threats against his life, Rev King lived with the notion that any day, the inevitable would become a reality. But his steadfast, relentlessness earned him the respect of millions all around the world. The Jim Crow laws were so embedded in the fabric of this nation and to have the courage to stand-up to the opposition was nothing but a God sent effort. The leadership of Rev. Dr. Martin Luther King, Jr. grew so quickly that the fever of Justice burned hotter and hotter as his message spread. Rev. King organized a number of black leaders in 1957 and laid the groundwork for the organization now known as the Southern Christian Leadership Conference (SCLC). For his efforts, he was elected president as he assisted communities in methods of legal non-violent avenues to protest against discrimination and injustices. Rev. King was the most prolific intellectual speaker of his day. His most famous *"I Have a Dream,"* speech made in 1963, concluding with the following words:

"Let freedom ring from stone mountain of Georgia, let freedom ring from look out mountain of Tennessee, let freedom ring from every hill and mole hill of Mississippi from every mountain side, let freedom ring and when this happens, when we allow freedom rings; when we let it ring, from every village and every hamlet from every state and every city, we will be able to speed up that day when all of God's children, black men and white men, Jews and Gentiles, Protestants and Catholics will be able to join hands and sing in the words of the old negro spiritual, Free at last!, Free at last!, Thank God'a mighty!, We're free at last!"

When I first heard those words of *"The Dream,"* and **"Being judged not by the color of ones skin but by the content of ones Character,"** I didn't realized, having been so much a part of the complacency with the segregated south, that things weren't as bad as he depicted in his speech. Years later, the significance of that speech did resonate itself with me after hearing it again. For it was a real dream, once I realize the significance of that historical day. I guess I assumed the integrity of a nation's laws would always protect all its citizens, *"We the People."* Not to be redundant, but I could not understand in hindsight; how a race of people could go to church every Sunday, pray to their God and despise our race as it appeared

Devour Us Not

"New-York Tribune," of January 11, 1903

ever so clearly after that speech. But like most of my generation, the animosity even from an early age was to forgive them. For I felt it was my obligation as a Christian to do so or was it perhaps the openly desire to just be accepted. People often made assumptions about, Rev. Dr. Martin Luther King, Jr.'s popularity among all people of color. Not true, some people were satisfied being second class citizens; as not to rock the boat or stir up the base; which was just pure ignorance. The fear of retaliation from agitated whites and fear of the whites with their hold on white supremacy was loosing its gripe by the new generation of blacks now being unified by the *"Drum Major,"* was cause for concerns. By this time, the slave mentality effect was diminishing with the frustrations of being feed up with this *"Jim Crow Law,"* way as the norm. I recalled living in Dallas when the State Fair of Texas only had one day for blacks to attend the fair, we called it *"N-word" Day at the Fair,"* but it was officially named *"Negro Day."* Whites could use any one of the twenty-nine others days to attend the fair. There was this huge parade in downtown Dallas of which I was an active participant for several years as a member of a drill team. At the Cotton Bowl, there would be a junior high school football game, followed by a high school game, generally Madison and Lincoln. Then, the big college game at night that featured Prairie View A & M against any number of other Black Colleges like Wiley, Bishop and Paul Quinn etc. But I must commend the people that were white that were in charge of the rides, food stands and games at the fair were some of the nicest people, of Anglo-Saxton heritage that I've every been around. They acted as if we were white, as if race appeared oblivious for just that one day. And I often pondered that in my mind; why can't that treatment be an everyday occurrence? What's so significant about treating a race of people like first class citizens? Of course this was all new for both whites and blacks as blacks during the 1970's begin to showcase their African heritage by singing chants of, *"I'm Black and I'm Proud,"* the Afro hair, once a sense of shame and disgrace (*the nappy hair*) was now so very kool as if before hair defines a person. The wearing of African attire, was now everyday wear, as blacks were unified and even in the military with the *"P-Check and the Dap."* Even though there were still many jobs restricted to exclude blacks in the military as well as civilian life. The blacks even change their race name from the *"N-word"* to *"Colored"* to *"Negro"* to *"Afro-American or to African-American,"* to the simplified sound of just *"Black."* In a very short time, America was slowly changing to match its creed, the never dieing dream; and the hopes of many who died before its reality.

He was a principal speaker at the historic, "March on Washington," in 1963, where he delivered one of the most passionate addresses of his career, *"I have a Dream."* Time magazine designated him as its, *"Person of the Year,"* for 1963. A few months later he was named the youngest recipient of the Nobel Peace Prize, in 1964. He was asked by now (*2011*) 99 year old Amelia Boynton Robinson, to come to Selma in 1965, *"Bloody Sunday."* Leader of several other protest marches in the heart of the south under the threat of danger at all times which he completely ignored. He became the first person of color to have a National Holiday named in his honor, January 15th his birthday in 1986, after Arizona and South Carolina to be one of the last States of the union to agree to this honor. Martin Luther King, Jr. was a great American, a clergyman, a civil rights activist, a martyr of two Christian churches, founder of the Southern Christian Leadership Conference, where he was the first President. He had influences that effected racial poverty, the Viet Nam War, and he was posthumously awarded the Presidential Medal of Freedom and the Congressional Gold Medal. And one of my most beloved quotes by Rev. Dr. Martin Luther King, Jr. is:

"Injustice anywhere is a threat to justice everywhere."

Now look how far we've come. Never in a million years did I and millions of other Americans alive and dead

would ever have believed that a man of color would win the popular vote and Electoral College vote to become the very first President of **known** African and white heritage. And let us not forget Robert M. Johnson, Vice President during the President Van Buren era with his common-law wife that was an octoroon named Julia Chinn. Her mere presence at White House functions must have made for quite a gossip piece. But believe it or not, some prominent people of color within the black community even suggested that he; meaning Barack; wasn't black enough or doesn't bear the scares of having Parentage of slave ancestry to claim the title *"A person of color."* But during the time Barack Obama was running for the Presidency, many comments were made about the race issue as it relates to the office that had never been held by a known person of color. Such as the comments made by Senator Harry Reid, stating that, *"Barack would have a good chance of winning because he had light-skin and had no black dialect unless he wanted to."*

Here we are in 2013, and the echoes of the post emancipation era, the deep embodiment of acceptable or not of race intolerance still exist. This continuous mode of thinking is so abstractly wrong until it injuriously taints this nation's self-proclaimed Christian image of itself. But thank God for the young Anglo's, thirty years and under that, *"Get it,"* and is a welcomed positive change for America. The ages of American Anglo's forced itself forward, to let the generation of whites over 60 whose overwhelmingly voted against President Obama prove to be a non-factor unlike previous elections. There are a number of *"Ole Folks Sayings"* and *"Biblical Phrases"* that equate to this historical victory that echo's *"We Shall Overcome,",* *"The first shall be last and the last shall be first,"* *"Plant a bad seed, you'll reap a bad harvest,"* *"What goes around, comes back around."* Despite this country's effort to ever prevent the outcome of this passed in the 2008 election. The almost complete obliteration of a race of people is not to be stopped or devoured. The consistent denial of an equal share of the American dream, the lock-outs, the sufferings and the many silent voices whose dreams of hope were never realized shall rise again. For the countless of lost souls of pure hearts that yearn the taste of justice, President Barack Obama has the weight of an entire race of people and a nation placed at his feet. With the prayers of a people and the forces of All-Mighty-God, *"no enemy formed against him shall prosper."* As the shift of profiteering Liberal's who've shown a blind eye to the proper justices that plague a nation of its creed. It is by the same notion that the hand of God will one day open the eyes of justice hence forth and forever. And the evil plague of racial injustice of a nation will hear the most alluring silence of hope and the voices of its entire people. God only knows what would have become of our nation had Rev. King lived? Could the cycle of injustice been broken much earlier? Could we as a race been further endowed into the fabric of wealth? All these questions and many, many more questions will never be known. For God's master plan, has to be fulfilled. Every man before departing this earth must fulfill God's purpose for his life. For it is God that governs the methods in which all things are created and judged.

Edward Herbert Wright was born on September 28, 1863 in New York City, New York. Horace Greeley (*an American newspaper editor, a founder of the Liberal Republican Party, a reformer, a politician, an outspoken opponent of slavery, and founder and editor of the New York Tribune*) advised him go West and he did so in 1884. Before then, he (*Wright*) graduated from public school and went on to the College in the City of New York. After graduating in 1881 at seventeen years of age, Wright taught in New Jersey for three years.

Chicago became Wright's next stop as he arrived in the city in 1884, penniless and looking for opportunities. In Chicago, sometimes having only 15-20 cent a day was all he had but found time to develop his skills. His desire to learn was for him the main motivating factor from the beginning for Wright. An industrious person, his work ethics landed him in Chicago by assisting a Pullman porter, working as a realtor in a real estate office, and working in the registry department of the postal service. His energy and forcefulness attracted the attention of others, including Republican politicians. Wright was later hired in the county clerk's office. He was six feet tall, dark-skinned, heavy, and slow-spoken. He married his wife, Sarah, in 1900 and had no children. Elected as county commissioner in November, 1898, retiring the first of December, 1900. He was also a South Town Clerk for two years. He was President of the Colored Republican League of Chicago.

Edward H. Wright and **W.G. Anderson** (*pictured on the left*) were the two Lawyers responsible for the release of Jack Johnson from the Cook County jail. Prior to Wright's involvement in the case, Jack Johnson, the first African-American to be crowned Heavyweight Champion of the World, had an array of white legal talents that failed in their attempt to have Johnson released. With the help of the right bondsman, Attorney's Wright and Anderson, despite against racial prejudice and bigotry performed admirable in securing his freedom.

Wright's reputation as a Habeas Corpus Lawyer, at the time was the only Negro to have served as President of the Cook County Board of Commissioners. Having boasted victories of similar cases while a member of the Chicago Bar, he was admired by his colleagues for his integrity. His astuteness and technical fact law successes, made him fearless and respected. Jack Johnson's troubles started with the four indictments under the Mann Act for importing women, and more importantly, white women for immoral purposes. Jack Johnson, like Edward H. Wright was admired for his talents in his profession as a boxer and therefore tolerated in his harem of white

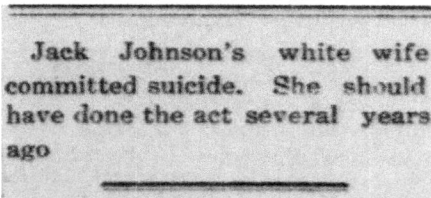

women draped all over him at every social setting. With that same enthusiasm, he was also despised for that very fact. Johnson's white divorcee wife,

Etta H. Duryea Johnson who were married January 18, 1911, committed suicide, September 12, 1912, as a result of his inexcusable thirst for many white women and among other things. She shot herself through the head and supposedly said to a neighbor these chilling words, *"God have pity on a lonely woman. I am a white woman and am tired of being a social outcast.*

I deserve all of my misery for marrying a black man. Even the Negroes don't respect me. I intend to end it all," as reported by, *"The Mt. Sterling Advocate,"* of September 18, 1912. So parents of some of the groupies,

"The Day Book," of November 12, 1912

labeled Jack Johnson as a *"damphool,"* (*damn fool*), and deserving the stiffest of penalties. Only because of his love for white women caused more hatred of him than his victories of white hopeful competitors. Case and point, the newspaper article from a Columbia, Kentucky newspaper defined the hate. Johnson's

"Miss Hattie Smith" - *"Bisbee Daily Review," of May 4, 1909*

wife pictured on the right original name was Hattie Smith, born in 1883 in Biloxi, Mississippi. She had dark olive tint skin and supposedly had some Negro blood in her bloodline. At age 26 she and Johnson were married in Las Vegas, New Mexico in 1906. Following the death of Etta, his second wife, Jack became involved

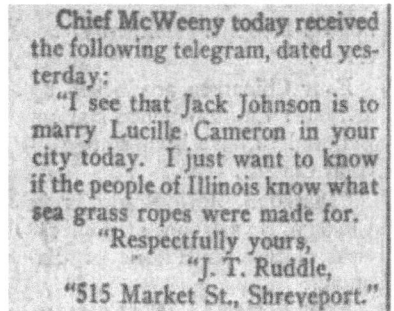

"Etta H. Duryea" - *"The Broad Ax," of Sep 14, 1912*

Chief McWeeny today received the following telegram, dated yesterday:

"I see that Jack Johnson is to marry Lucille Cameron in your city today. I just want to know if the people of Illinois know what sea grass ropes were made for.

"Respectfully yours,
"J. T. Ruddle,
"515 Market St., Shreveport."

"The Day Book," of Dec 4, 1912

with an eighteen year old white girl named Lucille Cameron whom he met while she was on a slumming trip that involved Johnson's wine room and café. This infuriated the whites from the girl's mother to the Mayor of Chicago, Mayor Harrison, to the Chief of Police, McWeeny, all with no legal rights to interfere. Johnson marries Lucille December 4, 1912; soon there after the Supreme Court filed on December 6, 1912 and advanced hearings for January 6, 1913 against Johnson for violation of the White Slaves Act and Lucille was a witness against him. Yet hypocritically, the infuriated whites never regarded the Platt of New York in the Hannah Elias case (*1904 Hannah Elias a 39 year old Negro divorcee supposedly extorted $685,000 from John R. Platt, a 84 year old white retired businessman in their 8 year affair*) or the Pillsbury case involving the Ida Dorsey affair or the James A. Stillman, a married white man, President of the

"Lucille Cameron"
"The Washington Herald," of Oct 23, 1912

"Jack Johnson"
"New-York Tribune," of Apr 6, 1915

National City Bank and Florence H. Leeds, a white New York Chorus Girl case where he was reportedly, father to two of her children. A cancerous act social order as to enact a law that should in the highest

stop the so call invasion of the sanctity and purity of white women from the *"Brutes,"* of our country to commingle is the issue. Hatred was also felt overseas like in Cuba, 1915, when a very attractive Cuban manicurist refused service to Jack Johnson's white wife, according to, *"The Washington Herald," of March 26, 1915.* Monica Valdez, the manicurist refuses to service Johnson's wife because she was married to a black man. A hair pulling and face punching saga was held at the Tonsorial Shop De Luxe where Monica was employed between Monica and Johnson's wife. Police had to be called in to disburse the excitement of the brawl. There was no arrest made, but Johnson demanded and received an immediate apology from the establishment. But Monica Valdez, however, refused to apologize and in her

departing ways, had a few choice words for the champ. In an overall calculated effort to have your cake and eat it too, white men have for centuries tried to no avail, prevent the Jack Johnson's and O.J. Simpson's of the world the inevitability. At the height of Johnson's popularity was July 4, 1910 in Reno, Nevada when he knocked out the once feared champ, James J. Jeffries of California. All the once theories of white hope, white male dominance, a black man would never ever beat a white man in nothing died that night in the fifteenth round. Followed by major riots in every large and small city in the country. Both black and white lives were lost as a result of white anger and black pride. And to add insult to injury, his white wife was first in the ring to greet him and bid him congratulations. Every bookie in country had Jeffries heavily favored. In Bloomfield Center, New Jersey, George Gray, a Negro Chauffeur, bet his white boss, Arthur Springfield an opposite chauffeured ride in a wheelbarrow in public view if Johnson were to be the victor. So confident was Springfield, like seemingly ever white American in the country that he agreed to the wager. As reported by, *"The Marion Daily Mirror," of July 7, 1910*, so outraged by the spectacle of a white man laboring for a Negro and still angered by the defeat, until a man from the crowd leaped into action and dumped an entire pail of fresh eggs on the head of George Gray, the Negro. At which time the humor of the bet faded with Gray being completely humiliated. This brought joy and laughter to the crowd of on-lookers which added a bit of sweeten their heartfelt misery was prevalent. In 1925, Johnson married **Irene Pineau** his last known wife. But on July 16, 1910, **Hattie McCray**, a white woman filed a divorce suit against Johnson. Hattie claimed they were married in Boston on September 28, 1907. Hattie also claimed she first met Johnson in a Philadelphia Café and they lived together as husband and wife in Atlantic City as reported by, *"Hopkinsville Kentuckian,"* of July 19, 1910. On November 16, 1910, **Miss Letha Ackley**, a white woman also claimed to have also been married to Jack Johnson and filed for a divorce. She claimed the decree was granted by Judge Brents according to, *"The Spokane Press," of November 16, 1910.* In 1912, Jack Johnson was even knocked unconscious in Pittsburgh when his vehicle was struck by a white man driving a truck, who initially acknowledged he didn't recognize Jack but later stated it was purposely done. **John Arthur Johnson** (*Jack Johnson's birth name*) was born in Galveston, Texas on a Sunday, March 31, 1878. A six feet and one quarter inch tall and weight of 195 pounds and was 32 years old when he won the Heavy-weight Championship of the world. He was the first Negro to hold the title from 1908 until 1915. His professional career started in 1901 with a career record of 74 wins

(40 KO, 30 decisions 3 disqualified), 13 losses (*7 KO, 5 decisions 1 disqualified*), 10 draws and 5 no contest. The champ was found guilty of violating the federal White Slave Law in transporting **Belle Schreiber** from Pittsburgh to Chicago in 1910. And fined $1,000 for smuggling a diamond necklace into the country. It took the jury about an hour to return a verdict. A motion by Attorney Parkin that Johnson be ordered to the county jail was overruled by Judge George A. Carpenter and the champ was released on bond for $10,000. Two counts of the indictment were dismissed on the grounds that no resolution could be solved between **Lucille Cameron Johnson** as his wife. In 1916 while in Spain with little money, trying to leave Spain for Brazil, the American Embassy refused to issue him a passport at the advice of Washington for fleeing Chicago. Johnson staged a fight in Barcelona with and unknown Negro boxer to raise money. Spaniards so use to bloody bull fights was not impressed with Jack Johnson display of boxing skills upon an unknown component was paid a meager $1,000 for his efforts. On October 18, 1912, Johnson was arrested on the grounds that his relationship with Lucille Cameron violated the Mann Act. After skipping bond, Johnson left the country and went to Montreal before fleeing to France. Spending seven years in exile, where he was reported living in Spain, Mexico, Cuba and South America. He returned to the United States on July 20, 1920 and served time starting in September 1920 at Leavenworth and released July 9, 1921. Jack Johnson had no children and died June 10, 1946 in an automobile accident at the age of 68.

Joe Gans was a Baltimore fighter who was the first African-American Boxing Champion in any weight class. Gans acknowledged that he really didn't know how old he was but assumed it was about 1874 he was born in Baltimore, Maryland and his name was **Joseph Gant** and parents were James and Maria. His fighting career began about 1890 where he netted a $4 purse in his first victory according to, *"The Salt Lake Herald-Republican," of August 11, 1910.* The first ten years he fought about 125 battles. Gans talents were much superior to most of his opponents and could have been crowned champion much sooner but

was involved in a crooked manager who fixed fights for profitability for himself. Soon his reputation began to suffer as a result of the boxing world becoming familiar with his superiority, knew when he was throwing a fight. But at an early age, Gans skills became much more defined as he had two bloody fights with Oscar *"Battling"* Nelson. After being knocked out by Terry McGovern, the boxing world had deemed Gans as being *"washed-up."* But it was as if, the McGovern fight, not staged, was a wake-up call. As Gans began a come-back so fierce, until it was known as *"the come-back of impossibility."* So from 1901 to 1908 he annihilated everyone in his path. Weighing only 133 pounds most times he was considered both a welterweight and a lightweight champion, with a total fight record of 196 bouts, 158 wins, 100 wins by KO, 12

Devour Us Not

losses, 20 draws and 6 no contest. Having a mild and cheerful demeanor, unlike Jack Johnson, Gans seldom sought the lights of fame and never tempted whites by dating or marrying outside his own race. Marrying three times, his first wife, **Mary Beulah** died in 1896, his second wife was **Miss Madge Wadkins** of Cincinnati, he married in 1900. His third wife was **Miss Martha Davis** of Baltimore he married in 1908. Joe Gans died of dread tuberculosis, at his home in Baltimore, Maryland on August 10, 1910 at the age of thirty-four.

"The Salt Lake Tribune," of December 16, 1906

Elizabeth Cady Stanton was born in Johnstown, New York on November 12, 1815. Known as a woman of great courage and a champion for the rights of women. Born to the parentage of strong, powerful and intellectual people, she was one of ten children in the family. Her father, a Congressman and Judge with Scottish ancestry. Elizabeth Cady Stanton was never sick in her eighty-six years until her death on October 26, 1902. At her side were her children; Mrs. M. F. Lawrence, Mrs. Stanton Blatch of New York, Henry and Robert L. Stanton of New York, Lawyers, Theodore Stanton of Paris and G. Smith, a real estate broker of Wardencliffe, Long Island. Her beginnings started with

"The Washington Times," of July 11, 1917

being in her father's law office which was located in the family's home listening to law quotes given by her father. Her mother, in a house with five girls and five boys created quite a loud and exciting environment. With Elizabeth being the eighth of the ten children and presumably one of the most noisiest. So, in an effort to create a quiet calm, her mother would often target the loudest children and send them into her father's office who'd demand quiet while dealing with his clients. Admittedly, most of her father's clients were women seeking divorce. These discussions planted a seed of interest that caused a normally noisy child into an inquisitive one. Elizabeth recalls what solidified her decision to focus on women rights that were unjust as reported by the, *"Blue-grass Blade," of November 9, 1902.* The law of the land was favoring sons in heir. Women, though wealthy prior to a marriage, once married wealth would become the husbands and later son's before daughter's. Noticing this injustice while in adulthood, her own brothers all died before she. When her last brother died, and she went to console her father his comments to her were, *"If you were only a boy!"* She was both hurt and disappointed in the lack of justice in considering the rights of women. After that comment she admits which hurt deeply, thought to herself, *"I'll be just as good as a boy!"* So the motto of her character was shaped on that statement. She once asked the Pastor of her church to teach her Greek along with a class of boys that at the time were five to eight years older than she. The Pastor consented and Elizabeth excelled to the top of the class, receiving the prize of a Greek Testament for her efforts. Elizabeth recalls being so excited about the prize until she headed straight to her father to hopefully change his heart about the boy wishing comment. Her father looked at the prize with love for her in his eyes, but, noticeably, Elizabeth acknowledges were not the spark of pride in her accomplishment and there was his every lasting comments still resonating with her. So yet again, which even more resonated itself, said, *"Oh how I do wish you were a boy!"* She recalls the hurt of the second comment that day as she ran to her room in tears which mentally caused everlasting tears for life. She admittedly, never got over it. She wanted to compete athletically with the boys in every sporting challenge. The thirst of her fight to prove her worthiness as equal to that of a boy was never quenched. She was responsible for fighting the New York Legislature Bill giving the rights of married women to claim property rights. While married to Henry B. Stanton in 1840, expanding her fight by becoming an antislavery worker. Rubbing shoulders with Frederick Douglass, Lloyd Garrison, Lucretia Mott and many others. Elizabeth Cady Stanton, in

New York called the first women rights conventions alone with Lucretia Mott (*Right*) a local Quaker, to discuss the rights of woman in July 19-20, 1848. One of the most debatable discussions were the rights of women to vote, equal wages and parental and guardianships. At the time an

"The Washington Times," of July 11, 1917   *"The Concordia Sentinel," Aug 28, 1920   "New-York Tribune," of May 2, 1920*

unmentionable topics. Elizabeth was even denied entry into Union College because of her sex. She then went to a seminary in Troy, New York for a couple of years and the following seven, she studied at home under the direction of her father becoming proficient in mathematics, law and the classics. Horace Greeley, a writer in the Chicago Inter-Ocean had a memorable debate with Mrs. Stanton about a woman's right to vote and right to serve in war are not mutually exclusive. So the question was asked of Mrs. Stanton what would be her course of action if asked to defend this nation in war or *"the ballot and the bullet go together," "If you want to vote, are you ready to fight?" Without a mille-second of hesitation replied, "I would do as you did, Mr. Greeley. I would send a substitute."* As a result of this comment the argument of Mr. Greeley opposition against the parables of service of war and voting for women changed the heart of Mr. Greeley as well as his deepest reverence for Elizabeth Cady Stanton as reported by, *"The Watchman and Southron," of July 15, 1903.* After the Civil War when the passage of the Fourteenth and Fifteenth Amendments to the United States Constitution, which give the rights to African-Americans, legal protection and voting privileges were opposed by Mrs. Stanton and Susan B. Anthony. The 14th and 15th Amendments did not apply to the two, because they were both women. Elizabeth was President of the National Woman's Suffrage from 1869-1893. She was the mother of seven children. It was said of Elizabeth that during her era, written into the marriage vows and repeated was the phrase *"I will obey."* But, Elizabeth being the feminist had it removed before she would repeat her vows.

William Lloyd Garrison was born in Newburyport, Massachusetts, December 10, 1805. Garrison was largely responsible for the liberation of slaves in America but few of this time know his story. Born in a prison of poverty and squalor tailored his life differently than most of his skin color. Daniel Palmer, Garrison's great-grandfather took forty years of his life to part ways from his birth place and settle in Nova Scotia, on the St. John River with his daughter, Mary who later

"The Broad Ax," of December 9, 1905

married Joseph Garrison and had three sons. Mary Palmer Garrison had many children. One of her sons was Abijah, the father of William Lloyd Garrison. Abijah, fell in love with a very well educated, strong willed, refined and beautiful woman named Fanny Lloyd. Soon they would marry and lots of children followed. Abijah drifting from place to place before finally leaving Nova Scotia in 1805 while his wife was very pregnant. And in December of that year, another son named William was born. Abijah became a Sailor and made many voyages of success. Attributed what he was know for, were gifts of both mind and body based on his life as a reckless sailor of excessive binged drinking. The drinking became more and more intensified as the years went on. Unable to bear the abandonment and drinking episodes, Fanny took actions. One night she broke up one of his drinking parties by smashing all the liquor bottles and kicked everyone out. This also included Abijah, who left his poverty-stricken home and was never heard of again. Like the life of a sailor traveling on the sometimes raging

seas, his abandonment had swallowed him up. Fanny, being of strong willed, with four children & the youngest still being breast-fed made ends meet with much hardship and struggle. Self-promoting herself as a hired nurse, spending copious hours away from her children. The landlord, Mrs. Martha Farnham, understanding her struggles would always care for her children in her absence. Both Fanny and Martha would make molasses candy for sale in an effort to achieve more food and other items of necessity needed for the house. She even accepted the scrapes from the wealthiest family's dinning table for which she was employed to help bridge the hunger of many skipped meals she and her children faced daily. With all of her gallant efforts of trying to keep the family together, with very little sympathy from anyone in the area and no relatives nearby, Fanny had to make a heart-wrenched decision. William was about eight years old when Fanny had no other choice but to separate her children and seek work in Lynn, Massachusetts, Essex County, located about 28 miles away. She left William and his younger sister Elizabeth with the Deacon Ezekiel Bartlett's family, while Fanny and the eldest son's James and Lloyd went to Lynn. Deacon Bartlett sawed wood as his trade and was about as poor as Fanny but accepted the children anyway. William being under aged saw the need and assisted the Deacon where ever his jobs took him. Admittedly, his under developed hands brought very little assistance but the Deacon admired the child's courage without being told to try and lean a hand. Fanny soon found employment in Lynn at shoe factory. But soon Fanny realized Lynn was no different than Newburyport. So she packed up the boys and headed for Baltimore, Maryland where it was rumored jobs were plentiful. She had taken the time to write to William and Elizabeth, explaining the hardship she faced daily, and how God had managed to look over she and the boys. She oddly mentioned a kind-hearted Colored women whom she had become acquainted with. Explaining to them that just to gaze upon her face gives no resemblance of kindness. But she was a slave, despite all she had endured; her heart was as pure as any living soul she had encountered. She gave her name as *"Henny,"* and detailed the nature of her kindness. She urged William that if her eyes never viewed the sparkle in her children's eyes and for whatever reason, they come to where she is, she stated they must come to know her for her sake. Another shoe shop job became available for her but as fate would have it, hard luck waved its ugly head again, because, James, the favorite and eldest of her children ran away. Fed-up with the prison of poverty, reported to have went to sea and was never heard of again. Brokenhearted was Fanny, then broke her foot and was limited in her work responsibilities.

Lloyd now completely lost without James, his big brother whom he idealized was gone. He begged his mother to allow him to separate from her and return to Newburyport. Reluctantly, Fanny consented and he returned to Newburyport and lived with the Bartlett's. Lloyd was eleven years old when he returned to Newburyport where he managed to complete his schooling and had picked up the trade of cabinet making and was offered a job in Haverhill, Massachusetts some 15 miles away when he was about thirteen. After a period of time, Lloyd missing everyone in Newburyport, and an unsuccessful attempt was made to return to Newburyport, spoiled only by the cabinet maker noticing his absence. He managed to catch-up with Lloyd, brought him back to the shop but Lloyd gave such a sincere confession of his longing for his family until the cabinet maker released Lloyd from his apprenticeship and he returned to the Bartlett's. Returning to familiar surrounding made all the difference to Lloyd productiveness. He began to develop his craft and be successful. But once again the fate of hard luck hit the Garrison family yet again, Fanny had died in Baltimore and was already buried there on December 8, 1823 at the age of forty-five. William, many years after she passed away wrote the following words in dedication to her: "She was the masterpiece of womankind-in shape and height majestically fine; her cheeks the lily and the

"The Weekly Messenger," of February 4, 1899

Even-Handed Justice.

Lafayette Gazette.

The killing of the negro child by a white man in St. Martin parish, is, from all accounts, a most deplorable tragedy. If the killing of this negro boy is accidental, of course there can be no guilt attached to it. If it is not accidental no plea can be advanced which justifies the killing. We can not conceive how the wilful killing of a 12-year-old child by a man can be justifiable. That is all there is to it.

Politically speaking the negro is where he should be. He has no business in governmental affairs and his disfranchisement by the constitutional convention was, as all good people will concede, a most salutary measure. Experience proves and every law of nature shows that the Caucasian is immeasurably superior to the negro race. But now that the white men of this country are in charge of every branch of the government, the courts especially should deal out even-handed justice to all, regardless of their color or social standing. We are no negro lover, nor are we a sentimentalist, but we do believe that a plain sense of human justice should behoove every white citizen to exert himself toward the condign punishment of the guilty no matter what be the color or condition of the victim.

rose combines; her lips-more opulently red than wine; her raven locks hung tastefully entwined; her aspect fair as nature could design; and then her eyes! So eloquently bright! An eagle would recoil before her light." William Lloyd Garrison went own to complete his apprenticeship with the Herald Newspaper Office in seven years. Soon thereafter he became editor and publisher of his own paper. It was then that a strong friendship developed between him and

John G. Whittier
"The Evening Bulletin," of Sep 8, 1892

John G. Whittier which would later play a pivotal role in his life. However, after about six months as editor in a very unpopular time left William nearly penniless. So wanting to stay in the newspaper business, William left the home of his birth and headed to Boston. Initially things were very difficult and finding work next to impossible. But William persevered, landing a job at the Philanthropist as a typesetter and in 1828, he became the editor. His fresh views brought a new perspective to the city of Boston and gained William much needed notoriety and popularity. It was with these highlights had another very influential acquaintance, the likes of a liberty apostle named Benjamin Lundy. William Lloyd

Garrison once wrote, *"Before God and our country, we give our pledge that the liberation of the enslaved Africans shall always be uppermost in our pursuits."* A solemn vow of his perpetual consecration. William eventually left Boston in a short time and sot residence in Bennington, Vermont where he was employed as the editor of The Journal of the Times that ended in 1829.

On August 29, 1829, William was personally invited by **Benjamin Lundy** to assist with his newspaper in Baltimore, Maryland called, *"The Genius of Universal Emancipation."* Only 3 months into his new job, he wrote a article blasting Francis Todd, from his home town of Newburyport, for transporting 75 slaves aboard one of his vessels to New Orleans. Todd filed charges for *"Gross and malicious Libel"* and William was arrested and indicted by the Grand Jury of Baltimore. He was convicted and fined $50 and court cost for $100 total. Unable to raise the money was sentenced to 49 days in jail. A rich New York merchant named Arthur Tappan sent him the $100 fine monies and advanced him another $100 to get his paper back up which had been suspended because of his legal issues. But this proved not to be the key to success as William faced another failed attempted in journalism and he returned to Boston January 1, 1831, where his paper, *"The Liberator,"* made its first appearance. Now on his own, having parted ways amicably with his once partner Benjamin Lundy, The Liberator, proved to be the icing on the cake for his success and the Liberator which ran for thirty-five years. During some of the successful years, William wrote the following: *"I solicit no man's praise. I fear no man's*

Devour Us Not

"The Appeal," of January 12, 1901

censure. Our trust for victory is solely in God. We may be personally defeated, but our principles, never! I am in earnest. I will not equivocate, I will not retreat a single inch. And I will be heard."

William's out spoken words against slavery so infuriated the southern slave-holder until a reward of five thousand dollars for his body dead or alive by the legislature of the state of Georgia was passed. Many other southern states wanted to follow suit with mob violence becoming increasingly more aggressive with each passing year. Even the burning of Pennsylvania Hall in Philadelphia and the destruction of a competitor James G. Birney's printing press in Cincinnati, followed by the murder of Elijah P. Lovejoy in Alton, Illinois. But most Northerner's wholeheartedly supported Williams' views on slavery but when a mob composed of so-called Christians attacked him in the streets of Boston, even wrapping a rope around his neck and were dragging him within view of many onlookers, no one helped. It was only the quick thinking of the Mayor of the city assisted with police officers hauling William to city hall and then to the Leverett street jail for his protection. Thinking this fear tactic would cause William to back-off the slavery issue, never wavered his opinion about what he sincerely believed in. And that was the immediate Emancipation of an indigenous people. Wanting to take his message to another level, in 1832, William with several friends headed for the African Baptist Church on Belknap Street and organized the first Garrisonian Society for the abolition of slavery in the United States. The following game-changers were present: Oliver Johnson, Robert B. Hall, Arnold Buffum, William J. Snelling, John E. Fuller, Moses Thatcher, Joshua Coffin Stillman, B. Newcomb, Benjamin C. Bacon, Isaac Knapp and Henry K. Stockton. Also this clan of bold abolitionary team founded the New England Anti-Slavery Society and in 1833. He co-founded the American Anti-Slavery Society with his paper appearing to be the heart of the voice of America yarning freedom for all, speaking for those with no voice, his message marched on. On September 4, 1834, William married Helen Eliza Benson, the daughter of a retired abolitionist merchant named George Benson from Rhode Island. They had five son's and two daughter's.

William believed in non-violence but immediate emancipation of all slaves and not gradual as were the popular decision of the time. The Emancipation Proclamation eventually became the eye of reality for the enslaved. And after millions of slaves were theoretically free, except for special sections of the country, William's life's work of righteousness was complete. But for political reasons, not all slaves were free. But the goals and the efforts of William Lloyd Garrison and his band of relentless followers would not be stopped. In 1865, William discontinued the publication of The Liberator having spoken the words of the slaves. After the Civil War, for his service in help ridding the country of the social wrongs of slavery, the community raised a large sum of $30,000 and presented to William. Lecturing when ever called on his views for America. William was even threatening with death for burning the Constitution of the United States for its hypocrisy, but he loved his country with its entire fault. Until his death, on May 24, 1879 at the home of his daughter, Mrs. Henry Villard in New York City he was defiant. Never looked upon his mother's face since the age of eight, most of his lectures mentioned her strength and resolve. He would mention in visual clarity as though she had engaged in conversation with him, *"Henny,"* a Negro slave woman, of nothingness, befriending his mother and showering her with all she had and that was nothing but love. Any man under similar circumstances, having nothing in exchange to offer, should have been filled with bitterness and hate. But the manner in which his mother spoke of this woman that's what intrigued her so about Henny. The heart and innocence of a child, had more to offer than rich

merchants whom rather look pass you as if you were not a person of means. And William went to join his mother with these simple last words: *"My country is the world!" "My countrymen are all mankind!"* Said of him by the *"The Broad Ax," of December 9, 1905, "His breast was full of the milk of human kindness, that his love for his fellow creatures was as broad as the universe, that he wore himself out in the service of his country, and that among the greatest champions of the rights of man, who have been spawned upon the face of the earth, none of them were born greater than William Lloyd Garrison."* Even one hundred after his birth, William was still being honored all over the country for his courage and commitment to end slavery. And 1905, an event held in Cooper Union Hall in New York City, where chairman Robert E. Ely and Dr. Moncure D. Conway were speakers. Booker T. Washington urged all Americans, particularly Negroes to celebrate the Garrison 100th Anniversary calling him a great abolitionist and patriot. And the year, most newspapers like, "The Broad Ax," of Salt Lake City, Utah, "The Seattle Republican," of Seattle, Washington, "The Minneapolis Journal," of Minneapolis, Minnesota, "The New-York Tribune," of New York City, New York, "The Sedalia Weekly Conservator," of Sedalia, Missouri, "The Appeal," of St. Paul, Minnesota, "The Rising Sun," of Kansas City, Missouri, "The Leavenworth Echo," of Leavenworth, Washington and "The Palestine Daily Herald," of Palestine, Texas just to name a few all gave tribute to William Lloyd Garrison for what he stood for.

"Dora April Richardson"

Cassius Marcellus Clay was an emancipationist from Madison County, Kentucky. Cassius known as one of the first abolitionist slaveholders in the south died at the age of 92 of cystitis on July 22, 1903 in his home, the very place where he was born on October 19, 1810. The son of General Green Clay, a slaveholder and one of the wealthiest men in the south, left Cassius some 2,200 acres of land. A graduate of Yale in 1832 and was very much influenced by William Lloyd Garrison's speeches, became an abolitionist. And he then, as a student gave his own abolitionist speech at Yale. After his Kentucky Legislature tenure, he began to practice law in Lexington. In 1834 he edited the *"True American,"* newspaper which was known as an anti-slavery paper. But not being particularly popular, was the paper until it was destroyed by a mob. Not to be deterred, Cassius went to Cincinnati some 82 miles away and had the papers printed there. He then brought back the printed papers to Kentucky and distributed them there. Dr. Bailey, a well known abolitionist in Cincinnati ran the Cincinnati Herald and allowed Cassius to print the papers there. Also both Cassius and Dr. Bailey publicly denounced the country's involvement in the Mexican War. Ironically, Cassius served as a volunteer Officer in the Mexican War and was decorated for his bravery. But his political support went to Republican Abraham Lincoln, probably because his views on slavery, which were similarly to that of his own. Cassius really admired Lincoln as he expressed to a reporter who asked of him, "Who is the greatest man you have ever known?" He unequivocally replied, *"President Abraham Lincoln was the greatest man this country ever produced. As a diplomat he was greater than all his diplomats. As a General he was superior to any General in the Army, and he as a statesman, he far out ranked his cabinet. He was clogged in his administration by his cabinet, and he had some bad elements about him."*

"The Appeal," of June 1, 1895

But in 1896, Cassius supported the gold Democratic ticket. Because of a conspiracy to assassinate him broke out in the late 1890's, had his house fortified and he went into seclusion and his home was then named "White Hall." White Hall set amongst 360 areas of land. Cassius at age 84 in 1894 married a child wife of 15 years named Dora April Richardson who later separated and divorced him. William Richardson, his wife's brother was offered $500 to leave the country or accept the fate of death by Cassius for allegedly preventing Dora from anymore contact with Cassius. Dora eventually left White Hall after reports went out that Cassius was keeping her locked up in a room and preventing her from leaving. This was fueled by jealousy of her love for another man. Cassius filed for divorce in 1898 but on his dieing bed in 1903 begged for her return. But by this time Dora was married to Riley Brock. Strangely, the six area land where Dora and her then new husband resided was purchased and deeded to the Brock's as a wedding gift from Cassius. Cassius's first wife was Mary Jane Warfield Clay whom he divorced in 1878 after 45 years of marriage. They had nine children, Elisha Warfield, Green, Mary Barr, Sally, Laura, Brutus, Anne, Rhode and adopted named Henry. Before the saga of White Hall, Cassius was a very well respected Democratic politician, serving in the State Senate from 1889-1891, to include the unexpired term of his son Rhodes Clay due to his

Abraham Lincoln
"The Seattle Republican," Jan 3, 1913

Charles Francis Adams
"The Times Dispatch," Dec 16, 1906

Edward Dickinson Baker
"The San Francisco Call," Nov 24, 1895

William Lewis Dayton
"The Minneapolis Journal," Jun 10, 1906

untimely death in the Missouri Legislature in 1902. Former Secretary of the American Legislature at Florence Italy, and St. Petersburg, Russia. In 1861 when the Civil War began, President Lincoln nominated Cassius as Ambassador to Spain in which he respectfully declined. Cassius then went to Washington to meet with President Lincoln and express his desire to take a post in either England or France. Later finding those positions had been promised by Mr. Lincoln to **Charles Francis Adams**, the grandson of President John Adams and son of President John Quincy Adams, the England position and **William Lewis Dayton**, the France position. As recorded by, *"The Herald," of November 17, 1895*, Mr. Lincoln then urged Cassius to stay in Washington a few days so that he may find a position suitable to his liking. Later that evening while having dinner with **Senator Henry Shelton Sanford**, who had recently accepted the position of minister to Belgium were interrupted by **Senator Edward Dickinson Baker** of Oregon who was relaying a message from the President, asking Cassius if he'd accept the position in Russia. He accepted the position from 1861 - 1869. William Henry Seward, the Secretary of State, recalled Cassius back to United States to accept a Major Generalship promotion, but he

refused to accept it until President Lincoln sign the Emancipation Proclamation. Cassius upon his return to the United States went to President Lincoln's office to argue about how the European Nations favored against slavery and urged the President to follow suit or be isolated worldwide. President Lincoln, concern about Cassius own State and bordering Southern States encouraged Cassius to go to Kentucky to make a canvass of the Legislature. Cassius made a compelling speech in Frankfort, Kentucky and suggested the wiser decision that Kentucky and bordering Southern States follow suit and not secede from the union if the main element of that decision was based on the slavery issue. Before returning to Russia, Cassius was invited to give a similar speech at Albany University. He did, gladly, knowing it would irritate Secretary Seward and Thurlow Reed, who were adamantly opposed to emancipating the slaves. September, 1862 the Proclamation was issue and Cassius had successfully completed his mission, and then went back to Russia to complete his assignment.

Muhammad Ali, the former Heavyweight champion of the world was born Cassius Marcellus Clay, Jr. January 17, 1942 in Louisville, Kentucky. Later he changed his name to Muhammad Ali in 1964 after joining the Nation of Islam. Admittedly, his father, Cassius Marcellus Clay, Sr. born in 1912, nine years after the death of the

Abolitionist General Cassius M. Clay, the person for whom he was named, must have assuredly had bloodline connections. The first African-American to play college football in America and the first African-American to be selected as All-American in football was **William Henry Lewis.** According to, *"The Appeal, of March 4, 1911,"* William was born November 28, 1863 to slave parents in Berkley, Virginia. He entered Amherst College in Amherst, Massachusetts where he excelled in academics and athletics. Amherst a private liberal arts college, founded in 1821 was the third oldest institution of higher education in Massachusetts. After graduating from Amherst, he then attended the Harvard Law School in 1892 and for two years became the star All-American center for the Harvard football team. After his playing days he became a defensive coach for

twelve years at Harvard from 1895 to 1906 with a combined winning record of 114-15-5. His strategist defense plan successfully managed to stop the previously unstoppable Pennsylvania's *Guard Back,"* play. During his time as coach wrote several books on football. Some were *"Making a Football Team,"* and *"A Primer of College Football,"* as reported by, *"The San Francisco Call," of November 16, 1902.* In October 1910, then President William Howard Taft appointed Lewis as the United States Assistant Attorney General. At the time was the highest public office ever held by an African-American. But the appointment didn't go on without

its objections from the Democratic in the House and the Senate. At the time still angered by the sponsorship of the Republican Party for the Sutherland Amendment to the direct elections resolution, which was meant to protect the African-Americans? Now to elevate an African-American to the Governmental position ever held by a Negro was more than the narrow minded racist of the Democratic Party could stand. Senator Henry Cabot Lodge, of Massachusetts, a Harvard Grad and co-authored a Federal Election Bill that guaranteed federal protection for Negro voting rights was one of the major components fighting hard for Lewis confirmation. As

Devour Us Not

George W. Wickersham
"Richmond Planet," July 24, 1909

President William H. Taft
"The Seattle Republican,"
of October 6, 1911

Assistant Attorney General, a high annual salary of $5,000, at the time the highest in the Judiciary. A fight that lasted more than a few months against the southern opposition. Finally, June, 1911, Lewis was confirmed. After the swearing in Lewis first went to the White House to personally thank President Taft for his courage in bestowing upon him this high honor and reassuring him of his conscious efforts and commitment to give more than what's required. October 1911, another first for William was his acceptance to the American Bar Association (ABA). And notwithstanding was the noise of racism which caused William to yet again face a campaign by racist oppositions who would staged a protest to secede from the organization if William remained a member. They requested his resignation on the grounds that the committee members never before faced with an African-American with credentials high enough to even be a factor. They voted purely on his qualification, essentially what it should be based on and not race. Even though after his name was submitted by the Massachusetts Bar to the American Bar Association, no one at that time had any objections. The objection came after seeing William at the convention. In their defense they suggested that race had nothing to do with it. Interventions from the **Attorney General George W. Wickersham** who sent a letter to then all 4,700 members, proposing they reconsider their positions regarding Lewis acceptance. Wickersham was blasted by southern newspapers for lack of proper manners. Wickersham attempt to prevent a resolution that would change the way elections into membership for the American Bar Association was overwhelmed by majority members to include race and sex and subsequent impeded Negroes and Women. The nature of the debate was as follows:

"Whereas three persons of the colored race were elected to membership in this association without knowledge upon the part of those electing them that they were of that race and are now members of this association; Resolved, That as it has never been contemplated that members of the colored race should become members of the association the several local councils are directed that if at anytime any of them shall recommend a person of the colored race for membership, they shall accompany the recommendation with a statement of the fact that he is of such race," as reported by, *"The Sun,"* of October 21, 1914.

After Lewis tenure as Assistant United States District Attorney was completed, and after President Taft's term ended in 1913, Lewis went into private practice. The President recommended William Lewis for an appointment to the Massachusetts Supreme Court, but was denied by the Governor of Massachusetts, Eugene Foss. Any reasons as to why? A question one need not ever ask. While in Washington, Lewis had made several acquaintances, one in particular was former President Roosevelt who visited Cambridge often to see Lewis. President Roosevelt a Harvard graduate also would always seek the company of Lewis and his family to reminisce on old times. William Lewis died January 1, 1949.

Joseph Preston Norris-"The Sun," of June 29, 1913

Joseph Preston Norris, according to, *"The Sun," of June 29, 1913*, was the body servant of General Robert E. Lee, the Confederate Leader. Norris was the last body servant assigned to General Lee which was during the Civil War and was with him at the time of his death, October 12, 1870. Norris, a native of Lexington, Virginia was born on a plantation in slavery to a master named Samuel McDowell Read. Samuel was described as a prominent member of the community and in Legislature. Norris learned the trade of a blacksmith on the plantation, a trade that became useful during service with the Army before being assigned to General Lee. After being assigned to General Lee, he was responsible for the tidiness of the tent he occupied as well as keeping his boots shined, clothes clean and acting as a waiter during meal time. Norris admitted to being apart of the Confederate Army because almost every Negro in the south were doing it. In describing General Lee's demeanor, Norris said he never witness the General in a state of anger or having unfavorable words towards anyone regardless of race. After the war, he stated that General Lee became President of a college now named Washington and Lee University where he took a home on the campus. After the death of General Lee, Norris had saved his earnings and moved to the place of his birth in Lexington where he purchased a farm of forty areas of land. And recorded by, *"The Washington Times," of February 11, 1917*, Joseph was also a porter in the office of President Daniel Willard, of the Baltimore and Ohio Railroad. Immediately after the death of General Robert E. Lee, Joseph was employed by the railroad at the Camden Station before being transferred to the executive office where he worked for the President. Joseph admits at one time that General Stonewall Jackson was his Sunday school teacher. At the Presbyterian Church in Lexington, Virginia before the Civil War, then Stonewall Jackson taught all slaves on the matters of the Christian religion. Joseph Preston Norris died February 11, 1917, survived by his wife and one son.

Daniel H. McDowell
"The Evening Herald," of April 13, 1918

Daniel H. McDowell, known as *"Mac,"* was a waiter at the National Press Club. Born approximately 1843 on the same plantation as Joseph P. Norris, on the Samuel McDowell Read plantation in Lexington, Virginia. Daniel was so an admirer of Stonewall Jackson for his instructional abilities until he was one of many Negroes who attended the funeral of General Jackson in Lexington following his death at the battle of Chancellorsville.

"The Princeton Union," of May 18, 1899

Uncle Jesse Welch pictured on the right, died March 29, 1893 at the age of 102. He was employed as a *"chore boy and gardener,"* for Dr. Asher Goslin. He was born in Haywood County, North Carolina, March 24, 1791. Owned by John Welch, who came with him in 1801 to Missouri. Later, the family settled in Franklin near Boonville. Uncle Jesse became

Uncle Jesse Welch
"The Holt County Sentinel," of July 21, 1911

a contraband of Colonel Reavis, of Iowa during the Civil War. He was later transferred to Colonel George A. Hall of the 4th Missouri State Militia Cavalry and became a body servant to Major George W. Kelly. After the Civil War, Uncle Jesse came to Oregon with the Major in 1869 and later was employed by Dr. A. Goslin, as a gardener. Once during a speech for the State Horticultural Society, June, 1888 by Dr. Goslin on the subject of producing great strawberries, a question was asked. So at the conclusion of his expert opinion of growing strawberries, someone in the audience called for Uncle Jesse. Without missing a beat, Uncle Jesse, as widely known and well-liked as he was, jumped to his feet and said, *"Friend, Dr. Goslin raises his strawberries wid' a spoon, I does de' cultivatin."* The audience went plum crazy with laughter and that included Dr. Goslin.

"The Evening Herald," of April 13, 1918

Pictured on the left is **Uncle "Fielding" Walker** with his wife. He was one of General Robert E. Lee's many body servants' and was present at the surrender at Appomattox Court House. On the right is **Eli Jackson** who was the property of Captain Forbes, who was on the Staff of Major-General Longstreet. As apart of Eli's responsibilities, was the carrying of a satchel

"The Evening Herald," of April 13, 1918

Albert Hawkins
"St. Paul Daily Globe," of August 2, 1885

that contained invaluable military documents on missions for Major-General Longstreet. These missions would be entrusted in his care of Eli for the purpose of safe delivering them from one southern Army camp to another. These dangerous missions at times required the maneuverability of a skilled spy, putting at risk his own life as well as the location of the southern camps and the contents of the satchel.

Albert Hawkins was the coachman for President Grant while he was in the White House. He was honored in driving the hearse for Grant to his final resting place and spoke fond of him while working in the White House.

The White House, contrary to what is believed, has always had Negro servants performing various duties with every President's Administration since Washington. President Theodore *"Teddy"*

Mrs. Edith Roosevelt
"The Washington Times," Mar 6, 1904

"The Herald," of December 26, 1897

Roosevelt was the 26th President and became the youngest President ever in 1901 after the assassination of President McKinley. At the age of 42, he served until 1908. According to, *"The St. Louis Republic," of October 6, 1901,* Mrs. Edith Kermit Carrow Roosevelt, President Roosevelt's second wife (*married to President Roosevelt from 1886-1919*), announced she wanted all white servants and cooks in the White House. This is contrary to President Roosevelt's love for all people and that included Africans and African-Americans. One of his children, Kermit, had made so many trips to Khartum until he spoke fluent

"A young President Theodore and Edith Roosevelt"
"The Washington Times," of March 13, 1904

Swahili and often acted as an interpreter on their trips there. But among the white servant coming to the White House was a favorite that had been with the Roosevelt family since she left Ireland in 1841. Her name was Mrs. Dora Watkins that accompanied the Roosevelt's from their Oyster Bay, New York home to the White House. The dean of faculty for servants at the White House was a Negro named *"Uncle Jerry,"* who had been at the White House for more than 30 years. Mrs. Roosevelt even overhauled cookware and eating utensils. It was clear some of the Negro servants and cook were sent packing and fewer remained. The second cook, a Negro woman named Mary from Virginia remained as cook. But the mere announcement of such a vast example of racial prejudice sent shock-waves throughout Roosevelt's Administration and the country almost as much as the Presidents' invite of Booker T. Washington for dinner that came later. But Mrs. Roosevelt unfazed by it all then contacted Colonel Theodore A. Bingham, Superintendent of Public Buildings and constructed three new servant rooms in the garret, located on top of the building with much better ventilation. These quarters were designed for the white and Swede servants while the Negro servants remained in the old rooms located in the basement with poor ventilation. Unapologetic was Mrs. Roosevelt, after the President voiced his disapproval.

Benjamin Oliver Davis, Sr., was the first Negro to be appointed a 1Lt. *(temp promotion)* of the 8th United States Volunteer Infantry until being mustered out in March, 1899. In June, 1899, he enlisted as a private, assigned to Troop T. 9th Cavalry Regiment, formally known as an original Buffalo Soldier Regiment. He was promoted to Cpl. and Squadron SgtMaj.

Benjamin O. Davis
"The Colored American," of Oct 18, 1902

Benjamin O. Davis
"The Washington Bee," of Jun 1, 1901

of the 9th Cavalry. In less than 2 years, Davis went from the bottom to the top of the enlisted ladder, making him eligible to take the examination for an appointment as an Officer in the regular Army.

Devour Us Not

Davis was successful and on February 2, 1901 and commissioned a Second Lieutenant, signed by President William McKinley. He was third on the list of twelve who passed the examination with his average score of 91% and high marks in Military Science and International Law. The Second Lieutenant rank claimed an annual salary of $1,500 for an official uncounted with an increase of 10 cents after each five years of service according to, *"The Seattle Republican," of May 27, 1904.* Much discrepancy has been written about Benjamin Davis' age and whether or not he lied about his age to enter into the Army without his parent's permission. Below is a copy of the United States Federal Census of 1880 for the District of Columbia area which list his mother and father, Henrietta and Lewis, who were Government employee's, living with her mother, Charlotte Stewart and Benjamin is one month old, being born May in 1880. Davis attended schools in Washington D. C. where he was a Major in his high school cadet corps. Due to the out break of the Spanish-American War, Davis was granted the

United States Federal Census June 1, 1880

Benjamin Davis (Mulatto, born May 1880) living with his mother, Henrietta Davis (Mulatto, age 25) and Father, Lewis Davis (Mulatto, age 35) living in the home of his Grandmother Charlotte Stewart (Black, age 47)

temporary promotion. Even though Captain Charles Young of the 9th Cavalry was already in the unit, product of the 1889 graduating class of West Point. Davis has the dubious destintion of rising from the lowest rank to General as an African-American first and at the time considerate one of the youngest Officers in the Army. As a First Lieutenant, he was ordered as a temporary assignment to Fort D.A. Russell, in Wyoming. As a Captain in 1915 he was in charge of the Military Training Academy at Wilberforce University, Ohio, the first all Black University in the United States and Davis second tour at the University. He was then assigned to the Cavalry unit in the Republic of the Philippines in 1917. On September 1, 1920 as a Lieutenant Colonel, he was assigned to teach Military Science and Tactics at Tuskegee Institute, Alabama where he remained until 1924.

Davis became the first African-American General in the United States Army, by being promoted to Brigadier General October 25, 1940. Davis died November 26, 1970 at the age of 90 and is buried in the Arlington National Cemetery in Washington D. C. A distinguished Army career that extended 50 years was commemorated by a public retirement ceremony, presided by President Harry S. Truman.

Sergeant William Harvey Carney, as a member of the 54th Massachusetts Volunteers, Company C, attack on Fort Wagner, South Carolina, Saturday, July 18, 1863. Sergeant Carney was recognized by the War Department for his bravery. His actions placed him in a unique category as being the first African-American to be awarded the nations highest medal for valor, **"The Medal Of Honor,"** as recorded by, *"The Colored American," of June 2, 1900.* Even though his recognition took 37 years to

William Harvey Carney
"Tensas Gazette," of January 31, 1913

"The Colored American," of June 2, 1900

be received, which was rewarded on May 23, 1900, his actions were widely known and talked about for decades. In the movie, *"Glory,"* William's role was completely omitted from the facts related to his heroism. In part, there was a Color Sergeant designated to every company during that period of the Civil War. Their primary duty was to carry the flags of their individual unit into battle without the necessity of a weapon. Sergeant Carney was not the assigned Color Sergeant for the 54th, but when the assigned Color Sergeant fell in the attack on Fort Wagner, Sergeant Carney was observed throwing away his weapon, seizing the colors from the fallen Color Sergeant before the colors could touch the ground and dashing forward. In frontal view of gun shots and shells all around him until he reached the top of the parapet. Then he drove the staff of the flag into the ground and

laid behind it for cover and stayed there for nearly and hour before looking around and finding himself all alone in full view of the enemy and those proud colors waving like ripples of water on a lake in summer. Receiving three bullet wounds in his body, losing blood and finding himself alone, pulled up the staff as it waved in view of all both friendly and enemy and made his way to a designated reserve line. Once he reached a friendly line, Officers at that location asked to relieve him of the flag, but William refused to surrender the colors to anyone that was not apart of the 54th. He was then placed in an ambulance and driven to the rallying point where he gave up the colors amongst an enormous cheering from all who had witness Williams and the 54th colors flying all alone at the top of that parapet for nearly and hour. After the jeering stopped William acknowledged by suggesting as modest as one might expect from a heroic act, *"Boys, I only did my duty."*

"The San Francisco Call," of August 3, 1912

His actions were duly noted and reported to Governor John A. Andrews of Massachusetts. General Quincy Adams Gilmore, in command of the U.S. forces recommended the Medal of Honor. However, the written citation made to the War Department was not received and ultimately caused the delay. In the interim, Robert Blake's heroic action as a Union Sailor aboard the USS Marblehead in December, 1863 was awarded the Medal of Honor in April, 1864. And for three decades he was known as the first African-American to receive the Medal of Honor. It wasn't until **Mr. Thomas J. Calloway**, in connection with the Negro exhibit at the Paris Exposition of 1900, that was organized by W.E.B. Du Bois, came up with a brilliant plan to showcase a collection of photographs from Medal of Honor

Prof. Thomas J. Calloway
"The Colored American," of August 25, 1900

167   *Devour Us Not*

"The Washington Times," of December 25, 1904

recipients that were African-American men. The Congress of the United States was notified and a person connected with the War Department put the plan in action. Some sixteen living and dead heroes were found but conspicuously absent from the group was Sergeant Carney's name. An investigation ensued to included contact with Sergeant Carney to gather all the facts. All necessary and viable facts had been substantiated and were submitted to the Secretary of War. And after thirty-seven years of wait, May, 1900, William Harvey Carney received his rightful placed among the sixteen other Medal of Honor recipients with one distinguishable difference, he was the first.

"The Seattle Republican," of January 15, 1904

First U.S. Senators L/R Standing/Sitting: **Robert C. De Large**, M.C. of South Carolina (1868-1870), **Jefferson F. Long,** M.C. of Georgia (1870-1871), **Hiram Rhodes Revels** of Mississippi (1870-1871), **Benjamin S. Turner,** M.C. of Alabama (1871-1873), **Josiah T. Walls**, M.C. of Florida (1871-1876), **Joseph H. Rainey**, M.C. of South Carolina (1870-1879), **Robert Brown Elliot**, M.C. of South Carolina (1871-1874).

After Emancipation followed by the Reconstruction Period, the above former slaves, without having the proper political knowledge or backing in an effort to challenge the unfairness of civil liberties in allowing the difficulty of transitioning was what they faced. The above first Senators are from the Forty-first and Forty-second Congresses as the beginning of a new chapter in American history and a polarized political system. A

political voice is what was lacking for justice in shared responsibilities for a better America. These pioneers took the first step in assuring the rights not only for African-Americans but all Americans who are disenfranchised as a result of proper law interpretation. **Robert C. De Large** was a Republican representing the Charleston District of South Carolina where the black vote outnumbered the white vote 10 to 1. De Large was born in slavery listed as a Mulatto, De Large, a barber and farmer, was met with much opposition from a man named Christopher C. Bowman who accused De Large of voter fraud and not being an American citizen by virtue of his birth in England. Bowen and De Large received over 15,000 votes each while a third man named Robert S. Tharin received 800 votes and makes the claim that Bowen was a bigamist and a murderer among other things while De Large was from England. In the end, De Large did not triumphant and the election seat tainted by voter fraud was declared vacant and he left January 24, 1873. Returning to Charleston where he became a Trial Justice, followed by his death in 1874.

Jefferson Franklin Long, known for his remarkable intellectual brilliance as well as his wit, was the first Negro that Georgia sent to Congress. At the time of his election, Georgia hosted the largest Negro population than any other southern state. Jefferson was a merchant tailor in Macon, Georgia and beloved by all races. He was sworn in January 16, 1871 and served until March 3, 1871 totaling 47 days. He was filling a seat left vacancy by Samuel F. Gove, who was deemed *"not entitled."* Jefferson not an eligible candidate for reelection, returned to Macon where died February 4, 1901.

John Willis Menard known as a great public speaker was elected to Congress November 3, 1868 from Louisiana. Born in Illinois, educated at Iberia College and had acted as hospital steward and recruiting officer for the Government during the Civil War. By virtue of his certificate of election for receiving the most votes and a *"prima facia,"* right to the seat was a matter that set in motion the amount of depravity he faced for a seat he'd never hold. The *"Memphis Daily Appeal," of December 21, 1868,* reports that even Governor Henry Clay Warmoth withheld his certificate, purposely, to give the Committee of Elections an excuse to deem him ineligible. Since Menard's election, a re-districting had begun to redistribute the demographics. Menard was

elected to fill the seat of the late James Mann, a white Democrat whom had died in 1868 before his term had expired. A Mr. Jones having run against Mann and lost questioned the legitimacy of James Mann's seat before his death on the grounds that he was not a citizen of the State even though Mann had the proper certificate to hold the seat.

Mr. Jones contended there was never a vacancy because Mann was never entitled to the seat. Meanwhile, Caleb S. Hunt, a white Democrat, who ran and lost against John Menard claimed fraud and refused to accept a defeat to a Negro. Menard addressed the House of Representatives to plead his case, and in so doing gained some respect from those members. A vote was taken on the resolution of the minority of the Committee on Elections, declaring Caleb S. Hunt duly elected, but it was rejected- yeas 41 and nays 136. Then another vote was taken for Menard, the rightful elected and it too was rejected - yeas 57 and nays 130. Because of all the attention directed in a deliberated attempt to bare him entry into the political spotlight paved the way for others to seek that seat. John Willis Menard never served one day as Senator for which he was elected by a large margin by the

"The Tomahawk," of May 4, 1916

"The Daily Phoenix," of February 4, 1868

people of Louisiana. On February 25, 1870, after much debate on the subject, Charles Sumner championed the Negro effort in allowing **Hiram Rhodes Revels** admission to the Senate to fill the seat let vacant by the resignation of Jefferson Davis. H.R. Revels representing Natchez, Mississippi from February 25, 1870 - March 4, 1871. Revels was born in 1827 in North Carolina and was an ordained minister and a barber. Revels stricken with paralysis died January 15, 1901 at Aberdeen, Mississippi. **Benjamin S. Turner** represented the Selma district in Alabama. His platform was for universal amnesty, universal suffrage, and universal repudiation of the national debt. Born March 17, 1825 in Weldon, North Carolina and died March 21, 1894 in Selma.

Josiah T. Walls was a Republican elected from 1871 to 1873. He was a very successful vegetable farmer from Florida. And after leaving Congress in 1876, his estimated net worth from his vegetables reached between $7,000 and $8,000 in 1883. Born a slave in Virginia in 1842, he was a member of the Confederate Army. Josiah Walls died, May 15, 1905.

Joseph H. Rainey was the first Republican Negro member of the House of Representatives December 12, 1871 and was defeated by Samuel Lee, a Negro in 1874 who was defeated by John S. Richardson, white, in 1879. Rainey was the first African-American to serve in the United States House of Representatives, and the second Negro to serve in the United States Congress. Rainey, born as a slave and was freed by his father's purchase of his entire family. Later, Rainey became a barber and died at his residence in Georgetown, South Carolina, August, 1, 1887.

Robert Brown Elliot was born in England in 1842. He received his college degree from Eton

College in England. Elliot was also a member of the Forty-second and Forty-third Congress from South Carolina. He was elected as a Republican in United States House of Representatives from 1871-1874 from South Carolina. In 1879, at the Chicago Republican Convention, Elliot nominated John Sherman for President. Following Elliot, Secretary of the Treasury Sherman made Elliot Special Agent of the Department of Treasury at Charleston, South Carolina as reported by the, *"New-York Tribune," of June 2, 1907*. Elliot died in 1884.

During the Reconstruction Period, the acceptability of Negroes having the same rights as whites angered so many in the south where Negroes were treated the worst and every effort was put in place to disenfranchise the Negro. Laws were passed to even prevent the

Forbidden *"Marriages,"* between blacks and whites by establishing a degree or drop of tainted blood law. More particularly, black men desiring marriage to white women as an unnatural act. The Jim Crow Laws of assured hanging, if a black man even looked in the direction of a white woman was the law of the land. This seemed to legitimize its continuance of white male dominance. Not to mention the off-spring's that would surely result in a new Mulatto race would cause the dead to roll-over in their graves was unthinkable. But for centuries, it was finding for the offspring's of white men and black women, but to taint the purity of white women without the brutality of rape was unimaginable. So written laws had to be implemented to impede this atrocity.

The court in its decision in the case of the 1910 Frank S. Ferrall and Susie Patterson Ferrall in the Ferrall vs. Ferrall case (69 S.E. 60) suggest that a Negro ancestry of the third generation must be of pure Negro blood that is known and recognized in his place of residence or social groups before a marriage is nullified and voided as it relates to mixed race marriages. Frank S. Ferrall of Franklin County, North Carolina filed for divorce and refused to pay alimony or child support on the grounds of his acknowledgement that his wife had tainted Negro blood within the third generation of her bloodline. Evidence presented at trial showed his wife's grandfather, named Julius Coley was a Mulatto. So when this statute in part was revised in 1905, under the heading *"Who May Not Marry,"* applied to either Negroes or Indians to the third generation inclusive or an enactment expressed in similar terms had been the statute law of a state governing the question of that character. So accordingly, the courts upheld bringing the marriage within the prohibited degree of void or who may not marry, if one of the ancestors of the named generation had to have been of pure untainted Negro blood. But the jury looking upon her physical appearance rather than drop of blood percentage ruled in favor or beyond the third generation statute. But Judge Cooke of the county, over-ruled the verdict and cited the ignorance of the statute regardless of physical appearance or social connections does not supersede the law. In the Hare's case (113 N.C. 10 S.E. 55) involving the right of an applicant to be admitted to a white school, the courts ruling, using the same principals to race-mixed marriages, seemingly, schools at that time were separate but equal depended on the degree of tainted Negro blood as it relates to off-springs of such marriages in attending these white schools. The courts at that time as reported by, *"The Broad Ax," of Chicago, Illinois, January 21, 1911*, ruled that the words, *"the third generation inclusive,"* must be construed to prohibit interracial marriages of whites with persons who were not beyond the third generation from pure Negro Ancestry blood argument. A similar trial of the Supreme Court case in the nations capitol involving Isabel Irene Wall vs. James Oyster, where all white and all Negro schools were established but were compel to enroll the petitioner in the all

white school of Brookland White, September, 1910. The admission made by the petitioner, Isabel Wall, had not less than 1/16 of Negro blood, making her physical appearance unnoticeable for whites objections. But her application was denied, by a vote of 8 to 5 and the child was eventually expelled. Even though her parents and she were accepted in their communities as white, traces of tainted Negro blood were link within the 3rd generation drop rule.

Congress had not established what percentage or proportion of racial blood percentage shall characterize an individual as a Negro. So visual observation as grounds for defining a race was not sufficient enough to classify a mixed race. Or, a measuring guide to discriminate will still be covered by the tainted blood law. But in defending his ruling, Chief Justice Shepard, presiding over the Court of Appeals, stated school segregation statute in effect prohibits *"Colored,"* children regardless of how faint in appearance that drop of tainted blood is reflected in outer appearance. Rumors of her forefathers in the form of her great-grandparents being of African Ancestry, was the law. But further comments by the Chief Justice that claimed the ruling in some southern states defining **any** Negro blood classifies one as a Negro, might have included himself. But, regardless, young Isabel, as white as any of her previous white classmates had to attend a Colored school. But assistant to the District Attorney, Stanton C. Peelle, later defeated that argument. The case of State vs. Chavers (50 N.C. 11), involving the construction of a statute defining free Negroes as, *"all free persons as, descended from Negro ancestors to the fourth generation inclusive,"* the courts approved a charge that *"every person who had 1/16 Negro blood in his or her veins were indeed considered full Negroes within the meaning of the statue."* The ruling continued by suggesting no one can just cease to be a Negro,

unless they reached the 5th generation from their Negro ancestry. To erase the physical appearance of black features, was the laws attempt to satisfy the prohibited existence of interracial marriages. The issue of blood however, has been around since before Jesus. Jesus, per scripture, came from the tribe of Judah, 4th of the 12 tribes of Israel (*Hebrews 7:14*). The Gospel of Matthews give all 14 generation of Jesus. Judah had 5 sons by his Canaanite wives, 3 (Er, Onan & Shelah) by his 1st, Shuah and 2 (Pharez and Zarah, *1 Chronicles 2:4*) by his 2nd, Tamar, also daughter-in-law of Judah. Pharez is the 25th generation from the start of Jesus bloodline (*Matthew1: 3*). Ham, was the youngest son of Noah (*Genesis 10:6*) by his Ethiopian wife. Canaan, Ham's son, was cursed by Noah for seeing his nakedness and made a servant to his brethren (Uncle) Shem. It is from this curse that many suggest the reason Negroes were slaves in America. Some confuse the curse of Cain with that of Canaan. God, per scripture, cursed Cain for killing his brother, Abel. But it was Noah and not God that cursed Canaan and it had nothing to do with

"The Coalville Times," of Coalville, Utah, November 21, 1902

Canaan's color or tainted blood or why Negroes were targeted as slaves. The hypocrisy of attempting to stigmatize a Biblical label to slavery as to legitimize it as a Biblical prophesy in an attempt to profit from it without shame or guilt. But this blood drop rule is the basis to restrict everything black, to include liberty. Liberty is the desire of every human being of this and any country. Basic rights that's often ignored by people with it and craved by people who are denied it. But, consider during the period of slavery, many people of this country opposed it, mostly in silence. Then the United States banded the import of slaves to America in 1808. After some 11 million Africans, mostly from West Africa, had visited our shores by force from their homeland. And before that entire let us examine the hypocrisy of 1776, The Declaration of Independence. There were five members of Congress selected to write the document. The parties consist of John Adams from Massachusetts whose idea it was to separate America from England. Robert R. Livingston from New York, Benjamin Franklin of Pennsylvania, Roger Sherman of Connecticut and Thomas Jefferson, at age thirty-three from Virginia who ended up the sole author of the document. Why was Thomas Jefferson chosen by the five to write the document? Was it perhaps his prolific writings from his 1775 book titled, *"Necessary of Taking up Arms"* and most noticeably the statement, **"And we solemnly declare that we will preserve our liberties being with one mind resolved to die free men rather than to live as slaves."** Quite astounding words for one that never would have been a slave of that era anyway. But, as adamant as Jefferson was about the degrading concept of enslavement, he too like many of his constituency were slave-owners. Widely criticized during the declaration process for hypocrisy, he later freed all his slaves and therefore justifying that his beliefs were not just mere words. And let us not forget the Virginia newspaper, *"The Richmond Recorder"* attempts to smear his name about his relationship with Sally Hemings, a very young Mulatto girl that later became his concubine. This amazing saga reports that Sally was thirty years his juror. But despite this attempt of character deformation, Jefferson still won reelection. And his secret love for Sally Hemings continued until his death.

John Adams brought to the table the idea of separating the thirteen colonies from England. Was it perhaps his own failed business as a Lawyer or perhaps like almost everyone else the disconcertedness with higher taxes? But what ever the reasons were in his mind, the intent was, liberty for all, just as the written document intended, but it was not to be the reality for the Africans. As the attempt to get the declaration signed, lead to copious hours of debate, whether the document should include the liberty of slaves and the legal classifications of an African living in America. Of particular interest was that of the Southern states and their claim to economic stability of their states that relied totally on the backs of free labor offer by keeping the Africans in bondage. There was even a walk out in protest, headed by Edward Rutledge of South Carolina during the Congressional vote. But one Southerner, Lyman Hall of Georgia caused the delay of signers to reconsider with a proposal. Therefore, Thomas Jefferson, reluctantly had to remove the statement, **"He has waged a cruel war against human nature and itself in the persons of a distant people who never offended him captivating and carrying them into slavery in another hemisphere determined to keep open a market where men should be bought and sold, he has prostituted himself."** If those words were allowed to stay would have been the freeing of all slaves in

Devour Us Not

"Tensas Gazette," of January 24, 1913

1776, since the document was about, *"Free White Americans,"* as self-proclaimed by themselves, Africans were left out of the *"liberty for all."* But once all agreed to the signing of the *"Declaration of Independence,"* which gave liberty to all but the Africans, the quest for liberty for them would be a constantly denied. Most of the Africans would have to wait some eighty-seven years for emancipation on January 1, 1863. Which ironically adds insult to injury because on that day not one slave was freed? Not to mention some parishes and counties for whatever reason were not apart of the emancipation document. And some Southern states purposely delayed emancipation acknowledgement and public reading for more than two years in a collective effort to prolong slavery. And not to mention by President Lincoln's own admission was the main focus of the document, to preserve the union and eventually compensate slave-owners handsomely for lost of property. Because almost all the southern States were seceding from the union after Lincoln's election in 1860. Most would also surmise that after emancipation was a period worst than slavery. The *"Black Code,"* was introduced which redefined the Africans citizenship as property of their slave-owners by virtue of the origin of their homeland beginnings. And the *"Sharecropping,"* concept for 90% of the Africans who could not read or write was in essence a legitimized slavery system to further disenfranchise the Africans. Much to the delight of the Southerners while regaining their strong hold on the hopes and dreams of an already oppressed people, life must have appeared unbearable and hopeless.

The Southern States argued the term *"distant people,"* or African slaves were not considered Americans, rather, they were only the property of their property-owners and nothing more. So the Africans had no legal rights that any white man would acknowledge, hence the term *"no equality."* Until this day, going back to the Dred Scott decision by the Supreme Court of 1857, prove to be a devastating blow to liberty denied for a people. Thomas Jefferson's forever echoing words, **"we hold these truths to be self-evidence that all men are created equal, they're endowed by their creator with certain inalienable rights that among these are life, liberty and the pursuit of happiness,"** as God intended, but will find the ears of few when determining who does and does not deserve liberty. So many lives would have to be lost, dreams shattered and families separated before God's plan for a harmonious society would compromised. Take The Voting Rights Act of 1965, signed into law by President Johnson in 1965 with a clause stating unless Congress voted to extend the voting Rights Act it would expire after 5 years. So in 1970 under President Nixon, Congress renewed the act for 5 more years. And in 1975 under President Ford , Congress renewed it for 7 more years. In 1982 President Reagan extended it for 25 more years. In 2006 President Bush extended it for 25 more years. So what will 2031 bring for the Voting Rights Act of 1965 and why is there any doubt, regardless of years gone by that generational hate will always be apart of a society that discriminates?

The much too cowardly 1% dare not speak out against any equality African-Americans might obtain by law. So the wheels of injustice keeps rolling while the rich increases it might and the poor disappears in the dark. In all fairness, some voices are speaking out to listening ears to erase the sins of silence. Thank God for the pundit voices, the likes of the crew at **MSNBC; Rev. Al Sharpton, Chris Matthews, Ed Schultz, Rachel Maddow, Steve Kornacki, Chris Hayes, Toure', Alex Wagner, Krystal Ball, Lawrence O'Donnell, Tamron Hall, Bill Maher** and **Melissa Harris-Perry** just to name a few. These brave souls are well-informed at the cost of being typed cast, all in a collective reporting effort for righteousness. It's without fanfare, without their insistence in truth telling, many would be lead down a path of the ill-informed. But Fox news is constant steering you to the

"The Appeals," of January 22, 1916

light of just plain right. As if their reality *"story-tellings,"* are issues related to people who look like they do. There are great Americans in this mass config-uration of, *"race-haters," "money-greedies," "hopes & dream-snatcher's and po-folk crusher's."* And without a material interest in any of the stories being reported, the dampening of true reality of their gifts is abruptly nullified by their candor. Where would we be without their edge on America's voiceless? So grievously neglected are the true values of political news reporting gone, when the bias of negative race inadequacies that grace the lips of the misconceptions. Then Fox, fueled by a ludicrous right-wing agenda deployed

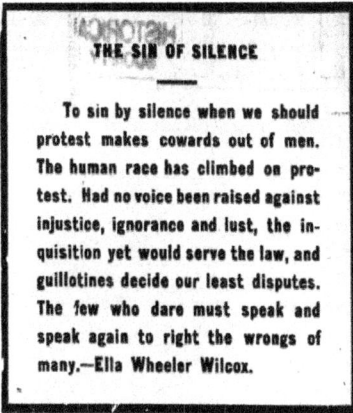

THE SIN OF SILENCE

To sin by silence when we should protest makes cowards out of men. The human race has climbed on pro-test. Had no voice been raised against injustice, ignorance and lust, the in-quisition yet would serve the law, and guillotines decide our least disputes. The few who dare must speak and speak again to right the wrongs of many.—Ella Wheeler Wilcox.

"Omaha Daily Bee," of June 24, 1906

to misrepresent the truth, the MSNBC squad quickly injects their brand of, *"got ya tactics,"* to dispel any of their falsehoods. As if we were not all created from one blood; what are their etchings? And even then, dare any opposition to its claim with unsub-stantiated exploits, invites a bold and accurate challenge from these folk. Again is where the MSNBC

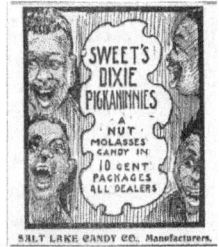

"The Salt Lake Tribune," of April 7, 1904

clan draws the line in the sand; taking the manifestations of half-truths, calculated fact-less brio, with the vital force of preeminence valuable leaven, others envy. Then MSNBC prevails with its journalistic integrity that infuriates the base of the opposition. Yet, take away the color base ignorance of injustice and clear it with facts, makes them undeniably my choice for news reporting. They also, reverses the lies with the aspirant focus and proven theory, that tailors the argument without question. Integrity, simply stated, is a measure that merit's the character of the MSNBC team for whom we owe so much in providing quality news reporting.

So this disease of blood-line heritages that promotes hate and intolerance, touches every aspect of a society. And knowing this plague of an issue exists, no one has come to a logical treatment for its demise. The San Francisco Call newspaper article of August 11, 1909 makes an observation along blood-drop laws as it relates to marriages. And in 1909 it reports the following states that had laws prohibiting interracial marriages between blacks and whites: Alabama, Arizona, Arkansas, California, Colorado, Delaware, Florida, Georgia, Idaho, Indiana, Kentucky, Louisiana, Maryland, Mississippi, Missouri, Nebraska, North Carolina, Oklahoma, Oregon, South Carolina, Tennessee, Texas, Utah, Virginia, and West Virginia. Marriages between whites and Indians were also not permitted in Arizona, North Carolina, Oregon, and South Carolina, while Arizona, California, Mississippi, Oregon and Utah did not permit whites and Chinese to marry. And California was the only state in the union that prohibited Japanese from marrying whites. Regardless of what avenue you take in life, some unjustified maneuvers are always at the forefront of some focus that restricts race harmony.

A court case of July, 1919, when a former cashier for the Capitol Savings Bank of Washington D.C. named Douglas B. Mc Carry, testified in a District Court on behalf of his son-in-law, Francis P. Dwyer who brought the

Devour Us Not

suit. McCarry's daughter as reported by, *"The Kansas City Sun," of July 19, 1919*, Clara McCarry-Dwyer, had at least one-eight Negro Blood in her veins, though appearance showed otherwise. Nebraska statute on mixed-race marriages based on drops of blood made the case for annulment of their 1916 marriage possible. Unbeknownst to Francis until the birth of their first child when his wife's Physician acknowledged the child, because of its skin pigmentations showed traces of Negro blood. Shocked, was Francis who also testified that he had never met his wife's father who's testimony on the witness stand was denied, favoring the Physician's professional opinion. Douglas, who looks as if he had no trace of Negro blood in his veins, testified to that effect as it relates to his Mother and father. After the baby was born, Francis abandoned his wife and child and joined the Army in disgust. And only filed the suit after his returned from military service.

"The Washington Herald," of April 5, 1914

In Taft Oklahoma located about 10 miles from Muskogee where a wealthy Negro girl named **Sarah Rector**, an oil-well business recipient of $15,000 a month and was considered one of the wealthiest females in the state. Born to the parentage of Joe and Rosa Rector on March 3, 1902, in Indian territory, Oklahoma owning 160 areas leased through her guardian T.J. Porter. Sarah's earlier life received land allotment like all children of that Indian Creek Nation. Before Oklahoma entered into statehood, slaves were owned by five civilized Indian tribes, the **Cherokee**, **Chickasaw**, **Choctaw**, **Creek** and **Seminoles**. After the Civil War, All civilized Indian tribes sign a treaty with the American government that they emancipate their many slaves; incorporate them within their nation's entitlements that make them entitled to land and all other properties and minerals. There was also the *"grafter,"* white men whose sole purpose was to swindle the land from the Negroes through a number of schemes and *"Dixie trickery."* The passing of the Dawes Allotment Act of February 8, 1887 that would bring Indians of the United States to an allotment and citizenship. Since the oil boom in Oklahoma, many Negro children like Sarah that

Sarah Rector at age 10-1912

were apart of that territory who received monthly payments from big oil businesses were preyed upon by whites in the area. Admittedly, *"The Tulsa Star," of February 7, 1914*, states many of these Negro children had been adopted by Court ordered, these unscrupulous white men for the sole purpose of financial gain and their own selfishness and greed. These white families had little love for those children who all had biological living parents living within the same counties in most cases. Reflective in their daily neglect, was the outer appearance of these children while these white families pocketed 10% each month of their allotment. Corrupt Judges who deemed Negro adults as being irresponsible and impoverished living condition disqualified them from adoptions or managing their own children. Mainly, because of the attitude of whites towards blacks and the all out effort to disenfranchise the Negroes was a commonality of monumental proportion. Sarah Rector's guardianship, Bob Fike, a white man in Muskogee, publicly acknowledged his hatred and prejudice for Negroes. Fike, over charged Sarah's estate for $57,000 for an apartment block building he owned on South Second Street called the *"White Elephant,"* located in none other than the black section of town. Yet, during this period, not a white child would ever be allowed to be adopted by a Negro and the wealth of these minors would have best serve the Negro communities. And for the same reason, Sarah Rector was being sorted out for marriage at the age 14 & 15 by both black and whites, despite marriage laws prohibiting such behaviors of mixed-race marriages in Oklahoma. Judges had acknowledged their roll in lending a blind eye for the sake of allowing no Negroes to feast in the wealth of oil money on Indian land where whites were excluded. In 1913, an effort was constructed by the

Oklahoma legislature to have Sarah declared as white as to eliminate the thought of Negro wealth that would anger its white residences. In 1914 the continuation for the life of the oil business which went bust during the 1930's followed by the depression and an immediate discontinuation of the guardianship adoption programs. With no considerations for the minor Negro children or Sarah, all in an effort to oppress Negroes continued in other forms of *"keepouts."* On March 3, 1920, when Sarah turned 18, court proceedings began to determine Sarah's competency as she becomes legal heir to over a million dollars in assets, making her the wealthiest Negro in America. She executed a deed of trust for her estate for M.G. Young and C.A. Looney naming them as guardians and her former guardian T.J. Porter turrets to serve under a $150,000 bond. In July, 1922, Joe Rector, the father of Sarah, died in Baylor Hospital, Dallas, Texas at the age of 45. Sarah Rector then marries Kenneth Campbell, September, 1922.

Leonard D. Ingram was another Freedman who was a youth millionaire. He like Sarah was allotted 160 areas located in the northern part of Muskogee where he lives with his Mother and step-father Charles Jones. One of the most extraordinary cases is that of Freedman Charles Roberts who had 51 children. Once arrested for guardianship in disbelief he had fathered that many children. Roberts claimed his family is the result of a plurality of wives granted under Creek law before the Federal government intervened. All 51 children held land allotments in the Indian territory. So intrigued by his story that his wife he married in 1867 and 19 of his children received a pass to visit President Roosevelt in Washington.

The Geraldine Hammett case as reported by, *"The Morning Tulsa Daily World,"* of March 14, 1922, investigates the kidnapping of Creek Freedmen by Sapulpa County Judge, H. S. Williams. In the case of Clifford Alec, like similar cases involving kidnappings was about to reach maturity as it relates to his inheritance, when he was kidnapped. He was founded in Ponca City, 95 miles from Sapulpa with his white and Negro kidnapers. While Alec appeared before the Judge, he explained the conditions of him being kidnapped which involved the kidnappers offering him $2,700 for his land deed which was worth $50,000. The Judge ordered Alec in jail until he reach maturity for his protection. The kidnapping of Nellie Naharkey in which Ted Reese, an oil man from Tulsa and W.R. McNutt, a Chauffeur, were charged but both deny. Sidney B. Nelson the former guardian of Nellie filed a petition of her anticipated age of maturity. John Bell was kidnapped by his former guardian Tobe Franklin who was arrested for the crime because he was reported to have been planning to swindle him out of his land. Bell was returned to his home and a new guardian was appointed as reported by, *"The Morning Tulsa Daily World,"* of May 27, 1922. The two cases of the kidnapping and disappearance of Jesse Harris and Geraldine

Hammett where the estates were never settled or the recovery of the two girls. Kidnapping of Owen Evans at 12 years old on October 13, 1909 according to, *"The Ogden Standard,"* of October 13, 1909, heir to his parents, Mr. and Mrs. Travis Evans large estate in Oklahoma went missing after a barber shop visit. He was recovered a short time later unharmed.

Mary Alexander *(Shiner)* Almarolia, pictured on the left was born in Washington D.C. near the Washington Navy yard on January 2, 1853. Her father was a slave named Michael Shiner. After the Civil War, he gained a considerable

amount of wealth through real estate investments in Southeast Washington and a manuscript of an unprinted book on the subject of slavery and treatment of the Negroes before and after the Civil War. Shiner's manuscript depicts first-hand accounts of slavery in Washington between the years of 1813 and 1868, containing 500 pages. The contents denote some prominent names in our nation's history to include President's and General's. There is also a recollection of the 1835 Washington riot that was scarcely reported. Michael Shiner was born a slave in Prince George's County, Maryland, in 1805. He was owned by the Pumphrey Family of Maryland and later sold to a family in the District of Columbia in 1830. In 1833, Shiner was freed by his Master and acquired employment in the Washington Navy Yard. Shiner's reputation as a *"slickster"* in acquiring his wealth through being street wise. Mary, at an early age married an Italian thirty years her senior named Alexander Almarolia. He owned a Dining Saloon. Mary Almarolia, despite being, what was a rarity then, a full blooded African and declaring never to marry a Negro. In 1893, Mary was serving a six month prison term for keeping the resort dining and dance hall open in violation of the original charges of keeping a disorderly house. At which time Charles Grayson, employed by Mary, as her driver whom he claimed also to be her Nephew was living in the same residence. After her death, he had supposedly stolen some property from Mary in her absence and sold it to O. Statler, William McLaughlin and Vincent Gaerarde. During Mary's six month stay in prison, the three individuals occupied the property and stated the pro-

1880 Federal U.S. Census- Washington D.C.
Almarolia, Alexander, Italian, age 68, Mary, Black, age 38, Lotta C., Mulatto, age 10 and Lewis, Mulatto, age 3

perty they received was sold to them by Charles Grayson who was known to have the property of Mary in his possession and knew the condition for which the property was being offered for sale. The furniture and all her properties were set out on the side walk during a snow storm by orders being enforced by a Constable in the form of an eviction notice. It was reported that Charles, not having any money to stop the eviction, went to the

"The Colored American," of August 4, 1900

jail to visit Mary who then gave him authorization to sell some of her property to prevent eviction and buy food for himself, Janie, her alleged Niece and her horses. Two years after this incident as reported by, *"The Morning Times," of August 30, 1895,* Mary had Charles Grayson locked up for grand larceny of selling stolen properties of hers while she was incarcerated. Charles Grayson is no stranger to trouble being arrested for the thief of parlor chairs from Mary Gordon of Washington. And prior to that arrest admittedly being involved in larceny in Alexandria, Virginia. He had also lived with his mother who supposedly was the half sister of Mary Alexander Almarolia. Mary and Alexander had a daughter named Lotta C. Almarolia born in 1870, and an adopted son named Lewis Alexander born in 1877. Her husband educated Mary and she was known as a linguist speaking and writing five different languages which included Spanish, Italian, French, German and English.

She also had an uncanny ability to grasp the administrative and bookkeeping aspect of business as she assisted her husband in his business affairs. Mary was also gifted in her charitable giving, allowing no color barriers to restrict her aid of the needy. Like sending a daily supply of a thousand loafs of bread to Police station and depending on the season, ice and coal were also supplied. Later, Mary's adoption of two infant children who were descendents of wealthy parents from the south living in the Washington D.C. area. Lewis Alexander, the eldest of the adopted boys at the time of Mary's death was twenty-seven, and Joseph Alexander was twenty-four years of age. The boys though legally adopted by Mary, took the last name of her middle name which was also her husband's first name. It was said of the two boys that they claimed to be brothers, but their appearance well suggest to the contrary and would be later solidified. The two bore no similarities of kinship other than having the same adopted last name. Lewis excelled in his studies and graduated from Bliss Electrical College at the age of twenty. He was then selected to become an instructor at the same college a year later. His notoriety for being an excellent electrician afforded him the opportunity to travel with theatrical companies and finally settled with the Electrical Decorating Company of New York and resided at 246 West Twenty-ninth Street, NY, his last known residence. However, Joseph or *"Joe as he was sometimes called,"* his brother being as different as their noticeable appearance, couldn't have been more different in his life choices. Incline not to study as hard and be aggressive in his achievements, ended up working for the Metropolitan Railroad as a switchman. When Mary died, on a Tuesday, August 9, 1904 and was buried at Mount Olivet Cemetery, the controversy surrounding her Will would be a matter of much debate.

"The Salt Lake Tribune," of April 14, 1913

Supposedly, her Will excluded her one natural born child, Lotta, and the entire estate, valued at over $75,000, was to be given to her two adopted sons, Lewis and Joseph. Also stipulated in the Will was four typed written letters to the boys suggesting only after the death of Mary, that a trunk be opened to reveal the true origin of their kinship written by the mother of one of the boys, linking him to an even more handsome fortune from his father's side of his Kentucky southern roots. Several prominent law authorities within the surrounding area, knowing of the circumstances by which the boys were mysterious adopted, gave noticed to only Lewis of this secretive revelation. The letter in questioned written by the biological mother of Lewis was for the purpose of safe guarding his identity and preserving hers and his father's good Christian name according to, *"The Washington Times," of August 21, 1904.* Lewis was reportedly announced as dead with even a gravestone declaring him legally dead at birth. Lewis being as modest as he was bright, decline to pursue any avenues

Devour Us Not

"The San Francisco Call," of June 23, 1912

that might share light as to his biological parents and the secrecy hovering over it. Nevertheless, a story as juice as this caused a frenzy of nosy gossipers to seek the know-it-all's about his life. Accordingly, during the 1874 year, a young handsome southern gentleman traveled to Washington for a lucrative real estate deal because of his prominent Kentucky roots, that he was privy to solely on that influence. There he fell in love with a gorgeous young Washington socialite and in 1875 were married in Kentucky. She immediately became pregnant and in eight months, prematurely gave birth to a son.

Having a child prematurely in the 1800's gave meaning to signs of weak genes and a source of bad blood and disgrace. So, being of prominent status as the southern gentleman was, he'd be thought of as having less than strong genes and be labeled a social outcast. The infuriation of his angry began to destroy their relationship as well as her relationship with his family. Residing in the Washington D.C. area where he had purchase a large estate, the mother of the child began to circulate the rumor of the child's sudden death immediately after his birth. Following all the death protocol of notifying the newspapers to announce the child's death, to the issuing of a certificate of death were performed. A coffin was even purchased and supposedly a doll was placed in it with human like features. A much publicized hearse was seen loading the small coffin from the house followed by a mourning mother trailing close behind but reluctantly too grieved to attend the funeral. The lowering of the casket into the ground before words were spoken over him by a Clergyman was all noticed to any inquiring eyes. And lastly a gravestone was erected in the child's honor, finalizing his official demise. Because the child was to be deceased there could be no noticeable baby cries coming from the house of a supposed mourning household. So then comes the mystic and tenderhearted, Mary Alexander Almarolia to the rescue where the child remain with her and the secret until Mary's death. Lewis premature death reach the father who came back to Washington in total disgust with his wife until soon divorced proceedings followed. The mother so devastated, first by the premature birth then followed by the immediate divorced. She dropped out of sight and reportedly died in 1883. The father, after returning to Washington, breathing the same air in the same city where his believed deceased son very much alive lived. He became very wealthy in his own right and intertwined with the political heavy weights not only in Washington but in New York, Louisville and some European countries. He eventually received a diplomatic appointment abroad under a Federal Democratic Administration. About five years prior to the death of Mary, the awareness of the true identity of Lewis became known to him and his father, with the father refusing to acknowledge the kinship. The Lawyers of Lewis did urged him not to pursue any recognition of his fathers name and his family. News that became the talk of the town brought forth a Niece of Mary's from Baltimore named Janie Grayson and her Nephew Charles Grayson. Lewis opinions on the contested Niece's position says the Will express provisions against such intervention siding along the lack of bloodline. She contested the Will on behalf of her biological child whose non-involvement became as much a mystery as the Will's content. The case went all the way to the Supreme Court of the District that started a year before Mary's death to gain a clear title her property as lot 1 in square 946 bounded by South Carolina Avenue, Tenth and D Street. Mainly because of her declining eye sight and health, Mary's once keen sense of business became a liability necessary for hiring a manager for her property. She named as defendants,

both William F. and Aylett T. Holtzman who were given management authority over the property in January, 1896. The named Trustees, Ella L. Castleman, who was the sister of the defendants. Also, Trustee's included the Secretary of War, Elihu Root. The property in question was inherited by Mary from her father, Michael Shiner who passed away in 1880. The Will acknowledged the 1867 purchased by her father from William B. Todd. During the managerial responsibility of the Holtzman's, who permitted the

SECRETARY OF WAR ELIHU ROOT

"Hopkinsville Kentuckian," of October 25, 1906

property to be sold to Ella L. Castleman for $165.50 in April of 1896, less than four months after assuming those responsibilities were performed in error. During Mary's illness, attempts were even made to steal the papers giving the true identity of Lewis Alexander to no avail. Other suspicious activity by the Holtzman's was a measure of distrust that had developed between the Holtzman's and Mary before her death. This was later explained to the executive of her Will, Irwin B. Linton. Judge Stafford, agreed with Mary Almarolia's Lawyers that the deeds were indeed fraudulent and the Holtzman's and all other parties named in the suit were ordered to pay compound interest on all monies involvement with the occupancy of the property and vacate it immediately, giving clear titled to the estate to Mary Alexander Almarolia, as principal owner.

General Oliver Otis Howard
"The Marion Daily Mirror," of March 23, 1911

General Oliver Otis Howard
"The Marion Daily Mirror," of Nov 30, 1907

ENTIRE FAMILY MURDERED

Five Killed as Result of White Woman Marrying Negro.

San Antonio, Tex., March 23.—A. L. Cassoway, 52, a negro; Elizabeth Cassoway, 37, his white wife, and their three children, 6 years, 3 years, and 15 months, were found murdered in their home here. They were evidently killed as they slept

Each of the victims had been struck repeatedly on the head with an ax, which was found in the room. Cassoway and his wife were married in Mexico, and the fact that the woman was white caused a bitter feeling against them in the neighborhood.

"The San Francisco Call," of Oct 9, 1902

Founder of Howard University was **General Oliver Otis Howard** according to the, *"Omaha Daily Bee" of March 20, 1886.* Born in Leeds, Maine, to Rowland B. and Eliza O. Howard on November 8, 1830. After graduating from Bowdoin College in 1850 at the age of 19, he entered the United States Military Academy of West Point, graduated fourth in his class of cadets in 1854. The following year he was married to Elizabeth

Devour Us Not

Ann Waite and had seven children. Howard fought in the Seminole Indian war of Florida in 1857 as a member of General Harvey's staff was assigned as the chief of Ordnance. Howard was called back to West Point as a mathematics Professor from September 21, 1857 to June 3, 1861. At the break out of the Civil War, he resigned his commission in the regular Army as a first Lieutenant to accept the commission as a Colonel in the Third Regiment of Maine Volunteers where he commanded a Regiment and a Brigade at the first Bull Run. Later he'd lose a right arm at the battle of Fair Oaks, May 31, 1862 and subsequently be awarded the nations highest award for bravery, for his act of heroism, *"The Medal of Honor."* And so impressed with his military maneuvers during a combat conflict, until his men presented him with a sword. He was accelerated promoted to Brigadier General, September 3, 1861, followed by another promotion to Major General on November 29, 1862. On December 13, 1862 he was placed in command of a Division at the Burnside defeat in Fredericksburg. As a part of Stonewall Jackson strategic military plan, he was made commander of the Eleventh Army Corps, May, 1863. In the latter part of that year, he received orders to be apart of the campaign that captured Atlanta while commanding the right wing during Major General William Tecumseh Sherman's Savannah Campaign, *"March to the Sea,"* during November and December of 1864. In May of 1865, he was placed in charge of the Freedman Bureau, which were the Army's Bureau of Refugees, Freedmen and Abandoned Lands until 1874. His significant role had major consequences in the Reconstruction period after the Civil War for getting freed slaves established. Much to the dismay of then President Johnson, who was oppose to the principals of the Freedmen's Bureau, Howard would stand his ground as in a military campaign. President Johnson, influenced by the sympathy of Southern whites wanted the Negro to have no legal rights to any chance of equality. As soon as Churches and Schools in the south were being constructed, the sooner southern whites would burn them down without remorse.

Because of Howard's religious beliefs, at one point of his military career, he wanting to be a military Chaplain. His principals for justice as it related to the fair and equitable treatment of freed slaves were often met with much opposition, from many who attempted everything to keep the Negroes enslaved. During such a pivotal time in American history, the Reconstruction Period was most challenging for him and the Negroes. But for the likes of people like General Howard who played a major role in the founding of Howard University for which he would later become President. The position he held from 1869 to 1874, which was then incorporated by Congress in 1867. General Howard had gone to Washington to suggest a theological seminary training at Howard for the training of Negro Ministers. Even though the school at the time was opened to all races and gender, Howard's influence prompted the initial naming of the school to Howard Normal and Theological Institute for the Education of Preachers and Teachers. January, 1867 the board of Trustees voted to change the name to Howard University. One of General Howard's quotes regarding the institution was, *"The opposition to Negro education made itself felt everywhere in a combination not to allow the freedmen any room or building in which a school might be taught."* General Howard was also assigned a special commissioner from 1873 to 1881, to go to be with the Indians in New Mexico and Arizona to serve on the frontier. And later he was placed back at his alma mater, West Point, as head of the Military. General Howard spent forty years on active duty and retired in 1894 at the age of 65 years of age. And at the age of 79, he died at his home in Burlington, Vermont on October 26, 1909.

"Los Angeles Herald," of July 5, 1908

From 1867 till 1926, all of Howard University President's had been white men much to the protest of the African-American community. It wasn't until the 1926 appointment of **Rev. Dr. Mordecai Wyatt Johnson**, who became the first African-American President and had the longest tenure of 34 years in Howard University's history, from 1926-1960. Mordecai Johnson, recipient of the N.A.A.C.P. award, *"The Spingarn Medal"* was born January 12, 1890, in Paris, Tennessee. Johnson was also secretary of the western region of the Student Young Men's Christian Association *(YMCA)*. And in 1917 he became pastor of the First Baptist Church in Charleston, West Virginia. He was also a founder of a Charleston, West Virginia chapter of the National Association for the Advancement of Colored People *(N.A.A.C.P.)*. He died September 10, 1976, at the age of 86, in Washington, D.C.

Some Initial President's of Howard University

Byron Sunderland (President from 1867-1869)- "New-York Tribune," of July 1, 1901 - General Oliver Otis Howard (President from 1869-1874) "Deseret Evening News," of November 2, 1907, John Gordon (President from 1903-1906)-"The Colored American," of November 7, 1903 Jeremiah E. Rankin (President from 1890-1903)- "The Colored American.," of January 13, 1900, Teunis S. Hamlin (Acting President 1903)-"The Colored American," of May 9, 1903 - Wilbur P. Thirkield (President from 1906-1912)-"The Washington Bee," of July 22, 1911.

Catherine Deaver Lealtad
"The Appeal," of Jun 15, 1912 "The Broad Ax," of April 20, 1912

Catherine Deaver Lealtad, at age 16, was the only African American attending Mechanic Arts High School in St. Paul, Minnesota. She was the Valedictorian of her 1912 Sr. Class of 80 students as reported by *"The Appeal," of Jun 15, 1912.* Catherine beat out the favorite, Marcellus L. Countryman, son of an Attorney for top honors. Catherine went on to graduate,

Catherine Deaver Lealtad
"The Appeal," of Jul 10, 1915

Valedictorian and *Cum Laude* from Macalester College in St. Paul and became its first African American graduate in 1915 *(finishing a 4 yr curriculum in 3 yrs)* with a duel major of Chemistry and History. She then received the Noyes Scholarship prize of $50 in her class of twenty-five. Macalester College later named the *"Catherine Deaver Lealtal 15 Year Service To Society Award"* in her honor. The award honors a Macalester alumni African-American, that used their Macalester education to distinguish themselves in service to their community. Catherine was born in Ohio, April 26, 1896 and was step-daughter to Father Alfred H. & Ida B. Lealtad. Her Step-Father, born in the West Indies, was Rector of St. Phillip's Episcopal Church at St. Paul Minnesota and St. Thomas at Minneapolis. Catherine later became a Physician and spoke several languages that included French and German. She also taught school in Cincinnati, and Jefferson City, Missouri. She was also

Devour Us Not

appointed Secretary to George F. Wells, who was the Chairman of the State Prohibition Committee and in charge of the Y.W.C.A. of New York. Catherine never married and had no children. She died in Queens, New York, January 30, 1989 at the age of 94. Her sister, Grace Magarfet, an organist at her father's church was dismissed by the St. Paul School District in 1917 after a signed petition was filed from whites who objected to their children being taught by a Negro. She was later reappointed to the Crowley school of St. Paul in 1918.

Bishop Daniel Alexander Payne

The first University for African-American in America was Wilberforce University   *"The Appeal," of February 28, 1891* in Ohio as reported by, *"The Daily Herald," of June 22, 1895.* Wilberforce was initially founded by the A.M.E. Church (African Methodist Episcopal) and Bishop D.A. Payne. Bishop Payne was elected as Bishop in 1852 of the A.M.E. Church in NY, City. **Bishop Daniel Alexander Payne** became President of Wilberforce University in 1863 until 1876. Bishop Payne was born February 24, 1811 in Charleston, South Carolina. His study of

theology began at the Lutheran College at Gettysburg, Pennsylvania. Receiving his licenses from the Franklin Synod of the Lutheran Church in 1837. Ordained in 1839 and joining the Quarterly Conference of Bethel A. M. E. Church of Philadelphia in 1841 according to, *"The Appeal," of February 28, 1891.* He received as a local preacher at the Philadelphia Annual Conference, a trial connection, the spring of 1842, followed by a full connection in 1843. Then shortly thereafter being called to the itinerant ministry in 1843. Becoming the first African-American President of Wilberforce University and first President of the A.M.E. Sunday School Union, Bishop Payne's message crossed all color lines. And in 1873 he

Richard S. Rust   became the oldest living Methodist Bishop in the world. Wilberforce University was also

"The Columbus Journal," of October 20, 1897   supposedly founded in Wilberforce, Ohio by trustees from both the Methodist Episcopal headed by **Richard S. Rust**, pictured on the left, and it's first President alone with the African Methodist Episcopal that included Bishop Daniel Alexander Payne. The A.M.E. Church being committed to the necessity of educating Negroes, until it became apart of their legacy as a religious organization. The first effort towards the focus of a university solely for the advancement of Negroes began September 21, 1844 when the Ohio Conference appointed a committee to select a seat for a seminary of learning on the *"manual labor plan."* And what was called the Union Seminary that later became Wilberforce Projected University. It's name, fittingly after the city for which it was built that gained it's name from a British Statesman who died in 1833, after dedicating his life towards the ending of the slave trade. William Wilberforce was relentless in his efforts and even Negroes in America when the news of his demised hit these shores mourned his death. The very day of the assassination of President Lincoln, Friday, April 14, 1865, Wilberforce University became a target as recorded by, *"The Xenia Sentinel," April 21, 1865,* of the continuation of violence against any and everything black. And the first school for higher learning for the Negro which threatens the very core of equality was burned to the ground. Even though there was insurance totaling $8,000, it wasn't enough to rebuild the University completely. Donations from many sources began to pour into the University for it's reconstruction like the wheels of unstoppable justice. But like many other schools and Churches alike for Negroes, they were often the target of the continuous efforts of an element that's sole purpose was to damage irreparably the advancement of Negroes and keep him in his place. His place of being poor, dependent, oppressed and much suffrage was not to be

"FIRST" for African-American Colleges, Religion and Politics.

"The Broad Ax," of Dec 27, 1902

Founder Bishop W.J. Gaines- Morris Brown College (1881) -"The Colored American," of Aug 23, 1902, **Founder Dr. James E. Sheppard -** North Carolina College at Durham-"The Washington Bee," of Mar 11, 1911. **Miss Cornelia Bowen**-Principal of Mt. Meigs Colored Institute, Waugh, Ala. "The San Francisco Call," of Jan 2, 1898 - **Founder Dr. S.J. Hunter**- Noxubee Industrial School (1898) now Mississippi State University -"The Minneapolis Journal," of Aug 26, 1906. **Walter Brown-** The First child and youngest Negro Caricaturist at age 6, born May 26, 1896 - "The Colored American," of Mar 21, 1903.

President Rev. I.B. Scott - Wiley College-Texas (1893-1896)-"The Colored American" of Dec 8, 1900, **Founder Booker T. Washington**-Tuskegee Institute-Alabama (1881-1915)-"The Kansas City Sun," of Nov 20, 1915, **President Rev. Charles H. Parrish**-Eckstein Norton Univ.(1892-1912)-Cane Spring, KY.-"The Appeal" of Aug 24, 1907, **Laura Spilman Rockefeller,** Spilman College named in her honor-"The Day Book," of Aug 2, 1912. **President & Founder - Inman E. Page**-Langston University, OK- (1898-1915) "The Tulsa Star," of Jul 24, 1915, First Negro Senator-**Hiram Rhodes Revels** of Mississippi (1870-1871), Richmond Planet," of Oct 18, 1890. **Lutie A. Lyttle-** First Negro-Female Lawyer-"The Saint Paul Globe," of Sep 16, 1897.

Founder D.C. Potts-Texas College-" The Houston Daily Post," of Feb 23, 1903, **Rev. Richard Allen**-Founder of A.M.E. Church-"The Kansas City Sun," May 13, 1916, **Founder William H. Councill**-Alabama A & M-"The Colored American" of Mar 21, 1903, **Founder Rev. John J. Smallwood-** (1892 - 1928) Temperance Industrial and Collegiate Institution, Claremont, VA.-"The Broad Ax" of Jan 2, 1904, **Founder Rev. W.H. Mixon-** Payne University- "The Broad Ax," of November 30, 1912., **John R Lynch-**First Negro to preside over a National Convention "The Washington Bee," of May 23, 1891. **John Newton-** "First Negro Voter in Nebraska, 1892"- "The Wichita Daily Eagle," of Mar 25, 1892.

Bishop Henry M. Turner-First Negro appointed Chaplain in the U.S. Army-"Warren Sheaf," of Jan 4, 1900. **Richard T. Greener-** "First Negro graduate of Harvard 1870- "The Colored American," of Feb 27, 1904. **Isaac Louis Manning (Uncle Isaac) & his sister Mrs. Jane Elizabeth James (Aunt Jane)-** First two Negroes to join the Mormon Church, "The Salt Lake Herald," of Oct 2, 1899. **Rev A.R. Griggs-** Founded first Colored Bapt. paper published in Texas-"Evening Star," of Sep 19, 1893. **Rev C.R. Uncles-**"First Negro Priest in America, " The Wichita Daily Eagle," of Jan 21, 1892. **Sophia Holmes-** First Negro Woman to be given a life position in the Federal Gov. award by a Special Act of Congress during the **President Lincoln Administration** , "The Broad Ax," of Dec 15, 1900.

Devour Us Not

"The Salt Lake Tribune," of February 6, 1910

"The Colored American," of November 24, 1900

Dr. Daniel H. Williams
"The Appeal," of Oct 15, 1910

Mrs. Alice D. Johnson Williams
"The Colored American," of Jul 14, 1900

Dr. Daniel H. Williams
"The Appeal," of Nov 29, 1913

Sir Moses Jacob Ezekiel
"The Times dispatch," Jun 21, 1903

the final rallying cry for an unbeatable race that would not be devoured. **Dr. Daniel Hale Williams,** a Negro, was a Physicians, Surgeon, Dentist and Pharmacist. Founder of the Provident Hospital and the first Doctor in the world to successfully conduct **open heart surgery**, according to, *"The Appeal," of May 30, 1914.* The operation of Mrs. Rena Barbour, a Negro woman, who had an enlarged abdomen that had resulted in a tumor while being employed as a domestic. Despite all advisories in the medical profession against the operating, citing the unsuccessful rate of similar medical procedures didn't wavier Dr. Williams to successfully conclude the difficult procedure. Dr. William's accomplishments include his appointment as the Surgeon-In-Chief at the Freedman's Hospital of Washington D.C. by then President Grover Cleveland. He was a Member of the Illinois State Board of Health, founder of the Provident Hospital of Chicago, elected as a Fellow of the American College of Surgeons, Director of the Louise Training School for Colored Boys, and a member of the Board of Directors of the Old Folks' Home of Chicago. Born of mixed blood in Hollidaysburg, Pennsylvania, January 18, 1858 to Daniel Hale Williams, Sr., a Negro and Sarrah Price, a white woman, according to his *Family Search Records.* Dr. Daniel Williams died on August 4, 1931 in Lake Idlewild, Michigan, at the age of 73. Alice, his wife, whom he married on April 2, 1898, when he was 41 years of age and she was 26 years of age, was born 1872 in Washington D.C. (*Her parents were famed sculptor, Sir Moses Jacob Ezekiel, her biological father. But Albert, who raised her when he married her mother, Mary Lee Johnson, was who she claimed as her real parents. Her famous sculptor father died in Rome, in 1917, but his remains were brought to Arlington Cemetery, Washington D.C. and buried at the foot of the Confederate Monument he designed in 1921*). Alice

died August 30, 1924 in Chicago, they had no children. Money is a necessity in a capitalist society and a major component towards progress. Hence the beginning of the National Negro Business League created by Booker T. Washington on August 1, 1900 when it held its first meeting in Boston. Recognizing the need for Negroes as major contributor's in the development of this country, Mr. Washington, appointed as President 15 consecutive times. Ahead of his time, saw a need woven in the fabric of capitalism for an aggressive plan towards expanding the knowledge of business to this demographic as reported by, "The Broad Ax," of August 31, 1912. Many efforts legally were employed to impede black entrepreneurs from succeeding. Booker T. Washington's plan, shook-up the business world as awakening the black communities to organize and develop small and large businesses. The plan was to be more independent with the hard labor skills they already possessed. As newspapers that were witnessed to the historical meeting, wrote what they witnessed, was met with skeptic results. First of it's kind ever to motivate a people to tap into a hidden desires for their own development strategize by their efforts of thinking, reasoning and planning. There was even a motion to make the business league permanent which passed unanimously. And year after year as memberships grew, the businesses and voting powers of Negroes were initially changing the imbalance that plagued the country immediately after the Civil War. Closely to its organizational mission was not for profit because it had no capital stock, rather, contrarily its mission was to educate its targeted base. And educate it did, it empowered a race of people who were often told they had not the skill or the intellect to succeed in business. Communities throughout the United States pool together like at no other time in American history wish infuriated the white base. As blacks begin to showcase their economical muscle by shopping within their own communities with owners who looked more like them, changed and angered America. Economics began to bring a race of people from the depths of their impoverishments as the opposition looked on with envy as the wheels of injustice began to figure out ways in which to limit or eliminate these progressions.

Warren C. Coleman as reported by the, *"New-York Tribune,"* of May 3, 1903, Mr. Coleman, in 1902 opened a *"Black Cotton Mill,"* meaning operated and ran solely by blacks. Contrary to White Cotton Mill owners who claim total failure if Negroes were employed as machinery technicians by virtue of the notion that even the sound of machinery humming would hepatize

the average Negro to sleep. Other racial slurs were slurred at Coleman for the gale to attempt to undermine the white analysis of Negro labor and management. Whites had performed experiments involving Negro labor of high-tech machinery with poor results. Whites in their effort to prove the incompetence of Negroes never materialized which caused the hiring of white worker to fill those positions. Then comes Warren C. Coleman

GEORGE PRIMROSE, Who will be at the Academy Thursday with his new minstrel show.

THE COLEMAN, COTTON MILL, CONCORD, N. C.

who built a mill in Concord, North Carolina, fueled with by the stereotypical negative rhetoric motivated him to dispel these fabrications with an experiment of his own. Within less than a year after opening and the hiring of mostly ex-slaves, but all Negroes, set out on making his point. His mill became the first of its kind in the United States and to suggest the eyes of the world were upon him was an understatement. Coleman, knowing the risk because of several other mills had failed in trying to unrifled the secret of how to make a successful business. This made him more determine than ever to succeed after conversing with the business owners who had made the daring attempt. Coleman's mill averaging $1,000 worth of yarn a week while gaining a very competitive profit, allowing him to have backorders in advance of three month increments. This profitability caused Coleman to upgrade his machinery, modernize his plant by install an electrical lighting system and erect tenement houses, a major factor in failed attempts by other owners, just to name a few of his innovative might to improve his business. Workers were earning from $4.50 to $30.00 a week, a far cry from $0.00 as a slave. Coleman admits, the idea to build a mill came from, in principle what Booker T. Washington had advocated in the starting of the National Negro Business League in 1900. The motivational speech heard in Atlanta a few years before, called for Negroes to seek knowledge, educating the young, both boys and girls and become more efficient and goal oriented. The goal of being independent and not relying on the whites who had historically used every effort within their desires to make it as difficult for Negroes as possible. The motivation was spreading throughout the south and eventually the country as the rallying cry for equality. Within a few years of operation, the stock in the mill had risen to over $100,000.

Remarkably, like almost every American and particularly ex-slaves, Coleman was penniless after the Civil War. He, however, from literally pennies made about $100,000 from a small modest store on Main Street in Concord, North Carolina. His mother, Roxanna Coleman was a mulatto and his father was a white man from a very prominent family in North Carolina and a General during the Civil War named Rufus C. Barringer. Born in a small cabin in Cabarrus County, March of 1849, he later married a woman named Jane in 1875, a woman 15 years his senior. Both white and black consumers would trade with Coleman at his store, mainly because of that white family tied influence that was widely known. His ability to manage and save his money as a junk collector, afforded Coleman the opportunity to purchase land in and around the Concord area. As the town began to populate his land and houses were being built and rented totaling by some estimates over a 100 houses. The opening of his cotton mill manufacturing plant began in 1897, along with several financiers. Sadly, April 30, 1904, Warren C. Coleman died as reported by the, *"Richmond Planet," of April 30, 1904* and Professor E.A. Johnson who was Dean of the Law Department for Shaw University and author of *"A History of the Negro*

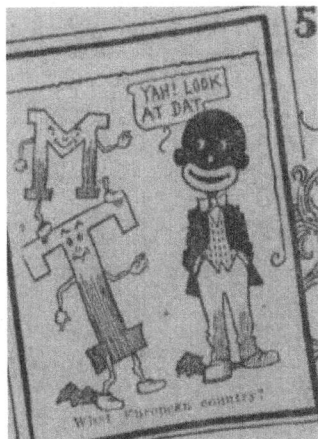

Race," was elected as President by the trustee board. Shortly thereafter the business was sold to Cannon Manufacturing company who changed the name. Even though the business was short lived, the success breeds others to at least dispel the rumors of Negroes not being business-minded to make an attempt by making the effort.

This is a story of **Miss Emma J. Wilson** as recorded in the, *"The New-York Tribune," of September 24, 1905*. Emma was born in slavery, 1855 in Mayesville, South Carolina, located about nine miles northeast of Sumter and property of a Presbyterian minister. Her recollection of slavery life was much different than most because of the kindness of her master and particularly his wife. Their son taught her to read with the full awareness of that family. Emma was quoted as saying, *"I believe everything I have made out of my life is due to her."* With their strong faith, those value were passed on to Emma as she was known as a praying woman. After the Civil War ended, her masters family moved away leaving her mother a small rented house on a small piece of land where she raised cotton and corn. Being of the times, boys were sent to school and girls seemingly less important were often being groomed for housekeeper. So while Emma's brothers were sent to school she was left to field and house chores. But Emma, from her days of learning to read was a lover of books and an almost self-educator. At night forcing her brothers to go over with her the teachings of that day, Emma showed an eagerness to learn. When Emma became a teenager, she elected to go to the Goodwill Parochial school which was about seven walking miles away. The fourteen mile daily trip was no matter for Emma as she enjoyed the liberty of book learning and educating herself for the betterment. Her teacher, a northerner took special interest in Emma for her obvious drive and brightness. Having the ability to recognize talent, she became somewhat of

"Negro girls learning to farm" -"New-York Tribune," of June 24, 1906   "Negro boys learning wood crafts"-"New-York Tribune," of September 24, 1905

a mentor to Emma and assisted her in attending a Presbyterian Scotia Seminary school for Negro girls in Concord, North Carolina. After winning a three year scholarship and the burden of lack of financing removed from her thoughts, all Emma wanted to do was to focus on her studies and thank the gentleman who made it possible for her scholarship. The scholarship was a gift from a wealthy man from Brooklyn, New York who wanted to reward a worthy person of color. After completing her studies she was confident, she was going to

Devour Us Not

some country in Africa to be a missionary worker. But upon arriving back in Mayesville, saw the need much greater at home. At that time, residence totaling at least a thousand, mostly Negro farmers had no nearby schools for Negro children as she had experienced. And with no immediate concerns alone that line to change, prompted Emma to take action. Because someone had taken an interest in her, she felt compel to return the favor. So, Emma started a local school using an old failed and deserted cotton mill manufacturing plant to educate the children of her community. In 1882, with only ten students, they had to make their own seats and blackboards with what ever materials they could find. Taking improvising to a new level. As the word began to spread of what Emma was single-handedly trying to accomplish, local authorities

Skinned
Him Alive

Bluefield, W. Va., July 10.—At Deville, Monday, a negro kidnapped a young girl, took her into the woods, tied her with ropes, repeatedly outraged her, and left her tied. He returned Tuesday with food, and again assaulted her. He repeated this Wednesday, and Thursday a searching party found the girl half dead. The men resuscitated her, and left her tied, and laid in wait. When the negro came he told the girl he was going to kill her. The party rushed out, seized him, and completely skinned him with sharp knives, and then tore the flesh from the bones, after which they repeatedly fired shots through different portions of the body. The negro died in terrible agony.

took the initiative to assist her by offering her $160 a year for her public school. She named the school, Mayesville Educational and Industrial Institution and established a board of Trustees and other financial backers. Soon the school had a farm of their own initially totaling sixty-seven areas which later grew to one hundred and forty-three areas that was used to grow a lot of what the kids ate such as potatoes, peas,

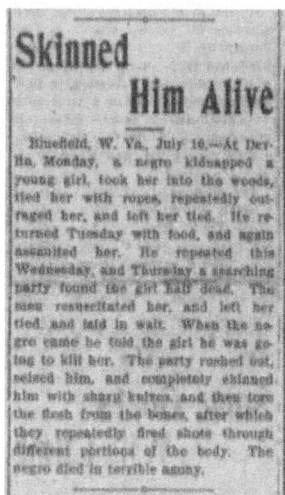

corn, cabbage and beans. Occasionally, farmers wives would bring by dishes of food, donate eggs and at ever they could afford to ensure the children were well nurtured. The school soon grew to five hundred and twenty-two students, many were orphans and over a 100 were boarders. A girls' dormitory housing seventy students and the boys' dormitory housing thirty students were soon constructed in which the students while being taught, helped in its completion. The schools curriculum, which coincided with the teachings of six trades and taking them through a competitive ninth grade educational level. This rigid curriculum was spread between only eight teachers. Emma was a constant visitor to the north on fund raising efforts for her school and students. One powerful speech was given the spring of 1914 at the Concord Baptist Church in Brooklyn, New York where she received many supporting dollars. She would also visit local authorities, constantly soliciting for other school necessities such as used books, classroom desks, tables and many other items her students could not make. Her tireless and diligent effort had major consequences into her personal life. Emma was never married and had no children of her own body. Her students were her children and their education was her life. Work that was a constant in her life since she first craved the will to learn while being deprived. No differences were shown in educational opportunities between genders as had been the case when she was a child. She explained that

education was a necessity for anyone who desired independence, regardless of gender. The school would triumph for several decades before disaster hit. The main building of the school caught fire about a week before Christmas, December, 1919, but the school quickly bounced back though donation were slow in coming. Having devoted a life time towards the education and training of many Negro children who would not have had the opportunity to acquire any skills other than farm labor. Emma's gift, that upheld a community forgotten, because of its inhabitants made the world stop and take notice. Amazing to what one person daring to challenge the will of a people with denial stamp from society. She never looked back in regret for her dreams. Her school among locals was called *"Little Tuskegee,"* modeled, admittedly by Emma as the blue-print for her educational purpose. One of Emma's famous student's was Mary McLeod Bethune, the founder of Bethune-Cookman University. Emma J. Wilson so beloved by the students of her Institution until when she died, she was buried on the campus of the school in modeling Booker T. Washington's campus at Tuskegee.

Alain Leroy Locke was the first African-American to receive a Rhodes Scholarship as reported by the, *"New-York Tribune," of March 17, 1907.* Alain Leroy Locke wrote an essay on Tennyson in the Bowdoin Literary competition securing him a first prize of $250. He also passed the rigorous examination, held at Lafayette College while a senior at Harvard University. Alain Leroy Locke was born in Philadelphia, Pennsylvania, September 13, 1885, his father was a well-known Lawyer in the area.

Alain Leroy Locke
"The Minneapolis Journal," of Mar 26, 1902

"New-York Tribune," of Mar 17, 1907

Cecil John Rhodes
"The Evening World," of Feb 15, 1909

Cecil John Rhodes, born in Herts, England on July 5, 1853, the fourth son of Rev. Francis W. Rhodes. A millionaire, South African businessman, for whom the scholarship was named, is one of the oldest and most prestigious international fellowship programs for graduates in the world. Alain being the first African-American recipient, it would be 56 years before the second African-American would be a recipient. Ironically, Cecil Rhodes had a reputation as a racist, believing in South African white supremacy system, *"apartheid."* Even though stipulated in his Will that race nor religion would be a factor in the selection process of future Rhodes Scholar recipients, Locke's selection raised eyebrows. Rhodes controlled two companies, De Beers Consolidated Mining Company and the Chartered Company which governed the African diamond product in the richest region of East Central Africa. He received his degree from the University of Oxford as an undergrad . He was never married and had no known children. He was eventually sent to Africa because of his illness with asthma as a youth. He then fell in love with the continent. Rhodes provided in his last Will and Testament, the world's first international scholarship study program to attend the University of Oxford for three years at three hundred pounds annually. Cecil John Rhodes died, March 26, 1902 of an apparent heart attack at the age of 48. After his death, the scholarship was established for all students of British colonies, Germany and the United States.

Devour Us Not

Even though Locke's race was known by both the Pennsylvania Trustees and Oxford committee in trying to interpret Mr. Rhodes intent as it relates to qualified Africans or American Negroes as reported by, *"The Hawaiian Gazette," of November 1, 1907.* The committee decided not to allow Locke to study at Oxford and be housed there like all other Oxford recipients. Rather, Locke, unlike the forty-four other scholars arriving from America, he was forced to a small low profile college named Hertford. There was a letter written by Gustaf R. Westfeldt, a well known business man in New Orleans, to the British Ambassador at Washington protesting the selection of Locke, sighting the selection would taint the prestige of the award and making it unpopular in the South. Many more objections were expressed fearing the start of what was feared, *"racial equality,"* as recorded by the, *"New-York Tribune," of May 2, 1907.* It was believed that most of the opposition of Locke's appointment came from American shores and not Britain. Locke finished his studies in England with much success.

Understanding the humility of life and what all having suffered causes one to do is but befitting of one so deserving. Locke's vision; unlimited by his abilities that would not be ignored otherwise; caused him to triumph regardless. He went on to receive his PhD and ended back at Harvard as a philosophy professor in 1918 and finally returned to Howard University as Chair of the Philosophy Department.

"Dorothy Merle Hendrickson"
"The Evening World," of June 12, 1922

Dorothy Merle Hendrickson became the first African-American woman to receive an M.A. degree in economics from Columbia, University. She entered the University in September, 1921 after receiving her undergraduate degree from Hunter College of Manhattan, New York with honors as reported by the, *"New-York Tribune," of June 18, 1920.* Ms. Hendrickson was also elected to the Phi Beta Kappa fraternity. Ms. Hendrickson's thesis was,

> **ABRAHAM LINCOLN.**
>
> In his great Illinois canvass with Stephen A. Douglas in 1858, he repeatedly declared that he was opposed "to a social and political equality between the black and white races;" that he "would to the very last stand by the laws of Illinois, which forbade the marriage of white people with negroes." In the same canvass he says: "I'm not, and never have been in favor of making voters or jurors of negroes; nor of qualifying them to hold office, nor to intermarry with whites; and I will say further, in addition to this there is a *physical difference between the black and white races* which I believe will *forever forbid the two races living on terms of political and social equality."*
>
> Again on the 21st of August, 1858, in a speech in Ottawa, Ill., he said: "I have no purpose to introduce political and social equality between the black and white races. There is a physical difference between the two which in my judgment, will *probably forbid their living together on the footing of perfect equality;* and inasmuch as it becomes a necessity that there must be a difference, *I am in favor of the race to which I belong having the superior position."*

" The Ouachita Telegraph," of September 11, 1874

"Guidance on the Employment Problem of Negro Graduates of Public School No. 119," as recorded by, *"The Evening world," of June 12, 1922.* Ms. Hendrickson, twenty-two years of age was also one of the youngest recipient of that degree at that time in American history. Also Higher Educational first are; **Alexander Lucius Twilight**, the first African-American to receive a college degree in America, class of 1823 from Middlebury College of Vermont. And he was also the first ever African-American elected Official in America as a State Legislator, serving in the Vermont General Assembly in 1836.

THE DAY WE CELEBRATE.

A THANKSGIVING SURPRISE PARTY.

"New-York Tribune," of Aug 2, 1922

Mary Jane Patterson, the first African-American woman to receive a college degree; Oberlin College, the first college to admit women in 1833, where Ms. Patterson received her degree in 1862 as recorded by, *"The Evening Times," of July 16, 1896.*

Mary Jane Patterson

The controversial figure of **Marcus Mosiah Garvey, Jr.** as it relates to the struggles of Africans in all parts of the world once said, *"Are the white people crazy to antagonize the Negroes by lynchings and unjust discrimination? White man, do you think you can stand up against the combined forces of India, China, Japan and Africa? "Don't you know when the war of the races comes you will be burned up?"* Garvey, once called the Moses of the African-Americans people, advocated a movement of all African Diasporas around the world to be sent back to their homeland for the colonization of Africa. Garvey who called himself, *"Provisional President of the Republic of Africa,"* who lived in Harlem, New York, but was actually born in St. Ann's Bay, Jamaica, August 17, 1887. Living in several countries in the Caribbean and in London, mainly working in publishing and newspaper editing work which was a part of his passion. He later organized the Universal Negro Improvement Association (UNIA), first in Jamaica in 1914 and revised the name to Universal Negro Improvement Association and African Communities (Imperial) League. Garvey developed a close relationship with Booker T. Washington and gives prudence to him for the platform to his cause. And to include the UNIA motto of, *"One God, One Aim and One Destiny,"* Garvey was also President of *"The Black Star Steamship Line."* An enterprise intended to provide a means for African-Americans to return to Africa in addition to providing exchange goods and trade with other countries where

Marcus Mosiah Garvey, Jr.

"Virginian-Pilot," of Nov 26, 1899

African Diaspora's were located. He also suggested the African-Americans denounce their citizenship even though he was not an American citizen. Because of Garvey's fraudulent management dealings, he was indicted for mail fraud and violating the Blue Sky Law of the State of Illinois. After taking millions from poor Negroes, his business ultimately failed as reported by, *"The New-York Tribune," of August 2, 1921.* Garvey, pictured above was from a parade held in the Negro section of Harlem where the, *"back to Africa rally,"* was being held in his honor with mixed reviews. There were circulations suggesting, *"Marcus Garvey must go,"* *"He is a menace to Negro freedom."* Marcus Garvey was supposed to have had meetings with the Ku-Klux-Klan during a meeting held June 25, 1922 as alleged by, *"The Broad Ax," of July 29, 1922.* The two hour conference was with acting imperial wizard Clark in Atlanta. Garvey's so-called purpose was *"white supremacy,"* and the over throw of all Negroes, Jews and Catholics. Garvey married his second wife one year after divorcing his first wife. The thirty-five year old Garvey married twenty-six year old Miss Amy E. Jacques, on a Thursday morning in Baltimore in 1922, according to, *"The Appeal," of August 5, 1922,* at the residence of Rev. J. R. L. Diggs, at 713 Mosher St. witnessed by Miss Cora Earl, Mr. B. M. Johnson, Captain Mulzack and Mrs. J. R. L. Diggs.

guilty for mail fraud and sentenced to 5 years in prison which he blamed the all Jewish jury. President Calvin Coolidge eventually commuted his sentence and he was deported back to his homeland of Jamaica in 1927. He died, June, 1940 and was buried in London. Then in 1964, his body was exhumed and brought to Jamaica for burial.

Four unsung hero that impacted the times as reported by, *"The Richmond Planet of January 5, 1895.* **R.E. Jones, MD**, a Negro, contributions to the progress of African-American history was probably known in his own community but his journey was not. Born in Greensboro, Alabama,

June 15, 1860 where he received his initial education at a private school and then at Tullibody Academy until age 16. Because of his age, several attempts to gain admittance to Medical schools were denied. So Dr. Jones began to teach school before entering the University of Michigan at Ann Arbor. He was the only Negro of 100 graduates that finished on July 1, 1881. After graduation, he secured employment in Detroit where he sent for his mother in August of 1882.
He was known as the first Negro Doctor making house calls while being transported in a horse driven buggy. Dr. Jones met and later married Miss Daisy Mc Linn of New Haven, Connecticut on November 10, 1884. Beloved by all his patients and neighbors, Dr. Jones initially purchased and remodeled a framed house on Leigh Street just beyond Brooke Ave. But, as his popularity and business picked up, Dr. Jones purchased a Brick home with an attached office in a modest part of town at 110 E. Leigh Street. Despite the uncertainty of his ethnicity and jubilant nature, Dr. Jones services were sought after mainly because of his Physician effectiveness and willingness to help. Born a child of privilege, essentially, a millionaire never once being too proud to care for the least of those in his community. Millions due him by nature of his inheritance remained secured in a bank untouched by him for most of his adult life.

S. J. Gilpin, a Negro shoemaker, was born of free parents on December 30, 1850 in Richmond, Virginia. He was educated in the public school system after the *"Richmond evacuation,"* during the Civil War order by General Lee. For about eighteen months under the supervision of Miss Elizabeth Mc Cannon he

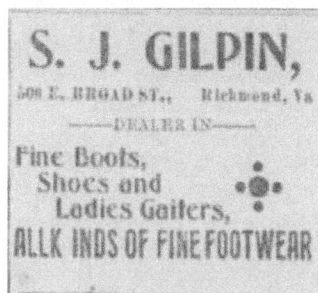

S. J. GILPIN,

508 E. BROAD ST., Richmond, Va

——DEALER IN——

Fine Boots,
Shoes and
Ladies Gaiters,

ALLK INDS OF FINE FOOTWEAR

received a good primary education. Gilpin became an entrepreneur in the shoe business, a trade he had learned from his father in 1873. A trade Gilpin kept up with much success for about fourteen years. And in 1875 he met and later married Miss Cordelia A. Reese and they had nine children. Being the proud papa that he was, had the first of his seven children born boys for which he later admits to being most proud. Changing courses shortly thereafter by gained a partner in 1889 named T.A. Miles. This turned out to be an unproven and unsuccessful venture under the firm name of Miles and Gilpin. After the failure of the partnership, Gilpin went

failure of the partnership, Gilpin went back to being a sole-proprietor and founded a location at 506 E. Broad Street and also became a board member of the Richmond Beneficial and Insurance Company. His business of **Gilpin Shoes** became very popular for a quality product. He watched his stock sore to $3,000 in value while becoming one of the most successful businessmen in the shoe district of his city.

Spottswood W. Robinson, a Negro, was born December 15, 1858 in King William County, Virginia. The only education he received was six months at the elementary level. Being poor, an autodidact was not a deterrent for being economically challenged for S.W. Robinson. He left his home while working with Dr. O.A. Crenshaw. Once they reach Richmond as a milk diary helper, after a year, Robinson left the employment of Dr. Crenshaw and sought employment with Mr. N. J. Smith and assisted him in his business from 1871 to 1879. After which he became an entrepreneur, he had an unsuccessful marriage and supported his widowed mother and a sister while working

S. W. ROBINSON

19 & 21 N. 18TH ST.
Dealer in
Fine Wines, Liquors, Cigars, &c

ALL STOCK SOLD AS GUARANTEED.
PROMPT ATTENTION.
Your Patronage is Respectfully Solicited.

continuously to succeed. His second wife, Miss Nannie Roberts, he married in 1892 and they had a son they named S.W. Robinson, Jr. Robinson's desire to be successful paid off as he soon became the most prosperous merchant in the city. His real estate was valued at $6,500. Robinson's success was attributed to his tenacity in placing all obstacles rendering failure aside and focusing on the job at hand.

J. H. Burke, a Negro, was a successful artist and sign painter,

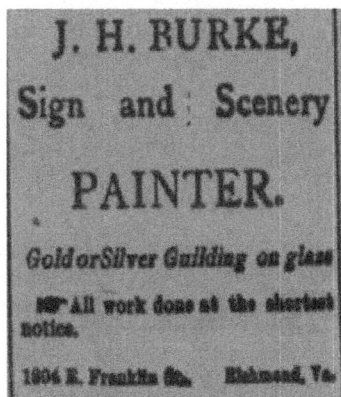

J. H. BURKE,

Sign and Scenery

PAINTER.

Gold or Silver Guilding on glass

All work done at the shortest notice.

1804 E. Franklin St., Richmond, Va.

born February 2, 1857 in Richmond, Virginia. He received his education in public schools and began showcasing his artistic talents around 1879. He was known for painted many portraits of local citizens before he began his sign painting career. Soon thereafter, the word of Burke's signs and artistic talents were being seen and discussed all over town in almost every newspaper advertising section, business window and on billboards

"The Pensacola Journal," of January 20, 1906

Miss Nannie Helen Burroughs was born in Washington D.C. in 1875. She was educated within the public school system of the Washington area. Known as a woman of high energy and a gifted speaker, before her efforts, many attempts were made unsuccessfully to organize as a Missionary and Educational body of the Baptist Women of the city of Washington D.C. Assisted by the leading Pastors of the time gave birth to a movement whose time had come. So, on October 4, 1909, Miss Burroughs founded the National Training School for Women and Girls, located in the Northeastern section of Washington D.C. called Lincoln Heights. The

Miss Nannie Helen Burroughs
"The Colored American," of Feb. 13, 1904

Miss Nannie Helen Burroughs
"The Washington Bee," of Nov.18, 1911

An incomplete Staff at the National Training School
"The Washington Bee," of November 18, 1911

picturesque six acres, which was viewed from top of a hill, was owned by the Women's Convention, Auxiliary to the National Baptist Convention. She also composed songs, two are, *"The Negro Has Fought Every Battle But His Own," &"The Prophecy,"* as reported by, *"The Washington Bee," of March 30, 1912.* The Washington Bee of March 18, 1911 records one of her speech when she spoke with the class of men at the First Highland Baptist Church stated, *"This thing that we call prejudice does not give me any concern whatsoever, because it is a thing that can be overcome. I am convinced that the Negro on well-doing in any position open to him is going to change public sentiment in his favor the world over. The call at this time is for men and women of the race who can render efficient service. We are on trial."*

At the time her school was formed, it was considered one of the largest body of Negro Christian educational institutions in the world. The school consisting of six departments; Domestic Science, Laundry, Dressmaking and Millinery, Gospel Music, Business and the Training of Teachers for Missionary Work. Miss Burroughs main objective was to create an Christian environment applicable to the needs of a people who seek this avenue of prosperity and based on the period of the times. And what the many religious leaders saw in this country at the time was a need for the morality. The religious aspect and industrial efficiency on Negro women in America to be

Miss Nannie Helen Burroughs
"The Appeal," of April 18, 1914

the focus point of African-American culture. The school of her dream was official dedicated on September 14, 1907, after five years in operation. The school based on her initial schooling becoming a stenographer in the office a Negro Christian Banner newspaper in Philadelphia. After a year, Miss Burroughs left and secured a job as a stenographer in Louisville, Kentucky working for a branch

"The Colored American," of Sep 28, 1901

of the missionary department of the National Baptist Convention. She rose to the position of Secretary for the Woman's Missionary Organization. While living in Louisville, Kentucky she was also a manager of an Old Folks' Baptist Home which was an institution based on religious Baptist principles. It was during this period; Miss Burroughs saw the need for her calling. Initially rejected by the Negro community,

"Graham Guardian," of Oct 29, 1920 accusing Miss Burroughs of limiting Negro women to domestic workers and being satisfied with mediocrity. But, Miss Burroughs was persistent in her presentation as she made her case by her vocal compelling brio. Starting with a dollar, the Baptist community gave her the privilege of using its platform of religious principles, but no volunteer funding would come from the church. As reported by the, *"El Paso Herald," of July 15, 1913,* several cities were being offered for such an innovated and pioneering idea. After much research, Miss Burroughs looked at her birth place for the school because of the accessibility and condenses Negro population other than in the south. Miss Burroughs spotted an old farm-house located on six areas for $6,500. She used mail subscriptions and other money raising efforts under the umbrella of the Negro Baptist Women. Word of Miss Burroughs efforts crossed all over the country and volunteer funds began to pour in. Within six years the school has invested some $42,000 into the growth of the school with most of the money coming from Negro churches.

With the increments of 50 cents per pledge, literally pennies were being received for the success of the school. But racial lines were being crossed in this effort as two Northern white women donated $3,500 to the erection of one of the schools building which was later deigned as a *"model home."* This house was used as a teaching example for training. So the premise of Miss Burroughs dreams of domesticating Negro women with its missionary plan of the three gospels *"B's,"* of the Bible, Bathtub and the Broom. Cleanliness of mind, body and home is next to Godliness. Miss Nannie Helen Burroughs died May 20, 1961, and today the school in which she founded is named in her honor.

E. Parker Read, M.D.

E. Parker Read, M.D., Ref. D. was President and founder of the East Indian Remedy Company that

manufactured preparations and sold exclusively by Dr. Read as a Senior Druggist, drug relief products. He was also founder, President, General Manager and Advertising Director of the National Co-operative Association of America, located in Philadelphia, Pennsylvania with capital assets valued at $100,000 in 1900 as recorded by *"The Colored American," of January 12, 1901*. Dr. Read was also a full-fledged Oculist and Optician, graduate of the Philadelphia Optical College with high honors. He was also at that time the only Negro member of the Druid's Medical Society of America (*A Native-American Medical Society that used spiritual forces in the world for healing. An understanding the worlds imbalances of diseases through practical Indian spiritual principles*). He was also appointed the Superintendent of mail at the Central Post Office of Philadelphia in 1901 at a hand-some salary of $2,500 a year. Among the many skill sets this Negro possessed was his ability to create money making ventures such as the over twenty-five real estate properties he a had acquired by 1901, creating the companies: The Assurance and Redemption Association of Petersburg, Virginia that was used to buy lapsed Insurance policies; The Consolidated Beneficial Society of Baltimore, Maryland, an Indian based Capital Life Insurance Company; The House Renters Protective Association, that was used to advise and protect the rights of tenants and renters; The Advocate Printing and Publishing Company of Philadelphia, Pennsylvania, that printed and published books; The National Co-Operative Industrial Protection and Investment Association, used to educate and advise Entrepreneurship, business risk and promote advertisement; Read & Christian Manufact-uring Company, the manufacturing of his brand of twenty-six different medical remedy products and The East Indian Remedy Company that manufactured hair preparation products and agent medical supplies. Dr. Read known as the finest chemist in the country was also the publisher of two books, *"Co-operation or Buy and Borrow of Ourselves,"* and *"Geographical Distribution of Animals and the Race of Men."* Born approximately 1865, the youngest of seven children, lost his mother at an early age, followed by the lost of his father during the Civil War. Dr. Read's limited history is no match for the enormous leap he made into prosperity. His five-story building at 1037 South Street, Philadelphia, Pennsylvania, bearing his name is but a testimony of what one can achieve despite the elements of restrictions.

Mrs. Elizabeth Lindsay Davis, a Negro, that was born in Peoria, Illinois. Educated in Princeton, graduating from Princeton Normal High School with high honors, majoring in *"Pedagogy,"* which is a holistic science of education being practically applied in child rearing. She became a school teacher in Missouri, Louisville, Kentucky, New Albany, Indiana and Quincy, Illinois. She married Dr. William H. Davis of Frederick City, Maryland in 1885.

Active in several women clubs as a part of an initial Negro women suffrage

Mrs. Josephine St. Pierre Ruffin
"Perrysburg Journal," of Aug. 17, 1900
Also one of the founders of N.A.C.W.

Mrs. Elizabeth Lindsay Davis
"The Broad Ax," of Nov. 12, 1921

President's of The National Association of Colored Women

Mary Church Terrell (1896-1900)
"Richmond Planet," of August 27, 1910

* Prof Josephine Silone Yates (1900-1904)*
"The Professional World," of December 26, 1902

* Mrs. Lucy Thurman (1904-1908)*
"The Colored American," June 9, 1900

* Margaret J. Murray Washington (1912-1916)*
"The Appeal," of November 16, 1901

* Mrs. Mary B. Talbert (1916-1920)*
"The Appeal," of April 22, 1905

* Miss Halle Quinn Brown (1920-1924)*
"The Appeal," of June 17, 1922

movement; where white and black women worked side by side in an America fight for justice. She became a chartered member of the I.B.W. Woman's Club. The I.B.W., which means Images of Black Women was one of the first women club's established in Chicago for Negro women. She also organized and became the President of the Phyllis Wheatley Club for the first 20 of its 21 years of existence. A club whose focus was for the viewing socially at the Negro home life and the woman's essential role in it. The Woman's Aid Club, designed to ensure the aged Negroes who could not afford to helped themselves, had proper housing and other essentials

necessary for their well-being. She worked tirelessly in the Provident Hospital and the Institution Church Social Settlement worked which help focus the attention on health care. The N.A.C.W., National Association of Colored Women Clubs

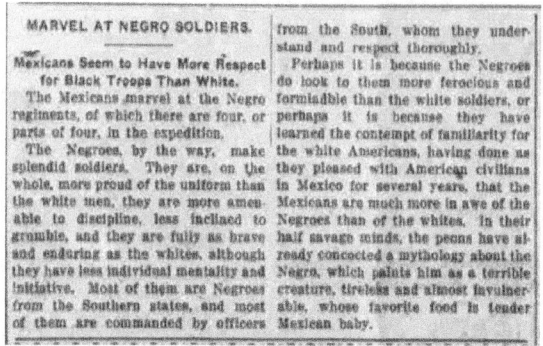

MARVEL AT NEGRO SOLDIERS.

Mexicans Seem to Have More Respect for Black Troops Than White.

The Mexicans marvel at the Negro regiments, of which there are four, or parts of four, in the expedition.

The Negroes, by the way, make splendid soldiers. They are, on the whole, more proud of the uniform than the white men, they are more amenable to discipline, less inclined to grumble, and they are fully as brave and enduring as the whites, although they have less individual mentality and initiative. Most of them are Negroes from the Southern states, and most of them are commanded by officers from the South, whom they understand and respect thoroughly.

Perhaps it is because the Negroes do look to them more ferocious and formidable than the white soldiers, or perhaps it is because they have learned the contempt of familiarity for the white Americans, having done as they pleased with American civilians in Mexico for several years, that the Mexicans are much more in awe of the Negroes than of the whites. In their half savage minds, the peons have already concocted a mythology about the Negro, which paints him as a terrible creature, tireless and almost invulnerable, whose favorite food is tender Mexican baby.

which merged with a number of other Negro women organizations in 1896 which was a major source of her public works. The Federal organizations called on Mrs. Davis as a state organizer for four years. Being affiliated with a prestige organization such as the N.A.C.W., that list members and Presidents; the likes of Mrs. Margaret Jane Murray Washington, one of the founders, 5th elected president and wife of Booker T. Washington of Tuskegee. Professor J. Silone Yates, Mrs. Mary Church Terrell of Washington D.C. who became the first African-American woman to be selected to speak before the Equal-Suffrage Convention in 1900. She was also one of the first African-American woman to receive a college degree and Mrs. Mary B. Talbert, recipient of the 1922 N.A.A.C.P. Spingarn Medal award for outstanding achievement in organizing fund raisers to help pay off the home of Frederick Douglass. Mrs. Lucy Thurman who was once the Michigan National Superintendent of work among Colored people inherited an organization from Mrs. Josephine Silone Yates that started in 1901 with five federated states national organizations and various local clubs to comprise the National Association for

Colored Women with membership enrollment totaling 10,000 women. At the end of her tenure, there were twenty-three federal states involved plus thirty-seven state club affiliates making the enrollment totaling 40,000 women. Also clubs were established in as far away as Africa and as close as Canada as the future for an international conference for women was planned. Miss Halle Quinn Brown founder of the Colored Women League which later merged with the N.A.C.W. and President of the Ohio State Federal Women's Club before

becoming the 7th President of the N.A.C.W. Because of the aggressive nature of the Negro women movement, prompted an aggressive approach from the white women clubs. But **Mrs. Elizabeth Lindsey Davis** who prominence became legendary during the women's movement is credited with creating the discussions on women in America. With the migration of Negroes from the south to Chicago, the needs for Negro involvement in home and communities, in Chicago at that time became the largest urban city populated with southern Negroes. A major concern in the country during the turn of the century, where issues as well as problems emerged. Without the success of these women clubs, even before the women could vote, the cultural importance of

their voice, if left silent, would have crippled a generation of females that would have been uncultured and uneducated household dwellers. Mrs. Davis' motto to the progress for people of color was: *"If You Can't Push! Pull!, if You Can't Pull!, Please Get Out of the Way!."* **The National Afro-American Council,** the first Civil Rights organization in America that lasted less than a decade. Originally the creation of Mr. Fortune in 1896 and 1897 but failed

in place to revive the organization under the name of the National Afro-American Council. The organization was then formed in August, 1898 as reported by, *"The Appeal," of June 28, 1902* in Rochester, New York by, Timothy Thomas Fortune of New York and Rev. Alexander Walters of New Jersey and others. Mr. Fortune was nominated for the first Presidency of the Council but declined and Bishop Walters was selected. The Council was also created to challenge mob laws, lynching's and their God given civil rights under the United States Constitution. The Councils' great axiom: *"To labor for man because he is man, is man's noblest work."* Noble words for the creation of the council and its ultimate objection. Also the council would not merely in carelessness accept

In the front middle L/R: *(1) Booker T. Washington, (2) Bishop Alexander Walters and (3) Ida B. Wells-Barrett* "The Appeal," of July 19, 1902 The National Afro-American Council at St. Paul, Minnesota July 9, 1902 .

the institution of passive compliance to the established laws which excluded Negroes. In compliance with the obligation of membership into the council meant also the exertion of an Supreme Court's attitude towards the Dred Scott's decision, stimulated the appeal for rights and race harmony. But the fulfillment of the active influence on behalf of the non-corrupt laws of the existing ones of the time which gave the membership into the council its valued importance. Use of that principal, caused many to join in search for proper justice for about a decade. The movement to challenge the governing institution, caused many clubs and groups of all sorts that addressed Africa-American, women and fairness issues that seemed oblivious to the already established form. The popularity and declining volunteer funding of the Council took a turn for the worst in 1907, causing its collapse couple with internal entanglements. The council then suggests the merging of its platform with several others up coming African-American organizations and groups, but failed in its attempt to resonate with its base.

Devour Us Not

"The St. Louis Republic," of November 11, 1900

President's of the National Afro-American Council

Bishop Alexander Walters (1898-1902)
"The Colored American," of Sep 8, 1900

Timothy Thomas Fortune (1902-1904)
"The Appeal," of Jun 28, 1902

William Henry Steward (1904-1905)
"The Appeal," of Jun 28, 1902

Bishop Alexander Walters (1905-1907)
"The Colored American," of Sep 8, 1900

Bishop Alexander Walters then became President of the National Independent Political League which help secure then equal rights they were entitled to as well as enforce the 13th, 14th and 15th amendments of the constitution. In 1905 W.E.B. Du Bois, the first African-American to receive a PhD from Harvard College, started what was called the *"Niagara Movement."* The Niagara Movement was named because of W.E.B. Du Bois' efforts in trying to meet with a number of prominent African-Americans to entertain issues concerning unfair treatment of black citizens. Because American hotels were segregated, Du Bois reserved a room at Niagara Falls in his name on the Canadian side to avoid the obvious issue under discussion. So the story of the issue resonated with other citizens with similar concerns. And by 1910, the group's enthusiasm had shifted, like many other like groups and joined with the N.A.A.C.P. Their first conference, however, was held in Buffalo, New York, August, 1905 giving praise for Negro accomplishments and how the race was becoming a major contributor to the overall success of the country. But the disgraceful events of 1908, at the time the resting place of President Lincoln, the Springfield, Illinois riots and the needless murder of Postmaster, Frazier Baker in 1898, prompted a number of whites liberal citizen's also to take up the cause. One of the more vocal components as reported by, *"The Appeal," of January 22, 1916,* were Moorfield Storey, a Boston Attorney and former President of the American Bar Association who became the first President of the N.A.A.C.P. Among very popular black's were also white's joining in the movement who were mostly descendents of abolitionist, were Professor Joel Elias Spingarn (*Chairman of the Board of Directors*) and his brother Arthur, Mary White Ovington (*Chairman of the Board of Directors*), Oswald Garrison Villard, grandson of William Lloyd Garrison (*Treasurer*), Dr. John Haynes Holmes (*Vice President*), W.E.B. Du Bois (*Director of Publicity and Research*), John E. Milholland, Archibald H. Grimke, Garnett R. Waller, Ida B. Wells-Barnett, Mary Church Terrell and Henry Moscowitz. Soon the National Independent Political League also merged with the new organization and addressed its name as the N.A.A.C.P., (*National Associate for the Advancement of Colored People)*. The organization was 104 years old in 2013 and the oldest and largest Civil Rights Organization in America that was founded in New York, 1909.

"The Washington Times," of March 4, 1906

President's and Initial Members of the N.A.A.C.P

First African-American President-James Weldon Johnson (1917-18)(1920-31)-"The Broad Ax," of February 9, 1918 * First Jewish-American President Professor Joel Elias Spingarn (1909-1929)*-"The Appeal," of January 23, 1915 * W.E.B. Du Bois-" The Broad Ax," of October 15, 1910, * Rev. Garnett Waller*-"The Colored American. " of May 25, 1901 * Archibald H. Grimke*-"The Colored American," of September 19, 1903 .

John H. Holmes-"The Evening World.," March 18, 1922 * Ida B. Wells-Barnett*-"The Morning Call," of February 22, 1895. * Mary Church Terrell -"The Colored American," August 13, 1904, * Mrs. Josephine Ruffin -"The Washington Bee," of May 3, 1902, * Inez Milholland -"The Washington Times," of November 26, 1916.

And the N.A.A.C.P. went on to incorporated in 1911. Significantly to the survival of the N.A.A.C.P. was the very noticeable initial white leadership to the organization, which in some minds legitimized the organization's existence. Of course, of the whites who did take up the cause, also faced opposition from their own race of which had a failing effort to discourage. But their support was a major factor in maintaining a visual vocal political element that otherwise would not have been as effective. And to their own acknowledgement of this fact, knew the task at hand that was paramount to the overall success of the movement. So the organization by virtue of its title, knew its purpose and like all organizations of its kind, the traditional turmoil's were

"The Washington Times," of March 4, 1906

eliminated. But the N.A.A.C.P. continued to challenge every law, issue or perception that involved Negroes not receiving proper justice unlike any organization in history, ever. The N.A.A.C.P. continued to grow and fight a thirty year fight against the fowl acts of lynching. Representative Leonidas C. Dyer of St. Louis, motivated and outraged by the East St. Louis riot of 1917, prompted him to author the known Dyer Anti-Lynching Bill H.R., 13. He was as relentless about its passing and enactment as pressures he and Congress received from all Negro organizations and clubs. The particulars of the bills and its focus concerning lynching involved also lynch mobs or riotous assembly responsibilities as deprivers invoking their own laws as reported by, *"The Appeal," of October 29, 1921.* The South with its notorious disregard for the rights of Negroes were the targeted fight base on factual numbers. But still angered by the Civil War and the desolation of the economic power based on slave labor was retaliated mostly by whites against blacks. During the Reconstruction Period, the most vulnerable times in which most Negroes were susceptible, the long arm of hate in gulped this nation with intent to devour.

First 11 Recipient's of the Spingarn Award

* Dr. Ernest Everett Just (Biologist)-1ˢᵗ recipient - 1915-"The Appeal," of March 6, 1915. * Col. Charles Young (U.S. Army)-2ⁿᵈ recipient in 1916-"The Kansas City Sun," of May 31, 1919. * Harry T. Burleigh (Composer)-3ʳᵈ recipient in 1917-"The Colored American," of January 16, 1904- * William Stanley Braithwaite (Poet) -4ᵗʰ recipient in 1918- "The Minneapolis Journal," of September 15, 1904- *Archibald H. Grimke (U.S. Consul) -5ᵗʰ recipient in 1919-"The Colored American," of September 19, 1903. * William E. B. Du Bois (Author) - 6ᵗʰ recipient in 1920- "The Broad Ax," of October 15, 1910.

* Charles S. Gilpin (Actor)-7ᵗʰ recipient in 1921-"New-York Tribune," of March 13, 1921. * Mrs. Mary B. Talbert (President of NACW)-8ᵗʰ recipient in 1922-"The Appeal," of November 16, 1901. * George Washington Carver (Botanist) 9ᵗʰ recipient in 1923-"The Colored American," of July 20, 1901. * Roland Hayes (Tenor Singer)-10ᵗʰ recipient in 1924-"New-York Tribune," of January 26, 1919. * James Weldon Johnson (Poet & 1ˢᵗ Black President of NAACP)-11ᵗʰ recipient in 1925-"The Broad Ax," of February 9, 1918.

Even though the Dyer Anti-lying Bill passed the United Stated House of Representatives, but because of the filibustering, it never got passed the senate. Much of the debate surrounding lynching's and the brutality associated with it came from and is credited by the N.A.A.C.P. 's relentless efforts. But it took one-hundred and five years for the Senate to issue an apology on behave of all victims, their survivors and descendants on June 14, 2005 for not passing the bill more than a century earlier. Joel Elias Spingarn was elected President from 1929-1939, prior to his tenure as President, when he was Chairman of the Board; he introduced a gold medal named the *"Spingarn Medal,"* to be awarded annually to an African-American who made significant achievements during the year. The first recipient of this award was Dr. Ernest Everett

Just, a biologist from Howard University, on February 12, 1915. Under Spingarn's leadership, the N.A.A.C.P. received much notoriety as the seeds of justice in motion by establishing offices and addressing issues. The seeds began to plant and establish itself in every major and small city around the country. The organization soon began to mount up a series of major court victories, challenging, *"Jim Crow,"* laws that were used to disenfranchise Negroes for decade. Its reputation as a no nonsense organization began to be the Negroes lifeline link to proper justice. The N.A.A.C.P. and its leadership began to change America and forced it to live up to its creed of equal justice for all. President James Weldon Johnson, the first elected Black President and his brother John, wrote the lyrics and music to the later adopted Negro National Anthem, *"Lift Every Voice and Sing,"* continued the momentum of the movement with great enthusiasm. During the 1940's the Fair Employment Practices Committee (FEPC) that would have a major effect in ensuring proper compliance in hiring practices was created. All the discriminatory practices that kept Negroes in the lower echelon of the pay scale were being challenged as blacks began to demand equal pay and higher paying jobs. This lead to the 1950's and the most challenging and dangerous period for Negroes being, *"The Modern Civil Rights Era."* Even though brick by brick as the walls of injustice began to tumble, that ever increasing element to keep the Negro back would be a constant. Soon the N.A.A.C.P. field reps began to be a target as well as their offices and homes. All persons of like interest in the

cause of liberty for all and fair play, they too became a target. As the strong hold of hate would try to stop educational progressions, voting opportunities, integration barrier's became increasingly numerous, soon felt their brick wall of opposition to equality crumble. And despite all that was done to Negroes during this long period that is still a struggle, the N.A.A.C.P. never wavered its fight for the rights of all people.

Professor William Henry Harrison Hart, pictured left, was a law professor at Howard University and founder of the Hart Farm School for Negro boys. The farm which was located in Prince George County, Maryland on the east bank of the Potomac River, twelve miles south of Washington, D.C. The initial purchase of 700 acres of

land from William M. Evarts, a white man, whose location was next to each other when Prof. Hart was the private secretary to Mr. Evarts and assisted in securing a grant for the purchase. The school was the initial personal vision of Prof. Hart to form a school whose primary designed was for neglected juveniles and deprived Negro boys between the ages of eight to eighteen. This lead the way towards an education in farming, self discipline and responsible manhood training for young males of all races without hope that begin November 11,

Devour Us Not

"The Saint Paul Globe," of Aug 28, 1904

1897. A daily practical application which included a Korean and a Puerto Rican among the first 42 students of indoor and outdoor training areas instruct them with, farm cultivating, planting, animal care and feeding, carpentry, blacksmith training and wheel-wrighting. Prof. Hart born October 30, 1857 to the parentage of William A.H. and Clementine B. Hart of Barbour County, Eufaula, Alabama. Coming up from Alabama, barefoot and eager to learn as reported by, *"The Colored American," of September 15, 1900 and 1870 Federal Census*. Professor Hart married a young white lady from Massachusetts named Mary M. Onley, 25 years his junior on March 27, 1905. They had four children losing two in infancy. Clementine, a daughter was born in 1907 and William, Jr. their son born in 1908. Professor Hart faith in his rural curriculum

1900 Photo of Teachers and Students of the "Hart Farm School" - "The Colored American," of Sep 15, 1900

prepares a youth to run a self-reliant farm for profitability in the most proficient manner while imbruing them with work ethnics necessary for life. The school is described as industrially magnetic which keeps the enthusiasm of the youth as they showcase their eagerness to learn. Monies appropriate by Congress, in the amount of $12,000 annually or $185 per child annually. Which was considerably less than white reform schools with no educational curriculum. The supervision, issuance and audit of these funds are made by the, *"Board of Children's Guardians."* The Comptroller for the Department of the Treasury was head of all financial issues pertaining to the State funded schools. Professor Hart was an Educator for more than thirty years. In the law department, Hart brought suit to a number of cases in a wide range of subject matters. Not only giving his heart and soul into in his school, he placed a lot of his own money into it. Professor Hart challenged a contract he signed on July 1, 1902, claiming amounts owed him of $8,856.70. He claimed & acknowledged the $12,000 annual amount offered by the Board of Children's Guardian for the care & maintenance for the 60 wards at a rate of $200 annually. Professor Hart claims only $3,741.40 was paid to him. In his deposition he states the allotted funds

"The Day Book," of Apr 18, 1917

did not allow for an accounting clerk to record the expenditures on behave of the school. Prof. Hart described the July 26, 1902 incident, in which the board withdrew the wards funds and several times between October 13, 1902 and the end of that fiscal year. They substituted the wards students totaling 43 others were sent to the school which was contractually flawed and only $3,741.40 was paid to Hart. He also detailed a fire which was purposely ignited by three youths that destroyed a number of buildings, losing an estimated replacement value of about $15,000. Since before the Federal involvement, Prof. Hart describes in detail other expenditures incurred as a result of the start-up cost in making the school functional, using his and volunteer funds from acquaintances. In presenting his case, recalling; Prof. Hart finished with honors at all levels of his educational journey with his primary major being Constitutional Law. This did much in the way of using parables in depicting the Board's discriminatory practices with his school. He made several references to the Board's salary

dealings in granting a Superintendent of a Reform School receiving $1,500.00 annual salary and $0.00 to his Superintendent. Prof. Hart combined a series of a number of incurred debt he had sustained in the first seven years of the school's existence that included his own wage base salary for seven years. And notwithstanding, was the repairs, normal upkeep totaling approximately $88,500 of which he was asking for the minus $8,856.70 plus interest of $16,725.09 added to the principal balance of $79,725.09. Prof. Hart surmises the total amount due him by the government was $96,368.39. Giving argument to the self reliant principals he instill in his students were the same values he used in engineering his school. Prof. Hart in conclusion of his argument on guideline given for the normal running of a Government sponsored school, that the provisions were made in the next budget hearing of the Treasury District Appropriation Bill. Allocations in similar amounts to that of any other white governmental sponsored school, as recorded by, *"The Washington Times," of December 30, 1903.* Prof. Hart's legal entanglements would continued as in July 21, 1903, he appeared before the Police Court on charges of making an assault on a nonaffiliated adult of the school named Michael Dorsey who was a saloon owner. The man testified that Prof. Hart, with several of his acquaintance watching, without provocation struck him several times in the face aboard a northbound seventh streetcar around 11:30 the night in question. Prof. Hart then took the stand and explained to the Judge with experience of a seasoned trial Lawyer detailed the incident quite differently. Prof. Hart describe a gang of intoxicated, loud and looking for trouble young men aboard the same streetcar occupied by himself and a youth he was taking before the Board of Children's Guardians the following morning. For the amusement of his buddies, Dorsey approached and assaulted the youth and Prof. Hart in a whaling of fist striking both he and the youth. Prof. Hart then explained for the protection of himself and the youth under his authority and in an effort to curtail the violent assault directed at them did admittedly strike Dorsey in the jaw. This seems to surprise the man of the force directed at him from Prof. Hart and hence stopped his aggression. The Judge having heard Prof. Hart's version of the incident dismissed the case without argument as recorded by, *"The Washington Times," of July 22, 1903.* Prof Hart's legal issues did not end there for the next case would be a land marked case of Hart vs. the State of Maryland in 1905. Prof. Hart had been arrested in Elkton, Maryland from what was known then as the Maryland *"Jim Crow,"* law or the Supreme Court case in 1896 of Plessy vs. Ferguson, which made it legal for all established accommodations from education to hotels to eating establishments to be *"separate-but-equally."* This law in which Prof. Hart describes in his research was a federal Law imposed on states providing for separate accommodations on railroad trains for blacks and whites for which he was arrested. The Plessy case

which initially focused on railcars, opened up a Pandora's Box in giving racist views to extending every walk of life where both races might encounter each other. Races views which infuriated Prof. Hart after his arrest. Prof. Hart's goal was to challenge the law for its stand in enforcing in his words, *"such an outdated law."* This meant if he were to travel, eat or request sleeping arrangements, he and his wife and children would have to have separate accommodations since his wife was white. Prof. Hart won his historical case against the streetcars of Maryland. And as a result of his victory, the 5 to 60 cent fare every citizen paid had no bearing into seating arrangements. Little is known about the sustainable success of the school as I'm assured the struggles of maintaining stability with the students and the board must to have been a daunting challenge. Professor William H.H. Hart died in Brooklyn Kings, New York, January 8, 1934, according to the, *"Free Family History and Genealogy Records."*

Mrs. Addie R. Clark, founded the Livingston School of Dress Making in Washington D.C. around 1902. Mrs. Clark, a South Carolinian was born a Mulatto in March, 1863. In 1884, she married a South Carolinian named Louis R. Clark, who was born March, 1852. They migrated north and soon settled in the

MRS. L. R. CLARK

DC area. They had no children so Addie developed a skill for dress making according to the 1900 Federal Census. She attended some of the finest schools in perfecting her skills. She attended the distinguished school of John Mitchell's of New York, S.E. Taylor's, and McDowell's & Royal. But very little is known about the vision of Addie and the prosperity of her schools' history other than they made some of the finest

dresses in all of North America with other schools located in

Baltimore, Maryland, and Lynchburg, Virginia. About 1904, Mrs. Clark had developed The Women's Bazaar, Millinery and Dressmaking, then formed her own company of Mrs. L.R. Clark & Co. in addition to establishing the Tailors and Dressmakers Organization of Washington D.C. Many of her students went on to become expert dressmakers all because of the efforts of Addie Clark.

Mrs. Harriet Beecher Stowe, was the author of *"Uncle Tom's Cabin in 1852"* and *"Dred-A Tale of the Great Dismal Swamp in 1956,"* just to name a few of her many works. Harriett was the third daughter and the sixth child of thirteen children born June 14, 1811 to Rev. Dr. Lyman and Roxana Foote Beecher of Litchfield, Connecticut as recorded by the, *"Warren Sheaf,"* of July 9, 1896. When Harriet was about four years of age, her deeply religious mother died, so her father sent Harriet to Guilford, Connecticut to be reared by her grandmother. Her father, a very out spoken clergyman on slavery and all the devious acts associated with it was the constant daily occurrence in the Beecher house and church. His sermons and prayers openly ask for expedient relief for the oppressed people of African descent. Harriet's earlier years were at an all girls school where

"The San Francisco Call," of January 21, 1905

Mrs. Harriet Stowe in 1836
"The Morning Call," of Aug 27, 1893

Mrs. Harriet Stowe in 1850
"Wichita Eagle," of Mar 2, 1890

Mrs. Harriet Stowe in 1890
"Wichita Eagle," of Mar 2, 1890

Prof. Calvin Ellis Stowe 1886
"Wichita Eagle," of Mar 2, 1890

her eldest sister, Catherine was in charge before moving back with her father whom had remarried and continued her education at Litchfield Academy. The views of her father had major consequences into Harriet line of thinking regarding the evils of slavery. Harriet developed an art for writing and at the tender age of 12, her first article made its way to the eyes of many within in her town. The article was titled, *"Can the Immortality of the Soul Be Proved From Its Light of Nature?"* Her father accepted a position in Cincinnati to be President of the Lane Theological Seminary.

The love-bug hits Harriet in 1836 and on January 6, 1836, she married a widower who was a Professor of Biblical Literature at Lane named Calvin Ellis Stowe. The Stowe's had seven children named, Eliza Taylor, Harriet Beecher, Henry Ellis, Frederick William, Georgiana May, Samuel Charles and Charles Edward. Calvin was also a Clergyman of the parish of Walnut Hills, a suburb of Cincinnati. Calvin having a commonality interest to that of her father, their home soon became a station, stop over point for the underground-railroad. The fears and secrecies surrounding their plight of resisting the institution of slavery, made her so-called imaginary story-telling that much more realistic. Harriet then began to put her observation and experiences with slavery to pin and paper. She soon published, *"The Mayflower,"* or *"Sketches of the Descendants of Pilgrims,"* in 1849. By 1850, with the aggressive nature in which the nation gripped fugitive slave laws, Harriet's family relocated to Brunswick, Maine where her husband accepted an appointment at Bowdoin College. Noticeably, free states were less enthusiastic about the issues of slaves as Harriet found it more difficult even among her friends and local Christian's who shared her compassion. It was this determination that she realized the magnitude of her responsibility to the American people and world to educate the atrocities of slavery. Harriet wrote a short story

"The Day Book," February 18, 1913

in which she received a $50 prize in 1832 titled, *"Uncle Lot."* Hence came *"Uncle Tom's Cabin,"* or sometimes called *"Life Among the Lowly."* Notwithstanding the nature of her creation, Harriet experienced a slow start to the book, mainly because of it's content and the period in which it was written. Harriet claims there were no original characters in the book but admits, Uncle Tom was in part based on a full-blooded Negro named Josiah Henson born a slave in Port Tobacco, Charles County, Maryland as written by, *"The National Tribune," of July 9, 1896.* And not to over state the fact that she was white, writing from a black prospective that first appeared in the National Era. The National Era was an anti-slavery weekly newspaper at Washington, D.C. from June 1851 until April, 1852 before being issued in book form. Within five years of it being printed in book form, more than 500,000 copies had been sold world wide in eighteen different languages. Second in total book sales at the time, only to the Holy Bible. All the excitement caught the attention of a Boston Publisher named John P. Jewett who proposed to pay a half a share in the profits if the author would share in the expenses of publishing it. But Professor Stowe instructed Harriet to accept a more practical offer of a flat 10 per cent royalty amount. She followed the brilliance of Uncle Tom's Cabin, with, *"A Key to Uncle Tom's Cabin,"* which showcased all the factual evidence to support the storyline. She also wrote to a more elemental version to attract a different demographic when she released *"A peep Into Uncle Tom's Cabin for Children."* Harriet Elisabeth Beecher Stowe died in Hartford, Connecticut, July 1, 1896 at the age of 85 according to, *"The North Platt Semi-Weekly Tribune," of July 3, 1896.* She was buried in the private cemetery of the Trustees of Phillip's Academy and the Andover Seminary where her husband, Professor C.E. Stowe, who died in 1886 and one of her children, Henry Ellis are buried.

"The Appeal," of August 25, 1900

Lillian Clayton Jewett was the founder of the Anti-lynching League from Boston. A white racist group named, *"The Green-Turtle Club of New Orleans,"* once placed a $2,000 bounty on her head for her interest in the rights of African-American citizens. After the murder of Postmaster Frazier Baker, February, 1898, discussed on page 31, Ms. Jewett at age 24 then, accompanied by her mother and a young man of the Boston Journalist named R.G. Larsen according to the, *"Kansas City Journal," of August 6, 1899,* went to Williamsburg County, Lake City, South Carolina. In August, 1899 they rescued the remaining Baker family members of his widow, Lavinia and five surviving children, Sarah, Lincoln, Willie, Cora and Rosa, then brought them all to Boston for their supposed safety. Ms. Jewett went before the congregation of St. Paul Baptist Church of Boston who assisted her in her efforts in purchasing train tickets and a supply of fresh clothing according to, *"The Appeal," of August 25, 1900.* But Ms. Jewett wasn't without her critics who suggested that her primary motivation for rescuing the Baker's was not for humanitarian reason but financially. It was suggested that she used the Baker family as depicted by Rev. J.L. Dart, a Negro minister of Charleston, South Carolina where the Baker's had been residing since the lynching, which appears to be a bit of hyperbolic. To most of the Negro Bostonians who had given her a number of titles, *"The White Angel of Freedom,"* while some newspapers dub her, *"The Female John Brown," "The New Harriet Beecher Stowe," "The Boston Joan of Arc," "The White Negress,"* and *"The Coming Emancipation of the Black Race."* Ms. Jewett hired some New York Lawyers named Herman Butterfield and P.A. Loomis to indict by Grand Jury, the Green Turtle Club for the offer for Ms. Jewett's head and the threats against her and all parties. According to, *"The Free Lance," of August 21, 1900,*

GIB DAT TO ME!
LOOK HERE CHILD,
DONT GIT ME
EXASPERATED!

"The San Francisco Call," of Jun 20, 1909

lawyers went to the Henmen Building of Louisiana to confront prominent Louisiana lawyers to the legality of their case. The confirmation of their case was based on a Louisiana law of section 5, act 8 of a special session of 1870 regarding conspiracy issues. But the Louisiana Lawyer's cautioned against pursuing such a case in the racist south of an organization with such a radical history. They also suggested that no Grand Jury south of the Mason and Dixon line would indict an organization such as the Green Turtle Club or the Regent of the Silver Shield of Alabama, all for a *"Negro Lover!"* The Green Turtle Club even went as far as to make a rope tied into a noose for her lawyers and a mock coffin for Ms. Jewett to be transported to Boston in its attempt to intimidate anyone who'd dare aid the Negro in his flight for justice against lynching. Ms. Jewett was born in Boston, Massachusetts and educated at Hollins Institute in Virginia and little else is known about this controversial figure in African-American history.

General Robert Smalls, a Republican, and known as *"The Hero of the Planter."* According to the, *National Republican," of March 6, 1886,* Smalls was born April 5, 1839 in Beaufort, South Carolina on the master Henry McKee's plantation and remain at the place of his birth for many years. Robert was born a Mulatto; his mother's name was Lydia Polite and probably the son of his master. In 1851, he left Beaufort by order of his master at age 12 as a hired to Charleston to work at the rigger's trade while also being employed as a seafaring, sailing along the South Carolina

General Robert Smalls
"The Appeal," of Jul 7, 1906

General Robert Smalls
"The Colored American," of Dec 1, 1900

and Florida coast. This experience of bars and harbors would pay major benefits for his legacy. As a stevedore, a dockworker, in Charleston for two years, Smalls joined the steamer CSS Planter, July, 1861 until May 13, 1862, then a Confederate transporter plying between Fort Sumter and the harbor of Charleston. The Planter, also known as the special dispatch boat of General Roswell Sabine Ripley. After two months, Smalls was promoted to *"wheelsman."* Wheelsman was another name for Pilot, but because of bigotry, the title of pilot was not given to Negroes publicly, even though the 1880 Federal Census lists him as a Pilot. As if the worthiness of prestige in navigating a water vessel was above the capability of Negroes, wheelsman was most commonly used which sounds less technical. On May 13, 1862, the whites of the Planter went ashore that included the Captain, Chief Engineer and shipmates. Left aboard the vessel was eight shipmates included Smalls that were restricted from disembarking. It was at this point when General Smalls headed a meeting of the men who were all Colored, to seize the vessel for themselves. This maneuver involved risky avoidance of enemy gunfire and or capture if their identity were known. Not to mention was the significance of their cargo which included guns and ammunition originally bound for Fort Ripley. Included in the seizing of the water vessel was

"The San Francisco Call," of July 14, 1907

Devour Us Not

"The San Francisco Call," of March 26, 1901

Smalls' wife, Hannah Jones (1826-1895), their two children, a daughter Elizabeth Lydia (Bampfield) (1858-Nov. 1, 1924) and a son who died as a youth (*Another daughter, Sarah S. (Williams) was born Dec.1864 and died Aug 22, 1920, there was also another son named William R. Smalls that was born Feb. 1892*), and one other crewman's wife and children. Among the silence of night around 2 am, the vessel with its new passengers headed for the sea. At the various check points, Smalls gave the proper check point signal of raising the flag of truce to gain access to the sea without detection. One misty morning which made visual recognition almost impossible, a Union frigate was observed off the bar. The Planter approached it waving its white flag of truce. But due to the mist, the flag became invisible, much to the surprise and fear of the crew of the Planter. This caused the Union ship to maneuver to the Planter's broadside and open its gun port. Just as Captain Nichols aboard the frigate was about to give the command to fire, an Officer on the quarter deck alertly identified the white flag among a clearing in the mist and sounded the alarm which caused Captain Nichols to cease his command orders. By this point the Planter was in such close proximity, until the Captain announced what was wanted or needed and the name of the vessel. These orders for whatever reason were not heard by Smalls as the two vessels were side by side by this point. The Captain became infuriated with the unresponsive notion from the Planter which caused him to command, *"Stop! or I will blow you out of the water."* An Officer named Watson and four seamen boarded the Planter as the Union ship was identified as the *"USS Onward."* Smalls family as well as the Planter were in route to Port Royal while he and his crew were being transferred to the gunship, *"USS Augusta,"* the flag ship off the bar commanded by Captain Parrot. With the Augusta in route to Port Royal to Commodore Du Pont, before commanding the southern squadron, the Planter was received and Robert Smalls name was entered on the Navy list as *"Pilot."* The Planter had become apart of the Union fleet and placed under an Officer named Phoenix from the ship Wabash. Although Naval regulations requiring Naval school attendance before payments and or services were recognized, were over-looked as Smalls service as a pilot warranted him a commission as a Second Lieutenant assigned to Company B, 1st South Carolina Volunteers, as an *"acting Pilot,"* commanded by General Rufus Saxton. This unit was in the preliminaries of its beginnings and later renamed, The 33rd Regiment, United States Colored Troops. Smalls was later assigned to Elisto joining the gunboat, *"The Crusader,"* under the command of Captain Ryan. Soon there-after, around June, 1862, Smalls found himself back on the Planter with a crew. As apart of the Crusaders fleet that were engaged in a battle with the Confederate Infantry and some light battery on Simmons Bluff and Wadmalaw Island forced a retreat. The Confederates were driven back as the result of fierce shelling from the Union. And when Smalls and his crew landed, they captured many enemy provisions and tents. Continuing his acting assignment of Pilot and Blockading Pilot between Charleston and Beaufort, he made repeated runs up and down the river engaging in small scrimmages. The locating and sinking strategic enemy locations and the torpedoing of many vessels Smalls himself had positioned himself. The Planter stood its ground in such battles as Rockville, John's Island and Adam's Run on the Dawho River where the vessel was highly contested and fired upon many times. Smalls was also ordered back to Port Royal and piloted his vessel up Board River to Pocotaligo where a fierce battle ensued, October, 1862. Smalls then became the Pilot of the Keokuk and on April 7, 1863 during the battle at Fort Sumter, where the vessel was struck ninety-six times and nineteen traveled clean through the other side of her. It wasn't until the following day that the vessel sunk near Light House Inlet. It was reported that Smalls being the last to leave, left moments before she went down. The following

"The San Francisco Call,"
of March 26, 1901

morning while aboard the, *"Ironsides,"* Smalls and the remaining fleet returned to Hilton Head. General Gilmore being commander of the southern fleet, promoted Smalls to the rank of Captain for his valor. It involved the Planter while Captain Nickerson was commanding her during a battle near Folly Island Creek. The Planter took on heavy fire from the Confederate when Captain Nickerson became demoralized and left the Pilot House. The quick thinking of Smalls, noticing the absence of Nickerson, took control of the vessel stirring her distances from Confederate gunfire. Not only did Smalls save the life of Nickerson and the crew but most importantly he saved the Planter. Smalls soon became Pilot in the quartermaster's department during the expedition on Morris Island and later Pilot of the Stono where he remain until Union troops took possession of the southern end of Morris Island followed by being assigned Pilot of the Light House inlet. As the Civil War neared its end; Captain Smalls was made Acting Captain of the Planter that was used by this time as a supply boat September of 1866, the historic vessel made its final voyage to Baltimore where she was put out of commission and the 147 foot vessel was appraised for its value of $9,000. Captain Smalls went on to receive his Honorable Discharge and the eight men crew received one half of the Planter's appraised value, netting each $1,125. A prize money Congressional Law passed by President Lincoln. Captain Smalls however received

$1,500 for his role in its capture. Smalls return to the place of his birth, Beaufort, SC where he was regarded as a hero among the citizen in the Negro communities. Children and Adults alike never seem to tire from his stories as those tales became the corner-stone of freedom they associated with Smalls that was handled down for many genera-tions. Because of his leadership and courage, he was urged to go into politics. Smalls won a number of local elections and in 1868 he was chosen as a member of the House of Representatives from his county of Beaufort. Smalls quickly began to make a name for him as he became the focal point in the Homestead Act passing and introduced the Civil

Samuel J. Bampfield
"The Colored American," of Jan 20, 1900

Rights Bill that passed the House eventually. In 1870, he was elected to the Senate of the State of South Carolina and reelected in 1872 where he served until he resigned March, 1875. His resignation was predicated by his 1874 general election victory that granted him a seat in the Forty-Fourth Congress. Smalls was then elected to the Forty-Fifth Congress in 1876 followed by his reelection in 1878 and again in 1880 with times resulting in a tissue ballot count out. Robert Smalls was delegate to the National Republican Convention twice. Once in Philadelphia that nominated General Grant for a second term and at Cincinnati which nominated Rutherford B. Hayes for President. Smalls was also appointed Collector of Customs for the Port of Beaufort, S.C. by President Roosevelt from 1889 to 1911. Pictured above is Mr. Samuel J. Bampfield (1850-1899), Postmaster of Beaufort, who married General Smalls eldest daughter, Elizabeth Lydia and had ten children with 2 dieing before 1900. Their children were: Julie (1878), Sarah (Nov 1879), Maria (Sep 1882), Yaddie B. (1883), Robert S. (Jul 1886), Elizabeth Jr. (Aug 1889), Albert B. (Jan 1891), Jennie (Aug 1893), Hellen (Apr 1896), Arianna (Jun 1897). He left Elizabeth a widow in 1899 with his untimely death and eight children to raise. She was appointed Postmistress in 1900 by virtue of her husband's death and reappointed in 1904. Robert Smalls died in Beaufort, South Carolina, July 23, 1915.

Lewis Bates, a Chicagoan and an ex-slave in 1895 was considered one on the wealthiest Negroes in the city, with wealth valued at $500,000. Bates, born in North Carolina around 1826, owned by John Bates of Richland County. Lewis was taken from his mother at a very young age and sold. Bates recalls being sold

and transported from one southern state to another many times. He eventually was sold to a trader who took him to St. Louis. While in St. Louis, he made an acquaintance with an elderly lady who had been leased out from another family explained to him that a wealthy Colored family owned a slave named Aunt Fannie who favored Bates in appearance and had similar background suggested it could possibly be his mother. Bates having developed a great relationship with his owner by this time explained to him what the elderly lady had told him and asked for his assistance.

Lewis Bates

1870 Federal Census - Cook Co., Chicago, IL. Lewis Bates listed as being in Prison and scratched off

The trader then knew some contacts in the area and conducted an unofficial investigation and discovered the woman identified by the old lady was correct and in fact involved his father as well. No sooner than the words reach the lips of his parent's owners, he negotiated a deal which allowed him to purchase Bates so the family could at least be as a family again. But Bates unsatisfied with the arrangement of slavery shortly departed his parents during the Fort Sumter battle. In the late hours of the night, just before dawn, Bates confiscated a small boat with bullets flying all about him, undetectably guided this boat to Chicago. Arriving safely and without the legitimacy of paperwork manage to find work. With the tenacity of a miser, Bates saved as much as $150 in only three months. With his newly earned capital, Bates sought out becoming self employed and purchased a horse and wagon. Continuing his thriftiness earning as much as $50 a week, he soon married Clara and secured freedom for his elderly mother. He purchased a home for her to make her life pleasant for the years of suffrage she endured. On October 8, 1871, came the great Chicago fire. Bates used that tragedy to earn as much as $60 a night hauling furniture and moving trunks for people affected by the fire. Bates commented once that during the great fire, people were so destitute that his profit could have been higher, but relied on his own ethical principles not to take advantage of the situation for greed. He made several free trips for some Colored people who had no money to give him to save what little possessions they had. Even though the fire only lasted three days, the aftermath and clean-up took years which netted Bates much profit. Bates, unusually so did not squander his money on foolish spending like so many Negroes found themselves after being deprived the finer things in life. Instead, Bates, working six days a week was steady in his efforts in acquiring as much wealth as honestly and hard-working as he knew how. He observed many business practices all around him, that taught him investment procedures in the Chicago real estate market. This method caused Bates to buy and sell properties for profits. He soon acquired two four story brick houses valued at $75,000 where he modestly lived in one of the single rooms. Among his other purchases was an exclusive for whites only, seven story, basement brick and terra cotta apartment house valued at over $100,000. Lewis wife and children died before he did, leaving only his sister, a widow by then, his only living heir left to claim his fortune.

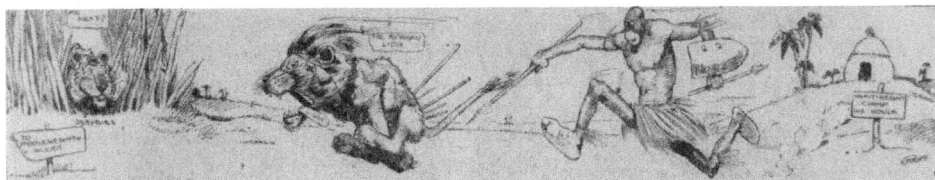

"The San Francisco Call," of October 17, 1909

Victoria C. Woodhull
"New-York Tribune," of March 5, 1905

Tennessee Claflin
"New-York Tribune," of March 5, 1905

As reported by, *"The Morning Call," of December 6, 1891*, in 1872, **Victoria California Woodhull** was proclaimed as President of the United States, a first, before women could even vote, by 500 delegates, representing 26 States and 4 Territories with her running mate for a time was **Frederick Douglass** who dropped out because he refused to run against Ulysses S. Grant and Henry Wilson. So Mrs. Mary L. Stowe of California was later nominated. She was an advocate for women suffrage, giving over 1200 speeches from 1870-1887, with supporters that included her sister, **Tennessee Claflin** also known as Lady Cook supporting her. She also founded a banking-house (Bank/Brokerage firm) a

THE PRESIDENTIAL TICKETS.—Presidential tickets are being brought out so rapidly now-a-days that it may be well enough to recapitulate the list to date:

Cincinnati—President, Horace Greeley; Vice-President, B. Gratz Brown.

Philadelphia—President, Ulysses S. Grant; Vice-President, Henry Willson.

Revenue Reform—William S. Groesbeck; Vice-President, Frederick Law Olmsted.

Labor Reform—President, David Davis; Vice-President, Joel Parker.

Temperance—President, James Black; Vice-President, James Russell.

Anti-Masonic—For President, Charles Francis Adams; Vice-President, C. H. Howard.

Nondescript—President, Victoria C. Woodhull; Vice-President, Frederick Douglass.

"The Daily Phoenix," of June 30, 1872

first, that profited $750,000 on Wall Street in 6 weeks and later started a journal, a first, for women in the U.S. called, *"Woodhull & Claflin's Weekly."* She used the paper to promote her views on equality, marriage and free-love. Contrary to rumors of female incompetence, proposed by the male demographics for women of that era, Victoria and her sister set out to change this by the use of their beauty and charm. Victoria, full of controversy, particularly coming from Ohio, penniless and starting a free-love abode and disclosing the Theodore Tilton's wife affair. Tilton, a poet, newspaper editor

Tennessee Claflin in 1909
"Los Angeles Herald," of Oct 29, 1909

Libby Richards Tilton

Theodore Tilton

Rev. Henry Ward Beecher
"The Washington Times," of March 10, 1907

and abolitionist was married to *"Libby"* or Elizabeth Richards, pictured above, who had an adulterous affair

Devour Us Not

BY PROXY

"The Day book," of January 10, 1916

and was charged with sending obscene matters through the mail, unlike other newspapers, the sisters described the affair in graphic detail. Details by today's standards would be considered as good journalistic reporting and writing but were fronded upon in the 1870's. More so if written by a woman, but they were acquitted on a technicality. The Beecher church followers had the sisters indicted for criminal libel and like the first trial, the good-looks and charm of the sisters, yet again prevailed the jury of men to rule in their favor. Then came the allegations of a woman that stated she had entrusted $60,000 or $70,000 for the sisters to invest. The sisters spent a short time in the Ludlow Street jail before the case came to trial in civil court. And a central figure in this case was Commodore Vanderbilt, a *"Big Money,"* Wall Street type and a crafty financier of the sisters

John Biddulph Martin   *Sir Francis Cook*   *Lulu "Lula" Maud Woodhull*
"The Wichita Daily Eagle," of May 17, 1890

who was reluctant to show up for the trial before the sisters charmed him to testify. It was his testimony that secured the sisters yet another victory. Shortly thereafter, Vanderbilt died among much controversy about his wealth that created another issue with his heirs and the sisters. This caused the sisters to leave the country for England in 1879. Minister Beecher

was acquitted after his trial of adultery and Libby and Theodore's divorced. Theodore left the United States for Paris where he lived until his death. Soon thereafter, the sisters were married to very wealthy Englishmen. Victoria married her third husband, John Biddulph Martin, head of a financial institution in England with financial wealth extended to the sixteenth century and owner of Martin's Bank of London, while Tennessee (*Lady Cook and Vicountess of Monserrat having a Palacic Moorish castle in Portugal*) married a wealthy Baronet named Sir Francis Cook in 1885. The sisters returned to the United States, April, 1890 much to the dismay of English-men who warned against it. In 1901, Mr. Martin died with Victoria inheriting all his wealth. Victoria, at the age of 15, she first married Dr. Canning Woodhull in 1853 and then she married Col. James H. Blood, July 10, 1865 in Hamilton County, Ohio. Victoria had a son named Bryon Woodhull, a daughter named Lulu *"Lula"* Maud Woodhull and another daughter named Gertrude Blood. Gertrude, as reported by the, *"Sacramento Daily Record-Union," of July 14, 1881*, married English Royalty, Lord Colin Campbell, son of the Duke of Argyl in 1881. Victoria was born in Licking County, Homer, Ohio, the 7th of 10 children on September 23, 1838 to Roxanna Hummel (*1804-1889*) and Reuben Buckman Claflin (*? -1885)* according to the, *"New-York Tribune," of September 11, 1871.*

Some reports have the girls receiving a good education and others report the girl's skills as being nothing but street wise hustlers wanting equality in everyway. A lot of the women and civil issues Victoria advocate were well ahead of her time which was reasons in some circles she was considered an evil-witch and eventually ostracized. The free-love concept; she believed a woman should not be stigmatized if she is divorced or never married. And sexual slaves being made of women by the forces of society that offered a woman no choice but conformity or be an outcast. She believed a woman should have the right to choose her life whether married or not, having kids or work outside the home without the labeled of being a obedient sex-slave. Sexual freedom,

With the options of choice for themselves was the essence of freedom. Her views sometimes even clashed with some of her supporter like Susan B. Anthony and Frederick Douglass. Mr. Douglass never indorsed his nomination as VP on her Presidential ticket. Mainly because of Douglass' recent marriage to a younger White woman after being married to a black woman for 44 years. And the unsubstantiated rumors of free-love advocated by Ms. Woodhull stirred up the *"Jim Crow Haters,"* who cringed at the mere thought of a black man eyes lusting upon a white woman also caused his participation to be obscure. But his acknowledgement of not wanting to run against Grant was a politically correct statement. Victoria appeared before the House Judiciary Committee presenting

Mammy Grace-"The Seattle Star," of February 12, 1909

OLD HOME OF COLONEL ROOSEVELT'S MOTHER AT ROSWELL, GA.
The group includes Col. and Mrs. Roosevelt, "Mammy" Grace, the old negro women who was nurse to the Colonel's Mother, and "Daddy" Williams, also an old servant of the Bulloch family.

Martha Bulloch Roosevelt "The St. Louis Republic," of September 29, 1901   *"New-York Tribune," of October 24, 1905*

those with an eloquent speech on women suffrage and the unjust double moral standard in America. Only the second woman in U.S. history to accomplish such a feat and created a firestorm of media coverage. Victoria died June 9, 1927, at the age of 88 in Bredon, England.

"Mammy Grace," also known as **"Mom Grace,"** a former slave who was also called, *"The Grand Old Lady,"* by President Theodore Roosevelt for being the nurse, sleeping at the foot of Martha's bed and maid of his mother, Martha *"Miss Mittle,"* Bulloch of Roswell, Georgia. Mammy Grace's birth name was Grace Robinson. Also *"Daddy,"* William *(Billy)* Jackson, a former slave, both Mammy and Daddy are pictured above that were beloved by the Bulloch family. His mother came from a family of wealthy slave-owners who bought and sold slaves as were the climate of that era. Mammy Grace, a trusted slave of Martha who even help dressed her on her wedding day (December 22, 1853) when she married the President's father according to the, *"Albuquerque Evening Citizen,"* of October 20, 1905. Oddly, President Roosevelt's first wife, Alice Hathaway Lee, gave birth to a daughter on February 12, 1884 and died of kidney failure on the same day of his mother of typhoid fever, February 14, 1884. President Roosevelt gave Mammy Grace a small piece of land near Roswell, Georgia after his mother's death. Mammy was believed to have been born around 1810 to slave parents. Little else is known about Mammy Grace and Daddy William, but they were loyal servants to the Roosevelt family all their lives.

Devour Us Not

A GOOD OLD DARKY.

MESSENGER TO THE GOVERNOR OF SOUTH CAROLINA.

William Nesbit Rose (pictured right) was born a mulatto approximately 1796 in South Carolina. He held the position of Messenger to the Governor of South Carolina and was a Veteran of three wars (*As a drummer in the Seminole War in 1836, the Mexican-American War in 1846-1848, the Civil War in 1861 - 1865 and also volunteered to go to Cuba*). He was the only Negro assigned to the Richmond Volunteer Rifle Company of the Confederate as an orderly and a musician. As an orderly he was authorized to wear non-commissioned officer's stripes, carry a sword and even march in closed ranks with whites, the only Negro of that period to be allowed to do so. He was part of the unit who brought back the body's of Brigadier General Pierce Butler Young from Mexico & Brigadier General Maxcy Greggs from Fredericksburg in 1862. There was even an annual medal called *"The Rose Medal,"* presented to a worthy soldier by William Rose himself during his tenure. As a lad, William was a slave in Charleston. William recalls his earlier years according to a newspaper article in, *"The El Paso Daily Herald,"* of October 6, 1899, in 1826 when he was a hired slave being sent to Columbia, S.C. to be an apprentice at a carpenters' trade school he was witness to many historical events. It was there he witnessed, when the Light

Put Your Heads Together : : : :

Dragoons (*A Military Unit*) of the city went to the North Carolina state line where British officer, General Marquis de Lafayette, who fought in the Revolutionary War, was met and escorted to Columbia. William, knowing he had Negro blood in his veins, but was never treated like others of his race. There was a period of time when the State was going through financial crisis, where no city official recommend salary cuts for him, even though other officials took pay cuts. As a result of this treatment, and his fair-skin, many ex-slaves, particularly during Reconstruction Period, despised him. The hate didn't come from the whites, who knew his ethnicity, but the Negroes threaten him on many occasions. In 1850, William play drums at Vice President John C. Calhoun's funeral. During the infamous Wade Hampton, III (*A Confederate Officer*) - Daniel H. Chamberlain (*A Northerner*) gubernatorial campaign of 1876, where federal troops were called in over the Reconstruction policies of the radical Republican led state government. Where the state of S.C. recorded its most fraudulent campaign in history, included the Hamburg Massacre riot in part because of voter fraud. William was then deemed *"A Hampton Man,"* by the decision of newly elected Governor Hampton's appointment of William as his messenger. William was messenger during less than two years as Governor Hampton term was cut short when he resigned as the 77th Governor of S.C. But William remained the messenger from 1876 -1901 under Governors' **William D. Simpson** the 78th , **Thomas B. Jeter** the 79th **Johnson Hagood** the 80th , **Hugh S. Thompson** the 81st, **John C. Sheppard** the 82nd, **John Peter Richardson, III** the 83rd, **Benjamin Ryan Tillman** the 84th **John Gary Evans** the 85th and **William H. Ellerbe** who died in office in 1899. After his death, he was relieved of his post. Relieved supposedly, because of his age, over 100 by this time. But during a Confederate Reunion in Charleston, voices were heard about the relieved position, and hundreds of veterans spoke to Governor **Miles B. McSweeney** who reinstated William as messenger before his inauguration. After his reappointment, William boosted about his longevity, as coming from his mother who had lived to be 111. But William died May 25, 1901 at 105 years of age and was buried with full Confederate military honors.

First African - American Educational Pioneers

"The Day Book,"
of Jun 7, 1912

* Edward A. Jones
Class of 1826 Amherst

* Alberta Virginia Scott
Class of 1898 Radcliffe

* Hortense Parker
Class of 1883 Mt Holyoke

* Anita Florence Hemmings
Class of 1897 Vassar

* Otelia Cromwell
Class of 1900 Smith

* Ella Elbert Smith
Class of 1888 Wellesley

* Zora Neale Hurston
Class of 1928 Barnard College

* Eva Beatrice Dykes
Class of 1921 PhD Radcliffe

* Alexander Lucius Twilight
Class of 1823 Middleburg

* Alexander Crummell
Class of 18** Cambridge

* David Jones Peck
Class of 1847 Rush Medical Sch.

* Edward Alexander Boucher
Class of 1874 Yale PhD 1876

@ Henry Ossian Flipper
Class of 1877 West Point

* John Brown Russwurm
Class of 1826 Bowdoin

* Mary Eliza Mahoney
Class of 1879 Nursing

* George Boyer Vashon
Class of 1844 Oberlin

* Jane Bolin
Class of 1931 Yale, 1st Judge

* Bessie Coleman
Class of 1920 Fed Aeronautique Internationale

* Rebecca Lee Crumpler
Class of 1864 NEFM

* Theodore Sedgewick Wright
Class of 1828 Princeton

*Artistry by Arnold P. Powers   @ Artistry by Newspaper Article, "The Colored American," of August 18, 1900

Alberta Virginia Scott was the first African-American female to graduate from Harvard College, class of 1898. Alberta actually received her degree from Radcliffe College, also known during that period as *"Harvard Annex for Women,"* of Cambridge, Massachusetts. Radcliffe was organized in 1879 by **Arthur Gillman** as a Collegiate Instructional match to the then Harvard all male College. According to the *"Kansas City Journal," of July 3, 1898,* the Massachusetts African-American women progress sites the two other accomplishments from Wellesley College, Miss Harriet Alleyne Rice and Mount Holyoke Female Seminary College in South Hadley, Massachusetts; Miss Hortense Parker and Miss Martha Ralston. Alberta's dream was to be an educator to

Devour Us Not

instruct children of southern states. Initially, most of its 75 Professors of Radcliffe came from Harvard, ensuring, the *"equal but separate,"* quality of education without the racial or sexist discriminatory elements. Mr. Gillman's approach was so insistent until he ensured of the 75 Professor's that the exact classes they taught at

Arthur Gillman
"Kansas City Journal," of Nov 27, 1899

the all male Harvard College, also carried over to the Radcliffe College. So the Diploma Alberta received from Radcliffe College President, **Mrs. Elizabeth Cary Agassiz**, pictured right was the exact equivalent of her male Harvard

"Bismarck Weekly Tribune," of February 2, 1894

constituents. Alberta was a member of two college clubs (Idler *Theatrical* & The German Club). At Radcliffe and during that period one of four black women *Two received diplomas from Wellesley College. In 1887,* **Harriett Alleyne Rice** *of Newport, Rhode Island who later became the 1ˢᵗ African-American Female Judge, also became a Osteopathic Physician after graduating of the American School of Osteopathy of Kirksville Missouri, "The Twice =A= Week Herald," of Oct. 24, 1905 & and in 1888-* **Ella Lavinia Smith** *was the 2nd* **Mrs. Maude Trotter Stewart** *and one from Smith College, 1890,* **Otelia Cromwell** graduates

MRS. ELIZABETH CARY AGASSIZ

"Meade County News," of Jul 15, 1915

of Massachusetts Colleges for women. Also, the Massachusetts Colleges were considered part of the, *"The Seven Sister College,"* group that include the following Colleges: *Mount Holyoke Female Seminary College,* that later became *Mount Holyoke College; Vassar College; Wellesley College; Smith College; Radcliffe College; Bryn Mawr College; & Barnard College.* Alberta Virginia Scott's Family lived in a picturesque house in Massachusetts at 37 Hubbard Avenue as a result of Smith Scott (*Alberta's father*) having received an inheritance after the Civil War. When Alberta was about six years old, Smith liquidated his assets from the Will and the family moved from Virginia and settled in Cambridge, Massachusetts. Alberta's childhood dream was to return to the south to teach African-American students. After briefly teaching high school in Indianapolis, she was recruited by Booker T. Washington in 1900 to teach at Tuskegee University. She only taught for less than a year before she attracted an aliment which caused her to return to Cambridge where she died August 30, 1902. Two other black women attended Wellesley in the last two decades of the nineteenth century. But only one other black woman was to earn a degree from the college over the next 25 years. Even Portia Washington, the daughter of Booker T. Washington, attended Wellesley for only a year in 1901. Some notable alumnae of Wellesley are Hillary Rodham Clinton and Madeleine Albright.

The *"Seven Sister Colleges," first African-American women graduates are:* **(1) Mount Holyoke Female Seminary College** in South Hadley, Massachusetts; 1883 Hortense Parker -1898 Martha Ralston. **(2) Vassar College** in Poughkeepsie, NY;- 1897 Anita Florence Hemmings. **(3) Wellesley College** in Wellesley, Massachusetts; - 1887 Harriet Alleyne Rice. **(4) Smith College** in Northampton, Massachusetts; - 1900 Otelia Cromwell, 1910 Masters from Columbia University & 1926 a Ph D from Yale. **(5) Radcliffe College** in Cambridge, Massachusetts; - 1898 Alberta Virginia Scott. **(6) Bryn Mawr College** in Bryn Mawr, Pennsylvania; - 1931 Enid Cook. **(7) Barnard College** in Morningside Height, Manhattan, NY. - 1931 Belle Tobias, 1932 earned a Masters from Wellesley College, Class of 1928 Zora Neale Hurston.

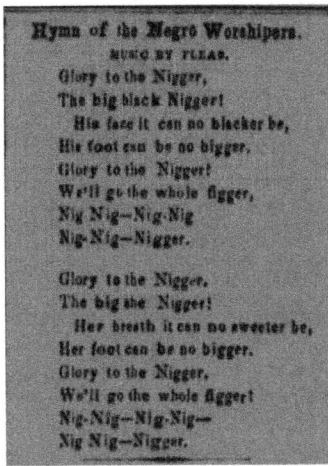

"The Jasper Weekly Courier," of May 21, 1862

Vassar College was the first of the seven sister colleges founded by Matthew Vassar in 1865 in Poughkeepsie, New York, according to, *"The Scranton Tribune of May 14, 1896."* Established as an all woman private college, it remained that way until 1969. Matthew Vassar was a wealthy man, acquiring most of his wealth through the sale of a form of "moonshine," (*a strong alcoholic drink*)," as suggested by, *"The Watchman and Southron," of January 24, 1882.* The prestige college had no color barriers restricting Negro students in 1893, but all was a buzz when **Anita Florence Hemmings** revealed her true ethnicity her senior year. With New York having passed a law into the gradual abolishment of slavery in the state in 1799, with all slaves being free July 4, 1827. So what caused the faculty of Vassar to panic with talk of dismissing Anita after the rumors of her ethnicity swirled. Anita or *"Annie,"* as she was generally called by her family, was the eldest of four children (*Freddie J. a chemist, born October, 1873, Elizabeth a manicurist born September, 1876) and Robert, Jr. born November 1882*) was born June, 1872 to the

parentage of Robert and Dora Hemmings as reported by the *"Evening Star," of August 17, 1897.* She was described as a very beautiful woman of clear olive skin and long dark straight hair. She was perhaps one of the prettiest women ever to attend Vassar. The daughter of two mulatto parents, whose ethnicity knowledge among her classmates were completely unknown until her junior year at Vassar. Anita's brother *"Freddy,"* had attended and graduated from the Institute of Technology as a chemist and made several visits to Vassar that he had reported to the local newspaper. Initially, Anita's name was not revealed, only that she was from Boston and a Negro or had some drops of African blood flowing in her veins. Assumptions were made after Anita was identified as the only graduating senior from Boston. Her identity was revealed by Anita to her roommate which she spread throughout the campus. The information reached the faculty who then took several days deliberating whether to allow her to graduate with the knowledge she was a part of the Negro race. Having achieved high honors and one of the most popular women on campus gave more concerns for the staff to make a sound decision. It wasn't as if Anita had broken any laws preventing her attendance at the college, rather it was having the audacity to forget her place and mingle with the Caucasian race and passing which mostly offended the high-society types. Hence, Anita Florence Hemmings became the first known graduate of the prestige Vassar College having African-American blood in her veins.

The founder of Mount Holyoke Female Seminary (1893 the college became Mt. Holyoke College) was **Mary Lyon** in 1836, according to, *"The San Francisco Call," of February 28, 1912.* Mary Lyon was born February 28, 1797 to poor parents. Her educational success was self-motivated, molding her initially into a country teacher earning as little as free board and 75 cents a week. Her tenacity to fight every level of prejudices for the period. Mary was even recorded as having the time to teach a forty year old kitchen helper who could not read, the opportunity to do so. Mary, its first President, never considered herself so high she couldn't offer any measure of assistance for a *"sister."*

Mary Lyon
"New-York Tribune," of February 4, 1900

Devour Us Not

Mary Lyon died March 5, 1849 before witnessing the first African-American graduate some forty-seven years after the college was founded. So, in 1883, **Hortense Parker** became the first African American to finish from Mount Holyoke Female Seminary College. And after the name change in 1898, Martha Ralston became the first African-American to finish under the name Mount Holyoke College. According to the 1870 / 1880 Federal Census, Hortense was born approximately 1859, the eldest daughter of John P. (1827-) and Miranda Bolden Parker (1834 -) who were married on May 12, 1848. In the Parker household were three sons named John P., Jr. (1850), Cassius C. (1854) and Horatio W. (1856). There were also two daughters listed named as Portia (1862) and Bianca (1872). Hortense would marry James Marcus Gilliam, and moved with him to St. Louis, Missouri where she died.

 Middleburg College once boost as among their alumni; 32 College Presidents and 9 State Governors during its first 100 years from 1800-1900, according to *"Middleburg Register," June 23, 1916*. But significant to black history, **Alexander Lucius Twilight** became the first African-American to receive a college degree in 1823.

In 1919, Charles Hamilton Houston becomes the first African American editor of the Harvard Law Review. In 1921 three black female scholars became the first African American women to earn PhD's. They were Georgiana Simpson (German Language and Literature, University of Chicago), Sadie Tanner Mossell Alexander (Economics, University of Pennsylvania), and Eva Beatrice Dykes (English Philology, Radcliffe College). Portia, was Booker T. and Fannie Washington's only child who attended Bradford Academy, of Haverhill where she became the first black graduate in 1905. Other first by African-American's include: **Alexander Crummell** graduating from Oxford, University in England, **David Jones Peck** receiving a medical degree from Rush Medical School in 1847 becoming the first African-American Physician, **Edward Alexander Bouchet** finishing from Yale in 1874 and followed up his success two years later by receiving his PhD also from Yale in 1876, Class of 1877 showcased **Henry Ossian Flipper** at the military academy, West Point. **John Brown Russwurm** was a member of the Class of 1826 that finish from Bowdoin College, **Mary Eliza Mahoney** became the first African-American nurse by finishing from the New England Hospital Nursing Program, in Boston, Massachusetts, 1879. **George Boyer Vashon** graduated from Oberlin College in 1844, **Jane Bolin** graduated from Yale Law School in 1931 and became the first African-American female Judge in 1939, **Bessie Coleman**, a Texas native, after being refused the opportunity in American aviation, received her pilot's license from the Federation Aeronautique Internationale, France, **Rebecca Lee Crumpler** became the first female Physician after graduating in 1864 from NEFM (New England Female Medical College). **Theodore Sedgewick Wright** became the first African-American to finish from Princeton in 1828.

Despite the efforts of so many in our pass to devour and hold us back as a people. We, the African-American of this country, can not and will not be denied our fundamental rights and prospective placement in American history. From the murders of innocent children in a church to the most recent murder of an innocent child named Trayvon Martin, we've come a long way, yet our destiny has not been fulfilled. Brighter days of our triumphs await us, but we will forever be stigmatized by our pass. But the dream shall never die in us because of the spirits of all whose history we share.

C_{hapter} II

"Our Family, the Powers (my father's surname) & the Carroll's (my mother's surname) add our names to the contribution for the making of America."

"The Evening World," of February 8, 1900

"Squire Carroll," aka Benjamin Franklin Carroll, Sr.

Chapter II is the Carroll family's contribution to African-American history in America. Where did the last name **"Carroll"**, come from, our family surname? Absalom Carroll, Sr. the man who started this clan of Carroll's in Texas, journey begin in Ireland around the 1740's, when he brought his family of five sons, **Britten, Absalom,**

Jr., Jon, James and **Moses** and settled in South Carolina. Absalom, Sr. and his wife died before their son's were adults. So the son's were then separated and sent to different families to be raised until they were adults. Absalom, Jr. in particular was sent to a very prominent family mainly to preserve his family's name in Colleton County, South Carolina where he remained until age 21. Absalom, Jr. married his fourth wife, Elinor Robinson after being a widower from the first three wives. He had returned to South Carolina from a joint venture for the Militia of North Carolina with his brother Britten.

Benjamin Franklin Carroll, Sr.
Feb 17, 1809 - Jul 9, 1869

Huldah Harper Carroll
Nov 26, 1816 - Jul 5, 1901

Absalom, Jr. also had one daughter by his third wife, before her death, named Susannah. There were nine children born to **Absalom** and **Elinor Robinson**; **Mary, Harriet, Benjamin Franklin, John Edward, Moses, Sarah, James Allen, Martha Ann** and **Absalom III**. Benjamin Franklin Carroll, Sr., was born February 17, 1809. He was the first born son and the link to my family-tree. Around 1818, Absalom Jr. moved his family to

James Alexander Texas & Alice Pevehouse Carroll
Jul 24, 1849 - Nov 10, 1936   Apr 10, 1847 - Apr 7, 1918

Benjamin Franklin Carroll, Jr.
May 4, 1841 - May 5, 1912

Wife of B.F. , Jr. Georgia Ann Stokes Carroll
Jan 12, 1849 - Feb 17, 1933

"The Morning Times," of March 1, 1896

Navarro County Alliance.
Special to the Gazette.

BLOOMING GROVE, TEX , April 19.—The convention of Navarro county Farmers' Alliances assembled here to-day for the transaction of business and to take action on questions of issue bearing on their interests. Evans Jones, president of the state alliance, is here and will give a public address to night. There are also attending J. J. Moody, district treasurer; William Smith, vice-president of the state alliance and president of the Navarro county alliance and B. F. Carroll, secretary. About forty Alliances were represented and considerable business was transacted. The committee on cotton seed will report to-morrow. The session will last two days. The prospects are favorable for a big crop this year.

Wayne County, Mississippi, then settled on the Bogue Hommer, an Indian name meaning, *"Red Bayou."* Only a year before, in 1817, had Mississippi become a state and land deals were attracting a number of Americans its way. Two of his daughter's were married, Susannah was married to Thomas Williams and Mary was married to Edward Harper, Jr. Absalom, Jr. and Elinor died sometimes during the 1820's and Benjamin Franklin, Sr. as a teen now finds himself head of the Carroll family which caused him to teamed up with a Methodist Minister from South

B.F. Carroll, Jr.- "Ft Worth Daily Gazette," of Apr 20, 1888

1814 Lauderdale County, MS Marriage Records

43

Leak, Frederick -- Mary Robb, Sept. 24, 1814
Leak, Thomas -- Mary Dewan, March 2, 1813
Lazarus, Thomas -- Betsy Putrey, --
Lewis, Joel -- Rebecca Porter, Jan. 16, 1812
Luyster, Garrett -- Mary Campbell, Feb. 3, 1817
Lyon, Joseph -- Aurea Cox, april 23, 1808
Long, James -- Jane H. Wilkinson, May 13, 1815

"M"

McCarty, Amos -- Ruth Elmore (wo. Ruth Elmore), March 17 1813
Miller, Alexander -- Polly McCurdY, 18 May, 1815
Mohun, Arthur -- Catherine Jenkins, July 5, 1813
Montgomery, Hugh -- Jane Montgomery (f. William Montgomery), Nov. 30, 1813
McComas, H. -- Nancy Willis, (mo. Bars Chotard), Jan.5'14
Madden, Emanuel -- Charity Carroll, Aug. 3, 1814
McGill, Jonas -- Penelope Coleman, Aug. 15, 1814
Mace, Richard -- Margaret McHenry, June 20, 1817
Morris, Benjamin -- Elizabeth D-----, Jan. 25, 1813
Michie, David -- Isabella Cochrane, Dec. 17, 1809
Miller, Thomas O. -- Parthena Rowan, March 23, 1818
McCarroll, Charles -- etsy Hughen, 1806
McGlaughlin ----- --- Keaton (f. William), March 9,'02
May, Otano -- Patsy Fague (f. Joseph Fague), April 11'00
Morgan, D.D. -- Eliza E. Middletonif. Elisha Middleton), May 03, 1805
Manning, Joseph -- Elizabeth Axwell, July 1, 1805
Miller, Abel -- Nancy Perkins, July 6, 1805
Miller, John -- Mary Kennison, March 29, 1806
Mulkey, Ellis -- Mary Floyd, Dec. 14, 1807

1839

Marvin Crain - 1 poll; Tax .37½
Thomas J. Clay - 1 poll; Tax .37½
William Clarke - 1 poll; 1 slave; Tax 1.00
Samuel Clarke - 1 poll; Tax .37½
Henry Clarke - 1 poll; Tax .37½
Micajah Crunch-- - 1 poll; 1 slave; $300. loaned at interest; Tax 2.00
Benjamin Carroll - 1 poll; 8 slaves; Tax 2.25
John B. Collins - 1 poll; Tax .37½
A. T. Cary - 1 poll; Tax .37½
Garrett Coker - 1 poll; Tax .37½
E. D. Cain - 1 poll; 1 slave; $5,607. merchandise sales; Tax 13.60
C. W. Clinton - 1 poll; 7 slaves; Tax 4.75
William Carson - 1 poll; Tax .37½
Benjamin Carpenter - 1 poll; 3 slaves; Tax 1.62½
Duncan Calhoun - 1 poll; Tax .37½
John M. Carrell - 1 poll; Tax .37½

Lauderdale County, MS. Tax Records
1841-1848

John Calhoun - 1 poll; 1 slave; Tax 1.10
Benjamin Carroll - 1 slave; value $5.; 11 cattle; 32 slaves; 1 poll; Tax 7.86
Thomas S. W. Clark - 1 poll; Tax .96
Hugh Calhoun - 1 poll; Tax .50
Meredith Chandler - 1 poll; Tax .50
E. J. Chatham - 1 clock, value $10; 1 poll; Tax .60
John Crane - 1 pistol; 1 slave; Tax 3.60
C. H. Crane - 1 poll; Tax .50
A. J. Crane - 1 poll; Tax .50

Carolina, named Edward Harper, Sr. The two families soon moved to Copiah County, Mississippi where on December 5, 1833 he married the minister's 17 year old daughter, **Huldah,** (*Born Nov 26, 1816*). The families later settled in Lauderdale County and it is at this point where the name of Charity Carroll's, a slave housemaid who had a daughter also named Charity. Charity, the mother, was alleged to have been purchased, assumingly by Absalom Carroll, Jr. during the early 1800's. Charity Carroll, the daughter, is alleged where the mixing of the races started within the Carroll family, most notably B.F. Carroll, Sr. Though it is unclear who purchased Charity Carroll's mother, undoubtedly she was a favorite and probably performed some type of household chores or Cook. Charity Carroll alone with her husband Emanuel Madden were Alabamians, but were permitted to married in Lauderdale County, August 3, 1814. Her story will be discussed later. Benjamin Franklin, Sr. was a black-smith, a trade he had learned from his father. He was also a Colonel for the State Militia of Mississippi and a Representative from Lauderdale County, Mississippi to the State Legislature from 1846-1847. Oral records from the Carroll's Bible suggested, Huldah, his wife, being very skilled in needle work, made his first suit by hand to appear as a Representative of Lauderdale County. The Carroll's had seven of their twelve children born in Mississippi, **Emily Caroline** born Jan 29, 1835, **Mary Eleanor Ann,** Nov 19, 1837, **Martha Elvira,** March 10, 1840, **Benjamin Franklin, Jr.,** May 4, 1841, **William Edward,** Mar 17, 1843, **Absalom Glenn,** February 15, 1845, and **Jefferson Davis,** Sep 10, 1847. To the left is a copy of Lauderdale County tax records, B.F. Carroll paid in taxes, that included slaves / cattle etc. from 1839-1848. The Carroll family also purchased about

Devour Us Not

200 acres of land that was known as the Carroll Plantation. In 1849, Benjamin Franklin & Huldah moved their family, 12 slaves and 13 cattle to Sabine Pass to Harrison County, Texas. Their first Texas born child, **James Alexander Texas Carroll** was born July 24, 1849. The Carroll Clan then settled in Navarro County in 1851. The following children were born in Dresden, Texas: **Euphemia Mathilda** born January 25, 1852, **Elizabeth Diana**, July 2, 1854, **Huldah Kiziah**, October 5, 1857 and **John Marshall**, June 23, 1859. Among the deceased children are **Absalom Glenn** who was kicked by a mule and died October 15, 1855 at the age of 10, **Mary Eleanor Ann** died July 11, 1865 at the age of 27 and may have been handicap because she never married or left home. But this *is* very suspect since every other death is recorded in exact terms with no probabilities. And Huldah Kizah died October 24, 1857 at 19 days old. Two son's fought in the Civil War, Benjamin Franklin, Jr. and William Edward. William Edward was a private in C.M. Winkler's company, who were one of the first volunteer units from Texas to sign up for the Civil War. The unit was named the 4th Texas Volunteer Infantry, and also known as *"The Navarro Rifles."* William was reported to have been killed in the battle of Chickamauga, Georgia on September 19, 1863 at the age of 20. While Benjamin Franklin Carroll, Jr. was assigned to Co. B 4th Texas Cavalry of the Parson's Brigade. He was reportedly captured at Lake Providence, Louisiana, but managed to escape his captives and make his way back to his unit before it disbanded. It was said that Benjamin Franklin Carroll, Sr., never got over the death of his beloved son William and died on July 9, 1869 with a broken heart, grieving his son's untimely death. It is unclear what happened to Charity's parents. But Charity's separation by whatever means, one can only imagine must have been horrific since their presence have not been found since the Carroll's departure from Mississippi. Also unclear, is what happen to Charity's husband and a male slave named *"Chant."* Chant, by some records was a master craftsman. A Slave based on the year

Judge James Carroll Sewell **Parthanian A. Carroll Sewell** **Parthanian Agnes Carroll** & **Jay Lamont Sewell, Sr.** **Georgia Carroll-Kyser**
Apr 13, 1912 - Nov 13, 1976 *Age 8 Dau. of James A. Texas Carroll* *Jul 12, 1887 - Apr 3, 1972* *Jun 6, 1886 - Aug 2, 1969* **(Movie Star)** *1919-2011*

Judge James C. Sewell also known as the **"Blind Judge."** *Parthanian Agnes Carroll, mother of the Blind Judge and daughter of the Carroll's first Texas born child, James Alexander Texas Carroll. Georgia Ann Carroll-Kyser nick named* **"Gorgeous Georgia Carroll,"** *was also the granddaughter to James Alexander Texas Carroll and Alice Pevehouse Carroll, and parents of Roger Mills Carroll and Aileen Rogers Carroll, born in Blooming Grove, Texas on November 18, 1919. She married Big-Band Leader Kay Kyser in 1945, they had 3 daughters, Kimberly, Carroll, (Carroll died in 1993) and Amanda. Georgia played in 14 films, to include a small part as Betsy Ross in James Cagney's musical, "Yankee Doodle Dandy," in 1942. Georgia died in Chapel Hill, North Carolina, at the age of 91, January 14, 2011.*

the Carroll (white) family refuses to acknowledge the existence of and their involvement to white / slave offspring's or their involvement in the slave trade of Navarro County for which Benjamin Franklin Carroll was a major contributor. But this ex-slave which built a *"gold box,"* used by the Carroll family to store their gold / silver coins and a *"wooden cabinet for clothing storage,"* pictured on the following page located in

the home of Jay Sewell *(pictured below)* today, the grandson of Parthania Agnes Carroll who was the daughter of James Alexander Texas Carroll and son of Judge James Carroll Sewell aka *"The Blind Judge."* So, the start of the Carroll name, given during the period of ownership by the slave era, was kept by Charity even after emancipation. Most likely out of respect for the treatment of partiality she had received from the Carroll family. So, this surname, *"Carroll,"* that has been apart of over 196 years of our family history.

Charity Carroll is the source of my family's beginning that has grown to an enormous number of Teachers, *"The San Francisco Call," of March 17, 1913* Lawyers, Doctors and law-abiding citizens. A great gratitude has to be given to this remarkable woman for her courage, accomplishments and her ability to endure the cruelties of slavery. The uncompromising humilities that must have existed daily during her life is worthy of sharing. Slavery in the south, particularly in Mississippi must have felt like the fiery pits of hell on earth each day for many slaves. Thought there is no evidence to support Charity was treated this way, but surely she had to observe others receiving this treatment. To have survived it was enough worth celebrating for eternity. Back breaking hard work in the cotton fields with no compensation for your labor, no nutritional foods for your body, compounded by unyielding weather conditions must have been unbearable. Your body and soul belong to the Master who owned you in every sense of the word. Your only salvation was to have been born a *"Mulatto,"* passing for white or be a *"House, "N-word,"* like it appeared Charity was. Otherwise, your life wasn't worth, as the old folks would say, *"a plug nickel."* People of color were considered property for all purposes and conditions to the Masters wants. Despite all the horrific things that did occur during that dark period in American and World history, there are some tales of miraculous survival and heroism that were mostly kept in silence. One such unlikely hero is that of a small statue woman who had to have had the Grace of God an all his angels watching over her for all 98 years of her life.

Above is the beloved cabinet made by Chant (A Slave) during the 1860's   ***Jay Sewell, JB & Catherine Porter, Mary Alice Powers & me (2010)***

Charity Carroll, is a story worth telling. Charity Carroll, just who was she? As described by Viola Jewel Gee Caruthers, one of a few number of family members old enough to have witnessed her presence during the time of my research for this book. She was the great-granddaughter of her eldest son, **"Big" Allen**, recalls her as being of small statue with short naturally gray curly hair and a spicy-tongue. Jewel once mentioned, that as a child,

Devour Us Not

"The Salt Lake Herald," of August 17, 1890

Charity asked her a question or an opinion on a matter of discussion or thought one day. Jewel recalls being only about five years of age, and not knowing how to respond properly and respectfully, simply replied with silence. Much to the chagrin of Charity who then replied, *"You unconcerned Heifer."* Jewel, then thought that was the exact reaction she would have gotten either way considering the nature of Charity's demeanor. But, Charity's wisdom was tested time and time again. And one can only imagine, she became wise through her obvious years and a keen sense of her surroundings. One extremely cleaver notation was from the Census of 1900. Clearly, years from the watchful eye of an overseer, she unequivocally responded truthfully to a very significant question. A measure of truth that would

* *

1900 Federal Census, Navarro County, Texas

prove to be of value towards the mystery of unidentified children that has been rumored since her known existence. Charity's acknowledgement from the 1900 Census above when she was 86 years of age, the marker and numeric numbers, *"11"* and *"4"* were used to represent the *"11"* children she had given birth to in her lifetime and the *"4"* that she could claim *("Big" Allen, Lewis, Robert & George)*. Little is know about Charity's child bearing years and the fact that her first known acknowledged child, *"Big"* Allen Carroll was born when

Charity was 29 years old. Also, Charity being born in Mississippi, March, 1814, when Benjamin Franklin Carroll, Sr. was about 5 years of age, born in 1809. Assuming Charity Carroll's mother was a house-worker, and the fact that she was granted permission to marry in 1814 further adds favorably to the possibility that the two probably played together as children. And Charity's mother, a cook and child care provider, adds yet another avenue into the favorable treatment of both. Unbeknown to most of the whites who would most assuredly have denounced the even thought of such an act

Lewis Carroll
1857 - Apr 7, 1937

Lil'Allen Carroll
1861 - Jan 12, 1941

of playing together was but a secret kept. But the concealment of what ever became of the other children Charity gave birth to remains but a secret taken to the graves of all involved. Charity having the advantage of working within the *"big-house,"* a term commonly used by slaves to describe the masters house, could have had many advantages. Gaining knowledge of reading, writing and business sense from overheard conversations was immeasurably and informative during that era. But, on Charity's court documents, during her latter years, only an *"X"* was used as her signature, assuming she could not write her name. Or was this just another secret to conceal her true intelligence that would have caused more problems and compromise whom ever had afforded her the opportunity to gain this knowledge. After all it was a punishable offense if any such informa-tion was revealed to the right people and death was assured. So, the relationship, if any between B.F. Carroll, Sr.

"The Times," of November 16, 1902

1880 Federal Census of "Big" Allen & Caroline Carroll

Eva Molina Carroll Gee
March 15, 1885 - October 16, 1981
Married George Gee on Dec 28, 1898

William Porter   &   Sarah Benjamin Porter
Apr 29, 1867 - Dec 6, 1954   Jan 3, 1874 - Aug 17, 1955
Married in 1892 and had 10 Children

and Charity Carroll eludes this family's curiosity, but will continue to be an interesting research motivator for us as an avenue to finding our true roots. **Big Allen Carroll**'s only known marriage was to a widowed women from Louisiana named **Caroline Benjamin** on Nov 7, 1878. Big Allen and Caroline had two children, **Martha** (Jul 15, 1883 - 1979) *(Married Llige Garrett Dec 24, 1898)* and **Eva Molina** (Mar 15, 1885 - Oct 16, 1981, *she married George Gee Dec 28, 1898*). Caroline Benjamin was first married to **George Benjamin** and had three children named **George, Jr.** (1865), **Sarah** (Jan 3, 1874 - Aug 17, 1955) and **Martha** (1879). Pelham, Texas found favor in **Sarah Benjamin** who then married **William Porter** (Apr 29, 1867 - Dec 6, 1954), in 1892 pictured above left. They had ten children named, **Ciary Davis** (Sep 20, 1893 - Sep 17, 1983)*(who married Josie Herron)*, **Laura Molena** (Nov 1, 1894 - Apr 15, 1939), *(Married Zeno Wendell Carroll)* , **Callie A.** (1896 - 1923), **Savanah Minnie**, (1897 - 1980), **Theo B.** (1900 - 1985), **William, Jr.**(Jan 13, 1903 - Feb 10, 1932), **Elmer Olem** (Jan 15, 1904 - Feb 18, 1993), **Cleo** (1906), **Helen** (Jan 1, 1907 - 1926) and **Prentice** (Dec 10, 1910 - Jul 3, 1967).

Laura Molena married **Zeno Wendell Carroll** and had 9 children named **Theresa Merrill** (Apr 24, 1918), **Leo** (1920), **Eunice Grace** (May 23, 1923), **Norma Uvanne** (Jul 1, 1926), **Carroll** (Nov 25, 1930), **Troy William** (Apr 22, 1932), **Ray Square** (Apr 22, 1932), **Frank** (Jul 22, 1935), **Walter Franklin** (Jul 22, 1935).

Ciary Davis Porter married **Josie Herron Porter** in Irene, Hill, Texas on December 17, 1914. They had two sons named **William Manuel** (Feb 9, 1916 - May 19, 1988), **Leroy Jerry** (Aug 26, 1917 - May 19, 1988). **William Manuel** married **Netta Mae Thomas** in 1938 & had 2 girls, **Carol A.** (1938) and **Dannie Maxine** Aug 23, 1939 -)

Dannie Maxine married **Donald L. Duster** (Feb 10, 1932 - Mar 11, 2013) **(Donald is *Ida B. Wells-Barnett's Grandson*)** on December 22, 1962 and had three children **Daniel**, **David** and **Michelle.**

Elmer Olem Porter married **Jennie M. Sweeney** on May 2, 1926 and had five children named **Cecilie Evelyn** (Nov 29, 1926), **Elmer Bernard** (Dec 18, 1929), **Virginia** (Jul 6, 1932), **Darlene Marian** (Jul 6, 1932) and **Wilburn James** (Dec 15, 1936).

Devour Us Not

Elmer Bernard married Alva Jean Blair and had four children, **Elmer Bernard**, Jr.(May 28, 1951), **Bruce Wilburn** (Apr 7, 1953), **Sheryl Constance** (Mar 8, 1955) and **William Ralph** (Feb 28, 1957). **Elmer Bernard Porter, Jr.** married Diann Ellison and had one child name **Nicole Dione** (May 18, 1978). The Federal Census of **1940,** Head - **Benjamin C. Duster** (May 14, 1892- Sep 18, 1945), Wife -**Alfreda Duster** (Sep 3, 1904 - April, 1983) (*Daughter of Ida B. Wells-Barnett*) and they had 5 children named **Benjamin - Duster, Jr.** (Mar 15, 1927 - Feb 11, 2011), **Charles Duster** (1930 -), **Donald Leon Duster** (Feb 10, 1932 - Mar 11, 2013) who married **Dannie Maxine Porter, Alfreda Duster (1935 -) and Troy Duster (1935 -).**

"Richmond Planet," of February 13, 1904

Lewis B. & **Bertha Harris Porter** were married in 1911 and had three children named were **S.C.** (Jun 12, 1911 - Dec 9, 1938), **Permilla Mag** (1913), **Robert** (1916) and. **J.B. Porter. J.B. Porter** was as born September 11, 1918 and married **Catherine Carroll** on May 11, 1939, pictured right. They had 2 children named, **J.B., Jr.** (Feb 5, 1942 - Jul, 1984) and **Voncile Elaine** (1940 - Oct 6, 1995). **Lewis Porter,** JB's father, was the only child of **Squire Columbus** (April 1, 1869 - Feb 2, 1949) & **Mary J. Jones** (1864) who were married Dec 16, 1888. Squire Columbus's father and mother were **Square Columbus** & **Margaret Carruthers Porter** who were married Jan 29, 1866. Their children were, **Laura** (Jul 3, 1863 - Mar 10, 1941) (married Allen), **Henry** (1865 - Aug 22, 1940), **William M.** (*WM or Billie who married Sarah Benjamin*) (April 29, 1867 - Dec 6, 1954), **Square Columbus, Jr.** (Apr 1, 1869 - Feb 2, 1949). So this was how the Porter's and the descendants of Ida B. Wells-Barnett link to this family. So back to Charity and the Carroll Clan. Charity Carroll's second child was named **Robert** or *"Bob,"* that was born in 1852 when she was about 38 years of age and shortly after the arrival and settlement in the Navarro County area. It is rumored that he was favored by the white Carroll's and is buried in the white cemetery. It was also rumored that the white Carroll's would often visit him which further acknowledges kinship. Occasionally, both families would eat Sunday dinner at Aunt Eva's house who was the daughter of *"Big"* Allen. This story was told many times with the whites being identified as relatives of Robert. The census records also list Robert as a *"Mulatto."* Her third son was named **Lewis**, born in 1857 when she was 43 years of age and **George** born in 1859 when she was 45 years of age.

Lil' Allen Carroll, my great-grandfather, Charity's adopted son, was born approximately 1861 with many rumors surrounding his beginnings. But to our knowledge the name Parthania, the daughter of James Alexander Texas Carroll who was also the Executor of her (*Charity's*) Will, we assumed had some withheld knowledge of the parentage of Lil' Allen. Charity's Will however, would not reveal any knowledge of the Carroll connection or the kinship questions regarding her 11 children or the four sons she claimed. She also alleged to have mothered a daughter named **Liddie**, born 1847, in Texas when Charity was about 33. She was also passing for white, working in the Polk's household as a cook on the 1880 census. But who was the parentage of Lil' Allen Carroll? To our knowledge, this information was never discussed with a person of color. Another rumor was, the daughter of B.F. Carroll, Sr., named **Mary Eleanor Ann Carroll**, born November 19, 1837 and died July 11, 1865 at the age of 27 that could supposedly not read or write. There was no acknowledgement of how she died listed anywhere during my research. She was rumored never to have married and probably was handicap. This was about the same time Lil' Allen Carroll shows up in the middle of the night at Charity's residence in 1865. Unable to speak by either traumatized over the uprooting or perhaps too young to know how. Either way, the coincidental nature of these dates arises the suspicious mind yet again as to the possibilities of her being somehow linked to Lil' Allen and or even possibly his mother. But all these unknown facts about passed events, Charity took to her grave. Charity was married and later widowed, but the name and dates of her marriage to her husband are unknown. There are rumors that it could have been a slave named *"Chant,"* who was a favorite of the Carroll Family and a skilled craftsman by evidence of the cabinet that is in the possession of Jay Sewell until this day. He was also the maker of a gold box that was used to store gold and silver coins belonging to the Carroll family. The life of this ex-slave remains a secret of this family's history. Charity's land was located in the Pelham community, 2 miles NE of Emmett County. The land is also described as a S.A. Kimble tract of land located on the west side of Richland Creek, three miles east of Irene, Texas, all 346 areas. The manner in which this land was acquired by Charity is partly unknown but her dealings and other land transactions were profound.

"New York Tribune," of August 30, 1903

Devour Us Not

Known only by an obvious savvy businessman then passed on to Charity. As more research is performed, undoubtedly, *"Truth, crushed to earth, shall rise again,"* quote by William Cullen Bryant. It was rumored that B. F. Carroll, Sr. before his death in 1869 left specific instructions for his sons to issue land and a house to Charity Carroll. Also mentioned in his Will, which remains a source of mystery as to its whereabouts

"The Hawaiian Star," of February 27, 1904   **William Cullen Bryant**-*Harper's Weekly-Sep 2, 1865*

and his living existing family protect its secrecy until this day. The white Carroll family admits to telling lies of death, hidden vital records and impeded our family from receiving documents and photos that they have admittedly in their possession. But there were instructions from Benjamin Franklin Carroll, Sr., to ensure her legal affairs where handled properly by his son's or whom ever within the Carroll family with legal authority to secure her (Charity) rights at her passing. In 1909, when Charity was 95 years of age, she established a Last Will and Testimony. James Alexander Texas Carroll, Justice of the Peace and the son of Benjamin Franklin Carroll, Sr., was established as her legal representative and acknowledged by Judge James M. Blanding. Present during these initial court proceedings were three of her four sons *(Big Allen had already passed)*, Lewis, George and Robert. James Carroll had the estate appraised by Robert S. Neblett, Asa H. Willie and Gordan Dorman who were all citizens of Navarro County and had no material interest in the property or the estate. These three did appraise the 346 acre of land at $5,000.00. Charity did outline her next of kin as descendants to receive their inheritance from her estate after of course her just debts had been paid. The descendants and amounts received were listed as follows: **Eva Gee, $200.00** *(Charity's eldest son, Big Allen's daughter who married George Gee)*, **George Gee** *(Eva's husband)*, **Robert (Bob) Carroll, $300.00** *(Charity's son)*, **Martha Garnett, $200.00** *(Charity's eldest sons' daughter who married E.L. Garnett)*, **Elige L. Garnett** *(husband of Martha)*, **Walter Carroll, $344.44** *(Son of allegedly, Liddie Carroll, who was Charity's daughter and his father, a white man named Daniel Hartzell)*, **Lewis C. Carroll, $516.68** *(Charity's son)*, **Alice McClendon $344.44** *(Charity's granddaughter who's mother was Jennie Carroll, allegedly another one of Charity's daughters)* and **George Carroll $344.44** *(Charity's son)*. Sum of all monies issued to her heir's totaled **$2,250.00**. After Charity's passing, much attention was being paid to the amount of wealth she had accumulated in part as a result of land given her by Benjamin Franklin Carroll, Sr. after his death in 1869. October 24, 1912, James Alexander Texas Carroll, acting as the Administrator of Charity Carroll's Will, brought the matter before the Probate Court, and given a Case Number 2199. It was at this time James Carroll presented six promissory notes dated December 30, 1909 from Sam F. Smith for 64 areas of land. This indebtedness for $255.50 each totaling $1,533.00 was to have been paid each year on the 1st of November, from 1913 to 1918, according to the petition. Also, the vendor was asking an additional charge to include 10% interest would be accessed. An individual emerged claiming $100 debt due the estate and was to be paid by September 11, 1911, that was not paid and had risen to $111.00. An open account from Roger Carroll also emerged claiming $200.00 debt owed to the estate valued at $2,000.00 and cash in Charity's bank totaling $786.73. This positive balance of $2, 450.73 was also presented in Probate Court. The total amount of her net worth at her death was *($2,450.73 + $5,000.00 = $7, 450.73)* $7,450.73, yet the sum of only $2,250.00 went to the listed Charity's heirs. The mystery of the so-called unpaid promissory notes was challenged by her sons to no avail. So, the remainder of her estate went to James Alexander Texas Carroll and his descendents, with little regards to the wishes of his father, Benjamin Franklin Carroll, Sr. Charity Carroll would live to be 98 years of age, passing away on September 1, 1912. Her remains were recently located after decades in obscurity and a marker was also placed at the site of her remains. This task was orchestrated by Catherine Porter, our family's 94 yr old matriarch. But her birth and death certificates are non-existent, like most of her life. Photographs and family history; secrets she was entrusted with; left this world with her in silence.

Lil' Allen Carroll, my great-grandfather was the beginning of my Mother's family and here is his story. Lil' Allen Carroll beginnings in this family were very suspicious as to the unresolved issue of his ethnicity. By his obvious Caucasian-like features, one would surmise the obvious bi-racial connections that he is the product of mixed parentage or all white possibly. Born approximately 1861, according to the 1880 Census where he is listed as being 19 years of age. The photograph to the right, pictures Lil' Allen Carroll and his only wife, Marry Davis Melton as adults. The year of this photograph is unknown. The stories of his existence with Charity Carroll as told by his children (Aunt Cora Rosie, Uncle Cornelius *(Nig)*, and Aunt Anna Dora *(Dump)* were all the same). But his true ethnicity until this day remains a mystery.

Lil' Allen Carroll "Pa" and wife Mary Davis Melton Carroll, "Ma"

When he *(Lil' Allen)* was a toddler, or barely walking age, while in route to Charity Carroll's residence during the black of night, was the start of this oral history of conspiracy. The safekeeping of this child was possibly entrusted in the hands of Charity Carroll to raise or possibly had some relationship with Charity and possibly could have been a daughter. As the oral history records, it supposedly

happened one summer night through the corn fields of Pelham and Hubbard, Texas while fleeing from a nearby farm. There was a rumored incident of bodily harm to be carried out the following day against him *(Lil' Allen)* because the knowledge of his mixed ethnicity was either discovered or presumed by presumably the wife of the master. His *(Lil' Allen)* mother was possibly working as a housemaid for a white farm owner and had a one-way relationship with someone of Caucasian ancestry. Whether this relationship was forced or not, consider the time period,

"Ma" - Marry Davis Melton Carroll
Oct 15, 1873 - Aug 6, 1951

"Ma"- Marry Davis Melton Carroll
Oct 15, 1873 - Aug 6, 1951

1860, right at the beginning of the Civil War in the state of Texas. The mother being fearful for his and or her life, because of the rumored threats of her possibly the unsolicited relationship, must have reach the

233   *Devour Us Not*

"The San Francisco Call," of March 26, 1901

"Pa" seated with Nancy on his lap, to his right is "Eute", to his left is "Mann"
L/R Standing : his Daughters, Rosie, Odessa, Anna Rosa "Dump", and Lillie in the hat.

"Little" Allen Carroll   22nd Oct 1902

Below is the Babylon School classroom picture sometimes during the early 1900's which included some children of Lil' Allen and Marry Carroll.

lady of the house with much anger. Accordingly, he was to be thrown in a hog pen to be trampled to death or even hung along with his mother before the truth of this child's identity reach within the families of the community. That night, she made her daring escape, never to be heard of again. Until this day, it is unknown whether the mother of Lil' Allen was related to Charity as possibly a daughter, daughter to one of her sons or a daughter to one of the white Carroll's as rumored. But Lil' Allen describes his mother as having a like resemblance to Aunt Odessa (*Dim*) or as he called her, *"Dimmie,"* one of his children.

1880 U.S. Census where Lil' Allen Carroll is listed as being 19 years old living with a brother

Having long brown hair and fair to brown-skinned facial tones and not very tall made her hasty transition of him quite difficulty as he later reportedly describing her efforts to get him to their intended destination. *"She would sometimes carry me and sometimes I would be running,"* he later recalled. Apparently, he didn't know his name or possibly was of the age he couldn't speak or perhaps, he was so traumatize over the ruckus of urgency that may have had a bearing on his inability to speak. So Charity named him after her eldest child, Allen, hence the names of *"Little or Lil"* and *"Big"* Allen stuck with them throughout their lives.

Ironically, the 1870 census show no traces of Charity or Little Allen Carroll living in Navarro County during that census visit. And we all know and agree that Charity and Lil' Allen Carroll never left Navarro County during either of their lifetime. And the overseer for the 1870 census taking for Navarro County was none other than **James Alexander Texas Carroll** *(Justice of the Peace)*, the first Texas born child of Benjamin Franklin & Huldah Carroll, Sr. Lil' Allen met and married Marry Davis Melton sometimes during 1881. Marry Davis was the daughter of Albert Davis and Sophie Henry Melton. Shortly before his *(Lil Allen)* marriage, on the 1880 Census, he lived with a half-brother named Joe Warren. Interestingly, the recorder first placed an "**M**" for race next to Joe Warren's name, but clearly later changed it to "**B**" for black to identify the race, which essentially making him a Mulotto, a person identified as having mixed-race blood. Even though the name of Joe Warren

can't be directly linked to any sources that would gain knowledge into Lil' Allen's parents, it would however have some common named associations in our research. Lil' Allen or "Pa" as he was affectionately called by his children and grandchildren, purchased 47.9 acres of land for $1,500.00. This purchase was made in 1902 from J.H. Farrold and Julia Farrold. The land was part of a tract of land inherited by then Julia Warren. Our research can't confirm if Julia Warren was related to Joe Warren, but it arouses the suspicion of the last name being a significant link. Oddly enough, it was rumored that Pa lost in his effort to secure enough funds to pay off the debt and subsequently lost the property assumingly through some type of trickery.

17 Children of "Ma" (Marry Davis Carroll) & "Pa" (Lil' Allen Carroll)

(1)   Fred Curtis "Fed"
Oct. 15, 1882 - Dec 10, 1955

(2)   Cornelius "Nig"
Dec 23, 1883 - Sep 26, 1987

(3)   Edward "Edd - Eute"
Mar 10, 1884 - Dec 2, 1962

(4)   Allen
Aug 2, 1885 - Aug 2, 1885

(5)   Elkin
Dec 1886 - Unk

(6)   Bertha "Betty"
Aug 12, 1887 - Jul 9, 1957

(7)   Lillie
May 1, 1890 - Jan 7, 1941

(8)   Alvin C "Al"
Jan 10, 1891 - Sep 16, 1939

(9)   Anna Dora "Dump"
Aug 17, 1894 - Oct 4, 1988

(10)   Bluett
Mar 12, 1895 - Oct 16, 1895

(11)   Lina "Line"
Sep 1897 - Aug 28, 1975

(12)   JD "Huttie"
Dec 25, 1898 - Jan 27, 1943

(13)   TC "Coty"
Feb 12, 1900 - Jun 7, 1982

(14)   Odessa "Dimmie"
Feb 12, 1905 - Nov 29, 1977

(15)   Clyde
Feb 14, 1906 - Mar 7, 1976

(16)   Carl Nora "Mann"
Mar 20, 1908 - Nov 18, 1975

(17)   Rose Nora "Rosie" "Pug"
Mar 20, 1908 - Nov 1, 2001

They had 17 children with 14 living to adulthood. Very little is known about "Pa" as an adult, but some of the stories that were told were that in the evening, while Pa would be seen from afar conversing with a number of other white men, the grandkids would yell out his name for supper. The grandkids, not knowing which one was Pa, would patiently wait to see which one would stand up before identifying him as their grandfather. He was described as short in height with blonde hair and blue eyes. He was also believed to have been a self-proclaimed Preacher as he would be seen from time to time visiting his children and grandchildren reading Bible verses and ministering the gospel. There was also a memorable moment as told by his granddaughters, Mary Alice Carroll Powers and Gracie Nancy Devroe. Nancy lived in the house with Ma & Pa until she moved to Houston. The way the story was told, apparently there were cookies that were taken from the kitchen without permission by Nancy that was noticed by Pa. In his assumptive apprehension of the responsible party, he inadvertently grabbed Mary Alice instead of Nancy who was laughing frantically underneath the bed with cookies in hand awaiting the opportunity to snack. Pa, yelled as he in one hand held the arm of Mary Alice and the other a switch (*a switch also was a tree branch with no leaves, used as a disciplinary tool*) stated, *"Con-founded, I'm gon' whoop yo' busy behind."* At the same time, Ma, knowing the responsible party for the cookie heist, yelled at Pa, stating, *"Ally! Ally!, You whooping the wrong gal!."* Initially this incident did not bring laughter but through the years, Nancy and Mary Alice both listed that incident as their most memorable moments with Pa.

Also, Pa would often ride the train from Purdon to Corsicana and various other places. The railroad like everything else during that era were segregated. The conductor would often direct Pa to the front of the train for *"Whites Only"* and indicated he'd see his *"lil' nigger,"* grandkids once he reaches his final destination. Pa, in response to the insult to his grand children would utter, in a quite voice as not to undermine the conductor's misidentified issue of his race, *"I don't know what I'm suppose to be."* Pa would also travel by train to visit an alleged brother named Abe to either Ennis or Oklahoma. However, the closest name to Abe would be Abram listed on the 1880 Census living with Charity Carroll as a son, born in 1867. And no other record of this brother until this day can be identified. But Pa managed to raise all his children and some grand children with the iron fist of discipline. Most of his children reportedly, climbed out the windows with their clothing in a pillow sack

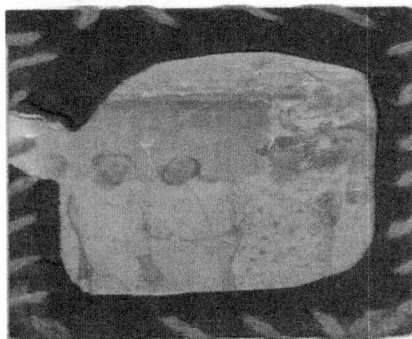

Lil Allen's Daughters, R/L Rosie, Odessa, Lillie, Anna Rose & Betty & Lina.

Lil'Allen's Wife, Marry Davis Carroll, grandson, James Phillip (L) & her son Cornelius, "Nig" on the right.

Devour Us Not

and headed for either Ennis, or Houston, Texas, fleeing from his alleged strict rearing. Lil' Allen died February 13, 1941 at the age of around 80. His death was due to an apparent heart attack and was pronounced dead before the doctor arrived. The story of Lil' Allen Carroll was dictated to me by his granddaughter and my mother, Mary Alice Carroll Powers. Jester, Texas prior name was

Switch, Texas located about eleven miles southwest of Corsicana. Purdon, its current name, was established in the 1930's by a man named **George Taylor Jester**, pictured on the left that was a businessman, banker and Lieutenant Governor of Texas. He purchased the land and established

"The Houston Daily Post," of May 18, 1898

the town as a St Louis and Southwestern Railway stop around the early 1890's before a Post Office opened. Soon a school was created followed by stores, a church and new homes. George was one of six children born to Levi and Diadema Jester in Macoupin County, Illinois, on August 23, 1847. His family moved to Texas in 1858 after his father died. George married Alice Bates from Mississippi and had three sons. George died on July 19, 1922 at his home in Corsicana where the Courthouse now sits.

JD Carroll, my grandfather, I never met, was my mother's father and 12th child of Lil' Allen and Marry Davis Carroll. Born on Christmas Day, 1898 in what is now known as Purdon, Texas. J.D. Carroll aka *"Hute" or "Huttie,"*

JD Carroll
Dec 25, 1899 - Jan 27, 1943

was raised in the home of his parent until he was an adult. On October 7, 1918, he married Viola Sneed at 15, and two children were born to this union, **Jimmie D.** & **Mary Alice**. On July 25, 1925 he married **Annie Zora Jones (aka Grand-**

Viola Sneed Carroll
Jan 29, 1903 - Aug 3, 1955

Jimmie D. Carroll
Jan 26, 1919 - Oct 2, 1990

Mary Alice Carroll
May 17, 1920 - Nov 5, 1946

Mama Carroll), where six girls were born to this union. These girls are **Mary Alice,** *(My Mother & her half sister shared the same name),* **Lucy Fern, Minnie Ruth, Ella Frances, Dorothy Lee** and **Gracie Ann.** After 18 years of marriage, J.D. suddenly passed away on January 27, 1943 from high blood pressure. My mother describes her dad's passing as leaving a great burden on her mother, widowed now with 6 daughters to raise alone at 35 years of age. My mother was 14 years old and the eldest of the girls, so the decision was made to move to Corsicana, Texas. There, my grandmother and her children lived with **Aunt Ella Sessions,** who was my grandmother's, mother's sister. There was much discontentment in Aunt Ella's household, so in the mid-forties, a distant relative named Elsa Carroll heard about the hardship grand-mama Carroll was having, offered her home to her before relocating to Los Angeles, California. At the time nobody knew of how they were related, but

they welcomed the change which was different. Grand-Mama Carroll did her best in raising the girls in that small framed house during the 1940's. My mother's sister, Lucy was almost killed in a train collision with the vehicle she was riding in while in route to pick cotton. Everyone in the pick-up truck that day was killed except for her sister Lucy. As a result of the accident, the railroad paid a small settlement to Grand-Mama Carroll where she had a house built on 8th Avenue in Corsicana. My mother later admitting that her life was never the same after her father passed. She described him as being a kind man who never spoke much. One of the last things she recalls him asking her was what she wanted to be when she grew up. She replied, *"A School-Teacher."* Because she so admired her cousin Frankie, until she wanted to be just like her. My mother also recalls the curiosity of her siblings all asking their father one day, why was there always a leader in an above formation of flying birds. So one day her dad shot the leader down while they were flying so they could see him. That was one of the most amazing things; she recalls they had ever witness, as they gazed at the big eyed bird with astonishment. JD then nursed the wounded bird back to health in the back yard until one day they went to check on him and he was gone. JD also never raised his voice at his wife or children and never administered any type of punishment. He was also close to his father. On several occasions my mother would see "Pa" (*Lil'Allen*) reading the bible to JD as he listened patiently even though Lil' Allen supposedly had no former education affording him the ability to read. There was an incident which really scared my mother and her sisters. During a portentous down pour while her father was in the field farming, water was everywhere, they feared the worse for her fathers' safety when he didn't return home timely. They recall waiting and waiting until the down pour had completely stopped. When they looked out the door so far away, they saw their dad hanging on a tree branch, with water appearing very deep all around him just'a shouting and a waving his hand letting them know he had survived. It made for plenty of hugs and kisses when he did reach the house. The purpose of his passing had a profound effect on my mother, because many relatives stated, my mother was his favorite child. So favorite until he named two daughters, Mary Alice. But that single event in their young life's left a huge void that has lasted a lifetime, they all recall. A very good man, hard working farmer who always made sure his family had the best the short time he was with them.

Annie Zora Jones *aka* **Grand-Mama Carroll,** (*Pictured on the left*) my grandmother, and the mother of my mother. She was born an only child on May 22, 1908 to the parentage of **Will** (*William*) **Jones** and **Callie Daulton Jones** in Coolidge, Texas as indicated in the below 1910 Census. Coolidge is a small southern Texas town in Limestone County located about 72 miles south of Dallas. Callie was the eldest daughter of **George Daulton** and **Emma (Emily) Willis** who were married on January 23, 1889. They were blessed with five daughter's, **Callie** (*Nov 1889*), **Mattie** (*Dec 1891*), **Lucy** (*Sep 1894*), **Alice** (*Feb 1897*) and **Ella** (*Mar 1899*). Emma later had **Ida** (*1910*) and **Artina** (*Aug 10, 1913 - Aug 14, 1975*).

1910 Federal Census for Limestone County, Coolidge, Texas

The JD & Annie Zora Jones Carroll Family Tree

12th Child - JD Carroll (Married on July 27, 1925) **Annie Zora Jones Carroll (Grand-Mama Carroll)**
(December 25, 1899 - January 27, 1943) *(May 22, 1908 - June 24, 2002)*

Mary Alice Powers
Sep 16, 1928

Lucy Fern Wilkerson
(Oct 11, 1930 - Jan 22, 1994)

Minnie Ruth McPherson
Dec 10, 1932

Dorothy Lee Newton
Dec 24, 1934

Ella Frances Langston
Feb 18, 1938

Gracie Ann Cook
Feb 1, 1942

James Cleotha Carroll
Sep 2, 1946

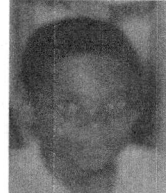

Billy Art Carroll
Feb 2, 1948

Mary Alice Carroll (Married on July 6, 1945) **James W. Powers, Jr.**
September 16, 1928 *(December 17, 1919 - March 13, 2009)*

Alice Patricia Dials
Sep 27, 1946

James W. Powers, III
Nov 28, 1947

Arnold Phillip Powers
Aug 12, 1949

Ann Phenia Powers
Jul 4, 1951

1900 Federal Census of Emma (Emily) Willis Daulton Johnson, mother of Callie Daulton Jones

Callie Daulton Jones Tubbs *(Nov 1889 - Feb 23, 1924)* was the mother of my grandmother *(Annie Zora Jones Carroll)* that has been the most difficult to research. Difficult, mainly because there is no official records of her birth. She died in Bardwell, Ellis County, Texas, at the age of 34 from cancer to the womb and was buried in Grady Cemetery, Bardwell, Texas. The reference is indexing project #B00152-7, Source film 1651039.

2012 -"Grady Cemetery" - Bardwell, Ellis County, Texas

My grandmother recalls sometime when she was about 15 years of age, making the year 1924, Aunt Ella Session, her mothers' sister, and later Aunt Lucy Smith and her husband, Sam Smith, came from Purdon, and picked her (*Annie*) up from her home in Bardwell, Texas. According to my grandmothers' testimony, all Aunt Ella and later Aunt Lucy told her that her mother was deceased and she was going to Purdon to live with them. My grandmother never knew what happen to cause her mothers death at age 34, other than she recalls her mother being a sickly woman. She never went to her mothers' funeral, and had no recollection where she was buried and never saw her father or stepfather again.

Callie Dalton (Daulton) was first married to Will (*William*) Jones on April 10, 1911 in Groesbeck, Texas, while living in Coolidge, Texas. The marriage did not last and later resulted in divorce. Soon there after Callie married Allen Tubbs and no children were born to this union. Callie was the oldest child of Emma Willis and George Daulton. Emma Willis was the illegitimate child of Eliza (Cherlious) Chinis and Anderson Willis. Anderson Willis is a remarkable story similar to so many other African-American stories of the South. Jeanette Adkins is the source of all information regarding this remarkable story. Jeanette, who is the great-granddaughter of Anderson Willis and daughter of Bird Willis, has pursued this injustice for more than forty years. Accordingly, Anderson Willis was born a slave in Virginia, approximately September, 1812.

"The Day book," of May 28, 1913

Anderson, according to now 87 (*2013*) year old, **Jeanette Adkins** recounts a chilling tale of grand thief and Dixie trickery. Anderson Willis was born a slave in Virginia even though written documentations can't be verified. His family supposedly originated from Ethiopia. But Willis was not his birth name, even though his parents and or siblings are unknown. Accordingly, when Anderson was about twelve, he was sold to a slave farm in Alabama whose owners' last named was *"Willis."* Anderson was a slave in Alabama and considered a favored, mainly because of his business-like sense in land dealings and the art of farming he had acquired. Anderson was also granted permission to marry **Harriet Smith** and they had 7 children named; **Jr.** *(1848)*, **Eastland** *(1850)*, **Bird** *(1854)*, **Bud** *(1855)*, **Mary Jane** (*1860*), **Berry** (*1861*) and **Sarah** *(1863)*. When the slaves were emancipated in 1865; even though Texas waited two years to allow the word to get to its slaves,

Anderson was given his and his family their freedom papers and monies from the Willis Plantation for his labor. So Anderson and his family packed up and moved to Freestone County, Texas sometimes during 1866. Upon his arrival, knowing the Reconstruction Period and the racism that it entailed, Anderson purchased nearly 3,000 areas of land. During a period where Freestone County officials, made every effort to impede blacks from land ownership. During this same period less than 1 in 100 black families' owned land. Laws were passed suggesting no black land-owner were allowed to hire whites as crop-sharers nor were whites encouraged to hire blacks. Anyone caught, would be either beaten, hung or worse, your whole family murdered. With the dominant white strong hold on the progress of blacks and playing to the ignorance thereof, Anderson became somewhat of a community leader. He employed many blacks, instructs them on farming tips, taught them to read and write and built a cohesiveness within a small black community. He also provided housing for many blacks who had no where to go or basic skills to even survive without whites ruling over them. Another trick the whites would perform was not to notify blacks of their land tax due date. This would cause a delinquency, prompting the immediate auction sale to valued land for pennies to their white relatives. These thieves would then conduct a quick kick out the black land owners from their land, leaving many landless and homeless. And this would also cause them to take their live stock as well.

According to the 1880 census, Anderson Willis had nine more children. **Eliza Chivis** (*Born approximately 1830*) was a young black woman living next door to Anderson whom he never married, but he had 12 children by her and they were; **Daniel** *(1869)*, **Elick** *(1870)*, **Alex** *(1871)*, **Emma** (*1872, My family linage starts with Emma*), **Dan** *(1873)*, **Henry** *(1874)*, **Rose** *(1875)*, **Sandy**(*1876*), **Bill** *(1877)*, **Minnie** *(1878)*, **Martha** *(1879)* and **Alice** *(1879)*. Considering the dire straits and conditions of blacks of that era, all manner of survival methods were being employed. A lot of precautionary methods were also being used by Anderson in a concerted effort not to offend the whites with his success. Anderson, having begun to quietly build houses for the homeless, schools for children, a graveyard and a Church, he named St. Hill Church all under the watchful eye of whites without much fanfare. After the death of Harriet between 1880-1889, Anderson then married **Mandy Hunt** *(Born in 1840)* in 1889, and had four children. In 1904 Anderson, at the age 92 got married to **Mary Augusta, "Gus,"** at 37 years of age and four more children were listed according to the 1910 Federal Census. These children listed were **Laura** *(1904)*, **Sandy** *(1905 son)*, **Roberta** *(1907) and* **Rose** *(1907)*. Anderson Willis died in 1917 at the age of 103.

On September 16, 1987, a federal judge in Waco, Texas dismissed a civil rights lawsuit filed by the Willis

THE QUEEN OF THE MAY.

SALT

"The Evening World," of May 1, 1888

family alleging the whites of swindled Anderson out of nearly 3,000 acres of land. The U.S. District Judge Walter S. Smith, Jr. had also ruled earlier that the 1984 lawsuit by Jeanette Adkins and other descendants of Anderson Willis was filed long after the statute of limitations (*for Texas is 25 years*) had expired.

SUPREME COURT OF THE UNITED STATES

February 27, 1989

ESTATE OF ANDERSON WILLIS, DECEASED, ET AL., PETITIONERS

v.

ESTATE OF JOHN RILEY, DECEASED, ET AL.

C.A. 5th Circuit Court

Justices of the Supreme Court decision were: Rehnquist, Brennan, White, Marshall, Blackmun, Stevens, O'Connor, Scalia, and Kennedy.

The Powers Clan *(My Father's Family)*

"Los Angeles Herald," of April 10, 1910

James W. Powers, Jr.
Dec 17, 1919 - Mar 13, 2009

Watson Powers
Feb 1865 - ?

Laura Warren Powers
June 1871 - ?

George Washington Powers
(Brother of Watson Powers)

Watson's parents were **Anderson Powers** from SC (1821) and **Rachel Smith Powers** (1831) from Georgia and had 10 children (6 lived), **Grant** (1856-1936), **Willie** (1863), **Watson** (1865), **Elberta** (1866), **John** (1869), **Rose** (1871). **Watson** moved from Alabama to Texas and married **Laura Warren** on Dec 24, 1894 and had four children, **James W. Powers, Sr.** (1893-1975), **Johnnie Mae** (1900), **Ethel L.** (1904-1956) and **Laura B** (1907). **Watson** also had another daughter named **Missouri Powers** born 1885 by a different relationship.

James W. Powers, Sr.
Jan 27, 1893 - Dec 21, 1975

Serphenia Williams Powers
Jun 21, 1894 - Feb 3, 1966

James W. Powers, Jr.
Dec 17, 1919 - Mar 13, 2009

Lillie Belle Jackson Matthews
Oct 25, 1902 - Nov 16, 1998

James, Sr. was married to **Serphenia (Williams)** twice (Feb 13, 1917) and had 1 son. **James W. Powers, Jr.** Serphenia was first married to **Andrew B. Matthews** on Oct 17, 1909 when she was 15 and had 2 children, **Eddie & Vassie**. Then **Serphenia** married **Mr. Carvell** sometimes during the 1930's who died shortly after their marriage and she then remarried **James W. Powers, Sr.** again.

Eddie Matthews & Gwen
Sep 3, 1910 - Feb 22, 1967

Vassie Beatrice Matthews
Mar 27, 1912 - Jan 7, 1955

Gwendolyn Matthews Robinson
Sep 3, 1944

Eddie Matthews, first married a woman named **Vivian** and later **Lillie Jackson**. In December, 1942 Eddie and Lillie were married and had one child named **Gwendolyn**. **Vassie** was poisoned to death in Omaha, Nebraska and the case was never solved or investigated. She was married to Melvin "Pencil" Johnson of Corsicana and possibly a man from Nebraska named Michaels who escorted her body back to Texas after her death. Vassie never had children.

Anita Powers Hooper, (Her family pictured left) who was my father's favorite cousin and daughter of Grant Powers, was born July 13, 1910 and died in Los Angeles, California October 2, 2001. Anita was married to **Nesbert Hooper** and had 5 children: **Jerry, Nesbert, Jr.** (aka "Stix Hooper" of The Crusaders Jazz Group), **Samuel, Tommy Grant** and **William** "Diddy."

Mary Alice Carroll-Powers And James W. Powers, Jr. & Alice Patricia Powers

My mother, **Mary Alice Carroll**, Grand-daughter of Allen & Mary Davis Carroll *aka Ma & Pa* and eldest Daughter of J.D. & Annie Zora (*Jones*) Carroll. JD and Annie were married July 27, 1925 and soon moved to Kerens, Texas and lived with JD's brother and wife, T.C. & Ora Carroll. My mother was born in Purdon, Texas on a landowner name Sammie Ward's land, September 16, 1928. Before long, the family moved to Babylon, Texas. Babylon, Texas, a small community about 14 miles SW of Corsicana, Texas.

Being born and raised during the depression years of the 1920's & 30's made life in the country very difficult where much of what you ate was self grown. They attended a one teacher, one classroom school in Babylon, Texas where the teacher was Leon Thomas. The use of second hand text books from the white schools was common for all Negro schools of that era. Students were all required to gather their own firewood for purpose of keeping warm a very large iron heater located in the center of the room. There was no separate room for lunch. All students brought their own lunch, those who could afford it. But the consistent amount of sharing was a common practice for all students never knowing the period where the roles would be reverse. My mother recalls her mother waking up early to prepare their lunch which contained a sausage, biscuit and tea cookies. There was no lunch pale so most of the children carried their lunch in a used syrup bucket of similar pale of dual purpose. Being in a system of impoverished means, books, desk etc were often used or outdated. They had no fancy paper or pens to write they'd get as Christmas gifts, one cedar pencil and tablet paper. They also used a bird feather as a writing utensil to write in ink. Throughout the year most of the students went to school and church bare feet. Shoes where considered a luxury item for the middle class and white folk. If they were lucky, shoes were made by her father that would be received at Christmas that consist of cardboard and cowhide sewn like an Indian moccasin. Her mother would be responsible for dresses made from the fabric of cotton sacks that was as perfect fit as if it were bought in a store.

They also lived on one of her father's brothers' farm; Uncle Eute Carroll, where they were taught farm-hand chores. Uncle Eute had no children, so a lot of the responsibilities were performed by the girls. And my mother being the eldest, a lot of the responsibility of work was placed at her feet. They picked cotton in addition to their performing their farm chores. Around the early 1930's, the family moved from Babylon to the Purdon Community and then to Dresden, Texas. Her father set out to farm on the Minnitree Ranch (*Mr. Minnitree was a wealthy white land-owner and crop sharer*). There was a large house with a water well on the back porch. Her sister Dorothy was born on Christmas Eve, 1934 and for the longest of time my mother was convinced Santa Claus had brought them a baby sister for Christmas. All the kids were happy to have a large bedroom to

Devour Us Not

share in comparison to the other residence which was studio style houses with no indoor running water or sewer system.

One day while growing up their father asks each of them what would each be when they became adults. My mother's response was to be a Teacher like her cousin Frankie who was their teacher in the Dresden Elementary School District. They had to recall walking 5 miles to school daily as snakes would often chase them. The school buses would pass right by them as they were not permitted (*The Jim Crow South*) to pick them up according to the Law. A lot of teasing, laughter and name calling were constant, particularly on rainy and snow days. Even the bus driver would it appear to purposely hit pot holes in the road on rainy days to drench the Negro kids with muddy water which made for an all day wet affair at school. Having no TV's or electronics for entertainment, the simplest of natural events were their only source of amusement. One memorable incident where wild geese were flying high above the sky heading to the south for winter was a matter of discussion. My mother recalls the girls proposing a question to their father who had an answer for all their inquiries about the geese one day. Their question made to him questioned the supposed leader as appearing larger than then others and justifiably caused the others to follow is lead in a *"V"* formation. The day came when their father took a rifle and shot down the leader. Without missing a beat another leader took the spot of the fallen leader as the formation shifted to maintain its almost perfect "V" alignment.

Her father being an excellent shot which was a necessity of rural living and being a family provider for the period retrieved the shot down bird that had fallen in the open field. He was slightly wounded in the foot and wing and offered no resistance when her father picked him up. He brought the bird back for the girls to view his characteristics in comparison to his ability to lead his flock. She recalls the large eyes and feet and wide wing span possessed by the bird as a teacher, her father seem to know all the parts of the geese. He made a temporary cage for the bird as he aided the bird back to health. He also used that moment as a chance to explain how larger than life, he appeared while leading but the moment he fell, the replacement bird likewise appeared larger than life. He further demonstrated that anyone can be a leader if you believe in yourself and can convince others to believe the same. He also causes the girls to share in the responsibility for aiding in the birds' health by requiring them to bring food and water. The bird as wild as he was offered no aggression against them in anyway. One day the girls went to bring food to the bird, and he was gone, flown south for the winter to rejoin his flock. So their father concluded their teachable moment of parables that they could be anything they wanted with confidence. Soon the family moved from that house with the well to a much smaller farm house in Dresden.

The new community in Dresden held no particular advantages, because they still had to walk 5 miles to school as the white kids would still tease them as the half empty school buses would passed them bye day after day. Their teacher was none other than my father, James W. Powers, Jr. Mr. Powers, as he was called by the students, was so distraught about the fact that they had to walk to school while half empty school buses passed them by until he then taught his students a song. The song was sung in the Superintendents' Office. The objective was for the Superintendent of Schools, representative of all the students black or white, to see with his own eyes. The eagerness to learn and enthusiasm these somewhat forgotten children of the Negro community displayed during their spot-light moment, opened his eyes to tears that day. He taught them a song to the tune of,

"Deep in the heart of Texas," where some of the verses were slightly altered to fit the occasion. The Superintendent was so impressed with the song and patriotic attire that grand-mama Carroll and other mothers in the community made by hand caused the Superintendent and the board to go against the law and authorized the buses to pick up the Negro kids with designated in the back sitting. But, at least it was a start to allow the Negro kids to be apart of the general educational conversation in that isolated rural area. My Dad mentioned in later years that the Superintendent pulled him to the side with tears in his eyes and mentioned how proud he was of the kids most of whom were in bare feet sang as if their little lives dependent on it. Unbeknownst to them at the time, that no one in the white community even knew the kids existed educationally. Simply because of their skin color, they were an invisible element that manages to sing their way into the heart of a person whom had forgotten they even existed educationally.

For a first year young teacher such as my Dad caused a community to come together and show much pride. He opened the doors of consideration for the suffrage of Negro kids. That same year was the first Christmas in the new community for the Carroll's. It was this Christmas where the girls had found their Santa Claus that was placed in the storage house awaiting Christmas by their Dad. Later on, in disappointment, their Dad stated, *"This will be your last Christmas."* And it was, they lost their father due to a heart attack on January 27, 1943. He was only 42 years of age. My mother recalls how hurt and distraught they were about their father and the echo's of his words before Christmas of 42. After his death, the family's bread-winner now gone, had to move from their little farm house in Dresden to Corsicana, Texas.

Corsicana was a large school district by comparison, but the pattern of using old text books was the only similarities to that of the small school in Dresden. My mother recalls she was about 14 years of age and being the eldest, she had to take a job at a local laundry to help her Mother take care of the family. She worked after school and on Saturday's and received $12.00 a week for her labor.

She later married her former teacher, **Mr. James W. Powers, Jr.**, on July 6, 1945 and had four children. **Alice Patricia Powers** (*Dials*) (*1946*), **James W. Powers, III** (*1947*), **Arnold Phillip Powers** (*1949*), **Ann Phenia Powers** (*1951*). My Mother was *"Queen of the Million Dollar Tea,"* Bishop College, pictured left, acquired her Masters Degree, and taught School for thirty years. She has 12 grandchildren, 18 great-grandchildren and 3 great-great grandchildren. She was the, *"Founder of the Carroll-Melton Family Reunion,"* in 1989. She accepted Christ at an early age and was baptized in the Babylon creek by Rev. Ford. Her favorite scripture is the 37th Psalms and her favorite songs are, *"How I got over"* and *"Oh they tell me of an unclouded day."*

Devour Us Not

"Valentine Democrat," of May 30, 1907

Alice Patricia Powers

James Virden

Robert Dials (Decd)

Keith Virden
Mar 23, 1965

Kera Dials Williams
May 6, 1970

Keeno Dials
Apr 4, 1973

Khristopher
Feb 19, 1988

Jamelyn
Jul 23, 2000

Keeno, Jr.
Jul 14, 2002

Harmonee
Apr 24, 2007

Kennedy
Sep 12, 2011

Khristopher
Jan 2013

James W. Powers, III

Mazie Moore (Decd)

Brenda Neal

Carolyn Thorpe (Decd)

Sherry Davis

James W. Powers, IV
Feb 26, 1969

Jamil Le Ann Powers
Jan 24, 1983

Melinda Powers
Jul 5, 1995

Nia Kristian
Jun 24, 2001

Kaliyah
Nov 24, 2002

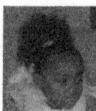

Ciara
Dec 24, 2005

Tiara
Dec 24, 2005

"The Morning Examiner," of January 3, 1909

Arnold P. Powers*Juana "Melinda" De Leon (Decd)
Aug 12, 1949   *Married Dec 15, 1973*   (Aug 16, 1946 - Oct 22, 1984)

Sharon D. Paris
Oct 23, 1959

(1) Arnold Phillip, Jr.
Oct 23, 1974

(2) Marricarr Kita
Dec 28, 1975

(3) Armando Kyron
(Mar 14, 1977 - May 23, 1998)

(4) Carlito LaPhonn
Apr 5, 1981

(5) Courtney Breon
Mar 11, 1986

(6) Drameagon D'Eric
Aug 1, 1987

(1) Deneisha
Jun 1, 1994

(1) Kelan
Apr 21, 1999

(1) Naudia
Mar 12, 2008

(2) Deja
Jun 2, 1996

(2) Cheridan
Mar 28, 2009

(3) Armani
Aug 15, 1996

(4) Carlito II
Feb 27, 2007

(4) Mia (Sdau)
Sep 19, 2003

(5) Kyi'Marri
Dec 24, 2004

(6)Laila Kelis
Oct 2, 2008

(1) Joshua

Ann Phenia Powers *Married 1970* **Alvin Moore (Decd)**   **Ann** *Married in 2000* **to Clarence Jeffery**
Jul 4, 1951

Stanley Alvin Moore
Jul 14, 1970

Devour Us Not

C_{hapter} III

"My life Story"

"The Hawaiian Star," of May 19, 1910   *Arnold "Phil" Powers at 6 months*   *Arnold "Phil" Powers today*

$\mathcal{I}$ am the third of four children born to **James W. Powers, Jr.** (*deceased*) and **Mary Alice Carroll** on Friday, August 12, 1949 at 5:45 am in Corsicana, Texas. Left is an article from the Philadelphia, Pennsylvania newspaper of June 5, 1917, stating what Corsicana, Texas is known for. I remember very little about Corsicana except East 7th Ave appeared to have been a major route for military vehicles. My brother and I would always

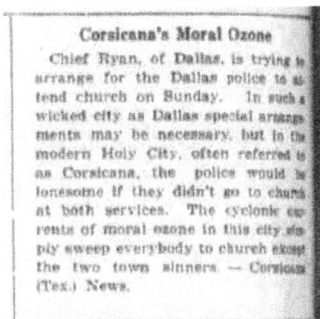

Corsicana's Moral Ozone

Chief Ryan, of Dallas, is trying to arrange for the Dallas police to attend church on Sunday. In such a wicked city as Dallas special arrangements may be necessary, but in the modern Holy City, often referred to as Corsicana, the police would be lonesome if they didn't go to church at both services. The cyclonic currents of moral ozone in this city simply sweep everybody to church except the two town sinners. — Corsicana (Tex.) News.

stand near the road and wave to the soldiers passing by. Shortly there after I recall moments of life in Houston, Texas. Accordingly, Aunt Dump had several entries in her dairy of baby sitting me. Several summers we would

1954 Corsicana, Texas James III, Pat and Phil

visit Corsicana I loved going to grand-mama's house because of Uncle's Billy and Cle. We knew we'd get roughed up and they were about our ages which made it fun and we got a chance to learn a new language. Like, *"Noam,"* which meant no ma'am, *"Gwown,"* which meant "Go head on" *"be back da reckly,"* which meant "I'll be back soon," *"chunk,"* which means to throw, *"Ya-som,"* which meant "Yes ma'am," *"a'ra,"* which meant a pause in dialog, *"I reckon,"* which means I recall and *"ourver,"* which means hour. I recall spending a lot of time with Aunt Ella which was my grand-mother's mother's sister and her interesting meal selections and touching her loaded pistol with admiration. It was a .22 caliber pocket size pistol made in Germany. There was an incident where Aunt Ella told me to go out back and catch a chicken. Her back yard, where she raised chickens was just full of them. Much to her amusement as she laughed for about 15 or 20 minutes at me, dust flying, chickens running for their lives, feathers and chicken-poop everywhere, my city-boy non-skilled at apprehending fowls were no joke to me. Then Aunt Ella came in the yard, it took her less than a minute to catch a chicken, rang its neck, with blood squirting everywhere as it flopped around until it died. She would then put the headless bird in a pre-heated pot full of water to soften its feathers before plucking them. I had never seen anything like that and I ate very little of that chicken that night. Between Aunt Dump and Aunt Ella, I ate, calf brains with scrambled eggs, large turkey eggs, cow tongue, pickled pig feet, Chitterlings, Possum, squirrel soup, fried rabbit, black birds dumplings soup with the buck shots cooked inside and probably more than that as my mind can only recollect. I must admit, it all tasted really good, excluding the lack of healthy choice effort.

Devour Us Not

Dalworth R. O. T. C.
Mr. James Powers, JR.
Director

Aunt Ella also had no washing machine, so the washing of her clothing and mine had to do with a large iron pot in her backyard. That pot must have been 6 feet in diameter and stood about half that size tall. She would place fire wood underneath it and put in lye soap that she made as its detergent. She had a long stick she would use to stir and lift the clothing up and down in that pot as the water would be boiling hot. She would

1954-Phil at age 5 singing "I've got a Woman."

always command me to stay back or if the boiling water and lye reached my skin, it would just pill right off. She would stir and lift those whites for hours it seemed before she'd declare them clean. Placing more and more firewood underneath the base of the pot to keep it boiling hot. But admittedly, those sheets would be the whitest of white and the freshness of morning dew flowers I'd ever encountered. Aunt Ella would also churned butter and always had a mouth full of snuff (*snuff is a smokeless brown powder like tobacco product made from pulverized tobacco leaves that was placed in a persons mouth between the front bottom lip and bottom gums for I assume an avoidance of nicotine that was not contained in snuff but an essential ingredients in other tobacco products*). In addition to chicken poop all over the yard, there would also be hefty spots of snuff spit everywhere. Aunt Ella would constantly be spitting brown spit all over the

Ground and at times drippings from her lip would also cling to her clothing. But she would always remind me to clean the bottom of my feet off thoroughly before entering the house. In the house however, she had a spittoon she'd use to the constant spitting ritual that lasted all during the night. When I was about five years of age (*pictured above left*), I recall having the gift of drawing and singing. I was the winner of a singing contest at the Club Matinee in Third-ward, Houston, Texas, where I sang, *"I got a women, way over town,"* By Ray Charles. I remember the crowd of mostly women showering me with coins and dollar bills being drown on stage during my performance. Having the child-like behavior applicable to my age, I'd stop singing and began to pick up the money. The more I stopped and started to pick up money and sang, the more frantic my dad became and the more the crowd laughed and cheered me on. After that episode of childish comic and adult vocal styling's all rolled up to one, the aftermath of kisses and hugs I'd received from big

Rev. A.A. Mc Cardell

breasted women wanting to embrace and rub my hair was quite an experience for a young lad such as myself. I recall my mother and father bragging about that contest for years as the money I acquired as the contest winner was enough to supply Easter outfits for all my siblings. Pictured on the right was a man of God, **Rev. A.A. Mc Cardell**, the Late Pastor of Pleasant Grove Baptist Church of Houston, Texas and the pastor who baptized me. I attended Edward L. Blackshear Elementary School of Houston in the first and

"The Day Book," of May 19, 1914

second grades which was right down the street from Aunt Dump's house where I would go some times after school. My favorite teacher was **Mrs. Holiday** in the second grade. Then there was a transitional move and we packed up and landed in Dallas where my dad was a teacher in Grand Prairie. Shortly after our arrival there was an act of kindness I'll never ever forget. I was about eight or nine years of age when we sold the local Dallas black newspaper, *"The Post Tribune,"* in downtown Dallas for 25 cents. One cold winery and rainy-day we were selling papers, as the unyielding rain had poured so until all twenty or so papers I carried were totally soaked as well as the clothing I was wearing. My brother and I were not properly dressed, meaning without the proper rain gear. As many people passed us by without notice and our voices were silent by this time as my brother and I had always been far apart in distance had huddled together for warmth. Finally, hoping our father would soon come to pick us up; two white men came up to us. I was assured with tears in their eyes, but after all it was raining. Their trembling voices, which confirmed the tears; asked us our names. It was so cold, until our lips could not move to respond. They kept using biblical phrases like *"Lord have mercy,"* and just *"Lord,"* as they took us out of the rain to the Dallas Police station. The policemen had to forcefully separate the newspapers from our fingers as the two white men gave us money more than the value of all the newspapers we had. We were also given warm coco and place near a heater to dry-out. We waited about four hours before our father arrived at the police station but seemed longer but not as long as the time we were in the rain. We could have taken shelter in hindsight, but I was about 8 or 9, wanting to accomplish my streak of selling all my papers before returning home gave no thought to my health. I thank God for those two nameless Godly white men, after hundreds of people black and white had passed us by. The events of that day and the exchange between the police and my dad were never addressed again as behind closed doors explanations were given to my mother. That day, announced the end our paper selling days, for we never went back downtown Dallas to sell papers. In the 3rd & 4th grades I attended Dalworth School and prior to that, I briefly attended to Colonial Elementary of Dallas. At Dalworth where my father was my teacher, it was a major shocker, massive coronary, but he never made any differences in me, for I was just another student. He formed a drill team where I was a member. During a short time we lived with my grandparents in Dallas. We would also visit them on holidays and in the summer. Most memorable thoughts about those visits was *"Wash."* Wash was a domesticated white rooster along with several hens my grandparents were raising in their backyard. Wash, all white in color, was as mean as Ole King Kong himself. The backyard was off limits. He would walk around pecking on the ground as if he didn't see you until he was out of your peripheral vision, then he would come up from behind and quickly attack. He had a beak as sharp as an ice pick and claws as sharp as razors. The initial introduction of Wash was made by my grandmother while we were all in the backyard. Unbeknownst to even her of his aggression and evilness. He even attacked my mother on the leg, drawing blood. As we hastily attacked the back-door leading into the house, like shoppers on a Friday after Thanksgiving sale. My grandmother looked on with astonishment. My Dad, who went for bad, dared to enter that backyard which made us even more fearful of Wash. When asked of my grandmother to explain the unusual behavior of a rooster thinking he was a dog, and to rid him of his backyard dominance, she replied, *"Honey, Wash is at home."* Giving prudence that the backyard and the now new meaning of whose guarding the henhouse; was off limits to us and anyone, as long as Wash was on duty and alive. Through the years no person, bird, cat or dog dared to enter the backyard under Wash's watch. Even one cold winter that killed all my grandparent's hens, Wash was still walking around the backyard in the snow playing cat and mouse with unsuspecting birds whom at their own peril attempt landing in the forbidden backyard where he ruled. But the

Devour Us Not

following extremely cold winter, we went to visit our grandparents, mindful of the restricted backyard situation, looked outside to see *"Ole Bad Wash,"* with the bottom of his legs facing the sky, in a dead cockroach pose, stiff as a board. We could not believe it, as bad as he was, Mother-nature had tried several times and failed finally succeeded in ridding us of the feared backyard dog, *"Wash."* To my knowledge, I've never encounter or known of anyone else who has had a chicken as bad as that idiot. And as the lost of Wash gave us a sense of relief and access to the backyard finally, we would occasional be on the look-out for Wash's reincarnation, still scaring each of us from time to time. The 5th & 6th grades I attended J.N. Ervin School in Highland Hills, Dallas, Texas, where we had purchased a new home. J.N. Ervin, like almost every other predominant black school had mostly used text books with names of obvious white kids as previous owners listed inside. The 7th & 8th grades I attended Dalworth School again. The summer of 1963 at the age of 13, the love bug hit me as I was a member of the Mt. Carmel Youth Choir of Dallas. Her name was **Carolyn Hunter**. I'm on the left, first boy in the first row of the picture shown below of our youth choir and Carolyn Hunter is the last girl on the right first row. The little fling lasted only for the summer because she went to Madison High and I was to attend a brand new school named Franklin D.

Mt. Carmel Baptist Church
3122 METROPOLITAN

Clerks
Mrs. Minnie H. Page
Mrs. Peggie Yarbough

Rev. Asa Horton
Minister

Junior Choir

Roosevelt, Mustangs where I was in the R.O.T.C. / Drill Team. In the white suit is my Dad, the organist and brother in the second row, second boy just above me. Roosevelt was an extremely large school by comparison and I was proud to have made the drill team with all the competition. That was the year that President Kennedy was shot. My recollection of that day is profound as I was in French class, when the news was announced over the intercom. Dallas Superintendent, Warren Travis White had initially made promises that all students of DISD could attend the parade to see President Kennedy, but later that week changed his mind. We hated him for that, considering the events that shocked the world that momentous day. There were a lot of conspicuous absences that day as the curious and bold dare defy the rules of shooting hooky for a last peak at a later fallen President. No one had an inkling into those days' events, but me, the faithful one, was last to leave the French classroom at the announcement of the shooting of the President reached the intercom. As every student was on liberty, out of control with sadness as the French Teacher's head laid in her hands on her desk sobbing. I even made a silent remark, apologizing for my exit and her sorrow as I quietly opened and closed the door behind me. There were no student hall patrols or policeman

available to stop the mass exit. Seemingly, which made my exit and others unnoticeable. The walk home; which we did not have a bus system in place was about 8 miles to Highland Hills. A very long walk, but really long that day considering what had happened and the labeling of Dallas as *"Black Dallas."* Black for the obvious sky turning unusually black that Friday before I reached home and the news of President Kennedy's assassination dominated the airwaves for the next decade it seemed. Among the mounting conspiracy theories that appear to number in the millions were spreading beyond the Dallas County line. Several black men, I recall were beaten by a mob of whites and policemen just for running in general and more specifically from the direction of the Dealey Plaza. The then Vice-President L.B. Johnson, Jack Ruby as well as the Dallas Chief of Police was even said

"The Times Dispatch," of June 11, 1905

to have played a roll and was deeply involved. But, one by one people came forward with eye witness accounts to seeing guns being pulled from the grassy knoll and to include smoke from a gun shot. And just like that one by one these same people began to disappear or were mysteriously found dead. There had to have been at least 20 such cases that's unsolved to this day. And the lone gun theory was a myth we all agreed. When we returned to school the following school day, no one said anything about the walkout or the conspicuous absences. But

CARVERDALE HIGH CLASS OF 1967

the amount of such conspiracy theories surrounding that assassination and the 911 issue of this era looms heavily over our nation to the amount of loyalty vice revenge, greed and dishonor people of the world will do for their cause. My 10th and 11th grade years were spent attending J.N Ervin HS, the Jaguars, then a brand new high school in Highland Hills, where I was in the R.O.T.C. and excelled in marksmanship. I was one of 10 cadets out of about 150 cadets to receive the Expert Rifle Badge in the Regiment. I also excelled in band where the only person to out perform me was Michael Massengale for first chair first seat, trombone section out of 10 other players. I also competed for Drum Major where I beat out all competition, but the job was given to Emerson Plummer. I was ticked off as Mr. Richards, the band director, explained to me that the backbone of a band was its brass section and I was more valued as a trombonist; as if to appease my anger. Our band went on to win

Devour Us Not

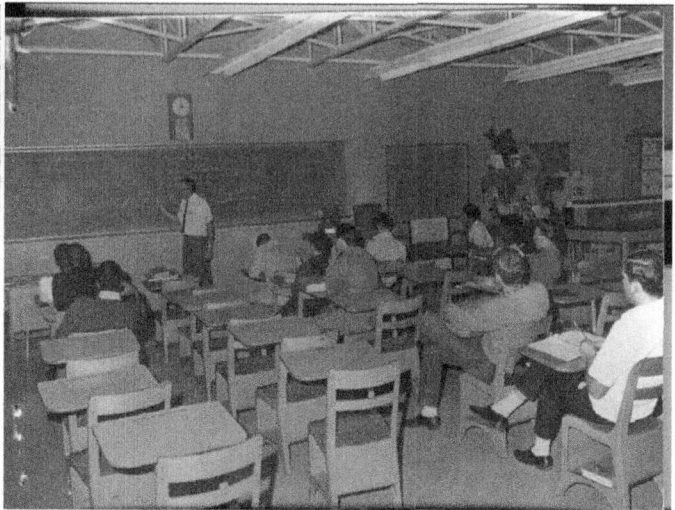

1966-67 Electronic Class-Cy-Fair Hi   "The Ogden Standard," of September 30, 1919   1966-67 Electronics class at Cy-Fair High at Cypress Fairbanks, Texas
(I'm 3ʳᵈ one back on the left)

the District competition taking 1st place where Emerson Plummer played a pivotal roll in the marching portion that help us secure that victory. I was glade I wasn't given that position of Drum Major in retrospect. For what he had to do had not been rehearsed, but his ability to think fast of an alternative, aided in securing that trophy. My senior year we moved back to Houston, Texas to a very small school named Carverdale Hi, the cobras. The kids there were very nice, being new in a small school made popularity very easy. An opportunity presented itself for black students to attend an all white high school in the district that offered college prep classes. Second time in my life I had an Anglo-Saxton call me *"Nigger."* It just rolled off their tongues like water off a duck's back. Of course they were much too cowardly to say it one on one, as there were always 15-20 of them versus just the three of us. The first time I was exposed to racism, however was in Corsicana, Texas. Uncle Billy and I had stopped by the service station on East 7ᵗʰ Avenue for a drink of water one hot summer day. There were two fountains in front of the local service station where we stopped for a drink. One had a sign above the fountain that read *"Colored Only,"* and the other read *Whites Only.* We approach the water fountain as Uncle Billy instructed me to wait until he finishes to get a drink. Well, curious me unfamiliar with the Jim Crow laws of Corsicana, saw a much cleaner bright shinning water fountain just waiting to cool my fat lips off with a fresh cool drink. I went for it and by the time that water hit my lips, there was a violent interruption before I could swallow. A large built white man from my point of view must to have been about 10 ft tall with overalls, was cursing me with words unknown to me before that day with some of which was *"Nigger."* He had grabbed me by the collar of my shirt and savagely slung me to the ground like a rag doll. I couldn't have been no more than 60 pounds, as Uncle Billy scooped me up and we ran across East 7th Avenue. After clearing the highway, Uncle Billy gave that white man the middle finger in protest to his actions. The events of that day were never discussed again and I never told my parents, fearing it would create a punishment for something I was surely guilty of. So, it was back to running and throwing rocks on that dusty road back to grand-mama's house with Sniff (*her dog*) running right alone side us barking as to alert everyone in the neighborhood it appeared of our arrival. As that incident manifested itself in my mind for years to come and it was years later I determined what I had done to cause the anger of that white man in overalls and boots, but was it necessary to violate my person by slinging

"The National Tribune," of July 4, 1889

me to the ground? The 1966-67 Electronics class at Cy-Fair Hi at Cypress Fairbanks, Texas *(a suburbia community located near Houston),* where the seating arrangements were not assigned. I never even knew their names and nor they ours. They (w*hite Students*) were all spread out when we first arrived but after our introduction, the picture was how it stayed for the entire year. I'm seated on the left with the other black students, the third one back. Never had a fight, though. The teacher, Mr. Sloan never made any attempt to force intermingling or incorporate altogether instructions. We later received individual instructions, separate from the white students. We were bused there in the morning and I returned to the predominate Black High School, Carverdale High in the afternoon. Ironic to that experience was the fact that the following year as a freshman at Prairie View A & M University and apart of the *"work study program,"* I was assigned to the Electronic Department. I, along with other upper-classmen were responsible for installing power supplies to the newly constructed electronics building. During that summer, to my surprise was Mr. Sloan seeking employment at the University. So consumed with his focused on his attempt to secure the job never recognized me, a former student of his. Mr. Foster, a black man, and the Head of Prairie View's Electronic Department, was so impressed with my knowledge of electronics during my interview process, prompted him to address me in determining the relationship of Mr. Sloan as it related to his black students. I don't know if what I said to him had a bases on whether or not he got the job but I never saw Mr. Sloan again.

I remember my first job at Wyatt's Cafeteria in Dallas, Texas. I was a dishwasher and busboy. I remember our manager spoke to us one day concerning eating our lunch on the dinning room floor verses eating out of sight in the heat and noise of the back where we washed the dishes. I was the first to except the challenge at the dismay and surprise of everyone who were black and dishwasher's who were fearful about the reactions of racist diners. My brother expressed my bravery in a different way that mirrored boldness. But still labeling me as *"crazy,"* like everyone else. The day I did it, I debated it and debated with my brother who still felt it would cause a riot-like atmosphere if I were to go through with it. The day came, still dressed in a smock, a clean one which I had changed for the purpose of going on the floor. I got a plate, went behind the line and dictated to the servers as to what my meal would contain. I walked passed the glass-port swinging door leading into dishwashing area with several blacks looking at my actions with much skepticism, as to whether or not I'd go through with it. A normal size restaurant with light dialog and the sounds of eating utensil's hitting the plate's hardware with uncoordinated cadence, typical of any eatery of sophisticated diners. Needless to say, once I broke pass that swinging door of dishwashers, the ire silence of shock as not to believe their eyes hit reality. I didn't dare look up or go - *"What ?"* to the constant eyes that were all on me. So I properly took my seat and bowed my head to bless my food which was in my opinion, *"the white flag indicator of peace"* which tend to take away the silence. Even before I could undo my napkin and take my first bite, much to my surprise, the silence was no more. Everyone went back to light dialog and forks hitting plates in that non-rhythmic fashion. I was elated but later, we were advised by management that my gesture caused some complaints

Devour Us Not

"The Wichita Daily Eagle," of August 1, 1897

which ended any followers into my initial daring stunt. But, after all, that was 1964, in Dallas, Texas! The summer of 1967, I attended Prairie View A&M University where I was in the band and as a Freshman, I was Section Leader first chair-first seat as I out performed all the upper classman, but there was no hating. PV's band, prior to our arrival was a military style, Khaki uniform wearing boring band. But our class changed the uniforms and I guess brought of the best in musicianship for us as a musical unit. I remain Section Leader from 1967-1969 in the Marching and Concert Band. During the summer of 1968, summer jobs were extremely difficult to obtain. My dad explained it as a matter of, *"hair."* He appeared to recent the long hair (*Afro-hair*) which was becoming for the first time, a black culture slowing evolving to our African roots. So my Dad, did express to me, I would either volunteer to cut my hair or he'd cut it for me. Several interviews turned out to be a bust in part, according to my dad's theory was the rebellious nature of my hair. Which was incidentally, despised by most whites fear of militant thugs that the hair suggested. More prudent to that theory was one Saturday during the summer of 1968, I went to a department store named *"Sakowitz,"* in downtown Houston, Texas to purchase a knit. I waited at the counter for about 30 minutes with one of their clothing items in my hand for purchase. I felt they wanted to humiliate me by the refusal of service. But I humiliate them to a certain extent by causing them to watch me to see what I'd do for thirty minutes. There was even a point when I whistled a popular tone as loud as I could to further my defiance which caused some other white customers to flee the store without a purchase fearing some altercation that was assured. But, the fall of 1968, after I was granted acceptance to enrollment into my sophomore year at PVU. My father somehow convinced the Dean of Men, then Leroy Marion, not to enroll me until I cut my hair. I was outraged because no other returnee were being asked to go against the, "styles of the day," and shave your head. I went to the barber shop three times with each time returning back to Dean Marion's office for his disapproval. Finally, the fourth time I was personally escorted by the Dean which left me with about an eighth of an inch of hair on my head as the Dean replied, *"Your Dad would be Proud."* After all my acts of rebellion, mostly against the white establishment, it was my Dad and the Dean who mostly invoked my anger at the world that day. I never got pass the anger toward them both.

April 4, 1968, 6:01pm, a date and time I'll never forget in my lifetime. I was a freshman, when the news hit the campus about the death of Martin Luther King, Jr. It immediately turned into a riot like almost every major city in America. We wanted to wreak havoc on every white person in view. So, among the sounds of screaming females and males alike, the words of *"They gon'a kill us all,"* windows being broken and one student, a bully football player, was even killed. A group of us headed for the main highway leading into the campus. A highway at that time normally full of commuters was but a few brave souls who then felt the wrath of our anger. As we threw rocks, bottles and sticks at every white-person-driven vehicle in sight. Then we headed for the restaurant right down the street from our campus that hosted an enormous sign in front for years that read, for,

"Evening Bulletin," of February 10, 1906

"*Whites Only.*" The display of anger directed at that eatery was more than just rage. For the years of disrespect with the audacity to open within walking distanced from a predominately historical black University was worth any punishment we'd receive for its total destruction. Needless to say, after that night, that restaurant never reopened again as we then headed back to the chaos on campus that night. For the remainder of that semester, all classes regardless of subject, focused on, where do we go from here? I'd be remised not to mention two of the most sincere and bravest act of courage I'd ever witnessed during my lifetime.

Bobby Kennedy, without an entourage, walked among a crowd in Indianapolis and broke the news of MLK's demise. Before he spoke, every major city in America was in flames, all but Indianapolis. Racial derogatory rhetoric being tossed around that should have swirled the air of hate never reached the lips of the hundreds who heard his words. When he spoke on the back of that flatbed of all the hundreds of blacks surrounding him, not a word was spoken as the mere appearance of presence drew an ire silence. No other white man in America on that day could have spoken to a crowd of blacks and deliver those words of sorrow. The events of that weekend and the hopes of a dreamer like MLK died in all of us as a people that 4th day of April, 1968. And to think it couldn't get any worse, Bobby was gone two months later, victimized by an assassin's bullet. The Kennedy and the King families will be forever beloved by us as a people and a grateful nation for all they gave us in their short lives. Thanks to both families for sharing them with our nation in its time of need. Secondly, fast forward several generations, 2008, John McCain and the *"No ma'am,"* comment. John, a 2008 Republican Nominee for the Presidency of the United States during a campaign stop, a white woman using a microphone to voice her opinion stated she couldn't trust Barack Obama because he was an Arab. John McCain going against his support base stated, *"No ma'am, no ma'am, he's a decent family man and citizen that I just happen to have disagreements with on fundamental issues, and that's what this campaign is all about."* Courage like this in the face of racial bigotry and contrary to the tolerance of the norm, brave men and women everyday face these challenges with defiance for the betterment of America. This is who we are as Americans and the essential part of what makes us great as a people, as a nation.

I was so disappointed in January 1970 when I received my *"Draft Notice,"* (pictured above). This was something I hadn't planned for, but in retrospect, it was probably the most important and best move of my life. But being drafted in a time when I was not registered to vote was a bit disconcerting. And not to mention the I withdrew from my classes in December of 1969 and received a draft notice in January 1970 was suspect at best. The misplacement, lost or stolen act of my student loan check plagued me for years. Rumors were being spread that if Dean Marion didn't like you, you were on your way to Viet Nam. So I'm in my junior year and

Devour Us Not

Pastimes in Georgia

Juana "Melinda," De Leon Altar Powers

suddenly I have to withdraw from all my classes or risk facing failures in all, and not to mention my student deferment in jeopardy. Unbeknownst to me was, November, 1969 the draft board was reinstated by President Nixon for the Viet Nam war for all males born between January 1, 1944 and December 31, 1950. This included me being born in 1949, but by-passed my brother who was born in 1947. *"Go figure."* The lottery system in an effort of supposed fairness, 360 individual days that included February 29 were placed in individual capsules and placed in a jar to be drawn to show a males birth date between the targeted years 1944-1950. So December 1, 1969, the first number drawn was September 14th which was assigned a draft number of 1. As a result of the first draft notice, all men with draft numbers from 1-195 were drafted. Needless to say my draft number was 142, my brother's draft number was 281. So, I reported to the selection board July 22, 1970 ready for induction, but totally in defiance of this decision. Not wanting to go in the Army, like my father, I chose the United States Marine Corps, just because of the uniforms. November 17, 1970, or thereabouts, as my mother drove me to the airport to catch a flight to MCRD, San Diego, California, she was in tears as Michael Jackson sang, *"I'll be there"* on the radio. My father had mentioned to me that I wouldn't last longer than a snowball in an oven in the Marine Corps. Mainly because I was a 6 ft 2 in. in height and boosting a 140 pound of mostly bones. But the comment hit me like a ton of bricks, but that became my silent motivation. As I used that negative energy to

Phil & Melinda Powers Marine Corps Ball 1973

excel. As a recruit I was the Platoon Gideon, and because of the War in Viet Nam, most of my platoon received infantry MOS (*Military Occupational Specialty*). I finished first in my class as a machine gunner and was meritoriously promoted to Lance Corporal (E-3), one month after graduating from boot camp. We were then all assigned to Staging Battalion, when President Nixon gave the orders not to send any more troops from stateside to Viet Nam. April, 1971, I was then transferred to Camp Lejeune, North Carolina where every major unit had an intramural football and basketball team. But upon my arrival, unlike the college atmosphere that a sports team can provide, there were so many racial issues on this base. We were told there was a dark-green Marine (*dark-green and light-green Marines was a term the Marine Corps used during the 1960's and 70's to decrease the amount of civilian racial unrest from tainting the ranks of the Corps*) and two light-green Marines that were hung there. This was 1971 in the sticks of North Carolina. There I tried to make the best of a situation as I became the 2nd Battalion 6th Marines, Golf Company Gideon Bearer and was then to sent to NCO School, Montford Point, North Carolina. There I finished first in my class and was recommended the NCO Sword and meritoriously promoted to Corporal (E-4) October 1971, eleven months after finishing boot camp. Unbeknownst to me at the time, that some 28 years prior to my arrival, the first dark-green Marines ever in 1942 were stationed there as their boot camp. The Marine Corps was the last branch of the service to integrate its forces and the first African-Americans in the Marine Corps boot camp was in Montford Point, North Carolina. No one ever mentioned to us that we were sleeping in the same barracks and ate in the same mess hall of this very historical hollowed ground. During my Camp Lejeune duty assignment, the unit traveled to Guantanamo Bay, Cuba, San Juan, Puerto Rico and Panama. I was then transferred and assigned to Marine Barracks, Republic of the Philippines. This would turn out to be a challenge of racial proportion. As one of the few times, racism would enter my Marine Corps career. There were two SSgt. who were ex-DI's and obviously southern born by

"The San Francisco Call," of September 23, 1905

the tone of their southern draw had a dislike for me. It had been rumored, they didn't want a black SOG *(Sergeant of the Guard)*, or perhaps they just didn't want me as an SOG. I was eligible for Sergeant that year, so when the time came to receive my promotion, all eligible candidates were promoted except me. When I went to inquire, I was told I wasn't eligible. I had been looking forward to that promotion, so I did some impartial investigation and discovered the truth. I was outraged, so being the fighter I was wrote my biggest supporter, my Mom. She advised my Congresswoman who was none other than **Senator Barbara Jordan**. There is about 15 hours time difference between times in the Philippines and Houston, Texas. All was a buzz in the Administration Office one day when I was called to the Office to explain that there was a Congressional Inquiry about my promotion and did I initiate it. I presented them with a letter I had received sighting my ineligibility for that promotion. I had been very specific in explaining all the Marine Corps regulations on Sergeant promotions which clearly depicted an over sight, purposely or not. There was no argument. An acknowledgement letter of apology to me and my Congresswomen was issued within days. And I was promoted before weeks end. In addition to receiving my promotion within days, I also received orders, transferring me away from the Barracks. An obvious retaliation gesture to still not wanting me to be a SOG. But I stood my ground and was forever grateful to my Mom and Congresswoman Barbara Jordan. I felt really bad for

1973- Melinda's Bridal Party that included her sister on the left.

not personally acknowledging her role in securing my promotion. Instead I told my mother to convey my gratitude to Senator Jordan. That promotion stayed on my mind my entire career. So when I retired in 1990, I finally sent a letter to her office, only to receive an acknowledgement letter and word she would not be able to attend. I'll never ever forget her efforts and angered at myself for missing the opportunity to thank her personally. But the Marine Barracks in the Philippines

D. I. SCHOOL STAFF   CLASS 2 – 7T
(L/R):GYSGT.R.O.THOMAS,GYSGT.C.D.PALMER,GYSGT.R.C.SHELLUM,MAJOR E.M.ST.CLAIR,
MSGT.L.M.PADILLA, GYSGT.J.R.EDWARDS, GYSGT.H.G.OVERSTREET, CPL.S.M.HERNANDEZ
GRADUATED 22 OCTOBER 1976

1976 - Drill Instructor School: *GySgt. Harold G. Overstreet pictured on the right 3rd from the DI sign was my Instructor Adviser, he later became the, 12th "SgtMaj. Of The Marine Corps." (SgtMaj. Of the Marine Corps established in 1957 & is the highest enlisted rank in the Marine Corps) (I'm on the top row, seventh DI from the left).*

"The Colored American," of September 10, 1904

had other memorable moments for me as it was there I met the love of my life, Juana *"Melinda"* De Leon Altar. She had to have been the most beautiful female, outside of my Moms, of course, I had ever seen and she saw an interest in me. Several Marines periodically, to include myself would visit Manila. Manila at the time was its capital and a large metropolitan modern city in the Philippines. We'd go to Manila every other weekend to get away from the hustle and bustle of Alongapo City which was about eight hours by bus. Makati Rizal Park was a favorite girl watching spot for us Marines and it was there I first noticed her. I was completely smitten by her beauty and that long dark-brown shining hair in length that reached her waist. That hair blew away from her face with every breath of strong wind as she'd quickly place it back with just a finger. She spoke very little English which was fine by me because I didn't speak very much English also. She felt good being with me and I with her. A year later we were married in Olongapo City. We have four children, **Arnold, Jr., Marricarr Kita, Armando Kyron** and **Carlito La Phonn**. December 15, 1973, had to have been the happiest day of my life, the day I got married to my Soul-Mate and a *"Trophy Wife."* The Mayor's wife of Olongapo City, R.P. attended our wedding along with her entourage to help us have a grand festival. We had several hired hands stayed up a couple of nights roasting two pigs below ground using hot coals and banana leaves. An odd thing happened after the cake was cut on the wedding day. We had a three tiered layered cake and at the top of the cake was a Bride and Groom toy. For no apparent reason, the Groom fell from the cake to the hard wooden floor below. Filipino's are very superstitious about weddings as all the guest gasp and embraced my wife and told her that tragedy would hit our marriage and she'd be a widow very soon. In hindsight, some of that was true, but not the way they envisioned it. But unlike death, racism would hit us first, as I tried to convey that sentiment to a limited racially exposed foreign national who had no clue. In Santa Ana, California, our first city in America after our foreign wedding, racism hit us. I was stationed at El Toro, with no car, no credit and a new wife. Lucky for me, the *"Marine Corps statement, "A Band of Brothers,"* concept really lived up to its billing. Until I bought a car, we had no other possessions besides clothing. So the only furniture we had was the light-weight rattan furniture we had purchased in the Philippines. So one Sunday afternoon, Melinda and I went window furniture shopping near Greenleaf Avenue apartments where we resided. There was no Sunday shopping in California that year, so viewing a couch in the window of that furniture store was more than we could bear as our desires swelled. The following Monday, I alone went into the store, explained to the sales clerk, that I was an American Service member, stationed at the nearby base of El Toro. The clerk was very cordial in explaining to me after the application was completed, to get the couch we so admired the day before, that there was a problem with my application. As he explained to me using words he assumed I didn't understand, to affect that I had *"no credit."* Having no credit was as bad as having *"bad credit,"* the two were not mutually exclusive; application denied. As I traveled back home and explained to my wife, the disappointment within those big brown eyes of hers broke my heart. In the interim and totally unbeknownst to me at the time, Melinda had befriended some white female civilians who had purchased furniture from that same company with bad credit. A couple of weeks had passed when one day I arrived home and the very couch that was so picturesque in that window was now in my living room. At the moment I enter the apartment, Melinda broke down into this hysterical cry. I was confused until Melinda sat me down and explained everything. Bear in mind, my wife was a foreign national with a green card, spoke very little English, had no job and was married to a Serviceman. During our pre-marital counseling, the word *"racism,"* being we were a bi-racial couple, came up quite frequently for which Melinda never comprehended. At the advice of the

1978- SDI GySgt Powers & PFC Conaway Graduation Day

Sgt. Sharon D. Paris

"Last Platoon" Sr Drill Instructor (SDI) GySgt A. Powers, GySgt. E.R. Dettloff, SSgt. G.C. Lutz Plt. 1085 graduated December 18, 1981

white female civilians, who encouraged Melinda to try again, but allow them to use their flirtatious demeanor of persuasion. The same sales clerk who lectured me on having no credit excepted my wife's application for approval bearing no obstacles. Melinda, had no experience in writing English, had the two white females help her with the application. They delivered the couch before the paperwork was signed. After Melinda explained the story to me the pride I had when we went back into that store as a newlywed couple the following day to sign the paperwork was my perfect revenge. The same sales clerk never even looked up at me after the initial mouth dropping observation was discovered. He never even shook my hand at the end of the transaction, but made a conscientious effort to extend his hand to my wife only. Melinda never understood that incident of racism or the degrading racial climate we faced our entire marriage as a bi-racial couple with bi-racial children.

The summer of 1976, I received orders to San Diego to be a Marine Drill Instructor, my proudest moment as a Marine. I came there as a buck Sergeant and left two years later being promoted, meritoriously to Gunnery Sergeant with 7 years of Service. I was on top of the world and then the saddest day of my life hit. While stationed in Kaneohe Bay, Hawaii, was the day I lost my beloved; my wife with an aneurysm on October 22, 1984, a day before Junior's 10th birthday. It took 15 days for me to persuade the Filipino government that my

1981 - MCRD - SDI Arnold P. Powers, Plt 1085

sole purpose was to bury my wife in her homeland. I lost myself for years in me. And then there was the long flight to the Philippines on the same plane that carried my wife's body also carried me with my four kids all under the age of 11. Not understanding what had just happened, the kids knew nothing of death. I received a humanitarian transfer to the Naval Air Station, Dallas, Texas, MAG-41. It was there I became involved with a WM *(Woman Marine)* named Sgt. Sharon Paris, and we have

1982-1st.Lt.S.M. Hickey, GySgt. G.W. Como, SSgt. J. Flores, GySgt. A.P. Powers, SSgt. Gloniak, GySgt. R. Rillo, 1st Lt. R.M. Lottie

two children, **Courtney Breon** and **Drameagon D'Eric**. Then I received orders to Iwakuni, Japan, unaccompanied. Reluctantly, I wrote letters to Congressman **Mickey Leland**, **Dick Armey** and **Lloyd Benson** to no avail. After receiving order to Iwakuni with about 2 years before retirement, thank God for my Mother who had to sacrifice a lot by selling her home in Houston and move to Arlington and assumed parental guidance over the kids, after all the Congressional Inquiries failed. The debt of my already pain was aggravated by the USMC's position of forced orders to comply with. We *(My Mother and I)* had all of one week together before she assumed my parental position and I was on a flight to Iwakuni, Japan for a year. While doing an unaccompanied tour in Iwakuni, Japan, I had an opportunity to visit Hiroshima and also visit my wife's grave in the Philippines where my longtime friend, Jerome Brown, took me there. It was there I left part of my sorrow, with her silent approval of letting go and moving on. I finished up my career in the Marine Corps at NAS Dallas in 1990, as a Master Sergeant *(E-8 promoted in 1986)* and having trained about three thousand recruits during my Marine Corps tenure. But my last act of defiance was with my Commanding Officer, Col. Augusta Fetch, III, before I retired. I challenged his *(Col. Fitch)* authority by going to Dick Armey's office for assistance after he refused my recommendation for a Navy Commendation Medal. But his *(Dick Armey)* mediocre efforts was lackluster at best as he offered no challenge to the Marine Corps explanation of denial. But here is how the story went. I was eligible for a Navy Commendation Medal, which most Commanding Officers were down grading. Major Robert S. *"All Meat,"* Franks was my OIC *(Officer in Charge)* and recommended me for the medal. But he forewarned me of Col. Fitch's dislike for me and felt it would be a waste of time to submit. After his

"The Washington Times," of February 13, 1919   *IR-07, Arnold P. Powers, IRS Dallas, TX 1990 - 2008*   *1986 - Arnold P. Powers & Uncle Cle*

1988 - 1989   MALS-12 Iwakuni, Japan F-18 Squadron

comments, I questioned his reasoning in determining Col. Fitch's attitude. He stated because every time my name would be mentioned in an Officer's meeting, without words to describe his disgust of me, would express his anguish in facial expressions. I unknowingly rejected that idea that he (*Col. Fitch*) would not place his personal opinions of me over his professional judgment. How naive and wrong was I to assume an officer of the Marine Corps, a graduate of the University of Mississippi, would be so shallow. In hindsight, I also recall his comments to me at the 1987 Marine Corps Ball that should have been a wake up call (*The Marine Corps Ball, is an annual Ball similar to a Prom, that is use to commemorate the birth of the Corps every November 10th or thereabouts. The Marine Corps Birthday was Nov 10, 1776, a branch of the military which did not include African-American Marines among its units until 1942*). While dancing with a white WM, he said to me, *"Don't get cocky, Gunny."* At that instant, the WM for whom I was engaged in dance, terminated the dance and just walked away, with no explanation, as if some kind'a code had been given her from a disapproving parent. So it was no surprise in hindsight when my name was twice submitted for my accomplishments as the Burial NCOIC (*Non-Commissioned Officer In Charge*) and other duties for MAG-41, that he would reject as unworthy for

submission. I was so adamant about my belief that his actions were racially motivated and not professionally guided; that I convinced Major *"All Meat"* Franks to conduct a somewhat of a sting ops with me. He reluctantly agreed, based on principal and the Colonel's narcissistic attitude. Narcissistic, because he'd constantly make slight of the Helicopter Pilots (*Major Franks was a Helicopter pilot*) because he (*Col. Fitch*) was a fixed wing, F-4 pilot. And supposedly the Naval flight school selects its Helicopter and fixed wing pilots based on their smarts in flight school training. We conveniently waited a month, and resubmitted the same information but used GySgt. Marcum, a white Marines' name instead of my name, because he headed the position a year before I assumed it. Without even verifying the dates, which would have reveled, GySgt. Marcum's duties elsewhere, Col. Fitch signed off on the medal and in formation, GySgt. Marcum received the medal for my efforts, only because the CO could not get passed his racial hatred of me. GySgt. Marcum came

1984-May HAMS-24 Inspector Generals Drill Team, Plt Cmdr. 1st Lt W.H. Orawczyk (pictured Left), Plt Sgt.'s GySgt A. Powers & Ssgt. T.A. Scott (pictured right). **"BEST IN THE BRIGADE,"** *Kaneohe Bay, Hawaii*

up to me afterwards and said, *"Now, what did I do to deserve this medal?"* I was so angered until I just walked away. After that, I went back to Major Franks who advised me not to expose him (*Col. Fitch*) until I had left the Marine Corps for retirement. And that he would collaborate any rendition of the truth of what happened and his involvement. After I retired in 1990, I couldn't get to Dick Armey's office in Arlington, Texas fast enough, to file a Congressional Inquiry to the Military Awards Board. Because of the *"Officer and a Gentlemen"* mystic bestowed upon all Marine Officers, even though I explicitly explained the sting effort, they *(the board)* went

Marine Corps Recruit Depot
San Diego, California

March 9, 1977
"L" Co. Plt. 3140

MCRD- San Diego, California-Third Recruit Training Battalion Commander, LtCol. R.J. Modrzejewski "MEDAL OF HONOR," recipient (Third from Top left), SSgt. A. P. Powers located last DI on the right, top row.

straight to Col. Fitch, who had also retired by that time and his explanation was that the act did not warrant a medal, sticking to his original ball-face lie. That's when Dick Armey made no attempt to challenge the decision of the Awards Board, only because they went to Col. Fitch, *"Case Closed."* But the day after my 41st birthday, 1990, I began working for the Internal Revenue Service where I retired after 18 years as of January 1, 2009. I

"The Day Book," of June 4, 1914

retired from the IRS as an IR-07 (*Frontline Manager*). I'm a Christian and a member of the Concord Baptist Church of Dallas, Texas, Pastor Bryan L. Carter, Sr. Pastor. As I retired among the waters of Cedar Hill, Texas, today I have five living children, Arnold, Jr., Marricarr, Carlito, Courtney and Drameagon and one deceased child Armando Kyron. I have 10 Grand-children, Deneisha, Kelan, Joshua, Naudia, Deja, Cheridan, Armani, Carlito II, Kyi'-Marri' and Leila. If I had to surmise my life, I'll describe it as *"having character,"* for the lack of character in a man's life is like a letter without a stamp. That letter will never reach its destination or its intended purpose without it.

Favorites: *I love to travel, having visited such places as: Beaulieu Sur Mer, Monte Carlo & Nice, **Monaco**, Paris, **France**, Brac, **Cayman Island**, Osaka, Hiroshima, Kobe & Iwakuni, **Japan**, **Panama**, San Juan (Ole & New), **Puerto Rico**, Guantanamo Bay, **Cuba**, Kailua, Kaneohe Bay, **Hawaii**, Seoul, Inchon and Osan **Korea**, Olongapo & Manila, **Republic of the Philippines** and Naha, **Okinawa**.*

Authors: ***Walter Mosley** (Blonde Faith), **Randall Robinson** (The Debt), **Elliott Jaspin** (Buried in the Bitter Waters), **Angela Y Davis** (If They Come In The Morning), **Baz Dreisinger** (Near Black), **Ishmael Reed** (Mumbo Jumbo), **Maya Angelou** (I Shall Not Be Moved), **Sidney Sheldon** (The Other Side of Midnight), **Henry Louis Gates, Jr.** (Life Upon These Shores), **Carla Kaplan** (Miss Anne in Harlem), **Ann Coulter** (Slander), **Randall Kennedy** (For Discrimination) & **Kareem Abdul-Jabbar** (Black Profiles In Courage).*

Musical Groups: *Earth, Wind & Fire, The Rippingtons, Nelson Rangel, Isaac Hayes, Barry White, Michael Jackson, Les Nubians, The Stylistics, The Temptations, George Duke & The Four Tops.*

Movies: *It's a Wonderful Life, The Wiz, An Officer and a Gentleman, Glory, Stars Wars, Malcolm X, Rosewood, Amistad, School Daze, Do the Right Thing, Pearl Harbor, The Cotton Club, The Count of Monte Cristo, Back to the Future, Schindler's List and Love in The Time of Cholera.*

Below is a cherished letter my Commanding Officer in Keneohe Bay, Hawaii, 1984, LtCol. Mike Sheedy, wrote to my son, Arnold, Jr., on his 10th Birthday, the day after his mother, my wife, had passed. Still stained with tear drops from a 10 year old child faced with shouldering the burden of being a motherless-child ever more. And such is life and balance according to God's mathematical plan which doesn't allow me or any other mortal human-beings to understand or question.

My Photo Gallery

1972 USO Show with Bob Hope, Philippines

Cpl Arnold P Powers Gideon Bearer
Golf Co. 2/6 Camp Lejeune, NC 1971

SSgt Arnold P Powers
MCRD San Diego, CA 1976

"B" Company COD Excellence - 821025
SSgt J. Flores (84), GySgt A. Powers,
Sgt C.S. Hoffman (82.8)

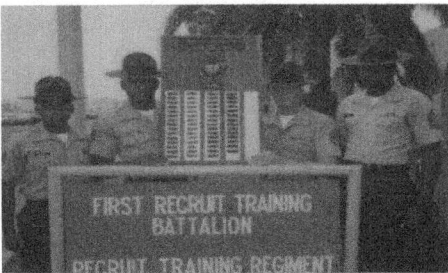

First Recruit Training Bn
MCRD San Diego, CA 1981

GySgt. Arnold P Powers (Far right)– Platoon Commander
Veterans Day Parade, Dallas, TX – 1986

Devour Us Not

My Photo Gallery II

1989-1990- MAG-41 NAS Dallas, TX (F-4 & CH-53) -Career Planner
CO. Col. Dewey-Among other Officer is LtCol. Jerry E. Patterson- Commissioner of the
General Land Office of Texas.

1973 -Marine Barracks Philippines -Barracks Gideon Bearer
picture on far left, leading the Platoon, Olongapo City, Philippines.

1981- B Co. MCRD San Diego, 1ˢᵗ Bn. with USMC Mascot "Chesty" who was Chocked to
death by an SDI who lost his Final Drill Competition.

1977-"Golden Boot" Award SSgt Powers-Sgt
Mills "Best Parade Platoon on the Depot"

1983 - 1ˢᵗ Battalion "B" Co. 1ˢᵗ Lt Lottie, Series Cmdr, 1ˢᵗ Lt Howard
Asst Series Cmdr, Chief Drill Instructor GySgt. Powers

1978- Platoon 3009, MCRD, Senior Drill Instructor SSgt. Powers,
DI SSgt. Bright, DI Sgt. Norrell

My Photo Gallery III

1977- SSgt Means III, Pvt Wiles, SSgt Powers & Sgt Fernando 1978- SDI SSgt Powers, SSgt Woodruff, Pvt Miller, Sgt Norrell & Cpl Vukelic

1981 - Drill Instructor School: *Class 1-82 Director: Maj. Walsh, Asst Dir: Capt. Clubine, CDI MGySgt. Dower (Dower trained Lou Gossett, Jr. for "An Officer and A Gentleman." The movie for which he won an Oscar for Best Supporting Actor as GySgt. Emil Foley) (I am on the second row, left hand side, second from the end)*

Devour Us Not

My Photo Gallery IV

1972 - "The Jungle" in Olongapo City, Republic of the Philippines

1969 - Pre-Military Draft - Houston, Texas

1972 - 1974 Marine Barack - Subic Bay, Philippines In Greens Utilities and Duty Belt

1972 - 1974 Marine Barack, Subic Bay, Philippines

1971 - 1972 - Camp Lejeune, North Carolina 2/6 Golf Co L/Cpl Powers

1971 - 1972 - Aboard a Naval Ship off the shores of Guantanamo Bay, Cuba

My Photo Gallery V

Cpl. Arnold P. Powers Camp Lejeune, N.C., 1971

1977 MCRD SSgt Woodruff, SSgt Powers, SSgt Frias & Sgt Norrell

L/Cpl Arnold P Powers, Camp Lejeune, NC 1971

Cpl Arnold P Powers, 1971, Camp Lejeune, NC

Cpl Arnold P Powers, Mac Base, Okinawa

1980 - Change of Command, El Toro, CA. for
Brigidier General Richard M. Cooke and Major General John V. Cox

1957 - 3917 Lovingood Dr. Dallas, TX / Highland Hills
The Powers Family First Dallas Home where we lived until 1966.

1988 - Career Planner for MAG-41, NAS Dallas

"The San Francisco Call," of March 10, 1912 , "The Sun," of Oct 13, 1906, "The Saint Paul Globe," of May 17, 1903, "Dayton Daily Empire." of August 10, 1860, "The Times Dispatch," of November 22, 1904, "The Corpus Christi Caller," of June 9, 1921, "The Morning Examiner," of March 27, 1910

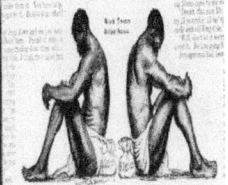

The St. Louis Republic., March 31, 1903, The St. Louis Republic., June 23, 1903, The Tacoma times., October 30, 1909 , The San Francisco call., March 13, 1898 , "The San Francisco Call," of November 21, 1897, Omaha daily bee., November 21, 1909, "The Wichita Daily Eagle," of August 01, 1897, The San Francisco call., July 2, 1905, "New-York Tribune," of July 31, 1910

Devour Us Not

"The Appeal,," of Aug 31, 1901 "The Appeal," of Aug 31, 1901 , "Omaha Daily Bee," of Sep 8, 1897, "Los Angeles Herald," of Feb 19, 1905, "The Washington Times," of Jun 20, 1910, "Evening Public Ledger," of Sep 1, 1915 , "Perrysburg Journal.," of Feb 20, 1897 , "The San Francisco Call," of Jul 10, 1898, "The National Tribune," of Feb 26, 1903 , "Evening Public Ledger, of Sep 2, 1915, "The Bemidji Daily Pioneer," of April 25, 1917, Perrysburg Journal," of Sep 7, 1895

C_{hapter} IV

INDEX

Index

A

Ackley, Letha, 152
Adams, Charles Francis, 160
Adams, John from Massachusetts, 173
Adams Run, 212
Adelina, Italian Opera Singer, 111
African Baptist Church on Belknap, 158
African Communities (Imperial) League, 193
A Key to Uncle Tom's Cabin, 210
Alabama, Barbour County, Eufaula, 206
Alabama, Dothan, 110
Alabama, Greensboro, 194
Alabama, Greenville, 110
Alabama, Huntsville, 108
Alabama, Macon County Black Belt District, 67
Alabama, Montgomery, 129, 145
Alabama, Pine Level, 130
Alabama, Selma, 170
Alabama, Tuskegee, 69, 130
Alcorn, James L. 43
Alford, James, 39
Alec, Clifford, 177
Alexander, Arthur, 119
Alexander, Lewis, 178, 179
Alexander, Joseph, 178
Ali, Muhammad, 161
Allen, Frank, 39
Allen, Judge, 49
Allen, Richard, Rev., 185
Allen, William, 17
Allman, Hazel, 59
Almarolis, Alexander, 178, 179, 180, 181
Almarolia, Lotta C., 179
Almarolia, Mary Alexander (Shiner), 177, 179, 180, 181
Alston, J.D. Dr., 146
Altgeld, Governor, 102
Alvord, William, 76
American Anti-Slavery Society, 158
American Bar Association, 162
Ames, Governor Adelbert, 41, 132
Amherst College of Amherst, Massachusetts, 161
Amos, General James, 40
Anderson, County, 39
Anderson, Hans Christian, 75
Anderson, Jeremiah, 76
Anderson, Osborn P. 76

Anderson, W.G., 150
Andrews, W.H. Captain, 133
Andrews, John A., Governor of Massachusetts, 72, 114, 167
Anthony, Susan B., 155, 217
Antioch College Model School, 120
Anti-Lynching League from Boston, 210
A Peep Into Uncle Tom's Cabin for Children, 210
Aranoff, Sol, 117
Arlington Heights, 58
Arkansas, Elaine, 122
Arkansas, Helena, 40, 41
Arkansas, Hoop Spur, 122
Arkansas, Little Rock, 40
Arkansas, Phillips County, 122
Arkansas, Stamps, 109
Arthur, Chester, President, 36
Ashantee, 74
Ashe, Julia, 56
Atkinson, Honorable William Yates, 92
Atlanta, GA., Theol, 8
Augusta Institute, 115
Avery Chapel at Memphis, 116
Ayers, Louisa, 120

B

Bacon, Benjamin C., 158
Bailey, Dr., 159
Baker, Edward Dickinson, 160
Baker, Frazier B, 31, 202, 210
Baker, George, 38
Bampfield, Samuel J., 213
Banks, Alf, Jr., 123
Bannister, Christiana Carteaux, 114
Bannister, Edward M., 113, 114
Barksdale, Ann, 47
Barksdale, W.D., 69
Bartlett, Ezekiel Deacon, 156
Bartlett, S.C., Rev., 139
Barnes, Tom, 38
Barnett, Audrey V., 35
Barnett, Albert G., 35
Barnett, Alfreda, 34
Barnett, Alfreda H., 35
Barnett, Beatrice J., 35

Barnett, Charles Aked, 34, 35
Barnett, Ferdinand L., 34, 35
Barnett, Florence B., 35
Barnett, Herman Kohlsaat, 34, 35
Barnett, Hulette E., 35
Barnett, Hulette M., 35
Barnett, Jr., Ida B. Wells, 34, 35, 129
Barnett, Jr., Attorney F. L. ,10, 35
Barnett-Wells, Ida B., 10, 25, 32, 33, 34, 35, 201, 202, 203
Barrett, John, 59
Barringer, Rufus C., 188
Bates, Clara, 214
Bates, Lewis, 213, 214
Baumfree, Isabella, 58
Baxter, Samuel Sheriff, 145
Baylor Hospital Dallas, Texas, 177
Bean, John, 145
Bedell, Grace, 27
Beecher, Rev., Dr. Lyman and Roxana Foote, 209
Beecher, Rev. Henry Ward, 215, 216
Beechwood Cemetery, New York, 126
Before Day Club, 50
Bell, Daniel, 108
Bell, D.F. Mr.& Mrs., 91
Bell, Essie, 108
Bell, John, 177
Bell, Sheriff, 141
Bennett, Sheriff, 47
Benson, George of Rhode Island, 158
Benson, Helen Eliza, 158
Berry, Samuel, 119
Berry, Thomas, 59
Bertschey, 30
Besler, Sheriff, 141
Bethune-Cookman University, 191
Bethune, Mary McLeod, 191
Biestline, Dick, 24
Bigby, John, 95
Big Sisters Society Organization, 54
Bingham, Henry, 95
Bingham, Theodore A., Colonel, 165
Bird, Point Missouri, 19
Birney's, James G. Press in Cincinnati, 158
Bischoff, J.W. Professor, 136
Bishop Taylor of Africa, 119
Bishop Thoburn of India, 119
Black Code, 174
Black Cotton Mill, 187
Black, Mr. Henry, 60
Black, Mrs. Henry, 60
Black Patti, 111
Black-snaking, 10
Blatch, Stanton of New York, 154
Bliss Electrical College, 179

Blood, Col. James H., 216
Blow, Peter, 61
Blow, Taylor, 62
Blue, Tom, 27
Board of Children's Guardians, 206
Bonner, District Attorney, 117
Boone, Alma, Mrs., 56
Booth, John Wilkes, 78
Boston, Anna, 47
Boston Art Club, 113
Boston Joan of Arc, 210
Bostwick. Anne, 47
Bowdoin College, 181, 209
Bowman, Christopher C., 170
Bowman, Hattie, 110
Bowen, Miss Cornelia, 185
Bramlette, Judge William, 42
Bradford, Sarah H., 72
Braithwaite, William Stanley, Poet, 204
Branch, John, 30
Brantley, James, 42, 43
Bratton, 40
Bray, Charley, 20
Breedlove, Alexander, 97
Breedlove, James, 97
Breedlove, Jr., Owen, 97
Breedlove, Louvenia, 97
Breedlove, Minerva, 97
Breedlove, Owen, 97
Breedlove, Sarah, 97
Breedlove, Solomon, 97
Bremer, Fredrika, 75
Brewer, Justice David J., 127, 129
Brents, Judge, 152
Brierfield Plantation House, 137
Bringhurst, Robert P. 102
Broad Ax, 5
Brookland White School, 172
Brooks, Allan, 117
Brough, Governor, 40
Brown, Amelia, 79
Brown, Annie, 79
Brown, Austin, 79
Brown, Charles, 79
Brown, Ed, 39, 95
Brown, Ernest, 38
Brown, Frederick, 76
Brown, Halle Quinn, Miss, 199, 200
Brown, Isham, 95
Brown, Jason, 76
Brown, John, 63, 74, 75, 77
Brown, Judge, 105
Brown, Justice Henry B., 127, 129
Brown, J. W., 117

Blood, Gertrude, 216
Brown, Lee, 58, 59
Brown, Ellen, 79
Brown, Ellen II, 79
Brown, Mrs. Celestine, 131
Brown, Oasawatomie, 76
Brown, Oliver, 76, 79
Brown, Owen, 76
Brown, Peter, 79
Brown, Ruth, 76
Brown, Salmon, 79
Brown, Sarah, 79
Brown, Sterling M. Trustee Rev., 136
Brown v. Board of Education, 127
Brown, Watson, 76, 79
Brown, Will, 9, 47
Brownlee, J.N., 88
Bruce, Blanche Kelso, 115
Bruce, Mrs. Blanche K., 68, 88
Bruce, Polly, 115
Bruce, Roscoe Conkling, ,68, 88, 115
Bruce Jr., Roscoe Conkling, 88
Bryant, William Collen, 225
Buckalow Plantation, 110
Buffum, Arnold, 158
Bulloch, Martha "Mittle", 217
Bull Run, First, 182
Bulls, Chicago, 55
Bunting, Justice of the Peace, 37, 38
Burke, Charles C. Saloon, 20
Burke, J.H., 195
Burleigh, Harry T., Composer, 204
Burns, Allen Deputy Sheriff, 110
Burmeister, Richard, Professor, 136
Burt, Armistead, 71
Burt, Sheriff, 69, 71
Burroughs, Nannie Helen Miss, 196, 197
Bush 41, President George, 55
Bush, Mrs., 55
Butchart, Sheriff W.W. "Ole W.W.", 130, 131
Butler, Peter, 38
Butterfield, Herman, a NY Lawyer, 210
Buvens, Henry J. 117
Buvens, Mary Ethel, 117
Byrd, Sergeant, S. T., 38

C

Caldwell, Negro Senator of Mississippi, 133
Calhoun, Jacob, 125
California, Alturas, 118
California, Cape Mendocino, 79
California, Lookout, 117
California, Modoc County, 117, 118
California, Rohnerville, 78

Claflin, Reuben Buckman, 216
Claflin, Tennessee, 215
Clark, Addie R., Mrs., 208
Calloway, Thomas J., 167
Campbell, Kenneth, 177
Canaan and Canaanites, 172
Canadian River Bridge, 45
Candler, Allen D. Governor of Georgia, 92, 93
Cann, McKinney, 69, 70, 71
Can the Immortality of the Soul Be Proved From Its Light of Nature?, 209
Cameron, Lucille, 151, 153
Campbell, Lord Colin, son of the Duke of Argyl, 216
Capital Life Insurance Company, 198
Cappage, 52
Captain Jinks of the Horse Marines, 111
Cardwell, A.P. 59
Carney, William Harvey Sergeant, 168
Cannon Manufacturing Company, 189
Carolina, South, 44
Carolyle, The of London, England, 75
Carpenter, Constable, 117
Carpenter, George A., Judge, 153
Carpetbaggers, 93
Carr, Colonel, 8
Carr, John, 103
Carson, Johnny Show, 134
Carson, Rose, 91
Carteaux, Madam, 114
Carusi, Charles Frances, 56
Carusi, Eugene, 56
Carver, George Washington, 68
Castleman, Ella L., 181
Cato, Ed, 50, 51, 52
Centeninial Philadelphia, 113
Channing, William, 75
Charleston, Missouri, 19
Chartered Company, 191
Cherokee Indians, 176
Chesterfield, Uncle Jerry Lord,35
Chicago, 6
Chicago Industrial Orphanage, 119
Chickasaw Indians, 176
Chickasawhay River, 104
Chief Justice Shepard, 172
Childs, Dr., of Washington DC, 122
Child, Lydia Marie, 75
Chilton, Charles, 133
Choctaw Indians, 176
Christian, Edward, 110
Christian Leadership Conference SCLC, 147
Church, African Zion Baptist, 69
Church, Anna (Wright), 120
Church, Annette, 120

Church, Col. Robert Reed, 120
Church, Robert Jr., 120
Church, St. George, 54
Civil Rights Act Law of 1875, 33
Clabaugh, Chief Justice, 56
Clark, Andrew, 104
Clark, General H.C.,17
Clark, G.W.H., Rev., 139
Clark, Jumbo, 21
Clark, L.R., Mrs., 208
Clark, Louis R., 208
Clark, Major, 104
Clark, Market Master, 107
Clark, Tom, 131
Clark, Tony, 39
Clay, Cassius Marcellus, 159
Clay, Anne, 160
Clay, Brutus, 160
Clay, Elisha Warfield, 160
Clay, General Green, 159
Clay, Green, 160
Clay, Henry (adopted), 160
Clay, Laura, 160
Clay, Mary Barr, 160
Clay, Mary Jane Warfield, 160
Clay, Rhodes, 160
Clay, Sally, 160
Clemens, Margaret, 53, 54, 55
Cleveland, Grover, President, 36
Cline, David, 110
Clopton, William, 42, 43
Coburn, J. Milton, Rev., 139
Coe, Joe, 13, 14
Collins, Jane, 53, 54, 55
Collins, St. Clair, 38
Collis, Charles Bailiff, 20
Coleman Cotton Mill of Concord, N.C., 187
Coleman, John W., 76
Coleman, Robert, 19
Coleman, Roxanna, 188
Coleman, Warren C., 187
Coley, Julius, 171
Colman, Ed, 123
Colorado, Denver, 56
Colorado, Limon, 24
Colored Women's League, 200
Columbia University, 192
Combs, A., painter & decorator, 126
Come unto me all ye that are weary and heavy laden, 114
Coming Emancipation of the Black Race, The, 210
Concord Baptist Church, 190
Conkling, Roscoe, Senator of New York, 115
Connecticut, Guilford, 209
Connecticut, Hartford, 210

Connecticut, Litchfield, 209
Connecticut, New Haven, 194
Conway, Edward H., 3
Conway, Moncure D. Dr., 159
Congressional Gold Medal, 130
Consolidated Beneficial Society of Baltimore, 198
Cook County, 5, 6
Cook, John E., 76, 77
Cook, Sir Francis, 216
Cooke, Judge, 171
Coolidge, Calvin President, 194
Cooper, Charles, 16
Cooper, Robert Archer, 70
Cooper Union Hall in New York City, 159
Copeland, James, 17
Copeland, John, 76
Coppin, L.J., Bishop, 79
Coppock, Barclay, 76
Coppock, Edwin, 76
Councill, William H., 185
County Judge Cooke, 171
Crozer, J. Lewis, 147
Crozer Theological Seminary in Pennsylvania, 147
Corbin, Mamie, 20
Cormack, Captain, 14
Corps, Marine, 40
Cortelyou, Chairman, 35, 36
Cotton, Bud, 94
Coubertin, Baron, 89
Coubertin Medal, 89
County, Spottsylvania, 3
Covey, Edward, 62
Cowan, Captain, 105
Cowboys, Dallas, 11
Cox, Judge, 126
Crawford, Anthony, 69, 70, 71
Cranford, Alfred, 91, 93
Cranford, Mattie, 91, 93, 95
Creek Indians, 176
Creek , Bubbly, 5
Crenshaw, O.A. Dr., 195
Crosby, Sheriff, 105
CSS Planter, 211
Curve, The, 90
Cynthiana, Kentucky, 21
Czolgosz, Leon, 30

D

Daley, Judge, 50, 51
Dartmouth College, 69
Dart, Rev. J.L. Minister of Charleston, S.C., 210
Datura, Texas, 14
Daugherty, Millie, 90
Davidson, Olivia, A.,67, 69
Davis, Alexander K., Lt. Governor, 132

Davis, Benjamin O., 165, 166
Davis, Edith, 136, 137
Davis, Elizabeth Lindsay Mrs., 198, 199, 200
Davis, Henrietta, 166
Davis, Henry, 39
Davis, Jefferson, President, 28, 29, 137, 170
Davis, Joseph S., 136, 137
Davis, Lewis, 166
Davis, Martha of Baltimore, 153
Davis, Martin, 21
Davis, Mrs. Jefferson, 28
Davis, Sheriff, 119
Davis, William H., Dr of Frederick City, 198
Dawes Allotment Act of February 8, 1887, 176
Day, Mary, 76
Dayton, William Lewis, 160
Dean, Mrs. D. H., 22
Dean, Hugh, 22
Deanewood, 29
De Beers Consolidated Mining Company, 191
Decker, H.H. City Attorney, 87
Declaration of Independence, 174
De Large, Robert C., 168, 169
Deneen, Governor, 119
Dexter Avenue Baptist Church, 130, 147
Diaspora, 23
Dickerson, Richard, 20, 21
Dickson, Amanda America, 124
Dickson, Charles Green, 125, 126
Dickson, David, 124
Dickson, Elizabeth Sholars, 124
Dickson, Julia, 124
Dickson, Julian Henry, 125
Dickson, Thomas, 124
Diggs, J.R.L., Rev., 193
Dixie Sex, 8, 130
Dixie Trickery, 138, 176
Dillon, Dr. H. T., 68
Distant People, 174
Dixie Trickery, 30, 40
Dockery, Gov, 16
Dodson, E. B., 106
Dolan, Jennie, 107
Dolan, John, 107
Domo, Black Major, 36
Dondino, Louis, 10
Donnegan, William, 21
Dorsey, Ida, 151
Dorsey, Michael, 207
Douglass, Charles, 62, 63
Douglass, Fred Literary Society, 90
Douglass, Frederick, 62, 63, 65, 75, 154, 200, 215, 217
Douglass, Jr. Frederick, 62, 63
Douglass, Lewis, Rosetta 62, 63

Dozier, Ada, 6
Dred-A Tale of Great Dismal Swamp, 209
Druid's Medical Society of America, 198
Du Bois, W.E.B., 34, 92, 93, 101, 167, 202, 203, 204
Du Bose, Charles W. Col., 124
Dubose, Judge, 90
Duff, Mr. of Boston, 114
Duke, Jailer, 109
Dulaney, William B., 36
Duncan, Horace, 17
Durant, Blakely, 112
Du Pont, Commodore, 212
Durbin, Winfield Governor, 58
Dwyer, Francis P., 175
Dyer Anti-lynching Bill, 204
Dyer, Leonidas C. of St. Louis, 204

E

Eagleswood, Military Academy, 75
Earl, Cora Miss, 193
Eastland, James, 103
Ebenezer Baptist Church, 147
Edmonson, Mable, 16, 18
El Dorado African Methodist Church, 145, 146
Elliot, Robert Brown, 168, 170, 171
Elliott, Jane, 133, 134, 135
Ellison, Reverend Gilbert, 96
Elias, Hannah, 151
Eliot, President of Harvard, 89
Elkhart, 39
Elloree County Jail, 91
Ely, Robert E., 159
Embree, Frank, 90, 91
Eminence Pike, 46
Emerson, Dr. John, 61
Emerson, Ralph Waldo, 75
England, Bredon, 217
England, Herts, 191
Equal-Suffrage Convention of 1900, 200
Erskine, Evelyn, 7
Ervin, J. Louis, 10
Eton College England, 170
Eubanks, Charles, 125
Evans, Jerry, 22
Evans, Lucy, 7
Evans, Owen, 177
Evarts, William M., 205
Evers, Medgar, 138
Ewert, Theodore Adjutant General Col., 145, 146, 147
Exposition, Pan-American, 29

F

Fahey, Tom, 56
Fair Employment Practices Committee, (FEPC), 205
Falls, Peb, 110

Farnham, Martha Mrs., 155, 156
Federal Civil Rights Act of 1964, 127
Federal Democratic Administration, 180
Female John Brown, 210
Ferguson, Judge John Howard, 128
Ferrall, Frank S., 171
Ferrall, Susie Patterson, 171
Field, Justice Stephen J, 127
Fields, Sam, 19
Fifty-Fourth Massachusetts, 114, 167
Fike, Bob, 176
Finley, Noah, 3, 4
First Congregational Church, 136, 137
First Highland Baptist Church, 196
Fisk University, 68
Florida, Gainesville, 21
Florida, Graceville, 110
Florida, Sebring, 119
Fleming, Sheriff, 48
Folk, Governor, 17
Folsoms Bridge, 46
Forbes, Captain, 164
Fort D.A. Russell in Wyoming, 166
Fort Sumter, 211
Fort Wagner, 167
Fort Ripley, 211
Fortson, Boyce, 47
Fortune, Timothy Thomas, 200, 201, 202
Foss, Eugene, 162
Foster, Colonel W. F., 67
Foster, George A., 30
Fox, Joe, 123
Fox, William, 19
Frances, Ezekiel, 38
Francis, W.F., 10
Franklin, Benjamin of Pennsylvania, 173
Franklin, Tobe, 177
Franks, Amanda, 108
Franks, Louis E., 125
Freedom Hospital, 58
Freeland, William, 62
Freeman, Roy, Deputy Sheriff, 47
Freedman Bureau, 182
Frost, Louise, 24
Frost, Robert W., 24
Fryer, Mrs. Lucy, 48
Fuller, John E., 158
Fuller, Justice Melville W., 127
Fuller, Margaret, 75
Fullerton, Lee, 86

G

Gaerarde, Vincent, 178
Gaines, W.J., Bishop, 185

Galbraith, Virgil, 18
Gallagher, 30
Gans, Joe or Joseph Gant, 153
Cappage, White man, 52
Garfield, James A., President, 36, 115
Garrett, Quaker Thomas, 72
Garrison, Abijah, 155
Garrison, Elizabeth, 156
Garrison, Fanny Lloyd, 155
Garrison Helen Eliza Benson, 158
Garrison, James, 156
Garrison, Lloyd, 156
Garrison, Mary Palmer, 155
Garrison, William Lloyd, 154, 155, 156, 157, 158, 159, 202
Garvey, Marcus Mosiah Jr., 193
Cato, Ed, 50
Geneva, Texas, 22
George, General J. Z., 115
Georgia, Barney, 46
Georgia, Bulloch County, 50
Georgia, Burke County, 115
Georgia, Chatham, 50
Georgia, Griffin, 92
Georgia, Hancock county, 124
Georgia, Hawkinsville, 47
Georgia, Lincolnton, 47
Georgia, Macon, 169
Georgia, McPherson, 95
Georgia, Newman, 92
Georgia, Palmetto, 92
Georgia, Pinehurst, 47
Georgia, Sparta, 124
Georgia, Savannah, 50, 51
Georgia, Statesboro, 52
Georgia, Valdosta, 46
Georgia, Washington county, 124
Georgia, Waynesboro, 96
Gibson, Sheriff G.D, 90
Gibson and Brendt of Augusta, 115
Gibson, Will, 131
Giles, Albert, 123
Gilmore, Quincy Adams, General, 167
Gilpin Shoes, 195
Gilpin, S.J., 194
Gilyard, Thomas, 86, 87, 88
Glass, Mary, 110
Goddess, Liberty Tower, 19
Godley, French, 15
Godley, Will, 87
Godley, William, 16
Goines, Lt. William C., 121
Goines, Phyllis, 121
Goodwill Parochial School, 189
Gordon, Jack, 47

Gordon, John, 183
Gordon, Mary of Washington, 179
Gordon, R.A., 94
Goslin, Asher, Dr., 164
Gove, Samuel F., 169
Governor, Thomas, 24
Goyette, S., 117
Graham, Dr. David, 9,10,
Grand View Cemetery, 102
Grant, Ulysses S., President, 35, 36, 104, 112, 164, 215
Grant, Mrs., 36
Grant Parish, 105
Gray, George, 152
Gray, Justice Horace, 127
Gray, T.R. of Jerusalem, Southampton County, 80
Grayson, Charles, 178, 179, 180
Grayson, Janie, 179, 180
Greeley, Horace, 75, 149, 155
Green, Benjamin, 138
Green, Nate, 8
Green, Peter A. Rev., 145
Green, Shadrach, 119
Green, Shields, 76
Green-Turtle Club of New Orleans, 210, 211
Greenleaf Scholarship Award, 89
Greenwood, Bot, 16
Grimke, Archibald H., 202, 203, 204
Grindle, Henry, 56
Grosbeck, Richard, 59

H

Haas, John, President of Capital Bank, 94
Haines College, 116,
Hall, Calvin, 118
Hall, Frank, 118
Hall, George A., Colonel of 4th MSM Cavalry, 164
Hall, James, 118
Hall, Martin, 118
Hall, Paul, 123
Hall, Robert B., 158
Hall, Tamron, 174
Hamlin, Teunis S., 183
Hammerberg, Carl, 10
Hammett, Geraldine, 177
Hampton Institute, 67
Hanson, Julia, 56
Harding, Colonel, 133
Harlan, James S., 128
Harlan, John Maynard, 128
Harlan, Justice John M., 128, 129
Harlan, Laura, 128
Harlan, Rev., Doc., Richard D., 128
Harlan, Ruth, 128
Harper's Ferry, 76

Harris, Clara, 124
Harris, Jesse, 177
Harris, Julia A., 7
Harris-Perry, Melissa, 174
Harrison, Benjamin, President, 36
Harrison, Major of Chicago, 151
Hart, Clementine, 206
Hart, Clementine B., 206
Hart Farm School, 205
Hart, Mary M. Onley, 206
Hart, William A.H., 206
Hart, William Henry Harrison, Jr., 206
Hart, William Henry Harrison, Prof., 205, 207, 208
Hartsborne Memorial College of Richmond, 121
Hartwell, H.H., Rev., 139
Harvard College, 139
Harvard Divinity School, 139
Harvard Law School, 161
Harvard University, 68, 69, 89, 121
Harvey, General Staff, 182
Havis, Greevy, 39
Hawkins, Albert, 164
Hawks, Annie Sherwood, 75
Hay, Mayor, 117
Haydon, Ulysses, 16
Hayes, Chris, 174
Hayes, Rutherford, President, 36, 128
Haynes, Tom, 38
Hays, John, 39
Hayson, W.B. Mr., 137
Haywood, a Negro, 77
Hazlett, Albert E., 75, 76
Hazlett, John, 94
Heard, Mrs. Josephine, 131
Heer, Dry Goods Co, 19
Helms, Jesse, 44
Hemnings, Sally, 7, 61, 173
Hemphill, Texas, 22
Hemphill, W.A., 94
Henderson, Charles Ernest Lafayette, 130, 131
Henderson, Phenia, 19
Hendrickson, Dorothy Merle, 192
Henman Building of Louisiana, 211
Henny, a Negro slave, 156, 158
Henshaw, Harry T., 30
Henson, Josiah, 210
Herb, C.A., 102
Hertford College, 192
Hickman, Laura Belle Durant, 112
Hickory Bill, 87
Hicks, Ed, 123
Hicks, Franks, 123
Hill, Judge W.H., 109
Hodges, Henry, 50

Hodges, Mrs., 51
Hoffman, Peter M. the coroner, 5
Holbert, Luther and wife, 103
Hollins Institute in Virginia, 211
Holmes, John Haynes Dr., 202, 203
Holsey, Harriet & Bishop Lucius, 125
Holsey, Kate, 125, 126
Holtzman, Aylett T. 181
Holtzman, William, 181
Hornback, Lawman, 46
Horner, Mrs. E.V.,18
Horton, Congressman, 31
Hose, Sam, 91, 92 , 93, 95
Houston, Charles, 88
Houston, Samuel, 27
Howard, Eliza Otis, 181
Howard, F.J., 9
Howard, Normal and Theological Institute for the Education
of Preachers and Teachers, 182
Howard, Oliver. Otis, General , 65, 181, 182, 183
Howard, Rowland B., 181
Howard University, 65, 121, 136, 182, 192
Howard & Co., 125
Howell, Clark, 94
Howson, Peter, 94
Howze, Alma, 104
Howze, Maggie, 104
Hoyt, Mr., Lawyer from Boston, 78
Hubbard, I.G., Rev., 139
Hudson, Tip, 95
Hughes, Langston, 117
Hummel, Roxanna, 216
Hunt, Caleb S., 169
Hunter College of Manhattan, 192
Hurricane Plantation House, 137

I

Iberia College, 169
I Have A Dream, 147
Illinois, Alton, 101
Illinois, Belknap, 119
Illinois, Cairo, 119, 120
Illinois, East St, Louis, 52, 53
Illinois, El Dorado, 145
Illinois, Harvey, 119
Illinois, Karnak, 119
Illinois, Saline County, 145
Illinois, Springfield, 3, 19, 20
Illinois, Vienna, 119
Illinois Volunteers, 131
Indiana, Evansville, 58, 59, 60
Indiana, Vincennes, 59
Ingram, Leonard D., 177

I Need Thee Every Hour, 75
Insor, Darby Plantation, 119
Institution Church Social Settlement, 200
Iowa, Des Moines, 108
Iowa, Riceville, 133
Irwin, John, 108
Ironside, 213
Isom, James, 46
Italy, Florence, 139, 160

J

Jackson, Andrew, 39
Jackson, Andrew, President, 35
Jackson, Daddy William (Billy), 217
Jackson, Ed, 141, 142
Jackson, Eli, 164
Jackson, Elmer, 8
Jackson, George, 19
Jackson, Grant, 141
Jackson, H.W., 94
Jackson, John, 140
Jackson, Mary, 107
Jackson, Nell, 140, 141, 142
Jackson, Robert, 38
Jackson, Stonewall General, 163, 182
Jackson, W.W., 94
Jacques, Amy E., 193
Jamaica, St. Ann's Bay, 193
James, Jesse, 38
James, Will, 119, 120
Jamison, John, 95
Jasper, John, Rev., 79
Jay, Mrs. Eva, 107
Jay, W. C., 106
Jefferson, City, 17
Jefferson, Thomas, President, 7, 35, 173
Jeffries, James J., 152
Jerry, Uncle, 37
Jesus Christ, 172
Jewell, Mr., 24
Jewett, John P., a Boston Publisher, 210
Jewett, Lillian Clayton, 210, 211
John's Island, 212
Johnson, Aaron, 22
Johnson, Albert & Mary lee, 186
Johnson, Alice P., 186
Johnson, Andrew, President, 182
Johnson, B.M., Mr., 193
Johnson, Dr. E.L., 103, 104
Johnson, E.A., Professor, 188
Johnson, Etta H. Duryea, 150
Johnson, Henry Lincoln, 121

Johnson, Irene Pineau, 152
Johnson, Jack, 150, 151, 152, 153
Johnson, James Weldon, 203
Johnson, Oliver, 139, 158
Johnson, Mordecai Wyatt, Dr. Rev.
Johnson, Robert, Rev., 79
Johnson, Sydney, 46
Johnson, Will, 22
Johnson, William, 29
Johnston, Dr. D.A., 40
Jones Boys, 92, 94
Jones, Charles, 177
Jones, Dr. William, 28
Jones, Hannah, 212
Jones, James H., 27, 28
Jones, Madam Sissieretta Etta, 111
Jones, R.E. MD, 194
Jones, Sherriff, 25
Joplin, 6, 85
Jordan, August, 59
Jordan, Jennie (Barlow), 47
Jordan, Michael, 55
Jordan, R.F., 47
Jungle, "The", 21
Just, Ernest Everett Dr., 204, 205

K

Kagi, John Henry, 76
Kansas City Railway yard, 86
Kansas, Coffeyville, 110
Kansas, Quindaro, 116
Karma, 1
Keckly, Elizabeth, 27, 28
Kelly Family, 108
Kelly, George W. Major, 164
Kelly, Sheriff Wilkes County, 47
Kendrick, Sheriff, 50
Kennard, Adam, 42
Kennedy, Miss Elizabeth, 111, 112
Kentucky, Boyle County, 128
Kentucky, Cynthiana, 21
Kentucky, Harrodsburg, 145
Kentucky, Frankfort, 161
Kentucky, Lebanon Junction, 108
Kentucky, Louisville, 161, 197
Kentucky, Madison County, 159
Kentucky, Paducah, 107
Kentucky, Shelbyville, 46
Kimball, Dr. 136
King, Alberta Williams, 147
King, Coretta Scott, 135, 147
King Edward IV of England, 111
King, Jr. Martin Luther, 4, 44, 130, 139, 147
Kinney, T.M., 18

Kirby, Rev. J.E., 8, 10, 11, 12
Kirkpatrick, Isaac, 109
Kirkpatrick, Puss, 109
Khartum, 165
Klan, Ku Klux, 42, 105, 193
Knapp, Isaac, 158
Knight, Edward, Mr., 137
Know, Robert, 122
Kratz, Sheriff Chris, 59

L

Lamble, Frank, 59
Langston, Charles Henry, 117
Langston, Ida, 117
Langston, John Mercer, 64, 65, 117
Lapseley, Mrs. Bessie, 131
Lark, George, 15
Lathrop, Abial, 31
Latter's, millionaires of Long Island, 54, 55
Lawrence, M.F. Mrs., 154
Lealtad, Catherine Deaver, 183
Leary, Sherrerd Lewis, 76
Ledbetter, Sheriff, 117
Lee, Robert E, Colonel, 77
Lee, Robert E., General, 163
Lee, Samuel, 170
Leeds, Florence H., 151
Leeman, William H., 76
Leslie, Officer Theodore, 86, 87, 88
Levee, 20
Le Vin, Detective Louis P., 93, 94
Lewis, Ed, 38
Lewis, Lenox, 39
Lewis, William Henry, 161, 162
Life of the lowly, 210
Lift Every Voice and Sing, 205
Lilly, Mr. O. R., 40, 122
Lightfoot, Thomas of Griffin, 94
Lincoln, President Abraham, 20, 28, 31, 58, 61, 101, 102, 139, 160
Lincoln Heights, 196
Lincoln, Judge, 17
Lincoln, Mary Todd, 27, 28
Lincoln University, 116
Linton, Irwin B., 181
Litchfield Academy, 209
Little, Arthur C., 56, 57
Little Ogeechee River, 124
Little Sisters of the Poor, 56
Livingston, Robert R of New York, 173
Livingston School of Dress Making, 208
Lloyd, Colonel Edward, 62
Lockart, Fred T., 115
Locke, Alain Leroy, 191
Lodge, Henry Cabot Senator, 161

Loeb, Secretary, 36
Loebeck, Agnes, 9
Loney, George H., Sheriff, 45, 46
Long, Jefferson Franklin, 168, 169
Longino, Governor A.H., 109
Longstreet, Major-General, 164
Loomis, P.A., 210
Looney, C.A., 177
Lorraine Hotel, 147
Louisiana, Algiers, 122
Louisiana, Colfax, 105
Louisiana, Columbia, 47
Louisiana, Delta, 97
Louisiana, Monroe, 47
Louisiana, Shreveport, 107
Lovejoy, Elijah P., 101, 102, 158
Lovejoy, Owen, 101, 102
Lovings, Carrie, 6
Lovings, Joseph, 6
Ludlow Street Jail, 216
Luke, St., 24
Lundy, Benjamin, 157
Lusk, Dianthe, 76
Lyons, Judson Whitlocke, 115

M

Maafa, 2, 23
Maddow, Rachel, 174
Madison, Eliza, 61
Madison, James, 35
Madison, Lizzie, 61
Madison, River, 22
Madison Square Garden, NY City, 111
Magie, Sheriff, 10
Maher, Bill, 174
Maine, Albion, 101
Maine, Brunswick, 209
Maine, Leeds, 181
Malone, A.E., 99
Malone, Annie Minerva Pope Turnbo, 98
Malta Building on W. 5th, 106
Mammy Grace Robinson, 217
Manly, Alexander, L., 37
Mann Act, 150, 153
Mann, James, 169
Manning, III, Governor Richard Irvine, 71
Mans Ideal of Character, 140
Mantoles, Saloon, 20
Manuel, Will, 22
Marines, Black Montford Point, 40
Marshall, Bayless, 107
Maryland, Baltimore, 156, 157
Maryland, Elkton, 207
Maryland, Port Tobacco, Charles County, 210

Massachusetts, Lynn in Essex County, 156
Massachusetts, Newburyport, 155
Massanutten Mountain, 110
Matthews, William, 94
Marshall, Eugene, 46
Marson, Willie, 39
Martin, John, 123
Martin, John Biddulph, 216
Martin, Mose, 47
Maryland, 36
Maryland, Baltimore, 136, 153
Maryland, Dorchester County, 72
Maryland, Long Green, 119
Maryland, Prince George's County, 178
Maryland, St. Michael, 62
Maryland, Talbot County, 62
Maryland, Tuckahoe, 62
Massachusetts, Bedford, 63
Massachusetts, Lexington, 138
Massachusetts, Nantucket Island, 63
Massey, Louis, 58, 59, 60
Mason, Max, 10
Matthews, Chris, 174
Matthews, Mariam, 119
Maye, Postal Inspector, 31
Mayesville Educational and Industrial Institution, 190
Mayflower, The, 209
Mavericks, Dallas, 55
McCall, James D., 68
McCannon, Elizabeth Miss, 194
McCarry-Dwyer, Clara, 176
McCarry, Douglas B., 175
McCauley, James a carpenter & Leona a teacher, 130
McCauley, Rosa Louise, 130
McCollough, Jim, 109
McCormick, Ms. Ida, 131
McCoy, Colonel, 59
McCray, Belfield, 109
McCray, Betsie, 109
McCray, Hattie, 152
McCray, Ida, 109
McDonald, John, 39
McDowell, Calvin, 90
McDowell, Daniel H., 163
McDowell's & Royal, 208
McFarland, Will a preacher, 122
McGhle, Isaac, 8
McGovern, Terry, 153
McKee, Master Henry Plantation, 211
McKinley, William, President , 29, 36, 115, 116, 166
McLaughlin, William, 178
Mc Lauren, 31
McLean, General, 28
McLendon, Sheriff, 90

McLinn, Daisy Miss, 194
McMillian, C.C., 21
McMurray, Miss Maudelie, 99
McNutt, W.R., a chauffeur, 177
McPherson, General James M., 112
McReynolds, Attorney General, 121
McWeeny, Chief of Police, 151
Medal of Honor, 167, 182
Menard, John Willis, 169
Merriam, Francis Jackson, 76
Michigan, Battle Creek treatment center, 137
Michigan National Superintendent of work, 200
Middlebury College of Vermont, 192
Milburn, John, 29
Miles and Gilpin, 194
Miles, T.A., 194
Milholland, Inez, 203
Miller, Kelly Professor, 137
Miller, William, 10
Milholland, John E., 202
Michigan, Battle Creek, 58, 136
Michigan, Detroit, 56
Minnesota, Duluth, 8, 9, 10, 130
Minnesota, St. Paul, 13, 112
Mississippi, Aberdeen, 170
Mississippi, Biloxi, 151
Mississippi, Carrollton, 109
Mississippi, Clinton, 132
Mississippi, Corinth, 131
Mississippi, Doddsville, 103
Mississippi, Durant, 110
Mississippi, Jackson, 38, 44, 105, 106, 109, 133
Mississippi, Meridian, 41
Mississippi, Mound Bayou, 138
Mississippi, Natchez, 170
Mississippi, Pickens, Holmes County, 110
Mississippi, Raymond, 132
Mississippi, Shepards town, 103
Mississippi, Shubuta, 103
Mississippi, Vicksburg, 21, 104, 133
Mississippi, Walhalla, 13
Mississippi, Warren County Davis Bend, 137
Mississippi, Yazoo County, 103
Mississippi, Yazoo River Valley, 138
Missouri, Bonne Terre, 116
Missouri, Fayette, 90
Missouri, Higbee, 90
Missouri, Howard County, 90
Missouri, Joplin, 85, 86, 88
Missouri, Lebanon, 116
Missouri, Pierce City, 87
Missouri, Springfield, 87
Missouri, St. Louis, 62, 98
Mitchell, James Attorney of Mt. Vernon, 146

Mitchell, John of New York, 208
Mixon, W.H., Rev., 185
Mollman, Mayor, 52
Montgomery, Isaiah T., 137
Monticello, 7
Moore, Aaron, 42, 43
Moore, Frank, 123
Moore, M.M., Rev, 79
Moore, Rachael, 106
Moore v. Dempsey, 123
Morgan, Glement G., 89
Morris Island, 213
Morven, Church Camp Ground, 46
Moscowitz, Henry, 202
Moseley, Elmore, 21
Mosley, Robert J., 41
Moss, Theodore, 90
Mott, Lucretia a local Quaker, 154, 155
Mulzack, Captain, 193
Mount Olivet Cemetery, 56, 179
Mower, Judge, 21
Mulguard, Louis, 102
Munroe, R.I. Dist. Judge, 48
Murphy, Watts, 110
Murray, Anna, 62, 63
Murphy, Eliza, 56

N

N.A.A.C.P., 10, 34, 70, 101, 122, 123, 130, 203, 204, 205
N.A.A.C.W., 34
N.A.C.W., 200
Naharkey, Nellie, 177
Nalle, Charles, 73, 74
Napier, James Carroll, 116, 117
Napier, William C. and Jane E., 117
Narragansett Indian Chief, 114
Nash, Roy, 70, 71
Natelson, Nate, 10
National Afro-American Council, 200, 201, 202
National Association for the Advancement of Colored People, (N.A.A.C.P.) 202, 203
National Association of Colored Women, 199, 200
National Baptist Convention, 196
National Co-operative Association of America, 198
National Freedman Relief Association, 58
National Independence Political League, 202
National Negro Business League, 186
Neal, Ed, 14
Neal, John, 133
Nebraska, Omaha, 13
Neff, 30
Negro Christian Banner, 197
Negro National Anthem, 205
Nelle, 73, 74

Nelson, Austin, 45
Nelson, Laura, 45, 46
Nelson Lawrence, 45
Nelson, LD, 45
Nelson, Oscar "Battling", 153
Nelson, Sarry, 45
Nelson, Sidney B., 177
Nevada, Reno, 152
Newby, Dangerfield, 76
Newcomb, B., 158
New England Anti-Slavery Society, 158
New Hampshire, Manchester, 139
New Harriet Beecher Stowe, 210
New Jersey, Perth Amboy, Eagleswood, 75
Newman, M., 38
Newton County, 86
New Mexico, Las Vegas, 151
New York, Auburn, 72
New York, Brooklyn, 189
New York, Brooklyn, Kings, 208
New York, Elba Essex County, 78
New York, Great Nock, 55
New York, Hoosick, 75
New York, Johnstown, 154
New York, Long Island, 54
New York, New York City, 53, 63, 149
New York, Oyster Bay, 165
New York, Rochester, 63, 201
New York, Saratoga Spring, 90
New York, Schenectady County, 74
New York, Seneca Falls, 154
New York, Ulster County, 58
Niagara Movement, 202
Nichols, Captain, 212
Nichols, R., 117
Nigger, 26, 50
Niggerhead, 25, 26
Nigger Heaven, 25
Noah, 172
North Carolina, Concord, 187
North Carolina, Franklin County, 171
North Carolina, Weldon, 170
Northern, Governor William J., 95
Norris, Joseph Preston, 163
Nova Scotia, 155
Nugent, Pearl, 88

O

Oakley, Convict Farm, 38
Oates, Burrell, 117
Obama, President Barack, 44, 55, 56, 86, 149
Oberlin College, 64, 65, 120
Oblate Sisters, 56
O'Brien, Frances, F., 30

O'Donnell, Lawrence, 174
Ohio, Bellefontaine, 141
Ohio, Carthagenia, 112
Ohio, Chillicothe, 64
Ohio, Cincinnati, 106
Ohio, Hamilton County, 216
Ohio, Licking County, Homer, 216
Ohio, Springfield, 21
Ohio State Federal Women's Club, 200
Ohio, West Liberty, 140
Ohio, Yellow Springs, 120
Oklahoma, Okfuskee County, 45, 46
Oklahoma, Okemah, 45
Oklahoma, Wagoner, 49
Okapilco River Brook County, 46
Old Folks Baptist Home, 197
Olson, Bryson, 10
Omaha, Nebraska, 9
Ossenberg's Saloon, 59, 60
Ovington, Mary White, 202
Owen, Mabel, 57
Owens, Clair, 94
Oxford Committee, 192
Oyster, James , 172

P

Page, Inman E., 185
Palestine, Texas, 39
Palmer, Daniel, 155
Parker, Captain, 29
Parker, James Benjamin, 29, 30
Parker, James W., 83
Parker, Theodore, 138, 139, 140
Parkin, Attorney, 153
Parks, Rosa Louise, 129
Parrish, Charles, H., Rev., 185
Parrot, Captain, 212
Patterson, Mary Jane, 193
Patterson, Wade, 46
Payne, Beverly, 119
Payne, D.A., Bishop, 183, 184
Peabody, Elizabeth Palmer, 75
Peace, Lemuel, 49
Pease, Charles, 6
Peckham, Justice Rufus W., 127
Peelle, Stanton C., Attorney, 172
Pelley, Annie, 119
Pennsylvania Hall in Philadelphia, 158
Pennsylvania, Philadelphia
Perrin, Captain J.L., 70
Peters, John, 99
Pharez and Zarah, 172
Phelps, P.F., 94
Phi Beta Kappa, 192
Phillip's Academy, 210

Devour Us Not

Phillips Exeter Academy, 88
Phillips, Wendell, 74, 75
Philadelphia Optical College, 198
Pierce, City, Missouri, 19
Pinchback, Nina Eliza, 125, 126
Pinchback, Pickney B.S. Gov., 125
Pinton, William, 94
Pittman, W.S., 6
Pitts, Helen, 62, 63
Platt, John R., 151
Pleasant, Mary "Mammy" Ellen, 76
Plessy, Homer Adolph, 127, 128
Plessy v. Ferguson, 127, 128, 207
Polk, James, 35
Poro College, 98, 99
Porter Hall, 67
Porter, Preston "John", 24, 25
Porter, T.J., 176, 177
Potomac River, 76, 77
Potts, D.C., 185
Potts, William, 94
Powers, Father, 9
Prairie View A & M, 148
Presbyterian Church in Lexington, Virginia, 163
Presbyterian Scotia Seminary School, 189
Presidential Medal of Freedom, 130
Price, Daniel, 41, 42
Price, Sarrah, 186
Prince of Wales, 111
Prima facia, 169
Priscilla, 7
Pullman Palace Car Company, 126
Pumphrey Family, 178

Q

Quarles, Captain Ralph, 64

R

Rainey, Joseph H., 168, 170
Rankin, J.E. Dr. 137, 183
Rayfield, W.A., 68
Raymer, Abe, 21
Read and Christian Manufacturing Company, 198
Read, E. Parker MD Ref. D., 197
Read, Samuel McDowell, 163
Reagan, President, 44
Reavis, Colonel of Iowa, 164
Rector, Joe & Sarah, 177
Rector, Rosa, 176
Red Shirts, 42, 105
Reed, Dudley, 38
Reed, Seward, 161
Reed, Thurlow, 161
Reed, Will, 50, 51, 52
Reese, Cordelia A. Miss, 194

Regent of the Silver Shield of Alabama, 211
Revels, Hiram Rhodes, 168, 170
Rheaton, Mrs. Ella, 109
Rhode Island, Providence, 111
Rhodes, Cecil John, 191
Rhodes, Francis W., Rev., 191
Rhodes Scholarship, 191
Rice, Eugene, 46
Rice, Waddy, 133
Richmond, The Recorder, 173
Richardson, Dora April, 159, 160
Richardson, Ernest, 39
Richardson, Harry, 9
Richardson, John S., 170
Richardson, Rosa, 108, 109
Richardson, William, 160
Richmond Planet, 3
Ricketts, Dr., 140
Rickman, David, 141
Rifle, Leagues, 42
Riley, Butch, 21
Rimmer, Dr., 113
Robert, Dr. James T., 115
Roberts, Albert, 52
Roberts, Charles, 177
Roberts, Lee, 59
Roberts, Nannie Miss, 195
Robinson, Amelia Boynton, 148
Robinson, Bob "Blubber", 117
Robinson, Harriett, 61
Robinson, John D., 97
Robinson, Lelia Walker, 97
Robinson, James, 96
Robinson, Spottswood W., 195
Robunson, S.W. Jr., 195
Rockefeller, Laura Spilman, 185
Rockwall, Church, 22
Rogowski, A., 94
Roosevelt, Alice Hathaway Lee, 217
Roosevelt, Kermit, 165
Roosevelt, Theodore, President, 35, 36, 41, 53, 116, 121, 165, 177, 217
Roosevelt, Martha "Mittle" Bulloch, 217
Roosevelt, Mrs. Theodore, 36, 165
Root, Elihu, Secretary of War, 181
Rose, William, 218
Rosen, William, 10
Rosewood, 4,8
Rouse, Fred, 14
Rowell, Victoria, 56
Royal, Darrell, 42
Ruffin, Josephine Mrs., 199, 203
Rufus, Mary, 107
Rusk, Texas, 22

Russell, Governor, 37
Russia, Petersburg, 160
Rust, Richard S., 184
Rutherford, Alvin, 38

S

Sabine County, 22
Salley, Sheriff, 108
Salzner, Henry, 119, 120
San Augustine, Texas, 22
Sanders, George, 107
Sanford, Henry Shelton Senator, 160
Sanford, John F. A., 61, 62
Santa Ana, de Antonio Lopez, 27
Saxton, Rufus, General, 212
Scallawags, 93
Schreiber, Belle, 153
Schultz, Ed, 174
Schuman, Frank, 90
Scott, Clarence, 3
Scott, Dred, 12, 61, 62, 128, 174, 201
Scott, Emmett J., 68
Scott, I.B., Rev., 185
Scott, Marie, 49
Seminole Indian War of Florida, 182
Seward, Secretary of State, 161
Sewell, Albert, 95
Shanklin, John of Evansville, Malvina F., Indiana, 128
Sharecropping, 174
Sharkey, E.D., 94
Sharpton, Al, Rev., 174
Shavers, Ferdinand, 27
Sheldon, Leonard, 10
Shepard, Chief Justice, 172
Sheppard, J., 38
Sheppard, James E., Dr., 185
Sherman, William Tecumseh, General, 112, 182
Sherman, John, 170
Sherman, Roger of Connecticut, 173
Sherwood, Ellen, 106
Shields, Hugh, 90
Shiner, Michael, 177
Shiras, Jr. Justice George, 127
Shoemake, George Hook, 115
Shows, Charles, 39
Simmons, Arthur, 36
Simmons Bluff, 212
Simmons, Jr. Arthur, 36
Simpson, O.J., 152
Sively, Martin, 133
Sketches of the Descendants of Pilgrims, 209
Slocum, 39
Smalls, Elizabeth Lydia (Bampfield), 212
Smalls, General Robert, Hero of the Planter, 211

Smalls, Hannah Jones, 212
Smalls, Sarah S. (Williams), 212
Smalls, William R., 212
Smallwood, John J., Rev., 185
Smith, Amanda, 119
Smith, Anderson, 39
Smith, Elwell, 108
Smith, Fannie N. First wife, 67, 69
Smith, G. of Wardencliffe, Long Island, 154
Smith, George, 13
Smith, George of Atlanta, 94
Smith, Gerrit, 73, 75
Smith, Hampton, 46
Smith, Hampton Mrs., 46
Smith, Hattie, 151
Smith, Isaac, 38, 76
Smith, James E. General, 146
Smith, Mollie, 108
Smith, N.J. Mr., 195
Smith, Sampson, 47
Smith, "Sister", 119
Sneed, Jennie, 107
Snelling, William J., 158
South Carolina, Abbeville, 69
South Carolina, Abbeville Courthouse, 70
South Carolina, Beaufort, 211, 213
South Carolina, Elloree, 108
South Carolina, Georgetown, 170
South Carolina, Greenwood, 106
South Carolina, Mayesville, 189
South Carolina, Orangeburg, 91
South Carolina, Orangeburg County, 108
South Carolina, Williamsburg County, Lake City, 210
Speer, Jennie, 107
Spellman, Moses, 22
Spickard, Mrs. O. M., 38
Spingarn, Arthur, 202
Spingarn, Joel Elias, 202, 203, 204, 205
Spingarn Medal, 183, 200, 204, 205
Spottsylvania County, 3
Spurger, James, 39
Spring, Marcus, 75
Spring, Rebecca B., 75
Springfield, Arthur, 152
Springfield, Illinois, 19, 20
Springfield, Ohio, 20 Stanley, Governor W.E., 90, 91
St. John River, 155
Stanton, Elizabeth Cady, 154, 155
Stanton, Robert L. of New York, 154
Stanton, Theodore of Paris, 154
State vs. Chavers, 172
Statler, O., 178
St.Clair, Pierre, 94

St. Frances Colored Catholic Orphan Asylum, 125, 126
Steele, James, 59
Stephens, Governor Von V., 90, 91
Stephens, Judge W.F., 109
Stephenson, Henry,
Stevens, Aaron Dwight, 75, 76
Steward, William Henry, 202
Stillman, James A. 151
Stillman, Joshua Coffin, 158
Stockton, Henry K., 158
Stough, Judge Samuel C, 6
Storey, Moorfield, 202, 204
Stowe, Mrs. Harriet Beecher, Prof. Calvin Ellis, 209
Stowe, Mrs. Mary L., 215
Strange, Ann, 136
Strange, Charles, 136, 137
Strange, Isabella, 136, 137
Strange, J.V., 136
Strange, Paul, 107
Street, Sheriff, 118
Strickland, Lige of Palmetto, 91, 92, 93, 94
Stuart, Sam, 96
Stuart, William, 90
St. Andrews, New Brunswick, 113
St. Ann's Orphan Asylum for Girls, 56
St. Joseph Male Orphan, 56
St. Patrick Church, 56
Sturgis, Mayor William, 41, 43
Sturgis, Theodore, 41
Suggs, Will, 38
Sulkins, Earle, 21
Sullivan, James, 8
Sunderland, Byron, 183
Swain, Robert, 76
Swett, Leonard, 101
Sykes, Walter, 38

T

Taft, William H. President, 117, 121, 161, 162
Tailors and Dressmakers Organization of Washington DC, 208
Talbert, Mary B. Mrs., 199, 200
Talbott, Annie O., 56,
Taliferro, Mr. & Mrs. R. T., 109
Tallahatchie River, 138
Talley, Harriett, 107
Tandy, V.W., 98
Taney, Chief Justice Roger B., 62
Tappan, Arthur, 157
Tar and Feathers, 140
Taylor, Charles, 59
Taylor, George, 95
Taylor, Robert R., 68
Taylor, Recy, x

Taylor, S.E. of NY, 208
Taylor, Stewart, 76
Taylor, Zachery, 35
Telfair St., 452, 124
Tellaferro, Major, 61
Tennessee, Gallatin, 109
Tennessee, Jackson, 107
Tennessee, Memphis, 90, 91, 120
Tennessee, Nashville, 116
Tennessee, Petersburg, 107
Tennessee Riflemen, Colored Military Organization, 90
Tennyson in Bowdoin Literary competition, 191
Terrell, Judge Robert Heberton, 121, 122
Terrell, Mary Church, 120, 121, 122, 136, 137, 199, 200, 203
Texas, Chappell Hill, 106
Texas, Dallas, 117
Texas, Galveston, 152
Texas, Houston, 27
Texas, Huntsville, 27
Texas, Marshall, 107
Texas, Waco, 48
Tharin, Robert S., 169
Thatcher, Moses, 158
The Women's Bazaar, Millinery and Dressmaking, 208
Third Regiment of Maine Volunteers, 182
Thirkield, Wilbur P., 183
Thomas, Charles, 94
Thomas, H.E., 68
Thomas, John, 9
Thomas, Les Restaurant, 20
Thomas, Major, 91, 94
Thomas, Saloon, 20
Thomas, Tim Goalie, 55
Thomasson, Frank, 133
Thompson, Adolphus, 76
Thompson, Edward, 46
Thompson, Mrs. Maria, 108
Thornton, Anna, 106
Thurman, Lucy Mrs., 199, 200
Tidd, Charles P. 76
Till, Emmett Louis, 138
Tillman, B.E.,31
Tilton, Libby Richards, 215
Tilton, Theodore, 215
Todd, Frances, 157
Todd, Sam, 38
Todd, William B., 181
Tonsorial Shop De Luxe, 152
Toomer, Amanda, 126
Toomer, Fred, 125
Toomer, Harriet, 125
Toomer, Henry, 125
Toomer, Walter, 125
Toomer, Mamie, 125, 126

Toomer, Nathan, 125, 126
Toomer, Nathan Eugene Pinchback, 125
Toomer, Nina Eliza Pinchback, 126
Traphagen, Oliver, 130
Tremble, William, 59
Tribe of Israel, 172
Tribe of Judah, 172
Tribune, New York, 6
Trigg, Mayor, 87
Troup, Drug Store, 21
Troupeville, 46
Truman, Harry S., President, 16
Truth, Sojourner, 58
Tubman, Harriet, 72, 73, 74
Tullibody Academy, 194
Turnbo, Isabella Cook, 99
Turnbo, Robert, 99
Turner, Benjamin S., 168, 170
Turner, Bishop Henry M., 95
Turner, Dr. Valdo, 10
Turner, Elmo, 68
Turner, Haynes, 46
Turner, Henry M. Bishop, 79
Turner, Mary, 46
Turner, Nathaniel "Nat", 79, 85
Turner, Thomas M. Col, 124
Turpentine Still of Searight, 145
Tuskegee, Normal and Industrial Institute, 66, 67, 88, 166
Tusken, Irene, 9
Twilight, Alexander Lucius, 192
Tyler, John, 35
Tyler, Warren, 42, 43

U

Uncle Jerry, 164, 165
Uncle Lot, 210
Uncle Tom's Cabin, 209, 210
"Under the Oaks," 113, 114
Union, Will, 39
Universal Negro Improvement Association (UNIA), 193
USS Augusta, 212
USS Marblehead, 167
USS Onward, 212

V

Vagabond, 41
Valdez, Monica, 152
Vallelley, James F.H., 30
Vanderbelt, Mrs. W.K., 54
Vanderbilt, Commodore, 216
Vardaman, Senator of Mississippi, 121
Vaughn, T. of Newman, 94
Vann, Holly, 117

Vermont, Bennington, 75, 157
Vernon, William Tecumseh, 116
Vernon, Adam and Margaret, 116
Vernon, Emily, 116
Villard, Mrs. Henry of New York City, 158
Villard, Oswald Garrison, N.A.A.C.P.,70, 202
Virginia, Alexandria, 36, 111, 179
Virginia, Berkley, 161
Virginia, Chariton County, 115
Virginia, Charlestown, 75
Virginia, Cowan's Depot, 110
Virginia, King William County, 195
Virginia, Louisa County, 64
Virginia, Lynchburg, 136
Virginia, Petersburg, 21
Virginia, Portsmouth, 111
Virginia, Richmond, 194, 195
Virginia, South Hampton County, 61

W

Waddell, A. M. Col., 38
Wadkins, Madge of Cincinnati, 153
Wadmalaw Island, 212
Wagner, Alex, 174
Waldecker, Professor, 136
Walker, Fielding, Uncle, 164
Walker, Lelia, 97, 98
Waite, Elizabeth Ann, 181
Walker, Madam C.J., 97, 98, 99
Walker, Rev. J.J., 97
Wall, Isabel Irene, 172
Walls, Josiah T., 168, 170
Wallace, C.W., Rev., 139
Wallace, George, 11
Waller, Garnett R., 202, 203
Walters, Alexander Bishop, 34, 200, 201, 202
Walton, Dumbar, 125
Walton, Eva, 125
Walton, Isabella & Charles of Augusta, 125
Wamsley, Charles E., 24
Ware, Edward, 122, 123
Warmoth, Henry Clay Governor, 169
Warner, Blanchard, 47
Washington and Lee University, 163
Washington, Booker, T, 34, 66, 67, 68, 69, 159, 185, 187, 191, 200
Washington, Booker T. Memorial Association, 121
Washington, Colonel, 77
Washington, Ernest Davidson, 69
Washington, George President, 77, 100
Washington, Jane, 66
Washington, John, 66
Washington, Jr., Booker, T., 69

Devour Us Not

Washington, Lilla-Niece, 68
Washington, Margaret Jane Murray, 66, 68, 199, 200
Washington, Portia, 66, 69
Washington, D.C., 56, 115, 136, 177, 196
Washington, George, 35
Washington, Jesse, 48, 49
Washington, Mannie, 38
Watkins, Dora, Mrs., 165
Watts, Clem, 95
Watts, Governor, 110
Wayland Seminary School, 69
Welch, John, 164
Welch, Uncle Jesse, 164
West, Delonte, 55
Westfeldt, Gustaf R., 192
West, Jim, 46
West Point Railroad Train, 94
West Point, United States Military Academy, 181
West Roxbury Unitarian Church, 139
West, Sam H., County Prosecutor, 141
Western University, 116
West Virginia, Harper's Ferry, 75, 76, 77
West Virginia, Malden, 69
Wheatley, John, 100
Wheatley, Phillis, 99, 100
Wheatley, Phyllis Club, 199
Wheelsman, 211
White Angel of Freedom, 210
White Elephant, 176
White Hall, 160
White, Justice Edward D., 127
White League Organization, 132
White Negress, The, 210
White Owls, 42
White, Peter, 22
Whitfield, Mrs. Carrie, 131
Whittier, John G., 75, 157
Wickersham, George W., Attorney General, 162
Wideman, Conilia, 107
Wideman, Oliver, 106
Wideman, Patrina, 106, 107
Wilberforce, University, 28, 116, 166, 183, 184
Wild, Caralle, 87
Wilde, Ms Gazelle, 15, 16
Wilkes, Samuel, 93
Willard, Daniel President, 163
Williamburg, County, 31
Williams, age26, 22
Williams, Augustus L., 5
Williams, Cleve, 22
Williams, Daniel Hale, 186
Williams, Eugene, 5
Williams, H. S., Sapulpa County Judge, 177
Williams, Louis, 9

Williams, R.J., 94
Williams, Samuel H.,29
Wilmington, North Carolina, 37
Wilson, Carrie, 125
Wilson, Emma J., Miss, 189
Wilson, Henry, 215
Wilson, Joe Republican, 44
Wilson, President, 121
Windes, Thomas G., 6
Winn, Alex, 14
Winters, John, 103
Wolfe, Admiral and daughter, 75
Wolford, Frank, 117
Woman's Aid Club, 199
Woman's Missionary Organization, 197
Wood, Charles Winter, 66
Woodhull, Bryon, 216
Woodhull & Claflin's Weekly, 215
Woodhull, Dr. Canning, 216
Woodhull, Lulu "Lula" Maud, 216
Woodhull, Victoria California, 214
Woods, Eliza, 107
Wooten, Mrs. J.P., 107
Wordlow, Will, 123
World's Women's Christian Temperance Union, 136
Wright, Bob, 22
Wright, Edward Herbert, 149, 150
Wright, Mayor, 38
Wright, Miss Bogkin, 115
Wright, Mose, 138
Wright, Mrs. J. Howard, 54
Wright, Sarah, 150
Wright, Silas, P., 38
Wyatt, Judge, 54
Wyly, B.F., 94

X

X, Malcolm, i

Y

Yantis, B. D., 117
Yates, Governor, 145
Yates, Josephine Silone, Prof., 199, 200
Yates, Lizzie, 14
Young, Charles, Captain, 166
Young, Charles, Col. U.S. Army, 204
Young, Jesse, 39
Young, M.G., 177
Young, Virginia, 54

Z

Ziegler, J. T., 59

Newspaper Article

1. "The Republic" of, September 13, 1903 ,
2. "Los Angeles Herald," of January 17, 1909 ,
3. "The Day Book" February 21, 1912 ,
4. "The Republic," of Sep 13, 1903 ,
5. "The San Francisco Call," of June 23, 1907,
6. "The Saint Paul Globe, "of Jan 10, 1904 ,
7. "The Richmond Virginia Times," of Dec 7, 1902 ,
8. "The Broad Ax", July 8, 1922 ,
9. "The St. Louis Republic," of June 26, 1904 ,
10. "The Republic", of   September 13, 1903 ,
11. "The Voice of the People," of New Orleans, LA., April 2, 1914 ,
12. "The Washington Herald," of June 22, 1913 ,
13. "The Republican," of Seattle, WA, Sep 13, 1903,
14. "The National Tribune," of Washington D.C. April 7, 1898 ,
15. "The New York Times," of April 2, 1922 ,
16. "The Tulsa Star," of July 31, 1920 ,
17. "Los Angeles Herald, " of October 29, 1905 ,
18. "The Bee" Sept 25, 1919 ,
19. " The Omaha Daily Bee, Sep 25, 1919 ,
20. "The Sun. Jacksonville, Fla.," of Jan 6, 1906 ,
21. "Truth," of Salt Lake City Utah, February 1, 1908 ,
22. "Los Angeles Herald," Oct 29, 1905,
23. "The Anderson Intelligencer," of June 30, 1870 ,
24. "Los Angeles Herald," of November 25, 1906 ,
25. "Los Angeles Herald," November 25, 1906,
26. "The Tacoma Times," of August 14, 1915 ,
27. "The Day Book," of September 16, 1912,
28. "The Day Book," of Chicago, IL. Jan 4, 1915 ,
29. "Palestine, TX. Daily Herald," of December 28, 1903 ,
30. "The Day Book," of March 11, 1914 ,
31. "Palestine Daily Herald," of December 28, 1903 ,
32. "The Washington Herald," of Jan 3, 1915 .
33. "The San Francisco Call," of June 18, 1905 ,
34. "Evening Star," of January 22, 1902 ,
35. "The Broad Ax," of August 30, 1919,
36. "The Washington Herald," of June 15, 1913 ,
37. "The Broad Ax," of June 25, 1921,
38. "The Washington Times," of July 12, 1908 ,
39. "New-York Tribune," of July 24, 1904 ,
40. "The Broad Ax," of June 25, 1921 ,
41. "The San Francisco Call." of July 9, 1911 ,
42 "The Appeal," of Feb 11, 1905 ,
43. "Valentine Democrat," of August 27, 1908 ,
44. "The Broad Ax," of June 25, 1921 ,
45. "Los Angeles Herald." of Feb 2, 1908 ,
46. "Los Angeles Herald," of Dec 17, 1905 ,
47. "The Ocala Evening Star," of December 1, 1908,
48. "The Salt Lake Herald," of March 28, 1909 ,
49. "The Mathews Journal," of May 12, 1910,
50. "New-York Tribune," of Sep 5, 1915 ,
51. "The San Francisco Call", of November 17-19, 1900 ,
52. "Keowee Courier," of September 30, 1908 ,
53. "The Republic Sunday," of Sep 13, 1903 ,
54. "The San Francisco Call," of Nov. 16, 1900 ,
55. "The Day Book," of January 11, 1913 ,
56. "The Princeton Union," of Oct 20, 1921 ,
57. "Pittsburg Dispatch," of Sep 3, 1892,
58. "The Evening Herald," of Oct 26, 1896 ,
59. "The Appeal," of June 30, 1917 ,
60. "The Bourbon News," of September 16, 1910 ,
61. "The Houston Daily Post," Dec 17, 1899,
62. "The Salt Lake Herald," Aug 9, 1909 ,
63. "The Washington Times," Jun 12, 1921,
64. "The Washington Times," Sep 4, 1904,
65. "The Day Book" of July 11, 1914 ,
66. "New-York Tribune," of June 4, 1907
67. " The San Francisco Call," of August 31, 1900 ,

Acknowledgement Index

68. "The Red Cloud Chief," of Mar 10, 1905
69. "The Holmes County Farmer", of July 21, 1864 ,
70. "The Times Dispatch," of October 22, 1911,
71. "The Colored American," of Sep 14, 1901 ,
72. "The Salt Lake Herald," of July 18, 1909 ,
73. "The Colored American," of Dec 2, 1899,
74. "The St. Louis Republic," of October 6, 1901,
75. "The Hocking Sentinel," of Sep 19, 1901 ,
76. "The Appeal.," of Sep 21, 1901 ,
77. "The San Francisco Call," of March 26, 1901,
78. "The Broad Ax," of July 14, 1917.
79. "Los Angeles Herald, "of August 2, 1908 ,
80. "The Broad Ax," of February 10, 1917 ,
81. "The Broad Ax," of December 27, 1919,
82 "The Los Angeles Herald ,"of December 17, 1905 ,
83. "The Appeal," of Jan 30, 1892 ,
84. "The Broad Ax," of December 22, 1917,
85. "Ft. Worth Gazette," of Mar 12, 1893 ,
86. "The Washington Times," of July 26, 1904 ,
87. "Los Angeles Herald," of July 9, 1905 ,
88. "Carrizozo News," of Nov 20, 1908 ,
89. "The San Francisco Call," of July 10, 1898 ,
90. "The Day Book," of May 22, 1915 ,
91. "The St. Louis Republic," of May 10, 1903 ,
92. "The St. Louis Republic," of May 10, 1903 ,
93. "The St. Louis Republic," of May 10, 1903 ,
94. "Los Angeles Herald," of July 14, 1907 ,
95. "The Marion Daily Mirror," Nov 6, 1909,
96. "The York Tribune," of December 20, 1896 ,
97. "The Ogden Standard," of September 14, 1918.
98. "The Saint Paul Globe," of Nov 20, 1898 ,
99. "The Appeal," of July 15, 1916 ,
100. "The Saint Paul Globe, "of Mar 5, 1905 ,
101. "The Saint Paul Globe," of Mar 5, 1905 ,
102. "The San Francisco Call," of Mar 12, 1911 ,
103. "The Washington Times," of August 28, 1904 ,
104. "The San Francisco Call," of April 2, 1911 ,
105. "The San Francisco Call," of March 12, 1911 ,
106. "The Tacoma Times," of March 22, 1911,
107. "The San Francisco Call of Feb 25, 1912 ,
108. "The San Francisco Call," of January 2, 1898,
109. "The Omaha Sunday Daily Bee Magazine" of February 7, 1915
110. "The Washington Herald," of Aug 3, 1913 ,
111. "The Salt Lake Tribune," of February 7, 1909 ,
112. "The Evening World," of October 11, 1904 ,
113. "New York Tribune," of March 12, 1916 ,
114. " The Colored American," of July 18, 1903 ,
115. "The Times," of Dec 7, 1902 ,
116. " Frank Leslie's Illustrated Newspaper, June 27, 1857,
117. "The Washington Herald," of Jan 3, 1915 ,
118. "The Appeal," of Sep 3, 1892,
119. "The Times Dispatch, " Aug 29, 1909 ,
120. "The Wichita Daily Eagle," of Sep 28, 1892,
121. "The Times Dispatch, " Aug 29, 1909 ,
122. "The Wichita Daily Eagle," of Sep 28, 1892,
123. "The St. Louis Republic," of May 30, 1901,
124. "The Sun," of November 21, 1897 ,
125. "Fort Worth Weekly Gazette," of October 16, 1890
126. "The Washington Times," of March 16, 1911.
127. "The Washington Herald," of June 15, 1913 ,
128. "Bisbee Daily Review," of Mar 6, 1902 ,
129. "The Colored American.," of December 28, 1901
130. "The Appeal," of April 22, 1905 ,
131. "The Appeal," of April 22, 1905,
132. "The Evening World's Home Magazine," of Sep 22, 1904 ,
134. "The Appeal," of March 12, 1892 ,
135. "The Appeal," of Mar 12, 1892 ,
136. "Los Angeles Herald," of Mar 19, 1905 ,

Devour Us Not

137. *"The Colored American, July 21, 1901,*
138. *"The Colored American., January 19, 1901,*
139. *"The Colored American., March 24, 1900,*
140. *"The Colored American., June 29, 1901,*
141. *"The Colored American., April 6, 1901,*
142. *"The Colored American., July 20, 1902,*
143. *" The Colored American., May 6, 1905,*
144. *"The Appeal," of August 25, 1906,*
145. *"The Colored American" of June 20, 1903,*
146. *"The Appeal., March 12, 1892,*
147. *"The Colored American., December 28, 1901,*
148. *"The Broad Ax., May 31, 1913,*
149. *"The Appeal", March 9, 1912,*
150. *"The Appeal"., March 12, 1892,*
151. *"The Colored American, October 10, 1903,*
152. *"The Colored American, July 18, 1903,*
153. *"The Evening World," of Apr 8, 1908 ,*
154. *"The Colored American," of May 26, 1900,*
155. *"The Kansas City Sun," of Dec 2, 1916,*
156. *"Los Angeles Herald," of Dec 17, 1905 ,*
157. *"The San Francisco Call," of Apr 2, 1911 ,*
158. *"The Sun," of May 2, 1909 ,*
159. *"The Washington Bee," of Apr 3, 1909 ,*
160. *"The San Francisco Call," of Sep 29, 1907,*
161. *"The Colored American," of Jul 13, 1901 ,*
162. *"Salt Lake Tribune," of July 2, 1911 ,*
163. *"The Paducah Sun," of Sep 10, 1903 ,*
164. *"El Paso Herald," of Oct 7, 1916 ,*
165. *"The Day Book," of Oct 16, 1916,*
166. *"The Tacoma Times," of Jun 24, 1909 ,*
167. *"Los Angeles Herald," Jun 9, 1909 ,*
167. *"Deseret Evening News," Aug 11, 1910 ,*
169. *"Omaha Daily Bee," of Jan 31, 1915 ,*
170. *"The San Francisco Call," of May 7, 1899 ,*
171. *"Omaha Daily Bee," of January 31, 1915 ,*
172. *"The San Francisco Call," of November 6, 1910 ,*
173. *"The National Tribune," of Sep 28, 1893,*
174. *"The Spanish Fork Press," of Mar 5, 1908 ,*
175. *"The San Francisco Call," of October 5, 1900,*
176. *"The Republic Sunday," of Sep 13, 1903 ,*
177. *"The Colored American," of Jan 20, 1900,*
179. *"The Colored American," of Jan 21, 1900,*
180. *"The Colored American," of Feb 10, 1900,*
181. *"The Colored American," of Apr 6, 1901,*
183. *"The Colored American," of April 25, 1903,*
184. *"The Colored American," of Jun 2, 1900,*
185. *"The Salt Lake Herald," of Jul 21, 1895 ,*
186. *"The Day Book," of November 15, 1915,*
187. *"The Times," of Oct 17, 1901 ,*
188. *" New York, NY of, June 10, 1901 ,*
189. *"Los Angeles Herald," of Jun 18, 1905 ,*
190. *"The San Francisco Call," of Mar 24, 1912 ,*
191. *"El Paso Herald," of May 4, 1918 ,*
192. *"The Saint Paul Globe," of Nov 6, 1898 ,*
193. *"The Colored American," of April 4, 1903 ,*
194. *"The Day Book," of May 28, 1913 ,*
195. *"Bisbee Daily Review," of October 8, 1903 ,*
196. *"The Columbus Journal," of Feb 17, 1909,*
197. *"Akron Daily Democrat," of Dec 24, 1901,*
198. *"The Colored American," of Jun 20, 1903,*
199. *"The Colored American.," of Mar 24, 1900,*
200. *"The Appeal," of June 28, 1890 ,*
201. *"New-York Tribune," of October 9, 1910,*
202. *"El Paso Herald," of January 18, 1913 ,*
203. *"El Paso Herald," of January 18, 1913 ,*
204. *" Kansas City Journal," of January 10, 1899,*
205. *"The Herald," of May 8, 1913,*

206. *"The San Francisco Call," of Apr 24, 1899 ,*
207. *"The Washington Times" of September 14, 1911*
208. *"The St. Louis Republic," of September 10, 1900 ,*
209. *"The Day Book," of March 1, 1917 ,*
210. *"Evening Bulletin," of June 17, 1905 ,*
211. *"The Houston Daily Post," of May 16, 1899 ,*
212. *"The Day Book," of August 23, 1915 ,*
213. *"The Houston Daily Post," of August 3, 1900,*
214. *"Richmond Planet," of Sep 29, 1900,*
215. *"Richmond Planet," of Dec 19, 1908 ,*
216. *"The Broad Ax," of Jan 24, 1914,*
217. *"The Kansas City Sun," of May 31, 1919,*
218. *"The Kansas City Sun," of February 23, 1918 ,*
219. *"The Washington Bee," of October 17, 1908 ,*
220. *"The Kansas City Sun," of December 15, 1917 ,*
221. *"The San Francisco Call," of July 27, 1902,*
222. *"The Kansas City Sun," of November 28, 1914 ,*
223. *"The Appeal," of July 16, 1892 ,*
224. *"The Day Book," of August 19, 1916 ,*
225. *"The Salt Lake Herald-Republican," of August 29 , 1909,*
226. *"The Colored American," of June 7, 1902 ,*
227. *"The Broad Ax," of July 12, 1913,*
228. *"Omaha Daily Bee," of September 20, 1896,*
229. *"New-York Tribune," of January 31, 1909,*
230. *"Kansas City Journal," of November 9, 1897 ,*
231. *"The Intelligencer," of May 11, 1915,*
232. *"The North Platte semi-weekly Tribune," of February 11, 1916 ,*
233. *"The Valentine Democrat," of November 18, 1897 ,*
234. *"The Intelligencer," of May 11, 1915,*
235. *"The Marion Daily Mirror," of December 17, 1910 ,*
236. *"The San Francisco Call," of July 28, 1907,*
237. *"The Times Dispatch," of Oct 17, 1909 .*
238. *"Keowee Courier," of May 1, 1901 ,*
239. *"The Colored American," of November 17, 1900 ,*
240. *"The Times Dispatch, "of August 13, 1911 ,*
241. *"The Minneapolis Journal," of May 13, 1905,*
242. *"The Colored American," of October 8, 1904 ,*
243. *"The Rising Son," of September 30, 1904 ,*
244. *"The Jasper News," of December 24, 1908*
245. *"The Seattle Republican., December 2, 1904 ,*
246. *"The Seattle Republican," of March 8, 1907 ,*
247. *"The Day Book," of May 20, 1915 ,*
248. *"The Princeton Union," of May 25, 1893 ,*
249. *"The Appeal," of July 13, 1918 ,*
250. *"The Day Book," of February 6, 1914,*
251. *"The Colored American," of May 25, 1901 ,*
252. *"The San Francisco Call," of January 2, 1898 ,*
253. *"Hopkinsville Kentuckian," of September 9, 1913,*
254. *"The Adair County News," of Feb 7, 1922 ,*
255. *"The Washington Bee," of December 18, 1897 ,*
256. *"The McCook Tribune," of July 28, 1899 ,*
257. *"Evening Public Ledger," of September 20, 1915 ,*
258. *"New-York Tribune," of November 25, 1906 ,*
259. *"The Kansas City Sun," of June 19, 1920 ,*
260. *"The Appeal," of March 18, 1911,*
261. *"Evening Public Ledger," of September 29, 1915 ,*
262. *"The San Francisco Call," of September 7, 1905 ,*
263. *"The Seattle Republican," of June 14, 1901 ,*
264. *"The San Francisco Call," of September 7, 1905*
265. *, "The Paducah Sun," of January 6, 1904,*
266. *"The Colored American," June 9, 1900 ,*
267. *"The Colored American," of January 3, 1903*
268. *"The Colored American., October 24, 1903 ,*
269. *"The Washington Bee," of April 29, 1911 ,*
270. *"Richmond Planet." of, August 27, 1910 ,*
271. *"The San Francisco Call," of July 27, 1902,*
272. *"The Paducah Sun," of February 18, 1903 ,*
273. *"The Orangeburg News," of December 4, 1869 ,*

274. "Omaha Daily Bee," of June 23, 1898,
275. "The San Francisco Call," of April 25, 1899,
276. "The Breckenridge News," of January 30, 1907,
277. "The Day Book," of January 22, 1914,
278. "The Colored American," Oct 6, 1900,
279. "The Washington Times," of March 16, 1911,
280. "The New York Sun," of May 20 1894,
281. "Akron Daily Democrat," of August 3, 1901,
282. "The San Francisco Call," of October 15, 1897,
283. "Los Angeles Herald," of October 25, 1909,
284. "Richmond Dispatch," of August 12, 1902,
285. "Richmond Dispatch," of November 21, 1902.,
286. "The Ogden Standard," of February 17, 1910,
287. "Deseret Evening News," of April 7, 1906,
288. "Pittsburg Dispatch," of October 11, 1892,
289. "The Citizen," December 15, 1910,
290. "The Morning Times," of November 15, 1896,
291. "The Colored American," December 22, 1900.
292. "The Mercur Miner," of February 12, 1908,
293. "The San Francisco Call," of September 8, 1897
294. "Omaha Daily Bee," November 30, 1890,
295. "The Appeal," of February 7, 1903,
296. "Anadarko Daily Democrat," of May 17, 1902,
297. "The San Francisco Call," of April 28, 1901,
298. "The San Francisco Call," of June 4, 1911,
299. "New-York Tribune," of September 5, 1915,
300. "St. Louis Republic," of August 18, 1901,
301. "The Colored American," of August 11, 1900,
302. "El Paso Herald," of October 24, 1916,
303. "The Colored American," of Jan 25, 1902,
304. "The Day Book," of April 9, 1915,
305. "New-York Tribune.," of May 2, 1920,
306. "The San Francisco Call," of February 26, 1911,
307. "The Salt Lake Tribune," of May 29, 1910,
308. "The National Tribune," of August 22, 1901,
309. "The St. Joseph Observer," of February 16, 1918,
310. "The Jennings Daily Record," of August 6, 1902,
311. "The San Francisco Call," of August 6, 1911,
312. "Carrizozo News," of June 2, 1911.
313. "The Day Book," of June 16, 1913,
314. "The San Francisco Call," of March 9, 1913,
315. "St. Paul Daily Globe," of July 24, 1890,
316. "New-York Tribune," of January 11, 1903
317., "The Washington Herald," of June 22, 1913,
318. "The Broad Ax," of November 23, 1912,
319. "The San Francisco Call," of January 24, 1899,
320. "The Broad Ax," of Sep 11, 1920,
321. "The Broad Ax," of Nov 23, 1912,
322. "The Adair County News," of Columbia, KY. September 25, 1912,
323. "The Day Book," of September 12, 1912,
324. "The Day Book," of November 12, 1912,
325. "Bisbee Daily Review," of May 4, 1909,
326. "The Day Book," of Dec 4, 1912,
327. "The Broad Ax," of Sep 14, 1912,
328. "New-York Tribune," of Apr 6, 1915,
329. "The Washington Herald," of Oct 23, 1912,
330. "The Tacoma Times," of June 17, 1911,
331. "The Day Book," of May 3, 1916,
332. "The Spokane Press," of July 13, 1910,
333. "Bisbee Daily Review," of December 12, 1912,
334. "The San Francisco Call," of July 5, 1908,
335. "The Seattle Star," of December 31, 1909,
336. "Los Angeles herald., September 15, 1907,
337. "Blue-grass Blade," of November 9, 1902.,
338. "The Washington Times," of July 11, 1917,
339. "The Washington Times," of July 11, 1917,
340. "The Broad Ax," of December 9, 1905,
341. "The Washington Times," of July 11, 1917,

342. "The Evening Bulletin," of September 8, 1892,
343. "The Weekly Messenger," of February 4, 1899,
344. "The Appeal," of January 12, 1901,
345. "The Appeal," of January 12, 1901,
346. "The Tomahawk," of July 30, 1903.
347. "The Hayti Herald," of April 16, 1914,
348. "The Appeal," of June 1, 1895,
349. "The Seattle Republican," of Jan 3, 1913
350. "The Times Dispatch," Dec 16, 1906
351. "The San Francisco Call," Nov 24, 1895
352. "The Minneapolis Journal," Jun 10, 1906,
353. "The Sun," of September 29, 1912,
354. "The Tacoma Times," of March 7, 1911,
356. "Pullman Herald," of December 27, 1902,
357. "Richmond Planet," July 24, 1909,
358. "The Hazel Green Herald," of March 24, 1893,
359. "The Seattle Republican," of October 6, 1911,
360. "The Sun.," of June 29, 1913,
361. "Fayetteville Observer," of May 24, 1866,
362. "The Evening Herald," of April 13, 1918,
363 "The Princeton Union," of May 18, 1899,
364. "The Holt County Sentinel," of July 21, 1911,
365. "The Evening Herald," of April 13, 1918,
366. "The Evening Herald," of April 13, 1918,
367. "St. Paul Daily Globe," of August 2, 1885,
368. "The Washington Times," Mar 6, 1904,
369. "The Herald," of December 26, 1897,
370. "The Washington Times," of March 13, 1904,
371. "The Colored American," of October 18, 1902,
372. "The St. Louis Republic," of February 17, 1901,
373. "The Colored American," of June 2, 1900,
374. "Tensas Gazette," of January 31, 1913,
375. "The Colored American," of August 25, 1900,
376. "The Washington Times," of December 25, 1904,
377. "The Seattle Republican," of January 15, 1904,
378. "The Hawaiian Star," of January 16, 1909,
379. "The Athens Post," of Athens Tennessee, January 15, 1869,
380. "The Tomahawk," of May 4, 1916,
381. "The Daily Phoenix," of February 4, 1868,
382. "Crittenden Press," of August 23, 1906,
383. "The Washington Bee," November 16, 1907,
384. "Capital City Courier," of December 25, 1890,
385. "The Coalville Times," of Coalville, Utah, November 21, 1902,
386. "Tensas Gazette," of January 24, 1913,
387. "Omaha Daily Bee," of June 24, 1906,
388. "The Appeals," of January 22, 1916,
389. "The Salt Lake Tribune," of April 7, 1904,
390. "The Washington Herald," of April 5, 1914,
391. "The Mt. Sterling Advocate," of June 7, 1921,
392. "The Washington Times," of September 5, 1904,
393. "The Pensacola Journal," of February 19, 1905,
394. "The Washington Times," of August 28, 1904,
395. "The Washington Times," of August 21, 1904,
396. "The Colored American," of August 4, 1900,
397. "The Salt Lake Tribune," of April 14, 1913,
398. "The San Francisco Call," of June 23, 1912,
399. "Hopkinsville Kentuckian"., October 25, 1906,
400. "The Day Book," of March 10, 1916,
401. "The Marion Daily Mirror," of March 23, 1911,
402. "Marion Daily Mirror," of Nov 30, 1907
403. "The San Francisco Call," of Oct 9, 1902,
404. "The Day Book," of April 9, 1914,
405. "Los Angeles Herald," of July 5, 1908,
406. "New-York Tribune," of July 1, 1901,
407. "Deseret Evening News," of November 2, 1907,
408. "The Colored American," of November 7, 1903,
409. "The Colored American.," of January 13, 1900,
410. "The Colored American," of May 9, 1903,

411. "The Washington Bee," of July 22, 1911,
412. "The Appeal," of Jun 15, 1912
413. "The Broad Ax," of April 20, 1912
414. "The Appeal," of Jul 10, 1915,
415. "The Saint Paul Globe," of February 26, 1905,
416. "The Appeal," of February 28, 1891,
417. "The Columbus Journal," of October 20, 1897,
418. "The Colored American.," of August 23, 1902,
419. "The Washington Bee," of March 11, 1911,
420. "The Broad Ax," of December 27, 1902,
421. "The San Francisco Call," of January 2, 1898,
422. "The Houston Daily Post" of February 23, 1903,
423. "The Kansas City Sun" of May 13, 1916,
424. "The Colored American" of March 21, 1903,
425. "The Broad Ax" of January 2, 1904,
426. "The Broad Ax" of November 30, 1912.,
427. "The Salt Lake Tribune," of February 6, 1910,
428. "The Colored American," of November 24, 1900,
429. "Groesbeck Journal" of May 16, 1924,
430. "The San Francisco Call," of January 18, 1903,
431. "Omaha Daily Bee," of February 4, 1900,
432. "The Professional World," of December 25, 1903,
433. "New-York Tribune," of May 3, 1903,
434. "Daily Press," of Newport News, VA., October 21, 1906,
435. "The Colored American," of July 23, 1904,
436. "The San Francisco Call," of February 24, 1911,
437. "New-York Tribune," of June 24, 1906,
438. "New-York Tribune," of September 24, 1905,
439. "Perrysburg Journal," of Mar 13, 1897,
440. "The Daily Journal," of Jul 10, 1903,
441. "New-York Tribune," of Sep 24, 1905,
442. "Evening Public Ledger," of Aug 2, 1915,
443. "The Minneapolis Journal," of Mar 26, 1902,
444. "New-York Tribune," of Mar 17, 1907,
445. "The Evening World," of Feb 15, 1909,
446. "Evening Public Ledger," of August 2, 1915,
447. "The Evening World," of June 12, 1922,
448. "The Ouachita Telegraph," of September 11, 1874,
449. "New-York Tribune," of Aug 2, 1922,
450. "Virginian-Pilot," of Nov 26, 1899,
451. "The San Francisco Call" of August 5, 1905,
452. "The Richmond Planet ,"of January 5, 1895,
453. "The Richmond Planet ,"of January 5, 1895,
454. "Richmond Planet," of September 9, 1905,
455. "Omaha Daily Bee," of January 31, 1915,
456. "The Richmond Planet ,"of January 5, 1895,
457. "Richmond Planet",- Jul 2, 1910,
458. "Richmond Planet," of Aug 17, 1895,
459. "The Richmond Planet ,"of January 5, 1895,
460. "The Pensacola Journal," of January 20, 1906,
461. "The Colored American," of February 13, 1904,
462. "The Washington Bee," of November 18, 1911,
463. "The Washington Bee," of November 18, 1911,
464. "The Colored American," of Sep 28, 1901,
465. "Graham Guardian," of Oct 29, 1920,
466. "The Colored American," of Nov 2, 1901,
467. "Perrysburg Journal," of Aug 17, 1900,
468. "The Broad Ax," of November 12, 1921,
469. "The San Francisco Call," of Feb 12, 1911,
470. "Richmond Planet," of August 27, 1910,
471. "The Professional World," of December 26, 1902,
472. "The Colored American," June 9, 1900,
473. "The Appeal," of November 16, 1901,
474. "The Appeal," of April 22, 1905,
475. "The Appeal," of June 17, 1922,
476. "El Paso Herald," of May 31, 1919,
477. "The Broad Ax," of Nov 12, 1921,
478. "The Colored American," of Sep 8, 1900,
479. "The Appeal," of Jun 28, 1902,

480. "The San Francisco Call," of Feb 7, 1909
481. "The Saint Paul Globe," of March 7, 1897
482. "The Appeal," of July 19, 1902
483. "The St. Louis Republic," of November 11, 1900
484. "The Colored American," of Sep 8, 1900
485. "The Appeal," of Jun 28, 1902
486. "The Appeal," of Jun 28, 1902
487. "The Colored American," of Sep 8, 1900
488. "The Washington Times," of March 4, 1906
489. -"The Broad Ax," of February 9, 1918
490. "The Appeal," of January 23, 1915
491. "The Broad Ax," of October 15, 1910,
492. "The Colored American. " of May 25, 1901
493. "The Colored American," of September 19, 1903.
494. "The Saint Paul Globe," of Aug 28, 1904
495. "The Colored American," of Sep 15, 1900
496. "The Saint Paul Globe," of Aug 28, 1904
497. "The Colored American" of Sep 15, 1900
498. "The Day Book," of Apr 18, 1917
499. "The Day Book," of June 14, 1915
500. "The Washington Bee," of Jun 22, 1907
501. "The Colored American," of May 31, 1902
502. "The Colored American," of Feb 14, 1903
503. "The San Francisco Call," of Jan 21, 1905
504. "The Morning Call," of Aug 27, 1893
505. "Wichita Eagle," of Mar 2, 1890
506. "The Day Book," February 18, 1913
507. "The Appeal" of Aug 25, 1900
508. "The San Francisco Call," of Jun 20, 1909
509. "The Appeal," of Jul 7, 1906
510. "The Colored American," of Dec 1, 1900
511. "The San Francisco Call," of July 14, 1907
512. "The St. Louis Republic., March 31, 1903,
513. "The St. Louis Republic., June 23, 1903,
514. "The Tacoma times., October 30, 1909,
515. "The San Francisco call., March 13, 1898,
516. "The San Francisco Call," of November 21, 1897,
517. "Omaha daily bee., November 21, 1909,
518. "The Wichita Daily Eagle," of August 1, 1897,
519. "The San Francisco call., July 2, 1905,
520. "New-York Tribune," of July 31, 1910
521. "The San Francisco Call," of March 10, 1912,
522. "The Sun," of Oct 13, 1906,
523. "The Saint Paul Globe," of May 17, 1903,
524. "Dayton Daily Empire." of August 10, 1860,
525. "The Times Dispatch," of November 22, 1904,
526. "The Corpus Christi Caller," of June 9, 1921,
527. "The Morning Examiner," of March 27, 1910
528. "The Appeal,," of Aug 31, 1901
529. "Omaha Daily Bee," of Sep 8, 1897,
530. "Los Angeles Herald," of Feb 19, 1905,
531. "The Washington Times," of Jun 20, 1910,
532. "Evening Public Ledger," of Sep 1, 1915,
533. "Perrysburg Journal.," of Feb 20, 1897,
534. "The San Francisco Call," of Jul 10, 1898,
535. "The National Tribune," of Feb 26, 1903,
536. "Evening Public Ledger, of Sep 2, 1915,
537. "The Bemidji Daily Pioneer," of April 25, 1917,
538. "Perrysburg Journal," of Sep 7, 1895

"To stand in silence when they should be protesting makes cowards out of men."
Abraham Lincoln

"To be inhuman is to watch the inhumane treatment of others in silence."
Arnold P. Powers

"Tis better to be silent and be thought a fool, than to speak and remove all doubt."
Abraham Lincoln

"In the end, we will remember not the words of our enemies, but the silence of our friends."
Rev. Dr. Martin Luther King, Jr.

This Book has taken five years to complete, but it's really incomplete. There are still elements of our family's history that has been purposely hidden from us by the white Carroll's of Navarro County, Texas. The white's are not alone, just as many blacks for whatever reason has also concealed information for the purpose of understanding our history. These minor set backs will never impede my enthusiasm to uncover our history. The photo on the front cover is from a newspaper article from, "The Pensacola Journal," dated December 16, 1906. The individuals pictured on the upper left hand corner are Uncle Joe and Aunt Lucy. Real people described as "Good-Ole Antebellum Colored Folks." On the lower right hand side is an artistic rendition of Trayvon Martin, the murdered 17 year old of Sanford, Florida by my son, Arnold P. Powers, Jr. The Back Cover is from "The San Francisco Call," newspaper article dated, July 17, 1904.

Devour Us Not

Made in the USA
Las Vegas, NV
09 February 2022